Here are some basic map concepts that will help you to get the most out of the maps in this textbook.

- Always look at the scale, which allows you to determine the distance in miles or kilometers between locations on the map.

- Examine the legend carefully. It explains the colours and symbols used on the map.

- Note the locations of mountains, rivers, oceans, and other geographic features, and consider how these would affect such human activities as agriculture, commerce, travel, and warfare.

- Read the map caption thoroughly. It provides important information, sometimes not covered in the text itself, and poses a thought question to encourage you to think beyond the mere appearance of the map and make connections across chapters, regions, and concepts.

- Several "spot maps" are present, to allow you to view in detail smaller areas that may not be apparent in larger maps.

TWENTIETH-CENTURY
WORLD HISTORY
A CANADIAN PERSPECTIVE

TWENTIETH-CENTURY
WORLD HISTORY
A CANADIAN PERSPECTIVE

WILLIAM J. DUIKER
Pennsylvania State University

BESSMA MOMANI
University of Waterloo

THOMSON

NELSON

Australia   Canada   Mexico   Singapore   Spain   United Kingdom   United States

THOMSON

NELSON

Twentieth-Century World History: A Canadian Perspective

William J. Duiker and Bessma Momani

Associate Vice-President, Editorial Director:
Evelyn Veitch

Editor-in-Chief:
Anne Williams

Executive Marketing Manager:
Kelly Smyth

Publisher's Representative:
Pamela Duprey

Developmental Editor:
Linda Sparks

Photo Researcher and Permissions Coordinator:
Terri Rothman

Production Editor:
Tammy Scherer

Copy Editor:
Claudia Forgas

Proofreader:
Tara Tovell

Indexer:
Megan Sproule-Jones

Production Coordinator:
Ferial Suleman

Design Director:
Ken Phipps

Interior Design:
Tammy Gay

Cover Design:
Johanna Liburd

Cover Image:
Bob Stefko/The Image Bank/ Getty Images

Compositor:
Interactive Composition Corporation

Printer:
Transcontinental

Library and Archives Canada Cataloguing in Publication

Duiker, William J., 1932-

Twentieth-century world history: a Canadian perspective / William J. Duiker, Bessma Momani. — 1st Canadian ed.

Includes bibliographical references and index.

ISBN 0-17-625154-5

1. History, Modern—20th century. I. Momani, Bessma, 1973- II. Title. III. Title: World history.

D421.D86 2006   909.82
C2006-901063-3

To Kirsten and Zachary, as you face the challenges of the new century

W. J. D.

To my supportive husband and loving children

B. M.

Brief Contents

Contents

List of Boxes

List of Maps

Preface

The twentieth century was an era of paradox. At the dawn of the century, Western civilization was a patchwork of squabbling states that bestrode the world like a colossus. As the century came to an end, the West was prosperous and increasingly united on ideological fronts, yet there were signs that despite the recent financial crisis in Asia, global economic and political hegemony were beginning to shift to the East. The era of Western economic dominance would be challenged. The twentieth century had been an era marked by war and revolution but also by rapid industrial growth and widespread economic prosperity, a time of growing interdependence but also of burgeoning ethnic and national consciousness, a period that witnessed the rising power of science but also of religiosity and growing doubts about the impact of technology on the human experience.

Twentieth-Century World History: A Canadian Perspective attempts to chronicle the key events in this revolutionary century from a Canadian perspective, while seeking to throw light on some of the underlying issues that shaped the times. Did the beginning of a new millennium mark the end of the long period of Western dominance? If so, will recent decades of European and American superiority be followed by a "Pacific century," with economic and political power shifting to the nations of eastern Asia? Has the end of the Cold War led to a "new world order" marked by global cooperation, or are we on the verge of an unstable era of ethnic and national conflict? Will American calls for a pre-emptive attack on sovereign states and blatant disregard for multilateralism and the United Nations re-ignite imperialism, particularly in the Middle East? Why was a time of unparalleled prosperity and technological advancement accompanied by deep pockets of poverty and widespread doubts about the role of government and the capabilities of human reason? Although this book does not promise final answers to such questions, it can provide a framework for analysis and a better understanding of some of the salient issues of modern times.

While there are many books on the turbulent twentieth century, there is an added emphasis in this book on the non-Western history of the time. Shedding our Eurocentric perspective is not an easy task, but this book attempts to give a truly thorough understanding of world history.

One of the challenges in writing a history book is deciding whether to present the topic as an integrated whole or to focus on individual cultures and societies. The world that we live in today is in many respects an interdependent one in terms of economics as well as culture and communications, a reality that is often expressed by the familiar phrase "global village." At the same time, the process of globalization is by no means complete or equally beneficial, as ethnic, religious, and regional differences continue to exist and shape the course of our times, and as many strata of society have been harmed by globalization. The tenacity of these differences is reflected not only in the rise of internecine conflicts and poverty in such divergent areas as Africa, South Asia, the Middle East, and Eastern Europe but also in the emergence in recent years of such regional organizations as the Organization of African Unity, the Association of Southeast Asian Nations, and the European Economic Community. Political leaders in various parts of the world speak routinely (if sometimes wistfully) of "Arab unity," the "African road to socialism," and the "Confucian path to economic development."

A second challenge is a practical one. University students today are all too often not well informed about the distinctive character of civilizations such as China, India, Africa, and Arab and Islamic countries. Without sufficient exposure to the historical evolution of such societies, students assume very readily that the peoples in these countries have had historical experiences similar to their own and respond to various stimuli in a similar fashion to those living in Western Europe or North America. If it is a mistake to ignore the forces that link us together, it is equally erroneous to underestimate the factors that continue to divide us and to differentiate us into a world of diverse peoples.

As a response to this challenge, this book has adopted an overall global approach to the history of the twentieth century while at the same time attempting to do justice to the distinctive character and recent development of individual civilizations and regions in the world. The opening chapters focus on issues that have a global impact, such as the Industrial Revolution, the era of imperialism, and the two world wars. Later chapters centre on individual regions of the world, although one chapter is devoted to the international implications of the Cold War and its aftermath. The book is divided into five parts, which attempt to link events in a broad comparative and global framework. The chapter in the fifth and final part examines some of the common problems of our time—including environmental pollution, the population explosion, and the future of global governance—and takes a cautious look into the future to explore how such issues might evolve in the twenty-first century.

Another issue that requires attention is the balance of the treatment of Western civilization and its counterparts in the Third World. The modern world is often viewed essentially as the history of Europe and North America, with other regions treated as appendages of the industrial countries. It is certainly true that much of the twentieth century was dominated by events in Europe and North America, and in recognition of this fact, the opening chapters focus primarily on issues related to the rise of the West, including the Industrial Revolution and the era of imperialism. In recent decades, however, other parts of the world have assumed greater importance and attention, thus restoring a global balance that had existed prior to the scientific and technological revolution that transformed the West in the eighteenth and nineteenth centuries. Later chapters examine this phenomenon, according to regions such as Africa, Asia, the Middle East, and Latin America, and the importance that they merit today.

This book seeks balance in another area as well. Many textbooks tend to simplify the content of history courses by emphasizing an intellectual or political perspective or, most recently, a social perspective, often at the expense of providing sufficient details in a chronological framework. This approach is confusing to students whose high school social studies programs have often neglected a systematic study of world history. This text attempts to write a well-balanced work in which political, economic, social, and cultural history have been integrated into a chronologically ordered synthesis. A strong narrative, linking key issues in a broad interpretive framework, is still the most effective way to present the story of the past to young minds.

To enliven the book, a number of boxed inserts—which explore key people, events, and issues within chapters—cite important works in the field. Photos and illustrations, each positioned at the appropriate place in the chapter, serve to deepen the reader's understanding of the text and spark interest and debate. Maps and "spot maps," which provide details not visible in the larger maps, have been included as a full-colour plate insert (a world map appears at the beginning of the book). Each chapter begins with a summary of key points to be addressed in the chapter. Timelines also appear at the start of the chapters, comparing chronological developments in parallel regions of the world. Each chapter includes headers in question format that act as guideposts for the reader as well as text definitions to ensure an understanding of key events and concepts. At the end of each chapter, Critical Thinking Questions are included to spark debate on and enhance reader awareness of the broader themes presented in the chapter. Finally, Suggested Readings, at the end of the book, reviews the most recent literature on each period, while referring to some of the "classic" works in the field.

An instructor's manual and PowerPoint® slides are available for instructors' use. Our book-specific website, http://www.worldhistory.nelson.com, is available for both instructors and students.

U.S. Author's Acknowledgments

I would like to express my appreciation to the reviewers who have read individual chapters and provided me with useful suggestions for improvement: George Esenwein, University of Florida; Richard Follett, Covenant College; James Harrison, Siena College; George Kosar, Bentley College/Tufts University; Arlene Lazarowitz, California State University—Long Beach; Steven Leibo, SUNY Albany; Constance McGovern, Frostburg State University; Marco Rimanelli, St. Leo University; Mark Rosenberg, Bentley College; Todd Shepard, Oklahoma University; and Dmitry Shlapentokh, Indiana University, South Bend. Jackson Spielvogel, who is coauthor of our textbook *World History* (now in its fourth edition), has been kind enough to permit me to use some of his sections in that book for the purposes of writing this one. Several of my other colleagues at Penn State—including Kumkum Chatterjee, On-cho Ng, and Arthur F. Goldschmidt—have provided me with valuable assistance in understanding parts of the world that are beyond my own area of concentration. To Clark Baxter, whose unfailing good humour, patience, and sage advice have so often eased the trauma of textbook publishing, I offer my heartfelt thanks. I am also grateful to Sue Gleason and Kim Adams of Wadsworth Publishing, and to Amy Guastello, for their assistance in bringing this project to fruition, and to John Orr of Orr Book Services for production. For this edition, ImageQuest has been helpful in obtaining images for this book.

Finally, I am eternally grateful to my wife, Yvonne V. Duiker, Ph.D. Her research and her written contributions on art, architecture, literature, and music have added sparkle to this book. Her presence at my side has added immeasurable sparkle to my life.

William J. Duiker
The Pennsylvania State University

Canadian Author's Acknowledgments

I would like to express my appreciation to the reviewers who have provided me with thoughtful suggestions for improvement, including David Gosseen, University of British Columbia; David Leeson, Laurentian University; Jeorg Schendel, University of Toronto; Daniel Perreault, Champlain College; and John R. Hinde, University of Victoria. Many thanks to my colleagues, doctors Lynne Taylor, Andrew Hunt, and Geoff Hayes, who have provided insightful comments and suggestions. My greatest appreciation goes to Dr. Whitney Lackenbauer, assistant professor at St. Jerome's University in Waterloo, for writing Chapter 10. I would like to thank my research assistants Amanda Mohammed and Wafa Mohamad. Many thanks for the excellent copy editing by Claudia Forgas. I am also grateful to two great women, Linda Sparks and Anne Williams of Thomson Nelson, who made this project truly enjoyable.

Final words of thank you go to my loving and caring husband, Dr. Mohamed Elmaraghy, and to our children. My family's thoughtfulness and support throughout this challenging project will not be forgotten. Lastly, the inspiration to write this book comes from the immeasurable injustices of the twentieth century that continue to be forgotten or discarded from mainstream discourses. I dedicate this book to the oppressed seeking the ultimate form of self-respect and dignity: self-determination.

Bessma Momani
University of Waterloo

About the Authors

William J. Duiker is liberal arts professor emeritus of East Asian Studies at The Pennsylvania State University. A former U.S. diplomat with service in Taiwan, South Vietnam, and Washington, D.C., he received his doctorate in Far Eastern History from Georgetown University in 1968, where his dissertation dealt with the Chinese educator and reformer Cai Yuanpei. At Penn State, Dr. Duiker has written extensively on the history of Vietnam and modern China, including the widely acclaimed *The Communist Road to Power in Vietnam* (revised edition, Westview Press, 1996), which was selected for a Choice Outstanding Academic Book Award in 1982–83 and 1996–97. Other recent books are *China and Vietnam: The Roots of Conflict* (Berkley, 1987), *Sacred War: Nationalism and Revolution in a Divided Vietnam* (McGraw-Hill, 1995), and *Ho Chi Minh* (Hyperion, 2000). While his research specialization is in the field of nationalism and Asian revolutions, his intellectual interests are considerably more diverse. Dr. Duiker has travelled widely and has taught courses on the History of Communism and Non-Western Civilizations at Penn State, where he was awarded a Faculty Scholar Medal for Outstanding Achievement in the spring of 1996.

Bessma Momani is assistant professor in the departments of History and Political Science at the University of Waterloo, where she teaches courses on Twentieth-Century Non-Western History, Middle East Politics and History, and International Organizations. Dr. Momani is also a fellow at the Centre for International Governance and Innovation, a Canadian research centre examining global governance and multilateralism, located in Waterloo. Her areas of research specialization include Middle East economic liberalization, and International Monetary Fund (IMF) decision making, reform, and conditionality. Dr. Momani has a B.A. in Political Science from the University of Toronto, an M.A. in International Development Studies from the University of Guelph, and a Ph.D. in Political Science from the University of Western Ontario. Recently, she published *IMF-Egyptian Negotiations* (American University of Cairo Press, 2006). She has also published journal articles on international affairs in *Global Society, Asian Affairs, Review of International Political Economy, New Political Economy,* and the *Journal of International Relations and Development*. These articles have examined, among other things, IMF recruitment, the American politicization of the IMF, IMF organizational culture, Pakistan in the war on terrorism, and Argentina's financial crisis. In addition, Dr. Momani has examined Middle East economic liberalization and integration, and recently published an article on the challenges of advancing Egyptian trade and economic liberalization in the *Middle East Review of International Affairs* (2003). Currently, she is examining the economic integration of the Gulf Cooperation Council in the Persian Gulf, Turkish economic liberalization, and the American-sponsored Middle East Free Trade Area Initiative.

New World in the Making

Copyright © Cam Cardow, Syndicam Productions

Chapter 1

The Changing Social and Political Order

The Industrial Revolution was unquestionably one of the most important factors in laying the foundation of the modern world. It not only transformed the economic means of production and distribution, but also altered the political systems, the social institutions and values, and the intellectual and cultural life of all the societies that it touched. The impact has been not only massive but controversial as well. Where proponents have alluded to the enormous material and technological benefits that industrialization has brought in its wake, critics have pointed out the high costs involved, from growing economic inequality to the dehumanization of everyday life.

At the conclusion of this chapter, you will be able to

- explain how discoveries in science and technology changed economic production;
- identify the modernizing values, attitudes, and ideas that changed social and political organization throughout the world;
- describe the contemporary origins of two dominant paradigms of the twentieth century: liberalism and socialism;
- explain how transitions in the world of art reflected social and value changes.

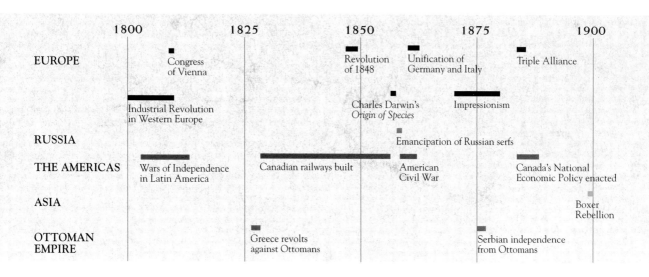

	1800	1825	1850	1875	1900
EUROPE	Congress of Vienna		Revolution of 1848	Unification of Germany and Italy	Triple Alliance
	Industrial Revolution in Western Europe		Charles Darwin's *Origin of Species*	Impressionism	
RUSSIA				Emancipation of Russian serfs	
THE AMERICAS	Wars of Independence in Latin America	Canadian railways built	American Civil War		Canada's National Economic Policy enacted
ASIA					Boxer Rebellion
OTTOMAN EMPIRE		Greece revolts against Ottomans		Serbian independence from Ottomans	

THE SPREAD OF THE INDUSTRIAL REVOLUTION

The **Industrial Revolution** began in England in the late eighteenth century and gradually spread to the European continent in the next several decades. Why England was the site of this momentous event has been the subject of debate among historians for many years. A number of factors certainly contributed to the transformation of British society from a predominantly agricultural to an industrial and commercial economy: improvements in agriculture, which enabled society to provide more food for less labour; abundant natural resources, including coal and iron, needed in the manufacturing process; and an increase in available capital, based on the growth of exports to foreign markets.

> The **Industrial Revolution** refers to the transition from a mainly rural and handicraft society to an urban one in which machinery was used to manufacture goods. The revolution started primarily in the second half of the eighteenth century in England and spread throughout most of Western Europe and abroad. The cultural, social, and economic effects of rapid industrialization put great strain on many people and on governments.

England benefited from its growing empire, which provided a source of cheap raw materials and opportunities for investment not available in the British Isles. Last but not least, technological inventions, such as the flying shuttle, the spinning jenny, and the power loom, led to significant increases in textile production, while the steam engine became a tireless source of power that depended solely on coal, a substance that at the time seemed to be available in unlimited quantities. By the mid-nineteenth century, Great Britain had become the world's first and richest industrial nation, the "workshop, banker, and trader of the world."

By the turn of the nineteenth century, industrialization had begun to spread to the continent of Europe, where it took a different path than had been followed in Great Britain. Governments on the Continent were accustomed to playing a major role in economic affairs and continued to do so as the Industrial Revolution got under way, subsidizing inventors, providing incentives to factory owners, and improving the transportation network. By 1850, a network of iron rails had spread across much of Western and Central Europe, while sea routes were improved by the deepening and widening of rivers and canals.

Across the Atlantic Ocean, the United States experienced the first stages of its Industrial Revolution in the first half of the nineteenth century. In 1800, America was still a predominantly agrarian society, as 85 percent of all workers were farmers. Sixty years later, only 50 percent of all workers were farmers, while the total population had grown from 5 to 30 million people. The Americans were also innovating by saving labour, an important consideration in a society that had few skilled artisans. The American company Harpers Ferry Arsenal, for example, built muskets with interchangeable parts. Because all of the individual parts of various musket models were identical (for example, all the triggers were the same), the final product could be put together quickly and easily.

In the United States, the lack of a good system of internal transportation initially seemed to limit economic development by making the transport of goods prohibitively expensive. This difficulty was gradually remedied, however. Thousands of miles of roads and canals were built linking east and west. The steamboat facilitated transportation on the Great Lakes, Atlantic coastal waters, and rivers. Most important of all in the development of an American transportation system was the railroad. Beginning in 1830, 160 kilometres of railroad tracks were laid, and this increased to more than 44 000 kilometres in 30 years. This transportation revolution turned the United States into a single massive market for the manufactured goods of the Northeast, the early centre of American industrialization, and by 1860, the United States was well on its way to being an industrial nation.

In Canada, railways also spurred and assisted industrial development, but laying down a transcontinental railway took on a nationalist purpose: to facilitate confederation. Under Prime Minister Sir John A. Macdonald's (1815–91) plan to unite the British colonies, a national railway system would connect Canada from British Columbia to the Maritimes. Ultimately, Macdonald wanted to secure Canada's political and economic position with regard to the United States by diversifying its economy through trade among provinces and with Great Britain—all in an effort to balance the growing economic hegemony of the American economy. Macdonald argued that a railway system would allow Western Canadian farmers to provide food for the growing number of industrial workers in Central Canada; in turn, Central Canadians would provide Western Canada with agricultural equipment. Macdonald envisioned that Canada would overcome divided terrain through the construction of a railway system, supporting an economy independent of the United States. Macdonald's vision of a united country would be realized through Confederation in 1867 and through the completion of the Canadian Pacific Railway, which connected Canada from east to west, in British Columbia in 1885.

THE SECOND INDUSTRIAL REVOLUTION

Throughout the Western world, new sources of energy and new technological achievements propelled a second Industrial Revolution that transformed the human environment and led people to believe that their material progress would improve world conditions and solve many human problems.

What New Products and New Patterns Shaped the Second Industrial Revolution?

After 1870, the first major change in industrial development was the substitution of steel for iron. New methods for rolling and shaping steel made it useful in the construction of lighter, smaller, and faster machines and engines as well as for railways, shipbuilding, and armaments. Steel also paved the way for the building of the first skyscraper, a development that would eventually transform the shape of many cities. In 1860, Great Britain, France, Germany, and Belgium produced 113 400 tonnes of steel; by 1913, the total was 29 million tonnes.

Electricity was a major new form of energy that was easily converted into other forms of energy, such as heat, light, and motion, and moved relatively effortlessly through space by means of transmitting wires. The first commercial-type electrical generators were not developed until the 1870s. By 1910, hydroelectric power stations and coal-fired steam-generating plants enabled entire districts of homes, shops, and industrial factories to be tied into a common source of power. Electricity spawned a whole series of new products. For example, the invention of the light bulb illuminated homes and cities.

A revolution in communications soon followed when Canada's Alexander Graham Bell (1847–1922) invented the telephone. In 1876, Bell made the first long distance telephone call between Brantford and Paris, Ontario. The invention of the telephone caused much debate between Canada and the United States as to where the telephone was actually invented, since the principles of the telephone were patented in Boston.

A generation later, Guglielmo Marconi sent the first radio waves across the Atlantic in 1901. After electricity was used for lighting and communication, it was eventually put to use in transportation and factory production. By the 1880s, streetcars and subways had appeared in major European cities. In factories, conveyor belts, cranes, machines, and machine tools could all be powered by electricity and located anywhere.

The development of the internal combustion engine had a similar modernizing effect. The processing of liquid fuels, like petroleum, made possible the widespread use of the internal combustion engine as a source of power in transportation. An oil-fired engine was made in 1897, by a German engineer named Dr. Rudolph Diesel, and by 1902, ships of the Hamburg-Amerika Line had

switched from coal to oil. By the beginning of the twentieth century, some naval fleets had been converted to oil burners as well.

The internal combustion engine, first honed by Belgian engineer Jean Joseph Etienne Lenoir and later improved by German-born Nicolaus August Otto, gave rise to the automobile and the airplane. In 1900, world production stood at 9000 cars; by 1906, Americans had overtaken the initial lead of the French. Henry Ford revolutionized the automotive industry with the mass production of the **Model T** car. By 1916, Ford's factories were producing 735 000 cars a year. In the meantime, air transportation had emerged with the Zeppelin airship in 1900. In 1903, the American Wright brothers made the first flight in a fixed-wing plane powered by a gasoline engine. It took World War I, however, to stimulate the aircraft industry, and it was not until 1919 that the first regular passenger air service was established.

> The **Model T** was an automobile designed by Henry Ford and mass-produced by Ford from 1908 to 1927 via the assembly line. Ford Company produced 15 million automobiles with a Model T engine for the masses.

The growth of industrial production depended on the development of markets for the sale of manufactured goods. Competition for foreign markets was keen, and by 1870, European countries were increasingly compelled to focus on promoting domestic demand. Between 1850 and 1900, real wages had increased in Great Britain by two-thirds and in Germany by one-third. A decline in the cost of food combined with lower prices for manufactured goods because of reduced production and transportation costs made it easier for Europeans to buy consumer products. In the cities, new methods for retail distribution—in particular, the department store—were used to expand sales of a whole new range of consumer goods made possible by the development of the steel and electric industries. The desire to own sewing machines, clocks, bicycles, electric lights, and typewriters was rapidly generating a new consumer value-system that has become a crucial part of the modern capitalist economy.

Meanwhile, increased competition for foreign markets and the growing importance of domestic demand led to a negative reaction to free trade. Despite nearly 50 years of free trade across Europe, by the 1870s, Europeans were returning to the practice of tariff protection in order to insulate domestic markets and promote products of national industries. The flow of cheap grain to Europe from the United States, due in part to its good harvests and budding railroad system, caused much concern for many European countries. Countries such as Austria-Hungary, Romania,

Portugal, and Greece had economies that still relied heavily on agriculture; therefore, they quickly adopted high tariffs and put protectionist policies in place. In fact, most of Europe sought to counter the American influx of grain on the world market—and Germany, then known for its strict protectionist policies, was no exception. At the same time, cartels were being formed to decrease internal competition. In a cartel, independent enterprises worked together to control prices and fix production quotas, thereby restraining the kind of competition that led to reduced prices. Cartels were especially strong in Germany, where banks moved to protect their investments by eliminating the so-called anarchy of competition. Germany's Rhenish-Westphalian Coal Syndicate, for example, controlled 98 percent of Germany's coal production by 1904.

The Eiffel Tower of Paris. When it was completed for the Paris World's Fair in 1889, the Eiffel Tower became, at 324 metres, the tallest monument in the world. The tower symbolized the triumph of the Industrial Revolution and machine-age capitalism. Constructed of wrought iron and comprising more than 2.5 million rivet holes, the structure was completed in two years and was paid for entirely by the builder himself, the engineer Gustave Eiffel.

Courtesy of William J. Duiker

The formation of cartels was paralleled by a move toward ever-larger manufacturing plants, especially in the iron and steel, machinery, heavy electric equipment, and chemical industries. Larger industrial plants led to pressure for greater production efficiency while competition led to demands for greater savings and profits. The result was a desire to streamline or rationalize production as much as possible. The development of precision tools enabled manufacturers to produce interchangeable parts, which in turn led to the creation of the production assembly line. In the second half of the nineteenth century, it was primarily used in manufacturing consumer goods, such as sewing machines, typewriters, bicycles, and finally, automobiles.

By 1900, many parts of Western and Central Europe had entered a new era, characterized by rising industrial production and material prosperity. The rest of Europe to the south and east, however, was little industrialized. Southern Italy, most of Austria-Hungary, Spain, Portugal, the Balkan kingdoms, and Russia were still largely agricultural, producing food and raw materials for the more industrialized parts of Europe. The presence of Romanian oil, Greek olive oil, and Serbian pigs and prunes in Western Europe served as reminders of an economic division of Europe that continued well into the twentieth century.

How Did a Capitalist World Economy Evolve?

The economic developments of the late nineteenth century, combined with the transportation revolution that saw the growth of marine transport, railroads, and the legacies of empires and colonial stakes, fostered a capitalist world economy. By 1900, Europeans were receiving beef and wool from Argentina and Australia, coffee from Brazil, nitrates from Chile, iron ore from Algeria, and sugar from Indonesia. Europeans were also invested abroad to develop railways, mines, electric power plants, and banks. High rates of return and furthering colonial and economic control of foreign lands provided plenty of incentive. Of course, foreign countries also provided markets for the surplus manufactured goods of Europe. With Europe's financial capital, industries, and military might, the continent dominated the capitalist world economy by the beginning of the nineteenth century.

Trade among various regions of the world, of course, had taken place for centuries. As early as the first millennium C.E., China and the Roman Empire had exchanged goods through intermediaries on both the maritime route across the Indian Ocean and over the famous Silk Road through the deserts of central Asia. Trade across the Eurasian supercontinent increased with the rise of the ninth-century Arab empire in the Middle East and then reached a peak during the thirteenth and fourteenth centuries, when the

Mongol Empire stretched from the shores of the Pacific to the borders of Eastern Europe. Trade routes also snaked across the Sahara to central and western Africa and along the eastern coast from the Red Sea to the island of Madagascar.

Not until the beginning of the sixteenth century, however, was a truly global economy created, when Portuguese adventurer Ferdinand Magellan sailed around the world. With the establishment of contacts between the Old World and the societies in the Western Hemisphere, trade now literally spanned the globe. New crops from the Americas, such as corn, potatoes, and manioc, entered the world market and changed eating habits and social patterns as far away as China. Tobacco from the New World and coffee and tea from Asia became the new craze in affluent circles in Europe and the Middle East.

In the view of some contemporary historians, it was this trading process that enabled Europe to launch the economic and technological advances that led to the Industrial Revolution. According to historian Immanuel Wallerstein, one of the leading proponents of this **world system theory**, the global trade patterns dominated by European countries in the core benefited European economic development while disadvantaging non-European countries in the periphery. This unequal trading pattern between the core and periphery determined future capitalist relations between the North and South. Expropriated capital, in the legitimized term of profits, from the East Asian spice trade and Latin American gold and silver, flowed into Northern European state treasuries and the pockets of private traders in London, Paris, and Amsterdam. The periphery's subordinate role in the global trading system and the core's heightened wealth and power were laying the groundwork for future capitalist relations.

> **World system theory** is a view that capitalism arose out of the feudal system of Europe, aiding in the rise of Western Europe to world supremacy between 1450 and 1670. Prosperous northwestern Europe was the core region of the world, benefiting the most from the capitalist world economy; the periphery represents regions of the world that exported raw materials to the core, benefiting least from the world economy.

THE STRUCTURE OF MASS SOCIETY

The new world created by the Industrial Revolution led to the emergence of a mass society by the end of the nineteenth century. A mass society meant new forms of expression for the lower classes as they benefited from the extension of voting rights, an improved standard of living, and

compulsory elementary education. But there was a price to pay. Urbanization led to overcrowding in the burgeoning cities and increasing public health problems. The development of expanded means of communication resulted in the emergence of new organizations that sought to mobilize the franchised population. A mass press, for example, swayed popular opinion by flamboyant journalistic practices.

As the number and size of cities continued to mushroom, governments by the 1880s came to the reluctant conclusion that private enterprise could not solve the housing crisis. In 1890, a British housing law empowered local town councils to construct cheap housing for the working classes. London and Liverpool were the first communities to take advantage of their new powers. Similar activity had been set in motion in Germany by 1900. Everywhere, however, these lukewarm measures failed to do much to meet the real housing needs of the working classes. Nevertheless, the need for planning had been recognized, and in the 1920s, municipal governments moved into housing construction on a large scale. In housing, as in so many other areas of life in the late nineteenth and early twentieth centuries, the liberal principle that the government that governs least governs best (discussed later in this chapter) had proved untrue. More and more, governments were stepping into areas of activity that they would never have touched earlier.

How Did Social Classes and Movements Respond to Changes of Mass Society?

At the top of European society stood a wealthy elite, constituting 5 percent of the population but controlling between 30 and 40 percent of its wealth. This nineteenth-century elite was an amalgamation of the traditional landed aristocracy that had dominated European society for centuries and the emerging upper middle class. In the course of the nineteenth century, aristocrats coalesced with the most successful industrialists, bankers, and merchants to form a new elite.

Increasingly, aristocrats and plutocrats fused as the members of the wealthy upper middle class purchased landed estates to join the aristocrats in the pleasures of country living while the aristocrats bought lavish town houses for part-time urban life. Common bonds were also created when the sons of wealthy middle-class families were admitted to the elite schools dominated by the children of the aristocracy. This educated elite assumed leadership roles in the government and the armed forces. Marriage also served to unite the two groups. Daughters of tycoons gained titles, and aristocratic heirs gained new sources of cash.

Below the upper class was a middle level that included such traditional groups as professionals in law, medicine, and the civil service as well as moderately well-to-do industrialists and merchants. The industrial expansion of the nineteenth century also added new groups to the middle class. These newcomers included business managers and new professionals, such as office workers, engineers, architects, accountants, and chemists, who formed professional associations as the symbols of their newfound importance. At the lower end of the middle class were the small shopkeepers, traders, manufacturers, and prosperous peasants. Their chief preoccupation was the provision of goods and services for the classes above them.

The moderately prosperous and successful members of the middle classes shared a certain lifestyle, one whose values tended to dominate much of nineteenth-century society. They were especially active in preaching their worldview to their children and to the upper and lower classes. This was especially evident in Victorian Britain, often considered a model of middle-class society. It was the European middle classes who accepted and professed the importance of progress and science. They believed in hard work, which they viewed as the primary human good, open to everyone and guaranteed to have positive results. They also believed in the good conduct associated with traditional Christian morality.

In Canada, the transmission of these British middle-class social values came from British migrants. Often, British migrants were professionals such as merchants and officials who had political and social power. Also, after the upheaval in the American 13 colonies, almost 40 000 to 50 000 settlers loyal to the British flag, termed **Loyalists**, came to Canada. These settlers intended on staying true to British values in all aspects of daily life and were instrumental in establishing the long-lasting British values in Canadian culture, values stemming from traditional Christian teachings of morality. It was believed by many of Canada's elite at the time that the superiority of Anglo-Saxon values would lead Canada to the same greatness of the British Empire.

> **Loyalists** were Americans who strongly supported the British monarchy and fled to Canada during the American Revolution to remain under British dominion.

At the time, such **Victorian values** were often scrutinized by members of the economic and intellectual elite, and in later years, it became commonplace for observers to mock the Victorian era—the years of the long reign of Queen Victoria in Great Britain—for its vulgar materialism, its cultural and artistic backwardness, and its conformist values. As the historian Peter Gay has recently shown, however, this harsh portrayal of the "bourgeois" character of the age distorts the reality of an era of complexity and contradiction, with diverse forces interacting to lay the foundations of the modern world.

> **Victorian values** refer to morals and principles that encouraged hard work, loyalty, and religious virtue which were commonly adhered to by people who lived during Queen Victoria's reign (1837–1901).

The working classes constituted almost 80 percent of the population of Europe. In rural areas, many of these people were landholding peasants, agricultural labourers, and sharecroppers, especially in Eastern Europe. Only about 10 percent of the British population worked in agriculture, however; in Germany, the figure was 25 percent.

There was no homogeneous urban working class. At the top were skilled artisans in such traditional handicraft trades as cabinet making, printing, and jewellery making. The second Industrial Revolution, however, also brought new entrants into the group of highly skilled workers, including machine-tool specialists, shipbuilders, and metalworkers. Many skilled workers attempted to pattern themselves after the middle class by seeking good housing and educating their children.

Semiskilled labourers, including such people as carpenters, bricklayers, and many factory workers, earned wages that were about two-thirds of those of highly skilled workers. At the bottom of the hierarchy stood the largest group of workers, the unskilled labourers. They included day labourers, who worked irregularly for very low wages, and large numbers of domestic servants. One of every seven employed persons in Great Britain in 1900 was a domestic servant.

Some urban workers did experience a betterment in the material conditions of their lives after 1870. A rise in real wages, accompanied by a decline in many consumer costs, especially in the 1880s and 1890s, made it possible for workers to buy more than just food and housing. Workers' budgets now included money for more clothes and even leisure at the same time that strikes and labour organizations were fighting for 10-hour days and Saturday afternoons off. The combination of more income and more free time produced whole new patterns of mass consumption.

Among the most exploitative aspects of the era, however, was the widespread practice of child labour. Working conditions for underage workers were often abysmal. According to a report commissioned in 1832 to inquire into the conditions of child factory workers in Great Britain, innocent children as young as six years of age began work before dawn. Those who were drowsy or fell asleep were hit on the head, doused with cold water, strapped to a chair, or flogged with a stick.

The position of women during the Industrial Revolution was also changing. During much of the nineteenth century, many women adhered to the ideal of

Discipline in the New Factories. Working conditions in the new factories were often degrading and exploitative. This image presents a foreman with a whip ready to bring in line female workers who fell asleep from over exhaustion. This structured factory was among the "better" working conditions compared with the slum-like sweatshops that spawned in the backyards of people's homes throughout England.

femininity popularized by writers and poets. But, the reality was somewhat different. Under the impact of the second Industrial Revolution, which created a wide variety of service and white-collar jobs, women began to work as clerks, typists, secretaries, and salesclerks. Compulsory education opened the door to new opportunities in the medical and teaching professions. In some countries in Western Europe, women's legal rights increased. Still, most women remained confined to their traditional roles of homemaking and child rearing. The less fortunate were still compelled to undertake marginal work at home as domestic servants or as pieceworkers in sweatshops.

Some improvements occurred as the result of the rise of Europe's first feminist movement. The movement had its origins in the social uprising of the French Revolution, when some women advocated equality for women based on the doctrine of natural rights. In the 1830s, a number of **maternal feminists** sought improvements for women by focusing on family and marriage laws to strengthen the property rights of wives and enhance their ability to secure a divorce. Later in the century, attention shifted to the issue of equal political rights for women. Many of these **liberal feminists** believed that the right to vote and participate in the workforce was the key to all other reforms to improve the position of women.

> **Maternal feminists** advocated suffrage for women based on the belief that women had a vested interest in the fabric of a family and should therefore play a role in public policy. In contrast, **liberal feminists** argued that the oppression of women in society was a result of its patriarchal nature and wanted greater female involvement in the workplace and government.

The British women's movement was the most vocal and active in Europe, but it was divided over tactics. Moderates believed that women must demonstrate that they would use political power responsibly if they wanted Parliament to grant them the right to vote. Another group, however, favoured a more radical approach. Emmeline Pankhurst (1858–1928) and her daughters, Christabel and Sylvia, in 1903 founded the Women's Social and Political Union, which enrolled mostly middle- and upper-class women. Pankhurst's organization realized the value of the media and used unusual publicity stunts to call attention to its insistence on winning women the right to vote and other demands. Its members pelted government officials with eggs, chained themselves to lampposts, smashed the windows of department stores on fashionable shopping streets, burned railroad cars, and went on hunger strikes in jail.

In Canada, women founded organizations like the Woman's Christian Temperance Union (WCTU) to fight for equality. The WCTU, founded in 1874 and made national in 1885, had suffrage as its main objective. Early Canadian feminists like Nellie McClung (1873–1951), known as "Our Nell" to those who supported her and "the Holy Terror" to those who opposed her, served as a leading member of the WCTU. Unlike some of the radical measures taken up by the feminist movement in Great Britain, women in Canada sought to secure the vote via social satire, which poked fun at the irrationality of not granting women the right to vote. In one such example, McClung staged a mock Parliament comprised of women discussing the upheaval that might be caused from granting Canadian men the vote.

Before World War I, demands for women's rights were being heard throughout Europe and North America, although only in Norway, some American states, Australia, and New Zealand did women actually receive the right to vote before 1914. In Canada and throughout the Western world, it would take the dramatic upheaval of World War I before male-dominated governments acknowledged this basic right.

THE CHANGING POLITICAL ORDER

While the Industrial Revolution shook the economic and social foundations of European society, similar revolutionary developments were reshaping the political map of many parts of the world. These developments were the product of a variety of factors, including not only the Industrial Revolution itself but also the Renaissance, the Enlightenment, and the French Revolution at the end of the eighteenth century. The influence of these new forces resulted in a redefinition of political conditions. The conservative order—based on the principle of hereditary monarchy and the existence of great multinational states such as Austria-Hungary, Russia, the Ottoman Empire, and, to a lesser extent, China—had emerged intact after the Industrial Revolution. However, by end of the eighteenth century, the conservative order had come under attack along a wide front. Arraigned against the conservative forces were a set of new, challenging Western political ideas.

What Are the Philosophical Roots of Liberalism and Nationalism?

One of these new political ideas was **liberalism**. Liberalism owed much to the Enlightenment of the eighteenth

century and the American and French Revolutions that erupted at the end of that century. It became increasingly important as the Industrial Revolution progressed because the emerging middle class largely adopted the idea as its own. Opinions diverged among people classified as Liberals, but all began with a common denominator, a conviction that in both economic and political terms, people should be as free from restraint as possible. Economic liberalism, also known as **classical economics**, was based on economist and philosopher Adam Smith's (1723–90) tenet of the invisible hand or laissez faire—the belief that the state should not interfere in the free play of natural economic forces, especially supply and demand. Political liberalism was based on the concept of a constitutional monarchy or constitutional state, with limits on the powers of government and a written charter to protect the basic civil rights of people. Nineteenth-century Liberals, however, were not egalitarian in the modern sense. Although they held that people were entitled to equal civil rights, the right to vote and to hold office would be open only to men who met certain property qualifications.

Liberalism is a belief, philosophy, or movement that advocates the pursuit of individual freedom as a means of progressing society as a whole.

Classical economics is an economic theory founded by Adam Smith which advocates private property, free markets, and the principle of competition. Smith argued that letting the market be guided by the invisible hand of people's natural behaviour would in turn result in the common benefit for all.

Nationalism was an even more powerful ideology for change in the nineteenth century. The idea arose out of an awareness of being part of a community that has common institutions, traditions, language, and customs. In some cases, that sense of identity was based on shared ethnic or linguistic characteristics. In others, it was a consequence of a common commitment to a particular religion or culture. Such a community came to be called a *nation,* and the primary political loyalty of individuals would be to the nation rather than to a dynasty or a city-state or some other political unit. Nationalism did not become a popular force for change until the French Revolution, when the concept arose that governments or states should coincide with nationalities. Thus a divided people such as the Germans wanted national unity in a German nation-state with one central government. Subject peoples, such as the Hungarians, wanted national **self-determination**, or the right to establish their own autonomy rather than be subject to a German minority in a multinational empire.

Self-determination is a doctrine that proposes people of a given territory or of a particular nationality should have the right to determine their own government and political future.

Liberalism and nationalism began to exert a measurable impact on the European political scene in the 1830s, when a revolt led by progressive forces installed a constitutional monarchy in France, and nationalist uprisings, often given active support by liberal forces, took place in Belgium (which was then attached to the Dutch Republic), in Italy, and in Poland (then part of the Russian Empire). Only the Belgians were successful, as Russian forces crushed the Poles' attempt to liberate themselves from foreign domination, while Austrian troops intervened in Italy to uphold reactionary governments in a number of Italian states.

In the spring of 1848, a new series of uprisings against established authority broke out in several countries in Central and Western Europe. The most effective was in France, where an uprising centred in Paris overthrew the so-called bourgeois monarchy of King Louis Philippe and briefly brought to power a new republic composed of an alliance of workers, intellectuals, and progressive representatives of the urban middle class.

Within a few months, however, it became clear that optimism about the imminence of a new order in Europe had not been justified. In France, the shaky alliance between workers and the urban bourgeoisie was ruptured when workers' groups and their representatives in the government began to demand extensive social reforms to provide guaranteed benefits to the poor. Moderates, frightened by rising political tensions in Paris, resisted such demands. Facing the spectre of class war, the French nation drew back and welcomed the rise to power of Louis Napoleon (1808–73), a nephew of the great Napoleon Bonaparte. Within three years, he declared himself Emperor Napoleon III.

Why Did Liberalism and Nationalism Fail in Germany and Italy?

Elsewhere in Europe—in Germany, in the Habsburg Empire, and in Italy—popular uprisings failed to unseat autocratic monarchs and destroy the existing conservative political order. But the rising force of nationalism was not to be stopped. Italy, long divided into separate kingdoms, was finally united in the early 1860s. Germany followed a few years later. Unfortunately, the rise of nation-states in Central Europe did not herald the onset of liberal principles or greater stability. To the contrary, it inaugurated a period of heightened tensions as an increasingly aggressive Germany

began to dominate the politics of Europe. In 1870, German Prime Minister Otto von Bismarck (1815–98) provoked a war with France. After the latter's defeat, a new German Empire was declared in the Hall of Mirrors at the Palace of Versailles, just outside Paris.

Many German Liberals were initially delighted at the unification of their country after centuries of division. But they were soon to discover that the new German Empire would not usher in a new era of peace and freedom. Under Prussian leadership, the new state quickly proclaimed the superiority of authoritarian and militaristic values and abandoned the principles of liberalism and constitutional government. Nationalism had become a double-edged sword, as advocates of a greater Germany began to impact domestic politics.

Liberal principles made similarly little headway elsewhere in Central and Eastern Europe. After the transformation of the Habsburg Empire into the dual monarchy of Austria-Hungary in 1867, the Austrian part received a constitution that theoretically recognized the equality of the nationalities and established a parliamentary system with the principle of ministerial responsibility.

But the problem of reconciling the interests of the various nationalities remained a difficult one. The German minority that governed Austria felt increasingly threatened by the Czechs, Poles, and other Slavic groups within the empire. The granting of universal male suffrage in 1907 served only to exacerbate the problem when nationalities that had played no role in the government now agitated in the parliament for autonomy. This led prime ministers after 1900 to ignore the parliament and rely increasingly on imperial emergency decrees to govern. On the eve of World War I, the Austro-Hungarian Empire was far from solving its minorities problem (see Map 1.1, Plate 1).

Why Was a Social Revolution and Not Liberalism in the Air in Russia?

To the east, in the vast Russian Empire, neither the Industrial Revolution nor the European Enlightenment had exerted much impact. At the beginning of the nineteenth century, Russia was overwhelmingly rural, agricultural, and autocratic. The Russian tsar was still regarded as a divine-right monarch with unlimited power, although the physical extent of the empire made the claim impracticable. For centuries, Russian farmers had groaned under the yoke of an oppressive feudal system that tied the peasant to poverty conditions and the legal status of a serf under the authority of a manor lord. An enlightened tsar, Alexander II (r. 1855–81), had emancipated the serfs in 1861, but under conditions that left most Russian peasants still poor and with little hope for social or economic betterment. In desperation, the ***muzhik*** ("peasants") periodically lashed out at their oppressors in sporadic rebellions, but all such uprisings were crushed with brutal efficiency by the tsarist regime.

Muzhik is the Russian word for "peasant."

In Western Europe, as we have seen, it was the urban middle class that took the lead in the struggle for change. In Russia, the middle class was still small in size and lacking in mobilization. A few, however, had travelled to the West and were determined to import Western values and institutions into the Russian nation. At mid-century, a few progressive intellectuals went out to the villages to mobilize their rural brethren on the need for change. Known as *narodniks* (from the Russian term *narod,* for "people" or "nation"), they sought to energize the peasantry as a force for the transformation of Russian society. Although many saw the answer to Russian problems in the Western European model, others insisted on the uniqueness of the Russian experience and sought to bring about a revitalization of the country on the basis of the communal traditions of their villages.

For the most part, such efforts achieved little. The *muzhik* was resistant to change and suspicious of outsiders. In desperation, some radical intellectuals turned to terrorism in the hope that assassinations of public officials would spark tsarist repression, thus demonstrating the brutality of the system and galvanizing popular anger. Chief among such groups was the Narodnaya Volya, Russian for "the People's Will," a terrorist organization that carried out the assassination of Tsar Alexander II in 1881.

The assassination of Alexander II convinced his son and successor, Alexander III (r. 1881–94), that reform had been a mistake, and he quickly returned to the repressive measures of earlier tsars. When Alexander III died, his weak son and successor, Nicholas II (r. 1894–1917), began his rule armed with his father's conviction that the absolute power of the tsars should be preserved.

But it was too late, for conditions were changing. Although industrialization came late to Russia, it progressed rapidly after 1890, especially with the assistance of foreign investment capital. By 1900, Russia had become the fourth-largest producer of steel, behind the United States, Germany, and Great Britain. At the same time, Russia was turning out half of the world's production of oil. Conditions for the working class, however, were abysmal, and opposition to the tsarist regime from workers, peasants, and intellectuals finally exploded into revolt in 1905. Facing an exhaustive war with Japan in Asia, Tsar Nicholas reluctantly granted civil liberties and agreed to create a legislative assembly, the duma, elected directly by a broad franchise.

But real constitutional monarchy proved short-lived. By 1907, the tsar had curtailed the power of the duma and fell back on the army and the bureaucracy to rule Russia.

What Brought Down the Ottoman Empire and Evoked Nationalism in the Balkans?

Like the Austro-Hungarian Empire, the **Ottoman Empire** was threatened by the rising nationalist aspirations of its subject peoples. Beginning in the fourteenth century, the Ottoman Turks had expanded from their base in the Anatolian peninsula and expanded into the Balkans, southern Russia, and along the northern coast of Africa. Soon they controlled the entire eastern half of the Mediterranean Sea. But by the nineteenth century, corruption and inefficiency had gradually weakened the once powerful empire so that only the interference of the great European powers, who were fearful of each other's designs in the area, kept it alive.

The **Ottoman Empire** was an empire controlled from present-day Turkey, geographically stretching from southeastern Europe through to the Middle East and to parts of North Africa. The Muslim Ottoman Turks ruled from the thirteenth century until the end of World War I.

But the emotional appeal of nationhood gradually began to make inroads among the various ethnic and linguistic groups in southeastern Europe. In the course of the nineteenth century, the Balkan provinces of the Ottoman Empire began to gain their freedom, although the intense rivalry in the region between Austria-Hungary and Russia complicated the process. Serbia had already received a large degree of autonomy in 1829, although it remained a province of the Ottoman Empire until 1878. Greece became an independent kingdom in 1830 after a successful revolt. By the Treaty of Adrianople in 1829, Russia received a protectorate over the principalities of Moldavia and Wallachia, but was forced to give them up after the Crimean War. In 1861, they were merged into the state of Romania. Not until Russia's defeat of the Ottoman Empire in 1878, however, was Romania recognized as completely independent, along with Serbia at the same time. Although freed from Turkish rule, Montenegro was placed under an Austrian protectorate, and Bulgaria achieved autonomous status under Russian protection. The other Balkan territories of Bosnia and Herzegovina were placed under Austrian protection; Austria could occupy but not annex them. Despite these gains, the force of Balkan nationalism was by no means stilled.

Meanwhile, other parts of the empire began to break away from central control. In Egypt, the ambitious governor

Muhammad Ali declared the region's autonomy from Istanbul and initiated a series of reforms designed to promote economic growth and government efficiency. During the 1830s, he sought to improve agricultural production and reform the educational system, and he imported machinery and technicians from Europe to carry out the first industrial revolution on African soil. In the end, however, the effort failed, partly because Egypt's manufacturers could not compete with those of Europe and also because much of the profit from the export of cash crops went into the hands of conservative landlords.

Measures to promote industrialization elsewhere in the empire had even less success. By mid-century, a small industrial sector, built with equipment imported from Europe, took shape, and a modern system of transport and communications began to make its appearance. By the end of the century, however, the results were meagre.

What Brought Down the Old Order in China?

In 1800 the Manchu, or Qing, dynasty (1644–1911) appeared to be at the height of its power. China had experienced a long period of peace and prosperity. Its borders were secure, and its culture and intellectual achievements were the envy of the world. But a little over a century later the Manchu dynasty, the last in a series that had endured for more than 2000 years, came to an end.

Historians once assumed that the primary reason for the rapid decline and fall of the Manchu dynasty was the intense pressure applied to a proud but somewhat complacent traditional society by the modern West. There is indeed some truth in that allegation. On the surface, China had long appeared to be an unchanging society patterned after the **Confucian** vision of a Golden Age in the remote past. The ancient philosopher Confucius (551–479 B.C.E.) emphasized such qualities as obedience, hard work, rule by merit, and the subordination of the individual to the interests of the community. This, in fact, was the image presented by China's rulers, who referred constantly to tradition as a model for imperial institutions and cultural values.

> **Confucian** philosophy stresses meritocracy, piety, and loyalty. Short of being regarded as a religion, Confucian way of life has been both discredited and used by rulers of China.

During the early 1900s, China tried desperately to reform itself. The **Empress Dowager** (1835–1908), who had long resisted change, now embraced a number of reforms in education, administration, and the legal system. The venerable civil service examination system was replaced by a new educational system based on the Western model. In 1905, a commission was formed to study constitutional changes, and over the next few years, legislative assemblies were established at the provincial level. Elections for a national assembly were held in 1910.

> The **Empress Dowager**, also known as *Empress Xiaoqin Xian,* was the monarchist ruler of China during the Manchu dynasty in the nineteenth and early twentieth centuries.

Unfortunately, reforms came too late to stop the domestic explosion known as the **Boxer Rebellion**. The Boxers, so called because of the physical exercises they performed, were members of a secret society operating primarily in rural areas in North China. Provoked by a damaging drought and high levels of unemployment caused in part by foreign economic activity—the introduction of railroads and steamships, for example, undercut the livelihood of boat-workers who traditionally carried merchandise on the rivers and canals—the Boxers attacked foreign residents and besieged the foreign legation quarter in Beijing until the foreigners were rescued by an international expeditionary force in the late summer of 1900. As punishment, the foreign troops destroyed a number of temples in the capital suburbs, and the Chinese government was compelled to pay a heavy compensation to the foreign governments involved in suppressing the uprising.

> The **Boxer Rebellion** was an uprising in 1900 led by a secret society in China; the Boxers attacked foreign interests and were soon defeated by Western powers.

Such foreign intervention helped shore up the dynasty temporarily, but the emerging new provincial elite, composed of merchants, professionals, and reform-minded gentry, soon became impatient with the slow pace of political change and were disillusioned to find that the new assemblies were intended to be primarily advisory rather than legislative. The government also alienated influential elements by financing railway development projects through lucrative contracts to foreign firms rather than by turning to local investors. The reforms also had little meaning for peasants, artisans, miners, and transportation workers, whose living conditions were being eroded by rising taxes and official corruption. Rising rural unrest, as yet poorly organized and often centred on secret societies such as the Boxers, was an ominous sign of deep-seated resentment to which the dynasty would not, or could not, respond.

To China's reformist elite, such signs of social unrest were a threat to be avoided; to its tiny revolutionary movement, they were a harbinger of promise. The first physical manifestations of future revolution appeared during the last decade of the nineteenth century by the young radical Sun Yat-sen (1866–1925). Born to a peasant family in a village south of Canton, Sun was educated in Hawaii and returned to China to practise medicine. Soon he turned his full attention to the ills of Chinese society, leading bands of radicals in small-scale insurrections to attract attention.

At first, Sun's efforts yielded few positive results other than creating a symbol of resistance and the new century's first revolutionary martyrs. But at a convention in Tokyo in 1905, Sun managed to unite radical groups from across China in the so-called **Revolutionary Alliance**. The new organization's program was based on Sun's Three People's Principles: nationalism through the destruction of Manchu rule over China, democracy, and a socialist-like program to improve social and economic conditions called the "people's livelihood." Although the Revolutionary Alliance was small and relatively inexperienced, it benefited from rising popular discontent with the failure of Manchu reforms to improve conditions in China.

> The **Revolutionary Alliance**, also known as *Tongmenghui*, was a party unified by Sun Yat-sen in the early 1900s to try to overthrow the Manchu dynasty with a republican government.

Empress Dowager. **The Empress Dowager was the most powerful figure in late-nineteenth-century China. Note the long fingernails, a symbol of the privileged class, in this photograph taken in her final years.**

In October 1911, Revolutionary Alliance followers of Sun Yat-sen launched an uprising in the industrial centre of Wuhan, in central China. The dynasty was now in a state of virtual collapse: the Empress Dowager had died in 1908, one day after her nephew Guangxu; the throne was now occupied by the infant Puyi, the son of Guangxu's younger brother. Sun's party, however, had neither the military strength nor the political base necessary to seize the initiative and was forced to turn to a representative of the old order, General Yuan Shikai. A prominent figure in military circles since the beginning of the century, Yuan had been placed in charge of the imperial forces sent to suppress the rebellion, but now he abandoned the Manchus and acted on his own behalf. In negotiations with representatives of the Revolutionary Alliance, he agreed to serve as president of a new Chinese republic. The old dynasty and the age-old system it had attempted to preserve were no more.

The Revolutionary Alliance found the bulk of its support in an emerging urban middle class and set forth a program based generally on Western liberal democratic principles. That class and that program had provided the foundation for the capitalist democratic revolutions in Western Europe and North America in the late eighteenth and nineteenth centuries, but the bourgeois class in China was too small to form the basis for a new post-Confucian political order. The vast majority of the Chinese people still lived on the land. Sun had hoped to win their support with a land reform program that relied on fiscal incentives to persuade landlords to sell excess lands to their tenants, but few peasants had participated in the 1911 revolution. In effect, then, the events of 1911 were less a revolution than a collapse of the old order. Undermined by imperialism and its own internal weaknesses, the old dynasty had come to an abrupt end before new political and social forces were ready to fill the vacuum.

What China had experienced was part of a historical process that was bringing down traditional empires across the globe, both in regions threatened by Western imperialism and in Europe itself, where tsarist Russia, the Austro-Hungarian Empire, and the Ottoman Empire all came to an end within a few years of the collapse of the Manchu dynasty. The circumstances of their demise were not all the same, but all four regimes shared the responsibility for their common fate because they had failed to meet the challenges posed by the times. All had responded to the forces of industrialization and popular participation in the political process with hesitation and reluctance, and their attempts at reform were too little and too late.

LIBERALISM TRIUMPHANT

In Western Europe and North America, liberal principles experienced a better fate. By 1871, Great Britain had a functioning two-party parliamentary system. For 50 years, the Liberals and Conservatives alternated in power at regular intervals. Both were dominated by a ruling class comprising a coalition of aristocratic landowners frequently involved in industrial and financial activities and upper-middle-class merchants. And each competed with the other in supporting legislation that expanded the right to vote. Reform acts in 1867 and 1884 greatly expanded the number of adult males who could vote, and by the end of World War I, all males over 21 and women over 30 had that right.

The growth of trade unions and the emergence in 1900 of the Labour Party, which dedicated itself to workers' interests, put pressure on the Liberals, who perceived that they would have to initiate a program of social welfare or lose the support of the workers. Therefore, they abandoned the classical principles of laissez faire and enacted a series of social reforms. The National Insurance Act of 1911 provided benefits for workers in case of sickness or unemployment, to be paid for by compulsory contributions from workers, employers, and the state. Additional legislation provided a small pension for those over 70 and compensation for those injured in accidents at work.

A similar process was under way in France, where the overthrow of Napoleon III's Second Empire in 1870 led to the creation of a republican form of government. France failed, however, to develop a strong parliamentary system on the British two-party model because the existence of a dozen political parties forced the premier to depend on a coalition of parties to stay in power. The Third Republic was notorious for its changes of government. Between 1875 and 1914, there were no fewer than 50 cabinet changes; during the same period, the British had 11. Nevertheless, the government's moderation gradually encouraged more and more middle-class and peasant support, and by 1914, the Third Republic commanded the loyalty of most French people.

By 1870, Italy had emerged as a geographically united state with pretensions to great-power status. Its internal weaknesses, however, gave that claim a particularly hollow ring. Sectional differences—a poverty-stricken south and an industrializing north—weakened any sense of community. Chronic turmoil between labour and industry undermined the social fabric. The Italian government was unable to deal effectively with these problems because of the extensive corruption among government officials and the lack of stability created by ever-changing government coalitions. Abroad, Italy's pretensions to great-power status proved equally hollow when Italy became the first European power to lose a war to an African state, Ethiopia, a humiliation that later led to the costly (but successful) attempt to compensate by conquering Libya in 1911 and 1912.

How Did the United States and Canada Develop into the North American States Known Today?

Between 1860 and World War I, the United States made the shift from an agrarian to a mighty industrial nation. American heavy industry stood unchallenged in 1900. In that year, the Carnegie Steel Company alone produced more steel than Great Britain's entire steel industry. Industrialization also led to urbanization. Whereas 20 percent of Americans lived in cities in 1860, more than 40 percent did in 1900.

By 1900, the United States had become the world's richest nation and greatest industrial power. Yet serious questions remained about the social quality of American life. In 1890, the richest 9 percent of Americans owned an incredible 71 percent of all the wealth. Labour unrest over unsafe working conditions, strict work discipline, and periodic cycles of devastating unemployment led workers to organize. By the turn of the twentieth century, one national organization, the American Federation of Labor, emerged as labour's dominant voice. Its lack of real power, however, is reflected in its membership figures: in 1900, it constituted but 8.4 percent of the American industrial labour force. And part of the U.S. labour force remained almost entirely disenfranchised. Although the victory of the North in the Civil War led to the abolition of slavery, the political, economic, and social opportunities for the African American population remained limited, and racist attitudes were widespread.

During the **Progressive Era** after 1900, the reform of many features of American life became a primary issue. National progressivism was evident in the administrations of Theodore Roosevelt and Woodrow Wilson. Under Roosevelt (1901–09), the Meat Inspection Act and Pure Food and Drug Act provided for a limited degree of federal regulation of corrupt industrial practices. Roosevelt's expressed principle, "We draw the line against misconduct, not against wealth," guaranteed that public protection would have to be within limits tolerable to big corporations. Wilson (1913–21) was responsible for the creation of a graduated federal income tax and the Federal Reserve

CONFEDERATION!

THE MUCH-FATHERED YOUNGSTER.

Who Was Canada's Daddy? This caricature shows key delegates (depicted from left to right: George Brown, Sir Francis Hincks, William McDougall, and Sir John A. Macdonald) who participated in the British North American union conferences all claiming to be the father of young Confederation. Sir John A. Macdonald was chosen as the first prime minister by the Fathers of Confederation.

System, which gave the federal government a role in important economic decisions formerly made by bankers. Like many European nations, the United States was moving into policies that extended the functions of the state.

The **Progressive Era** in the United States refers to a period of time under presidents Theodore Roosevelt, William Howard Taft, and Woodrow Wilson, who promoted better labour conditions for industrial workers and created administrative agencies that could better regulate rapid political, social, and economic changes.

To the north, delegates from Nova Scotia, New Brunswick, Prince Edward Island, and the then Province of Canada (comprising what are now Ontario and Quebec) met in a series of conferences to discuss forming a British North America. The new confederation would counter American supremacy and build a loyal monarchist nation. On July 1, 1867, the Dominion of Canada consisted of Nova Scotia, New Brunswick, and the Province of Canada. To convince new provinces to join the Dominion of Canada, first Prime Minister Sir John A. Macdonald had to build a viable nation. With the addition of two more provinces—Manitoba (in

1870) and British Columbia (in 1871)—the Dominion now extended from the Atlantic Ocean to the Pacific.

In 1878, Macdonald enacted his **National Policy** to help unite the nation. First and foremost, Canada would be connected from its western front to its eastern front through a national railway system, a step toward addressing hinterland provinces' concerns regarding isolation from Canada's centre. A transcontinental railway system would allow provinces to trade among themselves rather than look to the United States as a trading partner. Second, to protect infant Canadian industries and promote east-west trade, Macdonald instituted tariffs on imported goods, primarily coming from the United States. Canada could no longer depend on trade with the United States because U.S. tariff rates were constantly fluctuating, causing instability to the Canadian economy. Lastly, a national railway system would allow Canada to successfully defend itself if it were to have ever come under attack from the United States.

> The **National Policy** was an economic policy that originated under Sir John A. Macdonald's leadership; it included high tariffs, a transcontinental railway system, and the settlement of Canada's west to strengthen and unify an independent Canada.

Prime Minister Sir Wilfrid Laurier, who became the first French Canadian prime minister in 1896, tried to liberalize some of Macdonald's protectionist trade policies. Calling for liberal reforms like **free trade** and reciprocity with the Americans proved to be a political gamble. Echoing Macdonald's National Policy, Laurier continued to add on to the construction of the railway, making it at one point in time one of the world's longest railways, with the largest number of kilometres per capita. However, he was unable to convince Canadians suspicious of the American industrial giant, and the call for free trade failed, as did his bid for re-election in 1911. Nevertheless, Laurier was able to reconcile Canada's two major linguistic groups and resolve the issue of separate schools for French Canadians. Laurier's administration also witnessed increased industrialization and successfully encouraged immigrants from Central and Eastern Europe to help populate Canada's vast territories.

> **Free trade** is a mode of trade between two or more countries without protective border tariffs.

How Did Nationalism in Europe Lead to Change in Latin America?

In the three centuries following the arrival of Christopher Columbus in the Western Hemisphere in 1492, Latin America fell increasingly into the European orbit. Portugal dominated Brazil, and Spain formed a vast empire that included most of the remainder of South America as well as Central America and the Caribbean. Almost from the beginning, it was a racially stratified society composed of European settlers, indigenous peoples, and exploited black slaves brought from Africa to work on the sugar plantations. Intermarriage among the three groups resulted in the creation of a diverse population. Latin American culture, as well, reflected a rich mixture of Iberian, African, and indigenous themes.

Until the beginning of the nineteenth century, the various Latin American societies were ruled by colonial officials appointed by monarchical governments in Europe. An additional instrument of control was the Catholic Church, which undertook a major effort to Christianize the indigenous peoples and transform them into docile and loyal subjects of the Portuguese and Spanish empires. By 1800, however, local elites, mostly descendants of Europeans who had become permanent inhabitants of the Western Hemisphere, became increasingly affected by the spirit of nationalism that had emerged after the Napoleonic era in Europe. Preceding this sense of nationalism was a growing discontent among the people of Latin America living under Portuguese and Spanish rule. In the latter part of the eighteenth century, Brazilian elites in the captaincy of Minas Gerais revolted against the colonial rule of Portugal and its economic ties to Brazil. However, these efforts were quickly thwarted and the conspirators who took part in the Minas Conspiracy were either imprisoned or sent into exile. In later years, Napoleon's invasion of both Portugal and Spain (1808) and the subsequent removal of King Ferdinand VII served to weaken the power of colonial rule in the region and aided in encouraging the elites of Brazil to petition for its independence. Fearful of the violence that had erupted in the rest of Latin America, Pedro, Portugal's prince representing the throne in Brazil, chose to declare Brazil an independent nation, allowing for its birth as a sovereign country to be a relatively peaceful one.

In the rest of Latin America, Spain expanded its economic and political control of the economies of Latin America through the Bourbon reforms, which made it difficult for local industries to compete independently on the world market. Creoles, Europeans by blood living in New Spain, grew resentful toward the Spaniards' expanded control of Latin America. The Bourbon reforms resulted in higher taxes and lower living standards, plus it stunted trade as well as the potential growth of the Spanish colonies' economy. Creoles had become the region's elite and perceived themselves as the rightful purveyors of this position in society; however, the reforms had upset their way of life. They wanted to keep their aristocratic position and maintain racial divisions and inequality throughout the region. Creoles were alarmed by the revolts in Haiti, where a violent social and political revolution put an end to slavery and all colonial dependencies on France, making it a sovereign nation in 1804. This inspired the Creoles-led Cuba and Puerto Rico to remain loyal to the colonial powers of Spain. However, many Creoles still preferred independence from Spain to the current situation. Upon Napoleon's invasion of Spain and the appointment of his brother Joseph Bonaparte to the throne in 1808, many Creoles-led Spanish colonies did not recognize Joseph and remained openly opposed to his appointment. Constitutional monarchies were established throughout the region that gave rise to the creation of local *juntas*. When King Ferdinand VII returned to the throne and attempted to return to the status quo, the Creoles-led Spanish colonies revolted, and the struggle for independence began.

> **Juntas** were autonomous bodies that attempted to govern the Spanish colonies in the name of the deposed King Ferdinand VII.

During the first quarter of the nineteenth century, Creoles launched a series of revolts that led to the eviction of the monarchical regimes and the formation of independent states from Argentina and Chile in the south to Mexico in Central America.

One of the goals of the independence movement had been to free the economies of Latin America from European control and to utilize the riches of the continent for local benefit. Unfortunately, political independence did not lead to a new era of prosperity for the people of Latin America. Most of the powerful elites in the region were landowning agribusinesses that had few incentives to industrialize. As a result, the previous trade patterns persisted, with Latin America exporting raw materials and foodstuffs (wheat and sugar) as well as tobacco and hides in exchange for manufactured goods from Europe and the United States.

With economic growth came a boom in foreign investment. Between 1870 and 1913, British investments—mostly in railroads, mining, and public utilities—grew from £85 million to £757 million, which constituted two-thirds of all foreign investment in Latin America. As Latin Americans struggled to create more balanced and nation-led economies after 1900, they concentrated on increasing industrialization, especially by building textile, food-processing, and construction materials factories.

Nevertheless, the growth of the Latin American economy came largely from the export of raw materials, and economic modernization in Latin America simply added to the growing dependence of the region on the capitalist nations of the West. Modernization was basically a surface feature of Latin American society; past patterns still largely prevailed. Rural elites dominated their estates and their rural workers. Although slavery was abolished by 1888, former slaves and their descendants were still at the bottom of society. The natives remained poverty-stricken, debt servitude was still a way of life, and the region remained economically dependent on foreigners. Despite its economic growth, Latin America was still sorely underdeveloped.

The surface prosperity that resulted from the emergence of an export economy had both social and political repercussions. One result socially was the modernization of the elites, who grew determined to pursue their vision of modern progress. Large landowners of *latifundias* increasingly sought ways to rationalize their production methods to make greater profits. As a result, cattle ranchers in Argentina and coffee barons in Brazil became more aggressive entrepreneurs.

> **Latifundias** are large estates, or *haciendas,* owned by aristocrats with social and political power who are more concerned with retaining social status than land productivity and efficiency; they are laboured by paid peasants.

Another result of the new prosperity was the growth of a small but increasingly visible middle class—lawyers, merchants, shopkeepers, entrepreneurs, schoolteachers, professors, bureaucrats, and military officers. Living mainly in the cities, these people sought education and decent incomes and increasingly valued modernization, especially with regard to industrialization and education.

As Latin American export economies boomed, the working class expanded, which in turn led to the growth of labour unions, especially after 1914. Unions often advocated the use of the general strike as an instrument for changing working conditions and wages. By and large, however, the governing elites succeeded in stifling the political influence of the working class by restricting the right to vote. The need for industrial labour also led Latin American countries to encourage European immigrants. Between 1880 and 1914, three million Europeans, primarily Italians and Spaniards, settled in Argentina. More than 100 000 Europeans, mostly Italian, Portuguese, and Spanish, arrived in Brazil each year between 1891 and 1900.

As in Europe and the United States, industrialization led to urbanization, evident in both the emergence of new cities and the rapid growth of old ones. Buenos Aires (the "Paris of South America") had 750 000 inhabitants by 1900 and two million by 1914—one-fourth of Argentina's population. By that time, urban dwellers made up 53 percent of Argentina's population overall. Brazil and Chile also witnessed a dramatic increase in the number of urban dwellers.

Latin America also experienced a political transformation after 1870. Large landowners began to take a more direct interest in national politics, sometimes expressed by a direct involvement in governing. In Argentina and Chile, for example, landholding elites controlled the governments, and although they produced constitutions similar to those of Western countries, they were careful to ensure their power by regulating voting rights.

In some countries, large landowners made use of dictators to maintain the interests of the ruling elite. Porfirio Díaz, who ruled Mexico from 1877 to 1880 and 1884 to 1911, established a conservative, centralized government with the support of the army, foreign capitalists, large landowners, and the Catholic Church, all of whom benefited from their alliance. But there were forces for change in Mexico that sought to precipitate a true social revolution.

THE RISE OF THE SOCIALIST MOVEMENT

One of the negative consequences of the Industrial Revolution was the widening disparity in the distribution of wealth. If industrialization brought increasing affluence to an emerging middle class, to millions of others it brought grinding hardship and exploitation in the form of low-paying jobs in mines or factories characterized by long working hours under horrible conditions.

Beginning in the last decades of the eighteenth century, social and political groups began to both protest working conditions and seek the means to rectify the problem. Some found the answer in intellectual arguments that envisaged a classless society based on the elimination of private property. Others prepared for an armed revolt to overthrow the ruling order and create a new society controlled by the working masses. Still others began to form trade unions to fight for improved working conditions and reasonable wages. Only one group sought to combine all of these factors into a comprehensive program to change or destroy the governing forces and create a new egalitarian society based on the concept of **scientific socialism**. The founder of that movement was Karl Marx, a German Jew who had abandoned an academic career in philosophy to take up radical political activities in Paris.

Scientific socialism refers to a social, political, and economic order that arises from an international labour revolution against the inherent exploitative nature of capitalism.

Marxism made its first appearance in 1848 with the publication of a short treatise, *The Communist Manifesto*, written by Karl Marx (1818–83) and his close collaborator, Friedrich Engels (1820–95). In the *Manifesto*, the two authors predicted the outbreak of a massive uprising that would overthrow the existing ruling class and bring to power a new revolutionary regime based on an egalitarian society void of private property (see the box on page 20).

When revolutions broke out all over Europe in the eventful year of 1848, Marx and Engels eagerly but mistakenly predicted that the uprisings would spread throughout Europe and lead to a new revolutionary regime led by workers, dispossessed bourgeois, and Communists. When that did not occur, Marx belatedly concluded that urban merchants and peasants were too conservative to support the workers and would oppose revolution once their own immediate economic demands were satisfied. As for the worker movement itself, it was still too weak to seize power and could not expect to achieve its own objectives until the workers had become politically more sophisticated and better organized. In effect, revolution would not take place in Western Europe until capitalism had "ripened," leading to a concentration of capital in the hands of a wealthy minority and an "epidemic of overproduction" because of inadequate purchasing power by the impoverished lower classes. Then a large and increasingly alienated proletariat could drive the capitalists from power and bring about a classless utopia.

For the remainder of his life, Marx acted out the logic of these conclusions. From his base in London, he undertook a massive study of the dynamics of the capitalist system, a project that resulted in the publication of the first volume of the important work *Das Kapital* ("Capital"), in 1867. In the meantime, he attempted to prepare for the future revolution by organizing the scattered radical parties throughout Europe into a cohesive revolutionary movement called the International Workingmen's Association (usually known today as the First International), that would be ready to mobilize the workers to action when the opportunity came.

Unity was short-lived. Although all members of the First International shared a common distaste for the capitalist system, some preferred to reform it from within (e.g., many of the labour groups from Great Britain), whereas others were convinced that only violent insurrection would suffice to destroy the existing ruling class (e.g., Karl Marx and the anarchists around Russian revolutionary Mikhail Bakunin). Even the radicals could not agree. Marx believed that revolution could not succeed without a core of committed Communists to organize and lead the masses; Bakunin contended that the general insurrection should be a spontaneous uprising from below. In 1871, the First International disintegrated.

While Marx was grappling with the problems of preparing for the coming revolution, European society was undergoing significant changes. The advanced capitalist

THE COMMUNIST MANIFESTO

"A spectre is haunting Europe—the spectre of Communism." With these portentous words, penned in 1848, Karl Marx began his most famous work, *The Communist Manifesto.* With the assistance of his close collaborator, Friedrich Engels, Marx wrote the pamphlet at the request of a British labour union group seeking to publicize its activities among factory workers in London.

In writing the pamphlet, Marx and Engels hoped to promote their own efforts not simply to improve working conditions in Great Britain but also to arouse popular support for a vast revolution that would sweep away the capitalist system and create a new classless society. In their view, the motive force in human history was class struggle. Marx believed that whoever owned the sources of economic wealth in a given society—whether that wealth consisted of factories, raw materials, domesticated animals, or land—controlled the state and defined the culture and beliefs of that society. When the tensions between the oppressors and the exploited masses in a given society had become too glaring, the existing ruling class would be overthrown and a new form of society would emerge. That new society would in turn be dominated by a new ruling class based on new economic relationships, leading to the growth of new tensions that would result in its own eventual destruction. Only when the oppression of one class by another came to an end in the final stage of communism would the cycle be broken and a utopian society take shape.

According to Marx and Engels, then, human society passes through several stages en route to its final resting place in the classless society of utopian communism. European society during the Middle Ages had given rise to the landholding feudal class, but feudalism was now giving way to capitalism under the Industrial Revolution, which led to the introduction of new technology and the rise of the bourgeoisie as the dominant class in society. Capitalism was itself essentially oppressive, however, because it was based on the ability of the ruling capitalist class to exploit the workers (known in Marxist parlance as the *proletariat*). According to Marx, the political system of emerging capitalism—which he called *bourgeois democracy*—was a tool of the capitalist class, for although it promised freedom and equality, it actually permitted a level of economic inequality and exploitation equal to, if different in form from, that which had existed under feudalism.

In *The Communist Manifesto,* Marx and Engels set out these ideas in simple terms accessible to understanding by unsophisticated readers. "The proletariat," it said, "will use its political supremacy to wrest, by degrees, all capital from the bourgeoisie, to centralize all instruments of production in the hands of the State, i.e., of the proletariat organized as the ruling class." Once that had been achieved, a program would be adopted to abolish private ownership of property and bring to an end the exploitation of human by human. As a result, the state itself would begin to wither away. "In place of the old bourgeois society, with its classes and class antagonisms," it concluded, "we shall have an association, in which the free development of each is the condition of the free development of all."

Source: Karl Marx and Friedrich Engels, *The Communist Manifesto,* ed. A. J. P. Taylor (New York: Viking Penguin, 1967).

states such as Great Britain, France, and the Low Countries (Belgium, Luxembourg, and the Netherlands) were gradually evolving into mature, politically stable societies in which Marx's dire predictions were not being borne out. His forecast of periodic economic crises was correct enough, but his warnings of quick concentration of capital and the complete impoverishment of labour were not happening, as capitalist societies began to regulate and reduce some of the more flagrant inequities apparent in the early stages of capitalist development. These reforms occurred because workers and their representatives had begun to use the democratic political process to create a more socially just society,

organizing labour unions and political parties to improve working conditions and enhance the role of workers in the political system. Many of these political parties were led by Marxists, who were learning that in the absence of a social revolution to bring the masses to power, the capitalist democratic system could be reformed from within to improve the working and living conditions of its constituents. In 1889, after Marx's death, several such parties (often labelled "social democratic" parties) formed the Second International, dominated by reformist elements committed to achieving socialism within the bounds of the Western parliamentary system.

Marx had also underestimated the degree to which workers in most European countries would be attracted to the appeal of nationalism. Marx had viewed nation and culture as false idols diverting the interests of the oppressed from their true concern, the struggle against the ruling class. In his view, the proletariat would throw off its chains and unite in the sacred cause of "internationalist" world revolution. In reality, workers joined peasants and urban merchants in defending the cause of the nation against its foreign enemies. A generation later, French workers would die in the trenches defending France from workers across the German border.

A historian of the late nineteenth century might have been forgiven for predicting that Marxism, as a revolutionary ideology, was in decline. To the east, however, in the vast plains and steppes of central Russia, it was about to be reborn.

TOWARD THE MODERN CONSCIOUSNESS: INTELLECTUAL AND CULTURAL DEVELOPMENTS

The physical changes that were taking place in societies exposed to the Industrial Revolution were accompanied by an equally significant transformation in the arena of culture. Before 1914, most Westerners continued to believe in the values and ideals that had been generated by the impact of the Scientific Revolution and the **Enlightenment**. The ability of human beings to improve themselves and achieve a better society seemed to be well demonstrated by a rising standard of living, urban improvements, and mass education.

> The **Enlightenment** was a movement in the seventeenth and eighteenth centuries that promoted the use of reason in re-evaluating generally accepted ideas, norms, and principles of social institutions.

Between 1870 and 1914, however, a dramatic transformation in the realm of ideas and culture challenged many of these assumptions. A new view of the physical universe called **new physics**, an alternative view of human nature called *psychoanalysis,* and a radically innovative form of literary and artistic expression called *Modernism* shattered old beliefs and opened the way to a modern consciousness. Although the real impact of many of these ideas was not felt until after World War I, they served to provoke a sense of confusion and anxiety before 1914 that would become even more pronounced after the war.

> **New physics,** such as quantum theory, demonstrated a new view on matter and the limits of Sir Isaac Newton's classical physics.

What Did New Physics Challenge?

Science was one of the chief pillars underlying the optimistic and rationalistic view of the world that many Westerners shared in the nineteenth century. Supposedly based on hard facts and cold reason, science offered a certainty of belief in the orderliness of nature that was comforting to many people for whom traditional religious beliefs no longer had much meaning. Throughout much of the nineteenth century, Westerners adhered to the mechanical conception of the universe postulated by the classical physics of Sir Isaac Newton (1642–1727). In this perspective, the universe was a giant machine in which time, space, and matter were objective realities that existed independently of the parties observing them. Matter was thought to be composed of indivisible, solid material bodies called atoms.

These views were at first seriously questioned at the end of the nineteenth century. Some scientists had discovered that certain elements such as radium and polonium spontaneously gave off rays or radiation that apparently came from within the atom itself. Atoms were therefore not hard material bodies but small worlds containing such subatomic particles as electrons and protons that behaved in a seemingly random and inexplicable fashion. Inquiry into the disintegrative process within atoms became a central theme of the new physics.

Building on this work, in 1900, a Berlin physicist, Max Planck (1858–1947), rejected the belief that a heated body radiates energy in a steady stream but maintained instead that it did so discontinuously, in irregular packets of energy that he called "quanta." The quantum theory originated by Planck raised fundamental questions about the subatomic realm of the atom. By 1900, the old view of atoms as the basic building blocks of the material world was being seriously questioned, and Newtonian physics was in trouble.

Albert Einstein (1879–1955), a German-born patent officer working in Switzerland, pushed these new theories of thermodynamics into new terrain. In 1905, Einstein published a paper, "The Electrodynamics of Moving Bodies," setting forth his theory of relativity. According to relativity theory, space and time are not absolute but relative to the observer, and both are interwoven into what Einstein called a four-dimensional space-time continuum. Neither space nor time has an existence independent of human experience. Moreover, matter and energy reflect the relativity of time and space. Einstein concluded that matter was nothing but another form of energy. His epochal formula $E = mc^2$—each particle of matter is equivalent to its mass times the square of the velocity of light—was the key theory explaining the vast energies contained within the atom. It led to the atomic age.

How Did Freud's Psychoanalysis Also Challenge Views of Human Nature?

Although poets and mystics had revealed a world of unconscious and irrational behaviour, many scientifically oriented intellectuals under the impact of Enlightenment thought continued to believe that human beings responded to conscious motives in a rational fashion. But at the end of the nineteenth century, Viennese doctor Sigmund Freud (1856–1939) put forth a series of theories that undermined optimism about the rational nature of the human mind. Freud's thought, like the new physics, added to the

Edvard Munch (1863–1944) The Scream. 1893. National Gallery, Oslo, Norway.
© Erich Lessing/Art Resource, NY.

The Scream. Although Norwegian artist Edvard Munch probably never heard of Sigmund Freud, his painting *The Scream* (1893) graphically illustrates the Viennese psychotherapist's studies on human hysteria and neurosis. Fascinated by a withered Incan mummy shown at the Great Exposition in Paris in 1889, Munch was inspired in his painting to express the human condition as though, in his words, "the colors were real blood."

uncertainties of the age. His major ideas were published in 1900 in *The Interpretation of Dreams,* which laid the basic foundation for what came to be known as **psychoanalysis**.

> **Psychoanalysis** is a form of therapy developed by Sigmund Freud that probes into the unconscious mind in an effort to explore hidden emotions and feelings.

According to Freud, human behaviour is strongly determined by the unconscious—former experiences and inner drives of which people are largely oblivious. To explore the contents of the unconscious, Freud relied not only on hypnosis but also on dreams, which were dressed in an elaborate code that needed to be deciphered if the contents were to be properly understood.

Why do some experiences whose influence persists in controlling an individual's life remain unconscious? According to Freud, repression is a process by which unsettling experiences are blotted from conscious awareness but still continue to influence behaviour because they have become part of the unconscious. To explain how repression works, Freud elaborated an intricate theory of the inner life of human beings.

Although Freud's theory has had numerous critics, his insistence that a human being's inner life is a battleground of contending forces undermined the prevailing belief in the power of reason and opened a new era of psychoanalysis, by which a psychotherapist seeks to assist a patient in probing deeply into memory to retrace the chain of repression back to its childhood origins, thus bringing about a resolution of the inner psychic conflict. Belief in the primacy of rational thought over emotions would never be the same.

How Did Modernism Challenge Art and Culture?

The revolution in physics and psychology was paralleled by similar changes in literature and the arts. Throughout much of the late nineteenth century, literature was dominated by **Naturalism**. By addressing social problems, writers could contribute to an objective understanding of the world. The novels of the French writer Émile Zola (1840–1902) provide a good example of Naturalism. Against a backdrop of the urban slums and coalfields of northern France, Zola showed how alcoholism and different environments affected people's lives.

> **Naturalism** was a movement that accepted the material world as real and believed that literature should be realistic.

By the beginning of the twentieth century, the belief that the task of literature was to represent "reality" had lost much of its meaning because what was considered real was now believed to be subjective. By that time, the new psychology and the new physics had made it evident that many people were not sure what constituted reality anyway. The same was true in the realm of art; the changes that such cultural innovators produced have since been called **Modernism**.

> **Modernism** was a movement in art, literature, and intellectual discourse that challenged the so-called realism of Naturalists by proposing a more emotional and less rigid interpretation of the world.

The first group of painters to challenge perceptions of reality and experiment with radical new techniques of representation were the Impressionists. Originating in France in the 1870s, they rejected indoor painting and preferred to go out to the countryside to paint nature directly. The most influential of the Impressionists was Claude Monet (1840–1926), who painted several series of canvases on the same object—such as haystacks, the Rouen Cathedral, and water lilies in the garden of his house on the Seine River—in the hope of breaking down the essential lines, planes, colours, and shadows of what the eye observed. Post-Impressionists took these inspirations a step further with greater emotional expression in their art. Canada's beautiful and vast outdoor landscape proved to be a beautiful inspiration to its famous post-Impressionists: the Group of Seven.

Established in 1920, the Group of Seven were Canada's most notable landscape artists. The original Group of Seven were artists from Ontario, and most of them worked together at the firm Grip Ltd. as commercial artists. In each other's company, they discussed and debated an array of topics, including art and philosophy. Discussions on the Impressionist movement in Europe at the time, particularly in France, and a Scandinavian art show on display in Buffalo inspired these artists to begin to explore Ontario's north and its landscape.

The Group of Seven took sketching trips to Algonquin Park and the Algoma wilderness in Ontario. There, they climbed and explored the mountainous terrain by foot and discovered waterways by canoe, all the while stopping to paint hundreds of oil sketches of nature in different seasons on panels, which they eventually took back to their studios and reworked during the Canadian winter months.

The Group of Seven had a major impact on the post-Impressionist era in Canadian history. At first, they were dismissed by many among Canada's artistic elite. It was not until their work became recognized in places like Great Britain as having unique Canadian perception that others at

North Shore, Baffin Island, 1930, Lawren S. Harris (1885–1970). Purchased 1942. National Gallery of Canada/4561. © Family of Lawren S. Harris. Reproduced with permission.

Baffin Island. This depiction of Canada's largest island located in the Northwest Territories was painted in 1930 by Lawren Harris, one of the more famous Group of Seven artists. *Baffin Island* recently made history for being the priciest Group of Seven painting sold at an auction and the second most expensive painting ever sold in Canada. One of Canada's richest men, media mogul Ken Thomson, bought the painting for a mere $2.5 million in 2001.

home began to take notice of the Group's talent. The Group of Seven captured the spirit of the Canadian nationalism through their paintings of its landscape. Fuelled by the fervour of victory following World War I, these paintings became wildly reflective of Canada's national spirit.

By the end of the nineteenth century, then, traditional forms of literary, artistic, and musical expression were in a state of rapid retreat. Freed from conventional tastes and responding to the intellectual and social revolution that was getting under way throughout the Western world, painters, writers, composers, and architects launched a variety of radical new ideas that would revolutionize Western culture in coming decades.

CONCLUSION

During the course of the nineteenth century, Western society underwent a number of dramatic economic and social changes.

- Countries that were predominantly agricultural in 1750 had by 1900 been transformed into essentially industrial and urban societies.
- Machines were rapidly replacing labour-intensive methods of production and distribution.
- Social changes were equally striking—human beings were becoming more mobile.

- A mass society, based on the principles of universal education, limited government, and an expanding franchise, was in the process of creation.

The Industrial Revolution broke down many walls of aristocratic privilege and opened the door to a new era based on merit.

- Yet the distribution of wealth was as unequal as ever, and working and living conditions for millions of industrial workers had deteriorated.

Outside of the Western world—in Russia, the Balkans, the vast Ottoman Empire, and China—the Industrial Revolution had not yet made an impact or was just getting under way.

- Old autocracies in the Ottoman Empire and China found themselves under increasing pressure to change from ethnic minorities and poor peasants.
- Established political orders, such as the tsarist autocracy and the Manchu dynasty, however, continued to resist pressure for reform.
- While Marxism did not take hold in European countries initially, it grew in appeal in Russia.

- The Manchu dynasty collapsed amid social unrest, at the hands of groups such as the Boxers, and through foreign interference.

CRITICAL THINKING QUESTIONS

1. What advantages did England and America have that aided their industrialization? What cultural, regional, and political factors did they share?

2. Was Canada's industrialization a liberal model? What effect did Sir John A. Macdonald's National Policy have on our industrial development and on our national identity?

3. Why is child labour in practice in many parts of the Third World that are newly industrialized?

4. Why was a Marxist state averted in the Western world? What does this tell us about Marxism? Does this explain why liberalism was triumphant in the West?

5. Do art and culture mimic changes in the social and political order? Why is a lot of art and culture deemed avant-garde?

Chapter 2

The High Tide of Imperialism in the Non-Western World

During the nineteenth and early twentieth centuries, Western colonialism spread throughout much of the non-Western world. Spurred by the demands of the Industrial Revolution, a few powerful Western states—notably Great Britain, France, Germany, Russia, and the United States—competed greedily for consumer markets and raw materials for their expanding economies. By the end of the nineteenth century, virtually all of the traditional societies in Asia and Africa were under direct or indirect colonial rule.

At the conclusion of this chapter, you will be able to

- describe how the colonization of non-Western societies fed Europe's economic, political, and ego needs;
- explain how racism underpins the colonial philosophy;
- detail the "feeding frenzy" by imperialists in Africa and Southeast Asia;
- explain how colonization integrated the non-Western world into the world economy we know today.

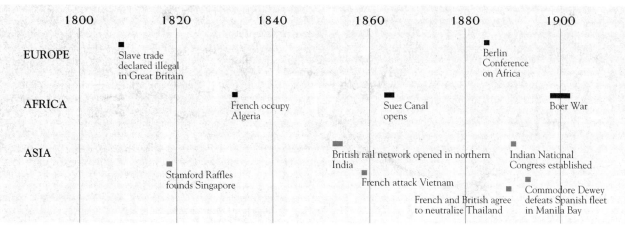

THE MYTH OF "EUROPEAN SUPERIORITY"

To some Western observers at the time, European superiority provided a clear affirmation of the innate advantage of Western civilization to its counterparts elsewhere in the world. Western historians began to view world history essentially as the story of the unstoppable rise of the West, from the glories of ancient Greece to the emergence of modern Europe after the Enlightenment and the Industrial Revolution. The extension of Western influence to Africa and Asia, a process that began with the arrival of European fleets in the Indian Ocean in the early sixteenth century, was thus a reaction of Western cultural superiority and represented a necessary step in bringing so-called civilization to the peoples of that area.

The truth, however, was quite different, for Western global hegemony was a relatively recent phenomenon. For centuries, Europe was only an isolated addition of a much larger world system of states stretching from the Atlantic Ocean to the Pacific. The centre of gravity in this trade network was not in Europe or even in the Mediterranean Sea but much farther to the east, in the Persian Gulf and in central Asia. The most sophisticated and technologically advanced region in the world was not Europe but China, whose proud history could be traced back several thousand years. As for the transcontinental trade network that linked Europe with the nations of the Middle East, South Asia, and the Pacific basin, it had not been created by Portuguese and Spanish navigators but, as we have seen, had already developed under the Arab empire, with its capital in Baghdad. Later the Mongols took control of the land trade routes during their conquest of much of the Eurasian continent in the thirteenth and fourteenth centuries. During the long centuries of Arab and Mongolian hegemony, the caravan routes and sea lanes stretching across the Eurasian continent and the Indian Ocean between China, Africa, and Europe carried not only commercial goods but also ideas and inventions such as the compass, printing, Arabic numerals, and gunpowder. Inventions such as these, many of them originating in China or India, would later play a major role in the emergence of Europe as a major player on the world's stage. Only in the sixteenth century, with the onset of the Age of Exploration, did Europe become important in the process. For the next three centuries, the ships of several European nations crossed the seas in quest of the spices, silks, precious metals, and porcelains of Asia.

In a few cases, Europeans engaged in bloody military campaigns as a means of seeking their objective. The islands of the Indonesian archipelago were gradually brought under Dutch colonial rule, and the British extended their political hegemony over the South Asian subcontinent. Spain, Portugal, and later other nations of Western Europe divided up the New World into separate colonial territories. For the most part, however, European nations were satisfied to trade with their Asian and African counterparts from coastal enclaves that they had established along the trade routes that threaded across the seas from the ports along the Atlantic and the Mediterranean Sea to their far-off destinations.

THE SPREAD OF COLONIAL RULE

In the nineteenth century, a new phase of Western expansion into Asia and Africa began. Whereas European aims in the East before 1800 could be summed up in the Portuguese explorer **Vasco da Gama**'s famous phrase "looking for Christians and spices," in the early nineteenth century, a new relationship took shape: European nations began to view Asian and African societies as a source of industrial raw materials and a market for Western manufactured goods.

No longer were Western gold and silver exchanged for cloves, pepper, tea, silk, and porcelain. Now European industrial goods were sent to Africa and Asia in return for oil, tin, rubber, and the other resources needed to fuel the Western industrial machine.

> **Vasco da Gama** was a Portuguese explorer who opened up trade between Western Europe and the East by way of the Cape of Good Hope; he took three voyages to India from 1497 to 1524. When asked what he was doing in India in 1498, da Gama described the aims of European exploration in South Asia in his famous response "looking for Christians and spices."

The reason for this change, of course, was the Industrial Revolution. Now industrializing countries in the West needed vital raw materials that were not available at home as well as a reliable market for the goods produced in their factories. The latter factor became increasingly crucial as capitalist societies began to discover that their home markets could not always absorb domestic output. When consumer demand lagged, economic depression threatened.

As Western economic expansion into Asia and Africa gathered strength during the last quarter of the nineteenth century, this became known as **imperialism**. Although the term *imperialism* has a broader meaning, it is more commonly used to refer to efforts of capitalist states in the West to exploit markets, cheap raw materials, and profitable sources for the investment of capital in foreign territory. In this interpretation, the primary motives behind the Western expansion were economic. The best-known promoter of this view was the British political economist John A. Hobson, who published a major analysis, *Imperialism: A Study,* in 1902. In this influential book, Hobson maintained that modern imperialism was a direct consequence of the modern industrial economy. In his view, the industrialized states of the West often produced more goods than could be absorbed by the domestic market and thus had to export their manufactures to make a profit. The best-known critic of this view was Vladimir Lenin (1870–1924), Russian leader of the Communist Party, who wrote *Imperialism: The Highest Stage of Capitalism* in 1916 and one year later led the Bolshevik Revolution. Lenin argued that imperialism was a necessary evil of the final stages of capitalism to exploit Third World countries of their resources and further feed the Western industrial machine that had already exploited the home front to its limits.

> **Imperialism** is the conquest of foreign territories or peoples for the purposes of expanding political and economic power, and exploiting the resources of such areas and peoples.

As in the earlier phase of Western expansion, however, the issue was not simply an economic one, since economic concerns were inevitably tinged with political ones and with questions of cultural racism. In nineteenth-century Europe, economic wealth, national status, and political power went hand in hand with the possession of a colonial empire, at least in the minds of observers at the time. To nineteenth-century global strategists, colonies brought tangible benefits in the world of balance-of-power politics as well as economic profits, and many nations became involved in the pursuit of colonies as much to gain advantage over their rivals as to acquire territory for its own sake.

With the change in European motives for colonization came a corresponding shift in tactics. Earlier, when their economic interests were more limited, European states had generally been satisfied to deal with existing independent states rather than attempt to establish direct control over vast territories. There had been exceptions where state power at the local level was on the point of collapse (as in India), where European economic interests were especially intense (as in Latin America and the East Indies), or where there was no centralized authority (as in North America and the Philippines). But for the most part, the Western presence in Asia and Africa had been limited to controlling the regional trade network and establishing a few footholds where the foreigners could carry on trade and missionary activity.

After 1800, the capitalist demands of industrialization in Europe created a new set of dynamics. Maintaining access to industrial raw materials, such as oil and rubber, and setting up reliable markets for European manufactured products required more extensive exploitation of colonial territories. As competition for colonies increased, the colonial powers sought to solidify their hold over their territories to protect their turf from rivals. During the last two decades of the nineteenth century, the quest for colonies became a scramble as all the major European states, now joined by the United States and Japan, engaged in a global land grab. In many cases, economic interests were secondary to perceived security concerns or cultural racism. In Africa, for example, the British engaged in a struggle with their rivals to protect their interests in the Suez Canal and the Red Sea. In Southeast Asia, the United States occupied the Philippines from Spain at least partly to keep them out of the hands of the Japanese, and the French took over Indochina for fear that it would otherwise be occupied by Germany, Japan, or the United States.

By 1900, virtually all the societies of Africa and Asia were either under full colonial rule or, as in the case of China and the Ottoman Empire, on the point of virtual collapse. Only a handful of states, such as Japan in East Asia, Thailand in Southeast Asia, Afghanistan and Iran in the

Middle East, and mountainous Ethiopia in East Africa, managed to escape political subjection to colonial rule. As the twentieth century began, European hegemony over the ancient civilizations of most of the now Third World seemed complete.

How Did India's History of Foreign Rule Aid Great Britain's Conquest of India?

The first of the major Asian civilizations to fall victim to European predatory activities was India. The first organized society had emerged in the Indus River valley in the fourth and third millennia B.C.E. After the influx of Aryan peoples into the Indian subcontinent around 1500 B.C.E., a new civilization, based on sedentary agriculture and a regional trade network, gradually emerged in north central India. The unity of the subcontinent was first established by the empire of the Mauryas in the third century B.C.E. Although the Mauryan state eventually collapsed, it had laid the foundation for the creation of a technologically advanced and prosperous civilization, and its concept of political unity was later reasserted by the Guptas, who ruled the region for nearly 200 years until they too were overthrown in about 500 C.E. Under the Guptas, **Hinduism**, a religious faith brought to the subcontinent by the Aryan people, evolved into the dominant religion of the Indian people.

> **Hinduism** is the dominant religion in India, based on a belief in reincarnation that mirrors results in one's previous life, and the desirability of escaping the cycle of reincarnation.

Beginning in the eleventh century, much of northern India fell under the rule of Turkic-speaking people who penetrated into the subcontinent from the northwest and introduced the people in the area to the religion of Islam. At the end of the fifteenth century, they were succeeded by the **Mughals**, a powerful new force from the mountains to the northern Mongolian region. The Mughal rulers, though foreigners and Muslims like many of their immediate predecessors, nevertheless brought India to a level of political power and cultural achievement that inspired admiration and envy throughout the entire region.

> The **Mughals** were members of a Muslim dynasty led by Babar "the Tiger"; they were descendants of the Mongols originally from the region of Turkestan.

In the eighteenth century, however, the Mughal dynasty began to weaken as Hindu forces in southern India sought to challenge the authority of the Mughal court in Delhi. This process of fragmentation was probably hastened by the growing presence of European traders, who began to establish enclaves along the fringes of the subcontinent. Eventually, the British and the French began to seize control of the regional trade routes and to meddle in India's internal politics. By the end of the century, nothing remained of the empire but a shell. The British filled the now **political vacuum** left by the decay of foreign rule. The British used a combination of modern firepower and cleverness to consolidate their power over the subcontinent.

> A **political vacuum** refers to a situation, short of chaos or anarchy, where there is an absence of political authority waiting to be filled.

Why Were European Colonial Powers Interested in Controlling Parts of Southeast Asia?

Southeast Asia had been one of the first destinations for European adventurers en route to the East. Lured by the riches of the **Spice Islands** (at the eastern end of present-day Indonesia), European adventurers sailed to the area in the early sixteenth century in the hope of establishing contacts with societies in the area and seizing control of the spice trade from Arab and Indian merchants. A century later, the trade was fast becoming a monopoly of the Dutch, whose sturdy ships and ample supply of capital gave them a significant advantage over their rivals.

> The **Spice Islands** is the area now known as *Indonesia*; it was once an important source of spices—including clove, nutmeg, and mace—which were highly traded among Europeans.

In 1800, only two societies in Southeast Asia were under effective colonial rule: the Spanish Philippines and the Dutch East Indies. The British had been driven out of the Spice Islands trade by the Dutch in the seventeenth century and possessed only a small enclave on the southern coast of the island of Sumatra and some territory on the Malay Peninsula. The French had actively engaged in trade with states on the Asian mainland but were eventually reduced to a small missionary effort run by the Society of Foreign Missions. The only legacy of Portuguese expansion in the region was the possession of half of the small island of Timor.

During the second half of the nineteenth century, however, European interest in Southeast Asia grew rapidly, and by 1900, virtually the entire area was under colonial rule

(see Map 2.1, Plate 2). The process began after the end of the Napoleonic Wars, when the British, by agreement with the Dutch, abandoned their claims to territorial possessions in the East Indies in return for a free hand in the Malay Peninsula. In 1819, the colonial administrator Stamford Raffles founded a new British colony on a small island at the tip of the peninsula. Called Singapore ("City of the Lion"), it had previously been used by Malay pirates to raid ships passing through the **Strait of Malacca**. When the invention of steam power enabled merchant ships to save time and distance by passing through the strait rather than sailing with the westerlies across the southern Indian Ocean, Singapore became a major stopping point for traffic to and from China and other commercial centres in the region.

> The **Strait of Malacca** is the shortest sea route connecting three of the world's most populated countries: China, India, and Indonesia.

During the next few decades, the pace of European penetration into Southeast Asia accelerated. At the beginning of the nineteenth century, the British had sought and received the right to trade with the Kingdom of Burma. A few decades later, the British took over the entire country and placed it under the colonial administration in India.

The British advance into Burma was watched nervously in Paris, where French geopoliticians were ever anxious about British operations in Asia and Africa. The French still maintained a clandestine missionary organization in Vietnam despite harsh persecution by the local authorities, who viewed Christianity as a threat to internal stability. In 1857, the French government decided to force the Vietnamese to accept French protection to prevent the British from obtaining a monopoly of trade in South China. A naval attack launched a year later was not a total success, but the French eventually forced the Vietnamese court to cede territories in the Mekong River delta. A generation later, French rule was extended over the remainder of the country. By the end of the century, French seizure of neighbouring Cambodia and Laos had led to the creation of the French-ruled Indochinese Union.

With the French conquest of Indochina, Thailand was the only remaining independent state on the Southeast Asian mainland. During the last quarter of the century, British and French rivalry threatened to place the Thai, too, under colonial rule. But under the astute leadership of two remarkable rulers, King Mongkut (familiar to millions in the West as the king in the film *The King and I*) and his son King Chulalongkorn, the Thai sought to introduce Western learning and maintain relations with the major European powers without undermining internal stability or inviting an imperialist attack. In 1896, the British and the

French agreed to preserve Thailand as an independent buffer zone between their possessions in Southeast Asia.

The final piece of the colonial edifice in Southeast Asia was put in place in 1898, when U.S. naval forces under Commodore George Dewey defeated the Spanish fleet in Manila Bay. President William McKinley, in racist and religious overtones, claimed he agonized over the fate of the Philippines but claimed that the Godly thing to do was to turn the islands into an American colony to prevent them from falling into the hands of the Japanese. In fact, the Americans (like the Spanish before them) found the islands convenient as a jumping-off point for the China trade. This American mixture of religious nationalism, racism, and capitalist ideology was part of the grander U.S. vision of **Manifest Destiny**.

> **Manifest Destiny** was a belief held by many American leaders and politicians in the mid- and late eighteenth century that the United States' control of the continent and beyond was an undeniable fate.

Needless to say, not all Filipinos were pleased to be placed under U.S. tutelage. Led by Emilio Aguinaldo, resistance forces fought bitterly against American imperialism to establish their independence from both Spain and the United States. But America's first guerrilla-warfare in Asia was an American success, and the resistance collapsed in 1901. President McKinley had his stepping-stone to the rich markets of China.

How Did Western Racism Shape Africa's History?

The last of the equatorial regions of the world to be exploited by European colonial rule was the continent of Africa. European navigators had first established contacts with Africans south of the Sahara during the late fifteenth century, when Portuguese fleets sailed down the Atlantic coast on their way to the Indian Ocean. During the next three centuries, Europeans established port facilities along the coasts of East and West Africa to facilitate their trade with areas farther to the east and to engage in limited commercial relations with African societies. Eventually, the horrific slave trade took on predominant importance to Europeans, and several million Africans were branded, chained, and loaded onto slave ships destined for abuse, racism, and hardship in the European New World.

Initially, exploited slaves bought and sold on Africa's west coast (present-day Ghana being one of the major slave ports at the time) were brought to the Caribbean, more specifically Barbados, which at the time had just entered the sugar cane industry after the demand for its tobacco ceased.

With a booming economy based on the sugar revolution of 1645, the need for labour grew, and Africans were deemed to be far better field hands than were their indigenous or European counterparts who had worked the fields as indentured labourers.

Shortly after slaves became commonplace in the Caribbean, a Dutch slave trader arriving in the American colony of Jamestown, Virginia, in 1619 exchanged a group of 20 Africans for food. These Africans were used as indentured servants much in the same way many Irish, Scottish, and indigenous peoples were used at this time. Indentured servants were not slaves since they were able to earn their freedom once they had worked for a set time.

However, in 1663 a Virginia court clarified and defined this relationship, and slavery became institutionalized by affiliating servitude with colour, thereby making all Africans slaves and all those born from slave mothers slaves as well; hence, the labour force would propagate and repopulate itself. By 1672 the King of England established the Royal African Company, which encouraged the slave trade from Africa across the Atlantic. The number of slaves who travelled the dreaded "Atlantic passage" would increase from 5000 annually during the late seventeenth century to 45 000 annually by the eighteenth century.

For a variety of reasons, Europeans made little effort to penetrate the vast continent of Africa and were generally content to deal with African intermediaries along the coast to maintain their trading relationship. Deeply ingrained in the Western psyche was the racist image of **"darkest Africa"**—a wrongful belief that the continent had no history and that its people lived out their days without cultural contact with the "outside world."

> **"Darkest Africa"** is a term that reflects the racist belief that the people of Africa had no contact with the outside world and were therefore "in the dark."

Although Africa was the original seedbed of humankind and the site of much of its early evolutionary experience, the drought of the Sahara during the fourth and third millennia B.C.E. had erected a major obstacle to communications between the peoples south of the desert and societies elsewhere in the world. The barrier was never total, however. From ancient times, caravans crossed the Sahara from the Niger River basin to the shores of the Mediterranean carrying gold and other tropical products in exchange for salt, textile goods, and other manufactured articles from the north. By the seventh century C.E., several prosperous trading societies, whose renown reached as far as medieval Europe and the Middle East, had begun to arise in the savannah belt in West Africa. Trading merchants brought not only commercial goods but also the Islamic religion and its practices.

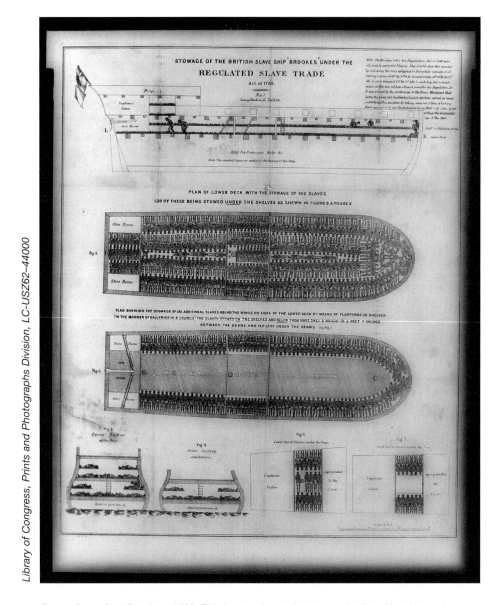

British Slave Ship Brookes, *1789*. This image shows the "packaging" of 454 slaves aboard a British slave ship called *Brookes* in 1789. The *Brookes,* however, had been known to carry as many as 609 enslaved Africans on a horrible passage across the Atlantic Ocean. The stench, starvation, and lack of breathing space were unimaginable and resulted in numerous deaths of innocent children, women, and men.

Farther to the east, the Sahara posed no obstacle to communication beyond the seas. The long eastern coast of the African continent had played a role in the trade network of the Indian Ocean since the time of the pharaohs along the Nile. Ships from India, the Persian Gulf, and as far away as China made regular visits to the East African ports of Kilwa, Malindi, and Sofala, bringing textiles, metal goods, and luxury articles in return for gold, ivory, and various tropical products from Africa. With the settlement of Arab traders along the eastern coast, the entire region developed a new synthetic culture known as **Swahili**. Although the Portuguese briefly seized or destroyed most of the trading ports along the eastern coast, by the eighteenth century the Europeans had been driven out and local authority was restored.

> **Swahili** is a mix of African tribal and Arab language and culture that developed by the twelfth century along the eastern coast of Africa.

© National Maritime Museum/Neg No: D9317

Hold of a Slave Ship, 1845. This watercolour painting depicts the liberation of Africans aboard a Portuguese/Brazilian slave ship called *Albaroz;* these Africans were originally destined to the horrors of slavery in the New World. The British Royal Navy liberated the ship's 300 African would-be slaves in the mid-1800s after Great Britain declared slavery illegal.

Why Didn't the Abolition of the Slave Trade End European Interest in West Africa?

The decline of the slave trade in the Atlantic during the first half of the nineteenth century, however, did not lead to an overall reduction in the European presence in West Africa. To the contrary, European interest in what they called **legitimate trade** in natural resources increased. Exports of peanuts, timber, hide, and palm oil increased substantially during the first decades of the century, and imports of textile goods and other manufactured products also rose.

> **Legitimate trade** refers to the trade of goods as opposed to that of enslaved people.

Stimulated by growing capitalist interests in the area, European governments began to push for a more permanent presence along the coast. During the first decades of the nineteenth century, the British established settlements along the Gold Coast (present-day Ghana) and in Sierra Leone, where they attempted to set up agricultural plantations for freed slaves who had returned from the Western Hemisphere or had been liberated by British ships while en route to the Americas. A similar haven for ex-slaves was developed with the assistance of the United States in Liberia. The French occupied the area around the Senegal River near Cape Verde, where they attempted to develop peanut plantations.

The growing European presence in West Africa led to tensions with African governments in the area. British efforts to increase trade with Ashanti, in the area of the present-day state of Ghana, led to conflict in the 1820s, but British influence in the area intensified in later decades. Most African states, especially those with a fairly high degree of political integration, were able to maintain their independence from this creeping European encroachment, called **informal empire** by some historians, but eventually, the British stepped in and annexed the region as the first British colony of the Gold Coast in 1874. At about the same time, the British extended an informal protectorate over warring tribal groups in the Niger delta.

Edouard Riou (1833–1900). after: The First Crossing of the Suez Canal by Royal Ships on November 17, 1869. *Bildarchiv Preussischer Kulturbesitz/Art Resource, NY*

The Opening of the Suez Canal. The Suez Canal, which connected the Mediterranean and the Red Sea for the first time, was constructed under the direction of French promoter Ferdinand de Lesseps. Still in use today, the canal is Egypt's greatest revenue producer. This sketch shows the ceremonial passage of the first ships through the canal upon its completion in 1869.

> **Informal empire** refers to the indirect influence of British colonialism on Africa's political, economic, and social systems, which ultimately served to benefit the British Empire and increase African dependency on Great Britain.

Why Would Imperialist Powers Be Interested in Controlling the Suez Canal and Egypt?

Ever since the voyages of the Portuguese explorers at the close of the fifteenth century, European trade with the East had been carried on almost exclusively by the route around the Cape of Good Hope (Southern tip of Africa). But from the outset, there was some interest in shortening the route by digging a canal east of Cairo, where only a low, swampy isthmus separated the Mediterranean from the Red Sea. The Ottoman Turks, who controlled the area, had considered constructing a canal in the sixteenth century, but nothing was accomplished until 1854, when the French entrepreneur Ferdinand de Lesseps signed a contract to begin construction of the Suez Canal. The project brought little immediate benefit to Egypt, however; the costs of construction imposed a major debt on the Egyptian government and forced a growing level of dependence on foreign financial support. When an army revolt against growing foreign influence broke out in 1881, the British stepped in to protect their investment (they had bought Egypt's canal company shares in 1875) and set up an informal protectorate that would last until World War I.

The weakening of Turkish Ottoman rule in the Nile valley had a parallel farther to the west, where autonomous regions had begun to emerge under local viceroys in Tripoli, Tunis, and Algiers. In 1830, the French, on the pretext of reducing the threat of piracy to European shipping in the Mediterranean, occupied most of Algeria and claimed to annex it into the Kingdom of France. By the mid-1850s, more than 150 000 Europeans had settled in the fertile region adjacent to the coast, at the expense of local Arabs, while Berber resistance continued in the desert to the south. In 1881, the French imposed a protectorate on neighbouring Tunisia. Only Tripoli and Cyrenaica

(Ottoman provinces that make up modern-day Libya) remained under Turkish rule until the Italians took them over in 1911–12.

Why Was the European Scramble for African Territory Not Motivated by Economic Reasons?

At the beginning of the 1880s, most of Africa was still independent. European rule was still limited to the fringes of the continent, and a few areas, such as Egypt, lower Nigeria, Senegal, and Mozambique, were under various forms of loose protectorate. But the trends were gloomy, as the pace of European penetration was accelerating and the constraints that had limited European greed were fast disappearing.

The scramble began in the mid-1880s, when several European states engaged in what today would be called a feeding frenzy to seize a piece of African territory. By 1900, virtually all of the continent had been placed under one form or another of European rule. The British had consolidated their authority over the Nile valley and seized additional territories in East Africa. The French retaliated by advancing eastward from Senegal into the central Sahara, where they eventually came eyeball to eyeball with the British at Fashoda on the Nile. They also occupied the island of Madagascar and other coastal territories in West and central Africa. In between, the Germans claimed the hinterland opposite Zanzibar, as well as coastal strips in West and Southwest Africa north of the Cape, and King Leopold II of Belgium claimed the Congo.

What had happened to spark the sudden imperialist hysteria that brought an end to African independence? Economic interests in the narrow sense were not at stake as they had been in South and Southeast Asia: the level of trade between Europe and Africa was simply not sufficient to justify the risks and the expense of conquest. Clearly, one factor was the growing rivalry among imperialist powers. European leaders might be provoked into an imperialist takeover not by economic considerations but by the fear that another state might do so, leaving them at a disadvantage.

Another consideration might be called the *missionary factor* as European missionary interests lobbied with their governments for a colonial takeover to facilitate their efforts to convert the African population to Christianity. In fact, considerable moral complacency was inherent in the process. The concept of the white man's burden persuaded many that it was in the so-called interests of the African people to be introduced more rapidly to the "benefits of Western civilization." Even the highly respected Scottish missionary David Livingstone had become convinced that missionary work and economic development had to go hand in hand, pleading to his fellow Europeans to introduce the three *C*s (Christianity, commerce, and civilization) to the continent.

There were other less bigoted reasons as well. Advances in Western technology and European superiority in firearms made it easier than ever for a small European force to defeat superior numbers. Furthermore, life expectancy for Europeans living in Africa had improved. With the discovery that quinine (extracted from the bark of the cinchona tree) could provide partial immunity from the ravages of malaria, the mortality rate for Europeans living in Africa dropped dramatically in the 1840s. By the end of the century, European residents in tropical Africa faced only slightly higher risks of death by disease than individuals living in Europe.

As rivalry among competing powers heated up, a conference was convened at Berlin in 1884 to avert war and reduce tensions among European nations competing for the spoils of Africa. It proved reasonably successful at achieving the first objective but less so at the second. During the next few years, African territories were annexed without provoking a major confrontation between Western powers, but in the late 1890s, Great Britain and France reached the brink of conflict at Fashoda, a small town on the Nile River in the Sudan. The French had been advancing eastward across the Sahara with the transparent objective of controlling the regions around the upper Nile. In 1898, British and Egyptian troops seized the Sudan and then marched southward to head off the French. After a tense face-off between units of the two European countries at Fashoda, the French government backed down, and British authority over the area was secured. Except for Djibouti, a tiny portion of the Somali coast, the French were restricted to equatorial Africa.

What Motivated British Interests in South Africa?

Nowhere in Africa did the European presence grow more rapidly than in the south. During the eighteenth century, Dutch settlers from the Cape Colony began to migrate eastward into territory inhabited by local Khoisan- and Bantu-speaking peoples entering the area from the north. Deadly warfare among the Bantus had largely depopulated the region, facilitating occupation of the land by the Boers, the Afrikaans-speaking farmers descended from the original Dutch settlers in the seventeenth century. But in the early nineteenth century, a Bantu people called the Zulus, under a talented ruler named Shaka, counterattacked, setting off a series of wars between the Europeans and the Zulus.

Eventually, Shaka was overthrown, and the Boers continued their advance northeastward during the so-called Great Trek of the mid-1830s. By 1865, the total European population of the area had risen to nearly 200 000 people.

The Boers' eastward migration was provoked in part by the British seizure of the Cape from the Dutch during the Napoleonic Wars. The British government was generally more sympathetic to the rights of the local African population than were the Afrikaners, many of whom saw white superiority as ordained by God and fled from British rule to control their own destiny. Eventually, the Boers formed their own independent republics, the Orange Free State and the South African Republic (usually known as Transvaal). Much of the African population in these areas was confined to reserves (see Map 2.2, Plate 3).

The discovery of gold and diamonds in the Transvaal complicated the situation. Clashes between the Afrikaner population and foreign (mainly British) miners and developers led to an attempt by Cecil Rhodes, prime minister of the Cape Colony and a prominent entrepreneur in the area, to subvert the Transvaal and bring it under British rule. In 1899, the **Boer War** broke out between Great Britain and the Transvaal, which was backed by the Orange Free State. Guerrilla resistance by the Boers was fierce, but the vastly superior forces of the British were able to prevail by 1902. To compensate the defeated Afrikaner population for the loss of independence, the British government agreed that only whites would vote in the now essentially self-governing colony. The Boers were placated, but the brutalities committed during the war (the British introduced an institution later to be known as the *concentration camp*) created bitterness on both sides that continued to fester for decades.

> The **Boer War** was a conflict in South Africa from 1899–1902, where the British defeated the Afrikaners (Dutch settlers), and established British rule in South Africa.

THE COLONIAL SYSTEM

Now that they had control of most of the world, what did the colonial powers do with it? As we have seen, their primary objective was to exploit the natural resources of the subject areas and to open up markets for manufactured goods and capital investment from the mother country. In some cases, that goal could be realized in cooperation with local political elites, whose loyalty could be earned (or purchased) by economic rewards or by confirming them in their positions of authority and status in a new colonial setting. Sometimes, however, this policy, known as **indirect**

rule, was not feasible because local leaders refused to cooperate with their colonial masters or even actively resisted the foreign conquest. In such cases, the local elites were removed from power and replaced with a new set of officials recruited from the mother country; this was known as **direct rule**.

> **Indirect rule** involves the purchase of local political elites by colonial powers to rule over a given area; **direct rule** involves the placement of officials from the colonizer's country in positions of power.

The distinction between direct and indirect rule was not merely academic and often had fateful consequences for the people ruled. Where colonial powers encountered resistance and were forced to overthrow local political elites, they often adopted policies designed to eradicate the source of resistance and destroy the traditional culture. Such policies often had quite corrosive effects on the indigenous societies and provoked resentment and resistance that not only marked the colonial relationship but even affected internal relations after the restoration of national independence. The bitter struggles after World War II in Algeria, the Dutch East Indies, and Vietnam can be ascribed in part to that phenomenon.

What Concepts and Ideas Underpinned the Philosophy of Colonialism?

To justify their conquests, the colonial powers appealed, in part, to the time-honoured maxim of "might makes right." In a manner reminiscent of the Western attitude toward the oil reserves in the Persian Gulf today, the European powers viewed industrial resources as vital to national survival and security and felt that no moral justification was needed for any action to protect access to them. By the end of the nineteenth century, that attitude received pseudoscientific validity from the concept of **social Darwinism**, which maintained that only societies that moved aggressively to adapt to changing circumstances would survive and prosper in a world governed by the Darwinist law of "survival of the fittest."

> **Social Darwinism** is the application of Darwin's principle of organic evolution to the social order: the idea that progress comes from the survival of the fittest and decline of the weak.

Some people, however, were uncomfortable with such a brutal view of the law of nature and sought a so-called moral justification that appeared to benefit the victim. Here again,

WHITE MAN'S BURDEN, BLACK MAN'S SORROW

One of the justifications for European colonialism was the notion that the "more advanced" white peoples had the moral responsibility to raise allegedly primitive societies in Africa and Asia to a higher level of civilization. Few captured this notion better than the British poet Rudyard Kipling (1865–1936) in his famous poem "The White Man's Burden." His appeal, addressed primarily to the United States, became one of the most famous set of verses in the English-speaking world:

> Take up the White Man's burden—
> Send forth the best ye breed—
> Go bind your sons to exile
> To serve your captives' need;
> To wait in heavy harness,
> On fluttered folk and wild—
> Your new-caught sullen peoples,
> Half-devil and half-child.

Yet that sense of moral responsibility was often misplaced or, even worse, laced with hypocrisy. Not only was it virtually self-evident that the underlying motive for colonial conquest was the drive for national or personal wealth and power, but it was also clear that the consequences of imperial rule all too often were detrimental to those living under colonial authority. Nowhere was this harsh reality more clearly displayed than in Africa, which had already suffered for centuries from the European slave trade.

Few observers described the destructive effects of Western imperialism on native Africans as well as Edward Morel, a British journalist who spent time in the Belgian Congo. In his book *The Black Man's Burden*, Morel pointed out that the power of what he called "modern capitalistic exploitation, assisted by modern engines of destruction" might manage to accomplish what even the slave trade and imperial conquest had failed to do. Colonial rule, he charged, kills not the body merely, but the soul. It breaks the spirit. It attacks the African at every turn, from every point of vantage. It wrecks his polity, uproots him from his land, invades his family life, destroys his natural pursuits and occupations, claims his whole time, and enslaves him in his own home.

The most harmful aspect of colonialism, in Morel's view, was the pervasive and corrosive character of capitalist exploitation, which relentlessly undermined the foundations of traditional society and allowed no recourse for African workers against long hours of "monotonous, uninterrupted labour," often involving a lengthy separation from home, family, and community. Violent resistance, he lamented, provided no answer because of the "killing power of modern armament."

Morel's book, combined with other searing attacks on the system, such as the British writer Joseph Conrad's famous novel *Heart of Darkness,* represented a terrible indictment of the colonial system and the alleged benefits extolled by its defenders.

Sources: Rudyard Kipling, "The White Man's Burden." *McClure's Magazine* 12 (February 1899).

the concept of social Darwinism pointed the way. According to Social Darwinists, human societies, like living organisms, must adapt to survive. Hence the advanced nations of the West were obliged to assist the backward nations of Asia and Africa so that they, too, could adjust to the challenges of the modern world. Few expressed this view as graphically as the English poet Rudyard Kipling, who called on the Anglo-Saxon peoples (in particular, the United States) to take up the white man's burden in Asia (see the box above).

Buttressed by such comforting yet racist theories, humane and sympathetic souls in Western countries could ignore the brutal aspects of the colonial process and foolishly persuade themselves that in the long run, the results would be beneficial to both sides. Some, like their antecedents in the sixteenth and seventeenth centuries, saw the objective primarily in religious terms. During the nineteenth century, Christian missionaries by the thousands went to Asia and Africa to bring the gospel to the "heathen masses." Others saw the objective as more secular—to bring the benefits of Western democracy and capitalism to the feudalistic and traditional societies of the East. Either way, sensitive Western minds could ignorantly console themselves with the belief that their governments were bringing civilization to the primitive peoples of the world. If commercial profit and national prestige happened to be by-products of that effort, so much the better. Few were as effective at making this case as the French colonial official Albert Sarraut. Admitting that colonialism was originally an "act of force" taken for material profit, he declared that the end result would be a "better life on this planet" for conqueror and conquered alike.

The French were most inclined to philosophize about colonialism, and adopted the terms **assimilation** and **association** to describe two methods of colonialism that they found to be useful. French policy in Indochina, for example, began as one of association but switched to assimilation under pressure from liberal elements who felt that colonial powers owed a debt to their subject peoples. But assimilation aroused resentment among the local population, many of whom naturally opposed the destruction of their native traditions.

> **Assimilation** implies an effort to transform colonial societies in the Western image; **association** implies collaborating with local elites while leaving native traditions alone.

Most colonial powers were less inclined to debate the theory of colonialism as the French were. The United States, in formulating a colonial policy for the Philippines, adopted a strategy of assimilation in theory but was not quick to put it into practice. The British refused to entertain the possibility of assimilation and generally treated their subject peoples as culturally and racially distinctive (as Queen Victoria declared in 1858, her government disclaimed "the right and desire to impose Our conditions on Our subjects"). Although some observers have qualified this attitude to a perception of racial superiority, not all agree. In his recent book *Ornamentalism: How the British Saw Their Empire,* historian David Cannadine argues that in fact, the British often attempted to replicate their own hierarchical system, based on the institutions of monarchy and aristocracy, and force it on the peoples of the empire.

How Did Colonialism Differ in India, Southeast Asia, and Africa?

In practice, colonialism in India, Southeast Asia, and Africa exhibited many similarities but also some differ-

ences. Some of these variations can be traced to political or social differences among the colonial powers. The French, for example, often tried to impose a centralized administrative system on their colonies that mirrored the system in use in France, while the British sometimes attempted to transform local aristocrats into the equivalent of the landed gentry at home in Great Britain. Other differences stemmed from conditions in the colonies and the colonizers' aspirations for them. For instance, Western economic interests were far more limited in Africa than elsewhere, and African colonies were therefore treated somewhat differently than those in India or Southeast Asia.

Courtesy of William J. Duiker

Blending East and West. After establishing colonies throughout the continents of Africa and Asia, the British began to erect monumental buildings to demonstrate their power and authority. Some of the buildings reflected a mixture of Western and indigenous styles. Shown here is the ornate railway station in Kuala Lumpur in Malaysia.

INDIA UNDER THE BRITISH RAJ

At the beginning of the nineteenth century, the once glorious empire of the Mughals had been debased and humiliated and was now reduced by British military power to a shadow of its former greatness. During the next few decades, the British sought to consolidate their control over the subcontinent, expanding from their base areas along the coast into the interior by way of both direct and indirect rule.

British governance over the subcontinent brought order and stability to a society that had been rent by civil war before the Western intrusion. By the early nineteenth century, British control had been consolidated and, some argued, had led to a relatively efficient government that could operate to the benefit of the average Indian (see Map 2.3, Plate 4). For example, heightened attention was given to education. Through the efforts of the British administrator and historian Lord Macaulay, a new school system was established to train the children of Indian elites, and the British civil service examination was introduced (see the box below).

British rule also brought an end to some Indian traditions. The practice of ***suttee*** was outlawed, and widows were legally permitted to remarry. The British also attempted to put an end to the brigandage (known as *thuggee,* which gave rise to the English word *thug*) that had plagued travellers in India since time immemorial. Railroads, the telegraph, and

---

INDIAN IN BLOOD, ENGLISH IN TASTE AND INTELLECT

Thomas Babington Macaulay (1800–59) was named a member of the Supreme Council of India in the early 1830s. In that capacity, he was responsible for drawing up a new educational policy for British subjects in the area. In his *Minute on Education,* he considered the claims of English and various local languages to become the vehicle for educational training and decided in favour of the former. It is better, he argued, to teach Indian elites about Western civilization so as "to form a class who may be interpreters between us and the millions whom we govern; a class of persons, Indian in blood and color, but English in taste, in opinions, in morals, and in intellect." As the later passages of his minutes demonstrate, Macaulay's racist overtures included a distaste for India's rich history and civilization.

Thomas Babington Macaulay, *Minute on Education*

We have a fund to be employed as government shall direct for the intellectual improvement of the people of this country. The simple question is, what is the most useful way of employing it?

All parties seem to be agreed on one point, that the dialects commonly spoken among the natives of this part of India contain neither literary or scientific information, and are moreover so poor and rude that, until they are enriched from some other quarter, it will not be easy to translate any valuable work into them. . . .

What, then, shall the language [of education] be? One half of the Committee maintain that it should be the English. The other half strongly recommend the Arabic and Sanskrit. The whole question seems to me to be, what language is the best worth knowing?

I have no knowledge of either Sanskrit or Arabic—I have done what I could to form a correct estimate of their value. I have read translations of the most celebrated Arabic and Sanskrit works. I have conversed both here and at home with men distinguished by their proficiency in the Eastern tongues. I am quite ready to take the Oriental learning at the valuation of the Orientalists themselves. I have never found one among them who could deny that a single shelf of a good European library was worth the whole native literature of India and Arabia. . . .

It is, I believe, no exaggeration to say that all the historical information which has been collected from all the books written in the Sanskrit language is less valuable than what may be found in the most paltry abridgments used at preparatory schools in England.

Source: Michael Edwards, *A History of India: From the Earliest Times to the Present Day* (London: Thames & Hudson, 1961), pp. 261–65.

the postal service were introduced to India shortly after they appeared in Great Britain. A new penal code based on the British model was adopted, and health and sanitation conditions were improved.

> **Suttee** refers to the burning of widows on the funeral pyres of their husbands; it is a practice banned in contemporary India.

But the Indian people paid dearly for the so-called peace and stability brought by the British raj (from the Indian term *raja,* for "prince"). Perhaps the most flagrant cost was economic. In rural areas, the British introduced the **zamindar** system, according to which local landlords were authorized to collect taxes from peasants and turn the taxes over to the government in the misguided expectation that it would not only facilitate the collection of agricultural taxes but also create a new landed gentry that could, as in Great Britain itself, become the conservative foundation of imperial rule. But the local gentry took advantage of their new authority to increase taxes and force the less fortunate peasants to become tenants or lose their land entirely. When

rural unrest threatened, the government passed legislation protecting farmers against eviction and unreasonable rent increases, but this measure had little effect outside the southern provinces, where it had originally been enacted.

> **Zamindars** were local Mughal Indian officials who were allowed to collect tax on agricultural land and keep part of locally paid taxes as their salaries.

British colonialism was also negligent in bringing modern science and technology to India. Some limited forms of industrialization took place, notably in the manufacturing of textiles and rope. The first textile mill opened in 1856; 70 years later, there were 80 mills in the city of Bombay alone. Nevertheless, the lack of local capital and the advantages given to British imports prevented the emergence of other vital new commercial and manufacturing operations, and the introduction of British textiles put thousands of Bengali women out of work and severely damaged the village textile industry.

Foreign rule also had an effect on the psyche of the Indian people. Although many British colonial officials

Probably Sir David Ochterlony (1758–1825) in Indian dress, smoking a hookah and watching a nautch in his house at Delhi. Watercolour. c. 1820. © The British Library, Oriental and India Office Collections/ Shelfmark: Add.Or.2

An English Nabob in Colonial India. When the British ruled India in the late eighteenth and nineteenth centuries, many Indians began to imitate European customs for prestige or social advancement. Sometimes, however, the cultural influence went the other way. Here an English nabob, as European residents in the colonies were often called, imitates the manner of an Indian aristocrat, complete with harem and hookah, the Indian water pipe. The paintings on the wall, however, are in the European style.

claimed they tried to improve the lot of the people under their charge, the government made few efforts to introduce democratic institutions and values to the Indian people. Moreover, British arrogance, narrow-mindedness, and contempt for native traditions cut deeply into the pride of many Indians, especially those of high caste who were accustomed to a position of superior status in India. Educated Indians trained in the Anglo-Indian school system for a career in the civil service, as well as Eurasians born to mixed marriages, rightfully wondered where their true cultural loyalties lay.

COLONIAL REGIMES IN SOUTHEAST ASIA

In Southeast Asia, economic profit was the immediate and primary aim of the colonial enterprise. For that purpose, colonial powers worked with local elites to facilitate the exploitation of natural resources and indirectly stunted the development of a middle class. Indirect rule reduced the cost of training European administrators and had a less corrosive impact on the local culture. In the Dutch East Indies, for example, officials of the Dutch East India Company (VOC) entrusted local administration to the indigenous landed aristocracy, known as the *priyayi*. The *priyayi* maintained law and order and collected taxes in return for a payment from the VOC. The British followed a similar practice in Malaysia. While establishing direct rule over areas of crucial importance, such as the commercial centres of Singapore and Malacca and the island of Penang, the British signed agreements with local Muslim rulers to maintain princely power in the interior of the peninsula.

> The **priyayi** were the local administrators who maintained law and order and collected taxes in return for a payment from the Dutch East India Company (VOC).

In some instances, however, local resistance to the colonial conquest made such a policy impossible. In Burma, faced with staunch opposition from the monarchy and other traditionalist forces, the British abolished the monarchy and administered the country directly through their colonial government in India. In Indochina, the French used both direct and indirect means. They imposed direct rule on the southern provinces in the Mekong Delta, which had been ceded to France as a colony after the first war in 1858–60. The northern parts of the country, seized in the 1880s, were governed as a protectorate, with the emperor retaining titular authority from his palace in Hue. The French adopted a similar policy in Cambodia and Laos, where local rulers were left in charge with French advisers to counsel them. Even the Dutch were eventually forced into a more direct approach. When the development of plantation agriculture and the extraction of oil in Sumatra made effective exploitation of local resources more complicated, they dispensed with indirect rule and tightened their administrative control over the archipelago.

Whatever method was used, colonial regimes in Southeast Asia, as elsewhere, were slow to create democratic institutions. The first legislative councils and assemblies were composed almost exclusively of European residents in the colonies. The first representatives from the indigenous population were wealthy and conservative in their political views. When Southeast Asians began to complain, colonial officials gradually and reluctantly began to broaden the franchise.

Colonial powers were equally reluctant to assist in furthering local economic development. As we have seen, their primary goals were to secure a source of cheap raw materials and to maintain markets for manufactured goods. So colonial policy concentrated on the export of raw materials— teakwood from Burma; rubber and tin from Malaysia; spices, tea, coffee, and palm oil from the East Indies; and sugar and copra from the Philippines.

In some Southeast Asian colonial societies, a measure of industrial development did take place to meet the needs of the European population and local elites. Major manufacturing cities, including Rangoon in lower Burma, Batavia on the island of Java, and Saigon in French Indochina, grew rapidly. Although the local middle class benefited in various ways from the Western presence, most industrial and commercial establishments were owned and managed by Europeans or, in some cases, by Indian or Chinese merchants. In Saigon, for example, even the manufacture of *nuoc mam,* the traditional Vietnamese fish sauce, was under Chinese ownership. Most urban residents were labourers, factory workers, or rickshaw drivers or eked out a living in family shops as they had during the traditional era.

Despite the growth of an urban economy, the vast majority of people in the colonial societies continued to farm the land. Many continued to live by subsistence agriculture, but the colonial policy of emphasizing cash crops for export also led to the creation of a form of plantation agriculture in which peasants were recruited to work as wage labourers on rubber and tea plantations owned by Europeans. To maintain a competitive edge, the plantation owners kept the wages of their workers at the poverty level. Many plantation workers were **shanghaied** to work on plantations, where conditions were often so inhumane that thousands died. High taxes, enacted by colonial governments to pay for administrative costs or improvements in the local infrastructure, were a heavy burden for poor peasants.

Shanghaied is an English term that originated from the practice of recruiting labourers, often from the docks and streets of Shanghai, by unscrupulous means such as the use of force, alcohol, or drugs.

The situation was made even more difficult by the steady growth of the population. Peasants in Asia had always had large families on the assumption that a high proportion of their children would die in infancy. But improved sanitation and medical treatment resulted in lower rates of infant mortality and a staggering increase in population. The population of the island of Java, for example, increased from about a million in the precolonial era to about 40 million at the end of the nineteenth century. Under these conditions, the rural areas could no longer support the growing populations, and many young people fled to the cities to seek jobs in factories or shops. The migratory pattern gave rise to the squatter settlements in the suburbs of the major cities.

In some cases, colonial rule did bring modern economic infrastructure to Southeast Asia and what is sometimes called a "modernizing elite" dedicated to the creation of an advanced industrialized society. The development of an export market helped create an entrepreneurial class in rural areas. On the outer islands of the Dutch East Indies (such as Borneo and Sumatra), for example, small growers of rubber, palm oil, coffee, tea, and spices began to share in the profits of the colonial enterprise.

A balanced assessment of the colonial legacy in Southeast Asia must take into account that the early stages of industrialization are difficult in any society. Even in Western Europe, industrialization led to the creation of an impoverished and powerless proletariat, urban slums, and displaced peasants driven from the land. In much of Europe and Japan, however, the bulk of the population eventually enjoyed better material conditions as the profits from manufacturing and plantation agriculture were reinvested in the national economy and gave rise to increased consumer demand. In contrast, in Southeast Asia, most of the profits were repatriated to the colonial mother country, while displaced peasants fleeing to cities such as Rangoon, Batavia, and Saigon found little opportunity for employment. Many were left with seasonal employment, with one foot on the farm and one in the factory. The old world was being destroyed, while the new had yet to be born.

COLONIALISM IN AFRICA

Colonialism had similar consequences in Africa, although with some changes in emphasis. As we have seen, European economic interests were more limited in Africa than elsewhere. Having seized the continent in what could almost be described as an act of hysteria, the European powers had to decide what to do with it. With economic concerns relatively limited except for isolated areas, such as gold mines in the Transvaal and copper deposits in the Belgian Congo, interest in Africa declined, and most European governments settled down to govern their new territories with the least effort and expense possible. In many cases, this meant a form of indirect rule reminiscent of the British approach to the princely states in the Indian peninsula. The British, with their tradition of decentralized government at home, were especially prone to adopt this approach.

In the minds of British administrators, the stated goal of indirect rule was to preserve African political traditions. The desire to limit cost and inconvenience was one reason for this approach, but it may also have been based on the racist belief that Africans were inherently inferior to the white race and thus incapable of adopting European customs and institutions. In any event, indirect rule entailed relying to the greatest extent possible on existing political elites and institutions. Initially, in some areas, the British simply asked a local ruler to formally accept British authority and to fly the Union Jack over official buildings.

Nigeria offers a typical example of British indirect rule. British officials operated at the central level, but local authority was assigned to native chiefs, with British district officers serving as intermediaries with the central administration. Where a local aristocracy did not exist, the British assigned administrative responsibility to clan heads from communities in the vicinity. The local authorities were expected to maintain law and order and to collect taxes from the native population. As a general rule, indigenous customs were left undisturbed; a dual legal system was instituted that applied African laws to Africans and European laws to foreigners.

One advantage of such an administrative system was that it did not severely disrupt local customs and institutions. In fact, however, it had several undesirable consequences. In the first place, it was essentially a fraud because all major decisions were made by the British administrators while the native authorities served primarily as the means of enforcing decisions. Moreover, indirect rule served to perpetuate the autocratic system that often existed prior to colonial takeover. It was official policy to instill respect for authority in areas under British rule, and there was a natural tendency to view the local aristocracy as the African equivalent of the traditional British ruling class. Such a policy provided few opportunities for ambitious and talented young Africans from outside the traditional elite and thus sowed the seeds for class tensions after the restoration of independence in the twentieth century. Furthermore, this contradicted the liberal notion of meritocracy and instead perpetuated inequities inherit in class structures.

The situation was somewhat different in East Africa, especially in Kenya, which had a relatively large European population attracted by the temperate climate in the central highlands. The local government had encouraged Europeans to migrate to the area as a means of promoting economic development and encouraging financial self-sufficiency. To attract them, fertile farmlands in the central highlands were reserved for European settlement while, as in South Africa, specified reserve lands of inferior quality were set aside for Africans. The presence of a substantial European minority (although, in fact, they represented only about 1 percent of the entire population) had an impact on Kenya's political development. The European settlers actively sought self-government and dominion status similar to that granted to such former British possessions as Canada and Australia. The British government, however, was not willing to run the risk of provoking racial tensions with the African majority and agreed only to establish separate government organs for the European and African populations.

The situation in South Africa, of course, was unique, not only because of the high percentage of European settlers but also because of the division between English-speaking and Afrikaner elements within the European population. In 1910, the British agreed to the creation of the independent Union of South Africa, which combined the old Cape Colony and Natal with the two Boer republics. The new union adopted a representative government, but only for the European population, while the African reserves of Basutoland (now Lesotho), Bechuanaland (now Botswana), and Swaziland were subordinated directly to the Crown. The union was now free to manage its own domestic affairs and possessed considerable autonomy in foreign relations. Remaining areas south of the Zambezi River, eventually divided into the territories of Northern and Southern Rhodesia, were also placed under British rule. British immigration into Southern Rhodesia was extensive, and in 1922, after a popular referendum, it became a Crown colony.

Most other European nations governed their African possessions through a form of direct rule. The prototype was the French system, which reflected the centralized administrative system introduced in France by Napoleon. As in the British colonies, at the top of the pyramid was a French official, usually known as a governor-general, who was appointed from Paris and governed with the aid of a bureaucracy in the capital city. At the provincial level, French commissioners were assigned to deal with local administrators, but the latter were required to be conversant in French and could be transferred to a new position at the needs of the central government.

The French wanted and tried to assimilate their African subjects into French culture rather than preserve their native traditions. Africans were eligible to run for office and to serve in the French National Assembly, and a few were appointed to high positions in the colonial administration. But, this was usually with the condition that locals forgo their native cultures, language, and religion. Ultimately, class divisions were distinguished by race divisions.

After World War I, European colonial policy in Africa entered a new and more formal phase. The colonial administrative network extended into outlying areas, where it was represented by a district official and defended by a small native army under European command. Colonial governments paid more attention to improving social services, including education, medicine, sanitation, and communications. The colonial system was now viewed more formally as a moral and social responsibility, a so-called sacred trust to be maintained by the civilized countries until the Africans became capable of self-government. Governments placed more emphasis on economic development and the exploitation of natural resources to provide the colonies with the means of achieving self-sufficiency. More Africans were now serving in colonial administrations, though relatively few were in positions of responsibility. During this period, race consciousness probably increased, as segregated clubs, schools, and churches were established. More European officials brought their wives and began to raise families in the colonies and wanted separation of social and racial groups.

At the same time, the establishment of European colonial rule often had the effect of reducing the rights and the status of women in Africa. African women had traditionally benefited from the prestige of matrilineal systems and were empowered by their traditional role as the primary agricultural producer in their community. Under colonialism, not only did European settlers take the best land for themselves, but in introducing new agricultural techniques, they tended to deal exclusively with males, encouraging the latter to develop lucrative cash crops, while women were restricted to traditional farming methods. While African men applied chemical fertilizer to the fields, women used manure. While men began to use bicycles and eventually trucks to transport goods, women still carried goods on their heads.

CONCLUSION

By the early twentieth century, virtually all of Africa and a good part of South and Southeast Asia were under some form of colonial rule. With the advent of the age of imperialism, a global economy was finally established, and the domination of Western civilization over those of Africa and Asia appeared to be complete.

- Western colonial powers were driven by an insatiable lust for profits. This locked contemporary Third World countries in what many social scientists today describe as a core-periphery "dependency relationship" with their colonial masters.

- The sources of imperialism lay not simply in the demands of industrial capitalism but also in the search for security, national greatness, and even cultural racism.
- Although the colonial peoples received little immediate benefit from the imposition of foreign rule, overall the imperialist era brought about a vast expansion of the international trade network and created at least the potential for societies throughout Africa and Asia to play an active role in the new global economic arena.

While colonialism did introduce the peoples of Asia and Africa to new technology and the expanding economic marketplace, it was unnecessarily brutal in its application and all too often failed to realize the exalted claims and objectives of its promoters.

- Existing economic networks were ruthlessly swept aside in the interests of providing markets for Western manufactured goods.
- Potential sources of native industrialization were stunted to avoid competition for factories in Amsterdam, London, Pittsburgh, and Manchester.

- Training indigenous peoples in Western democratic ideals and practices was ignored out of fear that the recipients might use them as weapons against the ruling authorities.
- Colonialism, then, was ultimately based on the self-interests of the citizens of the colonial powers.

CRITICAL THINKING QUESTIONS

1. Are there contemporary examples of countries still inherently propagating a "white-man's burden" philosophy?

2. How did the core-periphery dependency relationship solidify under colonialism?

3. Why did colonial powers ally with local elites to subdue the local masses?

4. What are the benefits and disadvantages of indirect versus direct forms of rule?

5. Can a colonial philosophy ever be deemed non-racist?

Cultures in Collision

Chapter 3

War and Revolution: World War I and Its Aftermath

In the early 1900s, some writers, artists, and intellectuals were thrilled by the potential power and force represented by the advent of the Industrial Age; they looked forward to a future cut off completely from the past, in which modern technology would create a new type of human being. World War I would erupt in a few years challenging the vision of a peaceful world order driven by technology and modern change. The ugliness and horror of war would erase the hope and naivety of people.

At the conclusion of this chapter, you will be able to

- understand the important part alliances played in the sequence of events leading to World War I;
- describe the highs and lows of war and how they shaped the social history of societies that contributed forces to World War I;
- identify the social and political changes that set the stage for the Bolshevik Revolution in Russia.

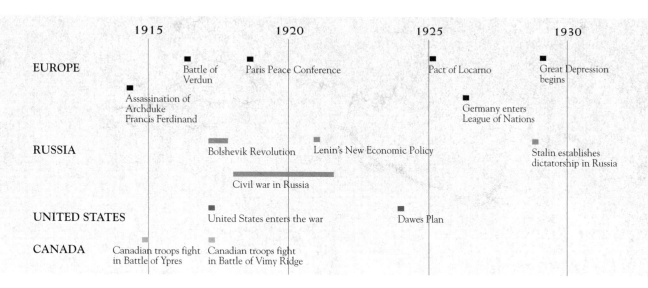

INTERNATIONAL RIVALRY AND THE COMING OF WAR

Between 1871 and 1914, Europeans experienced a long period of peace as the great powers managed to achieve a fragile balance of power in an effort to avert a re-creation of the destructive forces unleashed during the Napoleonic era.

But there were a series of crises that might easily have led to general war. Until 1890, Otto von Bismarck, the chancellor of Germany, exerted a restraining influence on Europeans. He realized that the emergence in 1871 of a unified Germany as the most powerful state on the Continent had upset the balance of power established at the Congress of Vienna in 1815, making many Europeans uneasy. Fearful of a possible anti-German alliance between France and Russia and possibly even Austria, Bismarck made a defensive alliance with Austria in 1879. In 1882, this German-Austrian alliance was enlarged with the entrance of Italy, angry with the French over convicting colonial ambitions in North Africa. The **Triple Alliance** of 1882 committed the three powers to support the existing political and social order while providing a defensive alliance against France. At the same time, Bismarck maintained a separate treaty with Russia and tried to remain on good terms with Great Britain.

> The **Triple Alliance** was a treaty formed in 1882 between Germany, Austria-Hungary, and Italy to defend one another if attacked by two or more superpowers.

When German Emperor Wilhelm II (1859–1941) dismissed Bismarck in 1890, he embarked on an activist foreign policy dedicated to enhancing German power by finding, as he put it, Germany's rightful "place in the sun." The treaty with Russia was cancelled as being at odds with Germany's alliance with Austria. But the result was what Bismarck had feared: it brought France and Russia together. Republican France leapt at the chance to draw closer to tsarist Russia, and in 1894, the two powers concluded a military alliance. During the next 10 years, German policies abroad caused the British to draw closer to France. By 1907, a loose confederation of Great Britain, France, and Russia—known as the **Triple Entente**—stood opposed to the Triple Alliance of Germany, Austria-Hungary, and Italy. Europe was divided into two opposing camps that became more and more inflexible and unwilling to compromise. When the members of the two alliances became involved in a new series of crises between 1908 and 1913 over the remnants of the Ottoman Empire in the Balkans, the stage was set for World War I.

> The **Triple Entente** was an alliance formed in 1907 between Great Britain, France, and Russia to thwart the perceived threat of German expansionism.

Who Were the Major Players in the Balkans Crises of 1908–1913?

In such an environment, where potentially hostile countries are locked in an awkward balance of power, it often takes only a spark to set off a firestorm. Such was the case in 1908, when a major European crisis began to emerge in the Balkans, where the decline of Ottoman power had turned the region into a tinderbox of ethnic and religious tensions.

The Bosnian crisis of 1908–09 began a chain of events that eventually spun out of control. Since 1878, Bosnia and Herzegovina had been under the protection of Austria, but in 1908, Austria took the drastic step of annexing the two Slavic-speaking territories. Serbia was outraged at this action because it dashed the Serbs' hopes of creating a large Serbian kingdom that would include most of the southern Slavs. But this possibility was precisely why the Austrians had annexed Bosnia and Herzegovina. The creation of a large Serbia would be a threat to the unity of their empire, with its large Slavic population. The Russians, desiring to increase their own authority in the Balkans, supported the Serbs, who then prepared for war against Austria. At this point, Wilhelm II demanded that the Russians accept Austria's annexation of Bosnia and Herzegovina or face war with Germany. Weakened from their defeat in the Russo-Japanese War in 1904–05, the Russians backed down but privately vowed revenge.

The crisis intensified in 1912 when Serbia, Bulgaria, Montenegro, and Greece organized the **Balkan League** and defeated the Turks in the First Balkan War. When the victorious allies were unable to agree on how to divide the conquered Turkish provinces of Macedonia and Albania, a Second Balkan War erupted in 1913. Greece, Serbia, Romania, and the Ottoman Empire attacked and defeated Bulgaria, which was left with only a small part of Macedonia. Most of the rest was divided between Serbia and Greece. Yet Serbia's aspirations remained unfulfilled. The two Balkan wars left the inhabitants embittered and created more tensions among the great powers.

> The **Balkan League** was an alliance organized by Prince Michael III of Serbia—it included Bulgaria, Serbia, Greece, and Montenegro—to drive the Turks out of the Balkans and form a single Slavic state.

By now Austria-Hungary was convinced that Serbia was a mortal threat to its empire and must at some point be crushed. Meanwhile, the French and Russian governments renewed their alliance and promised each other that they would not back down at the next crisis. Great Britain drew closer to France. By the beginning of 1914, two armed camps viewed each other with suspicion. The European "age of progress" was about to come to an inglorious and bloody end (see Map 3.1, Plate 5).

How Did Alliance Structures Prepare the Road to World War I?

On June 28, 1914, the heir to the Austrian throne, Archduke Francis Ferdinand, and his wife, Sophia, were assassinated in the Bosnian city of Sarajevo. The assassination was carried out by a Bosnian activist who worked for the Black Hand, a Serbian terrorist organization dedicated to the creation of a pan-Slavic kingdom. Although the Austrian government had no proof the Serbian government had been directly involved in the archduke's assassination, it saw an opportunity to "render Serbia innocuous once and for all by a display of force," as the Austrian foreign minister put it. Austrian leaders sought the backing of their German allies, who gave their assurance that Austria-Hungary could rely on Germany's "full support," even if "matters went to the length of a war between Austria-Hungary and Russia."

On July 23, Austrian leaders issued an ultimatum to Serbia in which they made such extreme demands that Serbia felt it had little choice but to reject some of them to preserve its sovereignty. Austria then declared war on Serbia on July 28. Still smarting from its humiliation in the Bosnian crisis of 1908, Russia was determined to support Serbia's cause. On July 28, Tsar Nicholas II ordered a partial mobilization of the Russian army against Austria. The Russian general staff informed the tsar that their mobilization plans were based on a war against both Germany and Austria simultaneously. They could not execute a partial mobilization without creating chaos in the army. Consequently, the Russian government ordered a full mobilization on July 29, knowing that the Germans would consider this an act of war against them. Germany responded by demanding that the Russians halt their mobilization within 12 hours. When the Russians ignored the ultimatum, Germany declared war on Russia on August 1.

Under the guidance of General Alfred von Schlieffen, chief of staff from 1891 to 1905, the German general staff had devised a military plan based on the assumption of a two-front war with France and Russia, which had formed a military alliance in 1894. The **Schlieffen Plan** called for only a minimal troop deployment against Russia. Most of the German army would execute a rapid invasion of France before Russia could become effective in the east or the British could cross the English Channel to help France. To achieve this rapid invasion, the Germans would advance through neutral Belgium, with its level coastal plain, where the army could move faster than on the rougher terrain to the southeast. After the planned quick defeat of the French, the German army would then redeploy to the east against Russia. Under the Schlieffen Plan, Germany could not mobilize its troops solely against Russia; therefore, on August 2, Germany issued an ultimatum to Belgium demanding the right of German troops to pass through Belgian territory and, on August 3, declared war on France. On August 4, Great Britain declared war on Germany, officially in response to this violation of Belgian neutrality but

in fact because of Great Britain's desire to maintain its world power. As one British diplomat argued, if Germany and Austria were to win the war, "What would be the position of a friendless England?" Thus by August 4, all the great powers of Europe were at war.

> The **Schlieffen Plan** was the most famous war plan during peacetime, named for the German general who devised it in 1892, in response to the Franco-Russian rapprochement and the fear that Germany might have to fight a war on two fronts at once; the plan directed the German army to begin any war by concentrating all possible forces against the French, for a rapid victory there would permit them to defeat the Russians afterward.

WORLD WAR I

Before 1914, many political leaders had become convinced that war involved so many political and economic risks that it was not worth fighting. Others believed that "rational" diplomats could control any situation and prevent the outbreak of war. At the beginning of August 1914, both of these pre-war illusions were shattered, but the new illusions that replaced them soon proved to be equally foolish.

How Were People Quickly Disillusioned by the Idea of a Quick and Easy War?

Europeans went to war in 1914 with overt enthusiasm. Government propaganda had been successful in stirring up national antagonisms before the war. Now, in August 1914, the urgent pleas of governments for defence against aggressors fell on receptive ears in every belligerent nation. Most people seemed genuinely convinced that their nation's cause was just. A new set of illusions also fed the enthusiasm for war. In August 1914, almost everyone believed that because of the risk of damage to the regional economy, the war would be over in a few weeks. People were told that European wars since 1815 had in fact ended in a matter of weeks. Both the soldiers who boarded the trains for the war front in August 1914 and the citizens who bombarded them with flowers as they departed believed that the soldiers would be home by Christmas.

In Canada, a similar level of support for the war was brewing. Once Great Britain declared war, Canada was automatically a participant since it was a British dominion at the time. Between 1914 and 1918 approximately 625 000 Canadian soldiers fought on the battlefields of Europe. Prime Minister Sir Robert Borden was able to secure unanimous consent from the Canadian government for its involvement in the war effort. Similarly, many Canadians overtly supported the war effort. People held impromptu parades and marches along Canadian streets where they believed in government propaganda that this war would be a victory of democracy over autocracy. Canadians believed that the war would be short; but they soon realized that the troops would not be home by Christmas. As the realities of war set in, the debate for and against conscription would prove to be a point of contention between French and English Canada. French Canadians did not support committing men to a war which seemed to have no near ending, while English Canadians felt a stronger sense of duty was owed to the monarchy of Great Britain and her battles. The growing opposition to the war in Canada started to take on a regional dimension.

German hopes for a quick end to the war rested on a military gamble. The Schlieffen Plan had called for the German army to make a vast encircling movement through Belgium into northern France that would sweep around Paris and encircle most of the French army. But the high command had not heeded Schlieffen's advice to place sufficient numbers of troops on the western salient to guarantee success, and the German advance was halted only

Librairie Larousse, Paris

The Excitement of War. Initially, World War I was greeted with enthusiasm; however, the fervour diminished quickly once the bloody realities of World War I began to set in and conscription was enforced.

30 kilometres from Paris at the First Battle of the Marne (September 6–12). The war quickly turned into a stalemate as neither the Germans nor the French could dislodge the other from the trenches they had begun to dig for shelter. Two lines of trenches soon extended from the English Channel to the frontiers of Switzerland (see Map 3.2, Plate 6). The Western Front had become bogged down in trench warfare that kept both sides immobilized in virtually the same positions for four years.

Warfare in the trenches of the Western Front produced unimaginable horrors. Battlefields were hellish landscapes of barbed wire, shell holes, mud, and injured and dying men. The introduction of poison gas in 1915 produced new forms of injuries, but the first aerial battles were a rare sideshow and gave no hint of the horrors to come with air warfare in the future. Soldiers in the trenches also lived with the persistent presence of death. Since combat went on for months, soldiers had to carry on in the midst of countless bodies of dead men or the remains of men dismembered by artillery barrages. Many soldiers remembered the stench of decomposing bodies and the swarms of rats that grew fat in the trenches.

In the first week of April 1915, soldiers were sent to fight in the City of Ypres, a medieval town in Belgium under the control of the Germans. Here, the British and allied forces had attempted to seize control from the Germans by pushing into German lines; however, their attempt failed and the Germans were able to maintain control over Ypres. The Battle of Ypres was the first time in World War I that chlorine gas was used, and is considered significant for the large scale of harm it inflicted. Here, the Germans fought the French using more than 5000 cylinders of chlorine gas. Unable to breathe, gasping for air and nearly choking, French troops were quickly defeated, eventually breaking and running to safety. In an effort to maintain a strong allied front, Canadian troops took over for the French. Faced with a second gas attack, Canadian soldiers held their ground, using their handkerchiefs soaked in muddy water and their own urine to protect themselves from breathing in the gases. As the armed Germans moved forward, Canadian soldiers, albeit using dysfunctional Ross rifles which constantly overheated and jammed, fought back fiercely, and won the battle against the Germans, successfully holding their place on the battlefield. This battle garnered international recognition for the Canadian military as superb fighters; however, the Battle of Ypres cost Canada over 6000 lives.

In contrast to the west, the war in the east was marked by much more mobility, although the cost in lives was equally enormous. At the beginning of the war, the Russian army moved into eastern Germany but was decisively defeated at the battles of Tannenberg on August 30 and the

Masurian Lakes on September 15. The Russians were no longer a threat to German territory.

The Austrians, Germany's allies, fared worse initially. After they were defeated by the Russians in Galicia and thrown out of Serbia as well, the Germans came to their aid. A German-Austrian army defeated and routed the Russian army in Galicia and pushed the Russians back 480 kilometres into their own territory. Russian casualties stood at 2.5 million killed, captured, or wounded; the Russians had almost been knocked out of the war. Buoyed by their success, the Germans and Austrians, joined by the Bulgarians in September 1915, attacked and eliminated Serbia from the war.

The successes in the east enabled the Germans to move back to the offensive in the west. The early trenches dug in 1914 had by now become elaborate systems of defence. Both lines of trenches were protected by barbed-wire entanglements 1 to 1.5 metres high and 27 metres wide, concrete machine-gun nests, and mortar batteries, supported farther back by heavy artillery. Troops lived in holes in the ground, separated from the enemy by a wasteland, but still, soldiers could hear the enemy's conversation across the fields.

The unexpected development of trench warfare baffled military leaders who had been trained to fight wars of movement and manoeuvre. Taking advantage of the recent American invention of the Caterpillar tractor, the British introduced tanks on the Western Front in 1915, but their effectiveness in breaking through enemy defences was not demonstrated. The only plan generals could devise was to attempt a breakthrough by throwing masses of men against enemy lines that had first been battered by artillery barrages. Periodically, the high command on either side would order an offensive that would begin with an artillery barrage to flatten the enemy's barbed wire and leave the enemy in a state of shock. After "softening up" the enemy in this fashion, a mass of soldiers would climb out of their trenches with fixed bayonets and hope to work their way toward the opposing trenches. The attacks rarely worked, as the machine gun put hordes of men advancing unprotected across open fields at a severe disadvantage. In 1916 and 1917, millions of young men were sacrificed in the search for the elusive breakthrough. In 10 months at Verdun, 700 000 men lost their lives over a few kilometres of terrain.

As another response to the stalemate on the Western Front, both sides looked for new allies who might provide a winning advantage. The Ottoman Empire, hoping to drive the British from Egypt, had already come into the war on Germany's side in August 1914. Russia, Great Britain, and France declared war on the Ottoman Empire in November. Although the Allies attempted to open a Balkan front by landing forces at Gallipoli, southwest of Constantinople, in April 1915, the campaign was a disaster. The Italians also entered the war on the Allied side after France and Great Britain promised to further their acquisition of Austrian territory.

By 1917, the war that had originated in Europe had truly become a world conflict. In the Middle East, the dashing but eccentric British adventurer T. E. Lawrence, popularly known as Lawrence of Arabia (1888–1935), incited an Arab revolt against their Ottoman overlords in 1917. In 1918, British forces from Egypt destroyed the rest of the Ottoman Empire in the Middle East. For these campaigns, the British mobilized forces from India, Australia, and New Zealand. The Allies also took advantage of Germany's preoccupations in Europe and lack of naval strength to seize German colonies elsewhere in the world. Japan seized a number of German-held islands in the Pacific, and Australia took over German New Guinea.

Most important to the Allied cause was the entry of the United States into the war. At first, the United States tried to remain isolationist, but that became more difficult as the war dragged on. The immediate cause of U.S. involvement grew out of the naval conflict between Germany and Great Britain. Great Britain used its superior naval power to maximum effect by imposing a naval blockade on Germany. Germany retaliated with a counter blockade enforced by the use of unrestricted submarine warfare. Strong U.S. protests over the German sinking of passenger liners—especially the British ship *Lusitania* on May 7, 1915, in which more than 100 Americans lost their lives—forced the German government to suspend unrestricted submarine warfare in September 1915 to avoid further antagonizing the Americans.

In January 1917, however, eager to break the deadlock in the war, German naval officers convinced Wilhelm II that the renewed use of unrestricted submarine warfare could starve the British into submission within five months, certainly before the Americans could act. To distract President Woodrow Wilson's administration in case it should decide to enter the war on the side of the Allied powers, German Foreign Minister Alfred von Zimmerman secretly encouraged the Mexican government to launch a military attack to recover territories lost to the United States in the American Southwest. Berlin's decision to return to unrestricted submarine warfare, combined with outrage in Washington over the Zimmerman telegram (which been decoded by the British and provided to U.S. diplomats in London), finally brought the United States into the war on April 6, 1917. Although American troops did not arrive in Europe in large numbers until 1918, U.S. entry into the war gave the Allied Powers a badly needed troop boost.

In the meantime, Canadian forces contributed a second notable, heroic effort at the **Battle of Vimy Ridge**. From

April 9 to 12, 1917, Canada's tactical training was put to use in one of the worst, yet one of the most important, Canadian battles fought during World War I. French and British troops attempted to make gains against their German counterparts several times yet failed in doing so, losing 200 000 British and French troops in the process. Canadian troops were brought in to defeat the Germans. The Germans had successfully built trenches, tunnels, and intricate fortifications, further protected by artillery and machine-gun platforms, that served to guard a number of German munitions factories. Four divisions of the Canadian Corps were brought in on April 9, 1917, in an attempt to defeat this German stronghold. Canadians studied the land through mock replicas and learned how to load and fire German artillery so that they could then use enemy equipment lost in battle by the Germans. Canadian troops advanced toward enemy lines with the help of British artillery men who fired shells in front of the Canadian troops, creating a surge of fire, which allowed Canadian troops to roll ahead and capture the hill from under German troops. The Battle of Vimy Ridge cost Canada over 3000 lives and is one of the more memorable battles in World War I.

In the **Battle of Vimy Ridge**, which took place in 1917 in northern France, Canadian soldiers defeated German troops and took hold of the strategic ridge and hills occupied by the Germans.

The year 1917 was not a good year for the Allied Powers. Allied offensives on the Western Front were disastrously defeated. The Italian armies were smashed in October, and in November 1917, the Bolshevik Revolution in Russia (discussed later in this chapter) led to Russia's withdrawal from the war, leaving Germany free to concentrate entirely on the Western Front.

For Germany, the withdrawal of the Russians from the war in March 1918 offered renewed hope for a favourable end to the war. The victory over Russia persuaded Erich von Ludendorff (1865–1937), who guided German military operations, and most German leaders to make one final military gamble—a grand offensive in the west to break the military stalemate. The German attack was launched in March and lasted into July, but an Allied counterattack, supported by the arrival of 140 000 fresh American troops, defeated the Germans at the Second Battle of the Marne on July 18. Ludendorff's gamble had failed. With the arrival of two million more American troops on the Continent, Allied forces began to advance steadily toward Germany.

On September 29, 1918, General Ludendorff informed German leaders that the war was lost and demanded that the government sue for peace at once. When German officials discovered that the Allies were unwilling to make peace with the autocratic imperial government, reforms were instituted to create a liberal government. But these constitutional reforms came too late for the exhausted and angry German people. On November 3, naval units in Kiel mutinied, and within days, councils of workers and soldiers were forming throughout northern Germany and taking over civilian and military administrations. Wilhelm II, capitulating to public pressure, abdicated on November 9, and the Socialists under Friedrich Ebert (1871–1925) announced the establishment of a republic. Two days later, on November 11, 1918, the new German government agreed to an armistice. The war was over.

The final tally of casualties from the war was appalling: nearly 5 million soldiers of the Allied side and 3.5 million from the Central Powers (as Germany and its allies were known). Civilian deaths were nearly as high. France, which had borne much of the burden of the war, suffered nearly 2 million deaths, almost one-tenth of the entire male population of the country.

How Were Conditions at Home?

As the war dragged on, conditions on the home front became a matter of concern for all the participants. The prolongation of the war had transformed it into a total conflict that affected the lives of all citizens, however remote they might be from the battlefields. The need to organize masses of men and materiel for years of combat (Germany alone had 5.5 million men in active units in 1916) led to increased centralization of government powers, economic regimentation, and manipulation of public opinion to keep the war effort going.

Because the war was expected to be short, little thought had been given to economic problems and long-term wartime needs. Governments had to respond quickly, however, when the war machines failed to achieve their knockout blows and made ever-greater demands for men and materials. The extension of government power was a logical outgrowth of these needs. Most European countries had already devised some system of mass conscription or military draft. It was now carried to unprecedented heights as countries mobilized tens of millions of young men for that elusive breakthrough to victory. Even countries that continued to rely on volunteers (Great Britain had the largest volunteer army in modern history—one million men—in 1914 and 1915) were forced to resort to conscription, especially to ensure that skilled labourers did not enlist but remained in factories that were important to the production of munitions. In the meantime, thousands of labourers were shipped in from the colonies to work on farms and in factories as replacements for Europeans mobilized to serve on the battlefield.

In Canada, World War I saw the debut of a strong interventionist state, including the start of a federal agency for marketing prairie wheat. Since the war had gone on for longer than expected, the need for wheat was critical to the war effort. By 1915, the Canadian government allotted 13 million bushels of wheat for the war effort. As the war raged on, more and more wheat was needed. Wheat farmers in Canada's west were no longer selling their wheat to British wholesalers; instead, they were selling wheat to the government of Great Britain. In fact, the British government requested as much of Canada's surplus wheat as it could offer, and, as a result, the Canadian government established the Board of Grain Supervisors that was responsible for fixing the price of grain and its overseas sales. By 1919, the **Canadian Wheat Board** was established, and it took over the responsibility of marketing grain from the Board of Grain Supervisors. Initially, the idea was meant to be a short-term war measure; however, the intervention of the government in agricultural affairs became lucrative and therefore solidified the government's place in the agricultural affairs of Canada.

> The **Canadian Wheat Board** was established in 1919 as a temporary wartime measure to market prairie wheat; it would later become an agency for controlling the marketing system for Canadian wheat, oat, and barley.

Similarly, throughout Europe, wartime governments expanded their powers over their economies. Free market capitalistic systems were temporarily shelved as governments experimented with price, wage, and rent controls; the rationing of food supplies and materials; the regulation of imports and exports; and the nationalization of transportation systems and industries. Some governments even moved toward compulsory employment. In effect, to mobilize the entire resources of the nation for the war effort, European countries had moved toward planned economies directed by government agencies. With total war mobilization, the distinction between soldiers at war and civilians at home was narrowed.

As World War I continued and both casualties and privations worsened, internal dissatisfaction replaced the patriotic enthusiasm that had marked the early stages of the conflict. By 1916, there were numerous signs that civilian morale was beginning to crack under the pressure of total war. War governments, however, fought back against the growing opposition to the war, as even parliamentary regimes resorted to an expansion of police powers to stifle internal dissent. At the very beginning of the war, the British Parliament passed the Defence of the Realm Act (DORA), which allowed the public authorities to arrest dissenters as traitors. The act was later extended to authorize public officials to censor newspapers by deleting objectionable material and even to suspend newspaper publication. In France, government authorities had initially been lenient about public opposition to the war, but by 1917, they began to fear that open opposition to the war might weaken the French will to fight. When Georges Clemenceau (1841–1929) became premier near the end of 1917, the lenient French policies came to an end, and basic civil liberties were suppressed for the duration of the war. When a former premier publicly advocated a negotiated peace, Clemenceau's government had him sentenced to prison for two years for treason.

The Call to War. With World War I recruitment posters like this one, Canadians were actively recruited to join the war effort. As the battles brought home more dead young men, the government had to be more active in recruiting them. How does this poster appeal to young men?

Library and Archives Canada/C-029484

Wartime governments made active use of propaganda to arouse enthusiasm for the war. The British and French, for example, exaggerated German atrocities in Belgium and found that their citizens were only too willing to believe these accounts. But as the war dragged on and morale sagged, governments were forced to devise new techniques for stimulating declining enthusiasm. One Canadian recruiting poster, for example, states "Your chums are fighting, why aren't you?" (see poster on page 51). But perhaps, one of the most memorable poems in Canada's history, "In Flanders Fields" by John McCrae, was an effective recruitment and propaganda tool that is still a large part of November 11 Remembrance Day ceremonies (see the box below).

Total war made a significant impact on society, most visibly by bringing an end to unemployment. The withdrawal of millions of men from the labour market to fight, combined with the heightened demand for wartime products, led to jobs for everyone able to work. The war also created new roles for women. Because so many men went off to fight at the front, women were called on to take over jobs and responsibilities that had not been available to them before.

Overall, the number of women employed in Great Britain who held new jobs or replaced men rose by 1 345 000. Women were also now employed in jobs that had been considered "beyond the capacity of women." These included such occupations as chimney sweeps, truck drivers, farm labourers, and factory workers in heavy industry. By 1918, some 38 percent of the workers in the Krupp armaments factories in Germany were women.

Canadian women also made a significant contribution to the war effort, keeping the economy stable by filling positions that were normally held by men in factories and offices. Alongside their counterparts on the home front, over 2500 Canadian women worked as nursing sisters in the Canadian Army Medical Corps. Margaret MacDonald was the director of the army of nurses and, as such, received two honours for her work during the war, namely, the Royal Red Cross from King George V and the Florence Nightingale Medal. All of the efforts on the part of women during the war played a pivotal role in raising awareness of the plight of women in Western society.

While male workers expressed concern that the employment of women at lower wages would depress their own

---

"IN FLANDERS FIELDS"

Canadian poet and medical officer John McCrae (1872–1918) published this now famous poem in England's *Punch* magazine December 8, 1915. Some have noted that the red poppies McCrae was referring to were in fact a symbol of the blood shed by his fellow army-men, which he witnessed. This official Flower of Remembrance in Canada, the United Kingdom, the United States, Australia, and New Zealand is still worn by Canadians to remember the fallen soldiers of the World Wars.

In Flanders Fields

In Flanders fields the poppies blow
Between the crosses, row on row,
That mark our place; and in the sky
The larks, still bravely singing, fly
Scarce heard amid the guns below.

We are the Dead. Short days ago
We lived, felt dawn, saw sunset glow,
Loved, and were loved, and now we lie
In Flanders Fields.
Take up our quarrel with the foe:
To you from failing hands we throw
The torch; be yours to hold it high.
If ye break faith with us who die
We shall not sleep, though poppies grow
In Flanders Fields.

John McCrae

© Photodisc/Getty Images

Source: Lieutenant Colonel John McCrae, MD (1872–1918), Canadian Army. First published in England's *Punch* magazine, December 1915.

wages, women began to demand equal pay legislation. For example, a law passed by the French government in July 1915 established a minimum wage for women home-workers in textiles, an industry that had grown dramatically thanks to the demand for military uniforms. Later in 1917, the government decreed that men and women should receive equal rates for piecework. Despite the noticeable increase in women's wages that resulted from government regulations, women's industrial wages still were not equal to men's wages by the end of the war.

Even worse, women's place in the workforce was far from secure. At the end of the war, governments moved quickly to remove women from the jobs they had encouraged them to take earlier. By 1919, there were 650 000 unemployed women in Great Britain, and wages for women who were still employed were lowered. The work benefits for women from World War I seemed to be short-lived as demobilized men returned to the job market.

Nevertheless, in some countries, the role played by women in the wartime economy did have a positive impact on the women's movement for social and political emancipation. The most obvious gain was the right to vote, which was granted to women in Manitoba in 1916 and then spread throughout the country. Similarly, women were granted the vote in Great Britain in January 1918 and in Germany and Austria immediately after the war. Contemporary media, however, tended to focus on the more noticeable, yet in some ways more superficial, social emancipation of upper- and middle-class women. In ever-larger numbers, these young women took jobs, had their own apartments, and showed their new independence by smoking in public and wearing shorter dresses, cosmetics, and new hairstyles. The social phenomenon of **Flappers**, newly emancipated young women who wore short hair and dresses, shook up a storm in the Western world.

Flappers were young, single, middle-class women who rejected convention; they wore their hair and dresses short, rolled their stockings down, used cosmetics, and smoked in public. They signalled their desire for independence and equality, but not through politics. The new female personality was endowed with self-reliance, outspokenness, and a new appreciation for the pleasures of life.

Who and What Countries Were Important to the Peace Settlement?

In January 1919, the delegations of 27 victorious Allied nations gathered in Paris to conclude a final settlement of World War I. Some delegates believed that this conference would avoid the mistakes made at Vienna in 1815 by aristocrats who rearranged the map of Europe to meet the selfish desires of the great powers. Harold Nicolson, one of the British delegates, expressed what he believed this conference would achieve instead: "We were journeying to Paris not merely to liquidate the war, but to found a New Order in Europe. We were preparing not Peace only, but Eternal Peace. There was about us the halo of some divine mission. . . . For we were bent on doing great, permanent and noble things."[1]

National expectations, however, made Nicolson's quest for "eternal peace" a difficult one. Over the years, the reasons for fighting World War I had been transformed from selfish national interests to idealistic principles. No one expressed the latter better than Woodrow Wilson. The American president outlined to the U.S. Congress **Fourteen Points** that he believed justified the enormous military struggle then being waged (see the box on page 54). Later, Wilson spelled out additional steps for a truly just and lasting peace. As the spokesperson for a new world order based on democracy and international cooperation, Wilson was enthusiastically cheered when he arrived in Europe for the peace conference being held in Paris.

The **Fourteen Points** of U.S. President Woodrow Wilson's post-war peace program included freedom of the seas, free trade, open diplomacy, and, most importantly, self-determination of occupied states.

Wilson soon found, however, that other states at the conference were guided by considerably more pragmatic motives. The secret treaties and agreements that had been made before and during the war could not be totally ignored, even if they did conflict with Wilson's principle of self-determination (see Chapter 4). National interests also complicated the deliberations of the conference. David Lloyd George (1863–1945), prime minister of Great Britain, had won a decisive electoral victory in December 1918 on a platform of making the Germans pay for the dreadful war.

France's approach to peace was determined primarily by considerations of national security. To Georges Clemenceau, the feisty French premier who had led his country to victory, the French people had borne the brunt of German aggression and deserved security against any possible future attack. Clemenceau wanted a demilitarized Germany, vast reparations to pay for the costs of the war, and a separate Rhineland as a buffer state between France and Germany—demands that Wilson viewed as vindictive and contrary to the principle of national self-determination.

Although 27 nations were represented at the **Paris Peace Conference** that took place at Versailles in 1919, the

A WORLD SAFE TO LIVE IN

For many Americans, World War I was an inevitable consequence of the sordid "balance of power" politics long practised in the Old World. President Woodrow Wilson expressed this view when, in January 1918, he proposed that the inter-war era should be based on the principle of the equality of nations. Among the Fourteen Points mentioned in his speech, the most famous was the fourteenth, which called for self-determination and territorial integrity for all states in the world. Although the idea won broad popular support, it was opposed by leaders of the imperialist powers, who viewed it as a threat to their colonial interests.

Woodrow Wilson's Fourteen Points

. . . WE ENTERED this war because violations of right had occurred which touched us to the quick and made the life of our people impossible unless they were corrected and the world secured once for all against their recurrence. What we demand in this war, therefore, is nothing peculiar to ourselves. It is that the world be made fit and safe to live in; and particularly that it be made safe for every peace-loving nation which, like our own, wishes to live its own life, determine its own institutions, be assured of justice and fair dealing by the other peoples of the world as against force and selfish aggression. All the peoples of the world are in effect partners in this interest, and for our own part we see very clearly that unless justice be done to others it will not be done to us. The programme of the world's peace, therefore, is our programme; and that programme, the only possible programme, as we see it, is this:

I. Open covenants of peace, openly arrived at, after which there shall be no private international understandings of any kind but diplomacy shall proceed always frankly and in the public view.

II. Absolute freedom of navigation upon the seas, outside territorial waters, alike in peace and in war, except as the seas may be closed in whole or in part by international action for the enforcement of international covenants.

III. The removal, so far as possible, of all economic barriers and the establishment of an equality of trade conditions among all the nations consenting to the peace and associating themselves for its maintenance. . . .

V. A free, open-minded, and absolutely impartial adjustment of all colonial claims, based upon a strict observance of the principle that in determining all such questions of sovereignty the interests of the populations concerned must have equal weight with the equitable claims of the government whose title is to be determined. . . .

XIV. A general association of nations must be formed under specific covenants for the purpose of affording mutual guarantees of political independence and territorial integrity to great and small states alike.

In regard to these essential rectifications of wrong and assertions of right we feel ourselves to be intimate partners of all the governments and peoples associated together against the Imperialists. We cannot be separated in interest or divided in purpose. We stand together until the end. . . .

Source: *Congressional Record,* 65th Congress, 2nd Session, pp. 680–81.

most important decisions were made by Wilson, Clemenceau, and Lloyd George. Italy was considered one of the so-called Big Four powers (originally the Big Five until Japan was left out of negotiations) but played a much less important role than the other three countries. Germany was not invited to attend, and Russia could not because it was embroiled in civil war. Canada attended the Paris Peace Conference and, as planned, signed the treaty independently of Great Britain, thus signalling its independence from the British Empire to the international community.

The **Paris Peace Conference** of 1919 led to the signing of the Treaty of Versailles by Germany and the Allies, stating the terms of peace and marking the conclusion of World War I.

In view of the many conflicting demands at Versailles, it was inevitable that the Big Three would quarrel. Wilson was determined to create an organization for international cooperation to prevent future wars. Clemenceau and Lloyd

George were equally determined to punish Germany. In the end, only compromise made it possible to achieve a peace settlement. On January 25, 1919, the conference adopted the principle of the **League of Nations** (the details of its structure were left for later sessions); Wilson willingly agreed to make compromises on territorial arrangements to guarantee the league's establishment, believing that a functioning league could later rectify bad arrangements. Clemenceau also compromised to obtain some guarantees for French security. He renounced France's desire for a separate Rhineland and instead accepted a defensive alliance with Great Britain and the United States, both of which pledged to help France if it were attacked by Germany.

> The **League of Nations** was an international organization established in 1919 at the Paris Peace Conference in order to prevent future wars through collective security arrangements. It became ineffective as early as 1931 with the failure to handle the Manchurian crisis. It was replaced by the United Nations in 1946.

Canada's approach to peace was determined by its ambition to be seen as a nation independent of the British Empire. Since Canada had contributed to the victory of World War I, it felt that it had earned the right to be seen as a nation separate from Great Britain in the international community. Canada, like other British dominions, sought a seat of its own at the League of Nations and was rightly granted one. Although still a part of the British family, Canada had gained control over its international affairs by the Statute of Westminster in 1931.

The final peace settlement at Paris consisted of five separate treaties with the defeated nations—Germany, Austria, Hungary, Bulgaria, and Turkey. The Treaty of Versailles with Germany, signed on June 28, 1919, was by far the most important one. The Germans considered it a harsh peace and were particularly unhappy with Article 231, the so-called war guilt clause, which declared Germany (and Austria) responsible for starting the war and ordered Germany to pay reparations for all the damage to which the Allied governments and their people had been subjected as a result of the war "imposed upon them by the aggression of Germany and her allies."

The military and territorial provisions of the treaty also rankled the Germans, although they were by no means as harsh as the Germans claimed. Germany had to lower its army to 100 000 men, reduce its navy, and eliminate its air force. German territorial losses included the return of Alsace and Lorraine to France and sections of Prussia to the new Polish state. German land west, and as far as 50 kilometres east, of the Rhine was established as a demilitarized zone

and stripped of all armaments or fortifications to serve as a barrier to any future German military moves westward against France. Outraged by the "dictated peace," the new German government complained but accepted the treaty.

The separate peace treaties made with the other Central Powers extensively redrew the map of Eastern Europe (see Maps 3.3, Plate 7, and 3.4, Plate 8). Many of these changes merely ratified what the war had already accomplished. Both Germany and Russia lost considerable territory in Eastern Europe; the Austro-Hungarian Empire disappeared altogether. New nation-states emerged from the lands of these three empires: Finland, Latvia, Estonia, Lithuania, Poland, Czechoslovakia, Austria, and Hungary. Territorial rearrangements were also made in the Balkans. Romania acquired additional lands from Russia, Hungary, and Bulgaria. Serbia formed the nucleus of a new South Slav state called *Yugoslavia,* which combined Serbs, Croats, and Slovenes. Although the Paris Peace Conference was supposedly guided by the principle of self-determination, the mixtures of peoples in Eastern Europe made it impossible to draw boundaries along neat ethnic lines. Compromises had to be made, sometimes to satisfy the national interest of the victors. France, for example, had lost Russia as its major ally on Germany's eastern border and wanted to strengthen and expand Poland, Czechoslovakia, Yugoslavia, and Romania as much as possible so that those states could serve as barriers against Germany and communist Russia. As a result of compromises, virtually every Eastern European state was left with a minorities issue that could lead to future conflicts. Germans in Poland; Hungarians, Poles, and Germans in Czechoslovakia; and the combination of Serbs, Croats, Slovenes, Macedonians, and Albanians in Yugoslavia all became sources of later conflicts. Moreover, the new map of Eastern Europe was based on the temporary collapse of power in both Germany and Russia. As neither country accepted the new eastern frontiers, it seemed only a matter of time before a resurgent Germany or Russia would seek to make changes.

The Ottoman Empire was also a casualty of the war. To gain Arab support against the Turks, the Western Allies had promised to recognize the independence of Arab areas now under Ottoman occupation. But imperialist habits died hard. Although Saudi Arabia eventually received full independence, much of the remainder of the region was assigned to Great Britain (Iraq, Jordan, and Palestine) and France (Syria and Lebanon) as mandates under the new League of Nations. The peace settlement had established the mandate system at the insistence of Woodrow Wilson, who opposed outright annexation of colonial territories by the Allies.

Within 20 years after the signing of the peace treaties, Europe was again engaged in deadly conflict. Some historians have suggested that the cause was the punitive nature of the peace terms imposed on the defeated powers, provoking anger that would lead to feelings of revenge in Germany and in Austria. Others maintain that the cause was less in the structure of the Versailles treaty than in its lack of enforcement. Successful enforcement of the peace necessitated the active involvement of its principal architects, especially in helping the new German state develop a peaceful and democratic republic. By the end of 1919, however, the United States was already retreating into political isolationism (albeit continuing its economic relations with Europe). The failure of the U.S. Senate to ratify the Treaty of Versailles meant that the United States never joined the League of Nations. The Senate also rejected Wilson's defensive alliance with Great Britain and France.

American withdrawal from the defensive alliance with Great Britain and France led Great Britain to withdraw as well. By removing itself from European affairs, the United States forced France to face its old enemy alone, leading the embittered nation to take strong actions against Germany that only intensified German resentment. By the end of 1919, it appeared that the peace was already beginning to unravel.

THE RUSSIAN REVOLUTION

The armistice of 1918 brought no peace to Russia. During the early years of the twentieth century, Russia entered the Industrial Revolution. As elsewhere, it was a wrenching experience, marked by rapid social change and political unrest. Demonstrations during the Russo-Japanese War of 1904–05 forced the tsar to agree to political reforms (including the creation of Russia's first legislative assembly, the duma) that for the first time limited his supreme authority. For a brief time, radicals harboured hopes that revolution was imminent, but the monarchy survived, though shaken, and the nation entered a brief period of relative stability.

Marxism made its first appearance in the Russian environment in the 1880s. Early Marxists were aware of the primitive conditions in their country and asked Karl Marx himself for advice. The Russian proletariat was oppressed—indeed, brutalized—but small in numbers and unsophisticated. Could agrarian Russia make the transition to socialism without an intervening stage of capitalism? Marx, who always showed more flexibility than the rigid determinism of his system suggested, replied that it was possible that Russia could avoid the capitalist stage by building on the communal traditions of the Russian village, known as the *mir*.

Mir is the Russian term for "rural peasant village" or "community."

But as Russian Marxism evolved, its leaders turned more toward Marxist orthodoxy. Founding member Georgy Plekhanov saw signs in the early stages of the Industrial Revolution that Russia would follow the classic pattern. He predicted, however, that the weak Russian bourgeoisie would be unable to consolidate its power, thus opening the door for a rapid advance from the capitalist to the socialist stage of the revolution. In 1898, Plekhanov's Russian Social Democratic Labour Party (RSDLP) held its first congress.

During the last decade of the nineteenth century, a new force entered the Russian Marxist movement in the figure of Vladimir Ulyanov, later to be known as *Vladimir Lenin*. Initially radicalized by the execution of his older brother for terrorism in 1886, he became a revolutionary and a member of Plekhanov's RSDLP. Like Plekhanov, Lenin believed in the revolution, but he was a man in a hurry. Whereas Plekhanov wanted to prepare patiently for revolution by education and mass work, Lenin wanted to build up the party rapidly as a vanguard instrument to galvanize the masses and spur the workers to revolt. In a pamphlet titled "What Is to Be Done?" he proposed the transformation of the RSDLP into a compact and highly disciplined group of professional revolutionaries that would not merely ride the crest of the revolutionary wave but unleash the storm clouds of revolt.

At the Second National Congress of the RSDLP, held in 1903 in Brussels and London, Lenin's ideas were supported by a majority of the delegates (thus the historical term **Bolsheviks**, or **majorityites**, for his followers). His victory was short-lived, however, and for the next decade, Lenin, living in exile, was a brooding figure on the fringe of the Russian revolutionary movement, which was now dominated by the **Mensheviks (minorityites)**, who opposed Lenin's single-minded pursuit of violent revolution.

The **Bolsheviks** were a small faction of the Russian Social Democratic Labour Party led by Vladimir Lenin and dedicated to violent revolution; they seized power in Russia in 1917 and subsequently renamed themselves *Communists*. The Bolsheviks were also known as **Majorityites**, a faction of the Second Congress of Russian Social Democratic Labour Party. The **Mensheviks**, the other faction of the party, were also known as **minorityites**.

World War I broke the trajectory of Russia's economic growth and laid the foundation for the collapse of the Old Order. There is a supreme irony in this fact, for Tsar Nicholas II appeared almost to welcome war with Germany as a means of uniting the people behind their sovereign. This was certainly the case with Russia. After stirring victories in the early stages of the war, news from the battlefield turned increasingly grim as the modern armies of the Kaiser slaughtered poorly armed Russian soldiers. The conscription of peasants from the countryside caused food prices to rise and led, by late 1916, to periodic bread shortages in the major cities. Workers grew increasingly restive at the wartime schedule of long hours with low pay and joined army deserters in angry marches through the capital of Saint Petersburg (then known as *Petrograd*).

It was a classic scenario for revolution—discontent in the big cities fuelled by mutinous troops streaming home from the battlefield and a rising level of lawlessness in rural areas as angry peasants seized land and burned the manor houses of the wealthy. Even the urban middle class, always a bellwether on the political scene, grew impatient with the economic crisis and the bad news from the front and began to question the competence of the tsar and his advisers. In late February 1917, government troops fired at demonstrators in the streets of the capital and killed several. An angry mob marched to the duma, where restive delegates demanded the resignation of the tsar's cabinet.

Nicholas II had never wanted to share the supreme power he had inherited with the throne. After a brief period of hesitation, he abdicated, leaving a vacuum that was quickly seized by leading elements in the duma, who formed a provisional government to steer Russia through the crisis. On the left, reformist and radical political parties—including the Social Revolutionaries (the legal successors of the outlawed terrorist organization Narodnaya Volya) and the two wings of the RSDLP, the Mensheviks and the Bolsheviks—cooperated in creating a shadow government called the *Saint Petersburg Soviet*. This shadow government supported the provisional government in pursuing the war but attempted to compel it to grant economic and social reforms that would benefit the masses.

The so-called February Revolution of 1917 had forced the collapse of the monarchy, but it showed little promise of solving the deeper problems that had led Russia to the brink of civil war. Finally convinced that a real social revolution was at hand, Lenin returned from exile in Switzerland in April (thanks to the Germans who allowed him passage across Germany in hopes of further destabilizing Russia) and, on his arrival in Petrograd, laid out a program for his followers: all power to the soviets (locally elected government councils), an end to the war, and the distribution of land to poor peasants. But Lenin's April Theses were too radical even for his fellow Bolsheviks, and his demands were ignored by other leaders, who continued to cooperate with the provisional government while attempting to push it to the left.

© Brown Brothers

Lenin Addresses a Crowd. Vladimir Lenin was the driving force behind the success of the Bolsheviks in seizing power in Russia and creating the Union of Soviet Socialist Republics. Here Lenin is seen addressing a rally in Moscow in 1917.

Who Were the Key Figures of the Bolshevik Revolution?

During the summer, the crisis worsened, and in July, riots by workers and soldiers in the capital led the provisional government to outlaw the Bolsheviks and call for Lenin's arrest. The "July Days," raising the threat of disorder and class war, aroused the fears of conservatives and split the fragile political consensus within the provisional government. In September, General Lavr Kornilov, commander in chief of Russian imperial forces, launched a coup d'état to seize power from Aleksandr Kerensky, now the dominant figure in the provisional government. The revolt was put down with the help of so-called Red Guard units, formed by the Bolsheviks within army regiments in the capital area (these troops would later be regarded as the first units of the Red Army), but Lenin now sensed the weakness of the provisional government and persuaded his colleagues to prepare for revolt. On the night of October 25 (according to the old-style Gregorian calendar still in use in Russia), forces under the command of Lenin's lieutenant, Leon Trotsky (1879–1940), seized key installations in the capital area. Kerensky fled from Russia in disguise. The following morning, at a national congress of delegates from soviet organizations throughout the country, the Bolsheviks declared a new socialist order. Moderate elements from the Menshevik faction and the Social Revolutionary Party protested the illegality of the Bolshevik action and left the conference hall in anger. They were derided by Trotsky, who proclaimed that they were relegated "to the dustbin of history."

With the Bolshevik Revolution of October 1917, Lenin was now in command. His power was tenuous and extended only from the capital to a few of the larger cities, such as Moscow and Kiev, that had waged their own insurrections. There were, in fact, few Bolsheviks in rural areas, where most peasants supported the moderate leftist Social Revolutionaries. On the fringes of the Russian Empire, restive minorities prepared to take advantage of the anarchy to seize their own independence, while "White Russian" supporters of the monarchy began raising armies to destroy the "Red menace" in Petrograd. Lenin was in power, but for how long?

The Russian Revolution of 1917 has been the subject of vigorous debate by scholars and students of world affairs. Could it have been avoided if the provisional government had provided more effective leadership, or was it inevitable? Did Lenin stifle Russia's halting progress toward a Western-style capitalist democracy, or was the Bolshevik victory preordained by the autocratic conditions and lack of democratic traditions in imperial Russia? Such questions have no simple answers, but some hypotheses are possible. The weakness of the moderate government created by the February Revolution was probably predictable, given the political inexperience of the urban middle class and the deep divisions within the ruling coalition over issues of peace and war. On the other hand, it seems highly unlikely that the Bolsheviks would have possessed the self-confidence to act without the presence of their leader, Vladimir Lenin, who employed his strength of will to urge his colleagues almost single-handedly to make their bid for power. Without Lenin, then, there would have been no political force with the sense of purpose to fill the vacuum in Petrograd. In that case, as in so many cases elsewhere during the turbulent twentieth century, it would probably have been left to the army to intervene in an effort to maintain law and order.

In any event, the October Revolution was a momentous development for Russia and for the entire world. Not only did it present Western capitalist societies with a brazen new challenge to their global supremacy, but it also demonstrated that Lenin's concept of revolution, carried through at the will of a determined minority of revolutionary activists "in the interests of the masses," could succeed in a society going through the difficult early stages of the Industrial Revolution. It was a repudiation of orthodox "late Marxism" and a return to Marx's pre-1848 vision of a multi-class revolt leading rapidly from a capitalist to a proletarian takeover (see the box "*The Communist Manifesto*" in Chapter 1). It was, in short, a lesson that would not be ignored by intellectuals throughout the world.

The Bolshevik seizure of power in Petrograd (soon to be renamed Leningrad after Lenin's death in 1924) was only the first, and not necessarily the most difficult, stage in the Russian Revolution. Although the Bolshevik slogan of "Peace, Land, and Bread" had earned considerable appeal among workers, petty merchants, and soldiers in the vicinity of the capital and other major cities, the party—only 50 000 strong in October—had little representation in the rural areas, where the moderate leftist Social Revolutionary Party received majority support from the peasants. On the fringes of the Russian Empire, ethnic minority groups took advantage of the confusion in Petrograd to launch movements to restore their own independence or achieve a position of autonomy within the Russian state. In the meantime, supporters of the deposed Romanov dynasty and other political opponents of the Bolsheviks attempted to mobilize support to drive the Bolsheviks out of the capital and reverse the verdict of "Red October." And beyond all that, the war with Germany continued.

Lenin was aware of these problems and hoped that a wave of socialist revolutions in the economically advanced countries of Central and Western Europe would bring the world war to an end and usher in a new age of peace, socialism, and growing economic prosperity. In the meantime, his first priority was to consolidate the rule of the working class and its party vanguard (now to be renamed the *Communist Party*) in Russia. The first step was to set up a new order in Petrograd to replace the provisional government that itself had been created after the February Revolution. For lack of a better alternative, outlying areas were simply informed of the change in government—a "revolution by telegraph," as Leon Trotsky termed it. Then Lenin moved to create new organs of proletarian power, setting up the Council of People's Commissars to serve as a provisional government. Lenin was unwilling to share power with moderate leftists who had resisted the Bolshevik coup in October, and he created security forces (popularly called the *Cheka,* or "extraordinary commission"), which imprisoned and sometimes executed opponents of the new regime. In January 1918, the Constituent Assembly, which had been elected on the basis of plans established by the previous government, convened in Petrograd. Primarily comprising delegates from the Social Revolutionary Party and other parties opposed to the Bolsheviks, it was critical of the new regime and immediately abolished.

In foreign affairs, Lenin's first major decision was to seek peace with Germany in order to permit the new government to focus its efforts on the growing threat posed by White Russian forces within the country. In March 1918, a peace settlement with Germany was reached at Brest-Litovsk, although at enormous cost. Soviet Russia lost nearly one-fourth of the territory and one-third the population of the pre-war Russian Empire. In retrospect, however, Lenin's controversial decision to accept a punitive peace may have been a stroke of genius, for it gained time for the regime to build up its internal strength and defeat its many adversaries in the Russian Civil War (1918–20). The White Russian forces were larger than those of the Red Army; they were supported by armed contingents sent by Great Britain, France, and the United States to assist in the extinction of the "Red menace"; but they were also rent by factionalism and hindered by the tendency of White Russian leaders to return conquered land to the original landowners, thus driving many peasants to support the Soviet regime. By 1920, the civil war was over, and Soviet power was secure.

How Was Socialism Gradually Brought in by the Bolsheviks?

With their victory over the White Russians in 1920, Soviet leaders now could turn for the first time to the challenging task of building the first socialist society in a world dominated by their capitalist enemies. In his writings, Karl Marx had said little about the nature of the final Communist utopia or how to get there. He had spoken briefly of a transitional phase, variously known as "raw communism" or "socialism," that would precede the final stage of communism. During this phase, the Communist Party would establish a "dictatorship of the proletariat" to rid society of the "capitalist oppressors," set up the institutions of the new order, and indoctrinate the population in the Communist ethic. In recognition of the fact that traces of "bourgeois thinking" would remain among the population, profit incentives would be used to encourage productivity (in the slogan of Marxism, payment would be on the basis of "work" rather than solely on "need"), but major industries would be nationalized and private landholdings eliminated. After seizing power, however, the Bolsheviks were too preoccupied with survival to give much attention to the future nature of Soviet society. "War communism"—involving the government seizure of major industries, utilities, and sources of raw materials and the requisition of grain from private farmers—was, by Lenin's own admission, just a makeshift policy to permit the regime to mobilize resources for the civil war.

In 1920, it was time to adopt a more coherent approach. The realities were sobering. Soviet Russia was not an advanced capitalist society in the Marxist image, blessed with modern technology and an impoverished and politically aware underclass imbued with the desire to advance to socialism. It was poor and primarily agrarian, and its small but growing industrial sector had been ravaged by years of war. Under the circumstances, Lenin called for caution. He won his party's approval for a moderate program of social and economic development known as the **New Economic Policy** (NEP). The program was based on a combination of capitalist and socialist techniques designed to increase production through the use of profit incentives while at the same time promoting the concept of socialist ownership and maintaining firm party control over the political system and the overall direction of the economy. The "commanding heights" of the Soviet economy (heavy industry, banking, utilities, and foreign trade) remained in the hands of the state, while private industry and commerce were allowed to operate at the lower levels. The forced requisition of grain, which had caused serious unrest among the peasantry, was replaced by a tax, and land remained firmly in private hands. The theoretical justification for the program was that Soviet Russia now needed to go through its own "capitalist stage" (albeit under the control of the party) before beginning the difficult transition to socialism.

> The **New Economic Policy** (NEP) was a modified version of the old capitalist system introduced in the Soviet Union by Vladimir Lenin in 1921 to revive the economy after the ravages of the civil war.

As an economic strategy, the NEP succeeded brilliantly. During the early and mid-1920s, the Soviet economy recovered rapidly from the doldrums of war and civil war. A more lax hand over the affairs of state allowed a modest degree of free expression of opinion within the ranks of the party and in Soviet society at large. Under the surface, however, trouble loomed. Lenin had been increasingly disabled by a bullet lodged in his neck from an attempted assassination, and he began to lose his grip over a fractious party. Even before his death in 1924, potential successors had begun to scuffle for dominance in the struggle to assume his position as party leader, the most influential position in the state. The main candidates were Leon Trotsky and a rising young figure from the state of Georgia, Joseph Dzhugashvili, better known by his revolutionary name, Stalin (1879–1953). Lenin had misgivings about all the candidates hoping to succeed him and suggested that a collective leadership best represented the interests of the party and the revolution. After his death in 1924, factional struggle among the leading figures in the party intensified. Although in some respects it was a pure power struggle, it did have policy ramifications as party factions debated about the NEP and its impact on the future of the Russian Revolution.

At first, the various factions were relatively evenly balanced, but Stalin proved adept at using his position as general secretary of the party to outmanoeuvre his rivals. By portraying himself as a centrist opposed to the extreme positions of his "leftist" (too radical in pursuit of revolutionary goals) or "rightist" (too prone to adopt moderate positions contrary to Marxist principles) rivals, he gradually concentrated power in his own hands.

In the meantime, the relatively moderate policies of the NEP continued to operate as the party and the state vocally encouraged the Soviet people, in a very un-Marxist manner, to enrich themselves. Capital investment and technological assistance from Western capitalist countries were actively welcomed. An observer at the time might reasonably have concluded that the Marxist vision of a world characterized by class struggle had become a dead letter.

THE SEARCH FOR STABILITY IN THE WESTERN WORLD

In the years following the end of the war, many people hoped that Europe and the world were about to enter a new era of international peace, economic growth, and political democracy. In all of these areas, the optimistic hopes of the 1920s failed to be realized.

Why Was the Treaty of Versailles Ultimately Fragile?

The peace settlement at the end of World War I had tried to fulfill the nineteenth-century dream of nationalism by creating new boundaries and new states. From the outset, however, the settlement had left nations unhappy. Conflicts over disputed border regions between Germany and Poland, Poland and Lithuania, Poland and Czechoslovakia, Austria and Hungary, and Italy and Yugoslavia poisoned mutual relations in Eastern Europe for years. Many Germans viewed the peace of Versailles as a dictated peace and vowed to seek its revision.

To its supporters, the League of Nations was the place to resolve such problems. The league, however, proved ineffectual in maintaining the peace. The failure of the United States to join the league (partially a consequence of public disillusionment with disputes at the Versailles conference) undermined the effectiveness of the league right from the start. Moreover, the league could use only economic sanctions to halt aggression. The French attempt to strengthen the league's effectiveness as an instrument of collective security by creating a peacekeeping force was rejected by nations that feared giving up any of their sovereignty to a larger international body. Similarly in Canada, Prime Minister William Lyon Mackenzie King (1874–1950) refused to contribute Canadian military forces to participate in overseas collective security activities, including assisting Ethiopia against Italian aggression in 1935.

The weakness of the League of Nations and the failure of both the United States and Great Britain to honour their collective military alliances with France led the latter to insist on a strict enforcement of the Treaty of Versailles. This tough policy toward Germany began with the issue of reparations—the payments that the Germans were supposed to make to compensate for the "damage done to the civilian population of the Allied and Associated Powers and to their property," as the treaty asserted. In April 1921, the Allied Reparations Commission settled on a sum of 132 billion marks (US$33 billion) for German reparations, payable in annual installments of 2.5 billion (gold) marks. Allied threats to occupy the Ruhr Valley, Germany's chief industrial and mining centre, induced the new German republic to accept the reparations settlement and to make its first payment in 1921. By the following year, however, facing rising inflation, domestic turmoil, and lack of revenues because of low tax rates, the German government announced that it was unable to pay more. Outraged by what they considered to be Germany's violation of one aspect of the peace settlement, the French government sent troops to occupy the Ruhr Valley. If the Germans would not pay reparations, the French would collect reparations in kind by operating and using the Ruhr mines and factories.

French occupation of the Ruhr Valley seriously undermined the fragile German economy. The German government adopted a policy of passive resistance to French occupation that was largely financed by printing more paper money, thus intensifying the inflationary pressures that had already begun at the end of the war. The German mark became worthless. Economic disaster fuelled political upheavals as Communists staged uprisings in October and Adolf Hitler's (1889–1945) band of Nazis attempted and failed to seize power in Munich in November 1923 in what became known as the *Beer Hall Putsch*. The following year, a new conference of experts was convened to reassess the reparations problem.

The formation of liberal-socialist governments in both Great Britain and France opened the door to conciliatory approaches to Germany and the reparations problem. At the same time, a new German government led by Gustav Stresemann (1878–1929) ended the policy of passive resistance and committed Germany to carry out the provisions of the Versailles treaty while seeking a new settlement of the reparations question.

In August 1924, an international commission produced a new plan for reparations. Named the **Dawes Plan** after the American banker who chaired the commission, it reduced reparations and stabilized Germany's payments on the basis of its ability to pay. The Dawes Plan also granted an initial US$200 million loan for German recovery, which opened the door to heavy American investments in Europe that helped create a new era of European prosperity between 1924 and 1929.

> The **Dawes Plan** was a post-war economic agenda that was named after the American banker Charles Dawes, who stabilized the German economy through the restructuring of German reparations and the stabilization of the German currency.

A new approach to European diplomacy accompanied the new economic stability. A spirit of international cooperation was fostered by the foreign ministers of Germany and France, Gustav Stresemann and Aristide Briand (1862–1932), who concluded the Pact of Locarno in 1925. One of the resulting treaties guaranteed Germany's new western borders with France and Belgium. Although Germany's new eastern borders with Poland were conspicuously absent from the agreement, the Pact of Locarno was viewed by many as the beginning of a new era of European peace. On the day after the pact was concluded, the headline

in the *New York Times* read "France and Germany Ban War Forever," and the *London Times* declared "Peace at Last."[2]

Germany's entry into the League of Nations in March 1926 soon reinforced the spirit of conciliation engendered at Locarno. Two years later, similar optimistic attitudes prevailed in the Kellogg-Briand Pact, drafted by U.S. Secretary of State Frank Kellogg and French Foreign Minister Aristide Briand. Sixty-three nations signed this accord, in which they pledged "to renounce war as an instrument of national policy." Nothing was said, however, about what would be done if anyone violated the treaty.

The spirit of Locarno was based on little real substance. Germany lacked the military power to alter its western borders even if it wanted to. Pious promises to renounce war without mechanisms to enforce them were virtually worthless. And the issue of disarmament soon proved that even the spirit of Locarno could not bring nations to cut back on their weapons. The League of Nations Covenant had recommended the "reduction of national armaments to the lowest point consistent with national safety." Numerous disarmament conferences, however, failed to achieve anything substantial as states proved unwilling to trust their security to anyone but their own military forces. By the time the World Disarmament Conference finally met in Geneva in 1932, the issue was already dead.

Did the End of World War I Return Things to Normal?

According to Woodrow Wilson, World War I had been fought "to make the world safe for democracy." In 1919, there seemed to be some justification for his claim. Four major European states and a host of minor ones had functioning political democracies. In a number of states, universal male suffrage had even been replaced by universal suffrage as male politicians rewarded women for their contributions to World War I by granting them the right to vote (except in Italy, Switzerland, France, and Spain, where women had to wait until the end of World War II). In the 1920s, Europe seemed to be returning to the political trends of the pre-war era—the broadening of parliamentary regimes and the fostering of individual liberties. But it was not an easy process; four years of total war and four years of post-war turmoil made the desire for a "return to normalcy," in Wilson's words, both difficult and troublesome.

After World War I, Great Britain went through a period of painful readjustment and serious economic difficulties. During the war, Great Britain had lost many of the markets for its industrial products, especially to the United States and Japan. The post-war decline of such staple industries as coal, steel, and textiles led to a rise in unemployment, which reached the 2 million mark in 1921. Britain experienced renewed prosperity between 1925 and 1929, but it proved relatively superficial. British exports in the 1920s never compensated for the overseas investments lost during the war, and even in these purportedly prosperous years, unemployment remained at a startling 10 percent. Coal miners were especially affected by the decline of the antiquated and inefficient British coal mines, which also suffered from a world glut of coal.

After the defeat of Germany and the demobilization of the German army, France became the strongest power on the European continent. Its biggest problem involved the reconstruction of the devastated areas of northern and eastern France. But neither the conservative National Bloc government nor a government coalition of leftist parties (the Coalition of the Left) seemed capable of solving France's financial problems between 1921 and 1926. The failure of the Coalition of the Left led to the return of the conservative Raymond Poincaré (1860–1934), whose government from 1926 to 1929 stabilized the French economy by means of a substantial increase in taxes during a period of relative prosperity.

When the imperial Germany of Wilhelm II came to an end with Germany's defeat in World War I, a German democratic state known as the Weimar Republic was established. From its beginnings, the Weimar Republic was plagued by a series of problems. It had no truly outstanding political leaders, and those who were relatively able—including Friedrich Ebert, who served as president, and Gustav Stresemann, the foreign minister and chancellor—died in the 1920s. When Ebert died in 1925, Paul von Hindenburg (1847–1934), a World War I military hero, was elected president. Hindenburg was a traditional military man, monarchist in sentiment, who at heart was not in favour of the republic. The young republic also suffered politically from attempted uprisings and attacks from both the left and right.

The Weimar Republic also faced serious economic difficulties. Germany experienced runaway inflation in 1922 and 1923, with grave social effects. Widows, orphans, the retired elderly, army officers, teachers, civil servants, and others who lived on fixed incomes all watched their monthly stipends become worthless or their lifetime savings disappear. Their economic losses increasingly pushed the middle class to the young German Communist Party or to rightist parties that were equally hostile to the republic.

What Precipitated the Great Depression?

After World War I, most European states hoped to return to the liberal ideal of a market economy largely free of state intervention. But the war had vastly strengthened business cartels and labour unions, making some government regulation of these powerful organizations necessary. At the same time, reparations and war debts had severely distorted the post-war international economy, making the prosperity that did occur between 1924 and 1929 at best a fragile one and the dream of returning to a self-regulating market economy merely an illusion. What destroyed the concept altogether was the **Great Depression**.

> The **Great Depression** was a worldwide economic downturn preceded by the crash of the U.S. stock market on October 29, 1929 (in what is referred to as "Black Tuesday"), which resulted in massive bankruptcy claims and severe unemployment.

Two factors played a major role in the coming of the Great Depression: a downturn in European economies and an international financial crisis created by the collapse of the American stock market in 1929. Already in the mid-1920s, prices for agricultural goods were beginning to decline rapidly as a result of the overproduction of basic commodities, such as wheat. In 1925, states in Central and Eastern Europe began to impose tariffs to close their markets to other countries' goods. And an increase in the use of oil and hydroelectricity led to a slump in the coal industry.

Much of the European prosperity in the mid-1920s was built on American bank loans to Germany, but in 1928 and 1929, American investors began to pull money out of Germany to invest in the booming New York stock market. When that market crashed in October 1929, panicky American investors withdrew even more of their funds from Germany and other European markets. The withdrawal of funds seriously weakened the banks of Germany and other Central European states. The Credit-Anstalt, Vienna's most prestigious bank, collapsed on May 31, 1931. By that time, trade was slowing down, industrialists were cutting back production, and unemployment was increasing as the ripple effects of international bank failures had a devastating impact on domestic economies.

Economic downturns were by no means a new phenomenon in European history, but the Great Depression was exceptionally severe and had immediate political repercussions. In Great Britain, the Labour Party, now the largest in the country, failed to resolve the crisis (at one point in the early 1930s, one British worker in four was unemployed) and fell from power in 1931. A new government dominated by the Conservatives took office and soon claimed credit for lifting the country out of the worst stages of the depression, primarily by using the traditional policies of balanced budgets and protective tariffs. British politicians largely ignored the new ideas of a Cambridge economist, John Maynard Keynes (1883–1946), whose 1936 book

The General Theory of Employment, Interest, and Money took issue with the traditional view that depressions should be left to work themselves out through the self-regulatory mechanisms of a free economy. Keynes argued that unemployment stemmed not from overproduction but from a decline in consumer demand, which could be increased by public works, financed if necessary through deficit spending to stimulate production. Such policies, however, could be accomplished only by government intervention in the economy, a measure that British political leaders were unwilling to undertake.

France did not suffer from the effects of the Great Depression as soon as other countries because its economy was almost evenly divided between urban and agricultural pursuits, and a slight majority of French industrial plants were small enterprises. Consequently, France did not begin to face the crisis until 1932, but then it quickly led to political repercussions. During a 19-month period from 1932 to 1933, six different cabinets were formed as France faced political chaos.

The European nation that suffered the most damage from the depression was probably Germany. Unemployment increased to over four million by the end of 1930. For many Germans, who had already suffered through difficult times in the early 1920s, the democratic experiment represented by the Weimar Republic had become a nightmare. Some reacted by turning to Marxism because Karl Marx had long predicted that capitalism would destroy itself through overproduction. As in several other European countries, communism took on a new popularity, especially with workers and intellectuals. But in Germany, the real beneficiary of the Great Depression was Adolf Hitler, whose Nazi Party came to power in 1933.

In Canada, the effects of the Great Depression reached many lives and homes. Hundreds of thousands of people lost their jobs as a result of the depression, and very few people were able to find new ones, especially during the early years. This had a significant psychological impact on Canadians; many of them had to turn to charities and handouts as a means to survive. Very few people held their jobs. Many women were hired in place of older men since they could be paid less for the same work, resulting in unemployment among dispensable male workers. Many men lost their jobs as a result of the depression and thus were very frustrated with their inability to provide for their families. This eventually put a strain on many marriages. Also, as many Canadians could not find work, marriages were often postponed until better times. Marriage rates dropped considerably, as did birth rates throughout Canada.

The full force of the Great Depression had struck the United States by 1932. In that year, industrial production fell to 50 percent of what it had been in 1929. By 1933,

there were 15 million unemployed. Under these circumstances, Democrat Franklin Delano Roosevelt (1882–1945) was able to win a landslide victory in the presidential election of 1932. Following the example of the American experience during World War I, his administration pursued a policy of active government intervention in the economy that came to be known as the **New Deal**.

> The **New Deal** describes the legislative program created by U.S. President Franklin D. Roosevelt's administration to rescue the United States' economy in the aftermath of the Great Depression; it embraced the idea of government intervention in the state's economic affairs.

Initially, the New Deal attempted to restore prosperity by creating the National Recovery Administration (NRA), which required government, labour, and industrial leaders to work out regulations for each industry. Declared unconstitutional by the Supreme Court in 1935, the NRA was soon superseded by other efforts collectively known as the Second New Deal. Its programs included the Works Progress Administration (WPA), established in 1935, which employed between two and three million people building bridges, roads, post offices, airports, and other public works. The Roosevelt administration was also responsible for new social legislation that launched the American welfare state. In 1935, the Social Security Act created a system of old-age pensions and unemployment insurance. At the same time, the National Labour Relations Act of 1935 encouraged the rapid growth of labour unions.

The New Deal undoubtedly provided some social reform measures and may even have averted social revolution in the United States; it did not, however, solve the unemployment problems of the Great Depression. In May 1937, during what was considered a period of full recovery, American unemployment still stood at 7 million; a recession the following year increased that number to 11 million. Only World War II and the subsequent growth of armaments industries brought American workers back to full employment.

THE SEARCH FOR A NEW REALITY IN THE ARTS

The mass destruction brought on by World War I precipitated a general disillusionment with Western civilization on the part of artists and writers throughout Europe. Avant-garde art, which had sought to discover alternative techniques to portray reality, now gained broader acceptance as Europeans began to abandon classical traditions in an attempt to come to grips with the anxieties of the new age.

WHAT IS ART?

Be they proponents of Dadaism, Surrealism, or Abstract art, many visual artists were depressed by World War I and its aftermath and became obsessed with redefining the meaning of art in order, as one put it, to "save mankind from the furious madness of these times." Did art have a social or religious responsibility, as traditionalists maintained, or did it exist independent of any external justification, simply as art for art's sake? How could art represent the psyche or unconscious dimensions of the human experience? Just what constituted a valid work of art now that past techniques and standards had been discarded? Who was to judge what was "good" or "bad" art?

A flagrant example of Dada's revolutionary approach to art was the decision by French artist Marcel Duchamp (1887–1968) to enter a porcelain urinal in a 1917 art exhibit held in New York City. By signing it and giving it a title, Duchamp proclaimed that he had transformed the urinal into a work of art. Duchamp's ready-mades (as such art would henceforth be labelled) declared that whatever the artists proclaimed to be art was art.

Such an intentionally irreverent act was meant to be a slap in the face of the established art world and to demystify the nearly sacred reverence that was traditionally attached to works of art. Essentially, Duchamp held the view that anything under the sun could be chosen as a work of art because the mental choice itself equalled the act of artistic creation. Therefore, art need not be a manual construct, only a mental conceptualization. Most important, Duchamp's liberating concept served to open the floodgates of the art world, obliging the entire twentieth century to swim in this free-flowing, exuberant, exploratory, and often frightening torrent.

Source: Robert Hughes, *The Shock of the New* (New York: Alfred Knopf, 1996), Chapter 2.

Although there were many different schools of artistic expression during the post-war era, a common denominator for all modernist art was its unrelenting crusade for absolute freedom of expression. Some artists opted for open revolt against the past, while others wished to liberate the darker impulses of the spirit from rational constraints to reveal the whole individual underneath. Others still, renouncing the apparent chaos of Western civilization, sought refuge in a new world of abstract painting. Some abandoned painting and sculpture altogether, preferring to focus on ameliorating social conditions through utopian architecture and interior designs for everyday living.

A number of the artistic styles that gained popularity during the 1920s originated during the war in neutral Switzerland, where alienated intellectuals congregated at cafés to decry the insanity of the age and to exchange ideas on how to create a new and better world. One such group was the Dadaists, who sought to destroy the past with a vengeance, proclaiming their right to complete freedom of expression in art (see the box above).

While Dadaism flourished in Germany during the Weimar era, a school of Surrealism was established in Paris to liberate the total human experience from the restraints of the rational world. By using the subconscious, Surrealists hoped to resurrect the whole personality and reveal a submerged and illusive reality. Normally unrelated objects and people were juxtaposed in dreamlike and frequently violent paintings that were intended to shock the viewer into

approaching reality from a totally fresh perspective. Most famous of the Surrealists was the Spaniard Salvadore Dalí (1904–89), who subverted the sense of reality in his painting by using near photographic detail in presenting a fantastic and irrational world.

Yet another modernist movement born on the eve of World War I was Abstract, or Nonobjective, painting. As one of its founders, Swiss artist Paul Klee (1879–1940), observed, "the more fearful this world becomes, . . . the more art becomes abstract."[3] Two of the movement's principal founders, Wassily Kandinsky (1866–1944) and Piet Mondrian (1872–1944), were followers of Theosophy, a religion that promised the triumph of the spirit in a new millennium. Since they viewed matter as an obstacle to salvation, the art of the new age would totally abandon all reference to the material world. Only abstraction, expressed as colourful forms and geometric shapes floating in space, could convey the bliss and spiritual beauty of this terrestrial paradise.

Just as artists began to experiment with revolutionary ways to represent reality in painting, musicians searched for new revolutionary sounds. Austrian composer Arnold Schoenberg (1874–1951) rejected the traditional tonal system based on the harmonic triad that had dominated Western music since the Renaissance. To free the Western ear from traditional harmonic progression, Schoenberg substituted a radically new "atonal" system in which each piece established its own individual set of relationships and structure. In 1923, he devised a 12-tone system in which he placed

For many post-war architects, the past was the enemy of the future. In 1925, the famous French architect Le Corbusier (1887–1965) advocated razing much of the old city of Paris, to be replaced by modern towers of glass. In his plan, which called for neat apartment complexes separated by immaculate areas of grass, there was no room for people, pets, or nature. Fortunately, it was rejected by municipal authorities.

During the post-war era, writers followed artists and architects in rejecting traditional forms in order to explore the subconscious. In his novel *Ulysses,* published in 1922, Irish author James Joyce (1882–1941) invented the "stream of consciousness" technique to portray the lives of ordinary people through the use of inner monologue. Joyce's technique exerted a powerful influence on literature for the remainder of the century. Other writers, such as Ernest

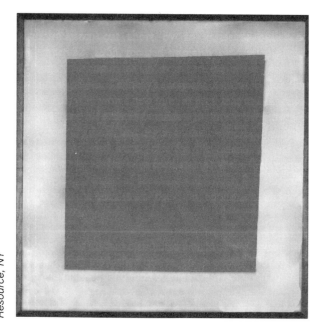

State Museum, St. Petersburg, Russia. © Erich Lessing/Art Resource, NY

Nonobjective Art. One artist who sought to break completely with the tradition of representative art was the Russian Kazimir Malevich (1878–1935), who painted geometric shapes that he felt expressed the dynamic rhythms of human experience. For Malevich, the square was the ideal geometric pattern because it is never found in nature, only in the mind, thus symbolizing his belief in the supremacy of pure thought. In this 1915 painting, *Red Square,* the colour red seems to be thrusting outward as if seething with the political turmoil of Russia on the eve of the 1917 revolution. The square subsequently became a common motif in twentieth-century art.

the 12 pitches of the chromatic scale found on the piano in a set sequence for a musical composition. The ordering of these 12 tones was to be repeated throughout the piece, for all instrumental parts, constituting its melody and harmony. Even today, such atonal music seems inaccessible and incomprehensible to the uninitiated. Yet Schoenberg, perhaps more than any other modern composer, influenced the development of twentieth-century music.

Other fields of artistic creativity, including sculpture, ballet, and architecture, also reflected these new directions. In Germany, a group of imaginative architects called the Bauhaus school created what is widely known as the International school, which soon became the dominant school of modern architecture. Led by the famous German architect Ludwig Mies van der Rohe (1886–1969), the Internationalists promoted a new functional and unadorned style (Mies was widely known for observing that "less is more") characterized by high-rise towers of steel and glass that were reproduced endlessly throughout the second half of the century all around the world.

© Peter Mauss/Esto

Chrysler Building, New York, 1929. America's greatest expression of modernist art was the city of New York itself, with its vertiginous vertical forest of shiny steel and glass skyscrapers. Most exuberant was William Van Alen's Chrysler Building, a monument to American ingenuity, industry, and power. Here the ornamentation suggests the hubcaps of a Chrysler automobile in the seven-tiered fringe, with radiator caps as gargoyles; the elegance and power of the building itself reflect the owner's luxurious vehicles and impressive fortune. The spire, which at the time made the building the tallest in the world, was completed about a week before the stock market crashed.

Hemingway (1899–1961), Theodore Dreiser (1871–1945), Mordecai Richler (1931–2001), and Sinclair Lewis (1885–1951), reflected the rising influence of mass journalism in a new style designed to "tell it like it is." Such writers sought to report the "whole truth" in an effort to attain the authenticity of modern photography.

For much of the Western world, however, the best way to find (or escape) reality was in the field of mass entertainment. The 1930s represented the heyday of the Hollywood studio system, which in the single year of 1937 turned out nearly 600 feature films. Supplementing the movies were cheap paperbacks and radio, which brought sports, soap operas, and popular music to the mass of the population. The radio was a great social leveller, speaking to all classes with the same voice. Such new technological wonders offered diversion even to the poor while helping to define the twentieth century as the era of the common people.

CONCLUSION

World War I shattered the image of a liberal, rational society in early-twentieth-century Europe. The incredible destruction and the deaths of millions of people undermined the whole idea of progress.

- New propaganda techniques had manipulated entire populations into sustaining their involvement in a meaningless slaughter.
- Allied leaders imposed their terms at the Paris Peace Conference at the end of the war.
- Some historians placed the blame for setting off World War I on Russia for its decision to order full military mobilization in response to events taking place in the Balkans.

In the first half of the nineteenth century, liberals had wrongly maintained that the organization of European states along national lines would lead to a peaceful Europe based on a sense of international fraternity.

- The system of nation-states that emerged in Europe in the second half of the nineteenth century led not to cooperation but to competition.
- Governments that exercised restraint to avoid war wound up being publicly humiliated; those that went to the brink of war to maintain their national interests were often praised for having preserved national honour.
- Not all ethnic groups had achieved the goal of nationhood, including Slavic minorities in the Balkans and the polyglot Austro-Hungarian Empire, the Irish in the British Empire, and the Poles in the Russian Empire, not to speak of the subject peoples living in colonial areas around the globe.

- A mounting sense of insecurity led to increased military expenditures. European military machines had doubled in size between 1890 and 1914.

The victorious world leaders who gathered at Versailles hoped to forge a peace settlement that would say goodbye to the militarization of Europe. But as it turned out, the turmoil wrought by World War I seemed to open the door to even greater insecurity.

- Revolutions in Russia and the Ottoman Middle East dismembered old empires and created new states that gave rise to unexpected problems.
- As economies continued to collapse, authoritarian governments in Europe rose; these governments not only restricted individual freedoms but also sought even greater control over the lives of their subjects, manipulating and guiding their people to achieve the goals of their totalitarian regimes.
- World War I brought an end to the age of European hegemony over world affairs, and Europeans inadvertently encouraged the subject peoples of their vast colonial empires to initiate movements for national independence.

CRITICAL THINKING QUESTIONS

1. Were recruitment efforts during World War I just state propaganda?

2. Had the Allies taken a less punitive stance against Germany at the Paris Peace Conference, would the horrors of World War II have been avoided?

3. Why were Lenin and the Bolshevik Revolution so appealing to the Russian masses?

4. Could the Great Depression have been prevented by better international economic cooperation and regulation?

CHAPTER NOTES

1. Harold Nicolson, *Peacemaking, 1919* (London: Constable, 1933), pp. 31–32.

2. Quoted in Robert Paxton, *Europe in the Twentieth Century*, 2nd ed. (San Diego, Calif.: Harcourt Brace Jovanovich, 1985), p. 237.

3. Quoted in Nikos Stangos, *Concepts of Modern Art: From Fauvism to Postmodernism*, 3rd ed. (London: Thames and Hudson, 1994), p. 44.

Chapter 4

Nationalism, Revolution, and Dictatorship: Africa, Asia, and Latin America from 1919 to 1939

After the Bolsheviks came to power in Moscow, Lenin and his colleagues were preoccupied with consolidating their control over the vast territories of the old tsarist Russian Empire. But Lenin had predicted that the colonial world was on the verge of revolt. Now, with the infant Soviet state virtually surrounded by capitalist enemies, Lenin argued that the oppressed masses of Asia and Africa were potential allies in the bitter struggle against the brutal yoke of world imperialism. For the next two decades, the leaders in Moscow periodically turned their eyes to the would-be Third World in an effort to ride what they hoped would be a mounting wave of revolt against foreign domination.

At the conclusion of this chapter, you will be able to

- describe how colonial rule determines the type of revolution that leads to its demise;
- detail the various means by which revolutionary forces gather populist support;
- explain the importance of national symbols and struggles as precursors to successful revolution;
- describe the differences between Leninism, Maoism, and classical Marxism.

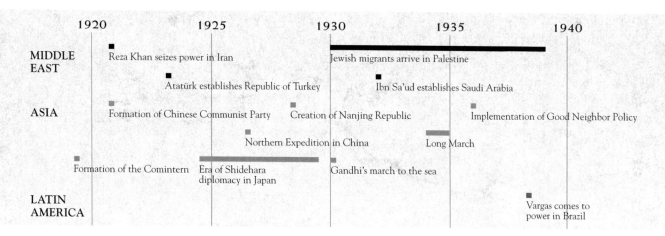

THE RISE OF NATIONALISM IN AFRICA, SOUTHEAST ASIA, AND THE MIDDLE EAST

Lenin's optimism that the colonial world was on the verge of revolt had a kernel of truth. Although the West had emerged from World War I relatively intact, its political and social foundations were severely undermined by the experience. Within Europe, doubts about the future viability of Western civilization were widespread, especially among the intellectual elite. These doubts were quick to reach the attention of perceptive observers in Asia and Africa and contributed to a rising tide of activism against Western political domination throughout the colonial and semi-colonial world. That activism took a variety of forms but was most notably displayed in increasing worker politicization, rural protest, and a rising sense of national sentiment among anti-colonialist intellectuals. Where independent states had successfully resisted the Western onslaught, the discontent fostered by the war and later by the Great Depression led to a loss of confidence in democratic institutions and the rise of political dictatorships.

As we have seen (see Chapter 1, pages 10–11), nationalism refers to a state of mind rising out of an awareness of being part of a community that has common institutions, traditions, language, and customs. Unfortunately, few nations in the world today meet such criteria. Most modern states contain a variety of ethnic, religious, and linguistic communities, each with its own sense of cultural and national identity. How does nationalism differ from tribal, religious, linguistic, or other forms of affiliation? Should every group that resists assimilation into a larger cultural unity be called nationalist?

Such questions complicate the study of nationalism even in Europe and North America and make agreement on a definition elusive. They create even greater dilemmas in discussing Asia and Africa, where most societies are deeply divided by ethnic, linguistic, and religious differences and the very concept of nationalism is a foreign phenomenon imported from the West. Prior to the colonial era, most traditional societies in Africa and Asia were unified on the basis of religious beliefs, tribal loyalties, or devotion to hereditary monarchies. Individuals in some countries may have identified themselves as members of a particular national group, while others viewed themselves as subjects of a king, members of a tribe, or adherents of a particular religion.

The advent of European colonialism brought the consciousness of modern nationhood to many of the societies of Asia and Africa, often as a reaction to colonialism. The creation of European colonies with defined borders and a powerful central government weakened tribal and village ties and reoriented individuals' sense of political identity. The introduction of Western ideas of citizenship and representative government engendered a new sense of participation in the affairs of government. At the same time, the appearance of a new elite class based not on hereditary privilege or religious sanction but on alleged racial or cultural superiority aroused a shared sense of resentment among the subjected peoples who felt a common commitment to the creation of an independent society. By the first quarter of the twentieth century, political movements dedicated to the overthrow of colonial rule had arisen throughout much of the non-Western world.

Modern nationalism, then, was a product of and a reaction to colonialism. But a sense of nationhood does not emerge full-blown in a society. Some would argue that it begins among a few members of the educated elite (most commonly among articulate professionals such as lawyers, teachers, journalists, and doctors) and spreads gradually to the mass of the population. Even after national independence has been realized, as we shall see, it is often questionable whether a true sense of nationhood has been created.

Can Resistance against Colonial Masters Create True National Consciousness?

If we view the concept of nationalism as a process by which people in a given society gradually become aware of themselves as members of a particular nation, with its own culture and aspirations, then it is reasonable to seek the beginnings of modern nationalism in the initial resistance by the indigenous peoples to the colonial conquest itself. Although essentially motivated by the desire to defend traditional institutions, such movements reflected a non-Western concept of nationhood in that they sought to protect the homeland from the invader. Thus traditional resistance to colonial conquest may logically be viewed as the first stage in the development of modern nationalism.

Such resistance took various forms. For the most part, it was led by the existing ruling class. In the Ashanti kingdom in West Africa and in Burma and Vietnam in Southeast Asia, the resistance to Western domination was initially directed by the imperial courts. In some cases, however, traditionalist elements continued to oppose foreign conquest even after resistance had collapsed at the centre. In Japan, conservative elements opposed the decision of the Tokugawa shogunate in Tokyo to accommodate the Western presence and launched an abortive movement to defeat the foreigners and restore Japan to its previous policy of isolation. In India, Tipu Sultan resisted the British in the Deccan after the collapse of the Mughal dynasty. Similarly, after the decrepit monarchy in Vietnam had bowed to French pressure and agreed to the concession of territory in the south and the establishment of a protectorate over the remainder of the country, a number of civilian and military officials set up an organization called Can Vuong (literally, "Save the King") and continued their resistance without imperial sanction.

Sometimes traditional resistance had a religious basis, as in the Sudan, where a revolt against the growing British presence had strong Islamic overtones, although it was initially provoked by Turkish misrule in Egypt. More significant was the famous Sepoy Mutiny of 1857 in India. The *sepoys* ("soldiers") were native troops hired by the East India Company to protect British interests in the region. Unrest within Indian units of the colonial army had been common since early in the century, when it had been sparked by economic issues, religious sensitivities, or nascent anti-colonial sentiment. Factors which lent themselves to the tensions between *sepoys* and their British superiors stemmed from the general distrust between the two within the East India Company. Lending itself to this mistrust was the evangelical nature of British Christianity, which sought to bring "light" to the non-Christian peoples of India. Many East Indian officers sought to convert Indian *sepoys* from Hindus and Muslims into Christians. This, alongside the British abolition of customs deemed "uncivilized" such as child marriages, *suttee,* and female infanticide, was seen as a threat to Indian tradition.

Sepoys (Persian for "soldiers") were native of India and employed by a European power, usually Great Britain.

Such attitudes intensified in the mid-1850s when the British instituted a new policy of shipping Indian troops abroad—a practice that, according to Hindu tradition, would expose Hindus to "pollution" by foreign cultures and lead to the loss of caste status. In 1857, tension erupted when the British adopted the new Enfield rifle for use by sepoy infantries. The new weapon was a muzzle-loader that used paper cartridges covered with animal fat and lard; because the cartridge had to be bitten off, doing so violated both Hindu and Muslim strictures against high-caste Hindus' eating animal products and Muslim prohibitions against eating pork. Protests among sepoy units in northern India turned into a full-scale defiance, supported by uprisings in rural districts in various parts of the country. But the revolt lacked clear goals, and rivalries between Hindus and Muslims, and discord among leaders within each community prevented coordination of operations. Although Indian troops often fought bravely and outnumbered the British by 240 000 to 40 000, they were poorly organized, and the British forces (supplemented in many cases by sepoy troops) suppressed the rebellion.

Still, the revolt frightened the British and led to a number of major reforms. The proportion of native troops relative to those from Great Britain was reduced, and precedence was given to ethnic groups likely to be loyal to the British, such as the Sikhs of Punjab and the Gurkhas, an upland people from Nepal in the Himalaya Mountains. To avoid religious conflicts, ethnic groups were spread throughout the service rather than assigned to special units. The British also decided to suppress the final remnants of the hapless Mughal dynasty, which had supported the uprising.

As noted earlier, such forms of resistance cannot properly be called nationalist because they were essentially attempts to protect or restore traditional society and its institutions and were not motivated by the desire to create a nation in the modern sense of the word. In any event, such movements rarely met with success. Peasants armed with pikes and spears were no match for Western armies possessing the most terrifying weapons then known to human society, including the Gatling gun, the first rapid-fire weapon and the precursor of the modern machine gun.

What Led to the First Stirrings of Modern Nationalism?

The first stage of resistance to the West in Asia and Africa must have confirmed many Westerners' racist conviction that colonial peoples lacked both the strength and the know-how to create modern states and govern their own destinies. In fact, however, the process was just beginning. The next phase began to take shape at the beginning of the twentieth century and was the product of the convergence of several factors. The primary sources of anti-colonialist sentiment were found in a new class of westernized intellectuals in the urban centres created by colonial rule. In many cases, this new urban middle class, composed of merchants, petty functionaries, clerks, students, and professionals, had been educated in Western-style schools. A few had spent time in the West. In either case, they were the first generation of Asians and Africans to possess more than a rudimentary understanding of the institutions and values of the modern West.

The results were paradoxical. On the one hand, this new class admired Western culture and sometimes harboured a deep sense of contempt for traditional ways. On the other hand, many strongly resented the hypocrisy of colonial policy, whereby the gap between ideal and reality, theory and practice, often reflected racial and cultural lines to the advantage of Europeans. Although Western political thought upheld democracy, equality, and individual freedom, these values were generally not applied in the colonies. Thanks to European colonialists, democratic institutions were nonexistent, and colonial subjects usually had access to only the most menial positions in the colonial bureaucracy.

Equally important, the economic prosperity of the West was only imperfectly reflected in the colonies. Normally, middle-class Asians did not suffer in the same manner as impoverished peasants or menial workers on sugar or rubber plantations, but they, too, had complaints. They usually "qualified" only for menial jobs in the government or business. Even when employed, their salaries were normally lower than those of Europeans in similar occupations. Racism was deeply embedded not only in the job market, but also in social structure. This cultural racism was expressed in a variety of ways, including "whites only" clubs and the forms of language used to address colonial subjects.

For example, Europeans would characteristically use the familiar form of direct address (normally used by adults to children) when talking to members of the local population in their own language.

Out of this mixture of hopes and resentments emerged the first stirrings of modern nationalism in Asia and Africa. During the first quarter of the century, in colonial and semi-colonial societies across the entire arc of Asia from the Suez Canal to the shores of the Pacific Ocean, educated subjected peoples began to organize political parties and movements seeking reforms or the end of foreign rule and the restoration of independence.

At first, many of the leaders of these movements did not focus clearly on the idea of nationhood but tried to defend the economic interests or religious beliefs of the people. In Burma, for example, the first expression of modern nationalism came from students at the University of Rangoon, who formed an organization to protest against official persecution of the Buddhist religion and British lack of respect for local religious traditions. Calling themselves *Thakin* (a polite term in the Burmese language meaning "lord" or "master," thus emphasizing their demand for the right to rule themselves), they protested against British arrogance, racism, and failure to observe local customs in Buddhist temples. For example, visitors are expected to remove their footwear in a temple, a custom of respect that was blatantly ignored by Europeans in colonial Burma. Eventually, however, they began to focus specifically on the issue of national independence.

A similar movement arose in the Dutch East Indies, where the first quasi-political organization dedicated to the creation of a modern Indonesia, the Sarekat Islam (Islamic Association), began as a self-help society among Muslim merchants to fight against domination of the local economy by Chinese interests. Eventually, activist elements began to realize that the source of the problem was not the Chinese merchants but the colonial presence, and in the 1920s, Sarekat Islam was transformed into a new organization—the Nationalist Party of Indonesia (PNI)—that focused on the issue of national independence. Like the *Thakins* in Burma, this party would eventually lead the country to independence after World War II.

How Did Nationalist Movements Build Mass Support for Statehood?

Building a new nation, however, requires more than a shared sense of grievances against the foreign invader. By what means was independence to be achieved? Was independence or modernization the more important objective? What kind of political and economic system should be adopted once colonial rule had been overthrown? What national or cultural concept should be adopted as the symbol of the new nation, and which institutions and values should be preserved from the past?

Questions such as these triggered lively and sometimes passionate debates among patriotic elements throughout the colonial world. If national independence was the desired end, how could it be achieved? Could the Westerners be persuaded to leave by nonviolent measures, or would force be required? If the Western presence could be beneficial in terms of introducing much-needed reforms in traditional societies, then a gradualist approach made sense. On the other hand, if the colonial regime was primarily violent and an impediment to social and political change, then the first priority was to bring it to an end.

Another problem was how to modernize ideas and institutions while preserving the essential values that defined the local culture. The vast majority of patriotic intellectuals were convinced that to survive, their societies must move with the times and modernize. Yet many were equally determined that the local culture could not, and should not, simply become a carbon copy of the West.

Traditional values were incorporated in national symbols for people to support. If the desired end was national independence, then the new political movements needed to enlist the mass of the population in the common struggle. But how could peasants, plantation workers, fishermen, and shepherds be organized to support concepts like democracy, industrialization, and nationhood? The problem was often one of communication, for most urban intellectuals had little in common with the population in the countryside.

How Did Gandhi Raise Consciousness of Indian Nationalism?

Nowhere in the colonial world were these issues debated more vigorously than in India. Before the Sepoy Mutiny, Indian consciousness had focused primarily on the question of religious identity. But in the latter half of the nineteenth century, a stronger sense of national consciousness began to arise, provoked by the conservative policies and racial arrogance of the British colonial authorities. (See Map 4.1, Plate 9.)

The first Indian nationalists were almost invariably upper-class and educated. Many of them were from urban areas such as Bombay, Madras, and Calcutta. Some were trained in law and were members of the civil service. At first, many tended to prefer reform to revolution and accepted the idea that India needed modernization before it could handle the problems of independence. An exponent of this view was Gopal Gokhale (1866–1915), a moderate nationalist who hoped that he could convince the British to bring about needed reforms in Indian society. Gokhale and other like-minded reformists did have some effect. In the 1880s, the government launched a series of reforms introducing a measure of self-government for the first time. All too often, however, such efforts were sabotaged by local British officials.

The slow pace of reform convinced many Indian nationalists that relying on British benevolence was futile. In 1885, a small group of Indians met in Bombay to form the Indian National Congress (INC). They hoped to speak for all of India, but most were high-caste English-trained Hindus. Like their reformist predecessors, members of the INC did not demand immediate independence and accepted the need for reforms to end traditional practices like child marriage and *suttee*. At the same time, they called for an Indian share in the governing process and more spending on economic development and less on military campaigns along the frontier.

The British responded with a few concessions, such as accepting the principle of elective Indian participation on government councils, but in general, change was glacially slow. As impatient members of the INC became disillusioned, radical leaders such as Balwantrao Tilak (1856–1920) openly criticized the British while defending traditional customs like child marriage to solicit support from conservative elements within the local population. Tilak's activities split the INC between moderates and radicals, and he and his followers formed the New Party, which called for the use of terrorism and violence to achieve national independence. Tilak was eventually convicted of subversion.

The INC also had difficulty reconciling religious differences within its ranks. The stated goal of the INC was to seek **self-determination** for all Indians regardless of class or religious affiliation, but many of its leaders were Hindu and inevitably reflected Hindu concerns. By the first decade of the twentieth century, Muslims began to call for the creation of a separate Muslim League to represent the interests of the millions of Muslims in Indian society.

> **Self-determination** is a doctrine that proposes people of a given territory or of a particular nationality should have the right to determine their own government and political future.

In 1915, the return of a young Hindu lawyer from South Africa transformed the movement and galvanized India's struggle for independence and identity. Mohandas Gandhi was born in 1869 in Gujarat, in western India, the son of a government minister. In the late nineteenth century, he studied in London and became a lawyer. In 1893,

he went to South Africa to work in a law firm serving Indian immigrants working as labourers there. He soon became aware of the racial prejudice and exploitation experienced by Indians living in South Africa and tried to organize them to fight for better civil rights.

On his return to India, Gandhi immediately became active in the independence movement. Using his experience in South Africa, he set up a movement based on nonviolent resistance (called **satyagraha**, meaning "hold fast to the truth") to try to force the British to improve the lot of the poor and grant independence to India. Gandhi was particularly concerned about the plight of the millions of "untouchables," whom he called *harijans,* or "children of God." When the British attempted to suppress dissent, he called on his followers to refuse to obey British regulations. He began to manufacture his own clothes (dressing in a simple *dhoti* made of coarse homespun cotton) and adopted the spinning wheel as a symbol of Indian resistance to imports of British textiles.

> **Satyagraha** (Indian for "hold fast to the truth") represents Gandhi's policy of determined but nonviolent resistance to British rule in India.

Gandhi, now increasingly known as India's **Mahatma** ("Great Soul"), organized mass protests to achieve his aims, but in 1919, the British repressed the populist uprising. British troops killed hundreds of unarmed protesters in the enclosed square in the city of Amritsar in northwestern India. When the protests spread, Gandhi was horrified at the violence and briefly retreated from active politics. Nevertheless, he was arrested for his role in the protests and spent several years in prison.

> **Mahatma** is literally translated as "Great Soul," and was the name given to Gandhi in place of his first name, Mohandas.

Gandhi combined his anti-colonial activities with an appeal to the spiritual instincts of all Indians. Though born and raised a Hindu, he possessed a universalist approach to the idea of God that transcended individual religion, although it was shaped by the historical themes of Hindu religious belief. At a speech given in London in September 1931, he expressed his view of the nature of God as "an indefinable mysterious power that pervades everything . . . , an unseen power which makes itself felt and yet defies all proof."

In 1921, the British passed the Government of India Act to expand the role of Indians in the governing process and transform the then advisory Legislative Council into a bicameral parliament, two-thirds of whose members would

Max Desfor/AP Wide World Photos

Nehru and Gandhi. Mahatma Gandhi (on the right), India's "Great Soul," became the emotional leader of India's struggle for independence from British colonial rule. Unlike many other nationalist leaders, Gandhi rejected the materialistic culture of the West and urged his followers to return to the native traditions of the Indian village. To illustrate his point, Gandhi dressed in the simple Indian *dhoti* rather than in the Western fashion favoured by many of his colleagues. Along with Gandhi, Jawaharlal Nehru was a leading figure in the Indian struggle for independence. Unlike Gandhi, however, his goal was to transform India into a modern industrial society. After independence, he became the nation's prime minister until his death in 1964.

be elected. Similar bodies were created at the provincial level. In an instant, five million Indians were enfranchised. But such reforms were no longer enough for many members of the INC, which under its new leader, Motilal Nehru (1861–1931), wanted to push aggressively for full independence. The British furthered their discriminatory policies by increasing the salt tax and prohibiting the Indian people from manufacturing or harvesting their own salt. On release from prison, Gandhi resumed his policy of civil disobedience by openly joining several dozen supporters in a 320 kilometre walk to the sea, where he picked up a lump of salt and urged Indians to ignore the law. Gandhi and many other members of the INC were arrested.

In the 1930s, a new figure entered the movement in the person of **Jawaharlal Nehru** (1889–1964), son of the INC leader Motilal Nehru. Educated in the law in Great Britain and a Brahmin (member of the highest social caste) by birth, Nehru personified the new Anglo-Indian politician: secular, rational, upper-class, and intellectual. In fact, he appeared to be everything that Gandhi was not. With his emergence, the independence movement embarked on dual paths: religious and secular, native and Western, traditional and modern. The dichotomous character of the INC leadership may well have strengthened the movement by

bringing together the two primary impulses behind the desire for independence: elite nationalism and the primal force of Indian traditionalism. But it portended trouble for the nation's new leadership in defining India's future path in the contemporary world. In the meantime, Muslim discontent with Hindu dominance over the INC was increasing. In 1940, the Muslim League called for the creation of a separate Muslim state, to be known as Pakistan ("Land of the Pure"), in the northwest. As communal strife between Hindus and Muslims increased, many Indians came to realize with sorrow (and some British colonialists with satisfaction) that British rule was all that stood between peace and civil war.

> **Jawaharlal Nehru** was the leader of a moderately socialist wing of the Indian National Congress who fought for Indian independence from Great Britain and eventually served as India's first prime minister when it gained independence in 1947.

THE NATIONALIST UPRISING IN THE MIDDLE EAST

In the Middle East, as in Europe, World War I hastened the collapse of old empires. The Ottoman Empire, which had been growing steadily weaker since the end of the eighteenth century, would not long survive the end of the war.

Mustafa Kemal: A Modernizer of Turkey, or an Imitator of the West?

Reformist elements in Istanbul, to be sure, had tried to resist the Ottoman Empire decline. The first efforts had taken place in the eighteenth century, when westernizing forces, concerned by the shrinkage of the empire, had tried to modernize the army. One energetic sultan, Selim III (r. 1789–1807), tried to establish a "new order" that would streamline both the civilian and military bureaucracies, but the emperor's janissary forces, alarmed at the potential loss of their power, revolted and brought the reformist experiments to an end. Further efforts during the first half of the nineteenth century, called the *Tanzimat Reforms,* were somewhat more successful and resulted in the removal of the **janissaries** from power and the institution of a series of bureaucratic, military, and educational reforms. New roads were built, the power of local landlords was reduced, and an Imperial Rescript issued in 1856 granted equal rights to all subjects of the empire, whatever their religious preference.

In the 1870s, a new generation of reformers seized power in Istanbul and pushed through a constitution aimed at forming a legislative assembly that would represent all the peoples in the state. But the sultan they placed on the throne, Abdülhamid II (r. 1876–1909), suspended the new charter and attempted to rule by traditional authoritarian means.

> **Janissaries** were members of an elite corps of troops personally loyal to the Ottoman leader, or sultan, and were made up of Christian boys who were taken from their parents and converted to Islam.

By the end of the nineteenth century, the defunct 1876 constitution had become a symbol of change for reformist elements, now championed by a group of reformers known as the **Young Turks**, which included would-be leader **Mustafa Kemal**. In 1908, Young Turk elements forced the sultan to restore the constitution, and he was removed from power the following year. But the Young Turks had appeared at a moment of extreme fragility for the empire. Internal rebellions, combined with Austrian annexations of Ottoman territories in the Balkans, undermined support for the new government and provoked the army to step in. With most minorities from the old empire now removed from Istanbul's authority (Armenians suffered an alleged genocide—see box on page 74), many ethnic Turks began to embrace a new concept of a Turkish state, shedding the Ottoman Empire role, based on all residents of the Turkish nation.

> **Young Turks** were a group of modernizing Turks that successfully brought westernization to the former Ottoman Empire.
>
> **Mustafa Kemal**, also known as Atatürk (meaning "father of the Turks"), was a World War I officer who led Turkey down a path of westernization, secularization, and modernization in the 1920s.

The final blow to the old empire came in World War I, when the Ottoman government chose the wrong side during the war and lost much of its territory in the peace settlement (see Chapter 3). As the tottering empire began to fall apart, the Greeks won Allied approval to seize the western parts of the Anatolian peninsula for their dream of re-creating the substance of the old Byzantine Empire. The impending collapse energized key elements in Turkey under the leadership of war hero Colonel Mustafa Kemal (1881–1938), who had commanded Turkish forces in their heroic defence of the Dardanelles against a British invasion during World War I. Now he resigned from the army and convoked a national congress that called for the creation of an elected government and the preservation of the remaining territories of the old empire in the new republic of Turkey. Establishing his new capital at Ankara, Kemal's forces drove the Greeks from the Anatolian peninsula and persuaded the British to agree to a new treaty. In 1923, the last of the Ottoman sultans fled the country, which was now declared a Turkish republic. The Ottoman Empire had finally come to an end.

During the next few years, President Mustafa Kemal (now popularly known as Atatürk, or "father of the Turks") attempted to transform Turkey into a Western secular republic. The trappings of a democratic system were put in place, centred on the elected Grand National Assembly, but the president was relatively intolerant of opposition and harshly suppressed critics of his rule. Turkish nationalism was emphasized, and the Turkish language was transformed from using an Arabic script to now using the Latin script. The Turkish language was instantly transformed from an eastern language base to a Western language base. People became technically illiterate by the stroke of Atatürk's pen. Education of the new script was emphasized. Atatürk also eliminated old aristocratic titles like *pasha* and *bey*, and all Turkish citizens were given family names in the Western style.

Atatürk also took steps to modernize the economy, overseeing the establishment of a light industrial sector producing textiles, glass, paper, and cement and instituting a five-year plan on the Soviet model to provide for state direction over the economy. Atatürk was no admirer of Soviet communism, however, and the Turkish economy could be better described as a form of state capitalism. He also encouraged the modernization of the agricultural sector through the establishment of training institutions and model farms, but such reforms had relatively little effect on the nation's predominantly conservative peasantry.

Perhaps the most significant aspect of Atatürk's reform program was his attempt to limit the religion of Islam and transform a Muslim Turkey into a secular state. The caliphate (according to which the Ottoman sultan was recognized as the temporal leader of the Sunni Islamic community) was formally abolished in 1924, and the shari'a (Islamic law) was replaced by a revised version of the Swiss law code. The **fez** was abolished because it was an Islamic compromise to the Western brimmed hat; the fez could be worn during prayers, which required men to bow their head to the ground. Similarly, women were discouraged from wearing their head coverings in the traditional Islamic custom. Women received the right to vote in 1934 and were legally guaranteed equal rights with men in all aspects of marriage and inheritance. Education and the professions were now open to citizens of both sexes, and some women even began to take part in politics. All citizens were given the right to convert to another religion at will.

WHO REMEMBERS THE ARMENIANS?

After the genocide of more than a million Armenians at the hands of the Ottoman Empire's Young Turks, Adolf Hitler once remarked "Who, after all, speaks today of the annihilation of the Armenians?" weeks before invading Poland. At the time, the failure of the international community to react to the Armenian genocide had paved the way for Hitler to believe the world would not notice or care about the crimes against humanity that he would commit. Today, the Armenians have fought relentlessly for recognition and commemoration of this human tragedy.

The annihilation of 1.5 million Armenians living in the Ottoman Empire between 1915 and 1923 is considered one of the twentieth century's first genocides. Often denied as completely fabricated by modern-day Turkey, the Ottoman Empire's largest remnant, the genocide was undertaken by the Young Turks. The Young Turks began as a movement in reaction to the absolute rule of Sultan Abdülhamid II. Led by Mehmed Talaat Pasha (1874–1921), the Young Turks movement's most prominent members included Ahmed Jemal Pasha (1872–1922) and Ismail Enver Pasha (1881–1922), all of whom belonged to the Committee of Union and Progress (CUP) prior to the formation of the movement.

Hailed as a turn for the better, the Young Turks had won a broad range of support among the people of the Ottoman Empire. People anticipated that the Young Turks would be more egalitarian than their predecessor, and so they found support among both the Turkish population and the Armenian population in the region. The Armenians, who at the time comprised approximately 10 percent of the overall population, were accustomed to being viewed and treated as second-class citizens by their Muslim Turkish government; however, the Young Turks seemed to offer hope with their notions regarding the equality of all Ottoman Empire's citizens.

Hopes of egalitarian rule were quickly dashed shortly after the Young Turks came into power. The central aim of the Young Turk movement became the formation of a pan-Turkic state wherein only Turks would reside, leaving the Christian Armenian minority to be seen as only a hindrance in the way. Armenians had lived in the region surrounded by the Black Sea, Mediterranean Sea, and Caspian Sea for nearly 3000 years and are known as the world's first societies to adopt the Christian faith. Having lived in the Ottoman Empire since the inclusion of Armenia in the sixteenth century, the Armenians were quickly deemed as a threat to Mehmed Talaat Pasha's goals, in the way of his desire to expand eastward throughout Asia Minor. Like many other ethnic groups such as the Greeks and the Serbs, the Armenians began to clamour for independence in the presupposition of the Ottoman Empire's final years of regional domination, and this proved to be a threat to the pan-Turkic ruling party of Talaat Pasha.

In one of the most notable atrocities committed during this time, April 24, 1915, marks the day when some 300 Armenian political figures, religious leaders, and professionals were massacred in Istanbul. Shortly following this incident, able-bodied Armenian men were disposed of by firing squads after being told their weapons and arms would be needed for the war effort by the national army. Women, children, and the elderly were led into the desserts of Syria in mass deportation style where along the way they were starved, raped, and murdered. Vast amounts of Armenian property and wealth were seized by Turkish forces and in turn used to pay off various sectors of the genocide's perpetrators and organizers. Those who survived and made it to Syria did so with the help of a few Turks and local Arabs who showed mercy in trying to help them escape their terrible fate.

As many as 1.5 million Armenians were systematically murdered, starved, raped, and deported at the hands of the Young Turks in an effort to rid the region of a supposed threat to the homogeneity of the Ottoman Empire and its anticipated expansion. Often rebuked as a false claim, the genocide was well documented by photographer Armin T. Wegner, a German soldier living in the Ottoman Empire at the time, who considered the fate of the Armenians one of the world's greatest tragedies and made it his mission to see to it that their story was told.

Getting international attention and recognition of this tragic event has been a struggle for survivors and their children. Because Turkey today is a member of NATO, allies are hesitant to condemn Turkey for its past wrongs. Through persistent lobbying of Armenian communities in the diasporas, however, recognition of the genocide is gaining international attention. As well, the internationally acclaimed film *Ararat* produced by Canadian Atom Egoyan, which traces the struggle of survivors to get international recognition of their cause amid Turkish downplaying of the tragic events, has renewed interest in this often forgotten tragedy.

© Mary Evans Picture Library/The Image Works

Atatürk. Mustafa Kemal Atatürk wanted to change Turkey's eastern orientation by boldly changing the script from an Arabic one to a Latin one. For Atatürk, changing the Turkish script also removed eastern and Muslim influence in Turkish society and represented a new orientation to the West.

A **fez** is a felt brimless cap, usually red, worn by men in the Ottoman Empire that was eventually outlawed by Atatürk; the cap is also known as *Tarboush* throughout the Middle East.

The legacy of Mustafa Kemal Atatürk was enormous. Although not all of his reforms were widely accepted in practice, especially by practising and devout Muslims, most of the changes that he introduced were retained after his death in 1938. In virtually every respect, the contemporary Turkish republic was the product of his determined effort to create a Western-oriented nation (see Map 4.2, Plate 9).

How Did Iran's Reza Khan Resemble Atatürk?

In the meantime, a similar process was under way in Persia. Under the Qajar dynasty (1794–1925), the country had not been very successful in resisting Russian advances in the Caucasus or resolving its domestic problems. To secure themselves from foreign influence, the shahs moved the capital from Tabriz to Tehran, in a mountainous area just south of the Caspian Sea. During the mid-nineteenth century, one modernizing shah attempted to introduce political and economic reforms but was impeded by resistance from tribal and religious—predominantly Shi'ite Muslim—forces. To buttress its rule, the dynasty turned increasingly to Russia and Great Britain to protect itself from its own people. (See Map 4.3, Plate 10.)

Eventually, the growing foreign presence led to the rise of an indigenous nationalist movement. Its efforts were largely directed against Russian advances in the northwest and growing European influence in the small modern industrial sector, the profits from which left the country or disappeared into the hands of the dynasty's ruling elite. Supported actively by local Shi'ite religious leaders, opposition to the regime rose steadily among both peasants and merchants in the cities, and in 1906, popular pressures forced the reigning shah to grant a constitution on the Western model.

As in the Ottoman Empire, however, the modernizers had moved before their power base was secure. With the support of the Russians and the British, the shah was able to retain control, and the two foreign powers began to divide the country into separate spheres of influence. One reason for the growing foreign presence in Persia was the discovery of oil reserves in the southern part of the country in 1908. Within a few years, oil exports increased rapidly, with the bulk of the profits going into the pockets of British investors.

In 1921, a Persian army officer by the name of **Reza Khan** (1878–1944) led a rebellion that seized power in Tehran. The new ruler's original intention had been to establish a republic, but resistance from traditional forces impeded his efforts, and in 1925, the new Pahlavi dynasty, with Reza Khan as shah, replaced the now defunct Qajar dynasty. During the next few years, Reza Khan attempted to follow the example of Atatürk in Turkey, introducing a number of reforms to strengthen the central government, modernize the civilian and military bureaucracy, establish a modern economic infrastructure, and secularize the country.

> **Reza Khan** was the self-made leader of Iran who came to power in the 1920s and whose national policies focused on nationalism and modernization.

Unlike Atatürk, Reza Khan did not attempt to all-out destroy the power of Islamic beliefs, but he did encourage the establishment of a Western-style educational system and forbade women to wear head coverings in public. To strengthen the sense of nationalism and reduce the power of

Islam, he restored the country's ancient name, Iran, and attempted to popularize the symbols and beliefs of pre-Islamic times. Like his Qajar predecessors, however, Reza Khan was hindered by strong foreign influence. When the Soviet Union and Great Britain decided to send troops into the country during World War II, he resigned in protest and died three years later.

How Are the Failures of Arab Self-Determination Related to the Status of Palestine?

As we have seen, the Arab uprising during World War I helped bring about the demise of the Ottoman Empire. Actually, unrest against Ottoman rule had existed in the Arabian peninsula since the eighteenth century, when the Wahhabi revolt attempted to purge the outside influences and cleanse Islam of corrupt practices that had developed in past centuries. The revolt was eventually suppressed, but the influence of the Wahhabi movement persisted, revitalized in part by resistance to the centralizing and modernizing efforts of reformist elements in the nineteenth century.

World War I offered an opportunity for the Arabs to throw off the shackles of Ottoman rule to create independent states—but foreign deception by the British and French prevented the rise of independent states. When the Arab leaders in Mecca declared their independence from Ottoman rule in 1916, they were lead to believe that they had British support, but they were sorely disappointed when much of the area was placed under British or French authority as mandates of the League of Nations. Instead, the Arab countries had to fight another set of imperialist powers, namely the British and French, for self-determination.

The land of Palestine became a separate international mandate under British control. Despite the fact that more than 90 percent of Palestine's inhabitants were Arabs, in November 1917 British Foreign Secretary Lord Balfour promised Great Britain's Jewish leaders in a letter that Palestine would be a national home given to the Jews after thousands of years of living in the diasporas. The **Balfour Declaration** was ambiguous on the legal status of the territory and promised that the decision should not, although clearly would, undermine the rights of the Arab Palestinian people living in the area. Needless to say, Arab nationalists were perplexed, stunned, and angered that colonist powers in far away lands were promising Arab-inhabited land to an outside group of people. How could a national home for the Jewish people be established in a territory where 90 percent of the population were Arab Palestinians who were predominantly Muslim?

The **Balfour Declaration** was a policy statement issued by British Foreign Secretary Arthur Balfour in November 1917, stating that Arab-inhabited Palestine could be a national home for the Jewish people.

In 1930, following the Balfour Declaration, Jewish settlers began to arrive in Palestine in response to the promises made by the British. As tensions between the new arrivals and existing Arab Palestinian residents began to escalate, the British tried to restrict Jewish immigration into the territory and rejected the concept of a separate state. Clashes continued to erupt by both Arab Palestinian nationalists outraged at the British for ignoring their rights and by Jewish militants and terrorists determined to create a state of Israel in the mandate of Palestine. The stage was set for the conflicts that would take place in the region after World War II.

In the Arabian Peninsula in the early 1920s, a leader of the Wahhabi movement, Ibn Sa'ud (1880–1953), successfully united bands of Arab tribes and drove out the remnants of Ottoman rule. The soon to be King Ibn Sa'ud was a descendant of the family that had led the Wahhabi revolt in the eighteenth century. Devout and gifted, he won broad support among several Arab clans and established the Kingdom of Saudi Arabia throughout much of the peninsula in 1932.

At first, the Saudi kingdom, consisting essentially of the vast deserts of central Arabia, was desperately poor. Its financial resources were limited to the income from Muslim pilgrims visiting the holy sites in **Mecca** and **Medina**. But during the 1930s, American companies began to explore for oil, and in 1938, Standard Oil made a successful strike at Dahran, on the Persian Gulf. Soon an Arabian-American oil conglomerate, popularly called *Aramco,* was established, and Western oilmen and unforeseeable wealth suddenly flooded the isolated kingdom.

Mecca and **Medina** are Islamic holy cities in Saudi Arabia; Prophet Mohammed fled Mecca for Medina to establish the first Muslim community.

Did Marxism and Nationalism Stick in Asia and Africa?

Before the Russian Revolution, to most observers in Asia and Africa, *westernization* referred to the influence of capitalist democracies of Western Europe and the United States, not to the influence of the doctrine of social revolution developed by Karl Marx. Until 1917, Marxism was regarded as a utopian idea rather than a concrete system of government. Moreover, Marxism appeared to have less application

to conditions in Asia and Africa. Marxist doctrine, after all, declared that a Communist society could arise only from the ashes of an advanced capitalism that had already passed through the stage of industrial revolution. From the perspective of Marxist historical analysis, most societies in Asia and Africa were still at the feudal stage of development; they lacked the economic conditions and political awareness to achieve a socialist revolution that would bring the working class to power. Finally, the Marxist view of nationalism and religion had little appeal to many patriotic intellectuals in the non-Western world. Marx believed that nationhood and religion were essentially false ideas that diverted the attention of the oppressed masses from the critical issues of class struggle and, in his phrase, the exploitation of one person by another. Instead, Marx stressed the importance of an "internationalist" outlook based on class consciousness and the eventual creation of a classless society with no artificial divisions based on culture, nation, or religion.

The situation began to change after the Russian Revolution in 1917. The rise to power of Lenin's Bolsheviks demonstrated that a revolutionary party espousing Marxist principles could overturn a corrupt, outdated system and launch a new experiment dedicated to ending human inequality and achieving a paradise on earth. In 1920, Lenin proposed a new revolutionary strategy designed to relate Marxist doctrine and practice to non-Western societies. Soviet Russia, surrounded by capitalist powers, desperately needed allies in its struggle to survive in a hostile world. To Lenin, the anti-colonial movements emerging in North Africa, Asia, and the Middle East after World War I were natural allies of the young regime in Moscow. **Leninism** was based on the principle that imperialist capitalist powers need markets, raw materials, and sources of capital investment in the non-Western world to thrive. If the tentacles of capitalist influence in Asia and Africa could be severed, imperialism itself would ultimately weaken and collapse.

Leninism is a revision of Marxism, which held that Russia need not experience a bourgeois revolution and an overthrow of mature capitalism before it could move toward socialism.

Establishing a Soviet and non-Western world alliance was not easy, however. Most nationalist leaders in colonial countries belonged to the urban middle class, and many disliked the idea of a comprehensive revolution to create a totally egalitarian society. In addition, many still adhered to traditional religious beliefs and were opposed to the atheistic principles of classical Marxism.

Since it was a challenge to expect bourgeois support for social revolution, Lenin sought a compromise by which Communist parties could be organized among the working classes in the pre-industrial societies of Asia and Africa. These parties would then forge informal alliances with existing middle-class nationalist parties to struggle against the remnants of the traditional ruling class and Western imperialism. Such an alliance, of course, could not be permanent because many bourgeois nationalists in Asia and Africa would reject an egalitarian, classless society. Once the imperialists had been overthrown, therefore, the Communist parties would turn against their previous nationalist partners to seize power on their own and carry out the socialist revolution. Lenin thus proposed a two-stage revolution: an initial national democratic stage followed by a proletarian socialist stage.

Lenin's strategy became a major element in Soviet foreign policy in the 1920s. Soviet agents fanned out across the world to carry Marxism beyond the boundaries of industrial Europe. The primary instrument of this effort was the Communist International, or **Comintern**, for short. Formed in 1919 at Lenin's prodding, the Comintern was a worldwide organization of Communist parties dedicated to the advancement of world revolution. At its headquarters in Moscow, agents from around the world were trained in the precepts of world communism and then sent back to their own countries to form Marxist parties and promote the cause of social revolution. By the end of the 1920s, almost every colonial or semi-colonial society in Asia had a party based on Marxist principles. The Soviets had less success in the Middle East, where Marxist ideology appealed mainly to minorities such as Jews and Armenians in the cities, or in sub-Saharan Africa, where Soviet strategists in any case did not feel conditions were sufficiently advanced for the creation of Communist organizations.

Comintern, the short form for *Communist International,* was a party formed in 1919 by Vladimir Lenin to help spread communism worldwide.

According to Marxist doctrine, the rank and file of Communist parties should be urban workers alienated from capitalist society by inhumane working conditions. In practice, many of the leading elements even in European Communist parties tended to be intellectuals or members of the lower middle class (in Marxist parlance, the "petite bourgeoisie"). That phenomenon was even more apparent in the non-Western world, where most early Marxists were intellectuals. Many were drawn into the movement for patriotic reasons and saw Marxist doctrine as a new and more effective means of modernizing their societies and removing the power of exploitative colonialism, such as Vietnamese revolutionary Ho Chi Minh (1890–1969); see the box on page 79. Others were attracted by the utopian dream of a classless society. For those who had lost their

faith in traditional religion, it often served as a new secular ideology, dealing not with the hereafter but with the here and now. All who joined found it a stirring message of release from oppression and a practical strategy for the liberation of their society from colonial rule.

Of course, Leninism's appeal was not the same in all non-Western societies. In Confucian societies such as China and Vietnam, where traditional belief systems had been badly discredited by their failure to counter the Western challenge, communism had an immediate impact and rapidly became a major factor in the anti-colonial movement. In Buddhist and Muslim societies, where traditional religion remained strong and actually became a cohesive factor within the resistance movement, communism had less success and was forced to adapt to local conditions to survive.

Sometimes, as in Malaysia (where the sense of nationhood was weak) or Thailand (which, alone in Southeast Asia, had not fallen under colonial rule), support for the local Communist Party came from minority groups such as the overseas Chinese community. To maximize their appeal and minimize potential conflict with traditional ideas, Communist parties frequently attempted to adjust Marxist doctrine to indigenous values and institutions. In the Middle East, for example, the Ba'ath Party in Syria and in Iraq adopted a hybrid socialism combining Marxism with Arab nationalism. In Africa, radical intellectuals talked vaguely of a uniquely "African road to socialism."

The degree to which these parties were successful in establishing alliances with existing nationalist parties also varied from place to place. In some instances, the local Communists were briefly able to establish a cooperative relationship with bourgeois parties in the struggle against Western imperialism. The most famous example was the alliance between the Chinese Communist Party and Sun Yat-sen's Nationalist Party (discussed in the next section). In the Dutch East Indies, the Indonesian Communist Party (known as the PKI) allied with the middle-class nationalist group Sarekat Islam but later broke loose in an effort to organize its own mass movement among the poor peasants. Similar problems were encountered in French Indochina, where Vietnamese Communists organized by the Moscow-trained revolutionary Ho Chi Minh sought to cooperate with bourgeois nationalist parties against the colonial regime. In 1928, all such efforts were abandoned when the Comintern, reacting to Chiang Kai-shek's betrayal of the alliance with the Chinese Communist Party, declared that Communist parties should restrict their recruiting efforts to the most revolutionary elements in society—notably, the urban intellectuals and the working class. Harassed by colonial authorities and saddled with strategic directions from Moscow that often had little relevance to local conditions,

WHO WAS HO CHI MINH?

In 1919, Vietnamese revolutionary Ho Chi Minh was living in exile in France, where he first became acquainted with the new revolutionary experiment in Bolshevik Russia. In France, he worked as a photo retoucher, but his primary interest was to liberate his country. At the Paris Peace Conference in 1919, Ho Chi Minh attempted to approach U.S. President Woodrow Wilson who was championing people's right to self-determination, to plea for Vietnamese independence. Ho Chi Minh was rebuffed by Wilson. Many charged this as an example of Western hypocrisy and that perhaps self-determination was not really part of the West's grand plan for Asia and many other parts of the non-Western world. Leninism further inspired Ho Chi Minh's struggle for justice in the non-Western world. In reacting to one of Lenin's books, Ho Chi Minh in 1919 wrote "What emotion, enthusiasm, clear-sightedness, and confidence it instilled in me I was overjoyed to tears. Though sitting alone in my room, I shouted aloud as if addressing large crowds 'Dear martyrs, compatriots This is what we need, this is the path to our liberation.' After that, I had entire confidence in Lenin, in the Third International." He became a leader of the Vietnamese Communist movement. Ho Chi Minh first led his people in the struggle against French imperialism in the region; later, his revolutionaries would fight the Americans in Vietnam. Both the French and Americans underestimated the revolutionary will of the Communist fighter. Despite the relative sophistication and technological superiority of the French and Americans, Ho Chi Minh and his guerillas were able to bring the superpowers to their knees.

Source: Marvin Gentleman, ed. *Vietnam History, Documents, and Opinions on a Major World Crisis* (New York: Fawcett, 1965), pp. 30–32.

Hulton Archive/Getty Images

Ho Chi Minh. Pictured here, Ho Chi Minh shakes hands with French Prime Minister Georges Bidault in Paris in the summer of 1946. Ho and his comrades were trying to negotiate with the French to avoid a war in Vietnam, resulting in a treaty known as the Franco-Vietminh Accords. However, the treaty failed to hold.

Communist parties in most colonial societies had little success in the 1930s and failed to build a secure base of support among the mass of the population.

REVOLUTION IN CHINA

Overall, revolutionary Marxism had its greatest impact in China, where a group of young intellectuals, including several faculty and staff members from prestigious Beijing University, founded the Chinese Communist Party (CCP) in 1921. The rise of the CCP was a consequence of the failed 1911 uprising of the Revolutionary Alliance followers of Sun Yat-sen (See Chapter 1).

In China, Sun and his Revolutionary Alliance colleagues had accepted General Yuan Shikai as president of the new Chinese republic in 1911 because they lacked the military force to compete with his control over the army. Moreover, many feared, perhaps rightly, that if the revolt lapsed into chaos, the Western powers would intervene and the last shreds of Chinese sovereignty would be lost. But some had misgivings about General Yuan's intentions.

Understanding little of the new ideas sweeping into China from the West, General Yuan ruled in a traditional manner, reviving Confucian rituals and institutions and eventually trying to found a new imperial dynasty.

Yuan's dictatorial inclinations led to clashes with Sun's party, now renamed the *Guomindang,* or **Nationalist Party**. When Yuan dissolved the new parliament, the Nationalists launched a rebellion. When it failed, Sun Yat-sen fled to Japan. Sun's successor Chiang Kai-shek and the Communists inspired by Mao Zedong (1893–1976) would shape China's political landscape through to the 1930s.

> The **Nationalist Party**, also known as *Guomindang,* was a conservative political party and is currently involved in the Republic of China breakaway island of Taiwan. Alongside the People First Party, the Nationalist Party forms what is called the *pan-blue coalition,* which is for the idea of reunifying Taiwan with mainland China.

Why Was the New Culture Movement Premature?

Although the failure of the 1911 revolution was a clear sign that China was not yet ready for radical change, discontent with existing conditions continued to rise in various sectors of Chinese society. The most vocal protests came from radical intellectuals who opposed Yuan Shikai's conservative rule but were now convinced that political change could not take place until the Chinese people were more familiar with trends in the outside world. Braving the displeasure of Yuan Shikai and his successors, progressive intellectuals at Beijing University launched the **New Culture Movement**, aimed at abolishing the remnants of the old system and introducing Western values and institutions into China. Using the classrooms of China's most prestigious university as well as the pages of newly established progressive magazines and newspapers, they presented the Chinese people with a mix of new ideas, from the philosophy of Friedrich Nietzsche and Bertrand Russell to the educational views of the American John Dewey and the feminist plays of Henrik Ibsen. As such ideas flooded into China, they stirred up a new generation of educated Chinese youth, who chanted "Down with Confucius and sons" and talked of a new era dominated by "Mr. Sai" (Mr. Science) and "Mr. De" (Mr. Democracy). No one was a greater defender of free thought and speech than the chancellor of Beijing University, Cai Yuanpei, who wrote,

> So far as theoretical ideas are concerned, I follow the principles of "freedom of thought" and an attitude of broad tolerance in accordance with the practice of universities the world over. . . . Regardless of what school

of thought a person may adhere to, so long as that person's ideas are justified and conform to reason and have not been passed by through the process of natural selection, although there may be controversy, such ideas have a right to be presented.[1]

> The **New Culture Movement** was a reform movement centred in Beijing University that sought to introduce Western values into China.

The problem was that appeals for liberal democracy and women's liberation were still foreign concepts to many Chinese people, particularly to many illiterate peasants who were understandably more concerned with survival. Consequently, the New Culture Movement did not win widespread support outside the urban areas. It certainly earned the distrust of conservative military officers, one of whom threatened to lob artillery shells into Beijing University to destroy the poisonous new ideas and their advocates.

Discontent among intellectuals, however, was soon joined by the rising chorus of public protest against Japan's efforts to expand its influence on the mainland. During the first decade of the twentieth century, Japan had taken advantage of the Manchu dynasty's decline to extend its domination over Manchuria and Korea. In 1915, the Japanese government insisted that Yuan Shikai accept a series of 21 demands that would have given Japan a virtual protectorate over the Chinese government and economy. Yuan was able to fend off the most far-reaching Japanese demands by arousing popular outrage in China, but at the Paris Peace Conference four years later, Japan received Germany's sphere of influence in Shandong Province as a reward for its support of the Allied cause in World War I. On hearing the news that the Chinese government had accepted the decision, on May 4, 1919, patriotic students, supported by other sectors of the urban population, demonstrated in Beijing and other major cities of the country. Although this May Fourth Movement did not result in a reversal of the decision to award Shandong to Japan, it did alert a substantial part of the politically literate population to the threat to national survival and the incompetence of the warlord government.

By 1920, central authority had almost ceased to exist in China. Two political forces now began to emerge as competitors for the right to bring order to the chaos of the early republican era. One was Sun Yat-sen's Nationalist Party. Driven from the political arena seven years earlier by Yuan Shikai, the party now reestablished itself on the mainland by making an alliance with the warlord ruler of Guangdong Province in South China. From Canton, Sun sought international assistance to carry out his national revolution. The other was the CCP. Following Lenin's strategy, the CCP sought to link up with the more experienced Nationalists. Sun Yat-sen needed the expertise and the diplomatic support that the Soviet Union could provide because his anti-imperialist rhetoric had alienated many Western powers. In 1923, the two parties formed an alliance to oppose the warlords and drive the imperialist powers out of China.

For three years, with the assistance of a Comintern mission in Canton, the two parties submerged their mutual suspicions and mobilized and trained a revolutionary army to march north and seize control over China. The so-called **Northern Expedition** began in the summer of 1926 (see Map 4.4, Plate 10). By the following spring, revolutionary forces were in control of all Chinese territory south of the Yangtze River, including the major river ports of Wuhan and Shanghai. But tensions between the two parties now surfaced. Sun Yat-sen had died of cancer in 1925 and was succeeded as head of the Nationalist Party by his military subordinate, Chiang Kai-shek. Chiang insincerely claimed support for the alliance with the Communists, but he actually planned to destroy them. In April 1927, he struck against the Communists and their supporters in Shanghai, killing thousands. The CCP responded by encouraging revolts in central China and Canton, but the uprisings were defeated and their leaders were killed or forced into hiding.

> The **Northern Expedition** was a military campaign led by Chiang Kai-shek from 1926 to 1929 whose goal was to unite China under the rule of the Nationalist Party and end the rule of the local warlords.

Who Supported and Opposed Chiang's Nanjing Republic?

In 1928, Chiang Kai-shek, leader of the Nationalist Party without the Communists, founded a new Republic of China at Nanjing, and over the next three years, he managed to reunify China by a combination of military operations and inducements to various northern warlords to join his movement. One of his key targets was warlord Zhang Zuolin, who controlled Manchuria, then under the control of Japan. When Zhang allegedly agreed to throw in his lot with the Chiang's Nationalists, the Japanese had Zhang assassinated by placing a bomb under his train as he was returning to Manchuria. The Japanese hoped that Zhang Zuolin's son and successor, Zhang Xueliang, would be more cooperative, but they had miscalculated. Promised a major role in Chiang Kai-shek's government, the younger Zhang began instead to integrate Manchuria politically and economically into the Nanjing republic.

Chiang Kai-shek saw the Japanese as a serious threat to Chinese national aspirations but considered them less dangerous than the Communists. After the Shanghai massacre of April 1927, most of the Communist leaders went into hiding in the city, where they attempted to revive the movement in its traditional base among the urban working class. Shanghai was a rich recruiting ground for the party: a city of millionaires, paupers, prostitutes, gamblers, and adventurers. Some party members, however, led by the young Communist organizer Mao Zedong, fled to the hilly areas south of the Yangtze River.

Unlike most other CCP leaders, Mao was convinced that the Chinese revolution must be based on the impoverished peasants in the countryside, a political revolutionary ideology later known as **Maoism**. The son of a prosperous peasant, Mao had helped organize a peasant movement in South China during the early 1920s and then served as an agitator in rural villages in his native province of Hunan during the Northern Expedition in the fall of 1926. At that time, he wrote a famous report to the party leadership suggesting that the CCP support peasant demands for a land revolution. But his superiors refused, fearing that adopting excessively radical policies would have destroyed the previous alliance with the Nationalists.

> **Maoism** is a political revolutionary ideology developed by Mao Zedong that places importance on the peasantry's role in Communist China.

Obviously after Chiang's Shanghai massacre in the spring of 1927, the CCP-Nationalist alliance ceased to exist. Chiang Kai-shek furthered his campaign against the Communists by attempting to root them out of their urban base in Shanghai. He eventually succeeded in 1931, when most party leaders were forced to flee Shanghai for Mao's rural hideout in the rugged hills of Jiangxi Province. Three years later, using their superior military strength, Chiang's troops surrounded the Communist base. Then, Mao's young communist People's Liberation Army (PLA) abandoned their guerrilla lair and embarked on the famous **Long March**, an arduous journey of 10 000 kilometres on foot through mountains, marshes, and deserts to the small provincial town of Yan'an in the dusty hills of North China. Of the 90 000 who embarked on the journey in October 1934, roughly 10 000 arrived in Yan'an a year later.

> The **Long March** was an immense military retreat undertaken by the Communist Army of the Chinese Soviet Republic, led by Mao Zedong, through China's harshest terrain. In an effort to escape the Nationalist Party army, almost 90 000 embarked on the journey from their base in South China in October 1934, but only about 10 000 reached Yan'an a year later.

Mao Zedong at Yan'an. In 1934, Mao Zedong led his bedraggled forces on the famous Long March from South China to a new location at Yan'an, in the hills just south of the Gobi Desert. Here Chairman Mao, standing to the right of one of his generals, poses for a photograph at his new headquarters. Note the thick padded jackets to keep out the cold.

© *Earl Leaf/Rapho*

Meanwhile, Chiang Kai-shek was trying to build a new nation, the Nanjing republic, without Mao and his Communist followers. When the Nanjing republic was established in 1928, Chiang publicly declared his commitment to his predecessor Sun Yat-sen's 1918 Three People's Principles (see Chapter 1, page 14). In keeping with Sun's program, Chiang announced a period of political indoctrination to prepare the Chinese people for a final stage of constitutional government. In the meantime, Chiang's Nationalists would use their dictatorial power to carry out a land reform program and modernize the urban industrial sector.

But it would take more than paper plans to create a new China. Years of neglect and civil war had severely frayed the political, economic, and social fabric of the nation. There were faint signs of an impending industrial revolution in the major urban centres, but most of the people in the countryside, drained by warlord exactions and civil strife, were still very poor and overwhelmingly illiterate. A westernized middle class had begun to emerge in the cities and would have formed much of the support for the Nanjing government. But this new westernized elite, preoccupied with bourgeois values of individual advancement and material accumulation, had few links with the peasants in the countryside or the rickshaw drivers in the streets.

Chiang was aware of the difficulty of introducing foreign ideas into a society still culturally conservative. While building a modern industrial sector, sponsored by his Western-educated wife, Mei-ling Soong, Chiang sought to propagate traditional Confucian values of hard work, obedience, and moral integrity while rejecting what he considered the excessive individualism and material greed of Western capitalism.

Unfortunately for Chiang, Confucian ideas—at least in their institutional form—had been widely discredited by the failure of the traditional system to solve China's growing problems. Critics noted, as well, that Chiang's government did not practise what it preached. Much of the national wealth was in the hands of the so-called four families, composed of senior officials and close subordinates of the ruling elite. Lacking the political sensitivity of Sun Yat-sen and fearing Communist influence, Chiang repressed all opposition and censored free expression, thereby alienating many intellectuals and political moderates.

With only a tenuous hold over the vast countryside, Chiang Kai-shek's government had little more success in promoting economic development. Although mechanization was gradually beginning to replace manual labour in a number of traditional industries (notably in the manufacture of textile goods), about 75 percent of all industrial production was still craft-produced in the mid-1930s. Then again, traditional Chinese exports, such as silk and tea, were hard-hit by the Great Depression. With military expenses consuming about half the national budget, distressingly little was devoted to economic development. Even during the decade of precarious peace after the Nationalists and Communists' Northern Expedition, industrial growth averaged only about 1 percent annually.

One of Sun Yat-sen's most prominent proposals was to redistribute land to poor peasants in the countryside. Whether overall per capita consumption declined during the early decades of the century is unclear, but there is no doubt that Chinese farmers were often victimized by high taxes imposed by local warlords and the endemic political and social conflict that marked the period. A land reform program was enacted in 1930, but it had little effect. Since the urban middle class and the landed gentry were Chiang Kai-shek's natural political constituency, he shunned programs that would lead to a radical redistribution of wealth.

JAPAN BETWEEN THE WARS

By the beginning of the twentieth century, Japan had made steady progress toward the creation of an advanced society on the Western model. Economic and social reforms launched during the Meiji era (1868–1912) led to increasing prosperity and the development of a modern industrial and commercial sector. Although the political system still retained many authoritarian characteristics, optimists had reason to hope that Japan was on the road to becoming a full-fledged democracy.

Why Was Japan's Young Democracy So Fragile?

During the first quarter of the twentieth century, the Japanese political system appeared to evolve significantly toward the Western democratic model. Political parties expanded their popular following and became increasingly competitive, while individual pressure groups such as labour unions began to appear in Japanese society, along with an independent press and a bill of rights. The influence of the old ruling oligarchy, the *genro,* had not yet been significantly challenged, however, nor had that of its ideological foundation, the **kokutai**, which had greater influence on the political nationalism of Japanese society.

> **Kokutai** refers to the sentiments of Japanese ultranationalists in the 1930s who pledged blind support for the government and military in the face of opposition from liberal-minded Japanese who questioned the emperor's position on national affairs.

In Japan, the realization of democratic institutions was able to survive throughout the 1920s. During that period, the military budget was reduced, and a suffrage bill enacted in 1925 granted the vote to all Japanese adult males. Women remained disenfranchised, but women's associations gained increased visibility during the 1920s, and women became active in the labour movement and in campaigns for various social reforms.

But the era was also marked by growing social turmoil, and two opposing forces within the system were gearing up to challenge the prevailing wisdom. On the left, a Marxist labour movement, which reflected the tensions within the working class and the increasing radicalism among the rural poor, began to take shape in the early 1920s in response to growing economic difficulties. Attempts to suppress labour disturbances led to further radicalization. On the right, ultranationalist groups called for a rejection of Western models of development and a more militant approach to realizing national objectives. In 1919, radical nationalist Kita

Ikki called for a military takeover and the establishment of a new system bearing a strong resemblance to what would later be called *fascism* in Europe (see Chapter 5, page 90).

Japan also continued to make impressive progress in economic development. Spurred by rising domestic demand as well as a continued high rate of government investment in the economy, the production of raw materials tripled between 1900 and 1930, and industrial production increased more than twelvefold. Much of the increase went into the export market, and Western manufacturers began to complain about the rising competition for markets from the Japanese.

As in Europe, rapid industrialization was accompanied by some exploitation and rising social tensions. A characteristic of the Meiji model was the concentration of various manufacturing processes within a single enterprise, the so-called *zaibatsu,* or "financial clique." Some of these firms were existing merchant companies that had the capital and the foresight to move into new areas of opportunity. Others were formed by enterprising samurai, who used their status and experience in management to good account in a new environment. Whatever their origins, these firms gradually developed, often with official encouragement, into large conglomerates that controlled a major segment of the Japanese industrial sector. According to one source, by 1937, the four largest *zaibatsu* (Mitsui, Mitsubishi, Sumitomo, and Yasuda) controlled 21 percent of the banking industry, 26 percent of mining, 35 percent of shipbuilding, 38 percent of commercial shipping, and more than 60 percent of paper manufacturing and insurance.

This concentration of power and wealth in the hands of a few major industrial combines resulted in the emergence of a form of dual economy: on the one hand, a modern industry characterized by up-to-date methods and massive government subsidies and, on the other, a traditional manufacturing sector characterized by conservative methods and small-scale production techniques.

Concentration of wealth also led to growing economic inequalities. As we have seen, economic growth had been achieved at the expense of the peasants, many of whom fled to the cities to escape rural poverty. That labour surplus benefited the industrial sector, but the urban proletariat was still poorly paid and ill-housed. Rampant inflation in the price of rice led to food riots shortly after World War I. A rapid increase in population (the total population of the Japanese islands increased from an estimated 43 million in 1900 to 73 million in 1940) led to food shortages and the threat of rising unemployment. Intense competition and the global recession in the early 1920s led to a greater concentration of industry and a perceptible rise in urban radicalism, marked by the appearance of a Marxist labour movement. In the meantime, those left on the farm continued to suffer. As late as the beginning of World War II, an estimated half of all Japanese farmers were tenants.

A final problem for Japanese leaders in the post-Meiji era was the familiar capitalist dilemma of finding sources of raw materials and foreign markets for the nation's manufactured goods. Until World War I, Japan had dealt with the problem by seizing territories such as Taiwan, Korea, and southern Manchuria and transforming them into colonies or protectorates of the growing Japanese Empire. That policy had succeeded brilliantly, but it had also begun to arouse the concern and, in some cases, the hostility of the Western nations. China was also becoming apprehensive; as we have seen, Japanese demands for Shandong Province at the Paris Peace Conference in 1919 aroused massive protests in major Chinese cities.

The United States was especially concerned about Japanese aggressiveness. Although the United States had been less active than some European states in pursuing colonies in the Pacific, it had a strong interest in keeping the area open for U.S. commercial activities. American anxiety about Tokyo's 21 demands on China in 1915 led to a new agreement in 1917, which essentially repeated the compromise provisions of the agreement reached nine years earlier.

In 1922, in Washington, D.C., the United States convened a major conference of nations with interests in the Pacific to discuss problems of regional security. The Washington Conference led to agreements on several issues, but the major accomplishment was the conclusion of a nine-power treaty recognizing the territorial integrity of China. The other participants induced Japan to accept these provisions by accepting its special position in Manchuria.

During the remainder of the 1920s, Japanese governments attempted to play by the rules laid down at the Washington Conference. Known as **Shidehara diplomacy**, after the foreign minister (and later prime minister) who attempted to carry it out, this policy sought to use diplomatic and economic means to realize Japanese interests in Asia. But this approach came under severe pressure as Japanese industrialists began to move into new areas of opportunity, such as heavy industry, chemicals, mining, and the manufacturing of appliances and automobiles. Because such industries desperately needed resources not found in abundance locally, the Japanese government came under increasing pressure to find new sources abroad.

> **Shidehara diplomacy** was a peaceful foreign policy followed by Japan in much of the 1920s (it was named after Japanese Foreign Minister Danshaku Shidehara Kijuro); it sought to achieve political objectives through diplomatic and economic means rather than through use of the military.

The fragile flower of democratic institutions was able to survive growing social turmoil throughout the 1920s, while Japan sought to operate within a cooperative framework with other nations. In the early 1930s, however, with the onset of the Great Depression and growing tensions in the international arena, nationalist forces rose to dominance in the government. The changes taking place in the 1930s were not in the constitution or the institutional structure, which remained essentially intact, but in the composition and attitudes of the ruling group. Party leaders during the 1920s had attempted to realize Japanese aspirations within the existing global political and economic framework. The dominant elements in the government in the 1930s, a mixture of military officers and ultranationalist politicians, were convinced that the diplomacy of the 1920s had failed and advocated a more aggressive approach to protecting national interests in a brutal and competitive world.

Historians argue over whether Japanese democracy was merely a fragile period of comparative liberalization within a framework dominated by the Meiji vision of empire and *kokutai* or whether the militant nationalism of the 1930s was an aberration brought on by the depression, which caused the emerging Japanese democracy to wilt. Perhaps both contentions contain a little truth. A process of democratization was taking place in Japan during the first decades of the twentieth century, but without shaking the essential core of the Meiji concept of the state. When the "liberal" approach of the 1920s failed to solve the problems of the day, the shift toward a more aggressive approach was inevitable.

NATIONALISM AND POPULISM IN LATIN AMERICA

Although the nations of Latin America played little role in World War I, that conflict nevertheless exerted an impact on the region, especially on its economy. By the end of the following decade, the region was also strongly influenced by another event of global proportions—the Great Depression. Throughout the remainder of the twentieth century, U.S. intervention in the region would forever change the political landscape in many countries.

What Were U.S. Interests in Latin America?

At the beginning of the twentieth century, the economy of Latin America was based largely on the export of foodstuffs and raw materials. Some countries stuck in mercantilist practices under colonialism continued to rely on the export earnings of only one or two products. Argentina, for example, relied on the sale of beef and wheat; Chile exported nitrates and copper; Brazil and the Caribbean nations sold sugar; and the Central American states relied on the export of bananas. Such exports brought large profits to a few, but for the majority of the population, the returns were meagre.

During World War I, the export of some products, such as Chilean nitrates (used to produce explosives), increased dramatically. In general, however, the war led to a decline in European investment in Latin America and a rise in the U.S. role in the local economies. That process was accelerated in the early years of the twentieth century when the United States intervened in Latin American politics to undertake construction of the Panama Canal, which dramatically reduced the time and distance needed for ships to pass between the Atlantic and Pacific Oceans.

During the first three decades of the twentieth century, the United States intervened numerously in the affairs of various countries of Latin America to protect its economic interests. President William Howard Taft's **dollar diplomacy** from 1909–13, for example, was based on the idea of protecting U.S. economic interests in the region, even if it meant overtaking and occupying Latin American countries. By 1913, under the internationalist President Woodrow Wilson, that policy was reversed. After all, dollar diplomacy had aroused considerable resentment on the part of governments throughout the region.

> **Dollar diplomacy** was a U.S. foreign policy that indicated the United States would use all means necessary to secure its private economic interests overseas; it was adopted by U.S. President William Howard Taft and Secretary of State Philander C. Knox from 1909 to 1913.

Yet, by the late 1920s, the United States had replaced Great Britain as the foremost source of foreign investment in Latin America. Unlike the British, however, U.S. investors placed funds directly into production enterprises, causing large segments of the area's export industry to fall into American hands. A number of Central American states, for example, were popularly labelled "banana republics" because of the power and influence of the U.S.-owned United Fruit Company. U.S. firms also dominated the copper mining industry in Chile and Peru and the oil industry in Mexico, Peru, and Bolivia.

Increasing economic interests served to reinforce the high level of U.S. imperialist political influence in Latin America, especially in Central America, a region that U.S. administrations considered vital to U.S. national security. U.S. troops occupied parts of both Nicaragua and

Honduras to protect U.S. economic interests there. The growing U.S. imperialist presence in the region provoked resentment among Latin Americans, who resented U.S. policies in the region. Washington also used its influence to keep ruthless dictators, such as Juan Vicente Gómez of Venezuela and Fulgencio Batista (1901–73) of Cuba, in power to preserve U.S. economic influence, sometimes through U.S. military intervention. In a bid to improve relations with Latin American countries, President Franklin D. Roosevelt in 1936 promulgated the **Good Neighbor Policy**, which rejected the use of U.S. military force in the region. To underscore his sincerity, Roosevelt ordered the withdrawal of U.S. marines from the island nation of Haiti in 1936. For the first time in 30 years, there were no U.S. occupation troops in Latin America.

> The **Good Neighbor Policy**, established by U.S. President Franklin D. Roosevelt, was a coming around of U.S. diplomatic policy; its objective was to improve the country's tarnished relationship with Latin America.

Because Latin American economies were dependent on the export of raw materials and food products, the Great Depression of the 1930s initially appeared to be a disaster for the region. The total value of Latin American exports in 1930 was almost 50 percent below the figure for the previous five years. Spurred by the decline in foreign revenues, Latin American governments began to encourage the development of new industries to replace dependence on imports. What came from the Great Depression was a reorientation of economic production to industrialization, in effect removing the past mercantilist practices and dependency on Europe and the United States. Breaking the chains of dependency allowed many Latin American economies to now flourish independently. Much of the empirical justification for world system theory (see Chapter 1, page 7) came from this happy divorce of the periphery (Latin America) from the core (Europe and the United States).

Why Were Latin American Governments Deemed Populist?

During the late nineteenth century, most governments in Latin America had been dominated by landed or military elites, who governed by the blatant use of military force. Latin America was, however, soon to be transformed. During the 1930s, populist governments were elected to power with broad reform agendas. **Populism** was especially evident in Argentina, Brazil, and Mexico—three countries that together possessed more than half of the land and wealth of Latin America (see Map 4.5, Plate 11).

> **Populism** is a political principle that supports the common people with social, political, and economic policies that better their position in relation to the advantaged elite.

The government of Argentina, once controlled by *latifundia* landowners who had benefited from the export of beef and wheat, eventually recognized the need to establish a local industrial base. In 1916, Hipólito Irigoyen (1852–1933), head of the Radical Party, was elected president on a program to improve conditions for the middle and lower classes through populist policies. First, significant political reforms were put in place, including extending the franchise, post-secondary education reforms, improving working conditions for women, and incorporating labour unions into national dialogue. Second, economic reforms were put in place, including government investment in railroads, petroleum, and shipping. Irigoyen's first term seemed to be a success; however, near the end of it, the party drew closer to the large landowners. Irigoyen was eventually reelected in 1928 for another term. But before he finished his term the army overthrew Irigoyen's government in 1930 and reestablished the power of the landed class. But the army's effort to return to the past and suppress the growing influence of labour unions failed, and in 1946, General Juan Perón (1895–1974)—claiming the support of the *descamisados* ("shirtless ones")—once again revived populist power (see Chapter 15, pages 271–72).

Brazil followed a similar path. In 1889, the army overthrew the Brazilian monarchy, installed by Portugal decades before, and established a republic. But it was dominated by landed elites, many of whom had grown wealthy through their ownership of coffee plantations. By 1900, three-quarters of the world's coffee was grown in Brazil. As in Argentina, the ruling oligarchy ignored the importance of establishing an urban industrial base. When the Great Depression ravaged profits from coffee exports, a wealthy rancher, Getúlio Vargas (1883–1954), seized power and served as president from 1930 to 1945. At first Vargas ruled more like a fascist dictator than a populist, using policy to torture and silence his opponents. However, after the Great Depression Vargas changed his style of governing to a populist one. Vargas's populist policies included protecting workers by declaring an eight-hour day and a minimum wage and expanding the franchise to include women. His industrial policy was also populist and successful; by expanding national protection of Brazilian industry, by the end of World War II, Brazil had become Latin America's major industrial power. In 1945, the army, concerned that Vargas was turning increasingly to leftist elements for support, forced him to resign.

Mexico, in the early years of the twentieth century, was in a state of turbulence. Under the rule of dictator Porfirio Díaz (see Chapter 1, page 19), the real wages of the working class had declined. Moreover, 95 percent of the rural population owned no land, and about a thousand families ruled almost all of Mexico. When a liberal landowner, Francisco Madero, forced Díaz from power in 1910, he opened the door to a wider revolution. Madero's ineffectiveness triggered a demand for agrarian reform led by Emiliano Zapata (1879–1919), who aroused the masses of landless peasants in southern Mexico and began to seize the haciendas of wealthy landholders.

For the next several years, Zapata and rebel leader Pancho Villa (1878–1923), who operated in the northern state of Chihuahua, became an important political force in the country by publicly advocating efforts to redress the economic grievances of the poor. But neither had a broad grasp of the challenges facing the country, and power eventually gravitated to a more moderate group of reformists around the Constitutionalist Party. The latter were intent on breaking the power of the great landed families and U.S. corporations, but without engaging in land reform or the nationalization of property. After a bloody conflict that cost the lives of thousands, the moderates consolidated power, and in 1917, they promulgated a new constitution that established a strong presidency, initiated land reform policies, established limits on foreign investment, and set an agenda for social welfare programs.

In 1920, Constitutionalist leader Alvaro Obregón (1880–1928) assumed the presidency and began to carry out his reform program. But real change did not take place until the presidency of General Lázaro Cárdenas (1895–1970) in 1934. Cárdenas won wide popularity with the peasants by ordering the redistribution of 44 million acres of land controlled by landed elites. He also seized control of the oil industry, which had hitherto been dominated by major U.S. oil companies. Alluding to the Good Neighbor Policy, President Roosevelt refused to intervene, and eventually Mexico agreed to compensate U.S. oil companies for their lost property. It then set up PEMEX, a governmental organization, to run the oil industry. By now, the revolution was a populist one under the leadership of the Institutional Revolutionary Party (PRI). Every six years, for more than half a century, PRI presidential candidates automatically succeeded each other in office.

How Did Populism Influence Latin American Culture?

The first half of the twentieth century witnessed a dramatic reflection of populism in Latin American culture. This was often expressed by demonstrating Latin America's unique

David Alfaro Siqueiros (1896–1974) © Estate of David Alfaro Siqueiros/SODRAC (2006). Encounter of the Armies. From Porfirianism to the Revolution. Mural. Completed 1964. © Schalkwijk/Art Resource, NY

Struggle for the Banner. Like Diego Rivera, David Alfaro Siqueiros (1896–1974) painted on public buildings large murals that celebrated the Mexican revolution and the workers' and peasants' struggle for freedom. Beginning in the 1930s, Siqueiros expressed sympathy for the exploited and downtrodden peoples of Mexico in dramatic frescoes such as this one. He painted similar murals in Uruguay, Argentina, and Brazil and was once expelled from the United States, where his political art and views were considered too radical.

identity through the adoption of indigenous themes and populist social issues. In *The Underdogs* (1915), for example, Mariano Azuela (1873–1952) presented a sympathetic but not uncritical portrait of the Mexican revolution as his country entered an era of unsettling change.

In their determination to commend Latin America's distinctive characteristics, some writers extolled the promise of the region's vast virgin lands and the diversity of its peoples. In *Don Segundo Sombra,* published in 1926, Ricardo Güiraldes (1886–1927) celebrated the life of the ideal **gaucho** ("cattle herder" or "cowboy"), defining Argentina's hope and strength through the enlightened management of its fertile earth. Likewise, in *Doña Bárbara,* Rómulo Gallegos (1884–1969) wrote in a similar vein about his native Venezuela. Other authors pursued the themes of solitude and detachment, and pride and independence, products of the region's relationship with the rest of the world.

> **Gaucho**, which means "cattle herder" or the Latin American equivalent of "cowboy," is often used as a symbol of Argentine nationalism.

Latin American artists followed their literary counterparts in joining the modernist movement in Europe, yet they too were eager to promote the emergence of a new regional and national essence. In Mexico, where the government provided financial support for painting murals on public buildings, the artist Diego Rivera (1886–1957) began to produce a monumental style of mural art that served two purposes: to illustrate the national past by portraying Aztec legends and folk customs and to popularize a political message in favour of realizing the populist goals of the Mexican revolution. His wife, Frida Kahlo (1907–54), incorporated Surrealist whimsy in her own paintings, many of which were portraits of herself and her family.

CONCLUSION

The inter-war period had a dramatic effect on nations and peoples throughout the non-Western world.

- In Europe, venerable empires collapsed and principles of nationalism were born.
- In Asia, nationalist movements arose, dedicated to freeing their societies from the ravages of Western colonialism.
- Gandhi would forever change the world with his dedication to nonviolence against the oppressor.
- In Turkey, the fall of the Ottoman Empire and the rise of Mustafa Kemal Atatürk would bring Turkey closer to Europe and the West.

- In the Middle East, Arab nationalists overthrew the Ottomans, only to be placed under the authority of the British or French.
- Chinese Nationalist Party leaders and Communists waged a war of blood and ideas on how China would progress.
- Japan would experiment with democracy and state-led economic development.
- Latin America would try to break its dependency on the outside world and follow a populist path.

The Great Depression of the 1930s undermined worldwide confidence in the capacity of the capitalist system to sustain modern progress even as it sowed the seeds of a second global conflict far more destructive than the first. It is to that devastating conflict that we must now turn.

CRITICAL THINKING QUESTIONS

1. Do globalization and the ongoing search by multinational corporations for cheaper labour and raw materials in the Third World validate Leninism?

2. Turkey has had difficulty winning European Union support for full membership, and many believe this is because Turkey is a Muslim country. Was Mustafa Kemal Atatürk unsuccessful at shedding Turkey of its eastern influence or can Europe ever think of Turkey as one of its own?

3. Does Japanese *zaibatsu* success show the virtues of government protection of "infant industries" at the start of a nation's economic growth?

4. Did the U.S. policy of dollar diplomacy with Latin America plant the seeds of populist revolution?

CHAPTER NOTE

1. Ts'ai Yuan-p'ei, "Ta Lin Ch'in-nan Han," in *Ts'ai Yuan-p'ei Hsien-sheng Ch'uan-chi* [*Collected Works of Mr. Ts'ai Yuan-p'ei*] (Taipei: Chuan chi wen hsueh, 1967), pp. 1057–58.

Chapter 5

The Crisis Deepens: The Outbreak of World War II

In September 1931, acting on the pretext that Chinese troops had attacked a Japanese railway near the northern Chinese city of Mukden, Japanese military units stationed in the area seized control throughout Manchuria. When the League of Nations issued a report condemning the Japanese seizure, Japan withdrew from the league. Although no one knew it at the time, this Manchurian incident would later be singled out by some observers as the opening shot of World War II. The failure of the League of Nations to take decisive action sent a strong signal to Japan and other potentially aggressive states that they might seek their objectives without the risk of united opposition by the major world powers. Despite its agonizing efforts to build a system of peace and stability that would prevent future wars, the league had failed dismally, and the world was once again about to slide inescapably into a new global conflict.

At the conclusion of this chapter, you will be able to

- state the similarities and differences between dictatorship, totalitarianism, and fascism;
- describe the efforts of Canadian battalions in noted battles;
- explain the pivotal roles that Japan, the Soviet Union, and the United States played during the war;
- name and describe the key agreements developed by Western powers for peace-time governance;
- understand the horrors of war and the sacrifices people made at home

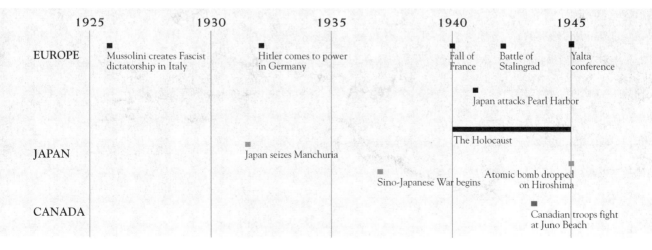

	1925	1930	1935	1940	1945
EUROPE	Mussolini creates Fascist dictatorship in Italy		Hitler comes to power in Germany	Fall of France · Battle of Stalingrad · Japan attacks Pearl Harbor · The Holocaust	Yalta conference
JAPAN		Japan seizes Manchuria	Sino-Japanese War begins	Atomic bomb dropped on Hiroshima	
CANADA				Canadian troops fight at Juno Beach	

RETREAT FROM DEMOCRACY: THE RISE OF DICTATORIAL REGIMES

In Europe, the first clear step to war took place two years after the attack in Mukden. On February 3, 1933, only four days after he had been appointed chancellor of Germany, Adolf Hitler met secretly with Germany's leading generals. He revealed to them his desire to remove the "cancer of democracy," create a new authoritarian leadership, and forge a new domestic unity. His foreign policy objectives were equally striking. Since Germany's living space was too small for its people, Hitler said, Germany must rearm and prepare for "the conquest of new living space in the east and its ruthless Germanization." From the outset, Hitler had a clear vision of his goals, and their implementation meant another war.

There was thus a close relationship between the rise of dictatorial regimes in the 1930s and the coming of World War II. The apparent triumph of liberal democracy in 1919 proved extremely short-lived. By 1939, two major states in Europe, France and Great Britain, as well as a number of smaller peripheral states such as Belgium, the Netherlands, Denmark, Norway, and Sweden remained democratic. Italy and Germany had installed fascist regimes, and the Soviet Union under Joseph Stalin was a repressive **totalitarian state**. A host of other European states adopted authoritarian systems, while a militarist regime in Japan moved that country down the path to war.

> A **totalitarian state** is characterized by mass party control over all aspects of economic, social, political, cultural, and intellectual life in an attempt to achieve the regime's transformation of society.

Dictatorship was by no means a new phenomenon, but the modern totalitarian state was. The totalitarian state extended the functions and powers of the central state far beyond what they had been in the past. If the immediate origins of totalitarianism can be found in the total warfare of World War I, when governments exercised controls over economic, political, and personal freedom to achieve victory, a more long-term cause stemmed from the growth of the state as the primary focus of human action at a time when traditional sources of identity, such as religion and the local community, were in a state of decline.

The modern totalitarian state transcended the ideal of passive obedience expected in a traditional dictatorship or authoritarian monarchy. It expected the active loyalty and commitment of its citizens to the regime and its goals and used modern mass propaganda techniques and high-speed communications to conquer citizens' minds and hearts.

That control had a purpose: the active involvement of the masses in the achievement of the regime's goals, whether they be war, a classless utopia, or a thousand-year Reich.

The modern totalitarian state was to be led by a single leader and single party. It ruthlessly rejected the liberal ideal of limited government power and constitutional guarantees of individual freedoms. Indeed, individual freedom was to be subordinated to the collective will of the masses, organized and determined for them by a leader or leaders. Modern technology also gave totalitarian states the ability to use unprecedented police powers to impose their wishes on their subjects.

Totalitarianism is an abstract concept that transcended traditional political labels. **Fascism** in Italy and Nazism in Germany grew out of extreme rightist preoccupations with nationalism, anti-socialism, and, in the case of Germany, racism. Communism in the Soviet Union emerged out of Marxism and the concept of the dictatorship of the proletariat. Thus totalitarianism could and did exist in what were perceived as extreme right-wing and extreme left-wing regimes. This fact helped bring about a new concept of the political spectrum in which the extremes were no longer seen as opposites on a linear scale but came to be viewed as similar to each other in key respects.

> **Fascism** refers to a totalitarian-like right-wing state combined with hyper-nationalism, racism, and rule of a feared dictator.

Where Was Europe's First Fascist Regime?

In the early 1920s, in the wake of economic turmoil, political disorder, and the general insecurity and fear stemming from World War I, Benito Mussolini (1883–1945) burst upon the Italian scene with the first Fascist movement in Europe that began with great popularity. Mussolini began his political career as a socialist but was expelled from the Socialist Party after supporting Italy's entry into World War I, a position contrary to the socialist principle of ardent neutrality in imperialist wars. In 1919, Mussolini established a new political group, the *Fascio di Combattimento,* or "League of Combat." It received little attention in the parliamentary elections of 1919, but Italy's three major political parties were unable to form an effective governmental coalition. When socialists began to speak of the need for revolution, provoking worker strikes and a general climate of class violence, alarmed conservatives turned to the Fascists, who formed armed squads to attack socialist offices and newspapers. By 1922, Mussolini's nationalist rhetoric and ability to play to middle-class fears of radicalism, revolution, and disorder were attracting ever more adherents. On October 29, 1922, after Mussolini and the Fascists threatened to march on Rome if they were not given power, King Victor Emmanuel III (r. 1900–46) capitulated and made Mussolini prime minister of Italy.

By 1926, Mussolini had established the institutional framework for his Fascist dictatorship. Press laws gave the government the right to suspend any publication that fostered disrespect for the Catholic Church, the monarchy, or the state. The prime minister was made "head of government" with the power to legislate by decree. A police law empowered the police to arrest and confine anybody for both non-political and political crimes without due process of law. In 1926, all anti-Fascist parties were outlawed. By the end of 1926, Mussolini ruled Italy as *Il Duce,* the leader.

Mussolini left no doubt of his intentions. Fascism, he said, "is totalitarian, and the Fascist State, the synthesis and unity of all values, interprets, develops and gives strength to the whole life of the people."[1] His regime attempted to mould Italians into a single-minded community by developing Fascist organizations. By 1939, about two-thirds of the population between eight and eighteen had been enrolled in some kind of Fascist youth group. Activities for these groups included Saturday afternoon marching drills and calisthenics, seaside and mountain summer camps, and youth contests. Beginning in the 1930s, all young men were given some kind of pre-military exercises to develop discipline and provide training for war.

Mussolini hoped to create a new Italian: hardworking, physically fit, disciplined, intellectually sharp, and martially inclined. In practice, the Fascists largely reinforced traditional social attitudes, as is evident in their regressive policies toward women. The Fascists portrayed the family as the pillar of the state and women as the foundation of the family. "Woman into the home" became the Fascist slogan. Women were to be homemakers and baby producers, "their natural and fundamental mission in life," according to Mussolini, who viewed population growth as an indicator of national strength. A practical consideration also underlay the Fascist attitude toward women: working women would compete with males for jobs in the depression economy of the 1930s. Eliminating women from the market reduced male unemployment.

How Was Hitler's Pre-Nazi Germany Exceedingly Racist?

As Mussolini began to lay the foundations of his Fascist state in Italy, a young admirer was harbouring similar dreams in Germany. Born on April 20, 1889, Adolf Hitler was the son of an Austrian customs official. He had done poorly in secondary school and eventually made his way to Vienna to become an artist. Through careful observation of the political scene, Hitler became an avid German nationalist who learned from his experience in mass politics in Austria how political parties could use propaganda and terror effectively. But it was only after World War I, during which he had served as a soldier on the Western Front, that Hitler became actively involved in politics. By then, he had become convinced that the cause of German defeat had been the Jews, for whom he now developed a fervent hatred.

Anti-Semitism was not new to Europe. Since the Middle Ages, Jews had been portrayed as the murderers of Christ and were often subjected to mob violence and official persecution. Their rights were restricted, and they were physically separated from Christians in residential quarters known as *ghettos.* By the nineteenth century, as a result of the ideals of the Enlightenment and the French Revolution, Jews were increasingly granted legal equality in many European countries. Nevertheless, Jews were not completely accepted, and this ambivalence was apparent throughout Europe, especially in France and in the Soviet Union.

During the nineteenth century, many Jews had left the ghetto and become assimilated into the surrounding Christian population. Some entered what had previously been the closed world of politics and the professions. Many Jews became successful as bankers, lawyers, scientists, scholars, journalists, and stage performers. In 1880, for example, Jews made up 10 percent of the population of Vienna but accounted for 39 percent of its medical students and 23 percent of its law students.

All too often, such achievements provoked envy and distrust. During the last two decades of the century, conservatives in Germany and Austria founded right-wing parties that used dislike of Jews to win the votes of traditional lower-middle-class groups who felt threatened by changing times. Such parties also played on the rising sentiment of racism in German society. Spurred by social Darwinist ideas that nations, like the human species, were engaged in a brutal struggle for survival, rabid German nationalists promoted the concept of the *Volk* ("nation," "people," or "race") as an underlying idea in German history since the medieval era. Portraying the German people as the successors of the "pure" Aryan race, the true and original creators of Western culture, nationalist groups called for Germany to take the lead in a desperate struggle to fight for European civilization and save it from the destructive assaults of such allegedly lower races as Jews, blacks, and Asians.

How Did Hitler Rise to Power and Consolidate Control?

At the end of World War I, Hitler joined the obscure German Workers' Party, one of a number of right-wing nationalist parties in Munich. By the summer of 1921, he had assumed total control over the party, which he renamed the *National Socialist German Workers' Party (NSDAP)*, or Nazi for short. Hitler worked constantly to develop the party into a mass political movement with flags, party badges, uniforms, its own newspaper, and its own police force or party militia known as the *SA*—the *Sturmabteilung*, or "storm troops." The SA added an element of force and terror to the growing Nazi movement. Hitler's own oratorical skills were largely responsible for attracting an increasing number of followers.

In November 1923, Hitler staged an armed uprising against the government in Munich, but the so-called Beer Hall Putsch was quickly crushed, and Hitler was sentenced to prison. During his brief stay in jail, he wrote **Mein Kampf** ("My Struggle"), an autobiographical account of his movement and its underlying ideology. Virulent German nationalism, anti-Semitism, and anticommunism were linked together by a social Darwinian theory of struggle that stressed the right of superior nations to *Lebensraum* ("living space") through expansion and the right of superior individuals to secure authoritarian leadership over the masses.

> **Mein Kampf** (German for "My Struggle") is an autobiographical account written by Adolf Hitler that includes an exploration of both Hitler's own political philosophy and national socialism.

After his release from prison in December 1924, Hitler worked assiduously to reorganize the Nazi Party on a regional basis and expand it to all parts of Germany; as a result, the party grew in size from 27 000 members in 1925 to 178 000 by the end of 1929. Especially noticeable was the youthfulness of the regional, district, and branch leaders of the Nazi organization. Many young Germans were fiercely committed to Hitler because he gave them the promise of a new life.

By 1932, the Nazi Party had 800 000 members and had become the largest party in the Reichstag. No doubt, Germany's economic difficulties were a crucial factor in the Nazi rise to power. Unemployment rose dramatically, from 4.4 million in 1931 to 6 million by the winter of 1932. The economic and psychological impact of the Great Depression made extremist parties more attractive. But Hitler claimed to stand above politics and promised to create a new Germany free of class differences and party infighting. His popular appeal to national pride, national honour, and traditional militarism struck chords of emotion in his listeners.

Increasingly, the right-wing elites of Germany—the industrial magnates, landed aristocrats, military establishment, and higher bureaucrats—came to see Hitler as the man who had the mass support to establish a right-wing, authoritarian regime that would save Germany from a Communist takeover. Under pressure, President Paul von Hindenburg agreed to allow Hitler to become chancellor on January 30, 1933, and form a new government.

Within two months, Hitler had laid the foundations for the Nazis' complete control over Germany. On February 27, he convinced Hindenburg to issue a decree suspending all basic rights for the full duration of the emergency, thus enabling the Nazis to arrest and imprison anyone without redress. The crowning step in Hitler's "legal" seizure of power came on March 23, when the Reichstag passed the Enabling Act by a two-thirds vote. This legislation, which empowered the government to dispense with constitutional forms for four years while it issued laws that dealt with the country's problems, provided the legal basis for Hitler's subsequent acts. In effect, Hitler became a dictator appointed by the parliamentary body itself.

With their new source of power, the Nazis acted quickly to consolidate their control. The civil service was purged of Jews and democratic elements, concentration camps were established for opponents of the new regime, trade unions were dissolved, and all political parties except the Nazis were abolished. When Hindenburg died on August 2, 1934, the office of Reich president was abolished, and Hitler became sole ruler of Germany. Public officials and soldiers were all required to take a personal oath of loyalty to Hitler as the "Führer [leader] of the German Reich and people."

Having destroyed the Weimar Republic, Hitler now turned to his larger objective: the creation of an Aryan racial state that would dominate Europe and possibly the world for generations to come. The Nazis pursued the vision of this totalitarian state in a variety of ways. Most dramatic were the mass demonstrations and spectacles employed to integrate the German nation into a collective fellowship and to mobilize it as an instrument for Hitler's policies. In the economic sphere, the Nazis pursued the use of public works projects and "pump-priming" grants to private construction firms to foster employment and end the depression. But there is little doubt that rearmament contributed far more to solving the unemployment problem. Unemployment, which had stood at 6 million in 1932, dropped to 2.6 million in 1934 and less than 500 000 in 1937. The regime claimed full credit for solving Germany's economic woes, although much of the success must be ascribed to decisions made at the initiative of local officials. Hitler himself had little interest in either economics or administration, and his prestige undoubtedly benefited enormously from spontaneous efforts undertaken throughout the country by his followers.

For its enemies, the Nazi totalitarian state had its instruments of terror and repression. Especially important was the SS (**Schutzstaffel**, or "protection echelon"). Originally created as Hitler's personal bodyguard, the SS, under the direction of Heinrich Himmler (1900–45), came to control all of the regular and secret police forces. Himmler and the SS functioned on the basis of two principles, ideology and terror, and would eventually play a major role in the execution squads and death camps for the extermination of the Jews.

> **Schutzstaffel** (German for "protection echelon"), also known as the SS, was an elite paramilitary group of the Nazi Party, whose members were chosen based on shared radical ideologies aligned with those of the Nazi Party.

Other institutions, including the Catholic and Protestant churches, primary and secondary schools, and universities, were also brought under the control of the state. Nazi professional organizations and leagues were formed for civil servants, teachers, women, farmers, doctors, and lawyers, and youth organizations—the *Hitler Jugend* ("Hitler Youth") and its female counterpart, the *Bund Deutscher Mädel* ("League of German Maidens")—were given special attention.

The Nazi attitude toward women was largely determined by ideological considerations. Women played a crucial role in the Aryan racial state as bearers of the children who would ensure the triumph of the Aryan race. To the Nazis, the differences between men and women were quite natural. Men were warriors and political leaders, while women were destined to be wives and mothers. Certain professions, including university teaching, medicine, and law, were considered inappropriate for women, especially married women. Instead, the Nazis encouraged women to pursue professional occupations that had direct practical application, such as social work and nursing. In addition to restrictive legislation against females, the Nazi regime pushed its campaign against working women with such poster slogans as "Get hold of pots and pans and broom and you'll sooner find a groom."

From the beginning, the Nazi Party reflected the strong anti-Semitic beliefs of Adolf Hitler. Many of the early attacks on Jews, however, were essentially spontaneous in character. The regime quickly took note, and in September 1935, the Nazis announced new racial laws at the annual party rally in Nuremberg. These Nuremberg laws excluded German Jews from German citizenship and forbade marriages and extramarital relations between Jews and German citizens. But a more violent phase of anti-Jewish activity was initiated on November 9–10, 1938, the infamous *Kristallnacht,* or "night of shattered glass." The assassination of a German diplomat in Paris became the excuse for a Nazi-led destructive rampage against the Jews, in which synagogues were burned,

7000 Jewish businesses were destroyed, and at least 100 Jews were killed. Moreover, 20 000 Jewish males were rounded up and sent to concentration camps. Jews were now barred from all public buildings and prohibited from owning, managing, or working in any retail store. Finally, under the direction of the SS, Jews were encouraged to "emigrate from Germany." After the outbreak of World War II, the policy of emigration was replaced by a more gruesome one.

Why Did Authoritarianism Spread in Eastern Europe and Later in Spain?

Nowhere had the map of Europe been more drastically altered by World War I than in Eastern Europe. The new states of Austria, Poland, Czechoslovakia, and Yugoslavia adopted parliamentary systems, and the preexisting kingdoms of Romania and Bulgaria gained new parliamentary constitutions in 1920. Greece became a republic in 1924. Hungary's government was parliamentary in form but controlled by its landed aristocrats. Thus at the beginning of the 1920s, political democracy seemed well established. Yet almost everywhere in Eastern Europe, parliamentary governments soon gave way to authoritarian regimes.

Several problems helped create this situation. Eastern European states had little tradition of liberalism or parliamentary politics and no substantial middle class to support them. Then, too, these states were largely rural and agrarian. Many of the peasants were largely illiterate, and much of the land was still dominated by large landowners who feared the growth of agrarian peasant parties with their schemes for land redistribution. Ethnic conflicts also threatened to tear these countries apart. Fearful of land reform, Communist agrarian upheaval, and ethnic conflict, powerful landowners, the churches, and even some members of the small middle class looked to authoritarian governments to maintain the old system. Only Czechoslovakia, with its substantial middle class, liberal tradition, and strong industrial base, maintained its political democracy.

In Spain, democracy also failed to survive. Fearful of the rising influence of left-wing elements in the government, Spanish military forces led by General Francisco Franco (1892–1975) launched a brutal and bloody three-year civil war. Foreign intervention complicated the situation. Franco's forces were aided by arms, money, and men from Italy and Germany, while the government was assisted by 40 000 foreign volunteers and trucks, planes, tanks, and military advisers from the Soviet Union. After Franco's forces captured Madrid on March 28, 1939, the Spanish Civil War finally came to an end. General Franco soon established a dictatorship that favoured large landowners, business owners, and the Catholic clergy.

Liberal democracies in the United States, Great Britain, and France were too embroiled in domestic issues to support the democratically elected Spanish Republic during the three-year civil war. The United States was practising a foreign policy of isolationism, after observing the consequences of World War I in Europe. By the 1930s, many Americans suffered under the effects of the Great Depression and still had little interest in the affairs of Europe. Although France tried to remain neutral, it allowed the sale of weapons to the Spanish Republic. France's Premier Leon Blum's willingness to support the Republic stemmed from the fear that Spain would become a fascist ally to Germany and Italy—France's other neighbours. Support for the Spanish Republic remained largely dependent on Blum's position in and out of office; however, for the most part, France remained relatively neutral and by 1936 no longer supplied the Republic with armament.

Did the Defeat of Trotsky Consolidate Stalin's Totalitarian Rule of the Soviet Union?

During the mid-1920s, Soviet society gradually recovered from the enormous damage caused by the Great War. As he consolidated his power at the expense of rivals within the party, Joseph Stalin took over from Vladimir Lenin and followed a centrist policy that avoided confrontation with his capitalist enemies abroad while encouraging capitalist forces at home under the careful guidance of the state. But Stalin—fearful that the rising influence of the small Russian bourgeoisie could undermine the foundations of party rule—had no intention of permitting the New Economic Policy (NEP) to continue indefinitely. In the late 1920s, he used the policy to bring the power struggle to a head.

Stalin had previously joined with the moderate Nikolay Bukharin and other members of the party to defend the NEP against **Leon Trotsky**, whose "left opposition" wanted a more rapid advance toward world revolution and socialism. Then, in 1928, Stalin reversed course: he now claimed that the NEP had achieved its purpose and called for a rapid advance to socialist forms of ownership. Beginning in 1929, a series of new programs changed the face of Soviet society. Private capitalism in manufacturing and trade was virtually abolished, and party and state control over the economy was extended. The first of a series of five-year plans was launched to promote rapid "socialist industrialization," and in a massive effort to strengthen the state's hold over the agricultural economy, all private farmers were herded onto collective farms.

> **Leon Trotsky** was an influential politician, Bolshevik revolutionary, and Marxist leader who was expelled from the Communist Party and Soviet Union following a power struggle with Joseph Stalin in the 1920s; he was later murdered while in Mexico by a Soviet agent.

The bitter campaign to collectivize the countryside aroused the antagonism of many peasants and led to a decline in food production and, in some areas, to mass starvation. Recent findings have shed light on the massive famine campaigns engineered by Stalin in places like the Ukraine (known as the "breadbasket of the Soviet Union") in an effort to consolidate Soviet power. Between 1932 and 1933, Stalin's calculated famines claimed the lives of 7 to 10 million Ukrainians. Stalin tried to break Ukraine's growing opposition to his collectivization policies by forcing them to turn over grain to the state. People were left starved by the time their quotas had been met, ordaining a famine that remains to be recognized as a great human tragedy of the twentieth century. The Soviets were able to disguise and downplay the severity of the tragedy, until recent archival evidence revealed the calamity involved. Collectivizing food production further divided the Communist Party and led to a massive purge of party members at all levels who opposed Stalin's effort to achieve rapid economic growth and the socialization of Russian society. A series of brutal purge trials eliminated thousands of "Old Bolsheviks" (people who had joined the party before the 1917 Revolution) and resulted in the conviction and death of many of Stalin's chief rivals. People throughout the Soviet Union were sent to prison, labour camps, or execution based on Stalin's purges that aimed at eliminating any and all opposition to his regime and its policies. Trotsky, who wanted to see the spread of a world socialist revolution and who opposed Stalin's increasing dictatorial-style of rule, was driven into exile and dispatched by Stalin's assassin in 1940. Of the delegates who had attended the National Congress of the Communist Party of the Soviet Union (CPSU) in 1934, fully 70 percent had been executed by the time of the National Congress in 1939.

By the late 1930s, as the last of the great purge trials came to an end, the Russian Revolution had been in existence for more than two decades. It had achieved some successes. Stalin's policy of forced industrialization had led to rapid growth in the industrial sector, surpassing in many respects what had been achieved in the capitalist years prior to World War I. Between 1918 and 1937, steel production increased from 4 to 18 million tons per year, and hard coal output went from 36 to 128 million tons. New industrial cities sprang up overnight in the Urals and Siberia. The Russian people in general were probably better clothed, better fed, and better educated than they had ever been

Pablo Picasso (1881–1973) © Picasso Estate/SODRAC (2006). Guernica. 1937. Museo Nacional Centro de Arte Reina Sofia, Madrid, Spain. © Erich Lessing/Art Resource, NY

Guernica. In 1937, Picasso painted *Guernica*, his diatribe against the violence of war, inspired by the bombing of a Basque town during the Spanish Civil War. It screams with pain and suffering and stands as one of the most expressive paintings in Western art. Guernica was to be the last great painting portraying the horrors of war, soon to be followed by war photography. How could painting compete any longer with those black-and-white frozen images of Auschwitz, with the quiet mountains of discarded eyeglasses, false teeth, and shoes?

before. The cost had been enormous, however. Millions had died by bullet or starvation. Thousands, perhaps millions, languished in Stalin's concentration camps. The remainder of the population lived in a society now officially described as socialist, under the watchful eye of a man who had risen almost to the rank of a deity, the great leader of the Soviet Union, Joseph Stalin.

The impact of Joseph Stalin on Soviet society in one decade had been enormous. If Lenin had brought the party to power and nursed it through the difficult years of the civil war, it was Stalin, above all, who had mapped out the path to economic modernization and socialist transformation. To many foreign critics of the regime, the Stalinist terror and autocracy were an inevitable consequence of the concept of the vanguard party and the centralized state built by Lenin. Others traced Stalinism back to Marx. It was he, after all, who had formulated the idea of the dictatorship of the proletariat, which now provided ideological justification for the Stalinist autocracy. Still others found the ultimate cause in the Russian political culture, which had been characterized by autocracy since the emergence of Russian society from Mongol control in the fifteenth century.

Was Stalinism an inevitable outcome of Marxist-Leninist doctrine and practice? Or as Mikhail Gorbachev later claimed, were Stalin's crimes "alien to the nature of socialism" and a departure from the course charted by Lenin before his death? Certainly, Lenin had not envisaged a party dominated by a figure who became even larger than the organization itself and who, in the 1930s, almost destroyed the party. On the other hand, recent evidence shows that

Lenin was capable of the brutal suppression of perceived enemies of the revolution in a way that is reminiscent in manner, if not in scope, of that of his successor, Stalin.

It is clear from the decade of the 1920s that there were other models for development in Soviet society than that adopted by Stalin; the NEP program, so ardently supported by Bukharin, is testimony to that fact. But it is also true that the state created by Lenin provided the conditions for a single-minded leader like Stalin to rise to absolute power. The great danger that neither Marx nor Lenin had foreseen had come to pass: the party itself, the vanguard organization leading the way into the utopian future, had become corrupted.

What Internal Conflicts Preceded the Rise of Militarism in Japan?

The rise of militant forces in Japan resulted not from a seizure of power by a new political party but from the growing influence of such elements at the top of the political hierarchy. During the 1920s, a multiparty system based on democratic practices appeared to be emerging. Two relatively moderate political parties, the Minseito and the Seiyukai, dominated the *diet,* or House of Representatives, and took turns providing executive leadership in the cabinet. Radical elements existed at each end of the political spectrum, but neither militant nationalists nor violent revolutionaries appeared to present a threat to the stability of the system.

In fact, the political system was probably weaker than it seemed at the time. Both of the major parties were deeply dependent on campaign contributions from powerful corporations (the *zaibatsu*), and conservative forces connected to the military or the old landed aristocracy were still highly influential behind the scenes. As in the Weimar Republic in Germany during the same period, the actual power base of moderate political forces was weak, and politicians unwittingly undermined the fragility of the system by engaging in bitter attacks on each other.

The road to war in Asia began in 1928 when Zhang Xueliang, son and successor of the Japanese puppet Marshall Zhang Zuolin (see Chapter 4, page 81), decided to integrate Manchuria into the Nanjing republic. Appeals from Tokyo to Washington for a U.S. effort to restrain Chiang Kai-shek were rebuffed.

Already suffering from the decline of its business interests on the mainland, after 1929 Japan began to feel the impact of the Great Depression when the United States and major European nations raised their tariff rates against Japanese imports in a desperate effort to protect local businesses and jobs. The value of Japanese exports dropped by 50 percent from 1929 to 1931, and wages dropped nearly as much. Hardest hit were the farmers as the price of rice and other staple food crops plummeted. At the same time, militant nationalists, outraged at Japan's loss of influence in Manchuria, began to argue that Shidehara diplomacy—peaceful cooperation with other nations to maintain the existing international economic order—had been a failure. It was undoubtedly that vision that had motivated the military coup d'état launched in Mukden in the early fall of 1931.

During the early 1930s, civilian cabinets managed to cope with the economic challenges presented by the Great Depression. By abandoning the gold standard, Prime Minister Inukai Tsuyoshi was able to lower the price of Japanese goods on the world market, and exports climbed back to earlier levels. But the political parties were no longer able to stem the growing influence of militant nationalist elements. Despite its doubts about the wisdom of the **Mukden Incident** in September 1931, the cabinet was too divided to disavow it, and military officers in Manchuria increasingly acted on their own initiative.

The **Mukden Incident**, or the Manchurian Incident, refers to an event in which a section of railroads owned by Japan's South Manchurian Railway was blown up; Japan blamed Chinese dissidents for the affair and used the event as a pretext for annexing Manchuria.

In May 1932, Inukai Tsuyoshi was assassinated by right-wing extremists. He was succeeded by a moderate, Admiral Saito Makoto, but ultranationalist patriotic societies began to terrorize opponents, assassinating businessmen and public figures identified with the policy of conciliation toward the outside world. Some, like the publicist Kita Ikki, were convinced that the parliamentary system had been corrupted by materialism and Western values and should be replaced by a system that would return to traditional Japanese values and imperial authority. His message "Asia for the Asians" had not won widespread support during the relatively prosperous 1920s but increased in popularity after the Great Depression, which convinced many Japanese that capitalism was unsuitable for Japan.

During the mid-1930s, the influence of the military and extreme nationalists over the government steadily increased. Minorities and left-wing elements were persecuted, and moderates were intimidated into silence. Terrorists tried for their part in assassination attempts portrayed themselves as selfless patriots and received light sentences. Japan continued to hold national elections, and moderate candidates continued to receive substantial popular support, but the cabinets were dominated by the military or advocates of Japanese expansionism. In February 1936, junior officers in the army led a coup in the capital city of Tokyo, briefly occupying the *diet* building and other key government installations and assassinating several members of the cabinet. The ringleaders were quickly tried and convicted of treason, but under conditions that strengthened even further the influence of the military in the halls of power.

THE PATH TO WAR IN EUROPE

Only 20 years after "the war to end all wars," the world plunged back into a new era of heightened international tension. The efforts at collective security in the 1920s—the **League of Nations**, the attempts at disarmament, the pacts and treaties—all proved ineffective in coping with the growth of Nazi Germany and the rise of a militarized Japan.

The **League of Nations** was an international organization established in 1919 at the Paris Peace Conference in order to prevent future wars through collective security arrangements. It became ineffective as early as 1931 with the failure to handle the Manchurian crisis. It was replaced by the United Nations in 1946.

Who Were to Be Hitler's Friends?

When Adolf Hitler became chancellor on January 30, 1933, Germany's situation in Europe seemed weak. The **Treaty of Versailles** had created a demilitarized zone on Germany's western border that would allow the French to move into the heavily industrialized parts of Germany in the event of war. To Germany's east, the smaller states, such as Poland and Czechoslovakia, had defensive treaties with France. The Versailles treaty had also limited Germany's army to 100 000 troops with no air force and only a small navy.

> The **Treaty of Versailles** was signed at the Paris Peace Conference in 1919; it officially ended World War I between the Central and Allied Powers.

Posing as a man of peace in his public speeches, Hitler emphasized that Germany wished only to revise the unfair provisions of Versailles by peaceful means and occupy Germany's rightful place among the European states. On March 9, 1935, he announced the creation of a new air force and, one week later, the introduction of a military draft that would expand Germany's army from 100 000 to 550 000 troops. France, Great Britain, and Italy condemned Germany's unilateral repudiation of the Treaty of Versailles but took no concrete action.

On March 7, 1936, buoyed by his conviction that the Western democracies had no intention of using force to maintain the Treaty of Versailles, Hitler sent German troops into the demilitarized Rhineland. According to the treaty, the French had the right to use force against any violation of the demilitarized Rhineland. But France would not act without British support, and the British viewed the occupation of German territory by German troops as reasonable action by a dissatisfied power. The London *Times* noted that the Germans were only "going into their own back garden."

Meanwhile, Hitler gained new allies. In October 1935, Benito Mussolini committed Fascist Italy to imperial expansion by invading Ethiopia. Angered by French and British opposition to his invasion, Mussolini welcomed Hitler's support and began to draw closer to the German dictator he had once called a buffoon. The joint intervention of Germany and Italy on behalf of General Francisco Franco in the Spanish Civil War in 1936 also drew the two nations closer together. In October 1936, Mussolini and Hitler concluded an agreement that recognized their common political and economic interests. One month later, Germany and Japan concluded the Anti-Comintern Pact (with Italy joining later) and agreed to maintain a common front against communism.

Why Did Stalin Support the Idea of Western Coalition Governments?

From behind the walls of the Kremlin in Moscow, Joseph Stalin undoubtedly observed the effects of the Great Depression with a measure of satisfaction. During the early

1920s, once it became clear that the capitalist states in Europe had managed to survive without socialist revolutions, Stalin decided to improve relations with the outside world as a means of obtaining capital and technological assistance in promoting economic growth in the Soviet Union. But Lenin had predicted that after a brief period of stability in Europe, a new crisis brought on by overproduction and intense competition was likely to occur in the capitalist world. That, he added, would mark the beginning of the next wave of revolution. In the meantime, he declared, "We will give the capitalists the shovels with which to bury themselves."

To Stalin, the onset of the Great Depression was a signal that the next era of turbulence in the capitalist world was at hand, and during the early 1930s, Soviet foreign policy returned to the themes of class struggle and social revolution. When the influence of the Nazi Party reached significant proportions in the early 1930s, Stalin viewed it as a pathological form of capitalism and ordered the Communist Party in Germany not to support the fragile Weimar Republic. Hitler would quickly fall, he reasoned, leading to a Communist takeover.

By 1935, Stalin became uneasily aware that Hitler was not only securely in power in Berlin but also represented a serious threat to the Soviet Union. That summer, at a major meeting of the Communist International held in Moscow, Soviet officials announced a shift in policy. The Soviet Union would now seek to form a united front with capitalist democratic nations throughout the world against the common danger of Nazism and fascism. Communist parties in capitalist countries and in colonial areas were instructed to cooperate with "peace-loving democratic forces" in forming coalition governments called **Popular Fronts**.

> **Popular Fronts** were political coalitions of Communists and moderate leftists; Stalin, in response to the growing threat of a fascist assault, advocated their formation to cooperate with mainstream forces that were anti-fascist.

In most capitalist countries, Stalin's move was greeted with suspicion, but in France, a coalition of leftist parties— Communists, Socialists, and Radicals—fearful that rightists intended to seize power, formed a Popular Front government in June 1936. The new government succeeded in launching a program for workers that some called the *French New Deal.* It included the right of collective bargaining, a 40-hour workweek, two-week paid vacations, and minimum wages. But such policies failed to solve the problems of the depression, and although it survived until 1938, the Popular Front was for all intents and purposes dead before then. Moscow signed a defensive treaty with France and reached an agreement with three non-Communist states in Eastern Europe (Czechoslovakia, Romania, and Yugoslavia), but talks with Great Britain achieved little result. The Soviet Union, rebuffed by London and disappointed by Paris, feared that it might be forced to face the might of Hitler's *Wehrmacht* alone.

How Did the Decision at Munich Give Hitler a Green Light?

By the end of 1936, the Treaty of Versailles had been virtually scrapped, and Germany had erased much of the stigma of defeat. Hitler, whose foreign policy successes had earned him much public acclaim, was convinced that neither the French nor the British would provide much opposition to his plans and decided in 1938 to move on Austria. By threatening Austria with invasion, Hitler coerced the Austrian chancellor into putting Austrian Nazis in charge of the government. The new government promptly invited German troops to enter Austria and assist in maintaining law and order. One day later, on March 13, 1938, Hitler formally annexed Austria to Germany.

The annexation of Austria, which had not raised objections in other European capitals, put Germany in position for Hitler's next objective—the destruction of Czechoslovakia. Although the latter was quite prepared to defend itself and was well supported by pacts with France and the Soviet Union, Hitler believed that its allies would not use force to defend it against a German attack.

He was right again. On September 15, 1938, Hitler demanded the cession to Germany of the Sudetenland (an area in western Czechoslovakia that was inhabited largely by ethnic Germans) and expressed his willingness to risk "world war" to achieve his objective. Instead of objecting, the British, French, Germans, and Italians—at a hastily arranged conference at Munich—reached an agreement that essentially met all of Hitler's demands. German troops were allowed to occupy the Sudetenland as the Czechs, abandoned by their Western allies, as well as by the Soviet Union, stood by helplessly. The **Munich Conference** was a signal of Western appeasement of Hitler. British Prime Minister Neville Chamberlain returned to England from Munich boasting that the agreement meant "peace in our time." Hitler had promised Chamberlain that he had made his last demand.

> The 1938 **Munich Conference** in Germany was arranged to discuss the fate of Czechoslovakia. The major European powers, following the principles of appeasement, surrendered part of Czechoslovakia to Nazi Germany.

At the Munich Conference, the leaders of France and Great Britain appeased Hitler's demands for Czechoslovakia. When Chamberlain defended his actions at Munich as necessary for peace, another British statesman, Sir Winston Churchill (1874–1965), characterized the settlement at Munich as "a disaster of the first magnitude." After World War II, political figures in Western Europe and the United States would cite the example of appeasement at Munich to encourage vigorous resistance to expansionism in the Soviet Union.

In fact, Munich confirmed Hitler's perception that the Western democracies were weak and would not fight. Increasingly, he was convinced of his own infallibility and had by no means been satisfied at Munich. In March 1939, Hitler occupied the Czech lands (Bohemia and Moravia), and the Slovaks, with his encouragement, declared their independence of the Czechs and set up the German puppet state of Slovakia. On the evening of March 15, 1939, Hitler triumphantly declared in Prague that he would be known as the greatest German of them all.

The Western states declared war, but it would take a year to mobilize forces and react to the Nazi threat. Hitler's naked aggression had made it clear that his promises were utterly worthless. When he began to demand the return to Germany of Danzig (which had been made a free city by the Treaty of Versailles to serve as a seaport for Poland), Great Britain recognized the danger and offered to protect Poland in the event of war. Both France and Great Britain realized that they needed Soviet help to contain Nazi aggression and began political and military negotiations with Stalin. Their distrust of Soviet communism, however, made an alliance unlikely.

Meanwhile, Hitler pressed on in the belief that Great Britain and France would not go to war over Poland. To preclude an alliance between the Western European states and the Soviet Union, which would create the danger of a two-front war, Hitler, ever the opportunist, approached Stalin, who had given up hope of any alliance with Great Britain and France. The announcement on August 23, 1939, of the Nazi-Soviet Nonaggression Pact shocked the world. The treaty with the Soviet Union gave Hitler the freedom he sought, and on September 1, German forces invaded Poland. Two days later, Great Britain and France declared war on Germany. Europe was again at war.

THE PATH TO WAR IN ASIA

In the years immediately following the Japanese seizure of Manchuria in the fall of 1931, Japanese military forces began to expand gradually into North China. Using the tactics of military intimidation and diplomatic bullying rather than all-out attack, Japanese military authorities began to carve out a new "sphere of influence" south of the Great Wall. Advocates of Japanese expansion in the 1930s justified their proposals by claiming both economic necessity and moral imperatives.

Not all politicians in Tokyo agreed with this aggressive policy—the young Emperor Hirohito, who had succeeded to the throne in 1926, was himself nervous about possible international repercussions—but right-wing terrorists assassinated some of its key critics and intimidated others into silence. The United States refused to recognize the Japanese takeover of Manchuria, which Secretary of State Henry L. Stimson declared an act of "international outlawry," but was unwilling to threaten the use of force. Instead, the Americans attempted to appease Japan in the hope of encouraging moderate forces in Japanese society. As one senior U.S. diplomat with long experience in Asia warned in a memorandum to the president:

> Utter defeat of Japan would be no blessing to the Far East or to the world. It would merely create a new set of stresses, and substitute for Japan the USSR—as the successor to Imperial Russia—as a contestant (and at least an equally unscrupulous and dangerous one) for the mastery of the East. Nobody except perhaps Russia would gain from our victory in such a war.[2]

For the moment, the prime victim of Japanese aggression was China. Chiang Kai-shek attempted to avoid a confrontation with Japan so that he could deal with what he considered the greater threat from the Communists. The Sino-Japanese War broke out when Chiang Kai-shek sought to appease the Japanese by granting them the authority to administer areas in North China. But as Japan moved steadily southward, popular protests in Chinese cities against Japanese aggression intensified. In December 1936, Chiang was briefly kidnapped by military forces commanded by General Zhang Xueliang, who compelled him to end his military efforts against the Communists in Yan'an and form a new united front against the Japanese. After Chinese and Japanese forces clashed at Marco Polo Bridge, south of Beijing, in July 1937, China refused to apologize, and hostilities spread.

Japan had not planned to declare war on China, but neither side would compromise, and the 1937 incident eventually turned into a major conflict. The Japanese advanced up the Yangtze valley and seized the Chinese capital of Nanjing, raping and killing thousands of innocent civilians in the process. But Chiang Kai-shek refused to capitulate and moved his government upriver to Hankou. When the Japanese seized that city, he moved on to Chongqing, in remote Sichuan Province. Japanese strategists had hoped to force Chiang to join a Japanese-dominated New Order in East Asia, comprising Japan, Manchuria, and China. Now

they established a puppet regime in Nanjing that would cooperate with Japan in driving Western influence out of East Asia. Tokyo hoped eventually to seize Soviet Siberia, rich in resources, and create a new "Monroe Doctrine for Asia" under which Japan would guide its Asian neighbours on the path to development and prosperity.

During the late 1930s, Japan began to cooperate with Nazi Germany on a plan to launch a joint attack on the Soviet Union and divide up its resources between them. But when Germany surprised Tokyo by signing the Nazi-Soviet Nonaggression Pact in August 1939, Japanese strategists were compelled to reevaluate their long-term objectives. Japan was not strong enough to defeat the Soviet Union alone, as a small but bitter border war along the Siberian frontier near Manchukuo had amply demonstrated. So the Japanese began to shift their gaze southward to the vast resources of Southeast Asia—the oil of the Dutch East Indies, the rubber and tin of Malaysia, and the rice of Burma and Indochina.

A move southward, of course, would risk war with the European colonial powers and the United States. Japan's attack on China in the summer of 1937 had already aroused strong criticism abroad, particularly from the United States, where President Franklin D. Roosevelt threatened to "quarantine" the aggressors after Japanese military units bombed an American naval ship operating in China. Public fear of involvement forced the president to draw back, but when Japan suddenly demanded the right to occupy airfields and exploit economic resources in French Indochina in the summer of 1940, the United States warned the Japanese that it would impose economic sanctions unless Japan withdrew from the area and returned to its borders of 1931.

Tokyo viewed the U.S. threat of retaliation as an obstacle to its long-term objectives. Japan badly needed liquid fuel and scrap iron from the United States. Should they be cut off, Japan would have to find them elsewhere. The Japanese were thus caught in a vise. To obtain guaranteed access to the natural resources that were necessary to fuel the Japanese military machine, Japan must risk being cut off from its current source of the raw materials that would be needed in case of a conflict. After much debate, the Japanese decided to launch a surprise attack on U.S. and European colonies in Southeast Asia in the hope of a quick victory that would evict the United States from the region.

THE COURSE OF WORLD WAR II

Using **blitzkrieg**, or "lightning war," Hitler stunned Europe with the speed and efficiency of the German attack. Panzer divisions (a panzer division was a strike force of about 300

Courtesy of William J. Duiker

Day of Humiliation. On June 23, 1940, France was forced to surrender after a brief six-week war with Nazi Germany. German Chancellor Adolf Hitler, shown in the middle of this photograph, attended the armistice ceremony, which took place in a railway car in the Compiègne Forest in northern France. Immediately to Hitler's left is Field Marshal Hermann Goering, chief of the German air force.

tanks and accompanying forces and supplies), supported by airplanes, broke quickly through Polish lines and encircled the bewildered Polish troops, whose courageous cavalry units were no match for the mechanized forces of their adversary. Conventional infantry units then moved in to hold the newly conquered territory. Within four weeks, Poland had surrendered. On September 28, 1939, Germany and the Soviet Union officially divided Poland between them.

> **Blitzkrieg** (German for "lightning war") describes a war conducted with great speed and force, as in Germany's advance at the beginning of World War II.

Although Hitler was apparently surprised when France and Great Britain declared war on September 3, he was confident of ultimate victory. After a winter of waiting (called the "phony war"), on April 9, 1940, Germany launched a *blitzkrieg* against Denmark and Norway. One month later, the Germans attacked the Netherlands, Belgium, and France. German panzer divisions broke through the weak French defensive positions in the Ardennes forest and raced across northern France, splitting the Allied armies and trapping French troops and the entire British army on the beaches of Dunkirk. Only by heroic efforts did the British succeed in a gigantic evacuation of

330 000 Allied (50 000 of which were French) troops. The French capitulated on June 22. German armies occupied about three-fifths of France while the French hero of World War I, Marshal Philippe Pétain, established a puppet regime (known as *Vichy France*) over the remainder. Germany was now in control of Western and Central Europe (see Map 5.1, Plate 12). Britain had still not been defeated, but it was reeling, and the wartime cabinet under Prime Minister Winston Churchill debated whether to seek a negotiated peace settlement.

As Hitler realized, an amphibious invasion of Great Britain could succeed only if Germany gained control of the air. In early August 1940, the *Luftwaffe* (German air force) launched a major offensive against British air and naval bases, harbours, communication centres, and war industries. The British fought back doggedly, supported by an effective radar system that gave them early warning of German attacks. Nevertheless, the British air force suffered critical losses and was probably saved by Hitler's change in strategy. In September, in retaliation for a British attack on Berlin, Hitler ordered a shift from military targets to massive bombing of cities to break British morale. The British rebuilt their air strength quickly and were soon inflicting major losses on *Luftwaffe* bombers. By the end of September, Germany had lost the Battle of Britain, and the invasion of the British Isles had to be abandoned.

At this point, Hitler pursued a new strategy, which would involve the use of Italian troops to capture Egypt and the Suez Canal, thus closing the Mediterranean to British ships and thereby shutting off Great Britain's supply of oil. This strategy failed when the British routed the Italian army. Although Hitler then sent German troops to the North African theatre of war, his primary concern lay elsewhere; he had already reached the decision to fulfill his long-time obsession with the acquisition of territory in the east. In *Mein Kampf*, Hitler had declared that future German expansion must lie in the east, in the vast plains of southern Russia.

Hitler was now convinced that Great Britain was remaining in the war only because it expected Soviet support. If the Soviet Union were smashed, Great Britain's last hope would be eliminated. Moreover, the German general staff was convinced that the Soviet Union, whose military leadership had been decimated by Stalin's purge trials, could be defeated quickly and decisively. The invasion of the Soviet Union was scheduled for spring 1941 but was delayed because of problems in the Balkans. Mussolini's disastrous invasion of Greece in October 1940 exposed Italian forces to attack from British air bases in that country. To secure their Balkan flank, German troops seized both Yugoslavia and Greece in April 1941. Hitler had already obtained the political cooperation of Hungary, Bulgaria, and Romania. Now reassured, Hitler ordered an invasion of the Soviet Union on June 22, 1941, in the belief that the Soviets could still be decisively defeated before winter set in. It was a fateful miscalculation.

The massive attack stretched out along a 2800-kilometre front. German troops, supported by powerful panzer units, advanced rapidly, capturing two million Russian soldiers. By November, one German army group had swept through Ukraine and a second was besieging Leningrad; a third approached within 40 kilometres of Moscow, the Russian capital. An early winter and unexpected Soviet resistance, however, brought a halt to the German advance. For the first time in the war, German armies had been stopped. A counterattack in December 1941 by Soviet army units newly supplied with U.S. weapons came as an ominous ending to the year for the Germans.

How Did Japan's Attack on Pearl Harbor Change the Dynamics of the War?

On December 7, 1941, Japanese carrier-based aircraft attacked the U.S. naval base at **Pearl Harbor** in the Hawaiian Islands. The same day, other units launched assaults on the Philippines and began advancing toward the British colony of Malaysia. Shortly thereafter, Japanese forces invaded the Dutch East Indies and occupied a number of islands in the Pacific Ocean. In some cases, as on the Bataan peninsula and the island of Corregidor in the Philippines, resistance was fierce, but by the spring of 1942, almost all of Southeast Asia and much of the western Pacific had fallen into Japanese hands. Japan formed the entire region into the Great East Asia Co-Prosperity Sphere and announced its intention to liberate Southeast Asia from Western rule. For the moment, however, Japan needed the resources of the region for its war machine and placed its conquests under its rule on a wartime footing.

> The surprise aerial attack on U.S. military base **Pearl Harbor** by Japan occurred on December 7, 1941; the Imperial Japanese Navy killed over 2000 Americans in the attack, prompting the United Stated to join in the World War II effort.

Japanese leaders had hoped that their strike at American bases would destroy the U.S. Pacific Fleet and persuade the Roosevelt administration to accept Japanese domination of the Pacific. The American people, in the eyes of Japanese leaders, had been made soft by material indulgence. But the Japanese had miscalculated. The attack on Pearl Harbor galvanized American opinion and won broad support for Roosevelt's war policy. The United States now joined with European nations and Nationalist China in a combined effort to defeat Japan's plan to achieve hegemony in the Pacific. Believing that U.S. involvement in the Pacific would render its forces ineffective in the European theatre, Hitler declared war on the United States four days after Pearl Harbor.

The entry of the United States into the war created a coalition, called the *Grand Alliance,* that ultimately defeated the **Axis Powers** (Germany, Italy, and Japan). Nevertheless, the three major **Allied Powers** that formed the Grand Alliance—Great Britain, the United States, and the Soviet Union—had to overcome mutual suspicions before they could operate as an effective alliance. In a bid to allay Stalin's suspicion of U.S. intentions, President Roosevelt declared that the defeat of Germany should be the first priority of the alliance. The United States, under its Lend-Lease program, also sent large amounts of military aid, including US$50 billion worth of trucks, planes, and other arms, to the Soviet Union. In 1943, the Allies agreed to fight until the Axis Powers surrendered unconditionally. This had the effect of making it nearly impossible for Hitler to divide his foes. On the other hand, it likely discouraged dissident Germans and Japanese from overthrowing their governments to arrange a negotiated peace.

The **Axis Powers** and the **Allied Powers** were coalitions of countries that were opposed to one another during World War II. The Axis Powers loosely comprised Germany, Italy, and Japan; and the Allied Powers comprised Great Britain, the United States, and the Soviet Union.

Victory, however, was only a vision for the distant future in the minds of Allied leaders at the beginning of 1942. As Japanese forces advanced into Southeast Asia and the Pacific after crippling the American naval fleet at Pearl Harbor, Axis forces continued the war in Europe against Great Britain and the Soviet Union. Reinforcements in North Africa enabled the Afrika Korps under General Erwin Rommel to break through the British defences in Egypt and advance toward Alexandria. In the spring of 1942, a renewed German offensive in the Soviet Union led to the capture of the entire Crimea, causing Hitler to boast that in two years, German divisions would be on the Indian border. By that fall, however, the war had begun to turn against the Germans. In North Africa, British forces stopped Rommel's troops at El-Alamein in the summer of 1942 and then forced them back across the desert. In November, U.S. forces landed in French North Africa and forced the German and Italian troops to surrender in May 1943. On the Eastern Front, the turning point of the war occurred at Stalingrad. After capturing the Crimea, Hitler's generals wanted him to concentrate on the Caucasus and its oil fields, but Hitler decided that Stalingrad, a major industrial centre on the Volga, should be taken first. After three months of bitter fighting, German troops were stopped, then encircled, and finally forced to surrender on February 2, 1943. The entire German Sixth Army of 300 000 men was lost, but Soviet casualties were estimated at nearly one million, more than the United States lost in the entire war. By spring, long before Allied troops returned to the European continent, even Hitler knew that the Germans would not defeat the Soviet Union.

The tide of battle in the Pacific also turned dramatically in 1942 (see Map 5.2, Plate 13). In the Battle of the Coral Sea in early May, U.S. naval forces stopped the Japanese advance and temporarily relieved Australia of the threat of invasion. On June 4, near Midway Island, American carrier planes destroyed all four of the attacking Japanese aircraft carriers and established U.S. naval superiority in the Pacific, even though almost all the American planes were shot down in the encounter. By the fall of 1942, Allied forces were beginning to gather for offensive operations into South China from Burma, through the Indonesian islands by a process of "island hopping" by troops commanded by U.S. General Douglas MacArthur, and across the Pacific with a combination of army, marine, and navy attacks on Japanese-held islands. After a series of bitter engagements in the waters off the Solomon Islands from August to November 1942, Japanese fortunes began to fade.

By the beginning of 1943, the tide of battle had begun to turn against the Axis. On July 10, the Allies crossed the Mediterranean and carried the war to Italy. After taking Sicily, Allied troops began the invasion of mainland Italy in September. Following the ouster and arrest of Benito Mussolini, a new Italian government offered to surrender to Allied forces. But the Germans, in a daring raid, liberated Mussolini and set him up as the head of a puppet German state in northern Italy while German troops occupied much of Italy. The new defensive lines established by the Germans in the hills south of Rome were so effective that the Allied advance up the Italian peninsula was slow and marked by heavy casualties. Rome finally fell on June 4, 1944. By that time, the Italian war had assumed a secondary role as the Allies opened their long-awaited second front in Western Europe.

Since the autumn of 1943, under considerable pressure from Stalin, the Allies had been planning a cross-channel invasion of France from Great Britain. Under the direction of U.S. General Dwight D. Eisenhower (1890–1969), five assault divisions landed on the Normandy beaches on June 6, 1944, in history's greatest naval invasion. An initially indecisive German response enabled the Allied forces to establish a beachhead. Within three months, they had landed two million men and a half-million vehicles that pushed inland and broke through the German defensive lines.

Canada's contribution to Normandy and D-Day remains one of the greatest efforts toward turning the tide of World War II. Of the nearly 107 000 men who stormed the beaches of Normandy on June 6, 1944, nearly 14 000 of them were Canadian. In this battle, 450 Canadian soldiers dropped behind enemy lines by parachutes and gliders. The Royal Canadian Navy contributed naval ships and approximately 10 000 sailors to the effort. Lancaster bombers and Spitfire fighters from the Royal Canadian Air Force were also part of the assault at Juno Beach on D-Day.

The role given to Canadian soldiers on D-Day was instrumental in taking one of five beaches, specifically Juno Beach, to allow for the liberation of France to begin. Canadian forces who landed on Juno Beach, part of an 80 kilometre stretch of difficult sandy shoreline, covered more ground on D-Day than any other Allied force.

In one of the greatest seaborne invasions ever, Canadians fought a fierce battle against incursions. The assault on Juno Beach proved successful in opening up a needed passage to occupied France; however, over 300 Canadian soldiers died in their struggle to defeat the

Germans. In severe hand-to-hand combat, Canadian troops from the 3rd Canadian Infantry Division fought their way across a heavy German defensive line with intense artillery fire and beach mines, crossing into the towns of Bernières, Courseulles, and St. Aubin and then pressed through, securing a significant bridgehead for Allied incursions.

After the breakout, Allied troops moved south and east, liberating Paris by the end of August. By March 1945, they had crossed the Rhine and advanced farther into Germany. In late April, they finally linked up with Soviet units at the Elbe River. The Soviets had come a long way since the Battle of Stalingrad in 1943. In the summer of 1943, Hitler gambled on taking the offensive by making use of newly developed "Tiger" tanks. At the Battle of Kursk (July 5–August 23), the greatest tank battle of World War II, the Soviets soundly defeated the German forces. Soviet forces now supplied with their own "T-34" heavy tanks, began a relentless advance westward. The Soviets reoccupied the Ukraine by the end of 1943, lifted the siege of Leningrad, and moved into the Baltic states by the beginning of 1944. Advancing along a northern front, Soviet troops occupied Warsaw in January 1945 and entered Berlin in April. Meanwhile, Soviet troops along a southern front swept through Hungary, Romania, and Bulgaria.

In January 1945, Hitler moved into a bunker 17 metres under Berlin to direct the final stages of the war. He committed suicide on April 30, two days after Mussolini was shot by partisan Italian forces. On May 7, German commanders surrendered. The war in Europe was over, yet the fighting continued.

The war in Asia continued, although with a significant change in approach. Allied war planners had initially hoped to focus their main effort on an advance through China with the aid of Chinese Nationalist forces trained and equipped by the United States. But Roosevelt became disappointed with Chiang Kai-shek's failure to take the offensive against Japanese forces in China and eventually approved a new strategy to strike toward the Japanese home islands directly across the Pacific. This island-hopping approach took an increasing toll on enemy resources, especially at sea and in the air.

As Allied forces drew inexorably closer to the main Japanese islands in the summer of 1945, President Harry S Truman (1884–1972), who had succeeded to the presidency on the death of Franklin Roosevelt in April, decided to use atomic weapons (only one of three bombs had been tested as part of the **Manhattan Project**, and their effectiveness was still undetermined) to capitulate the Japanese. Truman approved use of the most horrific kind— the nuclear bomb. The first bomb was dropped on the city of Hiroshima on August 6. Truman then called on Japan to

surrender or expect a "rain of ruin from the air." When the Japanese did not respond, a second bomb was dropped on Nagasaki. Japan surrendered unconditionally on August 14. As many as 100 000 people in Hiroshima and 40 000 people in Nagasaki were killed seconds after the only nuclear bombs to have been used in history. Many more Japanese died after high exposure to nuclear radiation, and for decades the residents of the two cities reported significant health problems.

> The **Manhattan Project** is the name given to a secretive U.S. scientific and military program that took place during World War II to develop the first nuclear bomb.

Truman's decision to approve the use of nuclear weapons to compel Japan to surrender has often been criticized, not only for causing thousands of civilian casualties but also for introducing a frightening new weapon that could threaten the future survival of the human race. Some analysts have even charged that Truman's real purpose in ordering the nuclear strikes was to intimidate the Soviet Union. Defenders of his decision argue that the human costs of invading the Japanese home islands would have been infinitely higher had the bombs not been dropped, and the Soviet Union would have had ample time to consolidate its control over Manchuria. More than half a century later, that debate has not yet come to an end.

World War II, in which 17 million combatants died in battle and perhaps 18 million civilians perished as well (some estimate total losses at 50 million), was finally over.

THE NEW ORDER

What did the Germans and Japanese do with the opportunity to create a new order in Europe and Asia? Although both countries presented positive images of the new order for publicity purposes, in practice both followed policies of ruthless domination of their subjected peoples. After the German victories in Europe, Nazi propagandists created glowing images of a new European order based on the equality of all nations in an integrated economic community. The reality was rather different. Hitler saw the Europe he had conquered simply as subject to German domination. Only the Germans, he once said, "can really organize Europe."

The Nazi empire, which at its greatest extent stretched across continental Europe from the English Channel in the west to the outskirts of Moscow in the east, was organized in two different ways. Some areas, such as western Poland, were annexed and transformed into German provinces. Parts of occupied Europe, such as Vichy France, Norway, and Denmark, however, were administered indirectly by German officials with the assistance of collaborationist regimes.

Racial considerations played an important role in how conquered peoples were treated. German civil administrations were established in Norway, Denmark, and the Netherlands because the Nazis considered their peoples to be Aryan, or racially akin to the Germans, and hence worthy of more lenient treatment. Latin peoples, such as the occupied French, were given military administrations. All the occupied territories were ruthlessly exploited for material goods and labour-power for Germany's production needs.

Because the conquered lands in the east contained the living space for German expansion and were populated in Nazi eyes by racially inferior Slavic peoples, Nazi administration there was considerably more ruthless. Heinrich Himmler, the leader of the SS, was put in charge of German resettlement plans in the region. His task was to replace the indigenous population with Germans, a policy first applied to the new German provinces created in western Poland. One million Poles were uprooted and dumped in southern Poland. Hundreds of thousands of ethnic Germans (descendants of Germans who had migrated years earlier from Germany to different parts of southern and Eastern Europe) were encouraged to colonize designated areas in Poland. By 1942, two million ethnic Germans had been settled in Poland.

The invasion of the Soviet Union inflated Nazi visions of German colonization in the east. Hitler spoke to his intimate circle of a colossal project of social engineering after the war, in which Poles, Ukrainians, and Russians would become slave labour while German peasants settled on the abandoned lands and Germanized them. Nazis involved in this kind of planning were well aware of the human costs. Himmler told a gathering of SS officers that the destruction of 30 million Slavs was a prerequisite for German plans in the east. "Whether nations live in prosperity or starve to death interests me only insofar as we need them as slaves for our culture. Otherwise it is of no interest."[3]

Labour shortages in Germany led to a policy of ruthless mobilization of foreign labour. After the invasion of the Soviet Union, the four million Russian prisoners of war captured by the Germans, along with more than two million workers conscripted in France, became a major source of heavy labour. In 1942, a special office was created to recruit labour for German farms and industries. By the summer of 1944, seven million foreign workers were labouring in Germany, constituting 20 percent of Germany's labour force. At the same time, another seven million workers were supplying forced labour in their own countries on farms, in industries, and even in military camps. The brutal character of Germany's recruitment policies often led more and more people to resist the Nazi occupation forces.

Who Did the Nazis Target for Mass Murder?

No aspect of the Nazi new order was more tragic than the deliberate attempt to exterminate the Jewish people of Europe. By the beginning of 1939, Nazi policy focused on promoting the "emigration" of German Jews from Germany. Once the war began in September 1939, the so-called Jewish problem took on new dimensions. For a while, there was discussion of the Madagascar Plan—a mass shipment of Jews to the African island of Madagascar. When war contingencies made this plan impracticable, an even more drastic policy was conceived.

The SS was given responsibility for what the Nazis called the **Final Solution** to the "Jewish problem"—the annihilation of the Jewish people. Reinhard Heydrich (1904–42), head of the SS's security service, was given administrative responsibility for the Final Solution. After the defeat of Poland, Heydrich ordered his special strike forces (*Einsatzgruppen*) to round up all Polish Jews and concentrate them in ghettos established in a number of Polish cities.

> The term **Final Solution** refers to the physical extermination of the Jewish people by the Nazis during World War II.

In June 1941, the *Einsatzgruppen* were given new responsibilities as mobile killing units. These death squads followed the regular army's advance into the Soviet Union. Their job was to round up Jews in the villages and execute and bury them in mass graves, often giant pits dug by the victims themselves before they were shot. Such constant killing produced morale problems among the SS executioners. During a visit to Minsk in the Soviet Union, Himmler tried to build morale by pointing out that

> They would not like it if Germans did such a thing gladly. But their conscience was in no way impaired, for they were soldiers who had to carry out every order unconditionally. He alone had responsibility before God and Hitler for everything that was happening, . . . and he was acting from a deep understanding of the necessity for this operation.[4]

Although it has been estimated that as many as one million Jews were killed by the *Einsatzgruppen*, this approach to solving the Jewish problem was soon perceived as inadequate. Instead, the Nazis opted for the systematic annihilation of the European Jewish population in specially built death camps. Jews from occupied countries would be rounded up, packed like cattle into freight trains, and shipped to Poland, where six extermination centres were built for this purpose. The largest and most famous was *Auschwitz-Birkenau*. Zyklon B (the commercial name for hydrogen cyanide) was selected as the most effective gas for quickly killing large numbers of people in gas chambers designed to look like shower rooms to facilitate the cooperation of the victims.

By the spring of 1942, the death camps were in operation. Although initial priority was given to the elimination of the ghettos in Poland, Jews were soon also being shipped from France, Belgium, and the Netherlands, and eventually from Greece and Hungary. Despite desperate military needs, the Final Solution had priority in using railroad cars to transport Jews to the death camps.

About 30 percent of the arrivals at Auschwitz were sent to a labour camp, and the remainder went to the gas chambers. After they had been gassed, the bodies were burned in crematoria. The victims' goods and even their bodies were used for economic gain. Women's hair was cut off, collected, and turned into mattresses or cloth. Some inmates were also subjected to cruel and painful "medical" experiments. The Germans killed between five and six million Jews, more than three million of them in the death camps. Virtually 90 percent of the Jewish populations of Poland, the Baltic countries, and Germany were exterminated. Overall, the **Holocaust** was responsible for the death of nearly two of every three European Jews.

> The **Holocaust** refers to the mass slaughter of European Jews by the Nazis during World War II.

The Nazis were also responsible for the death by shooting, starvation, or overwork of at least another nine to ten million people. Because the Nazis considered the Gypsies (like the Jews) an alien race, they were systematically rounded up for extermination. About 40 percent of Europe's one million Gypsies were killed in the death camps. The leading elements of the Slavic peoples—the clergy, intelligentsia, civil leaders, judges, and lawyers—were also arrested and executed. Probably an additional four million Poles, Ukrainians, and Belorussians lost their lives as slave labourers for Nazi Germany, and at least three to four million Soviet prisoners of war were killed in captivity. The Nazis also singled out homosexuals for persecution, and thousands lost their lives in concentration camps.

What Was Japan's Occupation Policy Like?

Once the Japanese takeover was completed, Japanese policy in the occupied areas of Asia became essentially defensive as Japan hoped to use its new possessions to meet its burgeoning needs for raw materials, such as tin, oil, and rubber, as well as an outlet for Japanese manufactured goods. To provide an organizational structure for the new Great East Asia Co-Prosperity Sphere, a Ministry for Great East Asia, staffed by civilians, was established in Tokyo in October 1942 to handle relations between Japan and the conquered territories.

The Japanese conquest of Southeast Asia had been accomplished under the slogan "Asia for the Asians," and many Japanese sincerely believed that their government was bringing about the liberation of the Southeast Asian peoples from European colonial rule. Japanese officials in the occupied territories made contact with nationalist elements and promised that independent governments would be established under Japanese tutelage. Such governments were eventually set up in Burma, the Dutch East Indies, Vietnam, and the Philippines.

In fact, however, real power rested with the Japanese military authorities in each territory, and the local Japanese military command was directly subordinated to the Army General Staff in Tokyo. The economic resources of the colonies were exploited for the benefit of the Japanese war machine, while indigenous people were recruited to serve in local military units or conscripted to work on public works projects. In some cases, the people living in the occupied areas were subjected to severe hardships. In Indochina, for example, forced requisitions of rice by the local Japanese authorities for shipment abroad created a food shortage that caused the starvation of more than a million Vietnamese in 1944 and 1945.

The Japanese planned to implant a new moral and social order as well as a new political and economic order in the occupied areas. Occupation policy stressed traditional values such as obedience, community spirit, filial piety, and discipline that reflected the prevailing political and cultural bias in Japan, while supposedly Western values such as materialism, liberalism, and individualism were strongly discouraged. To promote the creation of this new order, occupation authorities gave particular support to local religious organizations but discouraged the formation of formal political parties.

At first, many Southeast Asian nationalists took Japanese promises at face value and agreed to cooperate with their new masters. In Burma, an independent government was established in 1943 and subsequently declared war on the Allies.

But as the exploitative nature of Japanese occupation policies became increasingly clear, sentiment turned against the new order. Japanese officials sometimes unwittingly provoked resentment by their arrogance and contempt for local customs. In the Dutch East Indies, for example, Indonesians were required to bow in the direction of Tokyo and recognize the divinity of the Japanese emperor, practices that were repugnant to Muslims. In Burma, Buddhist pagodas were sometimes used as military latrines.

Like German soldiers in occupied Europe, Japanese military forces often had little respect for the lives of their subjected peoples. In their conquest of Nanjing, China, in 1937, Japanese soldiers had spent several days in killing, raping, and looting. Almost 800 000 Koreans were sent overseas, most of them as forced labourers, to Japan. Tens of thousands of Korean women were forced to be "comfort women" (prostitutes) for Japanese troops. In construction projects to help their war effort, the Japanese also made extensive use of labour forces composed of both prisoners of war and local peoples. In building the Burma-Thailand railway in 1943, for example, the Japanese used 61 000 Australian, British, and Dutch prisoners of war and almost 300 000 workers from Burma, Malaysia, Thailand, and the Dutch East Indies. An inadequate diet and appalling work conditions in an unhealthy climate led to the death of 12 000 Allied prisoners of war and 90 000 native workers by the time the railway was completed.

Such Japanese behaviour created a dilemma for many nationalists, who had no desire to see the return of the colonial powers. Some turned against the Japanese, and others lapsed into inactivity. Indonesian patriots tried to have it both ways, feigning support for Japan while attempting to sabotage the Japanese administration. In Indochina, Ho Chi Minh's Indochinese Communist Party established contacts with American military units in South China and agreed to provide information on Japanese troop movements and rescue downed American fliers in the area. In Malaysia, where Japanese treatment of ethnic Chinese residents was especially harsh, many joined a guerrilla movement against the occupying forces. By the end of the war, little support remained in the region for the erstwhile "liberators."

THE HOME FRONT: THREE EXAMPLES

World War II was even more of a global war than World War I. Fighting was much more widespread, economic mobilization was more extensive, and so was the mobilization of women. And the number of civilians killed was far higher: bombing raids, mass extermination policies, and attacks by invading armies killed almost 20 million.

During World War II, like many women in the home front, Canadian women played a significant role in Canada's war effort. It was considered the patriotic duty of many middle-class Canadian women to work while men were fighting overseas. Women often took on less than feminine jobs in plants, lumberyards, shipyards, and factories, and by midway through the war, nearly 200 000 women were involved in war work directly (although not in combat, many were nurses in European battlefields), and over a million women took part in the Canadian labour force. Shortly after the war ended, many Canadian women were expected to return to the domestic sphere as homemakers and mothers, to make room for men to take back their jobs. Their activity in the public sphere, however, did spawn many feminist questions about the position of women at home and how this remained unpaid work.

As the war raged on, women were not only expected to partake in the labour force, but were also expected to aid in the war effort through conservation at home. Items in short supply, like food and gasoline, were rationed to limited amounts for each family, and as imported items like sugar and tea were difficult to obtain, homemakers had to make due with less. Canadian homemakers were also expected to can and preserve food, although metal was also in limited supply, as it was directed to manufacturing wartime products.

During the war, the most troubling event that took place on Canada's home front was the internment of Japanese Canadians. Canada's response to Japan's attack on a U.S. navy base at Pearl Harbor incited one of the most hideous racist policies against Japanese Canadians primarily. By 1942, over 22 000 Japanese men, women, and children, 75 percent of whom were Canadian born, were removed from their homes and sent to internment camps. They were stripped of their belongings, homes, and businesses, which the Canadian government sold for profit of up to 200 percent. This policy affected the coastal communities of British Columbia, where the largest portion of Japanese Canadians had settled. The Canadian government claimed that it was prompted to remove residents of Japanese origin from within 160 kilometres of the West Coast for "national security" reasons.

The Japanese-Canadian community remained in these camps for several years. Following the surrender of Japan at the end of World War II, "loyalty commissions" were established to determine the so-called loyalty of Japanese Canadians. Those who refused to partake in the commissions were deemed a threat and deported to Japan, even though many of those deported did not even speak Japanese. Restrictions on the rights of Japanese Canadians lasted for several years after the end of the war. A formal Canadian Government apology to the Japanese community took nearly five decades.

Harry Rowed/National Film Board of Canada. Photothèque/Library and Archives Canada/PA-175991

Canadian Women on the Home Front. These Canadian Women worked in the Dominion Arsenals munitions factory during World War II. This photo reflects this company's policy of allowing women to invite boyfriends over for dinner during their shifts.

In Japan, society had been put on a wartime footing even before the attack on Pearl Harbor. A conscription law was passed in 1938, and economic resources were placed under strict government control. Two years later, all political parties were merged into the so-called Imperial Rule Assistance Association. Labour unions were dissolved, and education and culture were purged of all "corrupt" Western ideas in favour of traditional values emphasizing the divinity of the emperor and the higher spirituality of Japanese civilization. During the war, individual rights were severely curtailed as the entire population was harnessed to the needs of the war effort.

Japan was reluctant, however, to mobilize women on behalf of the war effort. General Hideki Tojo, prime minister from 1941 to 1944, opposed female employment, arguing that "the weakening of the family system would be the weakening of the nation. . . . We are able to do our duties only because we have wives and mothers at home."[5] Female employment increased during the war, but only in areas, such as the textile industry and farming, where women traditionally worked. Instead of using women to meet labour shortages, the Japanese government brought in Korean and Chinese labourers.

The home fronts of the major belligerents varied with the local circumstances. World War II had an enormous impact on the Soviet Union. Two of every five persons killed in World War II were Soviet citizens. Leningrad experienced 900 days of siege, during which its inhabitants became so desperate for food that they ate dogs, cats, mice, and even other humans. As the German army made its rapid advance into Soviet territory, the factories in the western part of the Soviet Union were dismantled and shipped to the interior—to the Urals, western Siberia, and the Volga region.

Soviet women played a major role in the war effort. Women and girls worked in industries, mines, and railroads. Overall, the number of women working in industry increased by almost 60 percent. Soviet women were also expected to dig anti-tank ditches and work as air-raid wardens. Finally, the Soviet Union was the only country to use women as combatants in World War II. Soviet women functioned as snipers and also as air crews in bomber squadrons. The female pilots who helped defeat the Germans at Stalingrad were known as the "Night Witches."

AFTERMATH OF THE WAR

In November 1943, Stalin, Roosevelt, and Churchill, the leaders of the Grand Alliance, met at Tehran, Iran, to decide the future course of the war. Their major strategic decision involved approval for an American-British invasion of the Continent through France, which they scheduled for the spring of 1944. The acceptance of this plan had important consequences. It meant that Soviet and British-American forces would meet in defeated Germany along a north-south dividing line and that Eastern Europe would most likely be liberated by Soviet forces. The Allies also agreed to a partition of post-war Germany until de-Nazification could take place. Roosevelt privately assured Stalin that Soviet borders in Europe would be moved westward to compensate for the loss of territories belonging to the old Russian Empire after World War I. Poland would receive lands in eastern Germany to make up for territory lost in the east to the Soviet Union.

In February 1945, the three Allied leaders met once more at Yalta, on the Crimean peninsula of the Soviet Union. Since the defeat of Germany was a foregone conclusion, much of the attention of the Yalta Conference focused on the war in the Pacific. Roosevelt sought Soviet military help against Japan. Development of the atomic bomb was not yet assured, and U.S. military planners feared the possibility of heavy casualties in amphibious assaults on the Japanese home islands. Roosevelt therefore agreed to Stalin's price for military assistance against Japan: possession of Sakhalin and the Kurile Islands, as well as two warm-water ports and railroad rights in Manchuria.

The creation of the **United Nations** was a major concern at Yalta. Roosevelt hoped to ensure the participation of the Big Three Powers—the United States, Great Britain, and the Soviet Union—in a post-war international organization before difficult issues divided them into hostile camps. After a number of compromises, both Churchill and Stalin accepted Roosevelt's plans for the United Nations

The Victorious Allied Leaders at Yalta. Even before World War II ended, the leaders of the Big Three of the Grand Alliance—Churchill, Roosevelt, and Stalin (shown seated from left to right)—met in wartime conferences to plan the final assault on Germany and negotiate the outlines of the post-war settlement. At the Yalta Conference (February 4–11, 1945), the three leaders concentrated on post-war issues. The American president, visibly weary at Yalta, died two months later.

© *The Art Archive/Imperial War Museum*

organization and set the first meeting for San Francisco in April 1945.

> In 1945, following the aftermath of World War II, the **United Nations** was established as an international organization with a mandate to promote worldwide peace; its members comprise nations from around the world.

The issues of Germany and Eastern Europe were treated less decisively. The Big Three reaffirmed that Germany must surrender unconditionally and created four occupation zones. German reparations were set at US$20 billion. A compromise was also worked out with regard to Poland. Stalin agreed to free elections in the future to determine a new government. But the issue of free elections in Eastern Europe would ultimately cause a serious rift between the Soviets and the Americans. The Allied leaders agreed on an ambiguous statement that Eastern European governments would be freely elected but were also supposed to be friendly to the Soviet Union. This attempt to reconcile the irreconcilable was doomed to failure.

Even before the next conference at Potsdam, Germany, took place in July 1945, Western relations with the Soviets had begun to deteriorate rapidly. The Grand Alliance had been one of necessity in which ideological incompatibility had been subordinated to the pragmatic concerns of the war. The Allied Powers' only common aim was the defeat of Nazism. Once this aim had been all but accomplished, the many differences that antagonized East-West relations came to the surface.

The **Potsdam Conference** of July 1945, the last Allied conference of World War II, consequently began under a cloud of mistrust. Roosevelt had died on April 12 and had been succeeded as president by Harry Truman. During the conference, Truman received word that the atomic bomb had been successfully tested. Some historians have argued that this knowledge stiffened Truman's resolve against the Soviets. Whatever the reasons, there was a new coldness in the relations between the Soviets and the Americans. At Potsdam, Truman demanded free elections throughout Eastern Europe. Stalin responded: "A freely elected government in any of these East European countries would be anti-Soviet, and that we cannot allow."[6] After a bitterly fought and devastating war, Stalin sought absolute military security, which in his view could be ensured only by the presence of Communist states in Eastern Europe. Free elections might result in governments hostile to the Soviet Union. By the middle of 1945, only an invasion by Western forces could undo developments in Eastern Europe, and in the immediate aftermath of the world's most destructive conflict, few people favoured such a policy. But the stage was set for a new confrontation, this time between the two major victors of World War II.

> The **Potsdam Conference**, held in Potsdam, Germany, was a gathering of triumphant World War II Allies whose goal was to decide how to govern surrendered Germany.

CONCLUSION

World War II was the most devastating total war in human history. Perhaps as many as 50 million people—soldiers and civilians—had been killed in only six years. In Asia and Europe, cities had been reduced to rubble, and millions of people faced starvation as once-fertile lands stood neglected or wasted. Untold millions of people had become refugees. What precipitated World War II?

- The rising fascist regime in Germany and a militarist state in Japan were bent on territorial expansionism.
- Germany and Japan were willfully determined to reverse the verdict of the Treaty of Versailles and divide the world between them.
- Neither Germany nor Japan possessed a strong tradition of political pluralism.

Whatever the causes of World War II and its controversial conclusion, the consequences were soon to be evident. The United States and the Soviet Union had arrived at different visions of the post-war world. No sooner had the war ended than their differences gave rise to a new and potentially even more devastating conflict: the Cold War.

CRITICAL THINKING QUESTIONS

1. Recently in Canada, several bookstores wanted to ban the sale of Hitler's book *Mein Kampf.* Should Hitler's book be deemed hate-literature and be banned or be deemed freedom of speech and be allowed to be distributed?

2. U.S. President Truman argued that the use of nuclear weapons on Japan were necessary to bring the war to an end and stop further deaths. Can the use of nuclear weapons ever be justified?

3. What can the horrors of the Holocaust teach us about war, politics, hate, and the dark side of human nature?

4. Many historians mark the start of World War II in 1939, in Europe, as opposed to in 1931, in Asia. Why is there an overwhelming Eurocentric view of a so-called

World War? Can the occupation of foreign lands ever be deemed liberation?

CHAPTER NOTES

1. Benito Mussolini, "The Doctrine of Fascism," in *Italian Fascisms from Pareto to Gentile,* ed. Adrian Lyttleton (London: Cape, 1973), p. 42.

2. John Van Antwerp MacMurray, quoted in Arthur Waldron, *How the Peace Was Lost: The 1935 Memorandum* (Stanford, Calif.: Hoover Archival Documentaries, 1992), p. 5.

3. International Military Tribunal, *Trial of the Major War Criminals* (Nuremberg: International Military Tribunal, 1947–49), vol. 22, p. 480.

4. Quoted in Raul Hilberg, *The Destruction of the European Jews,* rev. ed. (New York: Holmes & Meier, 1985), vol. 1, pp. 332–33.

5. Quoted in John Campbell, *The Experience of World War II* (New York: Oxford University Press, 1989), p. 143.

6. Quoted in Norman Graebner, *Cold War Diplomacy, 1945–1960* (Princeton, N.J.: Van Nostrand, 1962), p. 117.

Across the Ideological Divide

Chapter 6

In the Grip of the Cold War: The Breakdown of the Yalta Agreement

The Yalta Conference in February 1945, attended by U.S. President Franklin D. Roosevelt, Soviet Generalissimo Joseph Stalin, and British Prime Minister Winston Churchill, affirmed a common hope that the Grand Alliance, which had brought their countries to victory in World War II, could be sustained in the post-war era. The decisions reached at Yalta were meant to provide the basis for stable peace in the post-war era. Allied occupation forces—American, British, French in the west, and Soviet in the east—were to bring about the end of the Axis Powers' administration and pave the way for free elections to form democratic governments throughout Western Europe.

It had been hoped that the Allied victory would have put an end to ideological and political conflict among leading powers. However, within months after the German surrender, the attitude of mutual trust among the victorious Allies—if it had ever existed—rapidly disintegrated, and the dream of a stable peace was replaced by the spectre of nuclear annihilation. As the Cold War conflict between Moscow and Washington intensified, Europe was divided into two armed camps, and the two superpowers, glaring at each other across a deep ideological divide, held the survival of the entire world in their hands.

At the conclusion of this chapter, you will be able to

- describe how the distinct self-interests of the superpowers led to the collapse of the Grand Alliance and the rise of the Cold War;
- explain how and why the superpowers used Third World countries to indirectly fight their battles;
- understand why China and the Soviet Union, although both Communist states, often clashed and deceived each other for strategic gain.

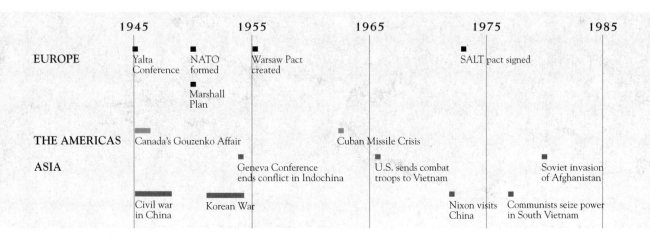

THE COLLAPSE OF THE GRAND ALLIANCE

The problem started in Europe. At the end of the war, Soviet military forces occupied all of Eastern Europe and the Balkans (except for Greece, Albania, and Yugoslavia), while U.S. and other Allied forces completed their occupation of the western part of the continent. It soon became clear that Moscow and Washington differed in their interpretations of the Yalta peace agreement. When Soviet occupation authorities turned their attention to forming a new Polish government in Warsaw, Stalin refused to accept the legitimacy of the Polish government in exile—headquartered in London during the war, it was composed primarily of representatives of the landed aristocracy who harboured a deep distrust of the Soviets—and instead installed a government composed of Communists who had spent the war in Moscow. Roosevelt eventually agreed to a compromise solution whereby two members of the exile government in London were included in a new regime dominated by the Communists. A week later, Roosevelt was dead of a cerebral haemorrhage.

Similar developments took place elsewhere in Eastern Europe as all of the states occupied by Soviet troops became part of Moscow's sphere of influence. Coalitions of all political parties (except Fascist or right-wing parties) were formed to run the government, but within a year or two, the Communist parties in these coalitions had assumed the lion's share of power. The next step was the creation of one-party Communist governments. The timetables for these takeovers varied from country to country, but between 1945 and 1947, Communist governments became firmly entrenched in East Germany, Bulgaria, Romania, Poland, and Hungary. In Czechoslovakia, with its strong tradition of democratic institutions, the Communists did not achieve their goals until 1948. In the elections of 1946, the Communist Party became the largest party but was forced to share control of the government with non-Communist rivals. When it appeared that the latter might win new elections early in 1948, the Communists seized control of the government on February 25. All other parties were dissolved, and Communist leader Klement Gottwald became the new president of Czechoslovakia.

Yugoslavia was a notable exception to the pattern of growing Soviet dominance in Eastern Europe. The Communist Party there had led resistance to the Nazis during the war and easily took over power when the war ended. Josip Broz, known as *Tito* (1892–1980), the leader of the Communist resistance movement, appeared to be a loyal Stalinist. After the war, however, he moved toward the establishment of an independent Communist state in Yugoslavia. Stalin hoped to take control of Yugoslavia, just as he had done in other Eastern European countries. But Tito refused to capitulate to Stalin's demands and gained the support of the people (and some sympathy in the West) by portraying the struggle as one of Yugoslav national freedom. In 1958, the Yugoslav party congress asserted that Yugoslav Communists did not see themselves as deviating from communism, only from Stalinism. They considered their more decentralized economic and political system, in which workers could manage themselves and local communes could exercise some political power, closer to the Marxist-Leninist ideal.

To Stalin (who had once boasted, "I will shake my little finger, and there will be no more Tito"), the creation of pro-Soviet regimes throughout Eastern Europe may simply have represented his interpretation of the Yalta peace agreement and a reward for sacrifices suffered during the war while satisfying Moscow's aspirations for a buffer zone against the capitalist West. Recent evidence suggests that Stalin did not decide to tighten Communist control over the new Eastern European governments until U.S. actions—notably the promulgation of the Marshall Plan (see below)—threatened to undermine Soviet authority in the region. If the Soviet leader had any intention of promoting future Communist revolutions in Western Europe—and there is some indication that he did—in his mind such developments would have to await the appearance of a new capitalist crisis a decade or more into the future. As Stalin undoubtedly recalled, Lenin had always maintained that revolutions come in waves.

How Did the Truman Doctrine Attempt to Limit the Spread of Communism?

In the United States, the Soviet takeover of Eastern Europe represented an ominous development. Public suspicion of Soviet intentions grew rapidly; Winston Churchill was quick to put such fears into words. In a highly publicized speech given to an American audience in March 1946, the former British prime minister declared that an "Iron Curtain" had "descended across the continent," dividing Germany and Europe itself into two hostile camps. Stalin responded by branding Churchill's speech a "call to war with the Soviet Union."

A civil war in Greece created another potential arena for confrontation between the superpowers. Communist guerrilla forces supported by Tito's Yugoslavia had taken up arms against the pro-Western government in Greece. Great Britain had initially assumed primary responsibility for promoting post-war reconstruction in the eastern

Mediterranean, but in 1947, continued post-war economic problems caused the British to withdraw from the active role they had been playing in both Greece and Turkey. U.S. President Harry S Truman, alarmed by British weakness and the possibility of Soviet expansion into the eastern Mediterranean, responded with the **Truman Doctrine**, promising money to countries that claimed they were threatened by Communist expansion. Truman presented the emerging dispute with Moscow to the U.S. Congress and the American people in a melodramatic manner on the advice of subordinates, who argued that only by so doing would the American people turn their full attention to the problem. Future presidents would frequently rely on this tactic to promote their foreign policy initiatives. If the Soviets were not stopped in Greece, the Truman argument ran, then the United States would have to face the spread of communism throughout the Western world.

> The **Truman Doctrine**, a pronouncement by President Harry S Truman in 1947, proposed that the United States provide economic aid to countries under the threat of Communist expansion.

The U.S. suspicion that Moscow was actively supporting the insurgent movement in Greece was inaccurate. Stalin was apparently unhappy with Tito's promoting of the conflict, not only because it suggested that the latter was attempting to create his own sphere of influence in the Balkans but also because it risked provoking a direct confrontation between the Soviet Union and the United States. The proclamation of the Truman Doctrine was soon followed in June 1947 by the European Recovery Program, better known as the **Marshall Plan**. Intended to rebuild prosperity and stability, this program included US$13 billion for the economic recovery of war-torn Europe. Underlying the program was the belief that the appeal of communism was spurred by poverty and inequality.

> The **Marshall Plan**, formally known as the *European Recovery Program,* was a U.S.-sponsored plan that provided financial aid to European countries to help them rebuild after World War II.

From the Soviet perspective, the Marshall Plan was nothing less than capitalist imperialism, a thinly veiled attempt to buy the support of the smaller European countries, which in return would be expected to submit to economic exploitation by the United States. The Soviets, however, were in no position to compete financially with the United States and could do little to counter the Marshall Plan except to tighten their control in Eastern Europe.

How Was Europe Divided Both Ideologically and Territorially?

By 1947, the split in Europe between East and West had become a fact of life. At the end of World War II, the United States had favoured a quick end to its commitments in Europe. But U.S. fears of Soviet aims caused the United States to play an increasingly involved role in European affairs. In an article in *Foreign Affairs* in July 1947, George Kennan, a well-known U.S. diplomat with much knowledge of Soviet affairs, advocated a policy of containment against further aggressive Soviet moves. Kennan favoured the "adroit and vigilant application of counter-force at a series of constantly shifting geographical and political points, corresponding to the shifts and manoeuvres of Soviet policy."[1] After the Soviet blockade of Berlin in 1948, containment of the Soviet Union became formal U.S. policy.

The fate of Germany had become a source of heated contention between East and West. Besides de-Nazification and the partitioning of Germany (and Berlin) into four occupied zones, the Allied Powers had agreed on little with regard to the conquered nation. Even de-Nazification proceeded differently in the various zones of occupation. The British had tried two million cases by 1948, while the Soviets went after major criminals and allowed lesser officials to go free. The Soviet Union, hardest hit by the war, took reparations from Germany in the form of booty. The technology-starved Soviets dismantled and removed to Russia 380 factories from the western zones of Berlin before transferring their control to the Western powers. By the summer of 1946, 200 chemical, paper, and textile factories in the East German zone had likewise been shipped to the Soviet Union. At the same time, the German Communist Party was reestablished under the control of Walter Ulbricht (1893–1973) and was soon in charge of the political reconstruction of the Soviet zone in eastern Germany.

Although the foreign ministers of the four occupying powers (the United States, the Soviet Union, Great Britain, and France) kept meeting in an attempt to arrive at a final peace treaty with Germany, they grew further and further apart. At the same time, the British, French, and Americans gradually began to merge their zones economically and by February 1948 were making plans for unification of these sectors and the formation of a national government. The Soviet Union responded with a blockade of West Berlin that prevented all traffic from entering the city's three western zones through Soviet-controlled territory in East Germany. The Soviets hoped to force the Western powers to stop the creation of a separate West German state.

The Western powers faced a dilemma. Direct military confrontation seemed dangerous, and no one wished to risk

World War III. Therefore, an attempt to break through the blockade with tanks and trucks was ruled out. The solution was the Berlin airlift: supplies for the city's inhabitants were brought in by plane. At its peak, the airlift flew 13 000 tons of supplies daily into Berlin. The Soviets, also not wanting war, did not interfere and finally lifted the blockade in May 1949. The blockade of Berlin had severely increased tensions between the United States and the Soviet Union and confirmed the separation of Germany into two states. The Federal Republic of Germany (FRG) was formally created from the three western zones in September 1949, and a month later, the separate German Democratic Republic (GDR) was established in East Germany. Berlin remained a divided city and the source of much contention between East and West.

The search for security in the new world of the Cold War also led to the formation of military alliances. The **North Atlantic Treaty Organization** (NATO) was formed in April 1949 when Belgium, Luxembourg, the Netherlands, France, Great Britain, Italy, Denmark, Norway, Portugal, and Iceland signed a treaty with the United States and Canada (see Map 6.1, Plate 14). All the powers agreed to provide mutual assistance if any one of them was attacked.

> The **North Atlantic Treaty Organization** (NATO) is a military alliance of Western states formed in 1949 in which the signatories agreed to provide mutual assistance to each other, considering an attack on one as an attack on all.

Hulton Archive/Getty Images

A City Divided. In 1948, U.S. planes airlifted supplies into Berlin to break the blockade that Soviet troops had imposed to isolate the city. Shown here is "Checkpoint Charlie," located at the boundary between the U.S. and Soviet zones of Berlin, just as Soviet roadblocks are about to be removed. The banner at the entry to the Soviet sector reads: "The sector of freedom greets the fighters for freedom and right of the Western sector."

A few years later, Greece, Turkey, and West Germany joined NATO.

The Eastern European states soon followed suit. In 1949, they formed the Council for Mutual Economic Assistance (COMECON) for economic cooperation. Then, in 1955, Albania, Bulgaria, Czechoslovakia, East Germany, Hungary, Poland, Romania, and the Soviet Union organized a formal military alliance, the **Warsaw Pact**. Once again, Europe was tragically divided into hostile alliance systems.

> The **Warsaw Pact**, a military alliance, was formed in 1955 and comprised European Communist states that agreed to provide mutual defence; it dissolved in 1991, and some former members even joined NATO.

By the end of the 1950s, then, the dream of a stable peace in Europe had been obliterated. There has been considerable historical debate over who bears the most responsibility for starting what would henceforth be called the *Cold War*. In the 1950s, most scholars in the West assumed that the bulk of the blame must fall on the shoulders of Joseph Stalin, whose determination to impose Soviet rule on the countries of Eastern Europe snuffed out hopes for freedom and self-determination there and aroused justifiable fears of Communist expansion in the Western democracies. During the next decade, however, a new school of revisionist historians—influenced in part by aggressive U.S. policies to prevent a Communist victory in Southeast Asia—began to argue that the fault lay primarily in Washington, where President Truman and his anti-Communist advisers abandoned the precepts of Yalta and sought to encircle the Soviet Union with a tier of puppet U.S. client states.

Both the United States and the Soviet Union took steps at the end of World War II that were unwise or might have been avoided. Both nations, however, were working within a framework conditioned by the past. Ultimately, the rivalry between the two superpowers stemmed from their different historical perspectives and their irreconcilable political ambitions. The United States and the Soviet Union were the heirs of that European tradition of power politics, and it should not come as a surprise that two such different systems would seek to extend their way of life to the rest of the world. Because of its need to feel secure on its western border, the Soviet Union was not prepared to give up the advantages it had gained in Eastern Europe from Germany's defeat. But neither were Western leaders prepared to accept without protest the establishment of a system of Soviet satellites that threatened the security of Western Europe.

This does not necessarily mean that both sides bear equal responsibility for starting the Cold War. Some revisionist historians have claimed that the U.S. policy of containment was a provocative action that aroused Stalin's suspicions and drove Moscow into a position of hostility to the West. As information from the Soviet archives and other sources has become available, it is increasingly clear that Stalin was suspicious of the West and long predated Washington's enunciation of the policy of containment. Although Stalin apparently had no master plan to advance Soviet power into Western Europe, he was probably prepared to make every effort to do so once the next revolutionary wave appeared on the horizon. Western leaders reacted to this possibility by strengthening their own lines of defence. On the other hand, it has been argued that in deciding to respond to the Soviet challenge in a primarily military manner, Western leaders overreacted to the situation and virtually guaranteed that the Cold War would be transformed into an arms race that could quite conceivably result in a new and uniquely destructive war.

How Did Canada Deal with the Soviet Union?

Caught literally and figuratively in between the duelling United States and the Soviet Union, Canada officially aligned itself with its neighbour to the south. But, throughout the Cold War it practised moderation and diplomacy with the Soviet Union. There were moments in the history of Canadian-Soviet relations that were somewhat strained, however; Canada treaded carefully. Canada and the United States were also partners of the **North American Air Defence Command** (NORAD) and members of NATO. NORAD consisted of three regions—Alaska, Canada, and the United States—with Canadian headquarters in Winnipeg.

> The **North American Air Defence Command** (NORAD) was a mutual defence system initiated as a means of protecting both Canadian and American airspace from a potential Soviet attack.

Through NORAD, Canada constructed what would come to be known as the "McGill Fence," a line of defence that consisted of the Pinetree Line, the Distant Early Warning (DEW) Line, and the Mid-Canada Line, all of which served to protect the airspace of Canada and the United States from any potential attacks by the Soviet Union.

Canada did not want to be seen as a protégé of the United States and its foreign policy. As an independent state, Canada tried to strike a balance during the Cold War period between its alliance with the United States and other Western states, and the Soviet Union. Canada's moderate position with regard to the Soviet Union was evidenced from the extensive economic and cultural trade that took place between the two nations. Canada sold grain to the Soviet Union, and both Air Canada and Aeroflot offered direct flights between Canada and the Soviet Union.

There were times, however, when relations between the two nations were strained at best, particularly during the **Gouzenko affair**. In 1945, a Soviet cipher clerk named Igor Gouzenko who worked at the Soviet Embassy in Ottawa defected to Canada and told the Canadian government of a Soviet spy ring infiltrating the Canadian defence system. In one case, Member of Parliament Fred Rose was revealed by Gouzenko as a Soviet spy. The discovery that the Soviet Union had infiltrated the Canadian government put serious strain on the bilateral relationship. Canada sentenced Rose to six years for conspiring with the Soviets and provided Gouzenko with protection and asylum status for his efforts.

> The **Gouzenko affair** comprises revelations by Igor Gouzenko, a Soviet cipher clerk in Ottawa, about the infiltration of Soviet spy rings in Canada, including the Canadian government.

THE COLD WAR IN ASIA

The Cold War was somewhat slower to make its appearance in Asia. At Yalta, Stalin formally agreed to enter the Pacific war against Japan three months after the close of the conflict with Germany. As a reward for Soviet participation in the struggle against Japan, Roosevelt promised that Moscow would be granted "preeminent interests" in Manchuria (interests reminiscent of those possessed by imperial Russia prior to its defeat by Japan in 1904–05) and the establishment of a Soviet naval base at Port Arthur. In return, Stalin promised to sign a treaty of alliance with the Republic of China, thus implicitly committing the Soviet Union not to provide the Chinese Communists with support in a possible future civil war. Although many observers would later question Stalin's sincerity in making such a commitment to the vocally anti-Communist Chiang Kai-shek, in Moscow the decision probably had a logic of its own. Stalin had no particular liking for the independent-minded Mao Zedong and did not anticipate a victory by the Chinese Communist Party in the eventuality of a civil war in China. Only an agreement with Chiang Kai-shek could provide the Soviet Union with a strategically vital economic and political presence in North China.

Despite these commitments, Allied agreements soon broke down, and the region was brought into the vortex of the Cold War by the end of the decade. The root of the problem lay in the underlying weakness of the Chiang Kai-shek regime, which both Moscow and Washington had eyes on controlling.

How Did the Chinese Civil War Gain Superpower Attention?

As World War II came to an end in the Pacific, relations between the government of Chiang Kai-shek in China and its powerful U.S. ally had become frayed. Although Roosevelt had hoped that republican China would be the keystone of his plan for peace and stability in Asia after the war, U.S. officials eventually became disillusioned with the corruption of Chiang's government and his unwillingness to risk his forces against the Japanese (he hoped to save them for use against the Communists after the war in the Pacific ended), and China became a backwater as the war came to a close. Nevertheless, U.S. military and economic aid to China had been substantial, and at war's end, the Truman administration wanted Chiang to support U.S. post-war imperialist goals in the region.

While Chiang Kai-shek wrestled with Japanese aggression and problems of post-war reconstruction, the Communists were building up their liberated base in North China. An alliance with Chiang in December 1936 had relieved them from the threat of immediate attack from the south, although Chiang was chronically suspicious of the Communists and stationed troops near Xian to prevent them from infiltrating areas under his control.

He had good reason to fear for the future. During the war, the Communists patiently penetrated Japanese lines and built up their strength in North China. To enlarge their political base, they carried out a "mass line" policy (from the masses to the masses), reducing land rents and confiscating the lands of wealthy landlords. By the end of World War II, according to Communist estimates, 20 to 30 million Chinese were living under the Communist administration, and their **People's Liberation Army** (PLA) included nearly 1 million troops.

> The **People's Liberation Army** (PLA) was Mao Zedong's army during the Chinese civil war.

As the war came to an end, world attention began to focus on the prospects for renewed civil strife in China. By 1946, full-scale war between Chiang Kai-shek's Nationalist government, now reinstalled in Nanjing, and the Communists resumed. The Communists, having taken advantage of the Soviet occupation of Manchuria in the last days of the war, occupied rural areas in the region and laid siege to Nationalist garrisons hastily established there. Now

Chiang Kai-shek's errors came home to roost. In the countryside, millions of peasants, attracted to the Communists by promises of land and social justice, flocked to serve in the Communists' PLA. In the cities, middle-class Chinese, who were normally against communism, were alienated by Chiang's brutal suppression of all dissent and his government's inability to slow the ruinous rate of inflation or solve the economic problems it caused. With morale dropping, Chiang's troops began to defect to the Communists. Sometimes whole divisions, officers as well as ordinary soldiers, changed sides. By 1948, the PLA was advancing south out of Manchuria and had encircled Beijing. Communist troops took the old imperial capital, crossed the Yangtze River the following spring, and occupied the commercial hub of Shanghai. During the next few months, Chiang's government and two million of his followers fled to Taiwan, which the Japanese had returned to Chinese control after World War II.

The Truman administration reacted to the spread of Communist power in China with acute discomfort. Washington had no desire to see a Communist government on the mainland, but it had little confidence in Chiang Kai-shek's ability to create a strong, united, and prosperous China. The United States started limiting military support to Chiang Kai-shek but refused to commit U.S. power to guarantee his government's survival. The U.S. administration's hands-off policy deeply angered many in the U.S. Congress, who charged that the White House was "soft on communism" and declared further that Roosevelt had betrayed Chiang at Yalta by granting privileges in Manchuria to the Soviets. In their view, Soviet troops had hindered the dispatch of Chiang's forces to the area and provided the Communists' PLA with weapons to use against their rivals.

In later years, evidence accumulated that the Soviet Union had given little assistance to the Chinese Communist Party in its struggle against the Chiang Kai-shek regime. In fact, Stalin periodically advised Mao against undertaking the effort. Although Communist forces undoubtedly received some assistance from Soviet occupation troops in Manchuria, the underlying reasons for their victory stemmed from conditions inside China, not from the intervention of outside powers.

Why Did Chinese-U.S. Tensions Set the Stage for the Korean and Vietnam Wars?

Communist leaders in China, from their new capital at Beijing, hoped that their accession to power in 1949 would bring about an era of peace in the region and permit their new government to concentrate on domestic goals. But the desire for peace was tempered by their determination to erase a century of humiliation at the hands of imperialist powers and to restore the traditional outer frontiers of the empire. In addition to recovering territories that had been part of the Manchu empire, such as Manchuria, Taiwan, and Tibet, the Chinese leaders also hoped to restore Chinese influence in former subjected areas such as Korea and Vietnam. (See Map 6.2, Plate 15.)

It soon became clear that these two goals were not always compatible. Negotiations with Moscow led to Soviet recognition of Chinese sovereignty over Manchuria and Xinjiang, although the Soviets retained a measure of economic influence in both areas. Chinese troops occupied Tibet in 1950 and brought it under Chinese administration for the first time in more than a century. But in Korea and Taiwan, China's efforts to re-create the imperial buffer zone threatened to provoke new conflicts with foreign powers.

The status of Taiwan was a consequence of the Cold War. As the civil war in China came to an end, the Truman administration appeared determined to avoid entanglement

Jack Wilkes/Time Life Pictures/Getty Images

Chiang Kai-shek and Mao Zedong Exchange a Toast. After World War II, the United States sent General George C. Marshall to China in an effort to prevent civil war between Chiang Kai-shek's government and the Communists. Marshall's initial success was symbolized by this toast between Chiang (on the right) and Mao. But suspicion ran too deep, and soon conflict ensued, leading to a Communist victory in 1949. Chiang Kai-shek's government retreated to the island of Taiwan.

in China's internal affairs and indicated that it would not seek to prevent a Communist takeover of the island, now occupied by Chiang Kai-shek's Republic of China. But as tensions between the United States and the new Chinese government escalated during the winter of 1949–50, influential figures in the United States began to argue that Taiwan was crucial to the U.S. defence strategy in the Pacific.

The outbreak of war in Korea also helped bring the Cold War to East Asia. Korea, long a Chinese tributary, was annexed into the Japanese Empire in 1908 and remained there until 1945. The removal of Korea from Japanese control had been one of the stated objectives of the Allies in World War II, and on the eve of Japanese surrender in August 1945, the Soviet Union and the United States agreed to divide the country into two separate occupation zones at the 38th parallel. They originally planned to hold national elections after the restoration of peace to reunify Korea under an independent government. But as U.S.-Soviet relations deteriorated, two separate governments emerged in Korea, Communist in the north and anti-Communist in the south.

Tensions between the two governments ran high along the dividing line, and on June 25, 1950, with the apparent approval of Joseph Stalin, North Korean troops invaded the south. The Truman administration immediately ordered U.S. naval and air forces to support South Korea, and the United Nations Security Council (with the Soviet delegate absent to protest the failure of the UN to assign China's seat to the new Communist government in Beijing) passed a resolution calling on member nations to jointly resist the invasion. By September, UN forces under the command of U.S. General Douglas MacArthur marched northward across the 38th parallel with the aim of unifying Korea under a single non-Communist government.

U.S. President Truman worried that by approaching the Chinese border at the Yalu River, the UN troops could trigger Chinese intervention but was led to believe that China would not respond. In November, however, Chinese "volunteer" forces intervened on the side of North Korea and drove the UN troops southward in disarray. A static defence line was eventually established near the original dividing line at the 38th parallel, although the war continued.

During the mid-1950s, China sought to build contacts with the non-socialist world. A cease-fire agreement brought the Korean War to an end in July 1953, and China signalled its desire to live in peaceful coexistence with other independent countries in the region. But a relatively minor conflict now began to intensify on Beijing's southern flank, in French Indochina. The struggle had begun after World War II, when Ho Chi Minh's Indochinese Communist Party, at the head of a multiparty nationalist alliance called the **Vietminh**, seized power in northern and central Vietnam after the surrender of imperial Japan. After abortive negotiations between Ho's government and the French over a proposed "free state" of Vietnam under French tutelage, war broke out in December 1946. French forces occupied the cities and the densely populated lowlands, while the primarily Communist Vietminh took refuge in the mountains. (See Map 6.3, Plate 16.)

> The **Vietminh** was a multiparty nationalist alliance in Vietnam that fought for Vietnamese independence from France and the United States.

For three years, the Vietminh waged a "people's war" of national liberation under the leadership of the popular Ho Chi Minh (see the box "Who Was Ho Chi Min?" in Chapter 4) that gradually increased in size and effectiveness. What had begun as an anti-colonial struggle by the Vietminh against the French became entangled in the Cold War in the early 1950s when both the United States and the new Communist government in China began to intervene in the conflict to promote their own national security objectives. China began to provide military assistance to the Vietminh to protect its own borders from hostile forces; the Americans supported the French.

With casualties mounting and the French public tired of fighting the "dirty war" in Indochina, the French, at the Geneva Conference, held in 1954, agreed to a peace settlement with the Vietminh. Vietnam was temporarily divided into a northern Communist half (known as the Democratic Republic of Vietnam) and a non-Communist southern half based in Saigon (eventually to be known as the *Republic of Vietnam*). Elections were to be held in two years to create a unified government. Cambodia and Laos, also under French rule, were both declared independent under neutral governments. French forces, which had suffered a major defeat at the hands of Vietminh troops, were withdrawn from all three countries.

China had played an active role in bringing about the settlement and clearly hoped that a settlement would lead to a reduction of tensions in the area, but subsequent efforts to bring about improved relations between China and the United States foundered on the issue of Taiwan. In the fall of 1954, the United States signed a mutual security treaty with Taiwan, guaranteeing U.S. military support in case of an invasion of Taiwan. When China wanted U.S. withdrawal from Taiwan as the price for improved relations, diplomatic talks between the two countries collapsed.

FROM CONFRONTATION TO COEXISTENCE

The 1950s opened with the world teetering on the edge of a nuclear war. The Soviet Union had detonated its first nuclear device in 1949, and the two blocs—capitalist and socialist—viewed each other across an ideological divide that grew increasingly bitter with each passing year. Yet as the decade drew to a close, a measure of sanity crept into the Cold War, and the leaders of the major world powers began to seek ways to coexist in an increasingly unstable world (see Map 6.4, Plate 17).

The first clear sign occurred after Stalin's death in early 1953. Nikita Khrushchev (1894–1971), once in power, attempted to reduce tensions with the West and improve the living standards of the Soviet people. In a clever public relations touch, Khrushchev publicized Moscow's appeal for a new policy of "peaceful coexistence" with the West. In 1955, he surprisingly agreed to negotiate an end to the post-war occupation of Austria by the victorious allies and allow the creation of a neutral country with strong cultural and economic ties with the West. He also called for a reduction in defence expenditures and reduced the size of the Soviet armed forces. Nevertheless, the Soviets had launched their first intercontinental ballistic missile (ICBM) in August 1957, arousing U.S. fears of a "missile gap" between the United States and the Soviet Union.

Despite periodic crises in East-West relations, there were tantalizing signs that an era of true peaceful coexistence between the two power blocs could be achieved. In the late 1950s, the United States and the Soviet Union initiated a cultural exchange program, helping the peoples of one bloc to become acquainted with the nature of life in the other. While the Soviet's Leningrad Ballet appeared at theatres in the United States, American films like *West Side Story* played in Moscow. In 1958, Nikita Khrushchev visited the United States and had a brief but friendly encounter with President Dwight D. Eisenhower at Camp David, an American presidential retreat in northern Maryland. Predictions of improved future relations led reporters to write about "the spirit of Camp David."

Yet the Soviets and Americans could rarely avoid the temptation to gain an advantage over the other in the competition for influence throughout the world, and this unstable relationship prevented any lasting accommodations between them. The superpowers also took every opportunity to promote their interests in the **Third World**, as the countries of Asia, Africa, and Latin America were now popularly called. The Soviets viewed the dismantling of colonial regimes in the area as a potential advantage for the Soviet Union and sought to exploit anti-American sentiment in Latin America especially. The Soviets established alliances with key Third World countries such as Indonesia, Egypt, India, and Cuba. In January 1961, at an informal summit meeting in Vienna, Khrushchev declared that the Soviet Union would provide active support to national liberation movements throughout the world. Superpower rivalry was about to be geared up in the Third World through continued **proxy wars**.

> The **Third World** refers to the countries of Asia, Africa, and Latin America that were neither Communist nor capitalist. These states preferred a non-aligned relationship with the superpowers and a mixed economic system.
>
> **Proxy wars** are conflicts in which two major powers use third parties as a substitute for fighting each other directly; such wars are meant to demonstrate a major power's strength and ideological will. Proxy wars dragged many Third World countries into the battles between the two superpowers at great cost to Third World peoples.

How Was the Cuban Missile Crisis Resolved?

The Cold War confrontation between the United States and the Soviet Union reached frightening levels during the Cuban Missile Crisis. In 1959, a Communist revolutionary named Fidel Castro (b. 1927) and his comrade Che Guevara (see the box "Who Was Che Guevara?" in Chapter 15) overthrew the Cuban dictator Fulgencio Batista and established a Soviet-supported totalitarian regime. After the utter failure of a U.S.-supported attempt (the **Bay of Pigs** incident) to overthrow Castro in 1961, the Soviet Union decided to place nuclear missiles in Cuba. The administration of John F. Kennedy (1917–63) was not prepared to allow nuclear weapons within such close striking distance of the American mainland, despite the fact that it had placed nuclear weapons in Turkey within easy range of the Soviet Union, a fact that Khrushchev was quick to point out. When U.S. intelligence discovered that a Soviet fleet carrying missiles was heading to Cuba, Kennedy decided to blockade Cuba to prevent the fleet from reaching its destination. In a conciliatory letter to

> The **Bay of Pigs** was a failed invasion of Cuban counter-revolutionaries supported by the United States to overthrow the Castro government.

Kennedy, Khrushchev agreed to turn back the fleet if Kennedy pledged not to invade Cuba:

> We and you ought not to pull on the ends of the rope in which you have tied the knot of war, because the more the two of us pull, the tighter that knot will be tied. And a moment may come when that knot will be tied too tight that even he who tied it will not have the strength to untie it. . . . Let us not only relax the forces pulling on the ends of the rope, let us take measures to untie that knot. We are ready for this.[2]

The intense feeling that the world might have been annihilated in a few days had a profound influence on both sides. A communication hotline between Moscow and Washington was installed in 1963 to expedite rapid communication between the two superpowers in time of crisis. In the same year, the two powers agreed to ban nuclear tests in the atmosphere, a step that served to lessen the tensions between the two nations.

Why Did the Communists of China and the Soviet Union Disagree?

Nikita Khrushchev had launched his slogan of peaceful coexistence as a means of improving relations with the capitalist powers; ironically, one result of the campaign was to undermine Moscow's ties with its close ally China. During the lifetime of Joseph Stalin, Beijing had accepted the Soviet Union as the official leader of the socialist camp. After Stalin's death, however, relations began to deteriorate. Part of the reason may have been Mao Zedong's contention that he, as the most experienced Marxist leader, should now be acknowledged as the most authoritative voice within the socialist community. But another determining factor was that just as Soviet policies were moving toward moderation, China's were becoming more radical.

Several other issues were involved, including territorial disputes and China's unhappiness with limited Soviet economic assistance. But the key sources of disagreement involved ideology and the Cold War. Chinese leaders were convinced that the successes of the Soviet space program confirmed that the socialists were now technologically superior to the capitalists, and they urged Soviet leader Nikita Khrushchev to go on the offensive to promote world revolution. Specifically, China wanted Soviet assistance in retaking Taiwan from Chiang Kai-shek. But Khrushchev was trying to improve relations with the West and rejected Chinese demands for support against Taiwan.

By the end of the 1950s, the Soviet Union had begun to remove its advisers from China, and in 1961, the dispute broke into the open. Increasingly isolated, China voiced its hostility to what Mao described as the "urban industrialized countries" (which included the Soviet Union) and portrayed itself as the leader of the "rural underdeveloped countries" of Asia, Africa, and Latin America in a global struggle against imperialist oppression. In effect, China had applied Mao's famous concept of people's war in an international framework.

THE SECOND INDOCHINA WAR

The United States did not like the terms of the peace settlement at Geneva in 1954, because Vietnam was divided temporarily into two separate zones, and specifically because the provision for future national elections opened up the possibility of placing the entire country under Communist rule. But the U.S. was not willing to introduce military forces to continue the conflict without the full support of the British and the French, who preferred to seek a negotiated settlement. In the end, Washington promised not to break the provisions of the agreement but refused to accept the results.

During the next several months, the United States began to provide aid to a new government in South Vietnam. Under the leadership of the anti-Communist politician Ngo Dinh Diem, the Saigon regime began to root out dissidents while refusing to hold the national elections called for by the Geneva Accords. It was widely anticipated, even in Washington, that the Communists led by Ho Chi Minh would win such elections.

By 1963, South Vietnam was on the verge of collapse. Diem's autocratic methods and inattention to severe economic inequality had alienated much of the population, and revolutionary forces, popularly known as the **Viet Cong** ("Vietnamese Communists"), expanded their influence throughout much of the country. In the fall of 1963, with U.S. support, senior military officers overthrew the Diem regime. But factionalism kept the new military leadership from reinvigorating the struggle against the Viet Cong forces, and by early 1965, the Viet Cong, their ranks now swelled by military units infiltrating from North Vietnam, were on the verge of seizing control of the entire country. U.S. President Lyndon Johnson (1908–73) decided to send U.S. combat troops to South Vietnam to support the anti-Communist government in Saigon.

The **Viet Cong** were Communist revolutionaries from southern Vietnam who wanted to unite Vietnam and overthrow Western domination in the North.

AP/Wide World Photos

A Bridge across the Cold War Divide. In January 1972, U.S. President Richard Nixon startled the world by visiting mainland China and beginning the long process of restoring normal relations between the two countries. Despite Nixon's reputation as a devout anti-Communist, the visit was a success, and the two sides agreed to put aside their bitter differences in an effort to reduce tensions in Asia. Here Nixon and Chinese leader Mao Zedong exchange a historic handshake in Beijing.

Chinese leaders observed the gradual escalation of the conflict in South Vietnam with mixed feelings. They were undoubtedly pleased to have a firm Communist ally—and indeed one that had in so many ways followed the path of Mao Zedong—just beyond their southern frontier. Yet they could not relish the possibility that renewed bloodshed in South Vietnam might enmesh China in a new conflict with the United States. Nor could they have welcomed the spectre of a powerful and ambitious united Vietnam that might wish to extend its influence throughout mainland Southeast Asia, which Beijing considered its own backyard.

Chinese leaders therefore tiptoed delicately through the minefield of the Indochina conflict, seeking to maintain good relations with their ally in North Vietnam while avoiding a confrontation with the United States. As the war escalated in 1964 and 1965, Beijing publicly announced that the Chinese people would give their full support to their fraternal comrades seeking national liberation in South Vietnam but privately assured Washington that China would not directly enter the conflict unless U.S. forces threatened its southern border. Beijing also refused to cooperate fully with Moscow in shipping Soviet goods to North Vietnam through Chinese territory.

Despite its dismay at the lack of full support from China, the Communist government in North Vietnam responded to U.S. escalation by infiltrating more of its own regular force troops into the south, and by 1968, the war was a virtual stalemate. The Communists were not strong enough to overthrow the Saigon regime, whose weakness was shielded by the presence of half a million U.S. troops, but President Johnson was reluctant to engage in all-out war on North Vietnam for fear of provoking a global nuclear conflict. In the fall, after the Communist-led Tet offensive aroused heightened anti-war protests in the United States, peace negotiations began in Paris.

In January 1973, North Vietnamese leaders signed a peace treaty in Paris calling for the removal of all U.S. forces from South Vietnam. In return, the Communists agreed to seek a political settlement of their differences with the Saigon regime. But negotiations between north and south over the political settlement soon broke down, and in early 1975, convinced that Washington would not intervene, the Communists resumed their campaign. At the end of April, under a massive assault by North Vietnamese military forces, the South Vietnamese government surrendered. A year later, the country was unified under Communist rule.

The Communist victory in Vietnam was a humiliation for the United States, but its strategic impact was limited because of the new relationship with China. During the next decade, Sino-American relations continued to improve. In 1979, diplomatic ties were established between the two countries under an arrangement whereby the United States renounced its mutual security treaty with Taiwan's Republic of China in return for a pledge from China to seek reunification with Taiwan by peaceful means. By the end of the 1970s, China and the United States had forged a "strategic relationship" in which each would cooperate with the other against the common threat of Soviet "hegemonism" (as China described Soviet policy) in Asia.

Meanwhile, relations between China and Canada had already begun to develop as early as 1968. At that time, Prime Minister Pierre Elliott Trudeau established diplomatic exchanges with China, and by 1970 had solidified a diplomatic relationship. Trudeau's meeting with Mao Zedong was an effort to nurture and develop better relations between Canada and the countries of the Asia-Pacific region as well as to separate itself on the world stage from the United States. Canada made a concentrated effort not to be viewed as a protégé of the United States. Reaction in the United States to Trudeau's efforts in China was typical to the strained bilateral relationship of the Trudeau era.

THE WEST AND THE SOVIET UNION

After October 1964, Nikita Khrushchev was replaced by a new leadership headed by party chief Leonid Brezhnev (1906–82) and Prime Minister Aleksey Kosygin (1904–80). The new Soviet leadership had no desire to see the Vietnam conflict sour relations between the great powers. On the other hand, Moscow was anxious to demonstrate its support for the North Vietnamese to deflect Chinese charges that the Soviet Union had betrayed the interests of the oppressed peoples of the world. As a result, Soviet officials voiced sympathy for the U.S. predicament in Vietnam but put no pressure on their allies to bring an end to the war. Indeed, the Soviets became Hanoi's main supplier of advanced military equipment in the final years of the war.

By the early 1970s, a new age in Soviet-Western relations had emerged, often referred to by the French term

détente ("relaxation"), meaning a reduction of tensions between the two sides. One symbol of the new relationship was the Antiballistic Missile (ABM) Treaty, often called SALT I (for Strategic Arms Limitation Talks), signed in 1972, in which the two nations agreed to limit their missile systems.

> **Détente** (French for "relaxation"), refers to the policy of reducing tensions between the Soviet Union and the United States that was adopted by the two countries in the 1970s.

The ABM Treaty would make it unprofitable for either superpower to believe that it could win a nuclear exchange by launching a preemptive strike against the other. *Détente* was pursued in other ways as well. When U.S. President Richard Nixon took office in 1969, he sought to increase trade and cultural contacts with the Soviet Union. His purpose was to set up a series of "linkages" in U.S.-Soviet relations that would persuade Moscow of the economic and social benefits of maintaining good relations with the West.

Similarly in Canada, Canadian-Soviet relations thawed during the Canada-Soviet Hockey Series in 1972, which put the sparring ideologies to the test on ice. The best players from Canada played the best from the Soviet Union in a series of seven exhibition games, and the two teams battled it out in an effort to win the hearts and minds of those who watched. The hockey series was quintessential of the Cold War—there were no outright battles, only psychological ones. Through the realm of hockey, the paranoia of Canadians regarding Soviet expansionism was put to rest; when Canada won the series, it scored an ideological victory.

Another symbol of improved Soviet-Western relations was the Helsinki Accords of 1975. Signed by the United States, Canada, and all European nations on both sides of the Iron Curtain, these accords recognized all borders in Central and Eastern Europe established since the end of World War II, thereby formally acknowledging for the first time the Soviet sphere of influence. The Helsinki Accords also committed the signatory powers to recognize and protect the human rights of their citizens, a clear effort by the Western states to improve the performance of the Soviet Union and its allies in that area.

An End to *Détente*?

Soviet influence was on the rise in Somalia, across the Red Sea in South Yemen, and later in Ethiopia. Soviet involvement was also on the increase in southern Africa, where an insurgent movement supported by Cuban troops came to

Map 1.1 Europe in 1871

German unification in 1871 upset the balance of power that had prevailed in Europe for more than half a century and eventually led to a restructuring of European alliances. By 1907, Europe was divided into two opposing camps: the Triple Entente of Great Britain, Russia, and France, and the Triple Alliance of Germany, Austria-Hungary, and Italy.

How was Germany affected by the formation of the Triple Entente?

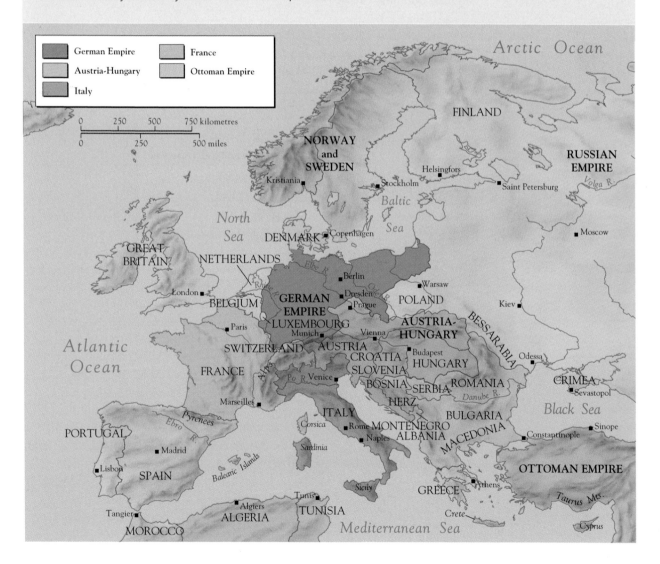

Map 2.1   Colonial Southeast Asia

European colonial rule spread into Southeast Asia between the early sixteenth and late nineteenth centuries.

What was the importance of the Strait of Malacca?

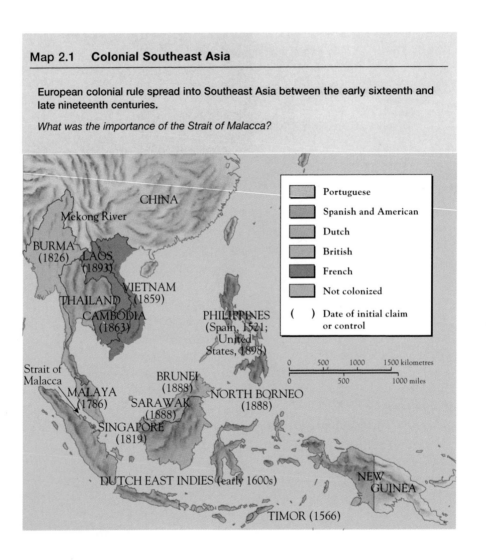

Plate 2

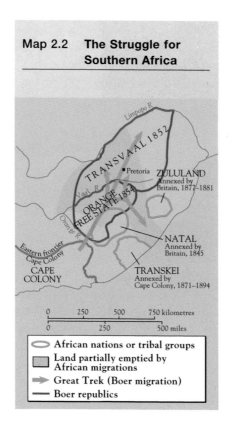

Map 2.2 **The Struggle for Southern Africa**

Limpopo R.

TRANSVAAL 1852

Vaal R.

Pretoria

ZULULAND
Annexed by
Britain, 1877–1881

ORANGE
FREE STATE 1854

Orange R.

NATAL
Annexed by
Britain, 1845

Eastern frontier
Cape Colony

CAPE
COLONY

TRANSKEI
Annexed by
Cape Colony, 1871–1894

| 0 | 250 | 500 | 750 kilometres |
| 0 | | 250 | 500 miles |

African nations or tribal groups

Land partially emptied by
African migrations

Great Trek (Boer migration)

Boer republics

Map 2.3   India under British Rule, 1805–1931

This map shows the different forms of rule that the British applied in India under their control.

Where are the major cities of the subcontinent located?

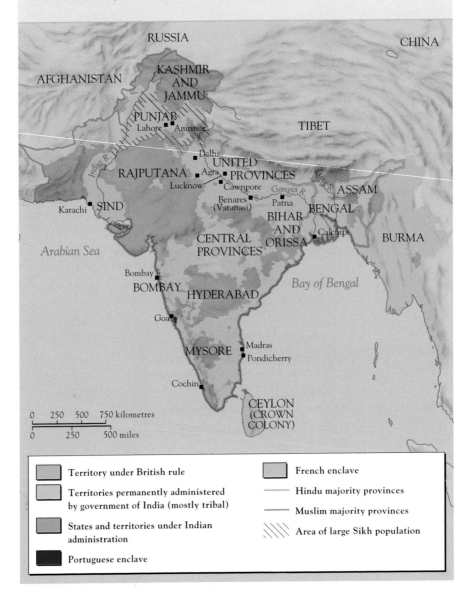

RUSSIA   CHINA

AFGHANISTAN

KASHMIR
AND
JAMMU

PUNJAB   TIBET
Lahore ■ Amritsar

                 ■ Delhi
RAJPUTANA   ■ Agra ■ UNITED
                    ■ PROVINCES
         Lucknow ■ Cawnpore   *Ganges R.*   ASSAM
                 Benares ■ Patna
Karachi SIND   (Varanasi)   BENGAL
                          BIHAR
Indus R.   CENTRAL   AND   ■ Calcutta
                 PROVINCES ORISSA   BURMA
Arabian Sea

Bombay
    ■
  BOMBAY   HYDERABAD   *Bay of Bengal*

Goa ■

       MYSORE   Madras
                ■ Pondicherry

Cochin ■

| 0 | 250 | 500 | 750 kilometres |
CEYLON
(CROWN
COLONY)

| 0 | 250 | 500 miles |

▢ Territory under British rule	▢ French enclave
▢ Territories permanently administered by government of India (mostly tribal)	— Hindu majority provinces
▢ States and territories under Indian administration	— Muslim majority provinces
▢ Portuguese enclave	⧄ Area of large Sikh population

Plate 4

NEL

Map 3.1   Europe in 1914

By 1914, two alliances dominated Europe: the Triple Entente of Great Britain, France, and Russia, and the Triple Alliance of Germany, Austria-Hungary, and Italy. Russia sought to bolster fellow Slavs in Serbia, whereas Austria-Hungary was intent on increasing its power in the Balkans and thwarting Serbia's ambitions. Thus, the Balkans became the flash point for World War I.

Which nonaligned nations were positioned between the two alliances?

Plate 5

Map 3.2 World War I, 1914–1918

This map shows how greatly the Western and Eastern Fronts of World War I differed. After initial German gains in the west, the war became bogged down in trench warfare, with little change in the battle lines throughout the war. The Eastern Front was marked by considerable mobility, with battle lines shifting by hundreds of kilometres.

How do you explain the difference in the two fronts?

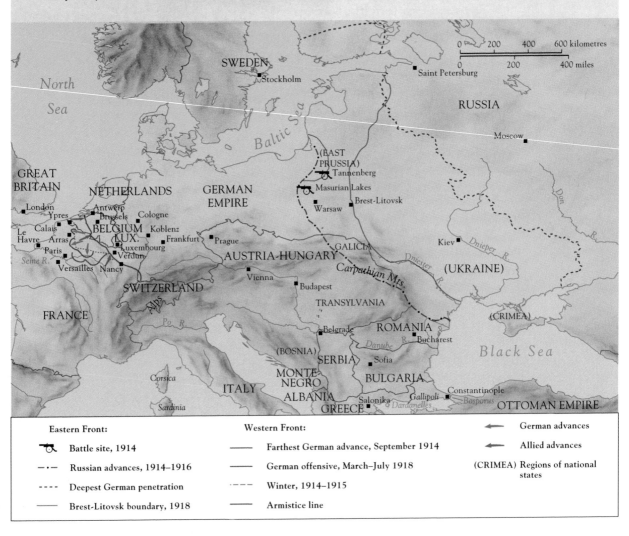

Eastern Front:	Western Front:	
⚔ Battle site, 1914	—— Farthest German advance, September 1914	← German advances
–·– Russian advances, 1914–1916	—— German offensive, March–July 1918	← Allied advances
---- Deepest German penetration	---- Winter, 1914–1915	(CRIMEA) Regions of national states
—— Brest-Litovsk boundary, 1918	—— Armistice line	

Plate 6

NEL

Map 3.3 **The Middle East in 1919**

French mandates
British mandates

Constantinople
TURKEY
Caspian Sea
SYRIA
LEBANON
Beirut
Mediterranean Sea
Damascus
PERSIA
Baghdad
PALESTINE
IRAQ
Jerusalem
TRANS-
JORDAN
Cairo
KUWAIT
EGYPT
SAUDI
ARABIA

0 250 500 750 kilometres
0 250 500 miles

Map 3.4   Territorial Changes in Europe and the Middle East after World War I

The victorious Allies met in Paris to determine the shape and nature of Europe following World War I. The imperialists carved the Middle East to reflect their geostrategic interests in the region.

What countries did imperialists carve in Europe and the Middle East?

Plate 8

NEL

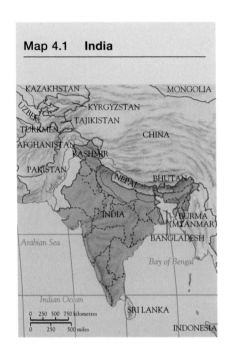

Map 4.1   India

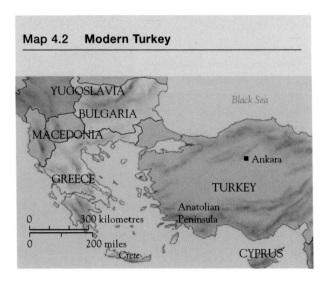

Map 4.2   Modern Turkey

Map 4.3 Iran under the Pahlavi Dynasty

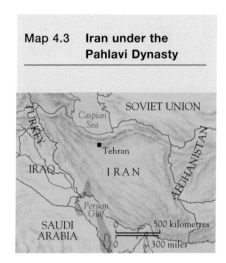

Map 4.4 The Northern Expedition and the Long March

This map shows the routes taken by the combined Nationalist-Communist forces during the Northern Expedition of 1926–28. Areas under the control of Chiang Kai-shek's Nationalist government in 1928 are indicated in dark shading. The blue arrow indicates the route taken by Communist units during the Long March led by Mao Zedong.

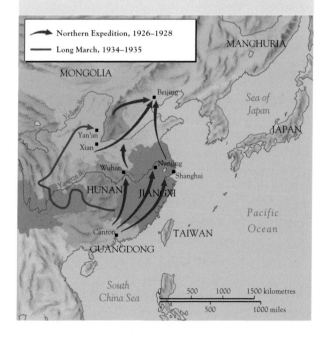

Plate 10

NEL

Map 4.5   Latin America in the First Half of the Twentieth Century

Shown here are the boundaries dividing the countries of Latin America after the independence movements of the nineteenth century.

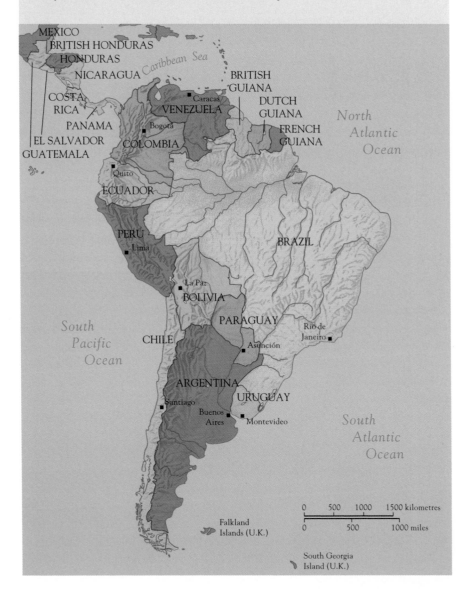

Plate 11

Map 5.1   World War II in Europe and North Africa

With its fast and effective military, Germany quickly overwhelmed much of Western Europe. However, Hitler overestimated his country's capabilities and underestimated those of his foes. By late 1942, his invasion of the Soviet Union was failing, and the United States had become a major factor in the war. The Allies successfully invaded Italy in 1943 and France in 1944.

Which countries were neutral, and how did geography help make their neutrality an option?

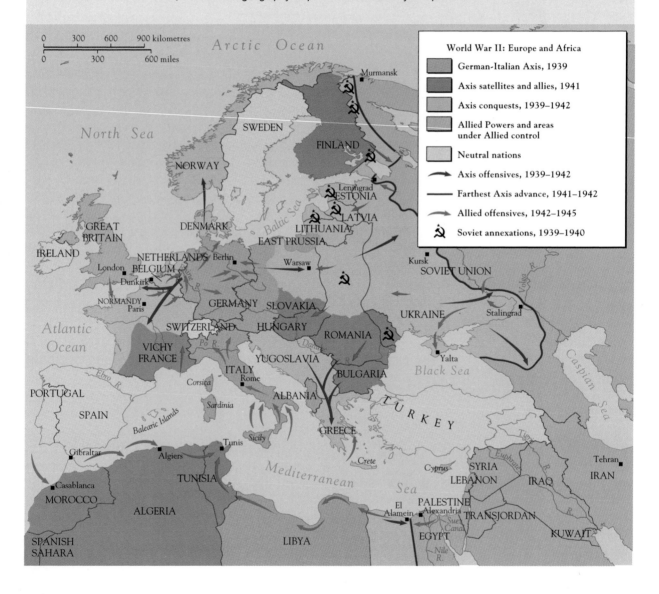

Plate 12

NEL

Map 5.2   World War II in Asia and the Pacific

In 1937, Japan invaded northern China, beginning its effort to create the "Great East Asia Co-Prosperity Sphere."
Further expansion induced America to end iron and oil sales to Japan. Deciding that war with the United States was
inevitable, Japan engineered a surprise attack on Pearl Harbor.

Why was control of the islands in the western Pacific of great importance both to the Japanese and to the Allies?

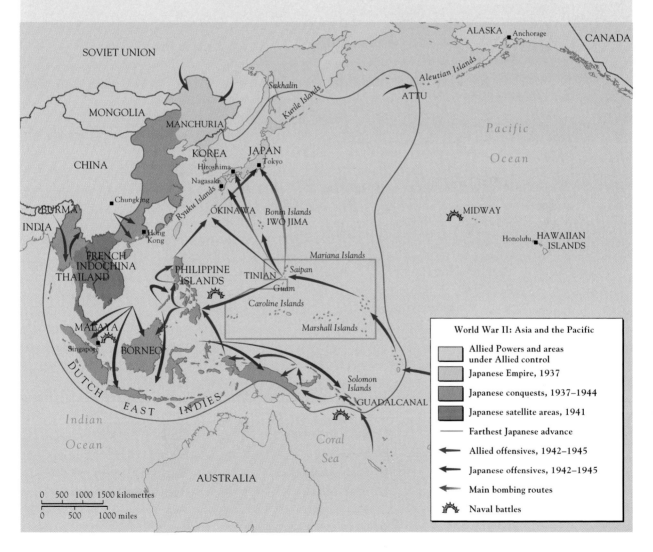

Map 6.1 The New European Alliance Systems during the Cold War

This map shows post-war Europe as it was divided during the Cold War into two contending power blocs, the NATO alliance and the Warsaw Pact. Major military and naval bases are indicated by symbols on the map.

Where on the map was the so-called Iron Curtain?

United States and NATO		Soviet Union and Warsaw Pact			
	Missile bases: NATO		Missile bases: Warsaw Pact		NATO member
	Troops: U.S.		Troops: Soviet		Non-NATO ally
	Nuclear bombers: U.S.		Nuclear bombers: Soviet		NATO member until 1969
	Naval port: U.S.		Naval port: Soviet		Warsaw Pact member
	Fleet: U.S.		Fleet: Soviet		Unrest or revolt in Eastern Europe
	Nuclear missile submarine: U.S.		Nuclear missile submarine: Soviet		

Plate 14

NEL

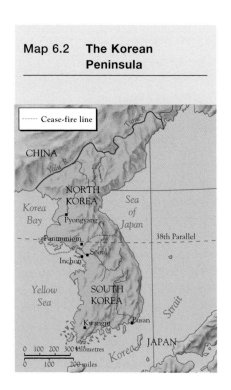

Map 6.2   The Korean Peninsula

Map 6.3   Indochina in 1954

Plate 16

NEL

Map 6.4 The Global Cold War

This map indicates the location of major military bases and missile sites possessed by the contending power blocs throughout the world at the height of the Cold War.

Which countries are the most heavily armed?

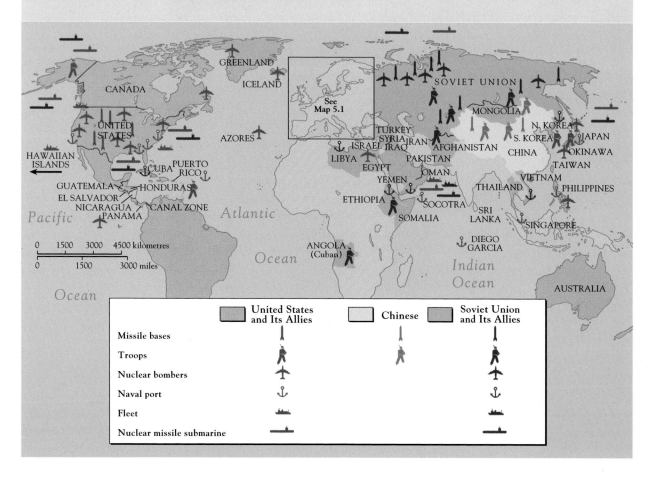

Plate 17

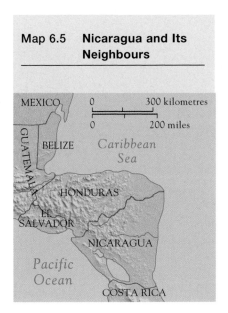

Map 6.5   Nicaragua and Its Neighbours

Plate 18   NEL

Map 7.1   Eastern Europe and the Soviet Union

After World War II, the boundaries of Eastern Europe were redrawn as a result of Allied agreements reached at the Tehran and Yalta conferences. This map shows the new boundaries that were established throughout the region, placing Soviet power at the centre of Europe.

How had the boundaries changed from the pre-war era?

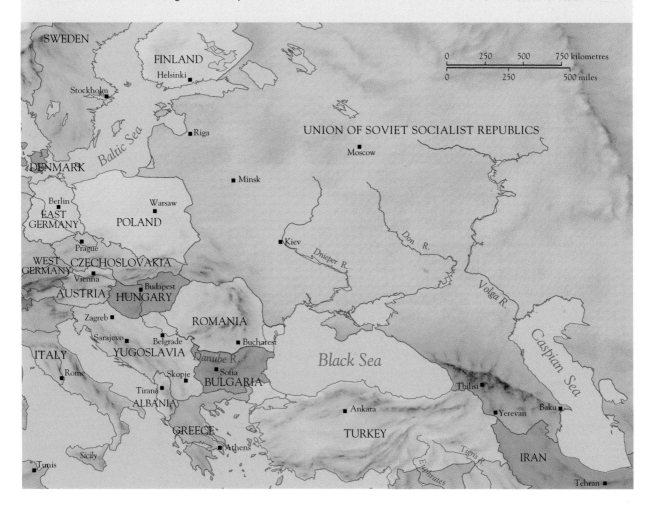

Map 7.2 Eastern Europe and the Former Soviet Union

After the disintegration of the Soviet Union in 1991, Soviet republics declared their independence. This map shows the new configuration of the states that emerged in the 1990s, including the boundaries after the dissolution of Czechoslovakia and Yugoslavia.

What new nations have appeared since the end of the Cold War?

Plate 20

NEL

Map 8.1   Europe after World War II

At the Yalta Conference in February 1945, Allied leaders altered the pre-war map of Europe, primarily in the east, where the boundaries of the Soviet Union were moved westward from the Baltic to the Black Sea.

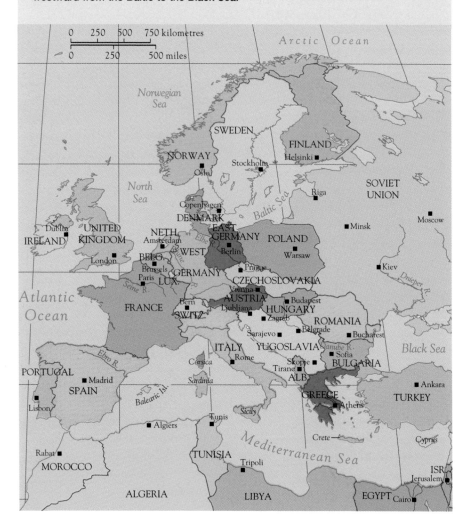

Map 8.2   Europe in 2000

After the collapse of the Communist order in Eastern Europe and the Soviet Union, a new order and a number of new states appeared in Central and Eastern Europe. At the same time, the European Union expanded and included 15 states by 2000.

What new countries emerged from the breakup of the Soviet Union?

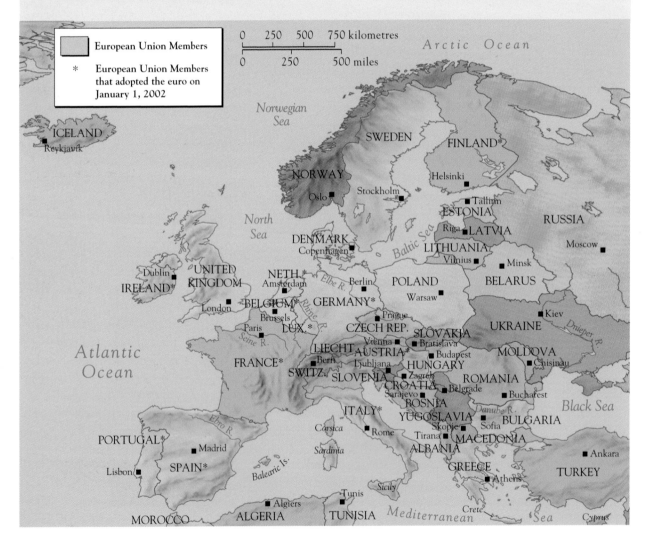

Plate 22

NEL

Map 11.1   The People's Republic of China

This map shows China's current boundaries. Major regions are indicated in capital letters. Areas in dispute are shown by darker shading.

In which regions are there movements against Chinese rule?

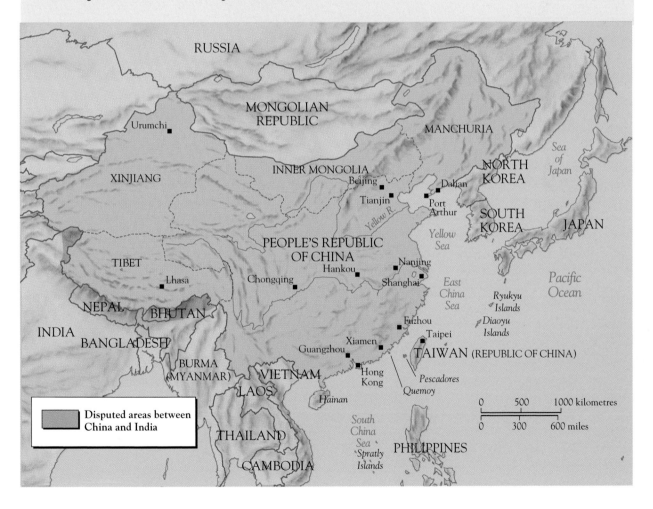

Plate 23

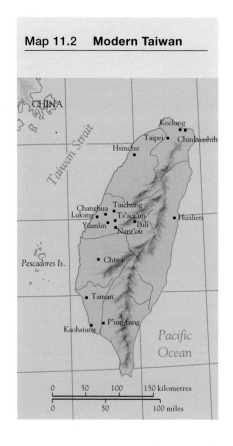

Map 11.2   Modern Taiwan

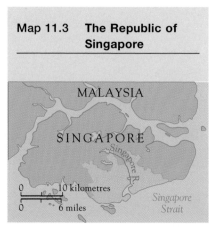

Map 11.3   The Republic of Singapore

Plate 24   NEL

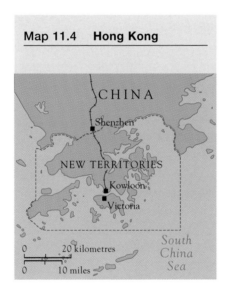

Map 11.4   Hong Kong

CHINA

Shenzhen

NEW TERRITORIES

Kowloon

Victoria

South
China
Sea

0   20 kilometres

0   10 miles

Map 12.1   Modern Africa

This map shows the independent states in Africa today.

Which is the most populated nation on the continent?

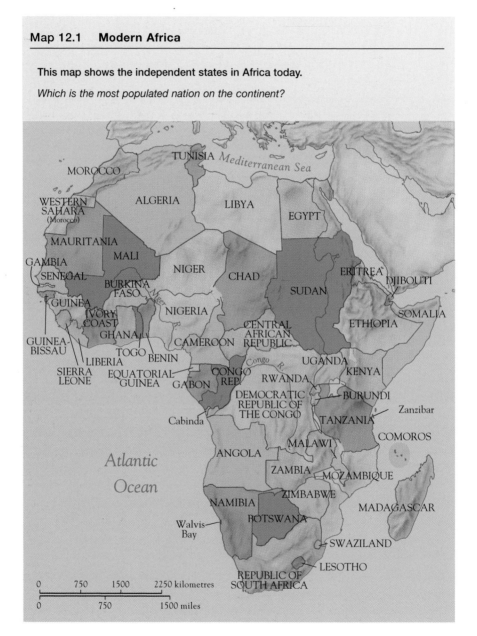

Plate 26

Map 13.1　The Modern Middle East

Shown here are the boundaries dividing the independent states in the contemporary Middle East.

Which are the major oil-producing countries?

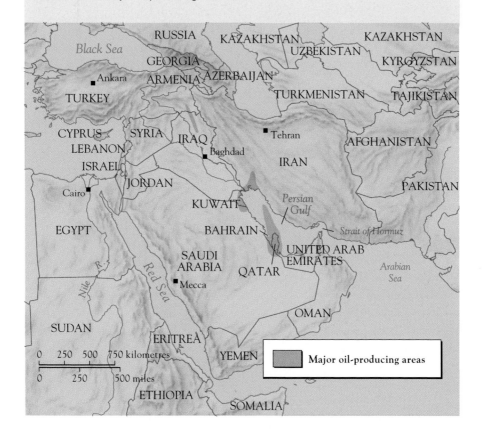

Major oil-producing areas

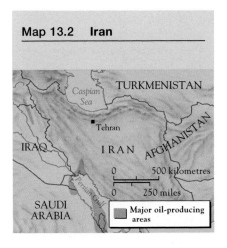

Map 13.2   Iran

TURKMENISTAN

Caspian
Sea

Tehran

IRAQ

IRAN

AFGHANISTAN

0   500 kilometres

0   250 miles

SAUDI
ARABIA

Persian Gulf

Major oil-producing
areas

Plate 28   NEL

Map 14.1 Modern South Asia

This map shows the boundaries of all the states in
contemporary South Asia. India, the largest in area and
population, is highlighted by darker shading.

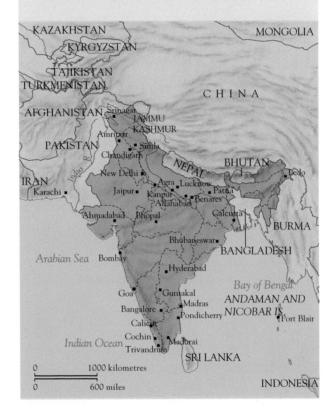

Map 14.2 Modern Southeast Asia

Shown here are the countries of contemporary Southeast Asia. The major islands that make up the Republic of Indonesia are indicated in italics.

Where is the new nation of East Timor?

Plate 30

NEL

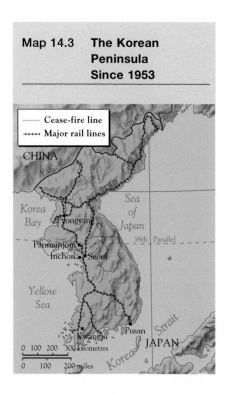

Map 14.3 The Korean Peninsula Since 1953

Cease-fire line
Major rail lines

CHINA

Tumen R.

Yalu R.

Korea Bay

Sea of Japan

Pyongyang

Panmunjom

Inchon   Seoul

38th Parallel

Yellow Sea

Korea Strait

Kwangju   Pusan

JAPAN

0 100 200 300 kilometres

0   100   200 miles

Map 15.1 Political Trends in Latin America in the 1960s and 1970s

Latin America experienced considerable political upheaval after World War II,
especially as a result of severe economic problems. The result was a move toward
military regimes as well as strong leftist movements, especially Marxism.

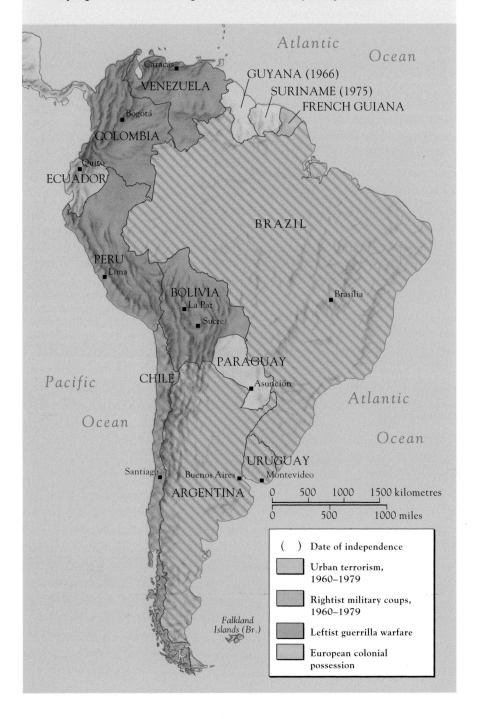

Atlantic Ocean

GUYANA (1966)
SURINAME (1975)
FRENCH GUIANA

VENEZUELA
Caracas

Bogotá
COLOMBIA

Quito
ECUADOR

BRAZIL

PERU
Lima

BOLIVIA
La Paz
Sucre

Brasília

PARAGUAY

Pacific Ocean

CHILE

Asunción

Atlantic Ocean

URUGUAY

Santiago
Buenos Aires
Montevideo

ARGENTINA

| 0 | 500 | 1000 | 1500 kilometres |

| 0 | 500 | 1000 miles |

Falkland Islands (Br.)

( ) Date of independence

Urban terrorism, 1960–1979

Rightist military coups, 1960–1979

Leftist guerrilla warfare

European colonial possession

Plate 32

power in Angola, once a colony of Portugal. Then, in 1979, Soviet troops were sent to neighbouring Afghanistan to protect a newly installed Marxist regime facing rising internal resistance from the **mujahideen**. Some observers suspected that the purpose of the Soviet advance into hitherto neutral Afghanistan was to extend Soviet power into the oil fields of the Persian Gulf. But others point to Soviet fears of an empowered Iran, after the 1979 Islamic Revolution, spreading its ideology to neighbouring Afghanistan and challenging Soviet hegemonic presence in Eurasian politics.

> The **mujahideen** are rebels engaged in a *jihad* ("struggle"); the Afghan mujahideen were financed primarily by the United States and Saudi Arabia in their struggle to overthrow the Soviet occupation of Afghanistan.

The Afghan mujahideen were supported and financed by the United States and Saudi Arabia, trying to overthrow the Communist-led regime. The Afghan civil war was a classic proxy war between the world superpowers. The 10-year civil war caused great social havoc and destruction, notably sending millions of refugees into neighbouring Pakistan and Iran. Noted as the Soviets' Vietnam, the war in Afghanistan left the Soviets humiliated. Afghanistan was in ruins and nearly a million Afghans lost their lives to the war.

In the United States, the reaction against the Soviets' appetite for more power included a return to the harsh rhetoric, if not all of the harsh practices, of the Cold War. U.S. President Ronald Reagan's (1911–2004) anti-Communist credentials were well known. In a speech given shortly after his election in 1980, he referred to the Soviet Union as an "evil empire" and frequently voiced his suspicion of its motives in foreign affairs. In an effort to eliminate perceived Soviet advantages in strategic weaponry, the White House began a renewed arms race. In 1982, the Reagan administration introduced the nuclear-tipped cruise missile, whose ability to fly at low altitudes made it difficult to detect by enemy radar. Reagan also became an ardent exponent of the Strategic Defense Initiative (SDI), nicknamed **Star Wars**. Its purposes were to create a space shield that could destroy incoming missiles and to force Moscow into an arms race that it could not hope to win.

> **Star Wars** is a U.S. defence system intended to destroy incoming missiles in space.

The Reagan administration also adopted a more activist, if not confrontational, stance in the Third World. That attitude was most directly demonstrated in Central America, where the revolutionary Sandinista regime had come to power with the overthrow of the Somoza dictatorship in 1979. Charging that the Sandinista regime was supporting a Marxist movement in nearby El Salvador, the Reagan administration began to provide financial aid to the government in El Salvador while simultaneously applying pressure on the Sandinistas by giving support to an anti-Communist guerrilla movement (called the *Contras*) in Nicaragua. (See Map 6.5, Plate 18.)

CONCLUSION

At the end of World War II, a new ideological conflict appeared as the two superpowers, the United States and the Soviet Union, began to compete for political domination throughout the world.

- The superpowers sought to extend their sphere of influence to Korea, Vietnam, Afghanistan, and Nicaragua.
- Both the Soviet Union and the United States became entangled in proxy war areas that in themselves had little importance in terms of real national security interests.

By the 1980s, however, there were tantalizing signs of a thaw in the Cold War.

- China and the United States, each hoping to gain leverage with the Soviet Union, had agreed to establish diplomatic relations.
- The United States decided to withdraw from South Vietnam, and the war there came to an end without involving the superpowers in a dangerous confrontation.
- The United States and the Soviet Union continued to compete for advantage all over the world, but came to realize that the struggle for domination could best be carried out in the political and economic arena rather than on the battlefield.

CRITICAL THINKING QUESTIONS

1. Had there been better diplomatic relations between the Soviets and Americans, would the Vietnam and Korean wars have been avoided?

2. Some point out that had Nikita Khrushchev and John F. Kennedy listened to war hawks in their inner circle, nuclear war would have broken out. How important are individual leaders to history? To what extent do national interests determine the behaviour of leaders, independent of who is in power?

3. If the United States and the Soviet Union had not participated in proxy wars, would they have been more inclined to fight each other directly?

4. Can antagonistic countries find an effective outlet for their rivalry through sporting events (consider the impact of events such as the Canada-Soviet Hockey Series in 1972, the Olympics, and Pakistan and India's cricket matches)?

CHAPTER NOTES

1. George Kennan (Mr. X), "The Sources of Soviet Conduct," *Foreign Affairs* 26, no. 2 (July 1947): pp. 575–76.

2. Quoted in Robert F. Kennedy, *Thirteen Days: A Memoir of the Cuban Missile Crisis* (New York: Norton, 1969), pp. 89–90.

The Rise and Fall of Communism in the Soviet Union and Eastern Europe

For three decades after the end of World War II, the Soviet sphere of influence appeared to be a permanent feature of the international landscape. But by the early 1980s, it became clear that there were cracks in the facade of the Kremlin wall. The Soviet economy was stagnant, the minority nationalities were restive, and Eastern European leaders were increasingly emboldened to test the waters of the global capitalist marketplace.

At the conclusion of this chapter, you will be able to

- describe the political barriers faced by those who wanted to reform the Soviet Union;
- identify the day-to-day challenges of living under a Soviet regime;
- explain how and why the Soviets exercised political control over satellite states in Eastern Europe;
- explain why the transition from the Soviet command economy to a market-led economy was difficult for Russia and its people.

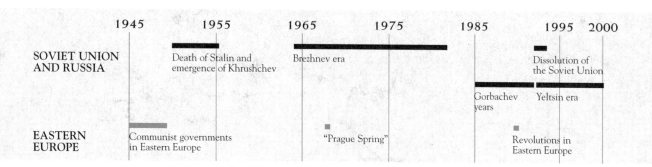

THE POST-WAR SOVIET UNION

World War II had left the Soviet Union as one of the world's two superpowers and its leader, Joseph Stalin, at the height of his power. As a result of the war, Stalin and his Soviet colleagues were now in control of a vast empire that included Eastern Europe, much of the Balkans, and territory gained from Japan in East Asia.

How Did Khrushchev Differ from His Predecessor Stalin?

World War II devastated the Soviet Union. Twenty million citizens lost their lives, and cities such as Kiev, Kharkov, and Leningrad suffered enormous physical destruction. As the lands that had been occupied by the German forces were liberated, the Soviet government turned its attention to restoring their economic structures. Nevertheless, in 1945, agricultural production was only 60 percent and steel output only 50 percent of pre-war levels. The Soviet people faced incredibly difficult conditions: they worked longer hours; they ate less; they were ill-housed and poorly clothed.

In the immediate post-war years, the Soviet Union removed goods and materials from occupied Germany and extorted valuable raw materials from its satellite states in Eastern Europe. More important, however, to create a new industrial base, Stalin returned to the method he had used in the 1930s—the extraction of development capital from Soviet labour. Working hard for little pay and for precious few consumer goods, Soviet labourers were expected to produce goods for export with little in return for themselves. The incoming capital from abroad could then be used to purchase machinery and Western technology. The loss of millions of men in the war meant that much of this tremendous workload fell to Soviet women, who performed almost 40 percent of the heavy manual labour.

The pace of economic recovery in the Soviet Union was impressive. By 1947, Russian industrial production had attained 1939 levels; three years later, it had surpassed those levels by 40 percent. New power plants, canals, and giant factories were built, while new industrial enterprises and oil fields were established in Siberia and Soviet Central Asia. Stalin's new five-year plan, announced in 1946, reached its goals in less than five years.

Although Stalin's economic recovery policy was successful in promoting growth in heavy industry, primarily for the benefit of the military, consumer goods remained scarce. The development of thermonuclear weapons, MIG fighters, and the first space satellite, **Sputnik 1**, in the 1950s may have elevated the Soviet state's reputation as a world power abroad, but domestically, the Soviet people were shortchanged. Heavy industry grew at a rate three times that of personal consumption. Moreover, the housing shortage was acute, with living conditions especially difficult in the overcrowded cities.

Sputnik 1 was the first orbital satellite created by the Soviet Union and was used to beam televised broadcasts; it essentially launched the superpowers' race for the control of space.

When World War II ended, Stalin had been in power for more than 15 years. During that time, he had removed all opposition to his rule and remained the undisputed master of the Soviet Union. Increasingly distrustful of competitors, Stalin exercised sole authority and pitted his subordinates against one another. One of these subordinates, Lavrenti Beria, head of the secret police, controlled a force of several hundred thousand agents, leaving Stalin's

colleagues completely cowed. As Stalin remarked mockingly on one occasion, "When I die, the imperialists will strangle all of you like a litter of kittens."[1]

Stalin's morbid suspicions added to the constantly increasing repressiveness of the regime. In 1946, government decrees subordinated all forms of literary and scientific expression to the political needs of the state. Along with the anti-intellectual campaign came political terror. By the late 1940s, there were an estimated nine million people in Siberian concentration camps. Distrust of potential threats to his power even spread to some of his closest colleagues. In 1948, Andrey Zhdanov, his presumed successor and head of the Leningrad party organization, died under mysterious circumstances, presumably at Stalin's order. Within weeks, the Leningrad party organization was purged of several top leaders, many of whom were charged with traitorous connections with Western intelligence agencies. In succeeding years, Stalin directed his suspicion at other members of the inner circle, including Foreign Minister Vyacheslav Molotov. Known as "Old Stone Butt" in the West for his stubborn defence of Soviet security interests, Molotov had been Stalin's loyal lieutenant since the early years of Stalin's rise to power. Now Stalin distrusted Molotov and had his Jewish wife placed in a Siberian concentration camp.

Stalin died in 1953 and, after some bitter infighting within the party leadership, was succeeded by Georgy Malenkov, a veteran administrator and ambitious member of the **politburo**. Malenkov came to power with a clear agenda. In foreign affairs, he hoped to promote an easing of Cold War tensions and improve relations with the Western powers. For Moscow's Eastern European allies, he advocated a "new course" in their mutual relations and a decline in Stalinist methods of rule. Inside the Soviet Union, he hoped to reduce defence expenditures and assign a higher priority to improving the standard of living. Such goals were laudable and probably had the support of the majority of the Russian people, but they were not necessarily appealing to key pressure groups within the Soviet Union—the army, the Communist Party, the managerial elite, and the security services (now known as the Committee for State Security, or the **KGB**). In 1955, Malenkov was removed from his position as prime minister, and power shifted to his rival, the new party general secretary, Nikita Khrushchev.

The **politburo** was a committee of inner circle political leaders—comprising the president and top party members only—that made important governing decisions.

The **KGB** was the Soviet Union's main intelligence gathering unit on both internal and external activities.

During his struggle for power with Malenkov, Khrushchev had outmanoeuvred him by calling for heightened defence expenditures and a continuing emphasis on heavy industry. Once in power, however, Khrushchev reversed his priorities. He now resumed the efforts of his predecessor to reduce tensions with the West and improve the standard of living of the Russian people. He moved vigorously to improve the performance of the Soviet economy and revitalize Soviet society. By nature, Khrushchev was a man of enormous energy as well as an innovator. In an attempt to release the stranglehold of the central bureaucracy over the national economy, he abolished dozens of government ministries and split up the party and government apparatus. Khrushchev also attempted to rejuvenate the stagnant agricultural sector, long the impediment to progress in the Soviet economy. He attempted to spur production by increasing profit incentives and opened "virgin lands" in Soviet Kazakhstan to bring thousands of acres of new land under cultivation.

Like any innovator, Khrushchev had to overcome the inherently conservative instincts of the Soviet bureaucracy, as well as of the mass of the Soviet population. His plan to remove the "dead hand" of the state, however laudable in intent, alienated much of the Soviet official class, and his effort to split the party angered those who saw it as the central force in the Soviet system. Khrushchev's agricultural schemes inspired similar opposition. Although the Kazakhstan wheat lands would eventually demonstrate their importance in the overall agricultural picture, progress was slow, and his effort to persuade the Russian people to eat more corn (an idea he had apparently picked up during a visit to the United States) led to the mocking nickname of "Cornman." Disappointing agricultural production, combined with high military spending, hurt the Soviet economy. The industrial growth rate, which had soared in the early 1950s, now declined dramatically from 13 percent in 1953 to 7.5 percent in 1964.

Khrushchev was probably best known for his policy of **de-Stalinization**. Khrushchev had risen in the party hierarchy as a Stalin protégé, but he had been deeply disturbed by his mentor's excesses and, once in a position of authority, moved to excise the Stalinist legacy from Soviet society. The campaign began at the Twentieth Congress of the Communist Party in February 1956, when Khrushchev gave a long speech criticizing some of Stalin's major shortcomings. The speech had apparently not been intended for public distribution, but it was quickly leaked to the Western press and created a sensation throughout the world. During the next few years, Khrushchev encouraged more freedom of expression for writers, artists, and composers, arguing that "readers should be given the chance to make their own judgments" regarding the acceptability of controversial

literature and that "police measures shouldn't be used."[2] At Khrushchev's order, thousands of prisoners were released from concentration camps.

> **De-Stalinization** refers to a process initiated by Nikita Khrushchev of removing Joseph Stalin's social and political influence—particularly the more repressive aspects—in many facets of Soviet life.

Khrushchev's personality, however, did not endear him to higher Soviet officials, who frowned at his tendency to crack jokes and play the clown. Nor were the higher members of the party bureaucracy pleased when Khrushchev tried to curb their privileges. Foreign policy failures further damaged Khrushchev's reputation among his colleagues. His plan to place missiles in Cuba was the final straw (see Chapter 6, page 122). While he was away on vacation in 1964, a special meeting of the politburo voted him out of office (because of "deteriorating health") and forced him into retirement. Although a group of leaders succeeded him, real power came into the hands of Leonid Brezhnev (1906–82), the "trusted" supporter of Khrushchev who had engineered his downfall.

How Did Brezhnev Consolidate Greater Political Control?

The ouster of Nikita Khrushchev in October 1964 vividly demonstrated the challenges that would be encountered by any Soviet leader sufficiently bold to try to reform the Soviet system. In democratic countries, pressure on the government comes from various sources within society at large—the business community and labour unions, interest groups, and the general public. In the Soviet Union, pressure on government and party leaders originates from sources essentially operating inside the system—from the government bureaucracy, the party apparatus, the KGB, and the armed forces.

Leonid Brezhnev, the new party chief, was undoubtedly aware of these realities of Soviet politics, and his long tenure in power was marked, above all, by the desire to avoid changes that might provoke instability, either at home or abroad. Brezhnev was himself a product of the Soviet system. He had entered the ranks of the party leadership under Joseph Stalin, and although he was not a particularly avid believer in party ideology—indeed, his years in power gave rise to innumerable stories about his addiction to "bourgeois pleasures," including expensive country houses in the elite Moscow suburb of Zhukovka and fast cars (many of them gifts from foreign leaders)—he was no partisan of reform.

Still, Brezhnev sought stability in the domestic arena. He and his prime minister, Aleksey Kosygin, undertook what might be described as a program of "de-Khrushchevization," returning the responsibility for long-term planning to the central ministries and reuniting the Communist Party apparatus. Despite some cautious attempts to stimulate the stagnant farm sector by increasing capital investment in agriculture and raising food prices to increase rural income and provide additional incentives to collective farmers, there was no effort to revise the basic structure of the collective system. In the industrial sector, the regime launched a series of reforms designed to give factory managers (themselves employees of the state) more responsibility for setting prices, wages, and production quotas. These so-called **Kosygin reforms** had little effect, however, because they were stubbornly resisted by the bureaucracy and were eventually adopted by relatively few enterprises within the vast state-owned industrial sector.

> **Kosygin reforms**, named after Leonid Brezhnev's right-hand man, were a series of policies designed to modernize the industrial sector.

A CONTROLLED SOCIETY

Leonid Brezhnev also initiated a significant retreat from the policy of de-Stalinization adopted by Nikita Khrushchev. Criticism of the "Great Leader" had angered conservatives both within the party hierarchy and among the public at large, many of whom still revered Stalin as a hero of the Soviet system and a defender of the Russian people against Nazi Germany. Many influential figures in the Kremlin feared that de-Stalinization could lead to internal instability and a decline in public trust in the legitimacy of party leadership—the hallowed "dictatorship of the proletariat." Early in Brezhnev's reign, Stalin's reputation began to revive. Although his alleged "shortcomings" were not totally ignored, he was now described in the official press as "an outstanding party leader" who had been primarily responsible for the successes achieved by the Soviet Union.

The regime also adopted a more restrictive policy toward free expression and dissidence in Soviet society. Critics of the Soviet system, such as physicist Andrey Sakharov, were harassed and arrested or, like the famous writer Aleksandr Solzhenitsyn (b. 1918), forced to leave the country. There was also a qualified return to the anti-Semitic policies and attitudes that had marked the Stalin era. Such indications of renewed repression aroused concern in the West and were instrumental in the inclusion of a statement on human rights in the 1975 Helsinki Accords, which guaranteed the

sanctity of international frontiers throughout the continent of Europe (see Chapter 6, page 124).

The political stamp of the Brezhnev era was formally enshrined in a new state constitution, promulgated in 1977. Although the preamble declared that the Soviet Union was no longer a proletarian dictatorship but rather a "state of all the people," comprising workers, farmers, and "socialist intellectuals," it confirmed the role of the Communist Party as "the predominant force" in Soviet society. Article 49 states that "persecution for criticism shall be prohibited," but Article 62 qualifies the rights of the individual by declaring that citizens "shall be obligated to safeguard the interests of the Soviet state and to contribute to the strength of its might and prestige."

There were, of course, no rival voices to compete with the party and the government in defining national interests. The media were controlled by the state and presented only what the state wanted people to hear. The two major newspapers, *Pravda* ("Truth") and *Izvestiya* ("News"), were the agents of the party and the government, respectively. Cynics joked that there was no news in *Pravda* and no truth in *Izvestiya*. Reports of airplane accidents in the Soviet Union were rarely publicized on the grounds that doing so would raise questions about the quality of the Soviet airline industry. The government made strenuous efforts to prevent the Soviet people from exposure to harmful foreign ideas, especially modern art, literature, and contemporary Western rock music. When the Summer Olympic Games were held in Moscow in 1980, Soviet newspapers advised citizens to keep their children indoors to protect them from being polluted with "bourgeois" ideas passed on by foreign visitors.

For citizens of Western democracies, such a political atmosphere would seem highly oppressive, but for the people in the Soviet republics, an emphasis on law and order was an accepted aspect of everyday life inherited from the tsarist period. Conformism was the rule in virtually every corner of Soviet society, from the educational system (characterized at all levels by rote memorization and political indoctrination) to child rearing (it was forbidden, for example, to be left-handed) and even to yearly vacations (most workers took their vacations at resorts run by their employer, where the daily schedule of activities was highly regimented).

A STAGNANT ECONOMY

Soviet leaders also failed to achieve their objective of revitalizing the national economy. Whereas growth rates during the early Khrushchev era had been impressive, under Brezhnev, industrial growth declined to an annual rate of

Courtesy of William J. Duiker

The KGB's Portals of Doom. Perhaps the most feared location in the Soviet Union was Lyubyanka Prison, an ornate pre-revolutionary building in the heart of Moscow. Taken over by the Bolsheviks after the 1917 revolution, it became the headquarters of the Soviet secret police, the *Cheka*, later to be known as the *KGB*. It was here that many Soviet citizens accused of "counterrevolutionary acts" were imprisoned and executed. The figure on the pedestal is that of Feliks Dzerzhinsky, first director of the *Cheka*. After the dissolution of the Soviet Union, the statue was removed.

less than 4 percent in the early 1970s and less than 3 percent in the period 1975–80. Successes in the agricultural sector were equally meagre. Grain production rose from less than 90 million tons in the early 1950s to nearly 200 million tons in the 1970s but then stagnated at that level.

One of the primary problems with the Soviet economy was the absence of incentives. Salary structures offered little reward for hard labour and extraordinary achievement. Pay differentials operated within a much narrower range than in most Western societies, and there was little danger of being dismissed. According to the Soviet constitution, every Soviet citizen was guaranteed an opportunity to work.

There were, of course, some exceptions to this general rule. Athletic achievement was highly prized, and a gymnast of Olympic stature would receive great rewards in the form of prestige and lifestyle. Senior officials did not receive high salaries but were provided with countless "perquisites," such as access to foreign goods, official automobiles with a chauffeur, and entry into prestigious institutions of higher learning for their children. For the elite, it was *blat* ("influence") that most often differentiated them from the rest of the population. The average citizen, however, had little material incentive to produce beyond the minimum acceptable level of effort. It is hardly surprising that overall per capita productivity was only about half that realized in most capitalist countries. At the same time, the rudeness of clerks and waiters toward their customers in Soviet society became legendary.

The problem of incentives existed at the managerial level as well, where the practice of centralized planning discouraged initiative and innovation. Factory managers, for example, were assigned monthly and annual quotas by the *Gosplan* (the "state plan," drawn up by the central planning commission). Because state-owned factories faced little or no competition, factory managers did not care whether their products were competitive in terms of price and quality, so long as the quota was attained. One of the key complaints of Soviet citizens was the low quality of most locally made consumer goods. Knowledgeable consumers quickly discovered that products manufactured at the end of the month were often of lower quality (because factory workers had to rush to meet their quotas at the end of their production cycle) and attempted to avoid purchasing them.

Often consumer goods were simply unavailable. Soviet citizens automatically got in line when they saw a queue forming in front of a store because they never knew when something might be available again. When they reached the head of the line, most would purchase several of the same item to swap with their friends and neighbours. Giving in to this "queue psychology," of course, was a time-consuming process and inevitably served to reduce the per capita rate of productivity.

Soviet citizens often tried to overcome the shortcomings of the system by operating "on the left" (the **black market**). Private economic activities, of course, were illegal in the socialized Soviet system, but many workers took to

Courtesy of William J. Duiker

How to Shop in Moscow. Because of the policy of state control over the Soviet economy, the availability of goods was a consequence not of market factors but of decisions made by government bureaucrats. As a result, needed goods were often in short supply. When Soviet citizens heard that a shipment of a particular product had arrived at a state store, they queued up to buy it. Here shoppers line up in front of a store selling dinnerware in Moscow.

"moonlighting" to augment their meagre salaries. An employee in a state-run appliance store, for example, would promise to repair a customer's television set on his own time in return for a payment "under the table." Otherwise, servicing of the set might require several weeks. Knowledgeable observers estimated that as much as one-third of the entire Soviet economy operated outside the legal system.

> The **black market** is an illegal market for buying and trading goods and services.

Another major obstacle to economic growth was inadequate technology. Except in the area of national defence, the overall level of Soviet technology was not comparable to that of the West or the advanced industrial societies of East Asia. Part of the problem, of course, stemmed from the issues already described. With no competition, factory managers had little incentive to improve the quality of their products. But another reason was the high priority assigned to defence. The military sector of the economy regularly received the most resources from the government and attracted the cream of the country's scientific talent.

Why Were There So Many Leaders of the Soviet Union in the 1980s?

Such problems would be intimidating for any government; they were particularly so for the elderly generation of party leaders surrounding Leonid Brezhnev, many of whom were cautious to a fault. While some undoubtedly recognized the need for reform and innovation, they were paralyzed by the fear of instability and change. The problem worsened during the late 1970s, when Brezhnev's health began to deteriorate.

Brezhnev died in November 1982 and was succeeded by Yury Andropov (1914–84), a party veteran and head of the KGB. During his brief tenure as party chief, Andropov was a vocal advocate of reform, but most of his initiatives were limited to the familiar nostrums of punishment for wrong-doers and moral exhortations to Soviet citizens to work harder. At the same time, material incentives were still officially discouraged and generally ineffective. Andropov had been ailing when he was selected to succeed Brezhnev as party chief, and when he died after only a few months in office, little had been done to change the system. He was succeeded, in turn, by a mediocre party stalwart, the elderly Konstantin Chernenko (1911–85). With the Soviet system in crisis, Moscow seemed stuck in a time warp. Each of the three elderly leaders, Brezhnev, Andropov, and Chernenko, died of natural causes within three years of each other—a problem of **gerontocracy**.

> **Gerontocracy** is the governmental rule of elder leaders (in the Soviet case, elder men) who follow old party traditions and policies.

FERMENT IN EASTERN EUROPE

The key to Moscow's security along the western frontier of the Soviet Union was the string of satellite states that had been created in Eastern Europe after World War II (see Map 7.1, Plate 19). Once Communist power had been assured in Warsaw, Prague, Sofia, Budapest, Bucharest, and East Berlin, a series of "little Stalins" put into power by Moscow instituted Soviet-type five-year plans that placed primary emphasis on heavy industry rather than consumer goods, on the collectivization of agriculture, and on the nationalization of industry. They also appropriated the political tactics that Stalin had perfected in the Soviet Union, eliminating all non-Communist parties and establishing the classical institutions of repression—the secret police and military forces. Dissidents were tracked down and thrown into prison, while national Communists who resisted total subservience to the nation were charged with treason in mass show trials and executed.

Despite such repressive efforts, however, Soviet-style policies aroused growing discontent in several Eastern European societies. Hungary, Poland, and Romania harboured bitter memories of past Russian domination and distrusted Stalin. For the vast majority of peoples in Eastern Europe, the imposition of the "people's democracies" (a euphemism invented by Moscow to refer to a society in the early stage of socialist transition) resulted in economic hardship and severe threats to the most basic political liberties.

The first indications of unrest appeared in 1953, when popular riots broke out against Communist rule in East Berlin. The riots eventually subsided, but the virus had begun to spread to neighbouring countries. In Poland, public demonstrations against an increase in food prices in 1956 escalated into widespread protests against the regime's economic policies, restrictions on the freedom of Catholics to practise their religion, and the continued presence of Soviet troops (as called for by the Warsaw Pact)

on Polish soil. In a desperate effort to defuse the unrest, in October the Polish party leader stepped down and was replaced by Wladyslaw Gomulka (1905–82), a popular figure who had previously been demoted for his "nationalist" tendencies. When Gomulka took steps to ease the crisis, the new Soviet party chief, Nikita Khrushchev, flew to Warsaw to warn his Polish colleague against adopting policies that could undermine the "dictatorship of the proletariat" (the Marxist phrase for the political dominance of the party) and even weaken security links with the Soviet Union. After a brief confrontation, during which both sides threatened to use military force to punctuate their demands, Gomulka and Khrushchev reached a compromise according to which Poland would adopt a policy labelled "internal reform, external loyalty." Poland agreed to remain in the Warsaw Pact and to maintain the sanctity of party rule. In return, Warsaw was authorized to adopt domestic reforms, such as easing restrictions on religious practice and ending the policy of forced collectivization in rural areas.

The developments in Poland sent shock waves throughout the region. The impact was the strongest in neighbouring Hungary, where the methods of the local "little Stalin," Mátyás Rákosi, were so brutal that he had been summoned to Moscow for a lecture. In late October in 1956, student-led popular riots broke out in the capital of Budapest and soon spread to other towns and villages throughout the country. Rákosi was forced to resign and was replaced by Imre Nagy (1896–1958), a national Communist who attempted to satisfy popular demands without arousing the anger of Moscow. Unlike Gomulka, however, Nagy was unable to contain the zeal of leading members of the protest movement, who sought major political reforms and the withdrawal of Hungary from the Warsaw Pact. On November 1, Nagy promised free elections, which, given the mood of the country, would probably have brought an end to Communist rule. Moscow decided on firm action. Soviet troops, recently withdrawn at Nagy's request, returned to Budapest and installed a new government under the more pliant party leader János Kádár (1912–89). While Kádár rescinded many of Nagy's measures, Nagy sought refuge in the Yugoslav Embassy. A few weeks later, he left the embassy under the promise of safety but was quickly arrested, convicted of treason, and executed. The dramatic events in Poland and Hungary graphically demonstrated the vulnerability of the Soviet satellite system in Eastern Europe.

The year of discontent was not without its consequences, however. Soviet leaders now recognized that Moscow could maintain control over its satellites in Eastern Europe only by granting them the leeway to adopt domestic policies appropriate to local conditions. Khrushchev had already embarked on this path when, during a visit to Belgrade in 1955, he assured Tito that there were "different roads to socialism." Eastern European Communist leaders now took Khrushchev at his word and adopted reform programs to make socialism more palatable to their subject populations. Even János Kádár, derisively labelled the "butcher of Budapest," managed to preserve many of Imre Nagy's reforms to allow a measure of capitalist incentive and freedom of expression in Hungary.

Czechoslovakia did not share in the thaw of the mid-1950s and remained under the rule of Antonín Novotný (1904–75), who had been placed in power by Stalin himself. By the late 1960s, however, Novotný's policies had led to widespread popular alienation, and in 1968, with the support of intellectuals and reformist party members, Alexander Dubcek (1921–92) was elected first secretary of the Communist Party. He immediately attempted to create what was popularly called "socialism with a human face," relaxing restrictions on freedom of speech and the press and the right to travel abroad. Reforms were announced in the economic sector, and party control over all aspects of society was reduced. A period of euphoria erupted that came to be known as the **Prague Spring**.

> **Prague Spring** refers to a brief period of political liberalization and liberating cultural expression in Czechoslovakia, led by Alexander Dubcek. It proved to be short-lived. Encouraged by Dubcek's actions, some Czechs called for more far-reaching reforms, including neutrality and withdrawal from the Soviet sphere of influence.

In the summer of 1968, when the new Communist Party leaders in Czechoslovakia were seriously considering proposals for reforming the totalitarian system there, the Warsaw Pact nations met under the leadership of Soviet party chief Leonid Brezhnev to assess the threat to the socialist camp. Shortly after, the military forces of several Soviet allied nations entered Czechoslovakia and imposed a new government subservient to Moscow. The move was justified by the spirit of "proletarian internationalism" and was widely viewed as a warning to China and other socialist states not to stray too far from Marxist-Leninist orthodoxy, as interpreted by the Soviet Union. The principle came to be known as the Brezhnev Doctrine (see the box on page 135). To forestall the spread of this "spring fever," the Soviet Red Army, supported by troops from other Warsaw Pact states, invaded Czechoslovakia in August 1968 and crushed the reform movement. Gustav Husak (1913–91), a committed Stalinist, replaced Dubcek and restored the old order.

...sewhere in Eastern Europe, Stalinist policies con-
...d to hold sway. The ruling Communist government in

East Germany, led by Walter Ulbricht, consolidated its position in the early 1950s and became a faithful Soviet satellite. Industry was nationalized and agriculture collectivized. After the 1953 workers' revolt was crushed by Soviet tanks, a steady flight of East Germans to West Germany ensued, primarily through the city of Berlin. This exodus of mostly skilled labourers ("soon only party chief Ulbricht would be left," remarked one Soviet observer cynically) created economic problems, and in 1961 led the East German government to erect the infamous **Berlin Wall** separating West from East Berlin, as well as even more fearsome barriers along the entire border with West Germany.

> The **Berlin Wall** was constructed in 1961 to separate German-controlled East Berlin and American-controlled West Berlin. The wall, which had become a symbol of the Cold War, was torn down in 1989.

After walling off the West, East Germany succeeded in developing the strongest economy among the Soviet Union's Eastern European satellites. In 1971, Walter Ulbricht was succeeded by Erich Honecker (1912–94), a party hard-liner who was deeply committed to the ideological battle against *détente*. Propaganda increased, and the use of the *Stasi,* the secret police, became a hallmark of Honecker's virtual dictatorship. Honecker ruled unchallenged for the next 18 years.

Poland, along with much of Eastern Europe, remained in the firm grip of Soviet communism until the 1970s. However, mass protest to rising food prices and the government's curtailment of religious freedom set the stage for a dramatic turn of events at the arrival of Pope John Paul II (1920–2005) to his homeland in 1979. There and then the Pope delivered 40 or more sermons in the course of 9 days to his fellow Poles on the significance of Christianity in the hearts and history of the Polish people. His speeches inspired the Solidarity movement made up of Polish intellectuals and workers opposed to communism and its atheistic principles. The Pope provided the movement, headed by Lech Walesa (b. 1943), with the moral support it needed to peacefully overthrow the demoralized Communist regime in Poland. The events in Poland had a domino effect on the rest of Eastern Europe. The Pope's visit in 1979, along with his subsequent visits in both 1983 and 1987, is credited with inspiring democracy in the region during this period.

CULTURE AND SOCIETY IN THE SOVIET SPHERE OF INFLUENCE

In his occasional pondering about the future Communist utopia, Karl Marx had predicted the emergence of a classless society to replace the exploitative and hierarchical systems of

THE BREZHNEV DOCTRINE

The Brezhnev Doctrine was introduced by Leonid Brezhnev in a speech in the summer of 1968 in response to the proposed liberalizing reforms of the Communist regime in Czechoslovakia. The doctrine essentially proclaimed to satellite Communist states that they were not to break allegiance with the Soviet Union. Shortly after the doctrine was announced, military forces of several Soviet bloc nations entered Czechoslovakia and imposed a new government subservient to Moscow.

A Letter to Czechoslovakia

To the Central Committee of the Communist Party of Czechoslovakia
Warsaw, July 15, 1968

Dear Comrades!

On behalf of the Central Committees of the Communist and Workers' Parties of Bulgaria, Hungary, the German Democratic Republic, Poland and the Soviet Union, we address ourselves to you with this letter, prompted by a feeling of sincere friendship based on the principles of Marxism-Leninism and proletarian internationalism and by the concern of our common affairs for strengthening the positions of socialism and the security of the socialist community of nations.

The development of events in your country evokes in us deep anxiety. It is our firm conviction that the offensive of the reactionary forces, backed by imperialists, against your Party and the foundations of the social system in the Czechoslovak Socialist Republic, threatens to push your country off the road of socialism and that consequently it jeopardizes the interests of the entire socialist system . . .

We neither had nor have any intention of interfering in such affairs as are strictly the internal business of your Party and your state, nor of violating the principles of respect, independence, and equality in the relations among the Communist Parties and socialist countries . . .

At the same time we cannot agree to have hostile forces push your country from the road of socialism and create a threat of severing Czechoslovakia from the socialist community. . . . This is the common cause of our countries, which have joined in the Warsaw Treaty to ensure independence, peace, and security in Europe, and to set up an insurmountable barrier against aggression and revenge. . . . We shall never agree to have imperialism, using peaceful or non-peaceful methods, making a gap from the inside or from the outside in the socialist system, and changing in imperialism's favour the correlation of forces in Europe . . .

That is why we believe that a decisive rebuff of the anti-communist forces, and decisive efforts for the preservation of the socialist system in Czechoslovakia are not only your task but ours as well . . .

We express the conviction that the Communist Party of Czechoslovakia, conscious of its responsibility, will take the necessary steps to block the path of reaction. In this struggle you can count on the solidarity and all-round assistance of the fraternal socialist countries.

Source: *Moscow News,* Supplement to No. 30 (917), 1968, pp. 3–6.

---

feudalism and capitalism. Workers would take part in productive activities but would share equally in the fruits of their labour. In their free time, they would help produce a new, advanced culture, proletarian in character and egalitarian in content.

How Was Culture Expressed in the Soviet Union?

Beginning in 1946, a series of government decrees made all forms of literary and scientific expression dependent on the state. All Soviet culture was expected to follow the party line. Historians, philosophers, and social scientists all grew accustomed to quoting Marx, Lenin, and above all, Stalin as their chief authorities. Novels and plays, too, were supposed to portray Communist heroes and their efforts to create a better society. Some areas of intellectual activity were virtually abolished; the science of genetics disappeared, and few movies were made during Stalin's final years.

Stalin's death brought a modest respite from cultural repression. Writers and artists banned during Stalin's years were again allowed to publish. Still, Soviet authorities, including Khrushchev, were reluctant to allow cultural freedom to move far beyond official Soviet ideology.

These restrictions, however, did not prevent the emergence of significant Soviet literature, although authors paid a heavy price if they alienated the Soviet authorities. Boris Pasternak (1890–1960), who began his literary career as a poet, won the Nobel Prize in 1958 for his celebrated novel *Doctor Zhivago,* published in Italy in 1957. But the Soviet government condemned Pasternak's anti-Soviet tendencies, banned the novel from the Soviet Union, and would not allow him to accept the prize. The author had alienated the authorities by describing a society scarred by the excesses of Bolshevik revolutionary zeal.

Aleksandr Solzhenitsyn caused an even greater furor than Pasternak. Solzhenitsyn had spent eight years in forced-labour camps for criticizing Stalin, and his *One Day in the Life of Ivan Denisovich,* which won him the Nobel Prize in 1970, was an account of life in those camps. Later, Solzhenitsyn wrote *The Gulag Archipelago,* a detailed indictment of the whole system of Soviet oppression. In response, Soviet authorities denounced Solzhenitsyn's writing and arrested and expelled him from the Soviet Union.

The limited cultural freedom that had arisen during the Khrushchev years was later rejected after his removal from power. Cultural controls were reimposed, de-Stalinization was halted, and authors were again sent to labour camps for expressing outlawed ideas. These restrictive policies continued until the late 1980s.

In the Eastern European satellites, cultural freedom varied considerably from country to country. In Poland, intellectuals had access to Western publications as well as greater freedom to travel to the West. Hungarian and Yugoslav Communists, too, tolerated a certain level of intellectual activity that was not liked but not prohibited. Elsewhere, intellectuals were forced to conform to the regime's demands. After the Soviet invasion of Czechoslovakia in 1968, Czech Communists pursued a policy of strict cultural control.

The socialist camp also experienced the many facets of modern popular culture. By the early 1970s, there were 28 million television sets in the Soviet Union, although state authorities controlled the content of the programs that the Soviet people watched. Tourism, too, made inroads into the Communist world as state-run industries provided vacation time and governments facilitated the establishment of resorts for workers on the coasts of the Black Sea and the Adriatic. In Poland, the number of vacationers who used holiday retreats increased from 700 000 in 1960 to 2.8 million in 1972.

Courtesy of William J. Duiker

Stalinist Heroic: An Example of Socialist Realism. Under Stalin and his successors, art was assigned the task of indoctrinating the Soviet population on the public virtues, such as hard work, loyalty to the state, and patriotism. Grandiose statuary erected to commemorate the heroic efforts of the Red Army during World War II appeared in every Soviet city. Here is an example in Minsk, today the capital of Belarus.

Spectator sports became a large industry and were also highly politicized as the result of Cold War divisions. Victory in international athletic events was viewed as proof of the superiority of the socialist system over its capitalist rival. Accordingly, the state provided money for the construction of gymnasiums and training camps and portrayed athletes as superheroes.

SOCIAL CHANGES IN THE SOVIET UNION AND EASTERN EUROPE

The imposition of Marxist systems in Eastern Europe had far-reaching social consequences. Most Eastern European countries made the change from peasant societies to modern industrialized economies. In Bulgaria, for example, 80 percent of the labour force was in agriculture in 1950, but only 20 percent was still there in 1980. Although the Soviet Union and its Eastern European satellites never achieved the high standards of living of the West, they did experience some improvement. In 1960, the average real income of Polish peasants was four times higher than before World War II. Consumer goods also became more widespread. In East Germany, only 17 percent of families had television sets in 1960, but 75 percent had acquired them by 1972.

According to Marxist doctrine, government control of industry and the elimination of private property were meant to lead to a classless society. Consequently, traditional ruling classes were stripped of their special status after 1945.

The desire to create a classless society led to noticeable changes in education. In some countries, the desire to provide equal educational opportunities led to laws that mandated quota systems based on class. In East Germany, for example, 50 percent of the students in secondary schools had to be children of workers and peasants. In 1964, the sons of manual workers constituted 53 percent of university students in Yugoslavia and 40 percent in East Germany, compared with only 15 percent in Italy and 5.3 percent in West Germany. Social mobility also increased. In Poland in 1961, half of the white-collar workers came from blue-collar families. A significant number of judges, professors, and industrial managers stemmed from working-class backgrounds.

Education became crucial in preparing for new jobs in the Communist system and led to higher enrollments in both secondary schools and universities. In Czechoslovakia, for example, the number of students in secondary schools tripled between 1945 and 1970, and the number of university students quadrupled between the 1930s and the 1960s. The type of education that students received also changed. In Hungary before World War II, 40 percent of students studied law, 9 percent engineering and technology, and

5 percent agriculture. In 1970, the figures were 35 percent in engineering and technology, 9 percent in agriculture, and only 4 percent in law.

By the 1970s, the new managers of society, regardless of class background, realized the importance of higher education and used their power to gain special privileges for their children. By 1971, fully 60 percent of the children of white-collar workers attended a university, and even though blue-collar families constituted 60 percent of the population, only 36 percent of their children attended institutions of higher learning. Even East Germany dropped its requirement that 50 percent of secondary students had to be the offspring of workers and peasants.

This shift in educational preferences demonstrates yet another aspect of the social structure in the Communist world: the emergence of a new privileged class, made up of members of the Communist Party, state officials, high-ranking officers in the military and secret police, and a few special professional groups. The new elite not only possessed political power but also received special privileges, including the right to purchase high-quality goods in special stores (in Czechoslovakia, the elite could obtain organically grown produce not available to anyone else), paid vacations at special resorts, access to good housing and superior medical services, and advantages in education and jobs for their children.

Men dominated the leadership positions of the Communist parties in the Soviet Union and Eastern Europe. Women did have greater opportunities in the workforce and even in the professions, however. In the Soviet Union, women comprised 51 percent of the labour force in 1980; by the mid-1980s, they constituted 50 percent of the engineers, 80 percent of the doctors, and 75 percent of the teachers and teachers' aides. But many of these were low-paying jobs; most female doctors, for example, worked in primary care and were paid less than skilled machinists. The chief administrators in hospitals and schools were still men.

Moreover, although women were part of the workforce, they continued to perform their traditional roles in the home. Most women, as in the West, confronted what came to be known as the **"double day."** After working eight hours in their jobs, they came home to face the housework and care of the children. They might spend two hours a day in long lines at a number of stores waiting to buy food and clothes. Because of the housing situation, they were forced to use kitchens that were shared by a number of families.

> **"Double day"** refers to the double shift most women work in a day, comprising their public/paid work outside the home and their private/unpaid work in the home.

Courtesy of William J. Duiker

Ghosts of Soviet Olympic Glory. A poignant legacy of the collapse of the Soviet Union is reflected in this abandoned skating rink and ski jump in Almaty, Kazakhstan. It was in this rink and on the adjacent ski jump in the mountains of central Asia that the Soviet Union trained its best athletes to win international competitions for gold medals and glory during the Cold War. Here we sense the ghosts of former skaters, subsidized darlings of the Soviet Union, as they attempt the difficult triple jump.

THE DISINTEGRATION OF THE SOVIET UNION

On the death of Konstantin Chernenko in 1985, party leaders selected the talented and vigorous Soviet official Mikhail Gorbachev to succeed him. The new Soviet leader had shown early signs of promise. Born into a peasant family in 1931, Gorbachev combined farm work with school and received the Order of the Red Banner for his agricultural efforts. This award and his good school record enabled him to study law at the University of Moscow. After receiving his law degree in 1955, he returned to his native southern Russia, where he eventually became first secretary of the Communist Party in the city of Stavropol and then first secretary of the regional party committee. In 1978, Gorbachev was made a member of the Central Committee of the Communist Party in Moscow. Two years later, he became a full member of the ruling politburo and secretary of the Central Committee.

During the early 1980s, Gorbachev began to realize the extent of Soviet problems and the crucial importance of massive reform to transform the system. During a visit to Canada in 1983, he discovered to his astonishment that Canadian farmers worked hard on their own initiative.

"We'll never have this for fifty years," he reportedly remarked.[3] On his return to Moscow, he established a series of committees to evaluate the inefficiencies in Soviet agricultural policies and recommend measures to improve the agricultural system.

How Did Gorbachev's *Perestroika* and *Glasnost* Lead to the Soviet Union's Demise?

With his election as party general secretary in 1985, Gorbachev seemed intent on taking earlier reforms to their logical conclusions. The cornerstone of his reform program was **perestroika** ("restructuring"). At first, *perestroika* meant only a reordering of economic policy, as Gorbachev called for the beginning of a market economy with limited free enterprise and some private property. Initial economic reforms were difficult to implement, however. Radicals demanded decisive measures; conservatives feared that rapid changes would be too painful. In his attempt to achieve compromise, Gorbachev often pursued partial liberalization, which satisfied neither faction and also failed to work, producing only more discontent.

> **Perestroika** (Russian for "restructuring") was Mikhail Gorbachev's attempt to modernize the Soviet command economy by decentralizing production and moving to a more market-based system.

Gorbachev soon perceived that in the Soviet system, the economic sphere was intimately tied to the social and political spheres. Any efforts to reform the economy without political or social reform would be doomed to failure. One of the most important instruments of *perestroika* was **glasnost** ("openness"). Soviet citizens and officials were encouraged to openly discuss the strengths and weaknesses of the Soviet Union. This policy could be seen in *Pravda*, the official newspaper of the Communist Party, where disasters such as the nuclear accident at Chernobyl in 1986 and collisions of ships in the Black Sea received increasing coverage. Soon this type of reporting was extended to include reports of official corruption, sloppy factory work, and protests against government policy. The arts also benefited from the new policy as previously banned works were now allowed to circulate and motion pictures began to depict negative aspects of Soviet life. Music based on Western styles, such as jazz and rock, began to be performed openly.

> **Glasnost** (Russian for "openness") was Mikhail Gorbachev's attempt to relax state constraints on intellectual thought, cultural expression, and media content.

Political reforms were equally revolutionary. In June 1987, the principle of two-candidate elections was introduced; previously, voters had been presented with only one candidate. Most dissidents, including Andrey Sakharov, who had spent years in internal exile, were released. At the Communist Party conference in 1988, Gorbachev called for the creation of a new Soviet parliament, the Congress of People's Deputies, whose members were to be chosen in competitive elections. It convened in 1989, the first such meeting since 1918. Now as an elected member of the Congress, Sakharov called for an end to the Communist monopoly of power and on December 11, 1989, the day he died, urged the creation of a new, non-Communist party. Early in 1990, Gorbachev legalized the formation of other political parties and struck out Article 6 of the Soviet constitution, which guaranteed the "leading role" of the Communist Party. Hitherto, the position of first secretary of the party was the most important post in the Soviet Union, but as the Communist Party became less closely associated with the state, the powers of this office diminished.

Gorbachev attempted to consolidate his power by creating a new state presidency, and in March 1990, he became the Soviet Union's first president.

One of Gorbachev's most serious problems stemmed from the nature of the Soviet Union. The Union of Soviet Socialist Republics was a truly multiethnic country, containing 92 nationalities and 112 recognized languages. Previously, the iron hand of the Communist Party, centred in Moscow, had kept a lid on the centuries-old ethnic tensions that had periodically erupted throughout the history of this region. As Gorbachev released this iron grip, tensions resurfaced, a by-product of *glasnost* that Gorbachev had not anticipated. Ethnic groups took advantage of the new openness to protest what they perceived to be ethnically motivated slights. As violence erupted, the Soviet army, in disarray since the Soviet intervention in Afghanistan in 1979, had difficulty controlling the situation. In some cases, independence movements and ethnic causes became linked, as in Azerbaijan, where the National Front became the voice of Muslim Azerbaijanis in the conflict with Christian Armenians.

The period from 1988 to 1990 witnessed the emergence of nationalist movements in all 15 republics of the Soviet Union. Often motivated by ethnic concerns, many of them called for sovereignty of the republics and independence from Russian-based rule centred in Moscow. Such movements sprang up first in Georgia in late 1988 and then in Moldavia, Uzbekistan, Azerbaijan, and the three Baltic republics.

In December 1989, the Communist Party of Lithuania declared itself independent of the Communist Party of the Soviet Union. Gorbachev made it clear that he supported self-determination but not secession, which he believed would be detrimental to the Soviet Union. Nevertheless, on March 11, 1990, the Lithuanian Supreme Council unilaterally declared Lithuania independent. Its formal name was now the Lithuanian Republic; the adjectives Soviet and Socialist had been dropped. On March 15, the Soviet Congress of People's Deputies, though recognizing a general right to secede from the Union of Soviet Socialist Republics, declared the Lithuanian declaration null and void; the Congress stated that proper procedures must be established and followed before secession would be acceptable.

During 1990 and 1991, Gorbachev struggled to deal with the problems unleashed by his reforms. On the one hand, he tried to appease the conservative forces who complained about the growing disorder within the Soviet Union. On the other hand, he tried to accommodate the liberal forces who increasingly favoured a new kind of decentralized Soviet federation. Gorbachev especially laboured to cooperate more closely with Boris Yeltsin (b. 1931), elected president of the Russian Republic in

June 1991. Conservative elements from the army, the party, and the KGB, however, had grown increasingly worried about the potential dissolution of the Soviet Union. On August 19, 1991, a group of these discontented rightists arrested Gorbachev and attempted to seize power. Gorbachev's unwillingness to work with the conspirators and the resistance in Moscow of Yeltsin and thousands of Russians who had grown accustomed to their new liberties caused the coup to disintegrate rapidly. The actions of these right-wing plotters served to accelerate the very process they had hoped to stop—the disintegration of the Soviet Union.

Despite desperate pleas from Gorbachev, all 15 republics soon opted for complete independence (see Map 7.2, Plate 20). Ukraine voted for independence on December 1, 1991. A week later, the leaders of Russia, Ukraine, and Belarus announced that the Soviet Union had "ceased to exist" and would be replaced by a much looser federation, the **Commonwealth of Independent States** (CIS). Gorbachev resigned on December 25, 1991, and turned over his responsibilities as commander in chief to Boris Yeltsin, the president of Russia. By the end of 1991, one of the largest empires in world history had come to an end, and a new era had begun in its lands.

> The **Commonwealth of Independent States** (CIS) was created in 1991, composed of many of the smaller, former Soviet states and Russia that wanted continued economic cooperation in a looser federation.

Why Were Reforms So Difficult to Implement in the New Russia?

In Russia, by far the largest of the former Soviet republics, a new power struggle soon ensued. Yeltsin, a one-time engineer who had been dismissed from the politburo in 1987 for his radicalism, was committed to introducing a free market economy as quickly as possible. In December 1991, the Congress of People's Deputies granted Yeltsin temporary power to rule by decree. But former Communist Party members and their allies in the Congress were opposed to many of Yeltsin's economic reforms and tried to place new limits on his powers. Yeltsin fought back. After winning a vote of confidence on April 25, 1993, Yeltsin pushed ahead with plans for a new Russian constitution that would abolish the Congress of People's Deputies, create a two-chamber parliament, and establish a strong presidency. A hard-line parliamentary minority resisted and in early October took the offensive, urging supporters to take over government offices and the central television station. Yeltsin

responded by ordering military forces to storm the parliament building and arrest hard-line opponents. Yeltsin used his victory to consolidate his power in parliamentary elections held in December.

During the mid-1990s, Yeltsin was able to maintain a precarious grip on power while seeking to implement reforms that would place Russia on a firm course toward a pluralistic political system and a market economy. But the new post-Communist Russia remained as fragile as ever. Burgeoning economic inequality and rampant corruption aroused widespread criticism and shook the confidence of the Russian people in the superiority of the capitalist system over the one that existed under Communist rule. A nagging war in the Caucasus—where the Muslim people of Chechnya sought self-determination and independence from Russia—drained the government budget and exposed the decrepit state of the once-vaunted Red Army. In presidential elections held in 1996, Yeltsin was reelected, but the rising popularity of a revived Communist Party and the growing strength of nationalist elements, combined with Yeltsin's precarious health and reported alcoholism, raised serious questions about the future of the country.

At the end of 1999, Yeltsin suddenly resigned his office and was replaced by Vladimir Putin (b. 1952), a former member of the KGB. Putin vowed to bring an end to the rampant corruption and inexperience that permeated Russian political culture and to strengthen the role of the central government in managing the affairs of state. During succeeding months, his proposal to centralize power in the hands of the federal government in Moscow was given approval by the parliament; in early 2001, he presented a new plan to regulate political parties, which had risen in number to more than 50. Parties at both extremes of the political spectrum, those representing Western-style liberal policies and a revived Communist Party, opposed the legislation, without success. Putin has not used his enhanced powers, however, to introduce market reforms and rein in the powerful forces that have impeded Russia's transition to an advanced capitalist society.

Putin also vowed to bring the breakaway state of Chechnya back under Russian authority and to adopt a more assertive role in international affairs. The new president took advantage of growing public anger at Western plans to expand the NATO alliance into Eastern Europe, as well as public anger against aggressive actions by NATO countries against Serbia in the Balkans (see Chapter 8, pages 149–50) to restore Russia's position as an influential force in the world. Moscow has also improved relations with neighbouring China and simultaneously sought to cooperate with European nations on issues of common concern. To ease national pride, Putin has entered negotiations with such former republics of the old

Soviet Union as Belarus and Ukraine to tighten forms of mutual political economic cooperation.

What had happened to derail Yeltsin's plan to transform Soviet society? To some critics, Yeltsin and his advisers tried to achieve too much too fast. Between 1991 and 1995, state firms that had previously provided about 80 percent of all industrial production and employment had been privatized, and the price of goods (previously subject to government regulation) was opened up to market forces. Only agriculture—where the decision to privatize collective farms had little impact in rural areas—was left substantially untouched. The immediate results were disastrous: industrial output dropped by more than one-third, and unemployment levels and prices rose dramatically. Many Russian workers and soldiers were not paid their salaries for months on end, and many social services came to an abrupt halt. With the harsh official and ideological constraints of the Soviet system suddenly removed, corruption—labelled by one observer as "criminal gang capitalism"—became rampant, and the government often appeared inept in coping with complexities of a market economy. Transition to a market-led economy was a difficult path for Russia and its people.

EASTERN EUROPE: FROM SOVIET SATELLITES TO SOVEREIGN NATIONS

The disintegration of the Soviet Union had an immediate impact on its neighbours to the west. First to respond, as in 1956, was Poland, where popular protests of high food prices had erupted in the early 1980s, leading to the rise of an independent labour movement called *Solidarity*. Headed by Lech Walesa, the Solidarity movement rapidly became an influential force for change and a threat to the government's monopoly of power. The union was outlawed in 1981, but martial law did not solve Poland's serious economic problems, and in 1988, the Communist government bowed to the inevitable and permitted free national elections to take place, resulting in the election of Walesa as president of Poland in December 1990. Unlike the situation in 1956, when Khrushchev had intervened to prevent the collapse of the Soviet satellite system in Eastern Europe, in the late 1980s, Moscow—inspired by Gorbachev's policy of encouraging "new thinking" to improve relations with the Western powers—took no action to reverse the verdict in Warsaw.

In Hungary, as in Poland, the process of transition had begun many years previously. After crushing the Hungarian revolution of 1956, the Communist government of János Kádár had tried to assuage popular opinion by enacting a series of far-reaching economic reforms (labelled

"communism with a capitalist face-lift"), but as the 1980s progressed, the economy sagged, and in 1989, the regime permitted the formation of opposition political parties, leading eventually to the formation of a non-Communist coalition government in elections held in March 1990.

The transition in Czechoslovakia was more abrupt. After Soviet troops crushed the Prague Spring in 1968, hard-line Communists under Gustav Husak followed a policy of massive repression to maintain their power. In 1977, dissident intellectuals formed an organization called Charter 77 as a vehicle for protest against violations of human rights. Regardless of the repressive atmosphere, dissident activities continued to grow during the 1980s, and when massive demonstrations broke out in several major cities in 1989, President Husak's government, lacking any real popular support, collapsed. At the end of December, he was replaced by Václav Havel (b. 1936), a dissident playwright who had been a leading figure in Charter 77.

But the most dramatic events took place in East Germany, where a persistent economic slump and the ongoing oppressiveness of the regime of Erich Honecker led to a flight of refugees and mass demonstrations against the regime in the summer and fall of 1989. Capitulating to popular pressure, the Communist government opened its entire border with the West. The Berlin Wall, the most tangible symbol of the Cold War, became the site of a massive celebration, and most of it was dismantled by joyful Germans from both sides of the border. In March 1990, free elections led to the formation of a non-Communist government that rapidly carried out a program of political and economic reunification with West Germany.

The dissolution of the Soviet Union and its satellite system in Eastern Europe brought a dramatic end to the Cold War. At the dawn of the 1990s, a generation of global rivalry between two ideological systems had come to a close, and world leaders turned their attention to the construction of a New World Order—one no longer characterized by ideological rivalry.

CONCLUSION

The Soviet Union had emerged from World War II as one of the world's two superpowers. Its armies had played an instrumental role in the final defeat of the powerful German war machine and had installed puppet Communist regimes throughout Eastern Europe.

- Soviet military and economic performance during the first post-war decade was sufficiently impressive.
- By the mid-1980s, however, fears that the Soviet Union would surpass the United States as an economic power had long since dissipated.

- The Soviet system appeared to be mired in a state of near paralysis. Economic growth had slowed, corruption had reached epidemic levels, and leadership had passed to a generation of elderly party bureaucrats.

It seems in retrospect that the Soviet command economy proved better at managing the early stages of the Industrial Revolution than at moving on to the next stage of an advanced technological society.

- The Leninist view of "democracy" failed to provide the quality of leadership needed to cope with the challenges of nation building.
- By the 1980s, behind the powerful shield of the Red Army, the Soviet system had become an empty shell.

The perceptive reformer Mikhail Gorbachev had recognized the crucial importance of instituting radical social, economic, and political changes in the Soviet Union.

- Initially, he hoped that through reform, he could save the socialist system.
- However, the momentum of *glasnost* and *perestroika* could not be stopped.

CRITICAL THINKING QUESTIONS

1. Did the United States overestimate the Soviet threat? After all, the Soviet people had much lower standards of living, and technological production was not up to par with the United States.

2. Should there be a minimum age and a maximum age for political leaders?

3. Some have argued that the West did not want the Prague Spring to succeed because it would have shown that a democratic socialist regime can flourish. What do you think?

4. The move to greater freedom of expression initiated by Nikita Khrushchev was eventually counteracted. Why didn't *glasnost* suffer the same fate?

CHAPTER NOTES

1. Vladislav Zubok and Constantin Pleshakov, *Inside the Kremlin's Cold War: From Stalin to Khrushchev* (Cambridge, Mass.: Harvard University Press, 1996), p. 166.

2. Nikita Khrushchev, *Khrushchev Remembers,* trans. Strobe Talbott (Boston: Little Brown and Company, 1970), p. 77.

3. Hedrick Smith, *The New Russians* (New York: Harper Perennial, 1991), p. 74.

Chapter 8

Post-War Europe: On the Path to Unity?

After World War II, to meet the needs of its people, Europe faced the challenge of either modernizing social, political, and economic systems along market-capitalist lines or succumbing to the socialist path of state-led economic and social systems. Populist pressures for economic redistribution, however, were subdued by economic prosperity. Between 1945 and 1970, Europe experienced an economic resurgence that seemed nothing less than miraculous and that helped contain demands for social redistribution. The economic prosperity of the post-war years helped pacify radical social elements and prompted leftist elements to work within the system for progressive change. Economic growth and virtual full employment continued so long that the first post-war recession, in 1973, came as a shock to Western Europe. The economic recession was short-lived, however, and economic growth returned. After the collapse of Communist governments in the revolutions of 1989, a number of Eastern European states sought to create market economies and join the military and economic unions first formed by Western European states.

At the conclusion of this chapter, you will be able to

- describe the importance of economic growth to democratization;
- identify the factors leading to the unification and disintegration of artificial states;
- identify the major changes to society in post-war Europe;
- explain why the European Union arose.

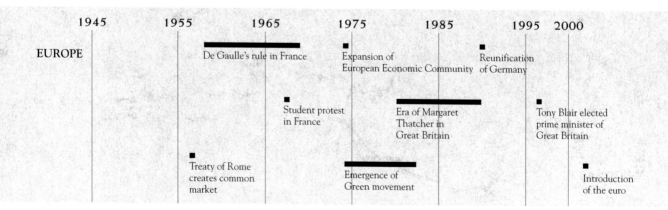

WESTERN EUROPE: RECOVERY AND RENEWAL

In the immediate post-war era, the challenge was clear and intimidating. The peoples of Europe needed to rebuild their national economies and re-establish and strengthen their democratic institutions. They needed to find the means to cooperate in the face of a potential new threat from the east in the form of the Soviet Union. Above all, they needed to restore their confidence in the continuing vitality and future promise of European civilization—a civilization whose image had been badly tarnished by two bitter internal conflicts in the space of a quarter century.

Why Was Democracy in Post-War Europe Tied to Economic Growth?

With the economic aid of the Marshall Plan, the countries of Western Europe (see Map 8.1, Plate 21) recovered relatively rapidly from the devastation of World War II. Between 1947 and 1950, European countries received US$9.4 billion to be used for new equipment and raw materials to be purchased from the United States and Canada. By the late 1970s, industrial production had surpassed all previous records, and Western Europe experienced virtually full employment. Social welfare programs included

© William Vandivert/Time Life Pictures/Getty Images

Armageddon, 1945. In the last months of World War II, the German capital of Berlin was exposed to a relentless bombing campaign by the Allied forces. As the war came to an end in May 1945, the once-stylish city was in ruins. Shown here is a view of Berlin's most fashionable street, Unter den Linden. In the foreground is Brandenburg Gate, soon to become the point of division between East and West Berlin.

affordable health care; housing; family allowances to provide a minimum level of material care for children; increases in sickness, accident, unemployment, and old-age benefits; and educational opportunities. Despite economic recessions in the mid-1970s and early 1980s, caused in part by a dramatic increase in the price of oil in 1973, the economies of Western Europe had never been so prosperous. Western Europeans were full participants in the technological advances of the age and seemed quite capable of standing up to competition from the other global economic powerhouses—namely, Japan and the United States.

At the end of World War II, the ability of democratic institutions to meet the challenge of the industrial era was at a critical juncture. As the war finally came to a close, many Europeans, attracted to the social equity promised by socialist ideals, turned their eyes to the Soviet model. In France and Italy, local Communist parties received wide support in national elections.

By the late 1940s, however, democratic institutions began to revive as economic conditions started to improve. Even Spain and Portugal, which retained their pre-war dictatorial regimes until the mid-1970s, established democratic systems in the late 1970s. Moderate political parties, especially the Christian Democrats in Italy and Germany, played a particularly important role in Europe's economic restoration. Overall, the influence of Communist parties declined, although reformist mass parties only slightly left of centre, such as the Labour Party in Great Britain and the Social Democrats in West Germany, continued to share power. During the mid-1970s, a new variety of communism, called *Eurocommunism,* emerged briefly when Communist parties tried to work within the democratic system as mass movements committed to better government. But by the 1980s, internal political developments in Western Europe and events within the Communist world had combined to undermine the Eurocommunist experiment.

FRANCE: EXPECTATIONS OF GRANDEUR

The history of France for nearly a quarter century after the war was dominated by one man, Charles de Gaulle (1890–1970), who possessed an unshakable faith in his own historic mission to re-establish the greatness of the French nation. De Gaulle was also skeptical about U.S. commitments to protect France, and Europe, from Soviet intervention. During the war, de Gaulle had assumed leadership of resistance groups known as the "Free French," and he played an important role in ensuring the establishment of a French provisional government after the war. But the creation immediately following the war of the Fourth Republic, with

a return to a multiparty parliamentary system that de Gaulle considered inefficient, led him to withdraw temporarily from politics. Eventually, he formed the Rally of the French People, a political organization based on conservative principles that blamed the party system for France's political mess and called for a stronger presidency, a goal—and role—that de Gaulle finally achieved in 1958.

At the time of his election as president, the fragile political stability of the Fourth Republic was shaken by a crisis in Algeria, France's large North African colony. The French army, having suffered a humiliating defeat in Indochina in 1954, was determined to resist demands for independence by Algeria's Arab majority. The elite and privileged French colonists living in Algeria also opposed giving the Arab majority their independence. But a strong anti-war movement among French intellectuals and church leaders led to bitter divisions in France that opened the door to the possibility of civil war. The panic-stricken leaders of the Fourth Republic offered to let de Gaulle take over the government and revise the constitution.

In 1958, de Gaulle drafted a new constitution for a Fifth Republic that greatly enhanced the power of the French president, who now had the right to choose the prime minister, dissolve Parliament, and supervise both defence and foreign policy. As the new president, de Gaulle sought to return France to a position of power and influence. In the belief that an independent role in the Cold War might enhance French stature, he pulled France out of the NATO high command. He sought to increase French prestige in the Third World by consenting to Algerian independence—after a bloody fight for Arab self-determination and justice that led to the death of a million Arab Algerians—despite strenuous opposition from the army. He offered French colonies in Africa membership in a new French community of nations under French tutelage. France invested heavily in the nuclear arms race and exploded its first nuclear bomb in 1960. Despite his successes, however, de Gaulle did not really achieve his ambitious goals of world power.

Although the cost of the nuclear program increased the defence budget, de Gaulle did not neglect the French economy. Economic decision making was centralized, a reflection of the overall centralization undertaken by the Gaullist government. Between 1958 and 1968, the French gross national product (GNP) experienced an annual increase of 5.5 percent. By the end of the Gaullist era, France was a major industrial producer and exporter, particularly in such areas as automobiles and armaments. Nevertheless, problems remained. The expansion of traditional industries, such as coal, steel, and railroads, which had all been nationalized, led to large government deficits. The cost of living increased faster than in the rest of Europe.

Public dissatisfaction with the government's inability to deal with these problems soon led to more violent action. In May 1968, a series of student protests and a general strike by the labour unions led to public protest. Although de Gaulle managed to restore order, the events of May 1968 seriously undermined popular respect for the aloof and imperious president. Tired and discouraged, de Gaulle resigned from office in April 1969 and died within a year.

During the 1970s, the French economic situation worsened, bringing about a political shift to the left. By 1981, the Socialists had become the dominant party in the National Assembly, and the veteran Socialist leader, François Mitterrand (1916–96), was elected president. Mitterrand's first concern was to resolve France's economic difficulties. In 1982, he froze prices and wages in the hope of reducing the huge budget deficit and high inflation. Mitterrand also passed a number of measures to aid workers: an increased minimum wage, expanded social benefits, a mandatory fifth week of paid vacation for salaried workers, a 39-hour workweek, and higher taxes for the rich. Mitterrand's administrative reforms included both centralization (nationalization of banks and industry) and decentralization (granting local governments greater powers). Their victory also convinced the Socialists that they could enact some of their nationalistic reforms. Consequently, the government nationalized the steel industry, major banks, the space and electronics industries, and important insurance firms.

WEST GERMANY: THE ECONOMIC MIRACLE

The unification of the three western zones into the Federal Republic of Germany (West Germany) became a reality in 1949. Konrad Adenauer (1876–1967), the leader of the Christian Democratic Union (CDU), served as chancellor from 1949 to 1963 and became the "founding hero" of the Federal Republic. Adenauer, who had opposed Adolf Hitler and his tyrannical regime, sought respect for Germany by cooperating with the United States and the other Western European nations. He was especially desirous of reconciliation with France—Germany's long-time rival. The beginning of the Korean War in June 1950 had unexpected repercussions for West Germany. The fear that South Korea might fall to the Communists led many in the West to worry about the security of West Germany and inspired calls for German rearmament. Although some people, concerned about a revival of German militarism, condemned this proposal, Cold War tensions were decisive. West Germany rearmed in 1955 and became a member of NATO.

The Adenauer era witnessed the resurrection of the West German economy, often referred to as the "economic miracle." Although West Germany had only 75 percent of the population and 52 percent of the territory of pre-war Germany, by 1955 the West German GNP exceeded that of

© Raimond-Dityvon/Viva/Woodfin Camp & Associates

Student Revolt in Paris, 1968. The discontent of university students exploded in the late 1960s in a series of student demonstrations. Perhaps best known was the movement in Paris in 1968. This photo shows the barricades erected on a Paris street on the morning of May 11 at the height of the revolt.

pre-war Germany. Real wages doubled between 1950 and 1965, even though work hours were cut by 20 percent. Unemployment fell from 8 percent in 1950 to 0.4 percent in 1965. To maintain its economic expansion, West Germany imported hundreds of thousands of "guest" workers—who remained decades without many of the rights and benefits of other German workers—primarily from Italy, Spain, Greece, Turkey, and Yugoslavia.

The capital of the Federal Republic had been placed at Bonn, a sleepy market town on the Rhine River, to erase memories of the Nazi era, when the capital was at Berlin. Still, the country was troubled by its past. The surviving major Nazi leaders had been tried and condemned as war criminals at the **Nuremberg trials** in 1945 and 1946. As part of the de-Nazification of Germany, the victorious Allies continued to try lesser officials for war crimes, but these trials diminished in number as the Cold War produced a shift in attitudes. By 1950, German courts had begun to take over the war crimes trials, and the German legal machine persisted in prosecuting cases. Beginning in 1953, the West German government also began to make payments to Israel and to Holocaust survivors and their relatives to make some restitution for, in the words of German president Richard von Weizsäcker, "the unspeakable sorrow that occurred in the name of Germany."

> The **Nuremberg trials** were convened by the International Military Tribunal to try suspected Nazis charged with "crimes against humanity."

After the Adenauer era ended in the mid-1960s, the Social Democrats became the leading party. By forming a ruling coalition with the small Free Democratic Party, the Social Democrats remained in power until 1982. The first Social Democratic chancellor was Willy Brandt (1913–92). Brandt was especially successful with his policy of "opening toward the east" (known as ***Ostpolitik***), for which he received the Nobel Peace Prize in 1972. On March 19, 1971, Brandt met with Walter Ulbricht, the leader of East Germany, and worked out the details of a treaty that was signed in 1972. This agreement, referred to as the Basic Treaty, did not establish full diplomatic relations with East Germany but did call for "good neighbourly" relations. As a result, it led to greater cultural, personal, and economic contacts between West and East Germany. Despite this success, the discovery of an East German spy among Brandt's advisers caused his resignation in 1974.

> ***Ostpolitik*** (German for "opening toward the east") was a West German policy of reconciliation with East Germany.

Brandt's successor, Helmut Schmidt (b. 1918), was more of a technocrat than a reform-minded socialist and concentrated on the economic problems brought about largely by high oil prices between 1973 and 1975. Schmidt was successful in eliminating a deficit of 10 billion marks in three years. In 1982, when the coalition of Schmidt's Social Democrats with the Free Democrats fell apart over the reduction of social welfare expenditures, the Free Democrats joined with the Christian Democratic Union of Helmut Kohl (b. 1930) to form a new government.

GREAT BRITAIN: SUNSET FOR THE EMPIRE

The end of World War II left Great Britain with massive economic problems. In elections held immediately after the war, the Labour Party overwhelmingly defeated Churchill's Conservative Party. It had promised far-reaching reforms, particularly in the area of social welfare—an appealing platform in a country with a tremendous shortage of consumer goods and housing. Clement Attlee (1883–1967), the new prime minister, was a pragmatic reformer rather than the leftist revolutionary that Churchill had chided during the election campaign. His Labour government proceeded to enact reforms that created a modern welfare state.

The establishment of the British welfare state began with the nationalization of the Bank of England, the coal and steel industries, public transportation, and public utilities such as electricity and gas. In the area of social welfare, the new government enacted the National Insurance Act and the National Health Service Act, both in 1946. The insurance act established a comprehensive social security program and nationalized medical insurance, thereby enabling the state to subsidize the unemployed, the sick, and the aged. The health act created a system of socialized medicine that forced doctors and dentists to work with state hospitals, although private practices could be maintained. This measure was especially costly for the state, but within a few years, 90 percent of the medical profession was participating. The British welfare state became the model for most European countries after the war.

The cost of building a welfare state at home forced the British to reduce expenses abroad. This meant dismantling the British Empire and reducing military aid to such countries as Greece and Turkey, a decision that inspired the enunciation in Washington of the Truman Doctrine (see Chapter 6, page 115). It was not only the British government's belief in the right of the colonies to self-determination but also economic necessity that brought an end to the British Empire.

Continuing economic problems brought the Conservatives back into power from 1951 to 1964. Although they favoured private enterprise, the Conservatives accepted the welfare state and even extended it, undertaking an ambitious construction program to improve British housing. Although the British economy had recovered from the war, it had done so at a slower rate than other European countries. This slow recovery masked a long-term economic decline caused by a variety of factors, including trade union demands for wages that rose faster than productivity and the unwillingness of factory owners to invest in modern industrial machinery and to adopt new methods. Underlying the immediate problems, however, was a deeper issue. As a result of World War II, Great Britain had lost much of its pre-war revenue from abroad and was left with a burden of debt from its many international commitments. At the same time, with the rise of the United States and the Soviet Union, Great Britain's ability to play the role of a world power declined substantially.

Between 1964 and 1979, Conservatives and Labour alternated in power. Both parties faced seemingly intractable problems. Although separatist movements in Scotland and Wales were overcome, a dispute between Catholics and Protestants in Northern Ireland was marked by violence as the rebel Irish Republican Army (IRA) staged a series of dramatic terrorist acts in response to the suspension of Northern Ireland's Parliament in 1972 and the establishment of direct rule by London. The problem of Northern Ireland remained unresolved. Nor was either party able to deal with Great Britain's ailing economy. Failure to modernize made British industry less and less competitive. Great Britain was also hampered by frequent labour strikes, many of them caused by conflicts between rival labour unions.

In 1979, after five years of Labour government and worsening economic problems, the Conservatives returned to power under Margaret Thatcher (b. 1925), the first woman prime minister in British history. Thatcher pledged to lower taxes, reduce government bureaucracy, limit social welfare, restrict union power, and end inflation. The "Iron Lady," as she was called, did break the power of the labour unions. Although she did not eliminate the basic components of the social welfare system, she did use austerity measures to control inflation. **"Thatcherism,"** as her economic policy was termed, improved the British economic situation, but at a great price. The south of England, for example, prospered, but the old industrial areas of the Midlands and north declined and were beset by high unemployment, poverty, and sporadic violence. Cutbacks in funding for education seriously undermined the quality of British schools, which had been long regarded as among the world's finest.

"Thatcherism" is a pro–free market approach to running Great Britain's economy associated with Margaret Thatcher's government (1979–90); most notably, it included the privatization of state-owned industries and the promotion of individual entrepreneurs.

In foreign policy, Thatcher took a hard-line approach against communism. She oversaw a large military buildup aimed at replacing older technology and re-establishing Great Britain as a world police force. In 1982, when Argentina attempted to take control of the Falkland Islands (one of Great Britain's few remaining colonial outposts, known to Argentineans as *Islas Malvinas*) 480 kilometres off its coast, the British successfully rebuffed the Argentineans, although at considerable economic cost and the loss of about 250 British lives. The Falkland Islands War, however, did generate popular support for Thatcher, as many in Great Britain revelled in memories of the nation's glorious imperial past.

Why Wasn't Western Europe Ready for Political and Diplomatic Unity?

As we have seen, the divisions created by the Cold War led the nations of Western Europe to form NATO in 1949. But military cooperation was not the only kind of unity fostered in Europe after 1945. The destructiveness of two world wars caused many Europeans to consider the need for additional forms of integration. National feeling was still too powerful, however, for European nations to give up their political sovereignty. Consequently, the quest for unity focused primarily on the economic arena rather than the political one.

In 1952, France, West Germany, the Benelux countries (Belgium, the Netherlands, and Luxembourg), and Italy formed the European Coal and Steel Community (ECSC). Its purpose was to create a common market for coal and steel products among the six nations by eliminating tariffs and other trade barriers. The success of the ECSC encouraged its members to proceed further, and in 1957 they signed a treaty in Rome to create the European Atomic Energy Community (EURATOM) to further European research on the peaceful uses of nuclear energy. At the same time, the same six nations signed another treaty, which created the **European Economic Community** (EEC), also known as the *Common Market*. The EEC eliminated customs barriers among the six member nations and created a large free-trade area protected from the rest of the world by a common external tariff. By promoting free trade, the EEC also encouraged cooperation and standardization in many aspects of the six nations' economies. All the member nations benefited economically.

> The **European Economic Community** (EEC) was established in 1957 by several Western European states to form an economic bloc that would harmonize economic, social, and regulatory policies. The successor to the EEC is the European Union, a political federation established in 1993.

Europeans moved toward further integration of their economies after 1970. The EEC was expanded in 1973 when Great Britain, Ireland, and Denmark gained membership in what its members now began to call the European Community (EC). By 1986, three more members—Spain, Portugal, and Greece—had been added. The economic integration of the members of the EC led to cooperative efforts in international and political affairs as well. The foreign ministers of the 12 members consulted frequently and provided a common front in negotiations on important issues.

EUROPE REUNITED: THE CURTAIN RISES

The fall of Communist governments in Eastern Europe during the revolutions of 1989 brought a tidal wave of change to Europe. The new structures meant an end to a post-war European order, and throughout 1989 and 1990, new governments throughout Eastern Europe worked diligently to scrap the remnants of the old system and introduce the democratic procedures and market systems they believed would revitalize their lands. But this process proved to be neither simple nor easy.

Most Eastern European countries had little or no experience with democratic systems. Then, too, ethnic divisions, which had troubled these areas before World War II and had been forcibly submerged under Communist rule, reemerged with a vengeance. Finally, the rapid conversion to market economies also proved painful. The adoption of "shock therapy" austerity measures produced much suffering. Unemployment, for example, climbed to over 13 percent in Poland in 1992.

Nevertheless, by the beginning of the twenty-first century, many of these states, especially Poland and the Czech Republic, were making a successful transition to both free markets and democracy. In Poland, Aleksander Kwasniewski, although a former Communist, was elected president in November 1995 and pushed Poland toward an increasingly prosperous free market economy. His success brought his re-election in October 2000. In Czechoslovakia, the shift to non-Communist rule was complicated by old problems, especially ethnic issues. Czechs and Slovaks disagreed over the makeup of the new state but were able to agree to a peaceful division of the country. On January 1, 1993, Czechoslovakia split into the Czech Republic and Slovakia (see Map 8.2, Plate 22).

Why Did Yugoslavia Disintegrate?

The most difficult transition to the post–Cold War era in Eastern Europe was undoubtedly in Yugoslavia. From its beginning in 1919, Yugoslavia had been an artificial creation of different ethnic and religious groups held by the glue of an authoritarian regime. After World War II, the socialist Marshal Josip Broz (Tito) had managed to hold its six republics and two autonomous provinces together. After his death in 1980, no strong leader emerged, and his responsibilities passed to a collective state presidency and the League of Communists of Yugoslavia. At the end of the 1980s, Yugoslavia was caught up in the reform movements sweeping through Eastern Europe. The League of Communists collapsed, and new parties quickly emerged.

The Yugoslavian political scene was complicated by the development of separatist movements. In 1990, the republics of Slovenia, Croatia, Bosnia-Herzegovina, and Macedonia began to lobby for a new federal structure of Yugoslavia that would fulfill their separatist desires. Slobodan Milosevic, who had become the leader of the Serbian Communist Party in 1987 and had managed to stay in power by emphasizing his Serbian nationalism, rejected these efforts. He asserted that these republics could be independent only if new border arrangements were made to accommodate the Serb minorities in those republics who did not want to live outside the boundaries of Serbia. Serbs constituted about 12 percent of Croatia's population and 32 percent of Bosnia's.

After negotiations among the six republics failed, Slovenia and Croatia declared their independence in June 1991. Milosevic's government sent the Yugoslavian army, which it controlled, into Slovenia, without much success. In September 1991, it began a full assault against Croatia. Increasingly, the Yugoslavian army was becoming the Serbian army, while Serbian irregular forces played a growing role in military operations. Before a cease-fire was arranged, the Serbian forces had captured one-third of Croatia's territory in brutal and destructive fighting.

The recognition of Slovenia, Croatia, and Bosnia-Herzegovina by many European states and the United States early in 1992 did not stop the Serbs from turning their guns on Bosnia. By mid-1993, Serbian forces had acquired 70 percent of Bosnian territory. The Serbian policy of **ethnic cleansing**—killing or forcibly removing Bosnian

Muslims from their lands—revived memories of Nazi atrocities in World War II. Nevertheless, despite worldwide outrage, European governments failed to take a decisive and forceful stand against these Serbian atrocities, and by the spring of 1993, the Muslim population of Bosnia was in desperate straits. As the fighting spread, European nations and the United States began to intervene to stop the bloodshed, and in the fall of 1995, a fragile cease-fire agreement was reached at a conference held in Dayton, Ohio. An international peacekeeping force was stationed in the area to maintain tranquility and monitor the accords.

> **Ethnic cleansing** is similar to genocide; it entails the mass killing of people based on their ethnicity to remove them from disputed or occupied lands.

Peace in Bosnia, however, did not bring peace to Yugoslavia. A new war erupted in 1999 over Kosovo, which had been made an autonomous province within Yugoslavia by Tito in 1974. Kosovo's inhabitants were mainly ethnic Albanian Muslims. But the province was also home to a Serbian minority that considered it sacred territory where Serbian forces in the fourteenth century had been defeated by the Ottoman Turks.

In 1989, Yugoslavian President Milosevic stripped Kosovo of its autonomous status and outlawed any official use of the Albanian language. In 1993, some groups of ethnic Albanians founded the Kosovo Liberation Army (KLA) and began a campaign against Serbian rule in Kosovo. When Serb forces began to massacre ethnic Albanians in an effort to crush the KLA, the United States and its NATO allies sought to arrange a settlement. When Milosevic refused to sign the agreement, the United States and its NATO allies began a bombing campaign that forced the Yugoslavian government into compliance. In the fall elections of 2000, Milosevic himself was ousted from power and later put on trial by an international tribunal for war crimes against humanity for his ethnic cleansing policies throughout the disintegration of Yugoslavia, which in 2003 changed its name to *Serbia and Montenegro*.

Why Did German Reunification Cause Internal Rifts?

For the peoples of Western Europe as well, the end of the Cold War brought changes in their lives. Perhaps the most challenging situation was faced in Germany, where the decision to unify the two zones created serious strains on the economy. Chancellor Helmut Kohl had benefited greatly from an economic boom in the mid-1980s. Gradually, however, discontent with the Christian Democrats increased, and by 1988, their political prospects seemed diminished.

But unexpectedly, the 1989 revolution in East Germany led to the reunification of the two Germanies a year later, leaving the new Germany, with its 79 million people, the leading power in Europe. Reunification, accomplished during Kohl's administration, brought rich political dividends to the Christian Democrats. In the first all-German federal election, Kohl's Christian Democrats won 44 percent of the vote, and their coalition partners, the Free Democrats, received 11 percent.

But the euphoria over reunification soon dissipated as the realization set in that the revitalization of eastern Germany would take far more money than was originally thought, and Kohl's government was soon forced to face the politically undesirable task of raising taxes substantially. Moreover, the virtual collapse of the economy in eastern Germany led to extremely high levels of unemployment and severe discontent. One reason for the problem was the government's decision to establish a 1:1 ratio between the East and West German marks. This policy raised salaries for East German workers, but it increased labour costs and provoked many companies into hiring workers abroad.

Increasing unemployment in turn led to growing resentment against foreigners. For years, foreigners seeking asylum or employment found haven in Germany because of its extremely liberal immigration laws. In 1992, more than 440 000 immigrants came to Germany seeking asylum, 123 000 of them from the former Yugoslavia alone. Attacks against foreigners by right-wing extremists—many of them espousing neo-Nazi beliefs—killed 17 people in 1992 and became an all too frequent occurrence in German life.

East Germans were also haunted by another memory from their recent past. The opening of the files of the secret police (the *Stasi*) showed that millions of East Germans had spied on their neighbours and colleagues, and even their spouses and parents, during the Communist era. A few senior *Stasi* officials were placed on trial for their past actions, but many Germans preferred simply to close the door on an unhappy period in their lives.

As the century neared its close, then, Germans struggled to cope with the challenge of building a new, united nation. To reduce the debt incurred because of economic reconstruction in the east, the government threatened to cut back on many of the social benefits West Germans had long been accustomed to receiving. This in turn sharpened resentments that were already beginning to emerge between the two zones. Although the Berlin Wall had been removed, the gap between East and West remained (see the box on page 151). In 1998, voters took out their frustrations at the ballot box. Helmut Kohl's conservative coalition was defeated in national elections, and a new chancellor, Social Democrat Gerhard Schroeder, came into office. Schroeder had no better luck than his predecessor, however, in reviving the

THE GREAT WALL OF GERMANY

The unification of the two Germanys after the fall of the Berlin Wall was widely hailed as a signal of the end of the Cold War in Europe. It even inspired fear among many Europeans living in neighbouring countries as the harbinger of the rise of a new and more powerful Germany. In fact, unification has given birth to a number of major political, economic, and social problems. Although the new Germany is administratively united, it remains divided in culture and outlook, as the following article suggests.

Remembrance of Things Past

There's a widespread feeling among East Germans that something new should have emerged out of unification, combining the best of both worlds.

"We suddenly saw that there is a different mentality, even a different language in some areas," says Western psychologist Uwe Wetter, "a different tradition, and cultural differences all around. But we tried to address these differences by giving our knowledge—what we thought was the best—to the Easterners. We thought that would be the way to handle the situation."

Many Easterners have not been able to re-establish the sense of identity. They pine for what they regard to be the sunny side of the former East German state: a sense of belonging, and a cozy feeling that they were being taken care of by the system. Some former East Germans continue to gather at frequently held nostalgia parties.

Stefan Winkler, from the eastern part of Berlin, is one of them: "I have mixed emotions about these nostalgia parties. I still have a GDR flag. I don't think it's for nostalgia reasons; it's more of a political statement. I think people tend to forget about the bad things after a while and only remember the good. There were a couple of really good things in East Germany. A lot of [East Germans] feel quite unsafe at the moment. Not only because they lost their jobs. It's also because many lost their identity—and that's where their nostalgia comes in."

(Hardy Graupner, *Deutsche Welle* [independent world radio], Cologne, November 1999.)

Source: *World Press Review,* January 2000, p. 9.

economy. In 2003, with nearly five million workers unemployed, the government announced plans to scale back welfare benefits that had long become a familiar part of life for the German people.

FRANCE: A SEASON OF DISCONTENT

Although France did not face the challenge of integrating two different systems into a single society, it encountered many of the same economic and social problems as its neighbour Germany. The policies adopted during the early 1980s by the Socialist majority under President Mitterrand failed to work, and within three years the Mitterrand government returned some of the economy to private enterprise. Mitterrand was able to win a second seven-year term in the 1988 presidential election, but France's economic decline continued. In 1993, French unemployment stood at 10.6 percent, and in the elections in March of that year, the Socialists won only 28 percent of the vote while a coalition of conservative parties won 80 percent of the seats in the National Assembly. The move to the right was strengthened when the conservative mayor of Paris, Jacques Chirac, was elected president in May 1995. The centre-right government remained in power as the new century opened.

As in Germany, resentment and xenophobia against foreign-born residents was a growing political reality. Spurred by rising rates of unemployment and large numbers of immigrant visible minorities from North Africa, many French voters gave their support to Jean-Marie Le Pen's National Front, which openly advocated a restriction on all new immigration and limited assimilation of immigrants already living in France.

GREAT BRITAIN: MOVE TO THE LEFT

In Great Britain, Conservative Prime Minister Margaret Thatcher dominated politics in the 1980s. The Labour Party, beset by divisions between moderate and radical wings, offered little effective opposition. Only in 1990 did Labour's fortunes seem to revive when Thatcher's government attempted to replace local property taxes with a flat-rate tax payable by every adult to his or her local authority. Although Thatcher argued that this would make local government more responsive to popular needs, many argued that this was nothing more than a poll tax that would enable the rich to pay the same rate as the poor. After anti-tax riots broke out, Thatcher's once legendary popularity plummeted to an all-time low. At the end of November, a revolt within her own party caused Thatcher to resign as prime minister. Her replacement was John Major, whose Conservative Party won a narrow majority in the general elections held in April 1992. But Major's lacklustre leadership failed to capture the imagination of many Britons, and in new elections in May 1997, the Labour Party won a landslide victory. The new Prime Minister, Tony Blair, was a moderate whose youth and energy immediately instilled a new vigour on the political scene. Adopting centrist policies, his party dominated the political arena into the new century.

EUROPE: THE MOVE TOWARD ECONOMIC UNITY

With the rise of NATO and other regional organizations such as EURATOM and the European Community, Western European governments took the initial moves toward creating a more unified continent. By 1992, the EC included nearly 350 million people and constituted the world's largest single trading bloc, transacting almost one-quarter of the world's commerce. In the early 1990s, EC members drafted the Treaty on European Union (known as the **Maastricht Treaty**, after the city in the Netherlands where the agreement was reached), seeking to create a true economic and monetary union of all members of the organization. The treaty would not take effect, however, until all members agreed. On November 1, 1993, the European Community became the European Union (EU).

> The **Maastricht Treaty**, signed in 1992, committed European community states to the creation of a common currency and to common citizenship rights. The treaty was ratified by national governments amid bitter debate and opposition.

One of its first goals was to introduce a common currency, called the euro. But problems soon arose. Voters in many countries opposed the austerity measures that their governments would be compelled to take to reduce growing budget deficits. Germans in particular feared that replacing the rock-solid mark with a common European currency could lead to economic disaster. Yet the logic of the new union appeared inescapable if European nations were to improve their capacity to compete with the North American Free Trade Agreement (NAFTA) and the powerful industrializing nations of the Pacific Rim. On January 1, 2002, eleven of the EC nations abandoned their national currencies in favour of the euro; notably out of the plan was the United Kingdom, which kept its pound.

In the meantime, plans got under way to extend the EU into Eastern Europe, where several nations were just emerging from decades of communism. In December 2002, the EU voted to add 10 new members, including Poland, the Baltic states, Hungary, Slovakia, and the Czech Republic, in 2004. Yet not all were convinced that European integration was a good thing. Eastern Europeans feared that their countries would be dominated by investment from their prosperous neighbours, while their counterparts in Western Europe expressed concerns at the possible influx of low-wage workers from the new member countries. All in all, a true sense of a unified Europe was still lacking among the population throughout the region, and the rising wave of anti-foreign sentiment and anger at government belt-tightening are issues that persist.

In 2004, the EU went one step further toward political integration by formulating a European constitution. Member states were required to ratify the constitution by putting it before their people in national referendums. Both the French and the Dutch people voted against the constitution, seriously challenging the future of European integration.

The NATO alliance continues to serve as a powerful force for European unity. Yet it too faces new challenges as Moscow's former satellites in Eastern Europe clamour for membership in the hope that it will spur economic growth and reduce the threat from a revival of Russian expansionism. In 1999, the Czech Republic, Hungary, and Poland joined the alliance, and the Baltic states have expressed an interest in doing so in the future. Some observers express concern, however, that an expanded NATO will not only reduce the cohesiveness of the organization but also provoke a new posture of antagonism in Europe.

ASPECTS OF SOCIETY IN POST-WAR EUROPE

Socially, intellectually, and culturally, Western Europe changed significantly during the second half of the twentieth century. Although many trends represented a continuation of pre-war developments, in other cases the changes were quite dramatic, leading some observers in the 1980s to begin speaking of the gradual emergence of a post-modern age.

How Were Europeans Increasingly Living "the Good Life"?

In the decades following the end of World War II, Western Europe witnessed remarkably rapid change. Such products of new technologies as computers, television, jet planes, contraceptive devices, and new surgical techniques all dramatically and quickly altered the pace and nature of human life. Called variously a technocratic society, an affluent society, or the consumer society, post-war Europe was characterized by changing social values and new attitudes toward the meaning of the human experience.

The structure of European society was also altered in major respects after 1945. Especially noticeable were changes in the nature of the middle class. Traditional occupations such as merchants and the professions (law, medicine, and the universities) were greatly augmented by a new group of managers and technicians, as large companies and government agencies employed increasing numbers of white-collar supervisory and administrative personnel. In most cases, success depended on specialized knowledge acquired from some form of higher education. Since their jobs usually depended on their skills, these individuals took steps to ensure that their children would be similarly educated.

Changes occurred in other areas as well. Especially noticeable was the dramatic shift from the countryside to the cities. The number of people in agriculture declined by 50 percent. Yet the industrial working class did not expand. In West Germany, industrial workers made up 48 percent of the labour force throughout the 1950s and 1960s. Thereafter, the number of industrial workers began to dwindle as the number of white-collar service employees increased. At the same time, a substantial increase in their real wages enabled the working classes to aspire to the consumption patterns of the middle class. Buying on the installment plan, introduced in the 1930s, became widespread in the 1950s and gave workers a chance to imitate the middle class by buying such products as televisions, washing machines, refrigerators, vacuum cleaners, and stereos. But the most visible symbol of mass consumerism was the automobile. Before World War II, cars were reserved mostly for the upper classes. In 1948, there were 5 million cars in all of Europe, but by 1957, the number had tripled. By the mid-1960s, there were almost 45 million cars.

Rising incomes, combined with shorter working hours, created an even greater market for mass leisure activities. Between 1900 and 1980, the workweek was reduced from 60 hours to about 40 hours, and the number of paid holidays increased. All aspects of popular culture—music, sports, media—became commercialized and offered opportunities for leisure activities, including concerts, sporting events, and television viewing.

Another very visible symbol of mass leisure was the growth of tourism. Before World War II, most persons who travelled for pleasure were from the upper and middle classes. After the war, the combination of more vacation time, increased prosperity, and the flexibility provided by package tours with their lower rates and low-budget rooms enabled millions to expand their travel possibilities. By the mid-1960s, some 100 million tourists were crossing European borders each year.

Social change was also evident in new educational patterns. Before World War II, higher education was largely the preserve of Europe's wealthier classes. Even in 1950, only 3 or 4 percent of Western European young people were enrolled in a university. European higher education remained largely centred on the liberal arts, pure science, and preparation for the professions of law and medicine.

Much of this changed in the 1950s and 1960s. European states began to foster greater equality of opportunity in higher education by eliminating fees, and universities experienced an influx of students from the middle and lower classes. Enrollments grew dramatically. In France, 4.5 percent of young people went to a university in 1950; by 1965, the figure had increased to 14.5 percent. Enrollments in European universities more than tripled between 1940 and 1960.

With growth came problems. Overcrowded classrooms, unapproachable professors, and authoritarian administrators aroused student resentment. In addition, despite changes in the curriculum, students often felt that the universities were not providing an education relevant to the modern age. This discontent led to an outburst of student revolts in the late 1960s. In part, these protests were an extension of the disruptions in American universities in the mid-1960s, which were often sparked by student opposition to the Vietnam War. Protesters also criticized other aspects of Western society, such as its materialism, and expressed concern about becoming cogs in the large and impersonal bureaucratic jungles of the modern world.

The most famous student revolt occurred in France in 1968. It erupted at the University of Nanterre outside Paris but soon spread to the Sorbonne, the main campus of the University of Paris. French students demanded a greater voice in the administration of the university, took over buildings, and then expanded the scale of their protests by inviting workers to support them. Half of France's workforce went on strike in May 1968. After the Gaullist government instituted a hefty wage hike, the workers returned to work, and the police repressed the remaining student protesters.

One source of anger among the student revolutionaries of the late 1960s was the lingering influence of traditional institutions and values. World War I had seen the first significant crack in the rigid code of manners and morals of the nineteenth century. The 1920s had witnessed experimentation with drugs, the appearance of hard-core pornography, and a new sexual freedom. But these changes appeared mostly in major cities and touched only small numbers of people. After World War II, they were more extensive and far more noticeable.

Sweden took the lead in the so-called sexual revolution of the 1960s, but the rest of Europe soon followed. Sex education in the schools and the decriminalization of homosexuality were but two aspects of Sweden's liberal legislation. Introduction of the birth control pill, which became widely available by the mid-1960s, gave people more freedom in sexual behaviour. Meanwhile, sexually explicit movies, plays, and books broke new ground in the treatment of once-hidden subjects.

The new standards were evident in the breakdown of the traditional family. Divorce rates increased dramatically, especially in the 1960s, while premarital and extramarital sexual experiences also rose substantially. The 1960s also saw the emergence of a drug culture. Marijuana use was widespread among college and university students.

How Did the Role of Women in European Society Change?

One area of significant change in post-war European society was the role of women. Although women were found in professional careers and a number of other vocations in the 1920s and 1930s, the place for most women was still in the home. Half a century later, there were almost as many women as men in the workplace, many of them employed in professions hitherto reserved for men.

One consequence of the trend toward greater employment outside the home for women was a drop in the birthrate. The percentage of married women in the female labour force in Sweden, for example, increased from 47 to 66 percent between 1963 and 1975. In many European countries, zero population growth was reached in the 1960s, and increases since then have been due solely to immigration. In Italy and Spain, the flood of women into the workplace resulted in a dramatic reduction in the number of children born annually, leading to fears of an absolute decline in total population. In newly united Germany, it has been estimated that nearly half a million immigrants will be required annually to maintain the current level of economic growth in the country.

But the increased number of women in the workforce has not changed some old patterns. Working-class women in particular still earn salaries lower than those paid to men for equal work. Women still tend to enter traditionally female jobs. A 1980 study of 25 European nations revealed that women still made up more than 80 percent of typists, nurses, tailors, and dressmakers in those countries. Many European women also still faced the double burden of earning income on the one hand and raising a family and maintaining the household on the other. Such inequalities led increasing numbers of women to rebel against their conditions.

The participation of women in World Wars I and II helped them achieve one of the major aims of the nineteenth-century feminist movement—the right to vote. After World War I, many governments acknowledged the contributions of women to the war effort by granting them the vote—Sweden, Great Britain, Germany, Poland, Hungary, Austria, and Czechoslovakia. Women in France and Italy finally gained the right to vote in 1945.

After World War II, European women tended to fall back into the traditional roles expected of them, and little was heard of feminist concerns. But with the student upheavals of the late 1960s came a renewed interest in feminism, or the women's liberation movement, as it was now called. Increasingly, women protested that the acquisition of political and legal equality had not brought true equality with men.

A leading role in the movement was played by French writer Simone de Beauvoir (1908–86). Born into a middle-class Catholic family and educated at the Sorbonne in Paris, she joined the existentialist movement, which was the leading intellectual movement of its time in Western Europe, and became active in political causes. In 1949, she published *The Second Sex,* in which she argued that living in male-dominated societies, women had been defined by their differences from men and consequently received second-class status. "What particularly signalizes the situation of woman is that she—a free autonomous being like all human creatures—nevertheless finds herself in a world where men compel her to assume the status of the Other."[1] De Beauvoir played an active role in the women's movement during the 1970s, and her book was a major influence on women throughout the Western world.

Feminists in Europe came to believe that women must transform the fundamental conditions of their lives. They did so in a variety of ways, forming numerous "consciousness-raising" groups to further awareness of women's issues and working to legalize both contraception and abortion. A French law passed in 1968 legalized the sale of contraceptive devices. In 1979, abortion became legal in France. Even in countries where the Catholic Church remained strongly opposed to contraception and legalized abortion, legislation allowing them passed in the 1970s and 1980s.

Why Did Green Movements Arise in Europe?

Beginning in the 1970s, environmentalism became a serious item on the political agenda throughout the Western world. By that time, serious ecological problems had become all too apparent in the crowded countries of Western Europe. Air pollution—produced by nitrogen oxide and sulphur dioxide emissions from road vehicles, power plants, and industrial factories—was causing respiratory illnesses such as bronchitis and asthma among people throughout Europe. It is estimated that 10 percent of children born in Europe suffer from asthma due to the poor quality of air caused by years of neglect and rapid industrialization during that time. The situation was considered far worse in the Central Eastern European (CEE) states, which once belonged to the Soviet Union, where far more attention was paid to industrialization and economic advancement than to the environment. As well, the acidity of rain stemming from the overall pollution of the atmosphere has had corrosive effects on buildings as well as on historical monuments such as the Parthenon in Athens. Many rivers, lakes, and seas had become so polluted with waste due to industrial growth that they posed serious health risks and, consequently, clean water has come to be considered one of the foremost concerns among Europeans. Dying forests (such as the famous Black Forest in southern Germany) and disappearing wildlife alarmed more and more people.

During the 1960s, the acidification (caused by toxic amounts of sulphur dioxide) of Scandinavian lakes caused major concern among researchers. With the help of the United Nations Economic Commission for Europe, Scandinavian researchers initiated the Convention on Long-range Transboundary Air Pollution (LRTAP) in 1979, which provided the countries of Eastern and Western Europe with a forum for the development of environmental regulation. By the 1980s, the convention became an effective vehicle for addressing environmental issues with regard to both lakes and forests. Since then it has evolved with far more ambitious goals as demonstrated in the 1999 Gothenburg Protocol, which aimed to reduce a wider range of environmental pollutants throughout Europe. By May 2000, a total of 31 countries in Europe signed the agreement aimed at the overall betterment of the European environment.

Growing ecological awareness gave rise to Green movements and Green parties throughout Europe in the 1970s. They came about in various ways. Some grew out of the antinuclear movement; others arose out of such causes as women's liberation and concern for foreign workers. Most started at the local level and then gradually extended their activities to the national level, where they became formally organized as political parties. Most visible was the Green Party in Germany, which was officially organized in 1979 and eventually elected 41 delegates to the West German Parliament, but Green parties also competed successfully in Sweden, Austria, and Switzerland.

Green movements, however, were challenged by business concerns that strict environmental regulations could sap economic growth and exacerbate unemployment. National rivalries and disagreements over how to deal with rising levels of pollution along international waterways such as the Rhine River also impeded cooperation. Nevertheless, public alarm over the potential effects of global warming has focused attention on the global character of environmental issues.

ASPECTS OF CULTURE IN POST-WAR EUROPE

During the German occupation of France, the French intellectual Jean-Paul Sartre (1905–80) developed a philosophy of resistance and individual freedom called *existentialism,* whose fundamental premise was the absence of a god in the universe, thereby denying any preordained destiny to humankind. Humans were thus deprived of any absolute purpose or meaning, set adrift in an absurd world. Often reduced to despair and depression, the protagonists of Sartre's literary works were left with only one hope—themselves, voluntarily reaching out and becoming involved in their community. In the early 1950s, Sartre became a devout Marxist, hitching his philosophy of freedom to one of political engagement to the Communist ideal.

One of Sartre's contemporaries, Albert Camus (1913–60), greatly influenced generations of young people in the post-war era with writings that focused on the notion of the absurd. In his seminal novel, *The Stranger* (1942), the protagonist, having stumbled through a lethargic existence, realizes just before dying that regardless of the absurdity of life, humans still have the opportunity to embrace the joyful dimensions of experience—in his case, the warmth and splendour of the Algerian skies. Neither a political activist nor an ideologue, Camus broke with Sartre and other French leftists upon the disclosure of the Stalinist atrocities in the Soviet gulags.

The existentialist worldview found expression in the Paris of the 1950s in the "theatre of the absurd." One of its foremost proponents was the Irish dramatist Samuel Beckett (1906–89), who lived in France. In his trailblazing play *Waiting for Godot* (1952), two nondescript men eagerly await the appearance of someone who never arrives. While they wait, they pass the time exchanging hopes and fears,

Courtesy of William J. Duiker

Glass Pyramid at the Louvre. The Louvre, residence of French kings since the sixteenth century and an art museum since the French Revolution, has traditionally represented classical symmetry and grandeur. In 1988, under the auspices of French President François Mitterrand, architect I. M. Pei added this imaginative and daring symmetrical pyramid of glass. It functions as an expedient entrance to the mammoth museum, while also allowing natural light to flood the lower floors. Its form incorporates the grandeur of Egypt with modernist simplicity.

with humour, courage, and touching friendship. This waiting represents the existential meaning of life, which is found in the daily activities and fellowship of the here and now, despite the absence of any absolute salvation to the human condition.

With the Soviet suppression of the Hungarian Revolution in 1956, many Europeans became disenchanted with political systems of any kind and began to question the validity of reason, history, progress, and universal truths. Leading the way toward the adoption of a new perspective was the French structuralist Claude Lévi-Strauss (b. 1908). An anthropologist, he examined world cultures as autonomous units, each different and worthy of respect, thus helping to reinforce the dismantling of the French colonial empire and empower the newly emerging post-colonial nations in Africa and Asia.

In the late 1960s, the negation of pre-war ideologies and the proliferation of structural methodology now applied to all branches of learning and fused into a new doctrine of skepticism called **deconstruction**. Deconstruction cast doubt on all Western political and philosophical traditions, leaving a world in which human beings have lost their status as free agents dealing with universal verities and are reduced to empty vessels programmed by language and culture.

> **Deconstruction** is a critical means of dissecting the nuances of written works by looking for hidden political and value assumptions.

For deconstructionists, language was like quicksand, constantly moving, its intermittent layers hiding unlimited and opposing meanings. A word does not signify an objective meaning but rather is open to different associations by each speaker or listener. Consequently, a given text can never have one single meaning, since the intention of the author and the understanding of the reader will never be precisely the same. By denying any ultimate meaning to language, deconstruction thus negated the existence of any objective truth.

The philosophical skepticism reflected in this new approach to literary criticism quickly manifested itself in European literature as authors grappled with new ways to present reality in an uncertain and nonsensical world. Whereas the modernists at the beginning of the century had celebrated the power of art to benefit humankind, placing their faith in the written word, much of the new "postmodern" literature reflected the lack of belief in anything, especially the written word (see Chapter 16, page 294).

Following in the footsteps of the modernists, French authors in the 1960s experimented so radically with literary forms and language that they pushed fiction well beyond its traditional limits of rational understanding. In the "new novel," for example, authors like Alain Robbe-Grillet (b. 1922) and Nathalie Sarraute (1900–99) delved deeply into stream-of-consciousness writing, literally abandoning the reader in the disorienting obsessions of the protagonist's unconscious mind.

Some authors, however, preferred to retrieve literary forms and values that modernists had rejected, choosing to tell a "good" chronological story, to entertain as well as to deliver a moral message. Graham Greene (1904–91) was one of Great Britain's more prolific, popular, and critically acclaimed authors of the century. He succeeded in combining psychological and moral depth with enthralling stories, often dealing with political conflicts set in exotic locales. A long-time critic of the United States, Greene forecast the American defeat in Vietnam in his 1955 novel *The Quiet American.* This and many of his other novels have been made into films.

Two other European authors who combined a gripping tale with seriousness of intent, written in fresh exciting narrative, were the German writer Günter Grass (b. 1927) and the Portuguese novelist José Saramago (b. 1922). Grass's 1959 novel, *The Tin Drum,* blasted German consciousness out of the complacency that had been induced by his country's post-war economic miracle, re-examining Germany's infatuation with Hitler and warning German readers of the ever-present danger of repeating the evils of the past. In *Crabwalk* (2002), Grass chronicled a 1945 Soviet submarine attack on a German ship carrying thousands of civilian refugees, thus breaking the taboo of silence by Germans, who had suppressed the memory of their own suffering during World War II.

In *The Cave* (2001), Saramago focused on global issues, such as the erosion of individual cultures stemming from the tyranny of globalization, which, in his view, had not only led to the exploitation of poor countries but also had robbed the world's cultures of their uniqueness, thus reducing humankind to living in caves where communication is impossible and the only place of worship is the ubiquitous shopping mall. Like Grass, Saramago believed strongly in the Western humanist tradition and viewed authors as society's moral guardians and political mobilizers.

CONCLUSION

During the immediate post-war era, Western Europe emerged from the ashes of World War II and achieved a level of political stability and economic prosperity unprecedented in its long history. By the 1970s, European leaders were beginning to turn their attention to bringing about their vision of further political and economic unity among the nations in the region.

- With the signing of the Maastricht Treaty in 1992, a schedule had been established to put the vision of unification into effect, which included the creation of a common currency and a united border.
- The road to unification has been bumpy, with long-standing economic disparities and cultural differences at times acting as obstacles.
- A truly united Europe still remains a long way off, as recently demonstrated in the 2005 rejection of the proposed European Constitution.

Europe retains a distinct cultural flavour and prides itself on its contribution to philosophy and art.

- Europeans have shown a greater interest and dedication to protecting the environment by supporting Green parties.
- Literary criticism and deconstruction are prominent in Europe's artistic circles.
- The European women's liberation movement has provided new critical and radical lenses for other women's movements to ponder.

CRITICAL THINKING QUESTIONS

1. Is it easier for a prosperous society such as post-war Western Europe to have democratic processes than it is for a less-prosperous society?

2. Why are a number of monumental populist protests—such as the student strikes in Paris in 1968, anti-Vietnam protests, and anti-globalization protests—led by students and young people?

3. Is xenophobia more apt to creep up to the surface when a country has economic difficulties?

4. Europeans work less and play more than Canadians, would Canada benefit from a legislated shorter work-week? Could we accomplish this and remain economically competitive?

5. The British people refused to adopt the euro because of great pride in their currency, the sterling pound. Could the British be holding on to the pound as a matter of nostalgia for their former status as an empire?

CHAPTER NOTE

1. Simon de Beauvoir, *The Second Sex*; trans. and ed. H. M. Parshley (New York: Knopf, 1953), p. xxxiv.

Chapter 9

Post-War United States: The Rise of a Hegemon

The United States emerged from World War II as one of the world's two superpowers. It remained deeply involved in international affairs and, as its Cold War confrontation with the Soviet Union intensified, the United States directed much of its energy toward combating the spread of communism throughout the world. Internally, Americans turned their attention to continuing the pre-war recovery from the Great Depression. Although American prosperity reached new proportions in the two decades after World War II, serious racial divisions and pockets of chronic poverty showed that the American dream still did not apply to everyone. After the end of the Cold War, a new international threat of terrorism appeared at the United States' doorstep.

At the conclusion of this chapter, you will be able to

- describe how the fight for racial equality in the United States challenged social institutions;
- detail the ebb and flow between conservatism and calls for change in American society;
- explain how post-war technological advances affected American society;
- describe the rise of Postmodernism;
- explain how the United States became an important force in shaping popular culture in the West.

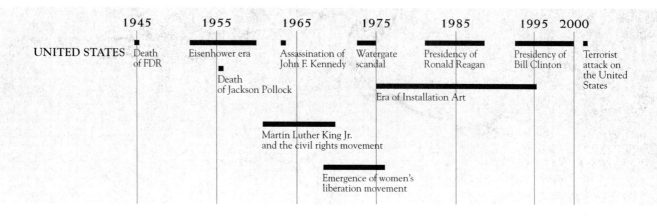

THE EMERGENCE OF THE UNITED STATES

Between 1945 and 1970, the legacy of Franklin D. Roosevelt's New Deal largely determined the parameters of American domestic politics. The New Deal gave rise to a distinct pattern that signified a basic transformation in American society. This pattern included a dramatic increase in the role and power of the federal government, the rise of organized labour as a significant force in the economy and politics, a commitment to the guarantor state, albeit a restricted one (Americans did not have access to universal health care as most other industrialized societies, like Canada, did), a grudging acceptance of the need to address deep-seated racism and inequity, and a willingness to experiment with deficit spending as a means of spurring the economy. The influence of New Deal politics was bolstered by the election of Democratic presidents—Harry S Truman in 1948, John F. Kennedy in 1960, and Lyndon B. Johnson in 1964. Even the election of a Republican president, Dwight D. Eisenhower, in 1952 and 1956, did not significantly alter the fundamental direction of the New Deal. As Eisenhower conceded in 1954, "Should any political party attempt to abolish Social Security and eliminate labor laws and farm programs, you would not hear of that party again in our political history."[1]

No doubt, the economic boom that took place after World War II fuelled public confidence in the new American way of life. A shortage of consumer goods during the war left Americans with both surplus income and the desire to purchase these goods after the war. Then, too, the growing power of organized labour enabled more and more workers to obtain the wage increases that fuelled the growth of the domestic market. Increased government expenditures (justified by the theory of English economist John Maynard Keynes that government spending could stimulate a lagging economy to reach higher levels of productivity) also indirectly subsidized the American private enterprise system. Especially after the Korean War began in 1950, outlays on defence provided money for scientific research in the universities and markets for weapons industries. After 1955, tax dollars built a massive system of interstate highways, and tax deductions for mortgages subsidized homeowners. Between 1945 and 1973, real wages grew at an average rate of 3 percent a year, the most prolonged advance in American history.

The prosperity of the 1950s and 1960s also translated into significant social changes. More workers left the factories and fields and moved into white-collar occupations, finding jobs as professional and technical employees, managers, proprietors, and clerical and sales workers. In 1940, blue-collar workers made up 52 percent of the labour force; farmers and farm workers, 17 percent; and white-collar workers,

31 percent. By 1970, blue-collar workers constituted 50 percent; farmers and farm workers, 3 percent; and white-collar workers, 47 percent. One consequence of this process was a movement from rural areas and central cities into the suburbs. In 1940, just 19 percent of the American population lived in suburbs, 49 percent in rural areas, and 32 percent in central cities. By 1970, those figures had changed to 38, 31, and 31 percent, respectively. The move to the suburbs also produced an imposing number of shopping malls and reinforced the American passion for the automobile, which provided the means of transport from suburban home to suburban mall and workplace. Finally, the search for prosperity led to new migration patterns. As the West and South experienced rapid economic growth through the development of new industries, especially in the defence field, massive numbers of people made the exodus from the cities of the Northeast and Midwest to the Sunbelt of the South and West. Between 1940 and 1980, cities like Chicago, Philadelphia, Detroit, and Cleveland lost between 13 and 36 percent of their populations, while Los Angeles, Dallas, and San Diego grew between 100 and 300 percent.

Although the country was becoming more affluent, it was also feeling more vulnerable as Cold War confrontations abroad had repercussions at home. The Communist victory in China aroused fears that Communists had infiltrated the United States. A demagogic senator from Wisconsin, Joseph McCarthy, helped intensify a massive "Red scare" with his (unsubstantiated) allegations that there were hundreds of Communists in high government positions. In this era of **McCarthyism**, a witch-hunt of academics, intellectuals, activists, actors, and artists stunted American ideals of free speech and liberty. Many actors, including Charlie Chaplin, were wrongly labelled by McCarthy as Communists, which effectively ended their Hollywood careers. But McCarthy went too far when he attacked alleged "Communist conspirators" in the U.S. Army, and he was censured by Congress in 1954. Shortly after, his anti-Communist crusade came to an end. The pervasive fear of communism and the possibility of a nuclear war, however, remained at a peak.

McCarthyism refers to an era in the United States, throughout the 1940s and 1950s, when the paranoia of Communist infiltration of U.S. political and cultural establishments led to socio-political repression.

While the 1950s have been characterized (erroneously) as a tranquil age, the period between 1960 and 1973 was clearly a time of upheaval that brought to the fore some of the problems that had been glossed over in the 1950s. The era began on an optimistic note. At age 43, John F. Kennedy became the youngest president in the history of the United

States and the first born in the twentieth century. His own administration, cut short by an assassin's bullet on November 22, 1963, focused primarily on foreign affairs, although it inaugurated an extended period of increased economic growth. Kennedy's successor, Lyndon B. Johnson (1908–73), who won a new term as president in a landslide in 1964, used his stunning mandate to pursue the growth of the **guarantor state**, first begun in the New Deal. Johnson's programs included health care for the elderly, a "war on poverty" to be fought with food stamps and a "job corps," the new Department of Housing and Urban Development to deal with the problems of the cities, and federal assistance for education.

> A **guarantor state** redistributes wealth to the under-privileged; in the United States, social security, low-income housing, and food stamps were common tools of redistribution.

Johnson's other domestic passion was the achievement of equal rights for African Americans. The civil rights movement began in earnest in 1954 when the U.S. Supreme Court took the dramatic step of striking down the practice of maintaining racially segregated public schools. According to Chief Justice Earl Warren, "Separate educational facilities are inherently unequal." A year later, during a boycott of segregated buses in Montgomery, Alabama, the eloquent Martin Luther King Jr. (1929–68) surfaced as the leader of a growing movement for racial equality.

By the early 1960s, a number of groups, including King's Southern Christian Leadership Conference (SCLC), were organizing demonstrations and sit-ins across the South to end racial segregation. In August 1963, King led the March on Washington for Jobs and Freedom. This march and King's impassioned plea for racial equality had an electrifying effect on the American people. By the end of 1963, a majority of Americans (52 percent) called civil rights the most significant national issue; only 4 percent had done so eight months earlier.

President Johnson took up the cause of civil rights. As a result of his initiative, Congress in 1964 enacted the Civil Rights Act, which ended segregation and discrimination in the workplace and all public accommodations. The Voting Rights Act, passed the following year, eliminated racial obstacles to voting in southern states. But laws alone could not guarantee a "great society," as systemic racism was deeply entrenched in American society and polity. Johnson soon faced bitter social unrest, both from African Americans and from the burgeoning anti-war movement.

In the North and West, African Americans had had voting rights for many years, but local patterns of segregation resulted in considerably higher unemployment rates for blacks (and Hispanics) than for whites and left blacks segregated in huge urban ghettos. In these ghettos, calls for militant action by radical black nationalist leaders, such as Malcolm X of the Nation of Islam, attracted more attention than the nonviolent appeals of Martin Luther King Jr. (see the box on page 162). In the summer of 1965, race riots erupted in the Watts district of Los Angeles that led to 34 deaths and the destruction of more than 1000 buildings. Cleveland, San Francisco, Chicago, Newark, and Detroit likewise exploded in the summers of 1966 and 1967. After the assassination of Martin Luther King Jr. in 1968, more than one hundred cities experienced rioting, including Washington, D.C., the nation's capital.

Anti-war protests also divided the American people after President Johnson committed American troops to a costly war in Vietnam (see the box on page 163). The anti-war movement arose out of the free speech movement that began in 1964 at the University of California at Berkeley as a protest against the impersonality and authoritarianism of the large university. As the war progressed and U.S. casualties mounted, protests escalated. Teach-ins, sit-ins, and the occupation of university buildings alternated with more radical demonstrations that increasingly led to violence. The killing of four students at Kent State University in 1970 by the Ohio National Guard caused a reaction, and the anti-war movement began to subside. By that time, however, anti-war demonstrations had helped weaken the willingness of many Americans to continue the war. But the combination of anti-war demonstrations and ghetto riots in the cities also prepared many people to embrace "law and order," an appeal used by Richard M. Nixon (1913–94), the Republican presidential candidate in 1968. With Nixon's election in 1968, a shift to the right in American politics had begun.

Why Did the United States Move to the Ideological Right?

Nixon eventually ended U.S. involvement in Vietnam by gradually withdrawing American troops after great loss of American and Vietnamese life and loss of domestic support for the imperialist-like war. A slowdown in racial desegregation appealed to southern whites, who ordinarily tended to vote Democratic. The Republican strategy also gained support among white Democrats in northern cities, where court-mandated busing to achieve racial integration had produced a white backlash. Nixon was less conservative on other issues, notably when, breaking with his strong anti-Communist past, he visited China in 1972 and opened the door toward the eventual diplomatic recognition of that Communist state.

However, Nixon was paranoid about conspiracies and began to use illegal methods of gaining political intelligence

WHO WAS MALCOLM X?

Malcolm X was born Malcolm Little in Omaha, Nebraska in 1925, and changed his surname to X to shed the slave master name *Little*. Malcolm X was a convicted criminal who became a minister of the United States' controversial Nation of Islam movement. After he departed from the controversial movement and rediscovered orthodox Islam in his pilgrimage to Mecca, Saudi Arabia, Nation of Islam members murdered Malcolm X in 1965. In the following excerpts of his autobiography, Malcolm X describes his first brush with racism, a conversation with his school teacher, and how his Muslim pilgrimage changed his perception of the "white man" and renewed his hopes for racial integration in the United States.

The Autobiography of Malcolm X

When my mother was pregnant with me, she told me later, a party of hooded Ku Klux Klan riders galloped up to our home in Omaha, Nebraska, one night. Surrounding the house, brandishing their shotguns and rifles, they shouted for my father to come out. My mother went to the front door and opened it. Standing there they could see her pregnant condition, she told them that she was alone with her three small children, and that my father was away, preaching in Milwaukee. The Klansmen shouted threats and warnings at her that we had better get out of town because "the good Christian white people" were not going to stand for my father's "spreading trouble" among the "good" Negroes of Omaha with the "back to Africa" preachings of Marcus Garvey. [p. 3]

Somehow, I happened to be alone in the classroom with Mr. Ostrowski, my English teacher . . . he was natural-born "advisor," about what you ought to read, to do, or think-about any and everything . . . I know that he probably meant well in what he happened to advise me that day . . . he told me, "Malcolm you ought to be thinking about a career. Have you been giving it thought?" . . . "Well, yes, sir, I've been thinking I'd like to be a lawyer." Lansing [Michigan] certainly had no Negro lawyers—or doctors either—in those days, to hold up an image I might have aspired to. All I knew for certain was that a lawyer didn't wash dishes, as I was doing. Mr. Ostrowski looked surprised . . . and leaned back in his chair and clasped his hands behind his head. He kind of half-smiled and said, "Malcolm, one of life's first needs is for us to be realistic. Don't misunderstand me now. We all here like you, you know that. But you've got to be realistic about being a n*****. A lawyer—that's no realistic goal for a n*****. You need to think about something you can be . . . ." It was a surprising thing that I had never thought of it that way before, but I realized that whatever I wasn't, I was smarter than nearly all of those white kids. But apparently I was still not intelligent enough, in their eyes, to become whatever I wanted to be. It was then that I began to change—inside. [p. 41]

During [pilgrimage to Mecca] the past eleven days here in the Muslim world, I have eaten from the same plate, drunk from the same glass, and slept in the same bed (or on the same rug)—while praying to the same God—with fellow Muslims, whose eyes were the bluest of blue, whose hair was the blondest of blonde, and whose skin was the whitest of white. And in the words and in the actions and in the same deeds of the "white" Muslims, I felt the same sincerity that I felt among the black African Muslims of Nigeria, Sudan, and Ghana. [pp. 71–72]

Since I learned the truth in Mecca, my dearest friends have come to include all kinds—some Christians, Jews, Buddhists, Hindus, agnostics, and even atheists! I have friends who are called capitalists, Socialists, and Communists! Some of my friends are moderates, conservatives, extremists—some are even Uncle Toms! My friends today are black, brown, red, yellow, and white! . . . I said to Harlem street audiences that only when mankind would submit to the One God who created all—only then would mankind even approach the "peace" of which so much talk could be heard. . . . [p. 410]

Source: From THE AUTOBIOGRAPHY OF MALCOLM X by Malcolm X and Alex Haley, copyright © 1964 by Alex Haley and Malcolm X. Copyright © by Alex Haley and Betty Shabazz. Used by permission of Random House, Inc.

about his political opponents. One of the president's advisers explained that Republican Party decision makers wanted to "use the available federal machinery to screw our political enemies." Nixon's zeal led to the infamous Watergate scandal— the attempted bugging of Democratic National Headquarters. Although Nixon repeatedly lied to the American public about his involvement in the affair, secret tapes of his own conversations in the White House revealed the truth. On August 9,

THE AGE OF AQUARIUS

The election of John F. Kennedy to the presidency in the fall of 1960 sparked a vast wave of enthusiasm among young people across the United States. In his inaugural address, the new president dramatically declared that the "torch of liberty" had passed to "a new generation of Americans," who were now admonished to ask not what their country could do for them, but what they could do for their country.

Within a few short years, however, the optimism engendered by the Kennedy presidency had dissipated, to be replaced by an era of discontent marked by anti-war protests on college campuses, urban riots, and a widespread distaste for the shallowness of life in the post-war United States. By the 1970s, many Americans had lost faith in their government and in its ability to adequately service their needs and realize their aspirations.

What had happened to tarnish the dream of the Kennedy years? In part, of course, the disillusionment was a direct consequence of the Vietnam War, a war for which President Kennedy himself bore part of the responsibility and which eventually aroused massive unrest on college campuses across the country. But it is clear that the public discontent over U.S. foreign policy in the 1960s was only one symptom of a deeper current of protest over domestic issues in the United States—over civil rights for racial minorities, over inequalities between men and women, and even over the materialistic lifestyle that characterized the country's capitalist civilization. According to one political scientist, Samuel P. Huntington, the "age of protest" actually began in February 1960, months before the Kennedy election, when four young African Americans demanded service at a lunch counter in Greensboro, North Carolina.

What puzzled many Americans was that the discontent of the 1960s and early 1970s took place during a period marked by the greatest material prosperity that the country had ever known. To seasoned observers, however, the ferment was a product of deep-seated cyclical changes that were an integral part of the rhythm of American society. Huntington notes that there has historically been a large gap between the nation's ideals of freedom and equality and the degree to which such aspirations have actually been achieved in American society. In that sense, Kennedy may have helped unleash the era of protest with his campaign pledge to "get this country moving again." That legacy continued to fester after his assassination in November 1963.

To participants, the fires of such intense social energy may seem unquenchable. Folk musician Bob Dylan—whose song "The Times They Are A-Changin'," published in 1964, became the anthem of the protest movement—wrote that the old order was rapidly fading, and anyone who was not ready to follow the new road had better get out of the way. In fact, however, such creedal passion cannot be sustained. As the historian Arthur F. Schlesinger Jr. has noted, life in America has always been a process of ebb and flow between innovation and conservatism, with each phase bearing the seeds of its own contradiction. Sustained public action is emotionally exhausting, breeding a desire to return to a calmer private life. But when social problems begin to fester and people grow weary of selfish motives and the concentration on material pleasures, the process begins again.

So it has happened periodically in American history. And so it was in the 1960s, when a generation of young Americans grew bored with the complacency of the Eisenhower years and welcomed the "Age of Aquarius," marked by "harmony and understanding, sympathy and trust abounding." All too soon, the dream died, and an exhausted country returned to its private concerns in the self-indulgent years of the 1980s.

Sources: Arthur F. Schlesinger Jr., *The Cycles of American History* (Boston: Houghton Mifflin, 1986); Samuel P. Huntington, *American Politics: The Promise of Disharmony* (Cambridge, M.A.: Belknap Press of Harvard University, 1981); Bob Dylan, *Lyrics, 1962–1985* (New York: Knopf, 1992); and "Aquarius," from the American rock musical *Hair,* words by James Rado and Gerome Ragni (New York: United Artists, 1968).

1974, Nixon resigned from office, an act that saved him from almost certain impeachment and conviction.

After Watergate, American domestic politics focused on economic issues. Gerald B. Ford (b. 1913) became president when Nixon resigned, only to lose in the 1976 election to the Democratic former governor of Georgia, Jimmy Carter (b. 1924), who campaigned as an outsider against the Washington establishment. Both Ford and Carter faced severe economic problems. The period from 1973 to the mid-1980s was one of economic stagnation, which came to be known as *stagflation*—a combination of high inflation and high unemployment. In 1984, median family income was 6 percent below that of 1973.

The economic downturn stemmed at least in part from a dramatic rise in oil prices. Oil had been a cheap and abundant source of energy in the 1950s, but by the late 1970s, half of the oil used in the United States came from the Middle East. An oil embargo imposed by the Organization of the Petroleum Exporting Countries (OPEC) cartel as a reaction to the Arab-Israeli War in 1973 and OPEC's subsequent raising of prices led to a quadrupling of the cost of oil. By the end of the 1970s, oil prices had increased twentyfold, encouraging inflationary tendencies throughout the entire economy. Although the Carter administration produced a plan for reducing oil consumption at home while spurring domestic production, neither Congress nor the American people could be persuaded to follow what they regarded as drastic measures.

By 1980, the Carter administration was facing two devastating problems. High inflation and a noticeable decline in average weekly earnings were causing a perceptible drop in American living standards. At the same time, a crisis abroad had erupted when 53 Americans were taken and held hostage by the Iranian government of Ayatollah Khomeini. Although Carter had little control over the situation, his inability to gain the release of the American hostages led to the perception at home that he was a weak president. His overwhelming loss to Ronald Reagan (1911–2004) in the election of 1980 brought forward the chief exponent of conservative Republican policies and a new political order.

How Did Reagan and Clinton Differ?

The conservative trend continued in the 1980s. The election of Ronald Reagan changed the direction of American policy on several fronts. Reversing decades of the expanding guarantor state, Reagan cut spending on food stamps, school lunch programs, and job programs. At the same time, his administration fostered the largest peacetime military buildup in American history. Total federal spending rose from US$631 billion in 1981 to more than US$1 trillion by 1986. But instead of raising taxes to pay for the new expenditures, which far outweighed the budget cuts in social areas, Reagan convinced Congress to support supply-side economics. Massive tax cuts were designed to stimulate rapid economic growth and produce new revenues. Much of the tax cut went to the wealthy. Between 1980 and 1986, the income of the lowest 40 percent of the workforce fell

9 percent, while the income of the highest 20 percent rose by 5 percent.

Reagan's policies seemed to create macroeconomic growth in the short run, and the United States experienced an economic upturn that lasted until the end of the 1980s. But the spending policies of the Reagan administration also produced record government deficits, which loomed as an obstacle to long-term growth and created greater gaps in wealth distribution. In the 1970s, the total deficit was US$420 billion; between 1981 and 1987, Reagan budget deficits were three times that amount. The inability of George H. W. Bush (b. 1924), Reagan's successor, to deal with the deficit problem or with the continuing economic downslide led to the election of a Democrat, Bill Clinton (b. 1946), in November 1992.

The new president was a southerner who claimed to be a new Democrat—one who favoured fiscal responsibility and a more conservative social agenda—a clear indication that the rightward drift in American politics had not ended by his victory. During his first term in office, Clinton reduced the budget deficit and signed a bill turning the welfare program back to the states while pushing measures to strengthen the educational system and provide job opportunities for those Americans removed from the welfare rolls. By seizing the centre of the American political agenda, Clinton was able to win reelection in 1996, although the Republican Party now held a majority in both houses of Congress.

President Clinton's political fortunes were helped considerably by a lengthy economic revival. Attributable to downsizing, major U.S. corporations began to recover the competitive edge they had lost to Japanese and European firms in previous years. At the same time, a steady reduction in the annual government budget deficit strengthened confidence in the performance of the national economy. Although wage increases were modest, inflation was securely in check, and public confidence in the future was on the rise.

Many of the country's social problems, however, remained unresolved. Although crime rates were down, drug use, smoking, and alcoholism among young people were on the rise, and the spectre of rising medical costs loomed as a generation of baby boomers neared retirement age. Americans remained bitterly divided over such issues as abortion, gay rights, gay marriage, and affirmative action programs to address systemic discrimination on the basis of gender, race, or sexual orientation.

President Clinton contributed to the national sense of unease by becoming the focus of a series of financial and sexual scandals that aroused concerns among many conservative Americans that the moral fibre of the country had been severely undermined. Accused of lying under oath in a judicial hearing, he was impeached by the Republican-led majority in Congress. Although the effort to remove

Million Worker March. Many Americans unhappy with the United States' current domestic socio-economic policies voiced their concerns at the Million Worker March in Washington. Factory workers dissatisfied with health care, wages, and social security took to the streets on Sunday, October 17, 2004, near Memorial Park. The allocation of government resources to war aims rather than to social needs of the American people prompted David Burrows (pictured here) to suggest that the blood of the American people is on President Bush's hands.

Manuel Balce Ceneta/AP/Wide World Photos

Clinton from office failed, his administration was tarnished, and in 2000, Republican candidate George W. Bush (b. 1946), the son of Clinton's predecessor, narrowly defeated Clinton's vice president, Albert Gore, in the disputed race for the presidency. Bush too sought to occupy the centre-right of the political spectrum while relying on support from his conservative base. In 2004, Bush won a second term in office, albeit by a slim majority, which indicated that despite the rise in conservatism in the United States, the country was very much divided on issues of morality and the direction of U.S. foreign policies.

TERRORIST ATTACK ON THE UNITED STATES

On September 11, 2001, terrorists hijacked four commercial jet planes shortly after taking off from Boston, Newark, and Washington, D.C. Two of the planes were flown directly into the twin towers of the World Trade Center in New York City, causing both buildings to collapse; a third slammed into the Pentagon, near Washington, D.C.; and the fourth crashed in a field in central Pennsylvania. About 3000 people were killed, including everyone aboard the four airliners.

The hijackings were carried out by a terrorist organization known as *al-Qaeda*, which had been suspected of bombing two U.S. embassies in Africa in 1998 and attacking a U.S. naval ship, the U.S.S. Cole, two years later. Its leader, Osama bin Laden, was a native of Saudi Arabia who opposed U.S. foreign policy in the Middle East, particularly support for the state of Israel, and who opposed U.S. presence in Saudi Arabia. U.S. President George W. Bush vowed to wage an offensive war on terrorism, and in October, with NATO support, U.S. forces attacked al-Qaeda bases in Afghanistan (see Chapter 16, page 287). The Bush administration had less success in gaining United Nations approval for an attack on the brutal regime of

AP/Wide World Photos

Terrorist Attack on the World Trade Center in New York City. On September 11, 2001, hijackers flew two commercial jetliners into the twin towers of the World Trade Center. Shown is the second of the jetliners about to hit one of the towers while smoke billows from the site of the first attack. Both towers soon collapsed, killing thousands.

Saddam Hussein in Iraq, which Washington falsely accused of amassing weapons of mass destruction.

SOCIAL AND TECHNOLOGICAL CHANGES IN THE UNITED STATES

As in Europe (see Chapter 8), major changes took place in American society in the decades following World War II. New technologies such as television, jet planes, medical advances, and the computer revolution all dramatically altered the pace and nature of American life. Increased prosperity led to the growth of the middle class, the expansion of higher education, and a rapid increase in consumer demand for the products of a mass society. The building of a nationwide system of superhighways, combined with low fuel prices and steady improvements in the quality and operability of automobiles, produced a more highly mobile society in which the average American family moved at least once every five years, sometimes from one end of the continent to the other.

What Is the U.S. Melting Pot?

One of the primary visual factors that helped shape American society in the post-war era was the increasing pace of new immigrants. As restrictions on immigration were loosened after World War II, millions of immigrants began to arrive from all over the world. Although the majority came from Latin America, substantial numbers came from China, Vietnam, and the countries of southern Asia. By 2003, people of Hispanic origin surpassed African Americans as the largest visible minority in the country. Although illegal immigration—especially from Mexico and the Caribbean islands—became a controversial issue in American politics, there was little doubt that the face of America was changing rapidly. Whether the country's traditional **"melting pot"** approach to immigrants can continue to function remains to be seen.

> **"Melting pot"** refers to a place where new immigrants are integrated into the mainstream of society by shedding parts of their ethnic and cultural background; the term is often used in reference to the United States.

What Ideas Do Feminist Movements Share?

Many of the changes taking place in American life reflected the fact that the role of women was in a state of rapid transition. In the years immediately following the war, many women were socially pressured to give up their jobs in factories to "make room for men returning home from war" and returned to their traditional role as homemakers, sparking the "baby boom" of the late 1940s and 1950s. Eventually, however, many women began to challenge their restrictive role as wives and mothers and began to enter the workforce at an increasing rate. Unlike the situation before World War II, many of them were married. In 1900, for example, married women made up about 15 percent of the female labour force. By 1970, their number had increased to 62 percent.

As in Europe, however, American women were still not receiving equal treatment in the workplace, and by the late 1960s, many began to assert their rights and speak as feminists. Leading advocates of women's rights in the United States were Betty Friedan and Gloria Steinem. A journalist and the mother of three children, Friedan (b. 1921) grew increasingly uneasy with her attempt to fulfill the traditional role of housewife and mother. In 1963, she published *The Feminine Mystique,* in which she analyzed the problems of middle-class women in the 1950s and argued that women were systematically being denied equality with men.

The Feminine Mystique became a best-seller and transformed Friedan into a prominent spokeswoman for women's rights in the United States.

As women became more actively involved in public issues, their role in education increased as well. Beginning in the 1980s, women's studies programs began to proliferate on college campuses throughout the United States. African-American women were also challenging liberal (mainly white) feminist ideals that viewed work as liberating. African-American women were already working in ghettoized professions that were hardly liberating! These new and vocalized feminist movements fought for greater awareness of the interplay between gender and race, and restated the importance of fighting racism as the pretext to African-American liberation. Women also became active in promoting women's rights in countries around the world, noting that Third World women were often further discriminated against; in many parts of the Third World they too work outside the home in less-than liberating professions, while making limited changes in the public sphere. Feminist movements grew from the liberal feminist perspective and started to help organize international conferences on the subject in Mexico City, Copenhagen, Nairobi, and Beijing—to get a more sophisticated and holistic argument about bettering women's lives.

What Have Been the Tensions between Economic Growth and Environmental Preservation?

Concern over environmental problems first began to engage public opinion in the United States during the 1950s, when high pollution levels in major cities such as Los Angeles, Chicago, and Pittsburgh, combined with the popularity of Rachel Carson's book, *Silent Spring,* aroused concerns over the impact that unfettered industrialization was having on the quality of life and the health of the American people. During the next several decades, federal, state, and local governments began to issue regulations directed at reducing smog in urban areas and improving the quality of rivers and streams throughout the country. In general, most Americans reacted favourably to such regulations, but by the 1980s, the environmental movement had engendered a backlash as some people complained that excessively radical measures could threaten the pace of economic growth and a loss of jobs in the workforce. By the end of the century, concern over the environment was deeply entangled with concerns over the state of the national economy. Still, it was clear that the quality of life in environmental terms was much improved for the vast majority of Americans compared with what had existed prior to World War II.

How Has the U.S. Military Machine Spurred Advances in Science and Technology?

Since the Scientific Revolution of the seventeenth century and the Industrial Revolution of the nineteenth, science and technology have played increasingly important roles in world civilization. Many of the scientific and technological achievements since World War II have revolutionized people's lives. When American astronauts walked on the moon, millions watched the event on their television sets in the privacy of their living rooms.

Before World War II, theoretical science and technology were largely separated. Pure science was the domain of university professors, far removed from the practical technological matters of technicians and engineers. But during World War II, university scientists were recruited to work for their governments to develop new weapons and devastating instruments of war. British physicists played a crucial role in developing an improved radar system in 1940 that helped defeat the German air force in the Battle of Britain. The computer, too, was a wartime creation. British mathematician Alan Turing designed a primitive computer to assist British intelligence in breaking the secret codes of German ciphering machines. The most famous product of wartime scientific research was the atomic bomb, created by a team of American and European scientists under the guidance of the physicist J. Robert Oppenheimer. Obviously, most wartime devices were created for destructive purposes, but computers and breakthrough technologies such as nuclear energy were soon adapted for peacetime uses.

The sponsorship of research by governments and the military during World War II led to a new scientific model. Science had become very complex, and only large organizations with teams of scientists, huge laboratories, and complicated equipment could undertake such large-scale projects. Such facilities were so expensive, however, that only governments and large corporations could support them, suggesting a rise in the **military-industrial complex**. Because of its post-war prosperity, the United States was able to lead in the development of the new science. Almost 75 percent of all scientific research funds in the United States came from the government in 1965. Unwilling to lag behind, especially in military development, the Soviet Union was also forced to provide large outlays for scientific and technological research and development. In fact, the defence establishments of the United States and the Soviet Union generated much of the scientific research of the post-war era. One of every four scientists and engineers trained after 1945 was engaged in the creation of new weapons systems. Universities found their research agendas increasingly determined by government funding for military-related projects.

> **Military-industrial complex** is a term that was first used by U.S. President Dwight D. Eisenhower to describe the close and elite connections between the U.S. defence industry, the seat of government, and the U.S. military; the phrase implies that growth of the American economy depends and benefits from military buildup and involvement in war.

There was no more stunning example of how the new scientific establishment operated than the space race of the 1960s. In 1957, the Soviets announced that they had sent the first space satellite, Sputnik 1, into orbit around the earth. In response, the United States launched a gigantic project to land a manned spacecraft on the moon within a decade. Massive government funding financed the scientific research and technological advances that attained this goal in 1969.

The post-war alliance of science and technology led to an accelerated rate of change that became a fact of life throughout Western society. The emergence of the computer has revolutionized American business practices and transformed the way individuals go about their lives and communicate with each other. Although early computers, which required thousands of vacuum tubes to function, were quite large, the development of the transistor and the silicon chip enabled manufacturers to reduce the size of their products dramatically. By the 1990s, the personal computer had become a fixture in businesses, schools, and homes around the country. The Internet—the world's largest computer network—provides millions of people around the world with quick access to immense quantities of information, as well as rapid communication and commercial transactions. By 2000, an estimated 500 million people were using the Internet. The United States has been at the forefront of this process, and the Clinton administration established the goal of providing instruction in computers to every school in the country.

TRENDS IN THE ARTS

Continuing the avant-garde quest to express reality in new ways, a group of New York artists known as *Abstract Expressionists* began to paint large nonrepresentational canvases in an effort to express a spiritual essence beyond the material world. Among the first was Jackson Pollock (1912–56), who developed the technique of dripping and flinging paint onto a canvas spread out on the floor.

Pollock's large paintings of swirling colours expressed the energy of primal forces as well as the vast landscapes of his native Wyoming.

During the 1960s, many American artists began to reject the emotional style of the previous decade and chose to deal with familiar objects from everyday experience. Some feared that art was being drowned out by popular culture, which bombarded Americans with the images of mass culture in newspapers, in the movies, or on television. In the hope of making art more relevant and accessible to the public, artists sought to pattern their work on aspects of everyday life to reach and manipulate the masses. Works such as those by Andy Warhol (1928–87), which repeated images such as soup cans, dollar bills, and the faces of the Mona Lisa and Marilyn Monroe, often left the viewer with a detached numbness and a sense of being trapped in an impersonal, mechanized world. Repetitious and boring, most such paintings did little to close the gap between popular culture and serious art.

Perhaps the most influential American artist of the post-war era was Robert Rauschenberg (b. 1925), whose works broke through the distinctions between painting and other art forms such as sculpture, photography, dance, and theatre. In his "collages" or "combines," he juxtaposed disparate images and everyday objects—photographs, clothing, letters, even dirt and cigarette butts—to reflect the energy and disorder of the world around us. He sought to reproduce the stream of images projected by flicking the channels on a TV set. His works represented an encapsulated documentary of American life in the 1960s, filled with news events, celebrities, war, sports, and advertisements.

Following in Marcel Duchamp's footsteps, Rauschenberg helped free future artists to find art in anything under the sun. Beginning in the late 1960s, a new school of conceptual art began to reject the commercial marketability of an art object and seek the meaning of art in ideas. Art as idea could be philosophy, linguistics, mathematics, or social criticism, existing solely in the mind of the artist and the audience. In a related attempt to free art from the shackles of tradition, a school of performance art used the body as a means of living sculpture. Often discomfiting or shocking in its intimate revelations, performance art offended many viewers. Such works expanded the horizons of modern creativity but also widened the gap between modern art and the public, many of whom now considered art as socially dysfunctional and totally lacking in relevance to their daily lives.

By the early 1970s, **Postmodernism** became the new art of revolt. It replaced Modernism, which was no longer considered sufficiently outrageous. Although some artists persevered in the Modernist tradition of formal experimentation, many believed that art should serve society, and therefore their work expressed political concerns, seeking to redress social inequities by addressing issues of gender, race, sexual orientation, ecology, and globalization. This new style was called *conceptual art,* because it was primarily preoccupied with ideas. Using innovative techniques such as photography, video, and even representational painting, such artists (many of them women, African Americans, gays, or lesbians) produced provocative works with the intent of addressing real social inequities and motivating the viewer to political action.

> **Postmodernism** is a critical art form that attempts to unseat Modernists' elitist values and assumptions through irony.

One of the most popular genres in the 1990s was installation art. The artist "installs" machine- or human-made objects, sometimes filling a large room, with the aim of transporting the viewer to another environment so as to experience new ideas and self-awareness. A powerful example is found in the untitled installation of 1997 by Robert Gober (b. 1954), in the centre of which a stereotypical statue of the Virgin Mary stands over an open drain while a wide steel pipe pierces her body. Such a violent violation of the Madonna can be viewed by Christians as the victory and resilience of faith despite the century's philosophical discourse denying the existence of God.

Musical composers also experimented with radically new concepts. One such innovator was American John Cage (1912–92), who by the 1950s had developed the extreme procedure of "indeterminacy," or the use of chance, in both musical composition and performance. Since Cage defined music as the "organization of sound," he included all types of noise in his music. Any unconventional sound was welcomed: electronic buzzers and whines, tape recordings played at altered speeds, or percussion from any household item. In wanting to make music "purposeless," Cage removed the composer's control over the sounds. Rather, he sought to let the sounds, unconnected to one another, exist on their own. His most discussed work, called "4'33"," was four minutes and thirty-three seconds of silence—the "music" being the sounds the audience heard in the hall during the "performance," such as coughing, the rustling of programs, the hum of air conditioning, and the shuffling of feet.

In the 1960s, minimalism took hold in the United States. Largely influenced by Aboriginal music, minimalist composers such as Philip Glass (b. 1937) focused on the subtle nuances in the continuous repetitions of a melodic or rhythmic pattern. Yet another musical development was microtonality, which expands the traditional 12-tone chromatic scale to include quarter tones and even smaller intervals. Since the 1960s, there has also been much experimental electronic and computer music. However, despite the excitement of such musical exploration, much of it is considered too cerebral and alien, even by the educated public.

One of the most accomplished and accessible contemporary American composers, John Adams (b. 1947), has labelled much of twentieth-century experimental composition as the "fussy, difficult music of transition." His music blends modernist elements with classical traditions using much minimalist repetition interspersed with dynamic rhythms. Critics applaud his opera *Nixon in China* (1987), as well as his oratorio *El Niño* (2000), for their dramatic effects and haunting music.

Of all the arts, music has been dealing with electronic devices the longest, so the computer represents just the latest technology in composing mathematically formed atonal works. Computer technology has also invented "hyperinstruments," which translate colours or movement into sounds. The "electric glove," for example, reacts to the motion of the fingers, producing changing tones—instant music.

Not to be undone, "hypertext" fiction offers a thoroughly postmodern, open-ended text, created by the reader,

© Monica Almeida/The New York Times

Robert Gober's Madonna Installation. Here the Virgin Mary is welcoming the faithful with outstretched arms, inviting them to unburden their suffering and tears down the drain at her feet. By combining such dramatically opposed visual objects, Gober succeeds in making the Madonna's pain palpably real, bringing her down to our level, overwhelming us with sadness and awe. For the unbeliever, Gober's installation is equally moving, representing as it does humankind's indomitable spirit. For despite the absurdity of one's existence, like this statue with its insides pierced, we are somehow still standing, still persevering in our quest for joy and meaning in life.

THE SEARCH FOR A NEW LITERATURE

Ever since James Joyce at the beginning of the twentieth century, Western authors have been searching for new literary means of expressing the complexities of modern life. Their often radical experiments culminated in the years after World War II. In this process, American literature has followed its own independent path, led by two authors, William Faulkner (1897–1962) and Ernest Hemingway (1899–1961). Although both wrote masterpieces before the war, they continued to write important works in the 1950s and influenced subsequent generations of authors with their unique styles. Under the impact of these two masters, post-war writing in the United States omitted authorial explanation and commentary and made its point by suggestion rather than assertion, by prying coherence and meaning from the text.

Faulkner's world was the Old South. Admired for their stylistic innovations regarding chronology and inner monologue, Faulkner's novels chronicled the history of an imaginary county in Mississippi from its early settlers to his own day. In novels such as *The Sound and the Fury* (1929), *Absalom, Absalom!* (1936), and *Intruder in the Dust* (1948), he expressed his outrage at the moral decay of the modern-day South and its failure to solve its social problems.

Hemingway's world was that of the American expatriate, roaming the world to find purpose and identity in a larger global culture. Using his patented laconic style (he once explained his stripped-down prose by referring to the principle of an iceberg, that "there is seven-eighths of it underwater for every part that shows"), his works—including *The Sun Also Rises* (1926), *For Whom the Bell Tolls* (1940), and *The Old Man and the Sea* (1952)—explored the psychological meaning of masculinity under the pressures of different aspects of modern life. Injured in a plane crash on safari in Africa, he committed suicide in 1961.

Fictional writing in the 1960s reflected growing concerns about the materialism and superficiality of American culture and often took the form of exuberant and comic verbal fantasies. As the decade intensified with the pain of the Vietnam War and the ensuing social and political turmoil, authors turned to satire, using "black humour" and cruelty, hoping to shock the American public into a recognition of its social ills. Many of these novels—such as Thomas Pynchon's *V* (1963), Joseph Heller's *Catch-22* (1961), and John Barth's *Sot-Weed Factor* (1961)—were wildly imaginative, highly entertaining, and very different from the writing of the first half of the century, which had detailed the "real" daily lives of small-town or big-city America.

In the 1970s and 1980s, American fiction relinquished the extravagant verbal displays of the 1960s, returning to a more sober exposition of social problems, this time related to race, gender, and sexual orientation. Much of the best fiction explored the moral dimensions of contemporary life from Jewish, African-American, feminist, or gay perspectives. Some outstanding women's fiction was written by foreign-born writers from Asia and Latin America, who examined the problems of immigrants, such as cultural identity and assimilation into the American mainstream.

Source: *The Norton Anthology of American Literature,* 4th ed. (New York: Norton, 1995); Naomi Lindstrom, *Twentieth Century Spanish American Fiction* (Austin: University of Texas, 1994).

who must direct the nonlinear chronology of the story on the computer. Actually, such a procedure was first developed during the 1960s by the Argentine author Julio Cortázar (1914–84). In his seminal novel *Hopscotch* (1966), the reader selects the chronology of the story by turning the pages forward or backward. For other trends in contemporary literature, see the box on page 170.

What Factors Have Shaped Popular Culture?

Popular culture in the twentieth century, especially since World War II, has played an important role in helping Western people define themselves. It also reflects the economic system that supports it, for it is this system that manufactures, distributes, and sells the images that people consume as popular culture. As popular culture and its economic support system have become increasingly intertwined, leisure industries have emerged. Modern popular culture is thus inextricably tied to the mass consumer society in which it has emerged. This consumer-oriented aspect of popular culture delineates it clearly from the folk culture of preceding centuries; folk culture is something people make, whereas popular culture is something people buy.

The United States has been an important force in shaping popular culture in the West and, to a lesser degree,

Che Guevara Meets Popular Culture. The export of American culture is the phenomenon of the twenty-first century, and this is best captured in this image of Che Guevara, the Cuban revolutionary, donning a Bart Simpson T-shirt. Bart is considered an American icon who has been woven into the fabric of American pop culture. Standing for everything which is American and thus capitalist, it seems that even a Communist like Che cannot resist liking such an appealing character.

throughout the world. Through movies, music, advertising, and television, the United States has spread its particular form of consumerism and the American dream, and even its values to millions around the world.

Motion pictures were the primary vehicle for the diffusion of American popular culture in the years immediately following the war and continued to dominate both European and American markets in the next decades. Hollywood became more than just a film production centre; it also became a producer and exporter of American culture and values (see the box below). Although developed in the 1930s, television did not become readily available until the late 1940s. By 1954, there were 32 million sets in the United States as television became the centrepiece of middle-class life. In the 1960s, as television spread around the world, American networks unloaded their products on Europe and developing countries at extraordinarily low prices. Only the establishment of quota systems prevented American television from completely inundating these countries.

The United States has also dominated popular music since the end of World War II. Jazz, blues, rhythm and blues, rock, rap, and hip-hop have been the most popular music forms in the Western world—and much of the non-Western world—during this time. All of them originated in the United States, and all are rooted in African American musical innovations. These forms later spread to the rest of the world, inspiring local artists, who then transformed the music in their own way.

HOLLYWOOD AND AMERICAN CULTURE

Hollywood, red carpet, paparazzi, movie stars, and glamour! There is no doubt that Hollywood films are the most well-known—in North America and most of the rest of the world. Through many setbacks and bad times, Hollywood has survived the twentieth century and continues to be one of the major ways that Americans consume their own culture—and export it to other nations.

Hollywood had become a powerful industry by the 1920s during the silent era of film with eight major studios—including familiar names like Paramount and Warner Bros.—that dominated and controlled the production, distribution, and exhibition of films in America. At the same time, various countries in Europe, such as France and Germany, also had strong film industries, but World War II brought a halt to film production in Europe during the war years while America was able to keep the cameras rolling. From this time on, American film would come to dominate most of the world market. Hollywood—whether consciously or not—was selling America's dream, myths, heroes, and stories to the world. The spread of American films has often been regarded as a form of "cultural imperialism"—not a physical attempt to take control of another nation but the promotion of one nation's culture in another, which acts as a more subtle kind of takeover.

The post–World War II era saw people from the city centres move to the suburbs, which had an impact on how they spent their leisure time. Initially, television was a threat to films as families chose to stay home for entertainment. Later, the films would move to the suburbs—especially in the 1980s—first, with cineplexes (multiple small-screen cinemas) and, second, with home video. Although external factors such as these had a major impact on films, so did internal changes within the industry itself. By 1948, the major studios' practice of controlling all three aspects of the industry—production, distribution, and exhibition—was

(continued)

declared an illegal monopoly by the U.S. Supreme Court (through a case called the *Paramount Case* or *Paramount Decrees*). The end of this practice brought about the eventual downfall of what had been dubbed "the studio system."

By the late 1960s and early 1970s, European art films were being shown in America as were new counterculture films with increasing numbers of scenes depicting violence and sexuality. Rather than banning films or editing them, the films were rated—letting audiences know for whom an individual film might be appropriate. This meant that topics like drugs, violence, and sex could be treated more openly and realistically in film while not being shown to audiences too young to understand them.

By the mid-1970s, audience taste for art films and low budget youth films was replaced with one for bigger budgets, famous stars, and slicker production values. In 1971, the gangster film *The Godfather* was a huge success, and in 1975 so too was the action-adventure film *Jaws*. Before *Jaws*, the summer was seen as the dead time of year for films; however, Spielberg's blockbuster film about a killer shark attracted audiences (as too maybe did the air-conditioned cinemas) and the summer blockbuster was born! Since *Jaws*, May to September has become the most important time of the year to release films (along with the Christmas holidays)—when kids are out of school. After all they are important consumers too!

American films reflect and often exploit American culture—America's desires, fears, anxieties, and myths. When society is obsessed with cars, films often have plots that revolve around cars—from *American Graffiti* (1973) to *The Fast and the Furious* (2001); when society is anxious about new scientific advances like those in genetic engineering, films often have plots centred on such topics—from *Jurassic Park* (1993) to *Gattaca* (1997). From the outset, American film has been dominated by glamorous actors that audiences find desirable or wish to emulate; audiences will often flock to a film just because it stars Ben Affleck, Clint Eastwood, or Julia Roberts—people we might want to be like or who we wish liked us! And in that way, American film has helped perpetuate U.S. culture as well as consumerism. For example, in the 1940s, ads appeared in film magazines promising that the Max Factor makeup worn by Rita Hayworth in her latest film would also make you beautiful; today, the same type of ad appears at Max Factor's website in relation to Cate Blanchett, who appeared in the film *The Aviator*. Such associations might lead some to think: maybe if I wear the lipstick Halle Berry advertises and the latest perfume from Britney Spears, I too will have Ashton Kutcher fall in love with me!

Film is also interconnected with other media. Today, ancillary (related but not essential) markets—video games, music, merchandising—are of increasing importance to the film industry. Films are often released in conjunction with a related meal deal at a fast food chain, a soundtrack, a stuffed animal, a video game, and a special edition DVD.

This emphasis on sales outside of the theatre seems to be affecting the kinds of films Hollywood is making. An emphasis on special effects, stunts, stars, explosions, and action sequences has less to do with changing American values (although that could be partially responsible too) and more to do with selling films to other countries—that is, cultural imperialism. Whether Hollywood producers have a desire to sell American values to other countries is debatable, but what is for certain is that the foreign box office and DVD/video rentals and sales produce lots of money. Critics have argued that Hollywood has thus reduced the amount of complicated plotlines, hard-to-follow dialogue, and/or issues that are familiar to Americans only in favour of the universal language of visual spectacle—something anyone from any culture can understand and appreciate! So if that pod-racing sequence in *The Phantom Menace* seemed like a long digression from the central storyline, it was most likely in the film to add another visually stunning action sequence (with minimal dialogue) and prime audiences (and their wallets) for the video game—*Star Wars Episode I: Racer*. So next time you buy a film-related meal at your favourite fast food chain, makeup, a T-shirt, a key chain, a video game, or a CD, think about how—in today's world—films are everywhere and connected to so many different aspects of culture and pop culture. Today you don't just see a film—you can eat it, wear it, listen to it, play it . . .

Source: Dr. Philippa Gates, Ph.D., Wilfrid Laurier University. Reprinted with permission.

In the post-war years, sports became a major product of both popular culture and the leisure industry. The development of satellite television and various electronic breakthroughs helped make spectator sports a global phenomenon. The Olympic Games could now be broadcast around the world from anywhere on earth. Sports became a cheap form of entertainment for consumers, as fans did not have to leave their homes to enjoy athletic competitions. In fact, some sports organizations initially resisted television, fearing that it would hurt ticket sales. However, the tremendous revenues possible from television contracts overcame this hesitation. As sports television revenue escalated, many sports came to receive the bulk of their yearly revenue from broadcasting contracts.

Sports became big politics as well as big business. Politicization was one of the most significant trends in sports during the second half of the twentieth century. Football (soccer) remains the dominant world sport and more than ever has become a vehicle for nationalist sentiment and expression. The World Cup is the most watched event on television. Although the sport can be a positive outlet for national and local pride, all too often it has been marred by violence as nationalistic fervour has overcome rational behaviour.

CONCLUSION

During the second half of the twentieth century, the United States emerged as the preeminent power in the world, dominant in its economic and technological achievements as well as in terms of its military hardware.

- The Soviet Union was a serious competitor in the arms race, but paled in its economic achievements.
- While the American economy has faced challengers from Asia and Europe since the 1970s, the American culture has proliferated with little rivalry.
- Socioeconomic problems in the United States include a growing gap in the distribution of wealth, an educational system that is not geared to a technology-driven economy, and a persistent racial divide.
- Post 9/11, Americans became increasingly concerned about the threat to national security. This has further

prompted many Americans to turn to religious conservatism and support right-wing political candidates.

U.S. dominance has had mixed consequences for other countries.

- The United States represents a vast consumer market and a source of capital; the dynamism of the U.S. economy has helped stimulate growth throughout the world.
- For many countries, however, the benefits of globalization have been slower to appear than originally predicted.
- The U.S. inclination to interfere in the affairs of other countries has aroused anger and frequently undermined efforts by local governments to deal with problems within their own borders.

CRITICAL THINKING QUESTIONS

1. The USA Patriot Act gave the federal government the power to monitor what books people check out at libraries. Is this type of power reminiscent of measures taken during the McCarthy era?

2. What were the 1960s really about? Was the time period more about political, cultural, or social change?

3. The United States' economic health is highly dependent on domestic military production and exports of military goods. Consequently, many leftist critics charge that it would be in the economic interest of the United States to provoke foreign wars. Do you agree or disagree?

4. Why is American culture one of the most valuable exports of the United States?

CHAPTER NOTE

1. Dwight D. Eisenhower, *The White House Years: Waging Peace, 1956–1961* (Garden City, N.Y.: Doubleday, 1965), p. 533.

Chapter 10

Canada: The Rise of a Middle Power

Canada emerged from World War II with a booming economy, which positioned it as a leading industrial nation, and with a newfound commitment to take its place as a "middle power" in the world. In the post-war era, the federal and provincial governments assumed increasing responsibility for social welfare. At the same time, Canada began to develop a stronger sense of its identity as distinct from both Great Britain and the United States. Since the 1970s, multiculturalism has been officially embraced as a powerful symbol of Canada's tolerance. This acceptance of cultural difference is held up as a national identifier, used to distinguish Canada from the American "melting pot." Canada's national unity has been threatened, however, by Quebec nationalism, regional divisions, and American economic, political, and cultural influence.

A notable feature of Canada's post-war history has been its close—but uneasy—relationship with the United States. Although Canada was a dedicated Western ally during the Cold War, Canadians worried about American economic and cultural domination, and also about the exorbitant political and military power wielded by the superpower to the south. Continentalist pressures culminated in the Canada-United States Free Trade Agreement of 1988 and the subsequent North American Free Trade Agreement (NAFTA), which ended the country's historic reliance on protectionism to safeguard its economic sovereignty. The trend toward North American integration continues to generate concern into the new millennium.

At the conclusion of this chapter, you will be able to

- understand why Canada has struggled to define its national identity;
- describe the regional divisions that have created political tensions in Canada;
- describe how Canada has risen as a middle power in the world;
- explain why Canada has a close but often difficult relationship with the United States.

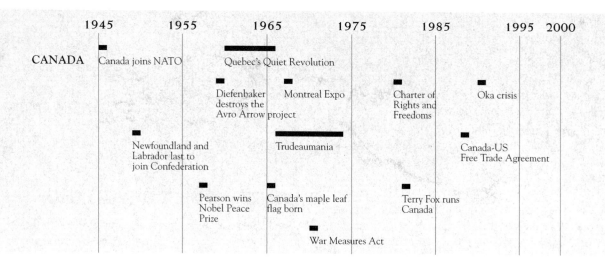

CANADIAN POLITICS AND THE RISE OF THE WELFARE STATE (1945–1968)

The Liberal Party dominated Canadian politics from 1935 to 1957. Prime Minister William Lyon Mackenzie King was fortunate to govern Canada during a post-war period of great economic prosperity due to industrial development. His government adopted platforms that reflected a new commitment to both social welfare and Keynesian principles in managing the economy. In the 1940s, public opinion polls showed strong popular support for social programs and Liberal policies, including the old age pension, unemployment insurance (later renamed *employment insurance*), and family allowances. By implementing these and other social programs, Canada began to emerge as a **welfare state**. King's government also brought in the Canadian Citizenship Act in 1947, which established distinct Canadian citizenship (up to that point, Canadians still carried British passports). When King stepped down as prime minister in 1948, he left a remarkably united country to his successor.

> The **welfare state** refers to a social system in which the state provides a safety net for its citizens through government-funded programs in the areas of health care, education, employment, and social security.

Liberal Louis St. Laurent (PM 1948–57) continued these social policies, celebrated Newfoundland and Labrador's decision to join Canada as its tenth province in 1949, and ensured that Canada pursued an internationalist foreign policy. The Liberals under "Uncle Louis" also pursued bold national projects, such as the Trans-Canada Highway, to bring the country together. These national projects did not always have the desired result, however. In 1956, the government announced plans for the Trans-Canada Pipeline, a gas pipeline that would connect Alberta to the industrial-belt provinces of Ontario and Quebec. The Liberal government's heavy-handed tactics to limit debate over the plan contributed to its fall and the election of John Diefenbaker's (1895–1979) Progressive Conservative Party in 1957.

Diefenbaker had the misfortune of taking over as prime minister at a time of economic recession. A Western Canadian lawyer with charisma and populist appeal, Diefenbaker won a resounding majority in the 1958 election owing to his "vision" of a new Canada and his policy of northern development. In 1960, the Diefenbaker government passed the Canadian Bill of Rights. Although a statutory document with no constitutional status, the bill was an important expression of Canadian support for human rights and civil liberties. Four years later, Diefenbaker's appeal

waned. Unemployment rose, federal budgets ran high deficits, and in May 1962 his government devalued the Canadian dollar. Internal divisions over Canadian defence policy led to his government's collapse in 1963. In a bitter election campaign, Diefenbaker accused the United States of colluding with the Liberal Party to defeat him. The Liberals focused on Diefenbaker's alleged incompetence and won a minority government under Lester B. Pearson (PM 1963–68).

What Innovative Social Policies Did Pearson's Government Enact?

Prime Minister Lester Pearson, who had been awarded the Nobel Peace Prize for his role in the creation of the first United Nations (UN) peacekeeping force in 1957, won two successive minority governments in 1963 and 1965. Although Canadian politics were rocked by scandal during the 1960s, Pearson's government was innovative, particularly in the field of social welfare. The Canada Pension Plan, Canada Assistance Plan, and a comprehensive, tax-supported universal health care program completed the emergence of Canada as a leading welfare state. Other notable successes included the Canada-U.S. Autopact, a treaty that ensured Canada a larger share of the continental auto market. By contrast, Liberal Minister of Finance Walter Gordon failed in his attempts to control foreign investment. To deal with divergent nationalist streams in Canada, the Liberal Party focused on the "politics of national unity" and promoted "cooperative federalism." Conservatives argued that the Liberals were too preoccupied with Quebec and allowed Canada's British identity to atrophy. This issue came to a head in the 1964 debate over the adoption of a distinctive Canadian flag to replace the Union Jack. Opponents on the left of the political spectrum, such as the New Democratic Party (NDP), criticized the Liberals for not sufficiently asserting Canada's economic and political independence. A resurgent Canadian nationalism, found in organizations such as the Committee for an Independent Canada, warned that Canada's future was threatened by continental integration. Perhaps the only thing that all Canadian politicians agreed upon was that dramatic changes were occurring in Quebec, although the answer to the question "What does Quebec want?" remained perplexing.

QUEBEC'S QUIET REVOLUTION

The nationalist challenges emanating from Quebec in the 1960s reflected the province's changing social and economic context. The majority of the province's population remained French-speaking, but other mainstays of French-Canadian identity had eroded by mid-century, which encouraged Quebeckers to seek new solutions to their problems: either within Canada or as an independent state.

Premier Maurice Duplessis (1890–1959) was an autocratic, conservative French-Canadian nationalist who dominated Quebec politics from 1944 until his death in 1959. Duplessis's Union Nationale Party's electoral success owed its appeal to "survival nationalism," which suggested that the "national" survival of French Canada required the defence of three traditional pillars: the rural and agrarian family, the Catholic Church, and the French language. As a defensive nationalism aimed at protecting French-Canadian collective rights, survival nationalism was ideologically conservative and isolationist. It also seemed out of touch with several striking realities in a province where two-thirds of the population was urban by the middle of the twentieth century. Duplessis saw provincial autonomy as a means to cultural distinctiveness, so he rejected federal social programs. Instead, he sided with big business and relied on the church to provide the social safety net in Quebec. As a result, provincial politics became increasingly out of touch with the modern world.

Which Groups Challenged Duplessis's "Survival Nationalism"?

Two main groups of critics challenged Duplessis during the 1950s and called for the abandonment of survival nationalism. One group espoused a liberal agenda focusing on individual rights, modernization, and democracy. This group included intellectuals such as Pierre Elliott Trudeau (1919–2000) and Gérard Pelletier, who argued that political and social priorities should be based on the rights of the individual, not collective attributes based on race, religion, or nationality. These liberals supported federalism and believed that Quebec should not be isolated from Canadian politics. A second stream of criticism was offered by Quebec neo-nationalists (new nationalists) who still focused on collective rights of French Canadians, but believed that nationalism needed to be reformed to reflect Quebec as a modern, urban society. They looked to the provincial government, not the federal government, as the main engine for social change in Quebec, because they saw the province as a distinct society within Canada.

The Quebec Liberal Party won the 1960 provincial election under the leadership of Jean Lesage (1912–80), a former federal Cabinet minister, on the campaign slogan "It's Time for a Change." The Lesage government largely adopted the stance of the neo-nationalists, and quickly announced a sweeping program to modernize the provincial government and "catch up" with the rest of North America. The provincial government declared that it was going to make French-speaking Quebeckers "masters in our own house." It took bold steps to achieve that end, such as replacing the church-run education system with a secular Ministry of Education, and nationalizing the hydroelectric resources of the province under Hydro-Québec, a government-owned corporation. As the provincial government grew and nationalism flourished during this period, clashes with the federal government became more frequent. English-Canadian politicians pondered the demands of Quebec's assertive provincial government, and wondered how much the federal government could concede without jeopardizing Confederation.

The Quebec Liberals lost the 1966 provincial election to the Union Nationale, whose leader Daniel Johnson (1915–68) ran on the slogan "Equality or Independence." The threat of **separatism**—that the province of Quebec might decide to leave Canada and form its own state—was now pondered in public discourse. The first separatist groups occupied the extreme left and right of the political spectrum, and enjoyed limited support. However, when French President Charles de Gaulle visited Quebec during Canada's 1967 centennial celebrations, he uttered the separatist slogan "*Vive le Québec libre!*" ("long live a free Quebec!") to a Montreal crowd. Had France pledged to support an independent Quebec state? Could separatism now become a mainstream political movement? Prime Minister Pearson issued an official rebuke and de Gaulle promptly returned to France, but the separatist movement gathered momentum.

> **Separatism** refers to the advocacy of separation or secession by a group of people from a larger political unit.

René Lévesque (1922–87) was elected leader of a separatist party, the Parti Québécois (PQ), in 1969. Lévesque had been a key member of the Quebec Liberals but became disillusioned with Canada and began to advocate a step-by-step approach to Quebec independence. He promoted sovereignty-association: that Quebec should be a separate country but maintain some association with Canada. Lévesque's PQ won few seats prior to 1976, but his moderate separatist movement grew steadily and enjoyed 30 percent of the popular support in the province by 1973.

THE TRUDEAU YEARS (1968–1984)

Pearson's successor as the leader of the Liberal Party, Pierre Trudeau, promoted a different future for Canada. Trudeau vigorously opposed Quebec nationalism, "special status" for

Trudeaumania. Pierre Trudeau enjoyed near-celebrity status when "Trudeaumania" swept the country in 1968; the hysteria generated by Trudeau was similar to that invoked by the Beatles at the time.

Quebec, and separatism. Although his father was French Canadian, Trudeau did not look to collective rights to frame his vision of Canada. He was a strong federalist, who believed that Quebec's place was in a strong, united Canada where individual rights would bind Canadians together and form the basis of a common sense of identity. A "Just Society" would provide equality of opportunity for all Canadians based on individual rather than collective rights. English Canadians supported his position on Quebec nationalism, while French Canadians saw him as an example of the important role that French Canadians could play in Ottawa. As Minister of Justice, Trudeau grabbed Canadians' attention with legislation that modernized divorce laws, decriminalized homosexual acts between consenting adults, and liberalized abortion laws. His quip that "the State has no business in the bedrooms of the nation" showed that he was clever, and his charisma was well suited to television: a key consideration in the "electronic age." In 1968 Trudeau rode a wave of sex appeal and hype, known as "Trudeaumania," to become prime minister.

Trudeau took steps to promote visions of a bilingual and multicultural Canada. His Official Languages Act of 1969 highlighted Canada's two official languages and gave every citizen the right to communicate with the federal government in either English or French. While Trudeau asserted that all Canadians should embrace linguistic equality, some English Canadians saw official **bilingualism** as an attempt to shove French down their throats and a waste of taxpayers' money. His government introduced a new policy of multiculturalism in 1971, which celebrated Canada's ethnic diversity and stressed every citizen's right to practise his or her culture. This popular policy not only secured votes for the Liberal Party, it also suggested that French-speaking Canadians were one culture among many, and should have no rights to special status.

> **Bilingualism** is the ability to communicate in two languages, such as in Canada's two official languages (English and French).

Bird/Montreal Star/Library and Archives Canada/PA-129838. Reprinted with permission of The Gazette (Montreal).

The October Crisis. In mid-October 1970, helicopters, tanks, and armed soldiers made an unusual appearance in the streets of Montreal. At the request of the Quebec government, Trudeau's government invoked the War Measures Act to deal with FLQ terrorists.

Trudeau quickly developed the image of a leader who would stand up to forces of disorder. He faced a serious threat to domestic security when the Front de libération du Québec (FLQ), a terrorist organization that promoted the overthrow of capitalist society and Quebec's separation from the rest of Canada, kidnapped a British diplomat and a Quebec Cabinet minister in 1970. The Trudeau government invoked the War Measures Act, suspending civil liberties and arresting hundreds of radicals in Quebec. The FLQ murdered Pierre Laporte, the Quebec Cabinet minister, but the movement's violent tactics generated very limited support, and it soon disappeared as a political force.

There were clear signs that Trudeaumania was on the wane in the early 1970s, and the 1972 federal election showed that it was dead. Trudeau campaigned on the slogan "The Land Is Strong," but, although reelected, he lost his majority. The Liberal government adopted a social agenda to secure the support of the social democratic NDP and enhanced social programs such as unemployment insurance. Massive spending increases ran up serious deficits at a time of economic decline. Rapid increases in energy costs fed inflation and rising unemployment. The government floundered trying to find a solution.

REGIONALISM AND SEPARATISM

By the mid-1970s, the Trudeau government faced regional discontent. Western Canadians, particularly in the Prairie provinces, had long harboured a culture of resentment toward the "Central Canadian establishment" in Montreal, Toronto, and Ottawa. Their sense of **Western alienation** also reflected distinct political and economic identities. For example, the expansion of Alberta's petroleum industry from 1947 to 1982 made it the fastest-growing province in that period, producing a westward shift of economic power in Canada. Politically, the province's population supported conservative parties: first the Social Credit Party and then the Conservative Party. By contrast, voters in Saskatchewan (one of the world's great wheat-producing regions) tended to support more left-leaning provincial governments. The Co-operative Commonwealth Federation (CCF), the first socialist government elected in North America, held power from 1944 to 1964 and enacted the first universal health care system in Canada in the early 1960s. Although controversial at the time, the Saskatchewan government showed that medicare was feasible, and Pearson's government passed federal medicare legislation in 1966. Although not all provinces were anxious to participate in the plan, all the provinces and territories joined in by 1972. Medicare has continued to the present day.

> **Western alienation** refers to the overall feeling of discontent in Western Canada, particularly in Alberta, from the centralistic decision-making approach of the federal government, the federal government's interference in the market, and the diversion of wealth from the West to Central Canada.

Why Was Western Canada Antagonistic toward the Trudeau Government?

The Trudeau government's economic policies did not endear the federal government to Western Canadians. Grain farmers pelted the prime minister with wheat at a 1969 rally, and the Conservative provincial government in Alberta fought Ottawa over energy issues. Why should the federal government be allowed to tax oil and gas profits away from Westerners? One of the rallying cries out West was "Let Those Eastern Bastards Freeze in the Dark!" Western Canadian voters resented that the populations of Ontario and Quebec ensured that Central Canadians alone could determine which party formed the federal government. This sense of Western alienation grew when Trudeau introduced the National Energy Program in 1980 to try to cope with rapidly rising oil prices. This energy strategy, designed to encourage domestic ownership in the petroleum industry and to reduce domestic energy prices, infuriated Western Canadians—particularly people in oil-rich Alberta.

Although economic difficulties led to the fall of Trudeau's government in 1979, he was reelected prime minister in February 1980 to deal with resurgent Quebec nationalism. In 1976, René Lévesque's PQ won the provincial election and formed a government committed to Quebec separation. The Lévesque government immediately brought in tough language legislation to protect and encourage the use of French by severely limiting English-language rights in the province. This idea of language as a collective right directly challenged the concept of bilingualism. The Lévesque government also promised to hold a **referendum** on Quebec separation in May 1980. As a federalist, Trudeau campaigned tirelessly for the "no" side in the referendum and received 60 percent of the vote, prevailing over Lévesque's "yes" (separatist) forces, which received 40 percent of the vote. Nevertheless, it was clear that Quebec was divided, and Montreal businesses relocated to Toronto amidst the uncertainty. In a year of political and economic turmoil, it seemed only runner Terry Fox (see the box below) could inspire Canadians with hope and a sense of common purpose.

> A **referendum** is a direct vote by the electorate on a proposed policy or law; voters are asked whether they accept or reject the proposal.

TERRY FOX: CANADIAN AMBASSADOR TO THE WORLD

Terrance Stanley Fox was born in 1958 in Winnipeg, Manitoba, and was raised just outside of Vancouver, British Columbia. At the age of 18, Terry Fox was diagnosed with bone cancer and had to have his right leg amputated just above the knee. While in the hospital, Terry Fox became inspired by the suffering of other cancer patients and decided he would run a marathon to raise awareness and money for cancer research in Canada. This marathon, which began on April 12, 1980, came to be known as the "Marathon of Hope." Terry Fox began his marathon in St. John's, Newfoundland, where he dipped his prosthetic right leg into the Atlantic Ocean, signalling the beginning of his journey. Terry Fox crossed much of Canada by foot, a painful journey that soon garnered the support of the entire nation captivated by one man's determination and humanitarianism.

Terry Fox made it all the way to Thunder Bay, Ontario, where he was forced to stop his run on September 1. After covering over 5000 kilometres of ground, cancer had spread to his lungs. In June of 1981, Terry Fox died of the disease. His efforts were not in vain, as the Marathon of Hope helped raise almost $17 million for cancer research. Annual Terry Fox Runs are held across Canada and around the world to raise awareness and funds for cancer research. To date, over $360 million has been raised worldwide to support Terry Fox's dream.

Source: P. Whitney Lackenbauer, Ph.D., St. Jerome's University. Reprinted with permission.

CONSTITUTIONAL DEVELOPMENTS (1982–1992)

In the wake of his 1980 referendum victory, Trudeau pushed for constitutional renewal in Canada. There was little controversy over his decision to "patriate" the Canadian Constitution—to end Canada's peculiar legal status as a constitutional colony of Great Britain. Patriation would allow the federal and provincial governments to change the Constitution themselves. Trudeau's strong support for a charter that would constitutionally protect individual rights and freedoms caused much more political controversy.

Why Was the Charter of Rights and Freedoms Controversial?

Trudeau saw the Charter of Rights and Freedoms as an instrument for nation building, because Canadians would have common rights, no matter where they lived. The Charter could serve as a set of common values for all Canadians. The provincial premiers worried that this would erode their powers and opposed the charter. Quebec's René Lévesque, in particular, saw the Charter as a direct challenge to collective rights. In November 1981, the premiers of all of Canada's provinces—except Quebec—reached a constitutional agreement. The following year, the Canada Act, 1982, received royal assent.

The Charter guaranteed basic individual and collective freedoms to Canadians, including rights of assembly, mobility, equality, voting, and legal rights. Because Charter rights are enshrined in the Constitution, government policies and resulting laws must not conflict with them. Ideally, this prevents politicians from trampling on individuals' rights. Canadians can take rights cases to the highest court in the country, the Supreme Court of Canada. As a result, the Canadian political system has changed significantly. It has moved away from parliamentary supremacy to constitutionalism, whereby judges may strike down laws that are deemed to violate individual rights under the Charter. At the same time, the Charter has become a symbol of Canadian tolerance and political identity.

By 1984, rising inflation, interest rates, and unemployment made the Liberal government very unpopular. The Conservatives chose a bilingual Quebecker, Brian Mulroney (PM 1984–93), as leader, who was swept into office. When support for the Mulroney government quickly crumbled, it took bold initiatives to increase its profile. Mulroney and the 10 provincial premiers discussed constitutional amendments, behind closed doors, and reached an arrangement—the 1987 Meech Lake Accord—that recognized Quebec as a "distinct society." The government also reached a free trade agreement with the United States—an agreement that would generate significant debate over Canada's future. Mulroney won a second majority government in the 1988 federal election on a pro-**free trade** platform. The majority of Canadian voters, however, split their votes between the Liberals and the NDP—parties that did not support free trade. The result was that Mulroney was reelected and free to ratify the Canada-United States Free Trade Agreement. Nonetheless, Mulroney would struggle to find support for compromise solutions in the years ahead.

> **Free trade** refers to trade or commerce between countries without restrictive import duties or trade quotas.

What Factors Led to the Fall of the Mulroney Government?

The ongoing constitutional saga and economic recession plagued the Conservative government during its second mandate. By 1990, opposition to the Meech Lake Accord outside of Quebec gained sufficient strength that the provinces of Manitoba and Newfoundland refused to ratify the accord. When Quebec reacted angrily, the Mulroney government and the provinces worked out a new agreement called the Charlottetown Accord. Although all major political parties and provincial governments supported this accord, most Canadians voted against it in a national referendum held in October 1992. This rejection also reflected the public's anger toward the Mulroney government, which had brought in unpopular legislation like the Goods and Services Tax (GST) and had proven unable to overcome the worst recession since World War II.

Quebec nationalism flourished as many Quebeckers concluded that constitutional renewal was impossible. Former Cabinet minister Lucien Bouchard (b. 1938) left the Conservative Party and formed the Bloc Québécois, a separatist party that campaigned at the federal level. In the 1993 federal election, Quebec voters sent more than 50 Bloc members of Parliament to Ottawa. The separatist PQ, led by Jacques Parizeau, again formed the Quebec provincial government in 1994 and the party remained in power for the next decade.

ABORIGINAL PEOPLES AND THE CANADIAN STATE

Aboriginal groups in Canada also embarked on their own struggles for political recognition and self-government in the post-war years. For more than a century, the Canadian government had imposed discriminatory policies designed to assimilate Aboriginal peoples into mainstream society. Although changes in the 1951 Indian Act removed the most blatantly racist clauses prohibiting Indian cultural and political expression, deep injustices remained. Aboriginal leaders fought for a voice in federal decision-making and underwent a cultural renaissance, inspired in part by the civil rights movements in the United States, decolonization around the world, and Quebec's Quiet Revolution.

Why Was the 1969 White Paper on Indian Affairs Controversial?

The Diefenbaker government made several gestures of goodwill to Canada's Aboriginal peoples. In 1958, Diefenbaker appointed the first Status Indian to the Canadian Senate: James Gladstone. In 1960, Aboriginal peoples were given the right to vote in federal elections. After a series of consultations with the Aboriginal community, the Trudeau government introduced the 1969 White Paper on Indian Affairs. This controversial policy proposal pledged to abolish the Indian Act and Indian treaties, to eliminate the Department of Indian Affairs, allocating responsibility to the provincial governments, and to remove the special status accorded to reserve lands. Trudeau called it "a breathtaking recipe for equality." He intended for Aboriginal peoples to disappear as a distinct legal group, and for them to become just another element in multicultural Canada. Furious with the government's abhorrent ignorance of their expressed wishes for special status, Canadian Aboriginal leaders presented their own "Red Paper," which promoted a different vision. They argued that Aboriginal peoples were "Citizens Plus," with all the rights of non-Aboriginal people and additional rights as First Peoples. They would no longer tolerate being treated as second-class citizens, and demanded that their voices be heard. The Liberal government soon retracted its White Paper in the face of this bitter resistance.

Economic development projects in the 1970s encouraged Canadian governments to accommodate Aboriginal peoples' concerns. In the early 1970s, Hydro-Québec initiated the James Bay Project, a monumental hydroelectric-power development that would flood the traditional territory of the James Bay Cree. The Quebec provincial government agreed to a negotiated settlement in the face of legal uncertainty over Cree claims to the area being developed. Negotiations produced the first modern-day "treaty": the James Bay and Northern Quebec Agreement of 1975. The Cree and Inuit received $225 million over 25 years, in exchange for use of 1 million square kilometres around James Bay. Aboriginal communities also received self-government guarantees and maintained hunting and fishing rights. Another controversial proposal, to build a gas pipeline from Alaska through Alberta to the United States, led the Trudeau government to establish a commission to investigate potential impacts on Aboriginal communities. After significant consultation with native groups, the federal commission deemed the proposed pipeline a social and environmental risk to Aboriginal communities and effectively sunk the multi-billion dollar plan.

The 1980s brought mixed results for Aboriginal groups. After considerable protest, Aboriginal rights were constitutionally recognized in the 1982 Constitution. Bill C-31 (1985) began to dismantle gender discrimination in the Indian Act, which had previously denied Indian status to Indian women who married non-Indian men. The Meech Lake Accord, however, raised major concerns among Aboriginal groups, who had not been consulted during the constitutional amendment negotiations. They were most upset by the proposed recognition of Quebec as a "distinct society"—recognition that was missing for Aboriginal peoples in the accord. An Aboriginal member of Manitoba's Legislative Assembly, Elijah Harper (b. 1949), blocked passage of the accord and effectively killed its ratification. This act was heralded as a peaceful victory for Aboriginal peoples.

Aboriginal leaders did participate in the constitutional amendment negotiations leading to the 1992 Charlottetown Accord, which acknowledged Aboriginal rights to self-government, language, and culture. This accord was unpopular among some Aboriginal women's groups, however, who believed it would entrench paternalistic political control in their communities. Although the accord was defeated in the 1992 referendum, Aboriginal demands for recognition of their inherent self-government and treaty rights remained.

The summer of 1990 was a period of confrontation. Kanesatake Mohawks living at Oka, just outside of Montreal, Quebec, were fed up with continued encroachments on their land by non-Aboriginal people. In this case, a golf course was proposed to be built on Kanesatake sacred burial ground. Mohawk Warriors erected roadblocks to prevent access to the forest containing the burial ground. A standoff ensued between the Mohawk Warriors and the Quebec Provincial Police, resulting in the shooting death of a police officer. Well known for its peacekeeping overseas, the Canadian military suddenly found itself peacekeeping at home. Although resolved without further bloodshed, the Oka Crisis generated significant national and international attention to the plight of Aboriginal peoples, and led to the establishment of a Royal Commission on Aboriginal Peoples—the largest and most expensive royal commission in Canadian history.

Aboriginal peoples made progress in land claims and self-government during the 1990s. Following the successful negotiation of a comprehensive land claim, a predominantly Inuit-controlled territory, Nunavut, was created in Canada's

Arctic. Nunavut is governed by Inuit leaders according to local customs, culture, and tradition, and showcases Aboriginal self-government and government partnerships.

CANADIAN POLITICS INTO THE TWENTY-FIRST CENTURY

In 1993, the Liberals under Jean Chrétien (b. 1934) were returned to office. The Conservatives were reduced to two seats, the NDP fared little better, and two new regional parties emerged on the federal political scene: the Bloc Québécois and the Reform Party (later the Canadian Alliance), the latter of which enjoyed strong support in Western Canada. Together, the Bloc and the PQ campaigned for Quebec separatism in another Quebec referendum in 1995. The "no" (federalist) side prevailed by a very narrow margin. A booming economy ensured continued Central Canadian support for the Liberals into the twenty-first century, but Canada's regional cleavages were clear. A new Conservative Party (uniting the Canadian Alliance and the Progressive Conservative Party) was formed to try to displace the Liberals as the dominant national party, and reduced Liberals to a minority government under Paul Martin (b. 1938) in 2003. National unity remained a central concern, as did the state of Canada's health care system.

What Factors Have Shaped Canada-U.S. Relations?

In the period leading up to World War II, Canada tended to see itself as a British or European nation rather than a North American one. Although Canada and the United States shared a common border, the two countries were really "distant neighbours" from 1763 until the 1930s, when the growing political, economic, and cultural influence of the United States quietly changed the nature of the relationship. The vast majority of Canadian imports came from the United States, American foreign investment in Canada exceeded that of Great Britain from 1922 onward, and trade agreements improved Canadian-American relations. Prime Minister King began to emphasize Canada's "North American character" and exalt the "undefended border" as a model for an uncertain world. Both countries pledged their cooperation in continental defence.

World War II consolidated Canada's economic and military relationship with the United States to an unprecedented degree. The Ogdensburg Declaration of August 1940 established a Permanent Joint Board on Defence and ushered in an era of intimate military ties. The Hyde Park Agreement of 1941 united the Canadian and American economies for wartime purposes. This economic integration proved so successful that the Canadians could not disengage, even after

The Oka Crisis. The image of a Canadian Forces soldier in confrontation with a Mohawk Warrior at Oka, Quebec, brought national and international attention to the importance of respecting land treaties and the plight of Aboriginal communities. The 78-day standoff also called into question Canada's self-proclaimed multicultural and inclusive society.

the war ended in 1945. The United States emerged from the war as the most powerful nation on earth, and now had the burden of defending the Western world on its shoulders. Canada, through its war effort, had gained self-confidence but was more closely tied to its North American neighbour than ever before.

How Has Canada Exercised Its Role as a Middle Power?

After the war, Canada sought a voice in the world commensurate with its middle power status. Canadian officials were reticent about the UN institution, especially the superpower veto, but **multilateralism** afforded Canada a means of balancing some of its southern neighbour's tremendous influence. Functionalism, the notion that countries should be represented in international organizations according to their expertise in various spheres, became a key concept in Canadian foreign policy. While Canada would never partake in the great power debates, it did play an important role in multilateral organizations such as the UN's Relief and Rehabilitation Administration, Food and Agriculture Organization, the International Atomic Energy Agency, and the International Civil Aviation Organization. Canada was also a founding member of UN specialized agencies such as

> **Multilateralism** refers to countries working together through cooperative instruments such as international organizations, regional associations, and international agreements.

the International Monetary Fund (IMF) and the World Bank in 1945, and played a prominent role in the negotiations that led to the General Agreement on Tariffs and Trade (GATT), the precursor to the World Trade Organization (WTO). Canadian contributions to the mandates and principles of the UN are also noteworthy. For example, McGill University Law Professor John Peters Humphery was one of the principal authors of the 1948 UN Declaration of Human Rights that set ideal goals of basic human rights for citizens of the world.

Although Canada supported the UN, its representatives witnessed deepening divisions between members from Western and Communist countries from 1945 onward. The ensuing Cold War had a dramatic impact on Canada's place in the world. Canada shared the same assumptions as the United States about the Soviet threat, and recognized that any American-Soviet conflict would inevitably involve Canadian territory and airspace. Canada vigorously pursued a North Atlantic pact, and was a charter member of the North Atlantic Treaty Organization (NATO) in 1949. Canadian troops fought in the Korean War as part of a Commonwealth division, and used diplomacy to try to restrain American military policy. As it became clear that the two neighbours would not always see eye to eye, Canadian Secretary of State for External Affairs Lester Pearson warned in the early 1950s that "the day of easy and automatic relation with the United States" was over. Nevertheless, Canada's economy grew increasingly dependent upon the United States. Massive American investment and corporate control of the Canadian natural resource and manufacturing sectors bound the country increasingly to U.S. markets, but also brought unprecedented prosperity. The Canadian economy grew by about 50 percent between 1946 and 1950.

Why Did American Cultural Imperialism Become a Concern for Canadians?

The issue of American cultural imperialism also emerged as an area of concern in Canada. As early as the 1930s, American popular media (such as radio, films, and cheap books) streamed north and threatened to overwhelm Canada's fledgling cultural industry. In 1951, the Canadian Royal Commission on National Development in the Arts, Letters and Sciences (the Massey Commission) reported that Canada's cultural sovereignty was extremely vulnerable to the massive influx of newspapers, books, and magazines from the United States and encouraged direct government intervention. As a result, the Canadian federal government began to take a more active and direct role in fostering Canadian cultural identity. Broader concerns remained. Had Canada made the shift from British colony to a nation, only to become a satellite of the United States? Some Canadian academics and parliamentarians began to think so. The 1956 Pipeline Debate and Opposition attacks on the Liberal government's critical stance toward British activities during the Suez Crisis generated nationalist concerns that Canada's identity and independence were in jeopardy.

How Did the Role of the Canadian Forces Affect Canadian Identity?

The Suez Crisis brought one positive outcome that became central to Canadian identity. During the crisis, Secretary of State for External Affairs Lester B. Pearson proposed that an international peacekeeping force, operating under the UN flag, should be sent to the region to maintain a brokered peace. Canadians soon embraced peacekeeping as a role for their national military that contributed to global peace during the Cold War. Missions in Palestine/Israel, Southeast Asia, the Congo, and Cyprus allowed Canadian peacekeepers to showcase Canada's moderating role as a middle power.

Why Have Canada-U.S. Relations at Times Been Strained?

Prime Minister John Diefenbaker was a fervent Canadian nationalist who vowed to restore and assert Canadian independence. Although Diefenbaker quickly committed Canada to the North American Air Defence Command (NORAD) with the United States, he soon adopted anti-American rhetoric in the face of public controversies over the cancellation of the Avro Arrow (a Canadian-designed interceptor aircraft) and the decision to buy American missiles instead of a Canadian-built weapons system. Diefenbaker resented American President John F. Kennedy's popularity, their personal relationship fell to pieces, and Canadian-American tensions grew in the early 1960s. The most serious divide was over Cuba. After the failed Bay of Pigs invasion, Canada maintained trade relations with the Fidel Castro's Communist country even though the Americans cut off all ties with Cuba. During the 1962 Cuban Missile Crisis, the United States received the immediate support of all of its allies' leaders except Diefenbaker, who refused to place Canadian military forces on alert status. During the 1962 Canadian federal election, Diefenbaker's anti-Americanism reached its zenith. He refused to accept nuclear weapons on Canadian soil, and accused the U.S. President and State Department of conspiring with the opposition to defeat him. The American administration was not sorry when Diefenbaker's government was defeated in 1963.

As the new prime minister, Lester Pearson renewed expectations that Canadian-American friendship would be restored. As the crisis in Southeast Asia worsened, the Americans used the Canadian representative on the international truce commission in Vietnam to gather information and issue threats of bombing by the United States. This worried the Canadian government, which found it increasingly difficult to support U.S. activities in Vietnam. Consequently, the relationship deteriorated by the mid-1960s. Pearson publicly requested a halt to American bombing in North Vietnam and a negotiated peace during a speech at Temple University in 1967. American President Lyndon Johnson was furious, and Canadian influence in Washington diminished. The American administration, to borrow the words of Dean Acheson, had enough of listening to Canada, which saw itself as "the stern daughter of the voice of God."

Economic concerns further complicated the bilateral relationship. In the late 1950s and early 1960s, the first recession of the post-war period, coupled with disconcerting reports on the state of foreign ownership of Canadian companies, led influential Canadians to advocate economic nationalism. The 1963 federal budget, drawn up by Minister of Finance Walter Gordon, was designed to counter continentalist forces. Although the more controversial elements of his budget (including a takeover tax) were eventually withdrawn, its anti-American tone and thrust toward a greater social welfare role for the federal government further distinguished Canada from its southern neighbour. In reality, the North American economy became even more inextricably intertwined during the Pearson years. Canada and the United States signed the Autopact in 1965, creating a conditional free trade zone for motor vehicles and parts. The Canadian manufacturing sector grew with this integration of North American automotive production, but ended up more dependent on the United States than ever before. Defence production sharing meant that the Vietnam War was profitable for Canada, even though the government did not send troops to fight in the war. Furthermore, Canada welcomed 20 000 American "draft dodgers" who evaded conscription south of the border, and 12 000 deserters from the U.S. army who fled north to a "safe haven" during the war. On the other hand, as many as 10 000 individual Canadians volunteered to serve in the U.S. armed forces and fight in Vietnam under U.S. command.

American-dominated mass media contributed to even more cultural convergence between the two countries in the 1960s. Most Canadian television ratings went to American programs and, in an attempt to define Canada as separate from its southern neighbour, government reports advocated "Canadian-content" stipulations for television, radio, and magazines. The real distinguishing features of Canadian culture in the 1960s, however, were political. If the United States was a "warfare state" committed to massive militarization, Canada began to see itself as a multicultural "welfare state" with a political spectrum that now extended to the labour left (with the creation of the NDP in 1960). Anti-Americanism remained an integral part of the Canadian identity, as the rock band The Guess Who made clear in their 1970 hit "American Woman."

When Pierre Trudeau became prime minister in 1968, he suggested that Canada's international priorities were going to change. Trudeau had been openly critical of his predecessor's foreign policies, and after a major policy review, his government decided to focus on sovereignty issues and dispense with the idea that Canada should be a "helpful fixer" to the world. Continental realities upset his agenda. U.S. President Richard Nixon spelled problems for Canada: his economic policy placed Canada in a precarious position, given its dependence on the American market. On a personal level, Nixon took quickly to disliking Canada and especially Trudeau. Canada's "third option" foreign policy sought out new markets for Canadian goods in Europe and Asia in an attempt to reduce dependency on the United States. Trudeau also advocated a more directed world economic system, and called for nuclear disarmament (the "suffocation of nuclear weapons") in the late 1970s. Furthermore, the Trudeau government established the Foreign Investment Review Agency (FIRA) in 1973 to regulate foreign takeovers of Canadian firms and outside investment. This infuriated American multinational corporations and the U.S. government.

When neoconservative Ronald Reagan became U.S. president and adopted a nationalist platform, his hard-line stance regarding the Cold War and open markets was a challenge to Canada. Trudeau's most dramatic nationalist initiative, the National Energy Program, was a response to the OPEC crisis of the 1970s. Introduced in 1980, the program created a crisis in Canadian-American relations. It was designed to "Canadianize" the oil industry through a wide range of measures, including federal grants to the industry, new taxes, and an expanded role for Petro-Canada (a government-owned corporation). The legislation defied the neoconservative agenda of Reagan's administration, and the American government (under pressure from the powerful U.S. oil lobby) reacted to the program as if it were a threat to the survival of free enterprise in North America. The United States resorted to multilateral institutions like GATT to pressure Canada to change the National Energy Program. When world oil prices fell after 1982, however, the program became irrelevant and the United States abandoned its proposed retaliatory measures. Canada slid into recession in the early 1980s, particularly owing to a weak manufacturing sector, and its economy ended up even more dependent on the American market. Before he departed politics, Trudeau appointed the Royal Commission on the Economic Union and Development Prospects for Canada. To everyone's surprise, its final report recommended free trade with the United States.

In 1984, the election of the Progressive Conservatives led by Brian Mulroney ushered in a decade of friendly relations with the United States. Mulroney's conservative policies paralleled similar developments in the United States during the Republican presidencies of Ronald Reagan and George Bush. Reagan and Mulroney had compatible personalities, and shared similar approaches to world affairs. Mulroney shared Reagan's antagonism toward the Soviet Union and communism, and supported U.S. activities. The Mulroney government perceived Canadian national interest in terms of improved trade and general economic relations with the United States. It pressed for a free trade agreement between the two countries and then a North American trade agreement, which was eventually concluded by the Liberal government of Jean Chrétien. Mulroney's government also committed the Canadian Forces to fight alongside the United States in the Gulf War (1991). Overall, Canadian foreign policy in the Mulroney years was the most continentalist and pro-American than it had been in more than a generation.

The debate in Canada in the late 1980s over the Canada-United States Free Trade Agreement focused primarily on potential impacts on Canadian sovereignty and values (economic, political, and cultural). Supporters stressed that free trade would encourage Canadian competitiveness and open larger markets for entrepreneurs (see the box below). Canadian opponents of free trade feared job

TED ROGERS, JR.: CANADIAN MEDIA MAGNATE

Prominent twentieth-century Canadian corporations have often been run by successful elite families such as the Bronfmans, Thomsons, and Reichmanns, and by successful individuals such as Ted Rogers. Rogers is one of Canada's most daring and successful entrepreneurs. Born in 1933, his early life was marred by the sudden death of his father. Ted Rogers Sr. (1900–39) was a distinguished radio pioneer who developed the alternating-current radio tube in 1925. Until that time, home radio sets had depended on noisy, leaky, rechargeable batteries, but with Ted Rogers Sr.'s invention, plug-in radios became practical and sound quality improved dramatically. When he died, the family business (radio station CFRB—"Canada's First Rogers Batteryless") was sold. In many ways, Ted Rogers Jr.'s career has been the story of a man trying to honour the memory and extend the legacy of a great father.

Ted Rogers Jr. was educated as a lawyer, but his heart was elsewhere; he was enthralled with broadcasting and bought his first business, an FM radio station (CHFI), in 1960. Within a few years, he expanded his media holdings, buying an AM radio station in Toronto and joining with some of Canada's wealthiest families to establish the first privately owned television station in Canada (CFTO).

In the late 1960s, television reception was very poor and Rogers realized that cable was his next big opportunity. Rogers became the leader in Canada's cable industry by the late 1970s, and the leading cable operator in the United States as well during the early 1980s. The company went public in 1979. Rogers entered the cell phone market in 1985 through Cantel, and continued to expand his communications holdings during the late 1980s and 1990s, through video stores, long distance service, magazines, and the Sun chain of newspapers. In 2000, Rogers acquired control of the Toronto Blue Jays baseball team, and more recently, in 2005, Rogers bought Toronto's SkyDome, renaming it the *Rogers Centre,* and began offering local phone service. Ironically, Canada's greatest communications entrepreneur rarely uses a computer or watches television, preferring to focus on business opportunities instead.

Like many other successful entrepreneurs, Ted Rogers is not afraid to risk it all. As he once declared, "You don't deserve to be called an entrepreneur unless you've mortgaged your house to the business." Throughout the many years of making deals and acquiring new businesses, Rogers has indeed mortgaged his house, and his company is well known for carrying a heavy debt load. He believes that in his industry, you have to invest heavily in the best new technology and that can be expensive. Still, by foreseeing and offering the newest technology to consumers, he has been able to "ride the wave of growth" again and again. The little boy who wanted to continue the legacy of his father has built a communications empire with revenues of $7 billion (2005). Ted Rogers plans to retire when he turns 75 in 2008, and it will be up to the next generation of Rogers to take on the unenviable task of extending the family legacy yet further.

Source: Cheryl Smith, Ph.D., University of Waterloo. Reprinted with permission.

TWENTIETH-CENTURY ENGLISH-CANADIAN LITERATURE

Canadian literature has played an important role in translating, reflecting, and even shaping domestic culture. It is not surprising, then, that trends in Canadian literature reflect the changing social values, political discourse, and cultural norms of Canadians.

At the dawn of the twentieth century, the search for an identity and a unique literary voice characterized the nation's early literature. Internal disputes, including the debate in 1899 over whether Canada should send troops to support the British army during the Boer War, had once again raised questions about the nature of the relationship between Canada and Great Britain. Novels of the early twentieth century, including Sara Jeannette Duncan's *The Imperialist* (1904), dealt with the theme of Canada's future role in the British Empire. Similarly, Canadian writers also engaged in the debate over the nature of Canada's relationship with the United States.

While some writers were exploring the themes of Canadian politics and international relations, others were examining the social changes taking place within the nation. For example, Stephen Leacock's *Sunshine Sketches of a Little Town* (1912) uses humour and irony to offer social commentary on the foibles and idiosyncrasies of the established small towns of Ontario. Such social commentary was not limited to life in Ontario, however, and the diversity of the Canadian landscape also became increasingly apparent as writers drew detailed portraits of life in various regions of the country. For example, both the unique natural beauty of Prince Edward Island and the insular nature of rural Maritimes society are portrayed in Lucy Maud Montgomery's highly successful *Anne of Green Gables* (1908).

The increasing settlement and development of the Canadian West led to the rise of a new literature specific to the prairies. Frederick Philip Grove was one writer who portrayed the experiences and hardships of immigrant settlers on the prairies in the early years of the century, while the trials of the Depression era were recorded by the likes of Sinclair Ross in *As For Me and My House* (1941). More recently, the history of the settlement of the West has been revisited by writers such as Guy Vanderhaeghe in *The Last Crossing* (2002).

The wilderness remained an important topic in Canadian literature throughout the twentieth century. For example, the Far North was a recurring theme, and the context for Farley Mowat's *People of the Deer* (1952). The wilderness and rural settlements were not, however, the only settings for Canadian literature. The increasingly vibrant cities of the nation were brought to life in works as different as Mordecai Richler's *The Apprenticeship of Duddy Kravitz* (1959), which portrays Montreal's Jewish community, and Margaret Atwood's *Cat's Eye* (1988), which paints a vivid and critical picture of a privileged but repressive Toronto neighbourhood of largely Anglo-Saxon inhabitants.

Margaret Atwood along with several other writers became associated with a new blossoming of Canadian literature in the later half of the century. These writers dealt directly with some of the most important issues shaping modern Canadian society, including questions of feminism and female sexuality, as explored by Alice Munro in *Lives of Girls and Women* (1971). Portrayals of the immigrant experience and the impact of cultural diversity on Canadian society were also dominant themes in twentieth-century literature. Examples include the works of immigrant writers such as Sri Lankan-born Michael Ondaatje, and those of Canadian born writers such as Nino Ricci, who explores questions of race, citizenship, and belonging in his tale of an Italian boy's immigration to Canada in *Lives of the Saints* (1990).

The works of writers such as Atwood, Ondaatje, and Ricci are popular not only at home but also around the globe. The number of Canadian writers nominated for international awards is evidence of the increasing respect and attention being paid to this country's literature. In 1995, for example, Carol Shields was awarded the prestigious Pulitzer Prize for *The Stone Diaries,* while Canadians short listed for the Booker Prize include Rohinton Mistry and Robertson Davies.

The twentieth century saw developments in many genres of English-Canadian literature. In addition to the success of writers such as Lucy Maud Montgomery, Canada has had many notable achievements in the field of children's fiction, including the award-winning *Alligator Pie* by Dennis Lee (1974), the popular story *The Paper Bag Princess* by Robert Munsch (1980), and the works of Jean Little, who was named a member

(continued)

of the Order of Canada in 1993. In addition, Canadian writers have devoted increasing attention to works of science fiction and fantasy. Although these were minor genres in the early years of Canadian literary development, the twentieth century produced notable works that include William Gibson's *Neuromancer* (1984) and Margaret Atwood's *The Handmaid's Tale* (1985). Ann Tracy's *Winter Hunger* (1990) is noteworthy for the manner in which it melds First Nations mythology with modern fantasy. The related genre of magical realism was further developed by Canadian writers such as Jack Hodgins and Yann Martel.

Throughout the twentieth century, English-Canadian writers from across Canada produced a wealth of literature that has both reflected and helped shape the nation's growing sense of identity. At the same time, the global success of many of these writers reveals that Canadian literature had attained a high level of international attention and appreciation by the end of the century, transcending political boundaries and addressing powerful elements of the common human experience.

Source: Elizabeth Galway, Ph.D., University of Lethbridge. Reprinted with permission.

losses, given lower labour costs in the United States, and worried that Canadian social welfare and health care systems were in jeopardy. The 1988 Canadian federal election was fought largely over the free trade issue. The Liberal and New Democratic parties denounced the agreement as a sellout to the United States. Although the parties that opposed free trade enjoyed a majority of public support in the 1988 election, the Progressive Conservatives won a majority of seats in Canadian Parliament and finalized the free trade agreement. When the Liberals under Jean Chrétien won the 1993 election, they did not repeal free trade. The debate over NAFTA, which applied most of the earlier Canada-U.S. agreement to trade with Mexico, generated less debate when enacted in January 1994.

By the time NAFTA came into effect, those who voiced Canadian concerns were largely the political left, organized labour, and non-governmental organizations, especially environmental groups. Now Canadian concerns paralleled those expressed by similar groups in the United States: that Mexico had an unorganized and therefore low-wage labour force, was not politically democratic, and had an abysmal environmental record. When the Clinton administration secured side agreements on labour standards and environmental issues, Canadians seemed to support increased trade liberalization. Persistent disputes over the Pacific Coast fishery, softwood lumber, and Canadian cattle have continued into the twenty-first century, as did concerns about American cultural dominance in the magazine and television industries.

Canadians continued to participate actively in world affairs in the 1990s. Canadian peacekeepers served in the former Yugoslavia, Haiti, and the ill-fated Somalia mission. Jean Chrétien's Liberal government (1993–2004) remained strongly committed to the UN and the resolution of international conflicts through negotiation. Under Foreign Affairs Minister Lloyd Axworthy, Canada took a leadership role on human security issues, seeking to improve human

welfare, protect the environment, promote human rights, and reduce the international sale of weapons—such as the Canadian-led international agreement banning the use of anti-personnel land mines.

The twenty-first century has brought new challenges to Canada-U.S. relations. Canadians were divided over the issue of participating in an American missile defence program, and, while overwhelmingly sympathetic to the United States after 9/11, waffled on whether to support the related American military response. When the United States and Great Britain unleashed their military might on Iraq in March 2003, Prime Minister Chrétien announced that his government would not support military action without a UN Security Council resolution. Canada watched the war from the sidelines. Instead, it sent troops to Afghanistan and joined in the international effort to provide humanitarian and reconstruction assistance to Iraq. Although Canada remained closely allied to the United States, its foreign and defence policies revealed that the relationship with its foremost partner remained thorny.

CONCLUSION

Canada is a vast and diverse country that has been challenged by political fragmentation, regionalism, and differing interpretations of nationalism. Canada's federal leaders and political parties have tried to govern Canada and promote their vision of nationalism in different ways.

- Rapid change in Quebec society and emerging discontent in the province produced a separatist movement that undermined Canadian unity and challenged federal policymakers.
- Canada's self-proclaimed image as a harmonious, mulitcultural society has been marred by the October Crisis, the Oka Crisis, and Western alienation.

- English-Canadian literature has explored contemporary Canadian sentiments and fears and contributed to a sense of national identity.
- Domestic debates around the future of Canada played out in the drama surrounding patriating the Constitution, the Charter of Rights and Freedoms, the Oka Crisis, and the Meech Lake and Charlottetown accords.
- Aboriginal peoples in Canada, historically marginalized, have fought for greater self-government and recognition.

Canada's relationship to the United States and with the world has been greatly influenced by Canadian sentiments and fears.

- Canadians often feared American economic and cultural control, leading to the establishment of regulated cultural industries and protected economic industries.
- Canadians have tended to see themselves as peacemakers and have wanted their governments to follow a foreign policy that promotes peace and security.
- Canadians have held high regard for international organizations, such as the UN, and federal governments have opted to use multilateralist channels to support or legitimize Canadian foreign policy choices.

CRITICAL THINKING QUESTIONS

1. Did French President Charles de Gaulle cross the line when he addressed a Montreal crowd and pronounced "*Vive le Québec libre!*"? Was he supporting Quebec separatism or simply supporting the self-determination of a common people within Canada?

2. Did the debate surrounding the Canada-United States Free Trade Agreement and NAFTA reflect Canadian fears of American control more than sound economics?

3. Could Canadian broadcasting withstand competition from American artists without Canadian content regulations?

4. In 2004, over 1.2 million votes were cast by Canadians in the CBC's search for the greatest Canadian. Among the nominees were Terry Fox, Pierre Trudeau, Tommy Douglas, Lester Pearson, and Don Cherry. What do these nominees tell us about Canadian views of public icons?

Chapter 11

China, Taiwan, and the "Little Tigers"

In the summer of 1949, Mao Zedong's Communists triumphed over Chiang Kai-shek's Nationalist forces in a bruising civil war that led to the latter's abandonment of the mainland and retreat to the island of Taiwan. By then, Mao had become the most powerful man in China, and people began to speculate on his future intentions. Were Mao and his colleagues really "agrarian reformers," more patriots than revolutionaries, who would bind the wounds of war and initiate a period of peace and prosperity? As Mao and his colleagues mounted the platform of Beijing's Gate of Heavenly Peace in early October 1949 to declare their intentions, the fate of a nation lay in the balance.

Across the Chinese shoreline, Taiwan, Hong Kong, and Singapore emerged as rival economies and nations. Resembling states, both Taiwan and Hong Kong developed independent paths that made them increasingly distinct from mainland China. Singapore's strict public laws have made this mainly Chinese-inhabited state a lure for foreign investment.

At the conclusion of this chapter, you will be able to

- detail the significant changes that took place in China under Mao Zedong and Deng Xiaoping;

- describe how and why Mao sought to indoctrinate and suppress average Chinese citizens;

- explain why both Mao and Deng emphasized economic reform in China;

- understand why Taiwan insisted on being independent of mainland China;

- describe the factors that contributed to the development of Hong Kong's and Singapore's thriving market-led economies.

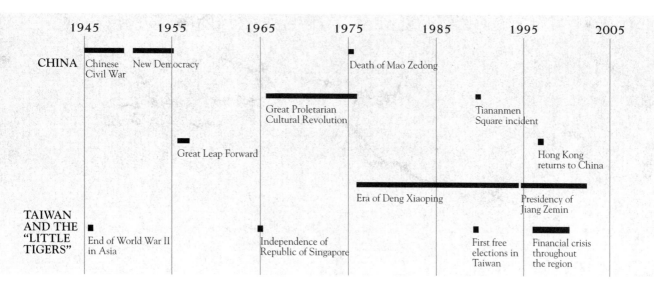

CHINA UNDER MAO ZEDONG

In the fall of 1949, China was at peace for the first time in 12 years. The newly victorious Chinese Communist Party (CCP), under the leadership of its chairman, Mao Zedong, turned its attention to consolidating its power base and healing the wounds of war. Its long-term goal was to construct a socialist society, but its leaders realized that popular support for the revolution was based on the party's platform of honest government, land reform, social justice, and peace rather than on the utopian goal of a classless society. Accordingly, the new regime followed the Soviet precedent in adopting a moderate program of political and economic recovery known as **New Democracy**.

> **New Democracy** was the moderate political and economic program instituted in China in 1949 to stimulate economic recovery; it was roughly patterned after Vladimir Lenin's New Economic Policy.

In its broad outlines, the new Chinese political system followed the Soviet pattern. Yet from the start, CCP leaders made it clear that the Chinese model would differ from the Soviet one. Whereas the Bolsheviks had severely distrusted non-revolutionary elements in Russia and established a minority government based on the radical left, Mao and his colleagues were more confident that they possessed the basic support of the majority of the Chinese people. Under New Democracy, the party would attempt to reach out to all progressive classes in the population to maintain the alliance that had brought it to power in the first place.

The primary link between the new regime and the population was the system of mass organizations, representing peasants, workers, women, religious groups, writers, and artists. The party had established these organizations during the 1920s to mobilize support for the revolution. Now they served as a conduit between party and people, enabling the leaders to assess the attitude of the masses and their local concerns while at the same time seeking support for the party's programs. Behind the façade of representative organizations stood the awesome power of the CCP.

Initially, this **"mass line"** system worked fairly well. True, opposition to the regime was ruthlessly suppressed, but on the positive side, China finally had a government that appeared to be "for the people." Although there was no pretence at Western-style democracy, and official corruption and bureaucratic mismanagement and arrogance had by no means been entirely eliminated, the new ruling class came preponderantly from workers and peasants and was more willing than its predecessors to listen to the complaints and aspirations of its constituents.

> The **"mass line"** was a tool instituted by Mao Zedong to organize and mobilize the masses to become faithful Communist Party followers.

Why Was New Democracy Initially Successful?

Under New Democracy—roughly patterned after Vladimir Lenin's New Economic Policy in Soviet Russia in the 1920s (see Chapter 3, page 59)—the capitalist system of ownership was retained in the industrial and commercial sectors. A program of land redistribution was adopted, but the collectivization of agriculture was postponed. Only after the party had consolidated its rule and brought a degree of prosperity to the national economy would the difficult transformation to a socialist society begin.

In following the Soviet precedent, Chinese leaders tacitly recognized that time and extensive indoctrination would be needed to convince the Chinese people of the superiority of socialism. In the meantime, the party would rely on capitalist profit incentives to spur productivity. Manufacturing and commercial firms were permitted to remain in private hands, but they were placed under stringent government regulations and were encouraged to form "joint enterprises" with the government. To win the support of the poorer peasants, who made up the majority of the population, the land reform program that had long been in operation in "liberated areas" was now expanded throughout the country. This strategy was designed not only to win the gratitude of the rural masses but also to undermine the political and economic influence of counterrevolutionary elements still loyal to Chiang Kai-shek.

In some ways, New Democracy was a success. About two-thirds of the peasant households in the country received property under the land reform program and thus had reason to be grateful to the new regime. Spurred by official tolerance for capitalist activities and the end of the civil war, the national economy began to rebound, although agricultural production still lagged behind both official targets and the growing population, which was increasing at an annual rate of more than 2 percent. But there were a number of blemishes in the picture. In the course of carrying out land redistribution, thousands if not millions of landlords and rich farmers lost their lands, their personal property, their freedom, and sometimes their lives. Many of those who died had been tried and convicted of "crimes against the people" in tribunals set up in towns and villages around the country. As Mao himself later conceded, many were innocent of any crime, but in the eyes of the party, their deaths were necessary to destroy the power of the landed gentry in the countryside.

How Was the Great Leap Forward Meant to Aid in the Transition to Socialism?

Originally, party leaders intended to follow the Leninist formula of delaying the building of a fully socialist society until China had a sufficient industrial base to permit the mechanization of agriculture. In 1953, they launched the nation's first five-year plan (patterned after earlier Soviet plans), which called for substantial increases in industrial output. Lenin had believed that the lure of mechanization would provide Russian peasants with an incentive to join collective farms, which, because of their greater size, could better afford to purchase expensive farm machinery. But the enormous challenge of providing tractors and reapers for millions of rural villages eventually convinced Mao Zedong and some of his colleagues that it would take years, if not decades, for China's infant industrial base to meet the burgeoning needs of a modernizing agricultural sector. He therefore decided to change the equation and urged that collectivization be undertaken immediately, in the hope that collective farms would increase food production and release land, labour, and capital for the industrial sector.

Accordingly, in 1955 the Chinese government launched a new program to build a socialist society. Beginning in that year, virtually all private farmland was collectivized, although peasant families were allowed to retain small plots for their private use (a Chinese version of the private plots adopted in the Soviet Union). In addition, most industry and commerce were nationalized.

Collectivization was achieved without provoking the massive peasant unrest that had taken place in the Soviet Union during the 1930s, perhaps because the Chinese government followed a policy of persuasion rather than compulsion (Mao remarked that Joseph Stalin had "drained the pond to catch the fish") and because the land reform program had already earned the support of millions of rural Chinese. But the hoped-for production increases did not materialize, and in 1958, at Mao's insistent urging, party leaders approved a more radical economic program known as the **Great Leap Forward**. Existing rural collectives, normally the size of a traditional village, were combined into vast "people's communes," each containing more than 30 000 people. These communes were to be responsible for all administrative and economic tasks at the local level. The party's official slogan promised "Hard work for a few years, happiness for a thousand."[1]

> The **Great Leap Forward** was the radical economic program established in China in 1958 by Mao Zedong to create vast people's communes; the program was meant to meet China's industrial and agricultural problems, but instead it was a disaster and led to starvation and crisis.

Mao hoped this program would mobilize the population for a massive effort to accelerate economic growth and ascend to the final stage of communism before the end of the twentieth century. It is better, he said, to "strike while the iron is hot" and advance the revolution without interruption. Some party members were concerned that this ambitious program would threaten the government's rural base of support, but Mao argued that Chinese peasants were naturally revolutionary in spirit. The Chinese rural masses, he said, are

> first of all, poor, and secondly, blank. That may seem like a bad thing, but it is really a good thing. Poor people want change, want to do things, want revolution. A clean sheet of paper has no blotches, and so the newest and most beautiful words can be written on it, the newest and most beautiful pictures can be painted on it."[2]

Those words were *socialism* and *communism*.

The Great Leap Forward was complicated by administrative bottlenecks, bad weather, and peasant resistance to the new system (which, among other things, attempted to eliminate work incentives and destroy the traditional family as the basic unit of Chinese society). All of this combined to drive food production downward, and over the next few years, as many as 15 million people may have died of starvation. Many peasants were reportedly reduced to eating the bark off trees and in some cases allowing infants to starve. In 1960, the commune experiment was essentially abandoned. Although the commune structure was retained, ownership and management were returned to the collective level. Mao was severely criticized by some of his more pragmatic colleagues (one remarked bitingly that "one cannot reach Heaven in a single step"), provoking him to complain that he had been relegated to the sidelines "like a Buddha on a shelf."

Moreover, the adoption of the Great Leap Forward betrayed a fundamental weakness in the policy of the mass line. While declaring his willingness to listen to the concerns of the population, Mao was also determined to build a utopian society based on Marxist-Leninist principles. Popular acceptance of nationalization and collectivization during the mid-1950s indicates that the Chinese people were not entirely hostile to socialism, but when those programs were carried to an extreme during the Great Leap Forward, many Chinese, even within the party, resisted and forced the government to abandon the program.

The failure of the Great Leap Forward split the CCP and led to the revolutionary disturbances of the following decade. Some of Mao's associates had opposed his radical approach and now sought to adopt a more cautious road to nation building. To Mao, such views were a betrayal of the party's revolutionary principles.

But Mao was not yet ready to abandon either his power or his dream of an egalitarian society. In 1966, he returned to the attack, mobilizing discontented youth and disgruntled party members into revolutionary units known as **Red Guards** who were urged to take to the streets to cleanse Chinese society—from local schools and factories to government ministries in Beijing—of impure elements who in Mao's mind were guilty of "taking the capitalist road." Supported by his wife, Jiang Qing, and other radical party figures, Mao launched China on a new forced march toward communism.

> **Red Guards** were the revolutionary units charged with carrying out the general policies of Mao Zedong's Great Proletarian Cultural Revolution.

The so-called **Great Proletarian Cultural Revolution** lasted for 10 years, from 1966 to 1976. One reason Mao had advocated the Great Leap Forward was to bypass the party and government bureaucracy, which in his view had lost their revolutionary zeal and were primarily concerned with protecting their power. Now he and his supporters feared that capitalist values and the remnants of "feudalist" Confucian ideas and practices would undermine ideological fervour and betray the revolutionary cause. Mao himself was convinced that only an atmosphere of constant revolutionary fervour (what he termed "uninterrupted revolution") could enable the Chinese to overcome the lethargy of the past and achieve the final stage of utopian communism. "I care not," he once wrote, "that the winds blow and the waves beat. It is better than standing idly in a courtyard."

> The **Great Proletarian Cultural Revolution** was a policy initiated by Mao Zedong, lasting from 1966 to 1976, in which revolutionary Red Guard units attacked people and institutions deemed not sufficiently committed to the socialist path.

His opponents, on the other hand, worried that Mao's "heaven-storming" approach could delay economic growth and antagonize the people. They argued for a more pragmatic strategy that gave priority to nation building over the ultimate Communist goal of spiritual transformation. But with Mao's supporters now in power, the party carried out vast economic and educational reforms that virtually eliminated any remaining profit incentives, established a new school system that emphasized "Mao Zedong Thought," and stressed practical education at the elementary level at the expense of specialized training in science and the humanities in the universities. School learning was discouraged as a legacy of capitalism, and Mao's famous *Little Red Book* (a slim volume of Maoist aphorisms to encourage good behaviour and revolutionary zeal) was hailed as the most important source of knowledge in all areas.

Many groups, including party bureaucrats, urban professionals, and many military officers, did not share Mao's belief in the benefits of "uninterrupted revolution" and constant turmoil. Many were alienated by the arbitrary actions of the Red Guards, who indiscriminately accused and brutalized their victims in a society where legal safeguards had almost entirely vanished. Whether the Cultural Revolution led to declining productivity is a matter of debate. Inevitably, however, the sense of anarchy and uncertainty caused popular support for the movement to erode, and when the end came with Mao's death in 1976, the vast majority of the population may well have welcomed its demise.

Of the many legacies left behind by Mao Zedong on the international stage, one continues to be the strength of Canadian-Chinese relations. Aided by Dr. Norman Bethune (1890–1939), a Canadian surgeon, diplomatic relations between Canada and China were strengthened during Mao Zedong's rule. A graduate of the University of Toronto and a physician who provided medical aid during World War I and the Spanish Civil War, Bethune made his way to China shortly after the Cultural Revolution began and was met by Mao in 1939 upon his arrival. In China, Bethune assisted in the establishment of medical hospitals and teaching centres. Bethune made it his mission to see that all the basic necessities of modern medicine were made available to those fighting in the region, his chief concern being that soldiers received medical attention wherever needed. Bethune became revered in China as the Canadian doctor who gave so much to those in need, and although Mao and Bethune had only met once, Bethune's work in China made a lasting impression on the leader. In honour of Dr. Bethune's work in China, Mao Zedong wrote a short essay celebrating his legacy, which later became required reading in the curriculum of Chinese school children.

In 1968, the Canadian government under the leadership of Prime Minister Pierre Elliot Trudeau sought to establish diplomatic ties with China, and was received graciously. By 1970, the two nations had formally recognized one another on the world stage, despite the fact that many other Western nations had yet to recognize the People's Republic of China. With little regard for Cold War rhetoric and paranoia, Trudeau established with China a strong relationship that today yields insurmountable gains for both Canada and China economically, politically, and socially.

CHINA UNDER DENG XIAOPING AND BEYOND

In September 1976, the death of Mao fundamentally changed the future of China. After a short but bitter succession struggle, the pragmatists led by Deng Xiaoping (1904–97) seized power from the radicals and brought the Cultural Revolution to an end. Mao's widow, Jiang Qing, and three other radicals (derisively called the "Gang of Four" by their opponents) were placed on trial and sentenced to death or to long terms in prison. The egalitarian policies of the previous decade were reversed, and a new program emphasizing economic modernization was introduced.

Under the leadership of Deng, who placed his supporters in key positions throughout the party and the government, attention was focused on what were called the **Four Modernizations**: industry, agriculture, technology, and national defence. Deng had been a leader of the faction that

Punishing Chinese Enemies during the Cultural Revolution. The Cultural Revolution, which began in 1966, was a massive effort by Mao Zedong and his radical supporters to eliminate rival elements within the Chinese Communist Party and the government. Accused of being "capitalist roaders," such individuals were subjected to public criticism and removed from their positions. Some were imprisoned or executed. Here Red Guards parade a victim wearing a dunce cap through the streets of Beijing.

opposed Mao's program of rapid socialist transformation, and during the Cultural Revolution, he had been forced to perform menial labour to "sincerely correct his errors." But Deng continued to espouse the pragmatic approach and reportedly once remarked, "Black cat, white cat, what does it matter so long as it catches the mice?" Under the program of the Four Modernizations, many of the restrictions against private activities and profit incentives were eliminated, and people were encouraged to work hard to benefit themselves and Chinese society. The familiar slogan "Serve the people" was replaced by a new one repugnant to the tenets of Mao Zedong Thought: "Create wealth for the people."

> The term **Four Modernizations** describes China's economic reform program under the leadership of Deng Xiaoping; the program sought to strengthen industry, agriculture, technology, and national defence.

Deng Xiaoping recognized the need to restore a sense of "socialist legality" and credibility to a system that was on the verge of breakdown and hoped that rapid economic growth would satisfy the Chinese people and prevent them from demanding political reforms. Deng and his government demonstrated a willingness to place economic performance over ideological purity. To stimulate the stagnant industrial sector, which had been under state control since the end of the era of New Democracy, they reduced bureaucratic controls over state industries and allowed local managers to have more say over prices, salaries, and quality control. Productivity was encouraged by permitting bonuses to be paid for extra effort, a policy that had been discouraged during the Cultural Revolution. State firms were no longer guaranteed access to precious resources and were told to compete with each other for public favour and even to export goods on their own initiative. The regime also tolerated the emergence of a small private sector. Unemployed youth were encouraged to set up restaurants, bicycle or radio repair shops, and handicraft shops.

The new leaders especially stressed educational reform. The system adopted during the Cultural Revolution, emphasizing practical education and ideology at the expense of higher education and modern science, was rapidly abandoned (Mao's *Little Red Book* itself was withdrawn from circulation and could no longer be found on bookshelves), and a new system based generally on the Western model was instituted. Admission to higher education was based on success in merit examinations, and courses on science and mathematics received high priority.

No economic reform program could succeed unless it included the countryside. Three decades of socialism had done little to increase food production or to lay the basis for a modern agricultural sector. China, with a population now numbering one billion, could still barely feed itself. Peasants had little incentive to work and few opportunities to increase production through mechanization, the use of fertilizer, or better irrigation.

Under Deng Xiaoping, agricultural policy made a rapid about-face. Under the new "rural responsibility system," adopted shortly after Deng had consolidated his authority, collectives leased land on contract to peasant families, who paid a quota as rent to the collective. Anything produced on the land above that payment could be sold on the private market or consumed. To soak up excess labour in the villages, the government encouraged the formation of so-called sideline industries, a modern equivalent of the traditional cottage industries in pre-modern China. Peasants raised fish or shrimp, made consumer goods, and even assembled living room furniture and appliances to sell to their newly affluent compatriots.

The reform program had a striking effect on rural production. Grain production increased rapidly, and farm income doubled during the 1980s. Yet it also created problems. In the first place, income at the village level became more unequal as some enterprising farmers (known locally as "ten thousand dollar" households) earned profits several times those realized by their less fortunate or less industrious neighbours. When some farmers discovered they could earn more by growing cash crops or other specialized commodities, they devoted less land to rice and other grain crops, thus threatening to reduce the supply of China's most crucial staple. Finally, the agricultural policy threatened to undermine the government's population control program, which party leaders viewed as crucial to the success of the Four Modernizations.

Since a misguided period in the mid-1950s when Mao had argued that more labour would result in higher productivity, China had been attempting to limit its population growth. By 1970, the government had launched a stringent family planning program—including education, incentives, and penalties for non-compliance—to persuade the Chinese people to limit themselves to one child per family. The program did have some success, and the rate of population growth was reduced drastically in the early 1980s. The rural responsibility system, however, undermined the program because it encouraged farm families to pay the penalties for having additional children in the belief that the labour of these offspring would increase family income and provide the parents with greater security in their old age.

Still, the overall effects of the modernization program were impressive. The standard of living improved for the majority of the population. Whereas a decade earlier the average Chinese had struggled to earn enough to buy a bicycle, radio, watch, or washing machine, by the late 1980s many were beginning to purchase videocassette recorders, refrigerators, and colour television sets. The government popularized the idea that all Chinese would prosper, although not necessarily at the same speed. The party announced that China was still at the "primary stage of socialism" and might not reach the state of utopian communism for generations.

Crucial to the modernization program's success was the government's ability to attract foreign technology and capital. For more than two decades, China had been isolated from technological advances taking place elsewhere in the world. Although China's leaders understandably prided themselves on their nation's capacity for "self-reliance," their isolationist policy had been exceedingly costly for the national economy. China's post-Mao leaders blamed the country's backwardness on the "ten lost years" of the Cultural Revolution, but the "lost years," at least in technological terms, extended back to 1949 and in some respects even before. Now, to make up for lost time, the government encouraged foreign investment and sent thousands of students and specialists abroad to study capitalist techniques.

By adopting this pragmatic approach in the years after 1976, China made great strides in ending its chronic problems of poverty and underdevelopment. Per capita income roughly doubled during the 1980s; housing, education, and sanitation improved; and both agricultural and industrial output skyrocketed. Clearly, China had begun to enter the Industrial Age.

During the 1990s, growth rates in the industrial sector remained high as domestic capital became increasingly available to compete with the growing presence of foreign enterprises. The government began to adopt a serious attitude to the need to close down inefficient state enterprises, and by the end of the decade, the private sector, with official encouragement, accounted for over 10 percent of the gross domestic product. A stock market opened, and China's prowess in the international marketplace improved dramatically.

As a result of these developments, China now possesses a large and increasingly affluent middle class. The domestic market for consumer goods has burgeoned, as indicated by the fact that over 80 percent of all urban Chinese now possess a colour television set, a refrigerator, and a washing machine. One-third own their homes, and nearly as many have an air conditioner. Like their counterparts elsewhere in Asia, urban Chinese are increasingly brand-name conscious, a characteristic that provides a considerable challenge to local manufacturers.

But as Chinese leaders discovered, rapid economic change never comes without cost. The closing of state-run factories has led to the dismissal of millions of workers each year, and the private sector, although growing at more than 20 percent annually, is unable to absorb them all. Discontent has been increasing in the countryside as well, where farmers earn only about half the salary of their urban counterparts (in recent years, the government tried to increase the official purchase price for grain but rescinded the order when it became too expensive). China's recent entry into the World Trade Organization (WTO) may help the nation as a whole, but is less likely to benefit farmers, who must now face the challenge of cheap foreign imports. Taxes and local corruption add to their complaints. In desperation, millions of rural people have left for the big cities, where many of them are unable to find steady employment and are forced to live in squalid conditions in crowded tenements or in the sprawling suburbs. Millions of others remain on the farm but attempt to maximize their income by producing for the market or increasing the size of their families. Although China's population control program continues to limit rural couples to two children, such regulations are widely flouted despite stringent penalties. Chinese leaders must now face the reality that the pains of industrialization are not limited to capitalist countries.

Similarly, as a result of rapid industrialization, China, much like its Western counterparts, has in recent years been forced to deal with the negative effects industrialization has had on the environment. Now standing as the third-largest economy in the world and home to 1.3 billion people (22 percent of the world's entire population), China is beginning to witness the toll of environmental neglect due to rapid industrialization. With over 110 million tons of waste being produced throughout cities and towns each year, the government has been forced to find ways to deal with the country's expanding population (China's one-child policy has succeeded at containing its overall population) in its urban centres. With more people living in the cities and more people driving cars, vehicle emissions stand as the largest contributor to pollution causing almost 300 000 deaths per year due to poor air quality. Although China is home to only 8 percent of the world's fresh water resources, three-quarters of these lakes and rivers are severely polluted, making water a growing concern among many Chinese. Further aggravating this situation is the increase in soil erosion throughout China in recent years, which has resulted in less arable land available for the growth of staples vital in providing China with the food it needs to feed its citizens. Government initiatives to deal with the problem include policies encouraging regulatory reforms in industry and production controlled by the government as well as providing information on ways to more effectively and efficiently deal with the juxtaposition of economic growth and environmental preservation.

Critics, both Chinese and foreign, also complained that Deng Xiaoping's program had failed to achieve a "fifth modernization": democracy. Official sources denied such charges and spoke proudly of restoring "socialist legality" by doing away with the arbitrary punishments applied during the Cultural Revolution. Deng himself encouraged the

Guang Niu/Reuters/Landov

No Fresh Air. Chinese residents of Beijing, and many other industrial cities, complain of the intense smog and pollution that has increased respiratory illnesses in the country. Pollution from coal and intensive industrialization has made Chinese cities among the dirtiest in the world.

Chinese people to speak out against earlier excesses. In the late 1970s, ordinary citizens began to paste posters criticizing the abuses of the past on the so-called Democracy Wall near Tiananmen Square in downtown Beijing.

Yet it soon became clear that the new leaders would not tolerate any direct criticism of the Communist Party or of Marxist-Leninist ideology. Dissidents were suppressed, and some were sentenced to long prison terms. The problem began to intensify in the late 1980s, as more Chinese began to study abroad and more information about Western society reached educated individuals inside the country. Rising expectations aroused by the economic improvements of the early 1980s led to increasing pressure from students and other urban residents for better living conditions, relaxed restrictions on study abroad, and increased freedom to select employment after graduation.

Why Did China's Political Elites Fear Demonstrations at Tiananmen Square?

As long as economic conditions for the majority of Chinese were improving, other classes did not share the students' discontent, and the government was able to isolate them from other elements in society. But in the late 1980s, an overheated economy led to rising inflation and growing discontent among salaried workers, especially in the cities. At the same time, corruption, nepotism, and favoured treatment for senior officials and party members were provoking increasing criticism. In May 1989, student protesters carried placards demanding Science and Democracy (reminiscent of the slogan of the May Fourth Movement, whose seventieth anniversary was celebrated in the spring of 1989), an end to official corruption, and the resignation of China's aging party leadership. These demands received widespread support from the urban population (although notably less in rural areas) and led to massive demonstrations in Tiananmen Square. Thousands of students gathered in Tiananmen Square in downtown Beijing to provide moral support to their many compatriots who had gone on a hunger strike in an effort to compel the Chinese government to reduce the level of official corruption and enact democratic reforms, opening the political process to the Chinese people.

The demonstrations divided the Chinese leaders. Reformist elements around party General Secretary Zhao Ziyang were sympathetic to the protesters, but veteran leaders such as Deng saw the student demands for more democracy as a disguised call for an end to CCP rule. After some hesitation, the government sent tanks and troops into Tiananmen Square to crush the demonstrators. Dissidents were arrested, and the regime once again began to stress ideological purity and socialist values. Although the crackdown provoked widespread criticism abroad, Chinese leaders insisted that economic reforms could only take place in conditions of party leadership and political stability.

Deng and other aging party leaders turned to the army to protect their base of power and suppress what they described as "counterrevolutionary elements." Deng was undoubtedly counting on the fact that many Chinese, particularly in rural areas, feared a recurrence of the disorder of the Cultural Revolution and craved economic prosperity more than political reform. In the months following the confrontation, the government issued new regulations requiring courses on Marxist-Leninist ideology in the schools, removed dissidents from the intellectual community, and made it clear that while economic reforms would continue, the CCP's monopoly of power would not be allowed to decay. Harsh punishments were imposed on those accused of undermining the Communist system and supporting its enemies abroad.

Why Did Chinese Leaders Return to Confucius?

In the 1990s, the government began to nurture urban support by reducing the rate of inflation and guaranteeing the availability of consumer goods in great demand among the rising middle class. Under Deng's successor, Jiang Zemin (b. 1926) who served as both party chief and president of China, the government promoted rapid economic growth while cracking down harshly on political dissent. That policy paid dividends in bringing about a perceptible decline in alienation among the population in the cities. Industrial production continued to surge, leading to predictions that China would become one of the economic superpowers of the twenty-first century. But problems in rural areas began to increase, as lagging farm income, high taxes, and official corruption sparked resentment among the rural populace.

Partly out of fear that such developments could undermine the socialist system and the rule of the CCP, conservative leaders have attempted to curb Western influence and restore faith in Marxism-Leninism. Recently, in what may be a tacit recognition that Marxist exhortations are no longer an effective means of enforcing social discipline; the party has turned to Confucianism as an antidote. Ceremonies celebrating the birth of Confucius now receive official sanction, and the virtues he promoted, such as righteousness, propriety, and social piety, are now widely cited as the means to counter antisocial behaviour.

Beijing's decision to emphasize traditional Confucian themes as a means of promoting broad popular support for its domestic policies is paralleled on the world stage, where it relies on the spirit of nationalism to achieve its goals. Today, China conducts an independent foreign policy and is playing an increasingly active role in the region. To some of its neighbours, including Japan, India, and Russia, China's new posture is cause for disquiet and gives rise to suspicions that it is once again preparing to assert its muscle as in the imperial era. A striking example of this new attitude took place as early as 1979, when Chinese forces briefly invaded Vietnam as punishment for the Vietnamese occupation of neighbouring Cambodia. In the 1990s, China aroused concern in the region by claiming sole ownership over the Spratly Islands in the South China Sea and over Diaoyu Island (also claimed by Japan) near Taiwan (see Map 11.1, Plate 23).

To Chinese leaders, however, such actions simply represent legitimate efforts to resume China's rightful role in the affairs of the region. After a century of humiliation at the hands of the Western powers and neighbouring Japan, the nation, in Mao's famous words of 1949, "has stood up" and no one will be permitted to humiliate it again. For the moment, at least, a fervent patriotism seems to be on the

Reach for the Sky. The 80-story television tower, shown here on the left, is an example of Shanghai's monumental effort to become one of the most modern cities in the world. Pudong was once an uninhabited mudflat on the eastern shores of the Huang Pu River. It is now a dynamic sector of the city teeming with hotels, office buildings, and entertainment centres.

rise in China, actively promoted by the party as a means of holding the country together. Pride in the achievement of national sports teams is intense, and two young authors recently achieved wide acclaim with the publication of their book *The China That Can Say No,* a response to criticism of the country in the United States and Europe. The decision by the International Olympic Committee to award the 2008 Summer Games to Beijing led to widespread celebration throughout the country.

Whether the current leadership will be able to prevent further erosion of the party's power and prestige is unclear. In the short term, efforts to slow the process of change may succeed because many Chinese are understandably fearful of punishment and concerned for their careers. And high economic growth rates can sometimes obscure a multitude of problems as many individuals will opt to chase the fruits of materialism rather than the less tangible benefits of personal freedom. But in the long run, the party leadership must resolve the contradiction between political authoritarianism and economic prosperity. One is reminded of Chiang Kai-shek's failed attempt during the 1930s to revive Confucian ethics as a standard of behaviour for modern China: dead ideologies cannot be revived by decree.

Unrest is also growing among China's national minorities: in Xinjiang, a predominantly Muslim society, and in Tibet, where the official policy of quelling separatism has led to the violent suppression of Tibetan culture and an influx of thousands of ethnic Chinese immigrants. In the meantime, the existence in China of the **Falun Gong** spiritual movement, which the government has attempted to suppress as a potentially serious threat to its authority, is an additional indication that with the disintegration of the old Maoist utopia, the Chinese people will need more than a pale version of Marxism-Leninism or a revived Confucianism to fill the gap.

Falun Gong is a spiritual movement founded in 1992 by Li Hongzhi that involves meditation and exercise to improve spiritual and physical well-being; it has been denounced by the Chinese government as a cult.

New party leaders installed in 2002 and 2003 appear to recognize the challenge. For example, Hu Jintao (b. 1942), who replaced Jiang Zemin as CCP general secretary (in 2002) and head of state (2003), appears to recognize the need for further reforms to open up Chinese society and bridge the yawning gap between rich and poor. In recent years, the government has shown a growing tolerance for the public exchange of ideas, which has surfaced with the proliferation of bookstores, avant-garde theatre, experimental art exhibits, and the Internet.

CHINA'S CHANGING CULTURE

Like their contemporaries all over Asia, Chinese artists were strongly influenced by the revolutionary changes that were taking place in the art world of the West in the early twentieth century. In the decades following the 1911 revolution, Chinese creative artists began to experiment with Western styles, although the more extreme schools, such as Surrealism and Abstract painting, had little impact.

The rise to power of the Communists in 1949 added a new dimension to the debate over the future of culture in China. Spurred by comments made by Mao Zedong at a cultural forum in Yan'an in 1942, leaders rejected the Western slogan of "Art for art's sake" and, like their Soviet counterparts, viewed culture as an important instrument of indoctrination. The standard would no longer be aesthetic quality or the personal preference of the artist but "Art for life's sake," whereby culture would serve the interests of socialism.

At first, the new emphasis on socialist realism did not entirely extinguish the influence of traditional culture. Mao and his colleagues saw the importance of traditional values and culture in building a strong new China and tolerated—and even encouraged—efforts by artists to synthesize traditional ideas with socialist concepts and Western techniques. During the Cultural Revolution, however, all forms of traditional culture came to be viewed as reactionary. Socialist realism became the only standard of acceptability in literature, art, and music. All forms of traditional expression were forbidden.

After Mao's death, Chinese culture was once again released from the shackles of socialist realism. In painting, the new policies led to a revival of interest in both traditional and Western forms. The revival of traditional art was in part a matter of practicality as talented young Chinese were trained to produce traditional paintings for export to earn precious foreign currency for the state. But the regime also showed a new tolerance for the imitation of Western styles as a necessary byproduct of development, thus unleashing an impressive outpouring of artistic creativity later dubbed the "Beijing Spring." A new generation of Chinese painters began to experiment with a wide range of previously prohibited art styles, including Cubism and Abstract Expressionism.

In music, too, the post-Mao era brought significant changes. Music academies closed during the Cultural Revolution for sowing the seeds of the bourgeois mentality were reopened. Students were permitted to study both Chinese and Western styles, but the vast majority selected the latter. To provide examples, leading musicians and composers, such as violinist Isaac Stern, were invited to China to lecture and perform before eager Chinese students.

TAIWAN: THE OTHER CHINA

After retreating to Taiwan following their defeat by the Communists, Chiang Kai-shek and his followers established a new capital at Taipei and set out to build a strong and prosperous nation based on Chinese traditions and the principles of Sun Yat-sen. The government, which continued to refer to itself as the *Republic of China (ROC)*, contended that it remained the legitimate representative of the Chinese people and that it would eventually return in triumph to the mainland.

The Nationalists had much more success on Taiwan than they had achieved on the mainland. In the relatively stable environment provided by a security treaty with the United States, signed in 1954, and the protectorate of the U.S. navy in the Taiwan Strait, the ROC was able to concentrate on economic growth without worrying about a Communist invasion. The regime possessed a number of other advantages that it had not enjoyed in Nanjing. Fifty years of efficient Japanese rule had left behind a relatively modern economic infrastructure and an educated populace, although the island had absorbed considerable damage during World War II and much of its agricultural produce had been exported to Japan at low prices. With only a small population to deal with (about seven million in 1945), the ROC could make good use of foreign assistance and the efforts of its own people to build a modern industrialized society. (See Map 11.2, Plate 24.)

The government moved rapidly to create a solid agricultural base. A land reform program, more effectively designed and implemented than the one introduced in the early 1930s on the mainland, led to the reduction of rents, while landholdings over 1 hectare were purchased by the government and resold to the tenants at reasonable prices. The results were gratifying: food production doubled over the next generation and began to make up a substantial proportion of exports.

In the meantime, the government strongly encouraged the development of local manufacturing and commerce. By the 1970s, Taiwan was one of the most dynamic industrial economies in East Asia. The agricultural proportion of the gross national product declined from 36 percent in 1952 to only 9 percent 30 years later. At first, the industrial and commercial sector was composed of relatively small firms engaged in exporting textiles and food products, but the 1960s saw a shift to heavy industry, including shipbuilding, steel, petrochemicals, and machinery, and a growing emphasis on exports. The government played a major role in the process, targeting strategic industries for support and investing in infrastructure. At the same time, the government stressed the importance of private enterprise and encouraged foreign investment and a high rate of internal savings. By the mid-1980s, more than three-quarters of the population lived in urban areas.

In contrast to the People's Republic of China (PRC) on the mainland, the ROC actively maintained Chinese tradition, promoting respect for Confucius and the ethical principles of the past, such as hard work, frugality, and piety. Although there was some corruption in both the government and the private sector, income differentials between the wealthy and the poor were generally less than elsewhere in the region, and the overall standard of living increased substantially. Health and sanitation improved, literacy rates were quite high, and an active family planning program reduced the rate of population growth. Nevertheless, the total population on the island increased to about 20 million in the mid-1980s.

In one respect, however, Chiang Kai-shek had not changed: increasing prosperity did not lead to the democratization of the political process. The Nationalists continued to rule by emergency decree and refused to permit the formation of opposition political parties on the grounds that the danger of invasion from the mainland had not subsided. Propaganda material from the PRC was rigorously prohibited, and dissident activities (promoting either rapprochement with the mainland or the establishment of an independent Republic of Taiwan) were ruthlessly suppressed. Although representatives to the provincial government of the province of Taiwan were chosen in local elections, the central government (technically representing the entire population of China) was dominated by mainlanders who had fled to the island with Chiang in 1949.

Some friction developed between the mainlanders (as the new arrivals were called), who numbered about two million, and the native Taiwanese; except for a few indigenous peoples in the mountains, most of the native population was ethnic Chinese whose ancestors had emigrated to the island during the Manchu dynasty. While the mainlanders were dominant in government and the professions, the native Taiwanese were prominent in commerce. Mainlanders tended to view the local population with a measure of condescension, and at least in the early years, intermarriage between members of the two groups was rare. Many Taiwanese remembered with anger the events of March 1947, when Nationalist troops had killed hundreds of Taiwanese demonstrators in Taipei. More than 1000 leading members of the local Taiwanese community were arrested and killed in the subsequent repression. By the 1980s, however, these differences in Taiwanese society had begun to diminish; by that time, an ever-higher proportion of the population had been born on the island and identified themselves as Taiwanese.

During the 1980s, the ROC slowly began to evolve toward a more representative form of government—a process that was facilitated by the death of Chiang Kai-shek in 1975. Chiang Ching-kuo (1909–88), his son and successor, was less concerned about the danger from the mainland and more tolerant of free expression. On his death, he was succeeded as president by Lee Teng-hui (b. 1923), a native Taiwanese. By the end of the 1980s, democratization was under way, including elections and the formation of legal opposition parties. A national election in 1992 resulted in a bare majority for the Nationalists over strong opposition from the Democratic Progressive Party (DPP).

But political liberalization had its dangers; some leading Democratic Progressives began to agitate for an independent Republic of Taiwan, a possibility that aroused concern within the Nationalist government in Taipei and frenzied hostility in the PRC. In the spring of 2000, DPP candidate Chen Shui-bian (b. 1950) won election to the presidency, ending half a century of Nationalist Party rule on Taiwan. His elevation to the position angered Beijing, which noted that in the past he had called for an independent Taiwanese state. Chen backed away from that position and called for the resumption of talks with PRC, but Chinese leaders remain suspicious of his intentions and reacted with hostility to U.S. plans to provide advanced military equipment to the island.

Whether Taiwan will remain an independent state or be united with the mainland is impossible to predict. Certainly, the outcome depends in good measure on developments in the PRC. In the meantime, economic and cultural contacts between Taiwan and the mainland are steadily increasing, thus making the costs of any future military confrontation increasingly expensive for both sides. However, the Taiwanese have shown no inclination to accept the PRC's offer of "one country, two systems," under which the ROC would accept the PRC as the legitimate government of China in return for autonomous control over the affairs of Taiwan.

SINGAPORE AND HONG KONG: THE LITTLEST TIGERS

Singapore and Hong Kong may be the smallest **"Little Tigers"** of East Asia, but by no means are they the least successful. Both are essentially city-states with large populations densely packed into small territories. Singapore, once a British Crown colony and briefly a part of the state of Malaysia, is now an independent nation. Hong Kong was a British colony until it was returned to PRC control, but with autonomous status, in 1997. In recent years, both have emerged as industrial powerhouses with standards of living well above the level of their neighbours.

> **"Little Tigers"** is a term that describes Taiwan, Singapore, Hong Kong, and South Korea, four states in East Asia that have experienced strong economic development.

The success of Singapore must be ascribed in good measure to the will and energy of its political leaders. When it became independent in August 1965, Singapore was in a state of transition. Its long-time position as an intermediary for trade between the Indian Ocean and the South China Sea was declining in importance. With only 1600 square kilometres of territory, much of it marshland and tropical jungle, Singapore had little to offer but the frugality and industriousness of its predominantly overseas Chinese population. But a recent history of political radicalism, fostered by the rise of influential labour unions, had frightened away foreign investors.

Within a decade, Singapore's role and reputation had dramatically changed. Under the leadership of Prime Minister Lee Kuan Yew (b. 1923), once the firebrand leader of the radical **People's Action Party**, the government encouraged the growth of an attractive business climate while engaging in massive public works projects to feed, house, and educate the nation's two million citizens. The major components of success have been shipbuilding, oil refineries, tourism, electronics, and finance—the city-state has become the banking hub of the entire region. (See Map 11.3, Plate 24.)

> The **People's Action Party** has been the dominant party in Singapore since 1959; Lee Kuan Yew led the party from its inception until 1992. The party has ruled the country by curbing political freedom and instituting draconian laws.

Like the other Little Tigers, Singapore has relied on a combination of government planning, entrepreneurial spirit, export promotion, high productivity, and an exceptionally high rate of saving to achieve industrial growth rates of nearly 10 percent annually over the past quarter century. Unlike some other industrializing countries in the region, it has encouraged the presence of multinational corporations to provide much needed capital and technological input. Population growth has been controlled by a stringent family planning program, and literacy rates are among the highest in Asia.

As in the other Little Tigers, an authoritarian political system has guaranteed a stable environment for economic growth. Until his recent retirement, Lee Kuan Yew and his People's Action Party dominated Singaporean politics, and opposition elements were intimidated into silence or arrested. The prime minister openly declared that the Western model of pluralist democracy was not appropriate for Singapore and lauded the Meiji model of centralized development. Confucian values of hard work, frugality, and the subordination of the individual to the community have been promoted as the ideology of the state. The government has had a passion for cleanliness and at one time even undertook a campaign to persuade its citizens to flush the public urinals.

But economic success is beginning to undermine the authoritarian foundations of the system as a more sophisticated citizenry begins to demand more political freedoms and an end to government paternalism. Lee Kuan Yew's successor, Goh Chok Tong (b. 1941), has promised a "kinder, gentler" Singapore, and political restrictions on individual behaviour are gradually being relaxed. In the spring of 2000, the government announced the opening of a speaker's corner, where citizens would be permitted to express their views, provided they obtained a permit and did not break the law. While this was a small step, it provided a reason for optimism that a more pluralistic political system will gradually emerge.

The future of Hong Kong is not so clear-cut. As in Singapore, sensible government policies and the hard work of its people have enabled Hong Kong to thrive. At first, the prosperity of the colony depended on a plentiful supply of cheap labour. Inundated with refugees from the mainland during the 1950s and 1960s, the population of Hong Kong burgeoned to more than six million. Many of the newcomers were willing to work for starvation wages in sweatshops producing textiles, simple appliances, and toys for the export market. More recently, Hong Kong has benefited from increased tourism, manufacturing, and the growing economic prosperity of neighbouring Guangdong Province, the most prosperous region of the PRC. Hong Kong has differed from the other societies discussed in this chapter in that it has relied on an unbridled free market system rather than active state intervention in the economy. At the same time, by allocating substantial funds for transportation, sanitation, education, and public housing, the government has created favourable conditions for economic development. (See Map 11.4, Plate 25.)

Unlike the other Little Tigers, Hong Kong remained under colonial rule until very recently. British authorities did little to foster democratic institutions or practices, and most residents of the colony cared more about economic survival than political freedoms. In 1983, in talks between representatives of Great Britain and the PRC, the Chinese leaders made it clear they were determined to have Hong Kong return to mainland authority in 1997, when the British 99-year lease over the New Territories, the food basket of the colony of Hong Kong, ran out. The British agreed, on the

condition that satisfactory arrangements could be made for the welfare of the population. The Chinese promised that for 50 years, the people of Hong Kong would live under a capitalist system and be essentially self-governing. Recent statements by Chinese leaders, however, have raised questions about the degree of autonomy Hong Kong will receive under Chinese rule, which began on July 1, 1997. A decision by the local government in 2003 to expand security restrictions aroused widespread public protests.

CONCLUSION

To the outside observer, since the Communist takeover of power on the mainland, China has projected an image of almost constant turmoil and rapid change. That portrayal is not an inaccurate one, for Chinese society has undergone a number of major transformations since the establishment of the People's Republic of China in the fall of 1949.

- Radical elements in the Communist Party grew restive at what they perceived as a relapse into feudal habits by "capitalist roaders" within the party and, led by Mao Zedong, they launched the Great Proletarian Cultural Revolution.
- To reach his desired political and social ends, Mao had sacrificed Communist ideals, and, as a result, risked the destruction of the very organization that had brought him to power in the first place—the Communist Party. To a large degree, Mao's Cultural Revolution was meant to renew the people's commitment to the Chinese Revolution.

With the death of Mao in 1976, the virulent phase of the Cultural Revolution appeared to be at an end, and a more stable era of economic development seemed to be under way.

- The Communist Party has been able to remain in power since Mao's death, perhaps for cultural reasons.
- Deng Xiaoping's economic modernization of China greatly strengthened the country's economy. (China's economic success has come at great expense to its environment, however.)

China has also seen significant changes.

- Literacy rates and the standard of living, on balance, have improved.
- Military threats from outside powers, such as Japan, the United States, and the Soviet Union, are no longer menacing Chinese borders.
- China has entered the opening stage of its own industrial and technological revolution.

The growing economic success of Taiwan, Hong Kong, and Singapore continues to marvel and defy standard notions of development.

• The economic success of the three countries has been attributed to a mix of autocratic rule, capitalism, and government ownership.
• Taiwan and Hong Kong may have strong historical ties to China, but both islands have followed their own paths and have carved out very different identities for themselves.

CRITICAL THINKING QUESTIONS

1. Why is Falun Gong seen by the Chinese government as a threat to the Chinese Communist Party?

2. Can economic advancements be made without democracy?

3. Could China's mass line system be considered a quasi-democratic approach to mobilizing party members?

4. Why has communism survived in China, albeit in a substantially altered form, when it collapsed in Eastern Europe and the Soviet Union?

5. Would Taiwan have survived without U.S. military support?

6. Can Hong Kong ever integrate with mainland China after almost a century of autonomous development and occupation by the British?

CHAPTER NOTES

1. Quoted in Stanley Karnow, *Mao and China: Inside China's Cultural Revolution* (New York: Viking Penguin, 1972), p. 95.

2. Quoted from an article by Mao Zedong in the June 1, 1958, issue of the journal *Red Flag*. See Stuart R. Schram, *The Political Thought of Mao Tse-tung* (New York: Praeger, 1963), p. 253. The quotation "strike while the iron is hot" is from Karnow, *Mao and China*, p. 93.

IV

Third World Rising

Courtesy of William J. Duiker

Chapter 12

Emerging Africa

At the end of World War II, Africa had already been exposed to over half a century of colonial rule. Many Europeans complacently assumed that colonialism was legitimate, claiming that it introduced "civilization" to the "backward peoples" of Africa (and Asia). However, to many Africans, colonialism was merely part of the Western drive for economic profit and political hegemony and was a plague that threatened ultimately to destroy their civilization.

In the three decades following the end of World War II, the peoples of Africa were gradually liberated from the formal trappings of European colonialism. The creation of independent states in Africa began in the late 1950s and proceeded gradually until the last colonial regimes were finally dismantled. But the transition to independence has not been an unalloyed success. The legacy of colonialism through continued European economic domination has combined with overpopulation and climatic disasters to frustrate the new states' ability to achieve political stability and economic prosperity. At the same time, arbitrary boundaries carved and imposed by the colonial powers along with ethnic and religious divisions within the African countries have led to bitter conflicts, which have posed a severe obstacle to the dream of continental solidarity and cooperation in forging a common destiny. Today, the continent of Africa, although blessed with enormous potential, is one of the most volatile and conflict-ridden areas of the world.

At the conclusion of this chapter, you will be able to

- identify the forces that led Africans to seek independence from colonial rule;
- explain why Pan-Africanism and socialism became popular in Africa;
- describe how Western ideals of nation-states fit with Africa's tribal, communal, and indigenous forms of rule;
- understand how Western values and structures have affected African societies.

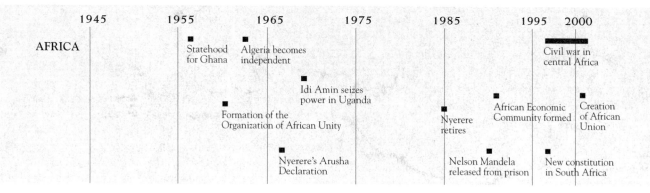

	1945	1955	1965	1975	1985	1995	2000
AFRICA		Statehood for Ghana	Algeria becomes independent				Civil war in central Africa
			Idi Amin seizes power in Uganda				
		Formation of the Organization of African Unity			Nyerere retires	African Economic Community formed	Creation of African Union
			Nyerere's Arusha Declaration		Nelson Mandela released from prison	New constitution in South Africa	

UHURU: THE STRUGGLE FOR INDEPENDENCE

After World War II, Europeans reluctantly recognized that the end result of colonial rule in Africa would be African self-government, if not full independence. Accordingly, the African population would have to be trained to handle the responsibilities of representative government. In many cases, however, little had been done to prepare the local population to lead their own governments—and the imposed foreign governing structures had destroyed local and tribal forms of self-rule. Early in the colonial era, during the late nineteenth century, African administrators had held influential positions in several British colonies, and one even served as governor of the Gold Coast. Eventually, several British colonies had legislative councils with limited African participation, although these councils' functions were solely advisory. But with the formal institution of colonial rule, senior positions were consistently reserved for the British.

After World War II, most British colonies introduced reforms that increased the representation of the local population. Members of legislative and executive councils were increasingly chosen through elections, and Africans came to constitute a majority of these bodies. Elected councils at the local level were introduced in the 1950s to reduce the power of the tribal chiefs and clan heads, who had controlled local government under indirect rule. An exception was South Africa, where European domination continued. In the Union of South Africa, the franchise was restricted to whites except in the former territory of the Cape Colony, where persons of mixed ancestry had voted since the mid-nineteenth century. Black Africans did win some limited electoral rights in Northern and Southern Rhodesia (now Zambia and Zimbabwe), although whites generally dominated the political scene.

A similar process of political change was taking place in the French colonies. At first, the French tried to assimilate the African peoples into French culture. By the 1920s, however, racist beliefs in Western cultural superiority had somewhat discredited this ideal. The French therefore undertook a more limited program of assimilating African elites into Western culture and using them as administrators at the local level as a link to the remainder of the population. This policy resembled the British policy of indirect rule, although it placed more emphasis on French culture in training local administrators. It had only limited success, however, because many Western-educated Africans refused to leave the urban centres to live in the countryside. Others, who were exposed to progressive ideas while studying abroad, rejected the prevailing forms of Western civilization and called for the restoration of national independence.

In 1944, the Free French movement under General Charles de Gaulle issued the **Brazzaville Declaration**, which promised equal rights, though not self-government, in a projected French Union composed of France and its overseas colonies. After the war, a legislative assembly for the new union was created, although its political powers were limited. At the same time, African representatives were elected to the French National Assembly in Paris. But even this new community of nations had separate categories of citizenship based on education and ethnic background, and decisions on major issues were still made in France or by French officials in French Africa.

> The **Brazzaville Declaration** was a 1944 proclamation by Charles de Gaulle promising equal rights—but not self-government—for colonial peoples; it was signed in Brazzaville, the capital of Republic of the Congo.

What Legacy Did Colonialism Leave?

The Western presence brought a few short-term and long-term benefits to Africa, such as improved transportation and communication facilities, and in some areas laid the foundation for a modern industrial and commercial sector. Improved sanitation and medical care in all probability increased life expectancy.

Yet the benefits of westernization were distributed very unequally, and the vast majority of Africans found their lives little improved, if at all. Only South Africa and French-held Algeria, for example, developed modern industrial sectors, extensive railroad networks, and modern communications systems. And both these societies had among the most racist regimes in Africa. In both countries, European settlers were numerous, most investment capital for industrial ventures was European, and whites comprised almost the entire professional and managerial class. Members of the native population were generally restricted to unskilled or semiskilled jobs at wages less than one-fifth of Europeans. Those who worked in industry or on infrastructure projects often suffered from inhumane working conditions. Several thousand African conscripts reportedly died on press gangs building new railroad systems. Needless to say, the benefits of colonialism did not serve the black Africans.

Many colonies concentrated on export crops—peanuts from Senegal and Gambia, cotton from Egypt and Uganda, coffee from Kenya, and palm oil and cocoa products from the Gold Coast. Here the benefits of development were somewhat more widespread. In some cases, the crops were grown on plantations, which were usually owned by Europeans. But plantation agriculture was not always suitable in Africa, and much farming was done by free or tenant farmers. In some areas, where land ownership was traditionally vested in the community, the land was owned and leased by the corporate village.

Even here, however, the vast majority of the profits from the export of tropical products accrued to Europeans or to foreign merchants. While few benefited from the increase in exports, the vast majority of Africans continued to be subsistence farmers growing food for their own consumption. The gap was particularly wide in places like Kenya, where the best lands had been discriminately reserved for European settlers. Ordinary subsistence farmers reaped few benefits from colonial rule.

What Groups Initiated the Fight for Independence?

The African response to the imposition of foreign rule and the loss of independence can be traced through several stages, beginning with resistance. In some cases, the opposition came from an organized state, such as Ashanti, which fought against the British takeover of the Gold Coast in the 1860s. Where formal states did not exist, the colonial takeover was often easier and more gradual; in a few instances, however, such as the Zulu attacks against the British in South Africa in the 1880s and Abdelkader's rebellion against the French in Algeria in the 1840s, resistance to white rule was quite fierce.

But formal nationalist movements and parties generally took time to arise in Africa. The first nationalist groups were formed in urban areas, primarily among people who had been exposed to Western civilization and who had held junior positions in the colonial bureaucracy. As the colonial system became more formalized in the early twentieth century, greater emphasis was placed on racial distinctions, and employment opportunities in government and other professional positions diminished for Africans, especially in the British colonies, where indirect rule was based on collaboration with the local tribal aristocracy. The result was a dissatisfied urban educated elite, who were all the angrier when they faced systemic discrimination.

Political organizations for African rights did not appear until after World War I, and then only in a few areas, such as British-ruled Kenya and the Gold Coast. At first, organizations such as the National Congress of British West Africa (formed in 1919 in the Gold Coast) and Jomo Kenyatta's Kikuyu Central Association in Kenya led by Jomo Kenyatta focused on improving African living conditions in the colonies rather than on national independence. After World War II, however, following the example of independence movements elsewhere, these groups became organized political parties with independence and self-determination as their objective. In the Gold Coast, Kwame Nkrumah

(1909–72) led the Convention People's Party, the first formal political party in black Africa. In the late 1940s, Jomo Kenyatta (1894–1978) founded the Kenya African National Union (KANU), which focused on economic issues but had an implied political agenda as well.

For the most part, these political activities were basically nonviolent and were led by Western-educated African intellectuals. Their constituents were primarily urban professionals, merchants, and members of labour unions. But the demand for independence was not entirely restricted to the cities. In Kenya, for example, the widely publicized Mau Mau movement among the Kikuyu people used armed violence as an essential element of its program to achieve **uhuru** ("freedom") from the British. Although most of the violence was directed against other Africans— only about 100 Europeans were killed in the violence, compared with an estimated 1700 Africans who lost their lives at the hands of the rebels—the spectre of Mau Mau violence alarmed the European population and convinced the British government in 1959 to promise eventual independence.

> **Uhuru** (Swahili for "freedom") is a term that symbolizes the drive for independence in Africa.

A similar process was occurring in Egypt, which had been a protectorate of Great Britain (and under loose Turkish authority until the breakup of the Ottoman Empire) since the 1880s. National consciousness had existed in Egypt since well before the colonial takeover, and members of the legislative council were calling for independence even before World War I. In 1918, a formal political party called the *Wafd* was formed to promote Egyptian independence. The intellectuals were opposed as much to the local palace government as to the British, however, and in 1952, an army coup overthrew King Farouk, the grandson of Khedive Ismail, and established an independent republic (see Chapter 13, pages 224–25).

In areas such as South Africa and Algeria, where the political system was dominated by European settlers, the transition to independence and self-determination was more violent. In South Africa, political activity by local Africans began with the formation of the **African National Congress** (ANC) in 1912. Initially, the ANC was dominated by Western-oriented intellectuals and had little mass support. Its goal was to achieve economic and political reforms, including full equality for educated Africans, within the framework of the existing system. But the ANC's efforts met with little success, while conservative white parties managed to stiffen the segregation laws. In response, the ANC became increasingly radicalized, and by the 1950s, the prospects for a violent confrontation were growing.

Political activity by South African blacks began with the founding of the **African National Congress** (ANC) in 1912. Banned by politically dominant European whites in 1960, the party was not officially un-banned until 1990. It is now the official majority party of the South African government.

In Algeria, resistance to ruthless French rule by Algerian Arabs had never ceased. After World War II, urban agitation intensified, leading to a widespread rebellion against colonial rule in the mid-1950s. At first, the French government tried to maintain its authority in Algeria, which was considered an integral part of metropolitan France. But when Charles de Gaulle became president in 1958 and Algerian Arabs fought back against the ruthless French occupation, he eventually reversed French policy. Algeria became independent under President Ahmed Ben Bella (b. 1918) in 1962. The armed struggle in Algeria hastened the transition to statehood in its neighbours as well. Tunisia won its independence in 1956 after social unrest but retained close ties with Paris. The French attempted to suppress the nationalist movement in Morocco by sending Sultan Muhammad V into exile, but the effort failed, and in 1956, he returned as the ruler of the independent state of Morocco.

Most black African nations achieved their independence in the late 1950s and 1960s, beginning with the Gold Coast, renamed *Ghana,* in 1957 (see Map 12.1, Plate 26). Nigeria, the Belgian Congo (renamed *Zaire* and in 1997 the *Democratic Republic of the Congo*), Kenya, Tanganyika (renamed *Tanzania* after merging with Zanzibar), and several other countries soon followed. Most of the French colonies agreed to accept independence within the framework of de Gaulle's French Community. By the late 1960s, only parts of southern Africa and the Portuguese colonies of Mozambique and Angola remained under European rule.

Independence came later to Africa than to most of Asia. Several factors help explain the delay. For one thing, colonialism was established in Africa somewhat later than in most areas of Asia, and the inevitable reaction from the local population was consequently delayed. Furthermore, with the exception of a few areas in West Africa and along the Mediterranean, coherent states with a strong sense of cultural, ethnic, and linguistic unity did not exist in most of Africa. Most traditional states, such as Ashanti in West Africa, Songhai in the southern Sahara, and Bakongo in the Congo basin, were collections of heterogeneous peoples with little sense of national or monocultural identity. Even after colonies were established, the European powers often practised a policy of "divide and rule," while the British encouraged political decentralization by retaining the authority of the traditional native chieftains. It is hardly surprising that when opposition to colonial rule emerged, unity was difficult to achieve.

THE ERA OF INDEPENDENCE

The newly independent African states faced great challenges, as they had been profoundly affected by colonial rule. The experience had been highly unsatisfactory in most respects. Although Western political institutions, values, and technology had been introduced, at least into the cities, the exposure to European civilization had been superficial at best for most Africans and tragic for many. At the outset of independence, most African societies were still primarily agrarian and traditional, and their modern sectors depended mainly on imports from the West.

What Did Pan-Africanism Offer to the African Peoples?

Most African leaders came from the urban middle class. They had studied in Europe or the United States and spoke and read European languages. Although most were profoundly critical of colonial policies, they appeared to accept the relevance of the Western model to Africa and gave at least lip service to Western democratic values.

Their views on economics were somewhat more diverse. Some, like Jomo Kenyatta of Kenya and General Mobutu Sese Seko (1930–97) of Zaire, were advocates of Western-style capitalism. Others, like Julius Nyerere (1922–99) of Tanzania, Kwame Nkrumah of Ghana, and Sékou Touré (1922–84) of Guinea, preferred an "African form of socialism," which bore slight resemblance to the Marxist-Leninist socialism practised in the Soviet Union and was more like the syndicalist movement in Western Europe. According to its advocates, it was descended from traditional communal practices in pre-colonial Africa.

Like the leaders of other developing countries, the new political leaders in Africa were strongly nationalistic and generally accepted the colonial boundaries. But as we have seen, these boundaries were artificial creations of the colonial powers. Virtually all of the new states included widely diverse ethnic, linguistic, and territorial groups. Zaire, for example, was composed of more than 200 territorial groups speaking 75 different languages.

Some African leaders themselves harboured attitudes that undermined the fragile sense of common identity needed to knit these diverse groups together. A number of leaders—including Nkrumah of Ghana, Touré of Guinea, and Kenyatta of Kenya—were enticed by the dream of **Pan-Africanism** and its concrete manifestation in the

Organization of African Unity (OAU), which was founded in Addis Ababa, Ethiopia, in 1963 (see the box below).

Pan-Africanism refers to a movement that supports African continental unity and solidarity, in which the common interests of black African peoples transcend regional boundaries.

The **Organization of African Unity** (OAU) was an international group of African states founded in 1963 to increase cooperation and solidarity among African states.

Pan-Africanism originated among African intellectuals during the first half of the twentieth century. A basic element was the conviction that there was a distinctive "African personality" that owed nothing to Western materialism and provided a common sense of destiny for all black African peoples. According to Aimé Césaire, a West Indian of African descent and a leading ideologist of the Pan-African movement, whereas Western civilization prized rational thought and material achievement, African culture emphasized emotional expression and a common sense of humanity.

The concept of a unique African destiny (known to its originators by the French term *négritude*, or "blackness"), was in part a natural defensive response to the social Darwinist concepts of Western racial superiority and African inferiority that were popular in Europe and the United States during the early years of the twentieth century. At the same time, it was stimulated by growing self-criticism among many European intellectuals after World War I, who feared that Western civilization was on a path of self-destruction.

TOWARD AFRICAN UNITY

In May 1963, the leaders of 32 African states met in Addis Ababa, the capital of Ethiopia, to discuss the creation of an organization that would represent the interests of all the newly independent countries of Africa. The result was the Organization of African Unity. An excerpt from its charter is presented here. Although the organization has by no means realized all of the aspirations of its founders, it provides a useful forum for the discussion and resolution of its members' common problems.

Charter of the Organization of African Unity

We, the Heads of African States and Governments assembled in the City of Addis Ababa, Ethiopia;

CONVINCED that it is the inalienable right of all people to control their own destiny;

CONSCIOUS of the fact that freedom, equality, justice, and dignity are essential objectives for the achievement of the legitimate aspirations of the African peoples;

CONSCIOUS of our responsibility to harness the natural and human resources of our continent for the total advancement of our peoples in spheres of human endeavour;

INSPIRED by a common determination to promote understanding among our peoples and cooperation among our States in response to the aspirations of our peoples for brotherhood and solidarity, in a larger unity transcending ethnic and national differences;

CONVINCED that, in order to translate this determination into a dynamic force in the cause of human progress, conditions for peace and security must be established and maintained;

DETERMINED to safeguard and consolidate the hard-won independence as well as the sovereignty and territorial integrity of our States, and to fight against neocolonialism in all its forms;

DEDICATED to the general progress of Africa; . . .

DESIROUS that all African States should henceforth unite so that the welfare and well-being of their peoples can be assured;

RESOLVED to reinforce the links between our states by establishing and strengthening common institutions;

HAVE agreed to the present Charter.

Source: John Woronoff, *Organizing African Unity*. © 1970 by Scarecrow Press, Inc., pp. 642–49.

Négritude (French for "blackness") refers to a philosophy shared by black Africans that a distinctive African personality—with no influence from Western values—exists that gives black Africans a common sense of purpose and destiny.

The idea had more appeal to Africans from French colonies than to those from British colonies because the former faced greater discrimination and oppression. Yet it also found adherents in the British colonies, as well as in the United States and elsewhere in the Americas. African American intellectuals such as W. E. B. Dubois and George Padmore and the West Indian politician Marcus Garvey attempted to promote a "black renaissance" by popularizing the idea of a distinct African personality. Their views were shared by several of the new African leaders, including Léopold Senghor (1906–2001) of Senegal, Kwame Nkrumah of Ghana, and Jomo Kenyatta of Kenya. Nkrumah in particular appeared to hope that a pan-African union could be established that would unite all of the new countries of the continent in a broader community.

The program of the Organization of African Unity had forecast a future Africa based on freedom, equality, justice, and dignity and on the unity, solidarity, and territorial integrity of African states. It did not take long for reality to set in. Vast disparities in education and income made it hard to establish democracy in much of Africa. Expectations that independence would lead to stable political structures based on "one person, one vote" were soon disappointed as the initial phase of pluralistic governments gave way to a series of military regimes and one-party states. Between 1957 and 1982, more than 70 leaders of African countries were overthrown by violence, and the pace has increased since then.

Hopes that independence would inaugurate an era of economic prosperity and equality were similarly dashed. Part of the problem could be (and was) ascribed to the lingering effects of colonialism. Most newly independent countries in Africa were dependent on the export of a single crop or natural resource. When prices fluctuated or dropped, they were at the mercy of the uncertainty characterizing the international market. In several cases, the resources were still controlled by foreigners, leading to the charge that colonialism had been succeeded by **neocolonialism**. To make matters worse, most African states had to import technology and manufactured goods from the West, and the prices of those goods rose more rapidly than those of the export products.

Neocolonialism refers to the Western domination of other nations through economic and corporate means, including international financial institutions, rather than through direct political and military means.

The new states also contributed to their own problems. Scarce national resources were squandered on military equipment or expensive consumer goods rather than on building up their infrastructure to provide the foundation for an industrial economy. Corruption, a painful reality throughout the modern world, became almost a way of life in Africa, as bribery (known variously as *dash, chai,* or *bonsella*) became necessary to obtain even the most basic services.

Finally, population growth, which has hindered economic growth more severely than anything else in the new nations of Asia and Africa, became a serious problem and crippled efforts to build modern economies. By the mid-1980s, annual population growth averaged nearly 3 percent throughout Africa, the highest rate of any continent. Drought conditions and the inexorable spread of the Sahara, known as **desertification**, have led to widespread hunger and starvation, first in West African countries such as Niger and Mali and then in Ethiopia, Somalia, and the Sudan. Despite global efforts to provide food, millions are in danger of starvation and malnutrition, and countless others have fled to neighbouring countries in search of sustenance.

Desertification is the process by which formerly useful agricultural land becomes unusable for agriculture; usually abetted by human mismanagement, it is occurring more so as the Sahara Desert expands southward.

In recent years, the spread of AIDS in Africa has reached epidemic proportions. According to one estimate, one-third of the entire population of sub-Saharan Africa is infected with the virus, including a high percentage of the urban middle class. Over 75 percent of the AIDS cases reported around the world are on the continent of Africa. Some observers estimate that without measures to curtail the effects of the disease, it will have a significant impact on several African countries by reducing population growth, which is currently predicted to increase throughout the continent by at least 300 million in the next 15 years.

Poverty is endemic in Africa, particularly among the three-quarters of the population still living off the land. Urban areas have grown tremendously, but as in much of Asia, most are surrounded by massive squatter settlements of rural peoples who have fled to the cities in search of a better life. The expansion of the cities has overwhelmed fragile transportation and sanitation systems and led to rising pollution and perpetual traffic jams, while millions are forced to live without water and electricity. Meanwhile, the fortunate few (all too often government officials on the take) live the high life and emulate the consumerism of the West (in a particularly expressive phrase, the rich in many

East African countries are known as ***wabenzi***, or "Mercedes-Benz people").

> ***Wabenzi*** ("Mercedes-Benz people") is a term given to East African elites who emulate the Western lifestyle.

Which African States Experimented with Socialist-Type Policies?

Concern over the dangers of economic inequality inspired a number of African leaders—including Kwame Nkrumah in Ghana, Julius Nyerere in Tanzania, and Samora Machel in Mozambique—to restrict foreign investment and nationalize the major industries and utilities while promoting social ideals and values. Nyerere was the most consistent, promoting the ideals of socialism and self-reliance through his **Arusha Declaration** of 1967. Taking advantage of his powerful political influence, Nyerere placed limitations on income and established village collectives to avoid the corrosive effects of economic inequality and government corruption. Sympathetic foreign countries provided considerable economic aid to assist the experiment, and many observers noted that levels of corruption, political instability, and ethnic strife were lower in Tanzania than in many other African countries. Unfortunately, corruption has increased in recent years, while political elements on the island of Zanzibar, citing the stagnation brought by decades of socialism, are agitating for autonomy or even total separation from the mainland. Tanzania also has poor soil, inadequate rainfall, and limited resources, all of which have contributed to its slow growth and continuing rural and urban poverty.

> The **Arusha Declaration**, made by Tanzanian president Julius Nyerere in 1967, was a pronouncement of the socialist principles Tanzania would follow to develop the nation's economy; it included a policy of self-reliance, respect for peasants, and a series of citizens' rights.

In 1985, Nyerere voluntarily retired from the presidency. In his farewell speech, he confessed that he had failed to achieve many of his ambitious goals to create a socialist society in Africa. In particular, he admitted that his plan to collectivize the traditional private farm (*shamba*) had run into strong resistance from conservative peasants. "You can socialize what is not traditional," he remarked. "The *shamba* can't be socialized." But Nyerere insisted that many of his policies had succeeded in improving social and economic conditions, and he argued that the only real solution was to consolidate the multitude of small countries in the region into a larger East African Federation.[1]

Courtesy of William J. Duiker

Manioc, Food for the Millions. Manioc, a tuber like the potato, was brought to Africa from the American hemisphere soon after the voyages of Columbus. Although low in nutrient value, it can be cultivated in poor soil with little moisture and is reportedly the staple food for nearly one-third of the population of sub-Saharan Africa. Manioc is also widely grown in tropical parts of Asia and South America and is familiar to westerners as the source of tapioca (it is also called *cassava* or *yuca*). In the illustration shown here, village women in Senegal rhythmically pound manioc to the chanting of those standing nearby.

The countries that opted for capitalism faced their own dilemmas. Neighbouring Kenya, blessed with better soil in the highlands, a local tradition of aggressive commerce, and a residue of European settlers, welcomed foreign investment and profit incentives. The results have been mixed. Kenya has a strong current of indigenous African capitalism and a substantial middle class, mostly based in the capital, Nairobi. But landlessness, unemployment, and income inequities are high, even by African standards (almost one-fifth of the country's 27 million people are squatters, and unemployment is currently estimated at 45 percent). The rate of population growth—more than 4 percent annually—is one of the highest in the world. Eighty percent of the population remains rural, and 40 percent live below the poverty line. The result has been widespread unrest in a country formerly admired for its successful development.

Beginning in the mid-1970s, a few African nations decided to adopt Soviet-style Marxism-Leninism. In Angola and Ethiopia, Marxist parties followed the Soviet model and attempted to create fully socialist societies with the assistance of Soviet experts and Cuban troops and advisers. Economically, the results were disappointing, and both countries faced severe internal opposition. In Ethiopia, the revolt by Muslim tribal peoples in the province of Eritrea led to the fall of the Marxist leader Mengistu Haile Mariam (b. 1937) and his regime in 1990. A similar revolt erupted against the government in Angola, with the rebel group National Union for the Total Independence of Angola (UNITA) controlling much of the rural population and for a time threatening the capital city, Luanda. With the death of the rebel leader Jonas Savimbi in 2002, the revolt finally appeared to be at an end.

What Forces Undermined Pan-Africanism?

Finally, Africans were disappointed that the dream of a united Africa was not realized. Most Africans felt a shared sense of continuing victimization at the hands of the West and were convinced that independence had not ended Western interference in and domination of African affairs. Many African leaders were angered when Western powers, led by the United States, conspired to overthrow the radical Congolese politician Patrice Lumumba in Zaire in the early 1960s. The episode reinforced their desire to form the Organization of African Unity as a means of reducing Western influence. But aside from agreeing to adopt a neutral stance during the Cold War, African states had difficulty achieving a united position on many issues, and their disagreements left the region vulnerable to external influence and even led to its being used by superpower interests to further conflict. During the late 1980s and early 1990s, border disputes festered in many areas of the continent and in some cases—as with Morocco and a rebel movement in the Western Sahara and between Kenya and Uganda—flared into outright war.

Even within many African nations, the concept of nationhood was undermined by the renascent force of regionalism or tribalism. Nigeria, with the largest population on the continent, was rent by civil strife during the late 1960s when dissident Ibo groups in the southeast attempted unsuccessfully to form the independent state of Biafra. Ethnic conflicts broke out among hostile territorial groups in Zimbabwe (the former Southern Rhodesia) and in several nations in central Africa. In Kenya, Luo tribal leader Tom Mboya was assassinated, presumably because rival groups feared that he would be selected to succeed the charismatic Kikuyu president Jomo Kenyatta.

Another force undermining nationalism in Africa was Pan-Islamism. Its prime exponent in Africa was Egyptian president Gamal Abdel Nasser. After Nasser's death in 1970, the torch of Islamic unity in Africa passed to Libyan president Muammar Qaddafi (b. 1942), whose ambitions to create a greater Muslim nation in the Sahara under his authority led to conflict with neighbouring Chad. The Islamic resurgence also surfaced in Ethiopia, where Muslim tribes in Eritrea (the former Italian colony of Eritrea had been joined with Ethiopia in 1952) rebelled against the Marxist regime of Colonel Mengistu in Addis Ababa.

What Recent Challenges Have Been Faced in South Africa, Nigeria, and Zaire?

Not all the news in Africa has been bad. Stagnant economies have led to the collapse of one-party regimes and the emergence of fragile democracies in several countries. Dictatorships were brought to an end in Ethiopia, Liberia, and Somalia, although in each case the fall of the regime was later followed by political instability or civil war. In Senegal, national elections held in the summer of 2000 brought an end to four decades of rule by the once dominant Socialist Party. New president Abdoulaye Wade, of the Senegalese Democratic Party, has promised to introduce comprehensive reforms to stimulate the economy.

Perhaps the most notorious end to a ruthless dictatorship is the demise of Idi Amin's regime in Uganda. Colonel Amin led a coup against Prime Minister Milton Obote in 1971. After ruling by terror and brutal repression of dissident elements, he was finally deposed in 1979. In recent years, stability has returned to the country, which in May 1996 had its first presidential election in more than 15 years.

Africa has also benefited from the end of the Cold War, as the superpowers have virtually ceased to compete for power and influence in Africa. When the Soviet Union withdrew its support from the Marxist government in Ethiopia, the United States allowed its right to maintain military bases in neighbouring Somalia to lapse, resulting in the overthrow of the authoritarian government there. Unfortunately, clan rivalries led to such turbulence that many inhabitants were in imminent danger of starvation, and in the winter of 1992, U.S. military forces occupied the country to oust a regime it did not favour, while claiming to be there to provide food to the starving population. Since the departure of American troops in 1993, the country has been divided into clan fiefdoms while Islamic groups struggle to bring a return to law and order.

Perhaps Africa's greatest success story is South Africa, where the white government—which long maintained a ruthless policy of racial segregation (**apartheid**) and restricted black sovereignty to a series of small "Bantustans" in relatively infertile areas of the country—finally accepted the inevitability of African involvement in the political process and the national economy. In 1990, the government of President F. W. de Klerk (b. 1936) released ANC leader Nelson Mandela (b. 1918) from prison, where he had been held since 1964. In 1993, the two leaders agreed to hold democratic national elections the following spring. In the meantime, ANC representatives agreed to take part in a transitional coalition government with de Klerk's National Party. Those elections resulted in a substantial majority for the ANC, and Mandela became president.

> **Apartheid** was a system of legal and social restrictions on black South Afrikaners that separated them from the whites who controlled the country.

In May 1996, a new constitution was approved, calling for a multi-racial state. The coalition government quickly collapsed, however, as the National Party immediately went into opposition, claiming that the new charter did not adequately provide for joint decision making by members of the coalition. The third group in the coalition, the Zulu-based Inkatha Freedom Party, agreed to remain within the government, but rivalry with the ANC intensified. Zulu chief Mangosuthu Buthelezi, drawing on the growing force of Zulu nationalism, began to invoke the memory of the great nineteenth-century ruler Shaka in a possible bid for future independence.

In 1999, a major step toward political stability was taken when Nelson Mandela stepped down from the presidency, to be replaced by his long-time disciple Thabo Mbeki. The new president faced a number of intimidating problems, including rising unemployment, widespread lawlessness, chronic corruption, and an ominous flight of capital and professional personnel from the country. Mbeki's conservative economic policies earned the support of some white voters and the country's new black elite but was criticized by labour leaders, who contend that the benefits of independence are not seeping down to the poor. Still, with all its problems, South Africa remains the wealthiest and most industrialized state on the continent, and many of its citizens still support the premise that a multi-racial society can succeed in Africa.

If the situation in South Africa provides grounds for modest optimism, the situation in Nigeria provides reason for serious concern. Africa's largest country in terms of population, and one of its wealthiest because of substantial oil reserves, Nigeria until recent years was in the grip of military dictatorship. During his rule, General Sani Abacha ruthlessly suppressed all opposition and in late 1995 ordered the execution of a writer despite widespread protests from human rights groups abroad. Ken Saro-Wiwa had criticized environmental damage caused by foreign interests in southern Nigeria, but the regime's major concern was his support for separatist activities in an area that had previously launched the Biafran insurrection in the late 1960s. In a protest against the brutality of the Abacha regime, Nobel Prize–winning author Wole Soyinka (b. 1934) published

from exile a harsh exposé of the crisis inside the country. His book, *The Open Sore of a Continent,* places the primary responsibility for failure not on Nigeria's long list of dictators but on the very concept of the modern nation-state, which was introduced into Africa arbitrarily by Europeans during the later stages of the colonial era. A nation, he contends, can only emerge from below, as the expression of the moral and political will of the local inhabitants; nationhood cannot be imposed artificially from above, as was the case throughout Africa.

In 1998, Abacha died, and national elections led to the creation of a civilian government under Olusegun Obasanjo. Civilian leadership has not been a panacea for Nigeria's problems, however. Northerners, who had traditionally dominated Nigerian politics, became irritated at the new president's efforts to address economic problems in the southern part of the country. In early 2000, religious clashes broke out in several northern cities as the result of a decision by provincial officials to apply Islamic law throughout their jurisdiction. President Obasanjo has attempted to defuse the unrest by delaying in carrying out the decision, but the issue raises tensions between Christian peoples in the southern part of the country and the primarily Islamic north while threatening the fragile unity of Africa's most populous country.

The religious tensions that erupted in Nigeria have spilled over into neighbouring states. In the nearby Ivory Coast, the death of President Félix Houphouët-Boigny in 1993 led to an outbreak of long-simmering resentment between Christians in the south and recently arrived Muslim immigrants in the north. National elections held in the fall of 2000, resulting in the election of a Christian president, were marked by sporadic violence and widespread charges of voting irregularities. In the meantime, pressure to apply the Islamic laws is spreading to Nigeria's northern neighbour Niger, where the president has opposed Islamic law on the grounds that it would unsettle his country. Christian churches have been attacked, and bars and brothels have been sacked or burnt to the ground.

Currently, the most tragic situation is in the central African states of Rwanda and Burundi, where a chronic conflict between the minority Tutsis and the Hutu majority has led to a bitter civil war, with thousands of refugees fleeing to the neighbouring Democratic Republic of the Congo (formerly Zaire). In a classic example of conflict between pastoral and farming peoples, the nomadic Tutsis had long dominated the sedentary Hutu population. It was the attempt of the Bantu-speaking Hutus to bring an end to Tutsi domination that initiated the recent conflict, marked by massacres on both sides. In the meantime, the presence of large numbers of foreign troops and refugees intensified centrifugal forces inside Zaire, where General Mobutu Sese

Seko had long ruled with an iron hand. In 1997, military forces led by Mobutu's long-time opponent Laurent Kabila managed to topple the general's corrupt government in Kinshasa. Once in power, Kabila renamed the country the *Democratic Republic of the Congo* and promised a return to democratic practices. The new government systematically suppressed political dissent, however, and in January 2001, Kabila was assassinated and was succeeded shortly afterward by his son. Peace talks are now under way.

It is clear that African societies have not yet begun to surmount the challenges they have faced since independence. Most African states are still poor and their populations illiterate. According to a World Bank report published in 2000, sub-Saharan Africa is the only major region in the world where the population is living less well than it did in the 1960s. But a significant part of the problem is, as Wole Soyinka contended, that the nation-state system is not indigenous to the African continent. Africans must find better ways to cooperate with each other and to protect and promote their own interests. A first step in that direction was taken in 1991, when the Organization of African Unity agreed to establish the African Economic Community (AEC). In 2001, the Organization of African Unity was replaced by the African Union, which is intended to provide greater political and economic integration throughout the continent in years to come. As a first step, West African states have set up a peacekeeping force to monitor fragile cease-fires in Liberia and neighbouring Sierra Leone, where civil wars have caused widespread devastation.

As Africa evolves, it is useful to remember that economic and political change is often an agonizingly slow and painful process. Introduced to industrialization and concepts of Western democracy only a century ago, African societies are still groping for ways to graft Western political institutions and economic practices onto a native structure still significantly influenced by traditional values and attitudes. As one African writer recently observed, it is easy to be cynical in Africa because changes in political regimes have had little effect on people's livelihood. Still, he said, "let us welcome the wind of change. This, after all, is a continent of winds. The trick is to keep hope burning, like a candle protected from the wind."[2]

CONTINUITY AND CHANGE IN MODERN AFRICAN SOCIETIES

Although generalizations are difficult on this most diverse of continents, it is clear that the impact of the West has been greater on urban and educated Africans and more limited on rural peasants. After all, the colonial presence was first and most firmly established in the cities. Many cities, including Dakar, Lagos, Johannesburg, Cape Town, Brazzaville, and Nairobi, are direct products of the colonial experience. Most African cities today look like their counterparts elsewhere in the world. They have high-rise buildings, blocks of residential apartments, wide boulevards, neon lights, movie theatres, and traffic jams.

The cities are also where the African elites live and work. Affluent Africans, like their contemporaries in other developing countries, have been strongly attracted to the glittering material aspects of Western culture. They live in Western-style homes or apartments and eat Western foods stored in Western refrigerators, and those who can afford it drive Western cars. It has been said, not wholly in praise, that there are more Mercedes-Benzes in Nigeria than in Germany, where they are manufactured.

Africans living in urban centres have become increasingly Western, in part, due to the educational system. In the pre-colonial era, education as we know it did not really exist in Africa except for schools in Christian Ethiopia and academies to train young males in Islamic law in Muslim societies in North and West Africa. For the average African, education took place at the home or in the village courtyard and stressed socialization and vocational training.

Traditional education in Africa was not necessarily inferior to that in Europe. Social values and customs were transmitted to the young by storytellers, often village elders who could gain considerable prestige through their performance. Among the Luo people in Kenya, for example, children were taught in a *siwindhe,* or the house of a widowed grandmother. Here they would be instructed in the ways and thinking of their people. A favourite saying for those who behaved stupidly was "you are uneducated, like one who never slept in a *siwindhe.*"[3]

Europeans introduced modern Western education into Africa in the nineteenth century, although some Africans had been literate in one or more Western languages by taking part in commerce. The French set up the first state-run schools in Senegal in 1818. In British colonies and protectorates, the earliest schools were established by missionaries. At first, these schools concentrated on vocational training with some instruction in European languages and Western civilization. Most courses were taught in the vernacular, although many schools later switched to English or French. Eventually, pressure from Africans led to the introduction of professional training, and the first institutes of higher learning were established in the early twentieth century. Most college-educated Africans, called "been-to's," however, received their higher training abroad.

With independence, African countries established their own state-run schools. The emphasis was on the primary level, but high schools and universities were established in major cities. The basic objectives have been to introduce vocational training and improve literacy rates. Unfortunately, both funding and trained teachers are scarce in most countries, and few rural areas have schools. As a result, illiteracy remains high, estimated at about 70 percent of the population across the continent. There has been a perceptible shift toward education in the vernacular languages. In West Africa, only about one in four adults is conversant in a Western language.

One interesting vehicle for popular education that emerged during the transition to independence in Nigeria was the Onitsha Market pamphlet. Produced primarily by the Ibo people in the southeast, who traditionally valued egalitarianism and individual achievement, the pamphlets were "how-to" books advising readers on how to succeed in a rapidly changing Africa. They tended to be short, inexpensive, and humorous, with flashy covers to attract the potential buyer's attention. One, titled "The Nigerian Bachelor's Guide," sold 40 000 copies. Unfortunately, the Onitsha Market and the pamphlet tradition were destroyed during the Nigerian civil war of the late 1960s, but they undoubtedly played an important role during a crucial period in the country's history. Recently, Onitsha has become the largest producer of video movies in sub-Saharan Africa.

Outside the major cities, where about three-quarters of the continent's inhabitants live, Western influence has had less of an impact. Millions of people throughout Africa (as in Asia) live much as their ancestors did, in thatch huts without modern plumbing and electricity; they farm or hunt by traditional methods, practise time-honoured family rituals, and believe in the traditional deities. Even here, however, change is taking place. Slavery has been eliminated, for the most part, although there have been persistent reports of raids by slave traders on defenceless villages in the southern Sudan. Economic need, though, has brought about massive migrations as some leave to work on plantations, others move to the cities, and still others flee to refugee camps to escape starvation. Migration itself is a wrenching experience, disrupting familiar family and village ties and enforcing new social relationships.

Nowhere, in fact, is the dichotomy between old and new, native and foreign, rural and urban so clear and painful as in Africa. Urban dwellers regard the village as the repository of

Courtesy of William J. Duiker

Building His Dream House. In Africa, the houses of rural people are often constructed with a wood frame, known as *wattle*, daubed with mud, and then covered with a thatch roof. Such houses are inexpensive to build and remain cool in the hot tropical climate. In this Kenyan village not far from the Indian Ocean, a young man is applying mud to the wall of his future home. Houses are built in a similar fashion throughout the continent, as well as in much of southern Asia.

all that is backward in the African past, while rural peoples view the growing urban areas as a source of corruption, prostitution, hedonism, and the destruction of communal customs and values. The tension between traditional ways and Western culture is particularly strong among African intellectuals, many of whom are torn between their admiration for things Western and their desire to retain an African identity. "Here we stand," wrote one Nigerian,

> infants overblown
> poised between two civilizations
> finding the balancing irksome,
> itching for something to happen,
> to tip us one way or the other,
> groping in the dark for a helping hand
> and finding none.[4]

How Have the Lives of African Women Changed?

One of the consequences of colonialism and independence has been a change in the relationship between men and women. In most pre-colonial African societies, men and women had distinctly different roles. Women in sub-Saharan Africa, however, generally did not live under the severe legal and social disabilities that we have seen in most other societies, and their relationship with men was complementary rather than subordinate.

Within the family, wives normally showed a degree of deference to their husbands, and polygamy was not uncommon. But because society was usually arranged on communal lines, property was often held in common, and production tasks were divided on a cooperative rather than hierarchical basis. The status of women tended to rise as they moved through the life cycle. Women became more important as they reared children; in old age, they often became eligible to serve in senior roles within the family, lineage, or village. In some societies, such as the Ashanti kingdom in West Africa, women such as the queen mother were eligible to hold senior political positions. Some observers argue that polygamy was beneficial for women because it promoted communal and cooperative attitudes within the community and divided up the task of motherhood among several wives.

Sexual relationships changed profoundly during the colonial era, sometimes in ways that could justly be described as beneficial. Colonial governments attempted to bring an end to forced marriage, bodily mutilation such as clitoridectomy (known as female circumcision), and polygamy. Missionaries introduced women to Western education and encouraged them to organize themselves to defend their interests.

But the new system had some unfavourable consequences as well. Like men, women now became a labour resource. As African males were taken from the villages to serve as forced labour on construction projects, the traditional division of labour was disrupted, and women were forced to play a more prominent role in the economy. At the same time, their role in the broader society was constricted. In British colonies, Victorian attitudes of sexual repression and female subordination led to restrictions on women's freedom, and the positions in government they had formerly held were closed to them.

Independence also had a significant impact on gender roles in African society. Almost without exception, the new governments established the principle of sexual equality and permitted women to vote and run for political office. Yet as elsewhere, women continue to operate at a disadvantage in a world dominated by males. Politics remains a male preserve, and although a few professions, such as teaching, child care, and clerical work, are dominated by women, most African women are employed in positions such as agricultural labour, factory work, and retail trade or as domestics. Education is open to all at the elementary level, but women comprise less than 20 percent of students at the upper levels in most African societies today.

Not surprisingly, women have made the greatest strides in the cities. Most urban women, like men, now marry on the basis of personal choice, although a significant minority are still willing to accept their parents' choice. After marriage, African women appear to occupy a more equal position than their counterparts in most Asian countries. Each marriage partner tends to maintain a separate income, and women often have the right to possess property separate from their husbands. While many wives still defer to their husbands in the traditional manner, others are like the woman in Abioseh Nicol's story "A Truly Married Woman," who, after years of living as a common-law wife with her husband, is finally able to provide the price and finalize the marriage. After the wedding, she declares, "For twelve years I have got up every morning at five to make tea for you and breakfast. Now I am a truly married woman [and] you must treat me with a little more respect. You are now my husband and not a lover. Get up and make yourself a cup of tea."[5]

In general, sexual relationships between men and women in contemporary Africa are relatively relaxed, as they were in traditional society. Sexual activity among adolescents is customary in most societies, and only a minority of women are still virgins at the time of marriage. Most marriages are monogamous. Males seem to be more likely to have extramarital relationships, often with bar girls or prostitutes (sometimes known as "walk-about women"), but adultery on the part of women is not rare.

There is a growing feminist movement in Africa, but it is firmly based on conditions in the local environment. Many African women writers, for example, refuse to be defined by Western dogma and opt instead for a brand of African feminism much like that of Ama Ata Aidoo (b. 1942), a Ghanaian novelist, whose ultimate objective is to free African society as a whole, not just its female inhabitants. After receiving her education at a girls' school in the Gold Coast and attending classes at Stanford University in the United States, she embarked on a writing career in which, as she notes, she has committed herself to the betterment of the African people. Every African woman and every man, she insists, "should be a feminist, especially if they believe that Africans should take charge of our land, its wealth, our lives, and the burden of our development. Because it is not possible to advocate independence for our continent without also believing that African women must have the best that the environment can offer."[6]

In a few cases, women are even going into politics. One example is Margaret Dongo of Zimbabwe, where a black African government under Robert Mugabe succeeded white rule in the former Southern Rhodesia in 1980. Now an independent member of Zimbabwe's Parliament, she is labelled "the ant in the elephant's trunk" for her determined effort to root out corruption and bring about social and economic reforms to improve the lot of the general population. "We didn't fight to remove white skins," she remarks. "We fought discrimination against blacks in land distribution, education, employment. If we are being exploited again by our black leaders, then what did we fight for?"[7]

In general, then, women in urban areas in contemporary Africa have been able to hold their own. However, they are still sometimes held to different standards than men (African men often expect their wives to be both modern and traditional, fashionable and demure, wage earners and housekeepers) and do not possess the full range of career opportunities that men do.

The same cannot necessarily be said about women in rural areas, where traditional attitudes continue to exert a strong influence, and individuals may still be subordinated to communalism. In some societies, clitoridectomy is still widely practised. Polygamy is also not uncommon, and arranged marriages are still the rule rather than the exception.

To a villager in Africa as elsewhere, an African city often looks like the fount of evil, decadence, and corruption. Women in particular have suffered from the tension between the pull of the city and the village. As men are drawn to the cities in search of employment and excitement, their wives and girlfriends are left behind, both literally and figuratively, in the native village. Nowhere has this been more vividly described than in the anguished cry of Lawino, the

Salt of the Earth. During the pre-colonial era, many West African societies were forced to import salt from Mediterranean countries in exchange for tropical products and gold. Today the people of Senegal satisfy their domestic needs by mining salt deposits contained in lakes like this one in the interior of the country. These lakes are the remnants of vast seas that covered the region of the Sahara in prehistoric times. Note that it is women who are doing much of the heavy labour, while men occupy the managerial positions.

Courtesy of William J. Duiker

abandoned wife in Ugandan author Okot p'Bitek's *Song of Lawino.* Lawino laments not just her husband's decision to take a modern urban wife, who dusts powder over her face to look like a white woman and has red-hot lips like glowing charcoal, but his rejection of his roots. Her husband in turn lashes out in frustration at what he considers the poverty, backwardness, and ignorance of the rural environment.

What Factors Have Driven Changes in African Culture?

Inevitably, the tension between traditional and modern, native and foreign, and individual and communal that has permeated contemporary African society has spilled over into culture. In general, in the visual arts and music, utility and ritual have given way to pleasure and decoration. In the process, Africans have been affected to a certain extent by foreign influences but have retained their distinctive characteristics. Wood carving, metalwork, painting, and sculpture, for example, have preserved their traditional forms but are now increasingly adapted to serve the tourist industry and the export market.

No area of African culture has been so strongly affected by political and social events as literature. Except for Muslim areas in North and East Africa, pre-colonial

Africans did not have a written literature, although their tradition of oral storytelling served as a rich repository of history, custom, and folk culture. The absence of written languages, of course, means a lack of a traditional African literature. The first written literature in the vernacular or in European languages emerged during the nineteenth century in the form of novels, poetry, and drama.

Angry at the negative portrayal of Africa in Western literature, African authors initially wrote primarily for a European audience as a means of affirming black dignity and purpose. Embracing the ideals of *négritude,* many glorified the emotional and communal aspects of the traditional African experience.

One of the first was Guinean author Camara Laye (1928–80), who in 1953 published *The Dark Child,* a touching and intimate initiation into village life in precolonial Africa. In the novel, which admitted the reader to the secret rituals and practices of daily life behind the protective hedges of an African village compound, the author openly regretted the lost ways of the African past while conceding that they were not appropriate to the Guinea of tomorrow.

Chinua Achebe of Nigeria was the first major African novelist to write in the English language. In his writings, he attempts to interpret African history from a native perspective and to forge a new sense of African identity. In his most famous novel, *Things Fall Apart* (1958), he recounts the story of a Nigerian who refuses to submit to the new British order and eventually commits suicide. Criticizing those of his contemporaries who have accepted foreign rule, the protagonist laments that the white man "has put a knife on the things that held us together and we have fallen apart."[8]

After 1965, the African novel took a dramatic turn, shifting its focus from the brutality of the foreign oppressor to the shortcomings of the new native leadership. Having gained independence, African politicians were now portrayed as mimicking and even outdoing the injustices committed by their colonial predecessors. A prominent example of this genre is the work of Kenyan Ngugi wa Thiong'o (b. 1938). His first novel, *A Grain of Wheat,* takes place on the eve of *uhuru,* or "freedom." Although it mocks local British society for its racism, snobbishness, and superficiality, its chief interest lies in its unsentimental and even unflattering portrayal of ordinary Kenyans in their daily struggle for survival.

Whereas Ngugi initially wrote in English for elite African and foreign readers, he was determined to reach a broader audience and eventually decided to write in his native Kikuyu. For that reason, perhaps, in the late 1970s, he was placed under house arrest for writing subversive literature. From prison, he secretly wrote *Devil on the Cross,* which urged his compatriots to overthrow the government

Courtesy of William J. Duiker

I Accuse! For many Africans, the end of European colonialism did not mark the opening of a new era of democratic achievement and economic prosperity. To the contrary, most African countries have been plagued with continuing problems of endemic poverty, internecine conflict, and authoritarian rule. In this photograph, an anonymous commentator from the city of Mombasa, in Kenya, braves official displeasure by pointing an accusing finger at African leaders who rule by dictatorial means. The focus of his anger is undoubtedly directed at Kenyan president Daniel arap Moi, one of the most authoritarian of recent African rulers. Moi agreed to retire in 2002.

of Daniel arap Moi. Published in 1980, the book sold widely and was eventually read aloud by storytellers throughout Kenyan society. Fearing an attempt on his life, in recent years Ngugi has lived in exile.

Many of Ngugi's contemporaries have followed his lead and focused their frustration on the failure of the continent's new leadership to carry out the goals of independence. One of the most outstanding is Nigerian Wole Soyinka. His novel *The Interpreters* (1965) lambasted the corruption and hypocrisy of Nigerian politics. Succeeding novels and plays have continued that tradition, resulting in a Nobel Prize in Literature in 1986. The winner of the Nobel Prize in Literature in 2003 was J. M. Coetzee (b. 1940), whose novels, such as *Disgrace* (1999), exposed the social and psychological devastation of apartheid on South Africans. His plea for tolerance and compassion echoed the moral commitment to human dignity on the part of many white African authors.

Colonialism camouflaged its economic objectives under the cloak of a "civilizing mission," which in Africa was aimed at illuminating the so-called Dark Continent with Europe's brilliant civilization. In 1899, the Polish-born English author Joseph Conrad (1857–1924) fictionalized his harrowing journey up the Congo River in the novella *Heart of Darkness.* Expressing views from his

Victorian perspective, he portrayed an Africa that was incomprehensible, irrational, sensual, and therefore threatening. Conrad, however, was shocked by the horrific exploitation of the peoples of the Belgian Congo, presenting them with a compassion rarely seen during the heyday of imperialism.

Over the years, Conrad's work has provoked much debate, and many African writers have been prompted to counter his vision by reaffirming the dignity and purpose of the African people. One of the first to do so was the Guinean author Camara Laye, who in 1954 composed a brilliant novel, *The Radiance of the King,* which can be viewed as the mirror image of Conrad's *Heart of Darkness.* In Laye's work, another European protagonist undertakes a journey into the impenetrable heart of Africa. This time, however, he is enlightened by the process, thereby obtaining self-knowledge and ultimately salvation.

Some recent African authors, like the Somali writer Nuruddin Farah (b. 1945), argue that it is time for Africans to stop blaming their present political ills on either colonialism or on their own dictators. In his writings, such as the novel *Sweet and Sour Milk,* Farah urges Africans to stop lamenting the contamination of African society from the West and take charge of their own destiny. In so doing, Farah joins other African writers in serving as the social conscience of a continent still seeking its own identity.

A number of women are among Africa's most prominent writers today. Traditionally, African women were valued for their talents as storytellers, but writing was strongly discouraged by both traditional and colonial authorities on the grounds that women should occupy themselves with their domestic obligations. In recent years, however, a number of women have emerged as prominent writers of African fiction. Two examples are Buchi Emecheta (b. 1940) of Nigeria and Ama Ata Aidoo of Ghana. Beginning with *Second Class Citizen* (1975), which chronicled the breakdown of her own marriage, Emecheta has published numerous works exploring the role of women in contemporary African society and decrying the practice of polygamy. In her own writings, Aidoo has focused on the identity of today's African women and the changing relations between men and women in society. Her novel *Changes: A Love Story* (1991) chronicles the lives of three women, none presented as a victim but all caught up in the struggle for survival and happiness. Sadly, the one who strays the furthest from traditional African values finds herself free but isolated and lonely.

One of the overriding concerns confronting African intellectuals since independence has been the problem of language. Unlike Asian societies, Africans have not inherited a long written tradition from the pre-colonial era. As a result, many intellectuals have written in the colonial language, a practice that sometimes results in guilt and anxiety. As we have seen, some have reacted by writing in their local languages to reach a native audience. The market for such work is limited, however, because of the high illiteracy rate and also because novels written in African languages have no market abroad. Moreover, because of the deep financial crisis throughout the continent, there is little money for the publication of serious books. Many of Africa's libraries and universities are almost literally without books. It is little wonder that many African authors, to their discomfort, continue to write and publish in foreign languages.

Contemporary African music also reflects a hybridization or fusion with Western culture. Having travelled to the New World via the slave trade centuries earlier, African drum beats evolved into North American jazz and Latin American dance rhythms, only to return to reenergize African music. In fact, today music is one of Africans' most effective weapons for social and political protest. Easily accessible to all, African music, whether Afro-beat in Nigeria, rai in Algeria, or reggae in Benin, represents the "weapon of the future," contemporary musicians say; it "helped free Nelson Mandela" and "will put Africa back on the map." Censored by all the African dictatorial regimes, these courageous musicians persist in their struggle against corruption, what one singer calls the second slavery, "the cancer that is eating away at the system." Their voices echo the chorus "Together we can build a nation, / Because Africa has brains, youth, knowledge."[9]

CONCLUSION

Nowhere in the developing world is the dilemma of continuity and change more agonizing than in contemporary Africa.

- Africans are intrigued by the spectacle of Western affluence yet repulsed by the bloody trail of slavery to colonialism.
- African intellectuals have been torn between advocating and supporting the image of Western materialism while preserving African traditions and cultures.
- Many Africans still yearn for the dreams of African empowerment embodied in Pan-Africanism and the program of the Organization of African Unity.
- African novelists have grappled with the effects of Western cultural imperialism and the need and desire for modernization. For the average African, of course, such intellectual dilemmas pale before the daily challenge of survival.

- Poverty, AIDS, and the fundamental gap between the traditional village and the modern metropolis are day-to-day concerns for Africans.

CRITICAL THINKING QUESTIONS

1. Has colonialism robbed Africans of a century of development?

2. South Africa today, despite the numerous legal and political changes made after the demise of apartheid, still struggles with racism and blacks remain generally disadvantaged. Can the roots of racism ever be removed in a society with a deep history of systemic discrimination?

3. South African president Thabo Mbeki has said that AIDS is an epidemic of the poor, noting that to fight AIDS one needs to fight poverty. To what degree does this view consider scientific evidence and reflect an understanding of the socioeconomic underpinnings of this deadly disease?

4. When the Western world failed to react quickly to the genocide in Rwanda, many charged that this lack of concern stemmed from the West's continued racist attitudes about black Africa. Is this accusation justified?

5. What responsibility does the West have in helping Africa deal with problems such as AIDS, tribal warfare, famine, and poverty?

CHAPTER NOTES

1. *New York Times,* September 1, 1996.

2. Dan Agbee, in *Newswatch* (Lagos), quoted in *World Press Review,* August 1991, p. 16.

3. Adrian Roscoe, *Uhuru's Fire: African Literature East to South* (Cambridge, U.K.: Cambridge University Press, 1977), p. 23.

4. Francis Ademola, *Reflections: Nigerian Prose and Verse* (Lagos, Nigeria: African Universities Press, 1962), p. 65, quoted in Mutiso, *Socio-Political Thought in African Literature,* p. 117.

5. Abioseh Nicol, *A Truly Married Woman and Other Stories* (London: Oxford University Press, 1965), p. 12.

6. Ama Ata Aidoo, *No Sweetness Here* (New York: Longman, 1995), p. 136.

7. Quoted in the *New York Times,* May 13, 1996.

8. Chinua Achebe, *Things Fall Apart* (New York: Anchor, 1994), p. 176. In the 1958 edition, this passage is on pp. 124–25.

9. Gilles Médioni, "Stand Up, Africa!" *World Press Review,* July 2002, p. 34. Reprinted in L'Express.

Chapter 13

Carving Up the Middle East

The Middle East has been greatly affected by the decolonization process as European powers carved up the region into states with artificial boundaries. The colonial decision to make the British Mandate of Palestine into the state of Israel would change future regional dynamics, as wars and conflicts would be fought over this holy place. Arab nationalism rose, first under the charismatic Egyptian leadership of Gamal Abdel Nasser, and then through Arabic music and news aired on satellite TV. The Iranian Revolution represented a new ideological force in the Middle East that perplexed both superpowers during the Cold War. Islamic movements and parties also ascended in many parts of the Middle East as a reaction to corrupt and autocratic regimes. At the same time, the youth and disaffected continue to yearn for social and political change.

At the conclusion of this chapter, you will be able to

- explain why the Middle East reshaped by European powers has become the site of numerous political conflicts and boundary wars;
- describe the central role of the Israeli-Palestinian conflict in understanding the Middle East;
- explain why Islamism arose in Iran and other Middle Eastern states;
- detail the regional and global implications of various wars in the Persian Gulf region;
- identify the various forms of Arab nationalism in the Middle East.

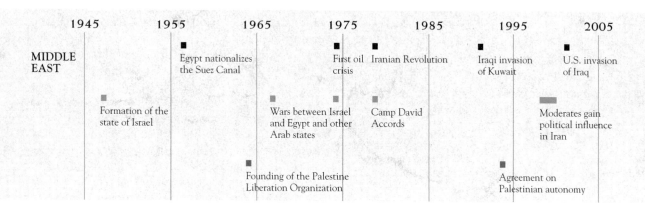

THE RESHAPED MIDDLE EAST

For the Middle East, the period between the two world wars was an era of transition. With the fall of the Ottoman and Persian empires, new modernizing regimes emerged in Turkey and Iran, and a more traditionalist but fiercely independent government was established in Saudi Arabia. Elsewhere, European influence continued to be strong; the British and French had mandates in Syria, Lebanon, Jordan, and Palestine, and British influence persisted in Iraq and southern Arabia and throughout the Nile valley. Although **Pan-Arabism** was on the rise, it was still in its infancy.

Pan-Arabism is a concept that calls for cross-border cooperation and political linkage among Arab peoples; it was promoted by Gamal Abdel Nasser, and resulted in the creation of the short-lived United Arab Republic that comprised Egypt and Syria.

During World War II, the Middle East became the cockpit of European rivalries, as it had been during World War I. The region was even more significant to the warring powers because of the growing importance of oil and the Suez Canal's position as a vital sea route. For a brief period, the Afrika Korps, under the command of the German general Erwin Rommel, threatened to seize Egypt and the Suez Canal, but British troops defeated the German forces at El-Alamein, west of Alexandria, in 1942. The British gradually drove the Germans westward until their final defeat and after the arrival of U.S. troops in Morocco under the field command of General George S. Patton. From that time until the end of the war, the entire region from the Mediterranean Sea eastward was under secure Allied occupation, but the colonial legacy in the region planted the seeds of continued conflict.

How Did the Status of Palestine Affect the Region?

As in other areas of Asia, the end of World War II led to the emergence of a number of independent states. Jordan, Lebanon, and Syria, all European mandates before the war, became independent. Egypt, Iran, and Iraq, though still under a degree of Western influence, became increasingly autonomous. Sympathy for the idea of Arab unity led to the formation of the **Arab League** in 1945, but different points of view among its members prevented it from moving beyond a diplomatic forum for Arab states to a more substantive organization.

The **Arab League** is an organization founded in 1945 to promote cooperation among Arab states in the Middle East.

The one issue on which all Arab states in the area could agree was the question of Palestine. Arab states wanted to preserve a united and independent Palestine that would guarantee the rights of its Arab majority. As tensions between Arabs and migrant Jews in Palestine intensified during the 1930s, the British attempted to limit Jewish immigration into the area while firmly rejecting proposals for independence of its Arab inhabitants. After World War II, the **Zionists** turned for support to the United States, and in March 1948, the administration of Harry S Truman

approved the concept of an independent Jewish state, despite the fact that only about one-third of the local population were Jews and the majority were Arab (later self-identified as Palestinian Arabs). The Soviets also supported the creation of Israel in hopes of it becoming a Communist or socialist state and in hopes of undermining British authority in the region. With growing international support for an independent Jewish state in Palestine (to be called *Israel*) that would be a place of refuge for persecuted European Jews, Zionists gained moral and political support from Western powers. A small number of Jewish terrorists took this international support as justification for "clearing" Palestinian Arabs from their homes. Most notably, in April 1948 Jewish militants massacred hundreds of Palestinians in the village of Deir Yassin, which heightened the fears of Palestinians in other villages. The story of the Deir Yassin massacre led to a chaotic exodus of Palestinians fearing for their lives. One month later, in May 1948, the Zionists declared independence of their new state of Israel, and many Western powers quickly recognized the new state.

Zionists are adherents of a political ideology that holds that modern-day Israel should be a land for the Jewish people as granted by their holy scriptures.

As Israel declared its independence, neighbouring Arab states attacked Israel in support of the stateless Palestinian Arabs. The war was won by the better trained and organized Israeli army. The first Arab-Israeli war also led to the further expulsion of hundreds of thousands of Palestinian refugees into neighbouring Arab states. Palestinian Arabs became landless refugees overnight and the socioeconomic and political hardships to be faced made a significant impact on the Palestinian community and neighbouring states. Jordan, which had become independent under a Hashimite ruler, was now flooded by the arrival of one million Palestinians seeking refuge. To the north, the state of Lebanon had been created to provide the local Christian community with a country of its own, but the arrival of the Palestinian refugees changed the balance between Christians and Muslims. In any event, the creation of Lebanon had angered the Syrians, who had lost it as well as other territories to Turkey as a result of European decisions before and after the war. The Middle East would never be the tranquil place it once was.

What Was Nasser's Ideology?

Egypt's King Farouk, who had acceded to power in 1936, had frequently declared support for the Palestinian Arab cause, and had committed Egyptian armies to the disastrous 1948 war against Israel. In 1952, King Farouk, whose corrupt habits had severely eroded his early popularity, was overthrown by a military and bloodless coup engineered by young military officers ostensibly under the leadership of Colonel Muhammad Nagib. The real force behind the scenes was Colonel Gamal Abdel Nasser (1918–70) who, like many of his fellow officers, had been angered by the army's inadequate preparation for the war against Israel four years earlier (see the box on page 226). In 1953, the monarchy was replaced by a republic.

In 1954, Nasser seized power and immediately instituted populist and statist-led policies, including **import-substitution industrialization** (ISI) and land reforms. He also adopted a policy of neutrality in foreign affairs, as one of the main figures behind the Non-Aligned Movement, and he sympathized with the Palestinian Arab cause. Like many other Third World leaders of the time, Nasser stood for decolonization of the Third World and wanted the remaining British presence in Egypt dissolved. The continued British presence in the Suez Canal created great populist anger in Egypt. Despite granting Egypt independence, Great Britain continued to occupy and control the Suez Canal to control trading routes to the Indian Ocean. To the admiration of many in the Third World, in 1956, Nasser suddenly nationalized the British and French Suez Canal Company. Seeing this move as a threat to their access to the Indian Ocean, the British and the French secretly conspired with Israel to launch a joint attack on Egypt. In an unprecedented move in the Cold War, both the United States and the Soviet Union denounced Israeli aggression and the British and French revival of colonial aspirations. The United Nations and both superpowers supported Egypt and the British and French eventually withdrew from the canal.

> **Import-substitution industrialization** (ISI) was an economic and industrial strategy that relied on state investment in the production of consumer goods that had previously been imported, with the expectation of spurring local industrial and economic development.

Nasser now turned to Pan-Arabism. In 1957, the socialist and Pan-Arab Ba'ath Party assumed power in Syria and opened talks with Egypt on a union between the two countries. Following a plebiscite, Egypt united with Syria to form the **United Arab Republic** (UAR) in 1958. Nasser was named president of the new UAR state. Egypt and Syria hoped that the union would eventually include all Arab states, but other Arab leaders, including young King Hussein of Jordan and the kings of Iraq and Saudi Arabia, were understandably suspicious. The latter two in particular feared Pan-Arabism on the assumption that they would be asked to share their vast oil revenues with the poorer states of the Middle East.

> The **United Arab Republic** (UAR) was a political union of Egypt and Syria led by Gamal Abdel Nasser in 1958 as part of the Pan-Arab movement; the union ended in 1961.

Nasser opposed the situation in which the wealth of the Middle East flowed into the treasuries of a handful of small feudal states created with artificial boundaries by former colonial powers. Europeans had carved up the oil-rich sheikdoms into small countries in order to divide and rule the oil-rich region—which further benefited the pockets of foreign oil interests. In Nasser's view, through Arab unity, this wealth could be put to better use to improve the living standard of all Arabs, who were predominantly poor. To achieve a more equitable division of the region's wealth, Nasser argued for nationalizing natural resources and major industries. Central planning would guarantee that resources were exploited efficiently, but private enterprise would continue at the local level.

In the end, however, Nasser's determination to extend state control over the economy brought an end to the UAR. Like many other parts of the Third World where ISI was tried, there were inefficiencies in the production structure, growing demands of organized labour, and corrupt practices of crony industrialists. When the government announced the nationalization of a large number of industries and utilities in 1961, a military coup overthrew the Ba'ath leaders in Damascus, and the new authorities declared that Syria would end its political union with Egypt.

The breakup of the UAR did not end Nasser's dream of Pan-Arabism. Nasser helped organize and supported the National Liberation Front (FLN) revolutionaries in Algeria's struggle for independence and autonomy from French control. In 1962, Algeria finally received its independence after a ruthless 130-year French occupation. Algeria's war of independence was a bloody one that led to the death of a million Algerians. Algeria's new president, FLN leader Ahmed Ben Bella, furthered close relations with Egypt, as did a new republic in Yemen. During the mid-1960s, Egypt continued to take the lead in promoting Arab unity and furthering populist Arab causes.

At a meeting of Arab leaders held in Jerusalem in 1964, the **Palestine Liberation Organization** (PLO) was set up under Egyptian sponsorship to represent the interests of the Palestinian struggle for self-determination. According to the charter of the PLO, only those born in Palestine (Arabs and Jews) and not immigrants from abroad (European Jews) had the right to form a state in the old British Mandate of Palestine. The PLO called for a unified, non-secular Marxist state in Palestine. A guerrilla movement called *Fatah,* led by

WHO WAS GAMAL ABDEL NASSER?

Gamal Abdel Nasser, born in Alexandria, Egypt, was a military officer who studied law and who participated in anti-British demonstrations throughout his youth. Nasser was influenced by a renowned Egyptian writer Tawfiq Al-Hakim who, in *The Return of the Spirit* (1933), wrote on Egypt's struggle for modernity while being in the shackles of colonialism. Nasser helped form a group of military men called the Free Officers, who were determined to overthrow the British-backed Egyptian monarchy. Nasser witnessed first hand the effects of the colonial presence in Egypt, and he felt isolated and left out of the politics of his own country. This colonizing experience inspired him and other Egyptians to challenge the puppet monarchy regime. In 1952, Nasser and his fellow revolutionaries overthrew the monarchy with little bloodshed and instituted a revolutionary-inspired regime. Nasser took formal control of the revolutionary government in 1954 and started a new phenomenon in the Arab world: Arab nationalism.

Inspired by the idea of Arab nationalism, Nasser envisioned a union of Arab states, and in 1958, successfully convinced Syria to unite under the United Arab Republic (though the union lasted only three years). Nasser's vision of Pan-Arabism was not wholly altruistic; Nasser argued that colonialist powers that had carved up the Middle East had placed artificial boundaries around oil-rich Arab sheikdoms to divide and conquer these oil-rich states and to cordon off the majority of the Arab population from the region's oil wealth. In other words, Nasser's Arab nationalism would involve distributing the region's oil wealth from the rich Arab states to the poorer Arab states. Needless to say, leaders of the oil-rich sheikdoms did not favour Nasser's vision.

Egypt's war against Israel in 1948 made Nasser hyper-aware of the bonds that tied the Arab world together. From the furthest end of North Africa to the Persian Gulf, the people not only shared a common language but also common concerns and sentiments. Nasser believed that what bound all Arabs together was the random chance that they could have been the victims of the Israeli-Palestinian quagmire at any moment in history since they had all equally been affected by colonialism and its reach. Nasser's role in the Arab-Israeli war awakened his consciousness as an Arab. His references to *al-watan al-arabi,* which translated into the "Arab nation," was commonplace in his speeches following the war in 1948 and more so after the 1956 nationalization of the Suez Canal.

Nasser, along with Josip Broz (Tito) of Yugoslavia and Jawaharlal Nehru of India, formed the Non-Aligned Movement to declare themselves neither Western capitalist (first world) nor Communist (second world). Nasser and other Third World leaders wanted to strike a new, alternative means of development without being used as pawns or proxy sites of Cold War conflict. The Non-Aligned Movement also worked to support countries seeking self-determination from colonial control.

As did many other populist leaders of the Third World, Nasser nationalized key industries, limited foreign economic control, promoted populist economic policies like land reform, and protected industries to modernize local economies. In another attempt to reclaim Egyptian territory, Nasser nationalized the Suez Canal amid popular protests against continued British presence in the canal. Nationalization of the canal was heralded throughout much of the Third World, but especially by the Egyptian people, to whom the canal really belonged.

© Bettmann/CORBIS

Nasser and Nehru. Egypt's president Gamal Abdel Nasser (pictured on the left) and India's Prime Minister Jawaharlal Nehru (pictured on the right), along with Yugoslavia's Josip Broz, established the Non-Aligned Movement in 1961. The organization grew out of a conference in Bandung, Indonesia, in 1955, aimed at organizing Third World countries into a bloc that could counterweight the socialist and capitalist blocs.

Yasir Arafat (1929–2004), began to launch attacks on Israeli territory, prompting Israel to raid PLO bases in Jordan in 1966.

> The **Palestine Liberation Organization** (PLO) was created in 1964 to promote Palestinian self-determination; it was dominated by Yasir Arafat until his death in 2004.

What Are the Disputed Areas of the Arab-Israeli Conflict?

During the late 1950s and 1960s, the dispute between Israel and other Middle East states had escalated in intensity. By the spring of 1967, relations between Israel and its Arab neighbours had deteriorated further as both sides were posturing for power and influence. In May 1967, Egypt asked the United Nations troops to leave the Sinai Peninsula. Both Israel and Egypt started amassing troops in the Sinai. Then, Nasser imposed a blockade against Israeli ships passing through the Suez Canal to the Gulf of Aqaba. In June 1967, Israel launched air strikes against Egypt and several of its Arab neighbours. Israeli armies then broke the blockade at the head of the Gulf of Aqaba and occupied the Sinai Peninsula. Israel's stronger army further occupied more Arab lands. To the east, Israeli forces occupied the West Bank of the Jordan River, including the occupation of the whole of Jerusalem, which was then under Jordanian control. To the north, Israel occupied Syria's Golan Heights along the Israeli-Syrian border.

Despite limited Soviet support for Egypt and Syria, in the brief six-day war of 1967, Israel had greatly defeated the Arab countries and now occupied areas that tripled the size of its territory (see Map 13.1, Plate 27). Israel's attack on Egypt and other Arab countries and Israeli occupation of Arab lands created added conflict in the region. Moreover, an additional one million Arab Palestinians, most of them living on the West Bank and to a lesser extent the Gaza Strip, were now occupied by a non-Arab, foreign power. Israel argued that it needed to acquire more land to enhance its security. But, to the Palestinian Arabs now living under Israeli occupation, their human security and right to self-determination would be further denied.

During the next few years, the focus of the Arab-Israeli dispute shifted as Arab states demanded the return of the occupied territories of the West Bank and Gaza, Egypt's Sinai, and Syria's Golan Heights. Meanwhile, some Israelis argued that the new lands improved the security of the state and should be retained and other Israelis argued that conquering the West Bank and Gaza fulfilled a religious prophecy of a greater Israel. Concerned that the dispute

might lead to a confrontation between the superpowers, the administration of Richard Nixon tried to achieve a peace settlement. The peace effort received a mild stimulus when Nasser died of a heart attack in September 1970 and was succeeded by his vice president, ex-general Anwar el-Sadat (1918–81). Sadat soon showed himself to be more Western-oriented than his predecessor, replacing Nasser's socialist policies with a new strategy based on free enterprise and encouragement of Western investment called *infitah* ("opening" or "liberalization"). He also agreed to sign a peace treaty with Israel on the condition that Israel end its occupation of Arab lands and return to its pre-1967 frontiers. Israel refused.

> *Infitah* (Arabic for "opening" or "liberalization") refers to Anwar el-Sadat's policy of deregulating government, liberalizing the economy, and generally making Egypt more hospitable to Western influence.

Rebuffed in his offer of peace, smarting from criticism of his moderate stand from other Arab leaders, and increasingly concerned over Israeli plans to build permanent Jewish settlements in the occupied territories, Sadat attempted to end Israeli occupation of Arab lands militarily by instigating a new confrontation with Israel. In 1973, on Israel's national holiday Yom Kippur, Egyptian forces suddenly launched an air and artillery attack on Israeli positions in the occupied Sinai just east of the Suez Canal. Syrian armies attacked Israeli positions in the Golan Heights to reclaim their occupied territories. After early Arab successes, the Israelis managed to recoup some of their losses on both fronts. As a superpower confrontation between the United States and the Soviet Union loomed, a cease-fire was finally reached.

In the next years, a fragile peace was maintained, marked by U.S. "shuttle diplomacy" (carried out by U.S. Secretary of State Henry Kissinger). After his election as U.S. president in 1976, Jimmy Carter began to press for a compromise peace based on Israel's return of occupied Arab territories and Arab recognition of the state of Israel (an idea originally proposed by Kissinger). By now, Sadat was anxious to reduce his military expenses—after all, Egypt had lost the greatest number of soldiers in the previous Arab-Israeli wars—and announced his willingness to visit Jerusalem to seek peace. The meeting took place in November 1977, with no concrete results, but Sadat persisted. In September 1978, he and Israeli Prime Minister Menachem Begin (1913–92) met with Carter at Camp David in the United States. Israel agreed to withdraw from the Sinai peninsula, but not from the remaining occupied territories.

The promise of the **Camp David Accords** was not fulfilled. One reason was the assassination of Sadat by an Islamic extremist in October 1981. But there were deeper causes, including the continued unwillingness of many Arab governments to recognize Israel without unconditional withdrawal from occupied territories and the Israeli government's encouragement of illegal Jewish settlements in the occupied West Bank as means of retaining future claims to the Arab lands.

> The **Camp David Accords** (initially titled "Framework for Peace in the Middle East"), signed in 1978, were brokered by U.S. President Jimmy Carter; Egypt recognized Israel and Israel ended its occupation of Egypt's Sinai peninsula.

During the early 1980s, the rise of Palestinian calls for an end to Israeli occupation and for an independent state increased, labelled the *intifada*, or uprising. The Israeli rightwing government under Prime Minister Yitzhak Shamir mistakenly conceived the uprising as a PLO concoction rather than a populist demand for self-determination. Shamir's response was to try to destroy the PLO headquartered in Lebanon, by invading Lebanon and occupying the capital Beirut for a little over two months (although the Israeli army continued to occupy southern Lebanon until 2000). The invasion provoked international condemnation and further destabilized the perilous and fractionalized Lebanon. As the 1990s began, U.S.-sponsored peace talks opened between Israel and a number of its neighbours. The first major breakthrough came in 1993, when Israel and the PLO reached an agreement calling for Palestinian autonomy in the occupied West Bank and Gaza, in return for PLO recognition of the legitimacy of the Israeli state and a two-state solution.

> *Intifada* literally means "to get rid of a yoke" in Arabic, and refers to a social and political uprising among Palestinians against Israeli occupation of the West Bank that started in the 1980s.

Progress in implementing the agreement, however, was slow. Both Palestinian and Israeli maximalists (each wanting the whole of Palestine or Israel for themselves) did not want peace and continuously undermined the tenuous agreement.[1] On the one hand, Palestinian extremists committed terrorist attacks in Israel. At the same time, Jewish settlers expanded and fortified their illegal settlements in the occupied West Bank and Gaza to further resist and undermine Palestinian authority in the area. In November 1995, an

Courtesy of William J. Duiker

Jerusalem's Holy Site. Pictured here is one of the most sacred places in the city of Jerusalem for both Jews and Muslims. Known as *Temple Mount* to Jews, this was the site of a temple built during the reign of Solomon, king of the Jews, in about 1000 B.C.E. The Western Wall of the temple is shown in the foreground. The site is known to Muslims as the *Dome of the Rock,* a part of a complex of many Mosques including the Al-Aqsa mosque called *Al-Haram al-Sharif,* where Prophet Muhammad ascended to heaven. Sacred to both religions, governing this site is now a major obstacle to a final settlement of the Israeli-Palestinian dispute.

Israeli extremist who opposed peace with the Palestinians assassinated peace advocate Prime Minister Yitzhak Rabin. National elections held a few months later led to the formation of a right-wing and hawkish new government under Benjamin Netanyahu (b. 1949), who stunted further negotiations on transferring autonomy to the Palestinian Authority under Yasir Arafat.

When Netanyahu was replaced by a new Labour government under Prime Minister Ehud Barak (b. 1942) the latter promised to revitalize the peace process. Negotiations continued with the Palestinian Authority and also got under way with Syria over a peace settlement in Lebanon and the possible return of the occupied Golan Heights. But in late 2000, peace talks were stalled over the future of the city of Jerusalem, a part of which was occupied and controlled by Israel since the 1967 war. Israel wanted to keep the city united under its tutelage. Palestinians wanted the city divided, with Arab-inhabited East Jerusalem under Palestinian autonomy and the presence of international monitors in the city's holy places. To add to the already tense situation, former Defence Minister Ariel Sharon (b. 1928), who was already viewed negatively by Palestinians—for his alleged support of a massacre of Palestinians in the Lebanese refugee camps Sabra and Shatila in 1982—visited the Muslim's holy place of Al-Haram al-Sharif in Jerusalem. This provocation led to massive riots by Palestinians, a harsh Israeli crackdown, and the election of the hawkish Ariel Sharon as prime minister.

The cycle of violence of Israeli military repression in the occupied territories followed by numerous terrorist attacks by Palestinian extremists caused great civilian deaths and casualties. In a few years, there was a dramatic increase in bloodshed on both sides. Although Saudi Arabia set forth a comprehensive peace plan—calling for full Arab recognition of the state of Israel in return for the latter's final withdrawal from the occupied territories of the West Bank, Gaza, and the Golan Heights—Israel refused and the prospects of peace again seemed dim.

Israel's Sharon government decided instead to build a wall along the occupied West Bank, encircling Jewish settlements and roadways within Israel; this action was argued to be a security measure, yet it undermined Palestinian rights. For Israelis, the wall served to better fortify themselves from terrorists acts. For Palestinians, the separation barrier cut communities and people from one another, adding great social burden to the existing hardship of living under military occupation while undermining the future of a contiguous Palestinian state.

What Precipitated the Iranian Revolution?

The Arab-Israeli dispute also provoked an international oil crisis. In 1960, a number of oil-producing states formed the **Organization of the Petroleum Exporting Countries** (OPEC) to gain control over oil prices and profit, while undercutting the influence of the foreign oil companies. In the 1970s, a group of Arab oil states established the Organization of Arab Petroleum Exporting Countries (OAPEC) to use as a weapon to force Western governments to stop supporting Israeli occupation of Arab lands. During the 1973 Yom Kippur War, some OPEC nations announced significant increases in the price of oil to foreign countries. The price hikes were accompanied by an apparent oil shortage and created serious economic problems in the United States and Europe as well as in the Third World. They also proved to be a windfall to oil-exporting countries, such as Libya, now under the leadership of the anti-American Colonel Muammar Qaddafi.

> The **Organization of the Petroleum Exporting Countries** (OPEC) is an oil cartel, working together to control prices and limit internal competition, dominated by Middle Eastern states such as Saudi Arabia.

Iran is one of the key oil-exporting countries. Under the leadership of Shah Mohammad Reza Pahlavi (1919–80), who had taken over from his father in 1941, Iran had become one of the richest countries in the Middle East. The corrupt and Western-backed shah regime, however, did not share much of the wealth with its people and grew increasingly out of touch with the Iranian people's growing conservatism. Prime Minister Mohammed Mossadegh had briefly attempted to nationalize the oil industry in 1951 and usurp the shah; but soon after, Mossadegh was overthrown by the CIA, which then reinstalled the shah to power. For the next 20 years, Iran became a prime ally of the United States in the Middle East.

At the macro-level, Iran appeared to be modernizing under the shah. Per capita income increased, literacy rates improved, a modern communications infrastructure took shape, and an affluent middle class emerged in the capital of Tehran. Under the surface, however, trouble was brewing. Despite an ambitious land reform program, many peasants were still landless and the clergy lost some of its political clout thereby alienating conservative elements of the society. Despite infrastructural investment into urban areas, unemployment among intellectuals was dangerously high, and the urban middle class was squeezed by high inflation. Similarly, housing costs had skyrocketed, provoked in part by the massive influx of foreigners attracted by oil money. (See Map 13.2, Plate 28.)

Some of the unrest took the form of religious discontent as millions of devout Shi'ite Muslims looked with distaste at the shah's pro-American foreign policies, greed, and excessive material accumulation. Conservative elements opposed rampant government corruption and the ostentation of the shah's court. In response to rising political opposition from conservatives, students, and leftists, the shah's U.S.-trained security police and intelligence service, the **Savak**, imprisoned and significantly tortured thousands of dissidents. As the shah tried to crack down on the opposition using repressive means, populist support for the opposition consequently grew.

> The **Savak** was the Shah Mohammad Reza Pahlavi's American-trained secret military police that spied on, tortured, and killed the shah's opponents; the terror it created led to further support for the opposition.

Leading the opposition was Ayatollah Ruholla Khomeini (1900–89), an austere Shi'ite cleric who had been exiled to Iraq and then to France because of his outspoken opposition to the shah's regime. From Paris, Khomeini continued his attacks in print, on TV, and in radio broadcasts. By the late 1970s, large numbers of Iranians began to respond to Khomeini's criticism of the corrupt and autocratic shah. Demonstrations by Khomeini's supporters were repressed with ferocity by the police. But workers' strikes (some of them in the oil fields, which reduced government revenue) grew in intensity. In January 1979, the shah appointed a moderate, Shapur Bakhtiar, as prime minister and then left the country for medical treatment.

Bakhtiar attempted to conciliate the rising opposition and permitted Khomeini to return to Iran, where Khomeini demanded the government's resignation. With rising public unrest and incipient revolt within the army, the government collapsed and was replaced by a hastily formed Islamic republic. The new government, which was dominated by Shi'ite *mullah* under the guidance of Ayatollah Khomeini, immediately began to introduce traditional Islamic law.

Though much of the outside world focused on the U.S. embassy in Tehran, where extremists held a number of foreign hostages, the Iranian Revolution involved much more. In the eyes of the ayatollah and his followers, the United States was "the great Satan," the powerful protector of Israeli occupation of Palestinians, and the enemy of Muslim peoples everywhere. Furthermore, it was responsible for the corruption of Iranian society under the shah. Now Khomeini demanded that the shah be returned to Iran for trial and that the United States apologize for its acts against the Iranian people. In response, the Carter administration stopped buying Iranian oil and froze Iranian assets in the United States.

The effects of the disturbances in Iran quickly spread beyond its borders. Shi'ite extremists briefly seized the holy places in Mecca and began to appeal to fellow Muslims to launch similar Islamic revolutions around the world. In July 1980, the shah died of cancer in Cairo. With economic conditions in Iran rapidly deteriorating, the Islamic revolutionary government finally agreed to free the hostages in return for the release of Iranian assets in the United States. During the next few years, the intensity of the Iranian Revolution moderated slightly, as the government displayed a modest tolerance for a loosening of clerical control over freedom of expression and social activities. But rising criticism of rampant official corruption and a high rate of inflation sparked a new wave of government repression in the mid-1990s; newspapers were censored, the universities were purged of disloyal or "un-Islamic" elements, and religious extremists raided private homes in search of blasphemous activities.

In 1997, the moderate Islamic cleric Mohammad Khatami was elected president of Iran. Khatami, whose surprising victory reflected a growing desire among many Iranians, particularly the youth, for a more pluralistic society open to the outside world, signalled the tantalizing possibility that Iran might wish to improve relations with the West. During the next few years, press censorship was relaxed, leading to the emergence of several reformist newspapers and magazines, and restrictions on women's activities were relaxed. But the new president faced severe pressures from conservative elements to maintain the purity of Islamic laws, and in April 2000, several reformist publications were ordered to close by the judiciary for having printed materials that "disparaged Islam." Although student protests erupted into the streets in 2003, hard-liners continued to reject proposals to expand civil rights and limit the power of the clerics. Initially, the 2003 Nobel Peace Prize awarded to Iranian lawyer and human rights advocate Shirin Ebadi—the first Muslim woman and first Iranian to receive the award—had renewed hope in Iran that progressive attitudes would help liberalize the conservative government. But, the 2005 presidential election of conservative Mahmoud Ahmadinejad raised doubts that the country's modernist forces would prevail.

What Three Crises Took Place in the Persian Gulf?

During the early phases of the Iranian Revolution, much of the Iranians' anger was directed against the United States for having supported the corrupt shah over the many years. But, Iran also had grievances closer to home. To the north, the immense power of the Soviet Union, driven by atheistic communism, was a concern. The Soviet invasion of Iran's neighbour Afghanistan was deemed to be a significant strategic threat. To the west was a militarized Iraq, now under the leadership of the ambitious Saddam Hussein (b. 1937). Problems from both directions appeared shortly after Khomeini's rise to power.

A year after Khomeini rose to power, Iraqi forces suddenly attacked along the Iranian border. Iraq and Iran had long had an uneasy relationship, fuelled by ideological differences (Iraq was a socialist-leaning secular state and Iran a theocracy) and a perennial dispute over borderlands adjacent to the Persian Gulf called *Shaat Al-'Arab,* the vital waterway for the export of oil from both countries.

During the mid-1970s, Iran gave some support to a rebellion of **Kurds** in the mountains of Iraq. In 1975, the government of the shah agreed to stop aiding the rebels in return for territorial concessions at the head of the gulf. Five years later, however, the Kurdish revolt had been violently and ruthlessly suppressed, and President Saddam Hussein, who had assumed power in Baghdad in 1979, accused Iran of violating the territorial agreement and launched an attack on his neighbour. The war was a bloody one, involving the use of poison gas against civilians and the employment of children to clear minefields, and lasted for nearly 10 years. Most horrific was Saddam Hussein's use of poison gas against the Kurdish town Halabja in 1988, killing thousands for supporting the Iranians during the war. The Iran-Iraq war created great human tragedy and destruction. Other countries, including the two superpowers, watched nervously in case the conflict should spread throughout the region. Finally, with both sides virtually exhausted, a cease-fire was arranged in the fall of 1988.

> The **Kurds** are an ethnic minority—located in Iraq, Iran, and parts of Turkey and Syria—that have sought self-determination. Numbering approximately 25 million people, the Kurds are the largest ethnic group without a state of their own.

The bitter conflict with Iran had not stopped Saddam Hussein's appetite for territorial expansion. In early August 1990, Iraqi military forces suddenly moved across the border and occupied the small oil-rich neighbouring country of Kuwait at the head of the gulf. The immediate pretext was the claim that Kuwait was pumping oil from fields inside Iraqi territory that had been neglected by the Iraqis when at war with Iran. Baghdad was also angry over the Kuwaiti government's demand for repayment of loans it had made to Iraq during the war with Iran. But the underlying reason was Iraq's contention that Kuwait was legally a part of Iraq. After all, Kuwait had been part of the Ottoman Empire until the opening of the twentieth century, when the local prince had agreed to place his patrimony under British protection. When Iraq became independent in 1932, it claimed the area on the grounds that the state of Kuwait had been created by British imperialism, but opposition from major Western powers and other countries in the region, who feared the consequences of a "greater Iraq" with more oil resources under its control, had prevented an Iraqi takeover.

The Iraqi invasion of Kuwait in 1990 sparked the United States to lead an international force to remove Iraqi control of the country. In doing so, the U.S.-led coalition destroyed a substantial part of Iraq's public infrastructure and armed forces. The U.S.-led forces, however, did not occupy Baghdad at the end of the war because they feared that doing so would lead to a breakup of the country. The United States did not want a divided Iraq, because it would compromise its geostrategic interests in the region. To the north were Kurds long seeking autonomy and independence from the repressive Saddam Hussein regime. Granting the Kurds autonomy or independence would have destabilized neighbouring Turkey, a long U.S. ally in NATO, which has a sizable Kurdish population on its eastern border. The majority of Iraq's population, mostly located in the oil-rich part of the country in the south, were Shi'ite like the Iranians. To unseat Saddam Hussein, a Sunni Muslim, from power would have strengthened Iran to whom southern Iraqi Shi'ites had loyalties. The United States hoped instead that the Hussein regime would be ousted by an internal revolt. In the meantime, harsh economic sanctions were imposed on the Iraqi government and people. The economic sanctions contributed to the deaths of hundreds of thousands of civilians caught between the international community's desire to both squeeze the Hussein regime and to incite popular uprising. The economic sanctions prevented necessary foods and medicine from entering Iraq, leading to a devastating human death toll. The anticipated overthrow of Saddam Hussein did not materialize, however, and his tireless efforts to evade the conditions of the cease-fire continued to bedevil the United States.

In 2002, the administration of George W. Bush accused Iraq, Iran, and North Korea of constituting an "axis of evil." The U.S. administration falsely held that Iraqi dictator Saddam Hussein had not only provided support to Osama bin Laden's terrorist organization but also sought to develop weapons of mass destruction. The United States threatened to invade Iraq and remove Hussein from power. The plan to overthrow the Iraqi regime on the unproven pretences of its being a potential threat, widely opposed by most of the world including most Western European states, had disquieted Arab leaders and fanned both anti-war and anti-American sentiment throughout the world. Despite broad opposition to the U.S. invasion of Iraq, in March 2003, American-led forces attacked Iraq and overthrew Hussein's regime. In the months that followed, occupation forces sought to restore stability to the now chaotic country exhibiting the signs of civil war along the many factional Iraqi lines. Despite the capture of Saddam Hussein, armed insurgents fought the U.S. occupation and the perceived U.S. puppet regime. In 2005, Iraq held historic elections to elect a legislative assembly and head of state that would write

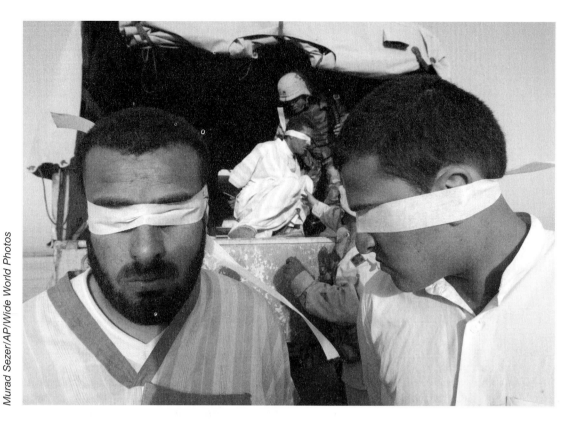

Murad Sezer/AP/Wide World Photos

The American Occupation of Iraq. In an ongoing effort to quell the violence in Iraq and bring stability to the country, American soldiers from the 4th Battalion 42 Field Artillery, seen here, unload men captured during an early morning raid in the village of Hamreen from a military vehicle on Sunday, August 31, 2003. While Americans are trying to stop insurgents fighting the American occupation of Iraq, the capture of Iraqis by American troops has only led other Iraqis to feel justified in joining the guerrillas' mission in ridding Iraq of its current occupier.

a constitution to be voted on by the people. It was hoped that the elections would end the insurgent fighting, but Sunni turnout in the election was poor due to those boycotting the process and to insecurity at the voting booths. Civilian casualties since the American invasion and occupation of Iraq have been calculated to be as high as 100 000 and as low as 20 000. The human suffering in Iraq continues.

POLITICS IN THE MIDDLE EAST TODAY

Few areas exhibit a greater disparity of individual and national wealth than the Middle East. Although millions live in abject poverty, a fortunate few rank among the wealthiest people in the world. The annual per capita income in Egypt is about US$600, but in the tiny states of Kuwait and United Arab Emirates, it is nearly US$20 000. Some of that disparity can be explained by the uneven

distribution of fertile and barren land, but the primary reason, of course, is oil. By design of colonialist powers carving up the Middle East with artificial boundaries, and by the excessive heat in oil-rich areas, oil reserves are distributed unevenly and located in areas where the population density is low. Egypt and Turkey, with more than 50 million inhabitants apiece, have almost no oil reserves. The combined population of oil-rich Kuwait, the United Arab Emirates, and Saudi Arabia is well under 10 million people. This disparity in wealth inspired Nasser's quest for Arab unity, but it has also posed a major obstacle to that unity.

The growing importance of petroleum has obviously been a benefit to several of the states in the region, but it has been an unreliable one. Because of the violent fluctuations in the price of oil during the past 30 years, the income of oil-producing states has varied considerably. The spectacular increase in oil prices during the 1970s, when members of OPEC were able to raise the price of a barrel of oil from about US$3 to US$30, could not be sustained, forcing a number of oil-producing countries to scale back their consumption of oil and search for alternative energies.

Not surprisingly, considering their different resources and political systems, the states of the Middle East have adopted diverse approaches to the problem of developing strong and stable economies. Some, like Nasser in Egypt and the leaders of the Ba'ath Party in Syria, attempted to create a form of Arab socialism, favouring a high level of government involvement in the economy to relieve the inequities of the free enterprise system. Others turned to the Western capitalist model to maximize growth, while using taxes or massive development projects to build a modern infrastructure, redistribute wealth, and maintain political stability and economic opportunity for all.

Socialist theories of economic development such as Nasser's were often suggested as a way to promote economic growth. State intervention in the economic sector would bring about rapid development, while land redistribution and the nationalization or regulation of industry would prevent or minimize the harsh inequities of the marketplace. In general, however, the socialist approach has had little success, and most governments, including those of Egypt and Syria, have shifted to a more free enterprise approach while encouraging foreign investment to compensate for a lack of capital or technology.

Although the amount of arable land is relatively small, most countries in the Middle East rely to a certain degree on farming to supply food for their growing populations. In some cases, as in Egypt, Iran, Iraq, and Turkey, farmers have until recently been a majority of the population. Often much of the fertile land was owned by wealthy absentee landlords, but land reform programs in several countries have attempted to alleviate this problem.

The most comprehensive and probably the most successful land reform program was instituted in Egypt, where Nasser and his successors managed to reassign nearly a quarter of all cultivable lands by limiting the amount a single individual could hold to five feddans (2.1 hectares) per person with a maximum of 50 feddans (21 hectares) per family. This, however, greatly upset the landed aristocracy and created an elite class that has been generally resentful of Nasser's populist legacies. Similar land reform programs in Iran, Iraq, Libya, and Syria had less effect. In Iran, large landlords at the local and national level managed to limit the effects of the shah's reform program. After the 1979 revolution, many farmers seized lands forcibly from the landlords, giving rise to questions of ownership that the revolutionary government has tried with minimal success to resolve.

Agricultural productivity throughout the region has been plagued by the lack of water resources. With populations growing at more than 2 percent annually on average in the

Courtesy of Bessma Momani

Mobile Phones. In many Middle Eastern countries telecommunications networks are underdeveloped, with long waiting lists to receive landlines. Peasants and the rising middle class resort to competitive cell phone providers for their connectivity.

Middle East (more than 3 percent in some countries), several governments have tried to increase the amount of water available for irrigation. Many attempts have been sabotaged by government ineptitude, political disagreements, and territorial conflicts, however. The best-known example is the Aswan High Dam, which was built by Soviet engineers in the 1960s and completed in 1970. The project was designed to control the flow of water throughout the Nile valley, but it has had a number of undesirable environmental consequences. Today, the dearth of water is reaching crisis proportions and is having a political impact as governments squabble over access to scarce water resources in the region. For example, disputes between Israel and its neighbours over water rights and between Iraq and its neighbours over the exploitation of the Tigris and the Euphrates have caused serious tensions in recent years.

Another way in which governments have attempted to deal with rapid population growth is to encourage emigration. Oil-producing states with small populations, such as Saudi Arabia and the United Arab Emirates, have imported labour from other countries in the region, mostly to work in the oil fields. By the mid-1980s, more than 40 percent of the population in those states was composed of foreign nationals, who often sent the bulk of their salaries back to their families in their home countries. The decline in oil revenues since the mid-1980s, however, has forced several governments to take measures to stabilize or reduce the migrant population. Since the Iraqi invasion, Kuwait, for example, has expelled Palestinians and restricted migrant workers from other countries to three-year stays.

ISLAMIC REVIVALISM

In recent years, many developments in the Middle East have been described in terms of a resurgence of Islam. But Islamic revivalism that has taken place in the contemporary Middle East is not a simple dichotomy between traditional and modern, native and foreign, or Western and non-Western. In the first place, many Muslims in the Middle East believe that Islamic values and modern ways are not incompatible and may even be mutually reinforcing in many ways. Second, the resurgence of what are sometimes called "fundamentalist" Islamic groups may, in a Middle Eastern context, appear to be a rational and practical response to corruption, illegitimate political leaders, and stifling political opposition. Finally, the reassertion of Islamic values can be a means of establishing cultural identity and fighting off the overwhelming impact of negative influences.

Initially, many Muslim intellectuals responded to Western influence by trying to reconcile the perceived differences between tradition and modernity and by creating an "updated" set of Islamic beliefs and practices that would not clash with the demands of the modern world. This process took place in most Islamic societies, but it was especially prevalent in Turkey, Egypt, and Iran. Mustafa Kemal Atatürk embraced the strategy when he attempted to secularize the Islamic religion in the new Turkish republic (See Chapter 4). The Turkish model was followed by Shah Reza Khan and his son Mohammad Reza Pahlavi in Iran and then by Nasser in post-war Egypt, all of whom attempted to make use of Islamic values while asserting the primacy of other issues such as political and economic development. Religion, in effect, had become the handmaiden of political power, national identity, and economic prosperity.

For obvious reasons, these secularizing trends were particularly noticeable among the political, intellectual, and economic elites in urban areas. They had less influence in the countryside, among the poor, and among devout elements within the community of religious scholars known as

Courtesy of Bessma Momani

Prayer and Fast Food. Pictured here in Amman, Jordan, is a Kentucky Fried Chicken outlet beside a Muslim mosque of worship. Jordan, particularly in its cities, offers a cosmopolitan blend of westernization, innovation, capitalism, and traditionalism. Jordan has successfully attracted foreign capital to invest in the kingdom for its moderate approach to society and politics.

the *ulama*. Many of the latter believed that Western secular trends in the major cities had given birth to regrettable and even repugnant social attitudes and behavioural patterns, such as political and economic corruption, sexual promiscuity, individualism, and the prevalence of alcohol.

This reaction began early in the century and intensified after World War I, when the Western presence increased. In 1928, devout Muslims in Egypt formed the Muslim Brotherhood as a means of promoting personal piety. Later, the movement began to take a more activist approach, trying to rid Egypt of the corrupt and autocratic regime. Despite Nasser's surface commitment to Islamic ideals and Arab unity, some Egyptians were fiercely opposed to his policies and regarded his vision of socialism as a betrayal of Islamic principles. Nasser reacted harshly and executed a number of his leading opponents.

The movement to return to Islamic purity strengthened after World War II and reached its zenith in Iran. It is not surprising that Iran took the lead in light of its long tradition of ideological purity within the Shi'ite sect as well as the uncompromisingly secular and corrupt character of the shah's reforms in the post-war era. In revolutionary Iran, traditional Islamic beliefs are all-pervasive and extend into education, clothing styles, social practices, and the legal system.

While the political aspects of the Iranian Revolution inspired distrust and suspicion among political elites elsewhere in the region, its cultural and social effects were profound. Although no other state in the Middle East adopted the approach to cultural reform applied in Iran, Iranian ideas have spread throughout the area and affected social and cultural behaviour in many ways. In Algeria, the political influence of an Islamic party had grown substantially and enabled the party to win a stunning victory in the national elections in 1992. But the military stepped in to cancel the second round of elections and violently cracked down on party supporters. Some supporters of the Islamic party resorted to

Courtesy of Bessma Momani

Egypt's First Presidential Elections. Historic elections were held in Egypt in 2005, amid U.S. pressure to liberalize the polity. Pictured here is a campaign billboard of incumbent President Hosni Mubarak, who won the elections. However, the largely populist Muslim Brotherhood was banned from participating in the elections. Not surprisingly, voter apathy was high and merely a quarter of the voting population went to the polls. The question of whether democratization of the Middle East should include religious parties like Egypt's Muslim Brotherhood looms on.

violence, killing moderates, artists, and intellectuals who were opposed to the Islamic party's ascent to power. The cycle of violence and campaign of both state and group terrorism has claimed the lives of thousands of Algerians.

A similar Islamic resurgence has been brewing in Egypt, where Islamic movements such as the Muslim Brotherhood have sought the overthrow of the corrupt (and after the Camp David Accords, pro-Western) Egyptian regime. The political process continues to be closed to Islamic parties in Egypt for fear that they might create a theocratic state like Iran.

Even in Turkey, generally considered the most secular of Islamic societies, a political party known as the *Islamic Welfare Party* took power in a coalition government formed in 1996. Worried moderates voiced their concern that the secular legacy of Kemal Atatürk was being eroded, and eventually the new prime minister, Necmettin Erbakan, agreed to resign under heavy pressure from the military. Turkey maintains close ties with the United States and is currently adopting reforms to extend human rights and freedom of expression in the hope of gaining entry into the European Union. But religious and economic discontent simmers beneath the surface.

CONTEMPORARY LITERATURE AND ART IN THE MIDDLE EAST

Contemporary literature of the Middle East has dealt with a number of new themes. The rise in national consciousness stimulated interest in historical traditions. Writers also switched from religious to secular themes and addressed the problems of this world and the means of rectifying them. Furthermore, literature was no longer the exclusive domain of the elite but was increasingly written for the broader mass of the population.

Iran has produced one of the most prominent national literatures in the contemporary Middle East. Since World War II, Iranian literature has been hampered somewhat by political considerations, since it has been expected to serve first the shah monarchy and more recently the Islamic republic. Nevertheless, Iranian writers are among the most prolific in the region and often write in prose, which has finally been accepted as the equal of poetry. Perhaps the most outstanding Iranian author of the twentieth century was short-story writer Sadeq Hedayat. Hedayat was obsessed with the frailty and absurdity of life and wrote with compassion about the problems of ordinary human beings. Frustrated and disillusioned with the government's suppression of individual liberties, he committed suicide in 1951. Hedayat later became a cult figure among his country's youth.

Despite the male-oriented nature of post-revolution Iranian society, many of the new writers have been women.

Since the revolution, the *chador,* or veiled garment, has become the central metaphor in Iranian women's writing. Advocates praise the veil as the last bastion of defence against Western cultural imperialism. Behind the veil, the Islamic woman can breathe freely, unpolluted by foreign exploitation and moral corruption. They see the veil as the courageous woman's weapon against Western efforts to dominate the Iranian soul. Similarly, the *chador* offered women mobility in public spaces that were unavailable to them. Other Iranian women, however, consider the veil a "mobile prison" or an oppressive anachronism from the Dark Ages. A few use the pen as a weapon in a crusade to liberate their sisters and enable them to make their own choices. As one writer, Sousan Azadi, expressed it, "As I pulled the *chador* over me, I felt a heaviness descending over me. I was hidden and in hiding. There was nothing visible left of Sousan Azadi."[2]

Like Iran, Egypt in the twentieth century has experienced a flowering of literature accelerated by the establishment of the Egyptian republic in the early 1950s. The most illustrious contemporary Egyptian writer is Naguib Mahfouz (b. 1911), who won the Nobel Prize in Literature in 1988. His *Cairo Trilogy,* published in 1952, chronicles three generations of a merchant family in Cairo during the tumultuous years between the two world wars. Mahfouz is particularly adept at blending panoramic historical events with the intimate lives of ordinary human beings with great compassion and energy. Unlike many other modern writers, his message is essentially optimistic and reflects his hope that religion and science can work together for the overall betterment of humankind.

No women writer has played a more active role in exposing the physical and social grievances of Egyptian women than Nawal El Saadawi (b. 1931). For decades, she has battled against the injustices of religious fundamentalism and a male-dominated society—even enduring imprisonment for promoting her cause. In *Two Women in One* (1985), El Saadawi follows the struggle of a young university student as she rebels against the life her father has programmed for her, striking out instead on an unchartered independent destiny.

The emergence of a modern Turkish literature can be traced to the establishment of the republic in 1923. The most popular contemporary writer is Orhan Pamuk (b. 1952), whose novels attempt to capture Turkey's unique blend of cultures. "I am living in a culture," he writes, "where the clash of East and West, or the harmony of East and West, is the lifestyle. That is Turkey."[3] In his novel *The Black Book* (1994), Pamuk resuscitates Istanbul's past from the multitude of Byzantine, Ottoman, and republican artefacts strewn in the muddy depths of the Bosphorus.

Although Israeli literature arises from a totally different tradition from that of its neighbours, it shares with them certain contemporary characteristics and a concern for the commoner. Early writers identified with the aspirations of the new nation, trying to find a sense of order in the new reality, voicing terrors from the past and hope for the future. Some contemporary Israeli authors, however, have refused to serve as promoters for Zionism and are speaking out on the repressive nature of Israel's occupation in the West Bank and Gaza. The internationally renowned novelist Amos Oz (b. 1939), for example, is a vocal supporter of ending the repressive occupation and making peace with the Palestinians. Oz is a member of Peace Now and the author of a political tract titled *Israel, Palestine, and Peace*. In an interview, Oz accused both Ariel Sharon and Yasir Arafat of being "immovable, handcuffed to the past and to each other."[4] With the Arabs feeling victimized by colonialism and the Jews by Nazi Germany, each side believes that it alone is the rightful proprietor of ancient Palestine. For Oz, the only solution is compromise of a two-state solution, which, however unsatisfactory for both sides, is preferable to mutual self-destruction.

Like literature, the art of the modern Middle East has been profoundly influenced by its exposure to Western culture. Reflecting their hopes for the new nation, Israeli painters sought to bring to life the sentiments of migrants arriving in a new state. Many attempted to capture the longing for community expressed in the Israeli commune, or *kibbutz*. Others searched for the roots of Israeli culture in the history of the Jewish people or in the horrors of the Holocaust. The experience of the Holocaust has attracted particular attention from sculptors, who work in wood and metal as well as stone.

The popular music of the contemporary Middle East has also been strongly influenced by that of the modern West, but to different degrees in different countries. In Israel, many contemporary young rock stars voice lyrics as irreverent toward the traditions of their elders as those of Europe and the United States do. An idol of many Israeli young people, rock star Aviv Gefen declares himself to be "a person of no values," and his music carries a shock value that attacks the country's political and social shibboleths with abandon. The rock music popular among Palestinians, on the other hand, makes greater use of Arab musical motifs and is closely tied to a political message of self-determination, ending the repressive Israeli occupation, and the dream of an independent Palestinian state.

Why Is Satellite TV Popular in the Middle East?

Prior to the introduction of the Arab world to satellite TV, there were few options available to the masses with regard to the dissemination of information. Throughout the 1950s and 1960s, radio waves were all that connected the Arab world to outside information. Programs aired and listened to by millions in the Arab world included *Saut El Arab* (or "Voice of the Arabs"—VOA) courtesy of Nasser and the Egyptian government, Radio Monte Carlo via *Maison de la Radio* in Paris, and the British Broadcasting Corporation (BBC) Arabic Service, all of which provided news and information in Arabic.

Since then the Arab world has experienced an onslaught of information courtesy of satellite news networks such as Al-Jazeera, Al-Manar, Abu-Dhabi, and Al-Hayat, some of which have done more for Pan-Arabism than Nasser's VOA could have ever dreamed of earlier. An estimated 70 to 80 percent of Arab viewers watch these networks, some of which have a relative amount of editorial independence never experienced before in Arab media.

Prior to the existence of networks such as Al-Jazeera, most news in the Middle East came directly from each state's Ministry of Information. Since its debut following the American war in Afghanistan, Al-Jazeera has made a name for itself as the voice of Pan-Arabism and Islamism in the region and around the world. Its greatest claim to fame has been its coverage of news related to 9/11, especially its presentation of videotapes recorded by the United States' number-one enemy, Osama bin Laden, leader of al-Qaeda and the mastermind of the attacks on the World Trade Center and the Pentagon. Al-Jazeera, based in Qatar and fully employed by a BBC-trained staff, reflects popular Arab opinion in its coverage of daily news from Palestine and Iraq, and brings into the homes of Arabs around the world the struggles of brethren next door and abroad.

In an effort to engage Arab audiences, Al-Jazeera plays on the emotions of its viewers through various programs such as talk shows and interviews with topics including women's issues, health, Palestine, Iraq, Islam, and democracy—and more specifically its lack thereof in the Arab Muslim world—all of which have rarely been discussed, if they were discussed at all, outside the parameters of state supervision.

Al-Jazeera is considered to be one of the most independent news networks in the Arab world, whose rivals include Al-Arabiya out of Saudi Arabia, owned by Prince al-Walid bin Talal of the Saudi royal family in association with MBC (Middle East Broadcasting Center). Al-Arabiya, while considered somewhat independent—taking not only its cue from Al-Jazeera but also its staff—is nonetheless under Saudi royal influence. Al-Jazeera and Al-Arabiya receive public funding from the government or officials closely associated with the government. As such, both networks have boundaries they do not cross, as is often the case with regards to domestically funded news outlets. These two rivalling stations are quick to criticize neighbouring countries and their policies; however, they don't necessarily provide the same critical analysis to their host state.

Along with the advent of competing news sources in the Arab world has come an influx of foreign programming. Not only is it easier for Arabs in the Persian Gulf to see how Arabs in North Africa live, but also it is easier for Arabs to see how the rest of the world lives, particularly the United States and Western Europe. In the past several years, viewers in the Arab world experienced a sharp increase in the sources of information and entertainment available to them in their homes.

Umm Kulthum, hailed by some as the Ella Fitzgerald of the Arab world, was not only an entertainer, she was a national symbol for Egyptians and the Arab world at large. She was most popular in the 1950s and 1960s. Born in a small rural village in Egypt circa 1908, her father was a religious man employed as an Imam at a local Mosque, and her mother was a homemaker. Umm Kulthum was discovered by her father, who brought her along to sing with him at wedding ceremonies after he overheard her singing by herself. By the early 1920s she left her small town in search of bigger dreams and landed a recording contract.

What set Umm Kulthum apart from the rest, then and now, was her strong affiliation with the masses. She understood her audience, and, as a result, she was conservative in her demeanour on stage and off, which commanded the respect of the most conservative Islamic factions in society as well as its most secular. She stood as a beacon for the Arab world and was by all accounts an ambassador for Gamal Abdel Nasser and his party's Pan-Arab agenda. She was received all over the Arab world as though she were a political figure of great stature. The masses saw themselves in Umm Kulthum, which would explain why over four million people poured into the streets of Cairo for her funeral in 1975.

Greater independence of the Middle Eastern media, courtesy of the explosion in number of Arab satellite channels, has led to an increase in access to risqué entertainment. While sexuality has been prevalent in the media for some time in North America and Western Europe, this has not been the case in the Middle East. As people in the United States were experiencing the sexual revolution of the 1960s and 1970s, people in the Middle East were embracing the values of people like Umm Kulthum, who stood for all that was traditional and conservative.

Today, Arab pop stars look a lot less like Umm Kulthum than they do Britney Spears. In an effort to mirror what the Western world deems popular, Arab pop stars have become much more sexually charged in their dress and demeanour. All of this is new in the Arab world and for the first time ever, long-held views on sexuality and conservatism are being challenged by what is seen on satellite TV. Very little effort is being made by the satellite networks to adjust their programming, since they have discovered that "sex sells." While religious preachers call for change, provocative singers like Egypt's Ruby, born Rania Hussein, continue wearing skimpy dresses and entertaining in an overtly sexual manner. Ruby's videos have raised many eyebrows in Egypt, even leading Hamdi Hassan of Egypt's Muslim Brotherhood to complain to the Egyptian Parliament that Ruby is far too risqué and should be banned. While satellite TV has brought many advantages to the Arab world, it has also brought challenges. Western influence stands to threaten conservatism in the Middle East as Arabs increasingly consume Western images and culture.

CONCLUSION

The Middle East is an unstable region in the world today. In part, this turbulence is due to the legacy of colonialism and the continued interference of outsiders attracted to controlling oil in the vicinity of the Persian Gulf.

- Colonialist powers left their greatest mark on the Middle East by carving up the region into artificial states with imposed boundaries.
- For Gamal Abdel Nasser, who led the overthrow of the monarchy, the Middle East needed to remove the influence and legacy of colonialism by creating independent republics.
- For Ayatollah Ruholla Khomeini and the Iranian Revolution, Iran and the rest of the Muslim world needed to get rid of the neocolonial influence of the United States and strong oil corporate interests by instating Islamic states.

Social and cultural changes in the Middle East are taking place amid a strong revival of Islamic sentiments.

- For many conservatives in the Middle East, Islam and its overall traditional preaching of social life offer comfort to a community inundated with Western images and culture.
- The youth of the Middle East, often promoting more progressive values than their elders, are pushing for social and political changes.

CRITICAL THINKING QUESTIONS

1. Progressive Israelis that have criticized their government's occupation of the West Bank and Gaza have been called "self-haters" by other Israelis. Similarly, in the United States, progressive Americans that have criticized the U.S. invasion and occupation of Iraq have

been called "anti-American." Is it un-patriotic to criticize one's own government when in conflict or at war?

2. Globalization and technology—such as the Internet and satellite TV—have forced the sexual revolution onto Arab regions that did not experience this grassroots movement in the past. What effect has the sexual revolution had on Arab societies?

3. Can a theocracy ever be truly democratic? Can religion and politics coexist in a democratic system?

4. The United States based its invasion of Iraq on the idea that Iraq was an imminent threat. Was this pre-crime accusation justified? In what type of situation might a pre-crime accusation be justified?

CHAPTER NOTES

1. Joseph Weatherby, *The Middle East and North Africa* (New York: Longman, 2001), pp. 197–98.

2. S. Azadi, with A. Ferrante, *Out of Iran* (London: Macdonald, 1987), p. 223, quoted in S. Sullivan, ed., *Stories by Iranian Women Since the Revolution* (Austin, Tex.: University of Texas Press, 1991), p. 13.

3. *The New York Times,* August 27, 2003.

4. Amos Oz, interview, *The NewsHour with Jim Lehrer,* PBS, January 23, 2002.

Chapter 14

The Emergence of Independent States from South to East Asia

Malaysia is a modernizing, multiethnic society that has blended its commitment to Islam with a promotion of democratic ideals and economic liberalization. Today Malaysia, like many other countries from South to East Asia, faces the challenge of integrating demands for both traditionalism and modernity. The success of Malaysia's modernization and economic growth is visible in the skyline of the capital Kuala Lumpur, where a pair of twin towers thrusts up above the surrounding buildings into the clouds. The Petronas Twin Towers rise over 450 metres, and were the world's tallest buildings until very recently. More than an architectural achievement, the towers typify the emergence of Asia as a major player on the international scene. It is probably no accident that the foundations were laid on the site of the Selangor Cricket Club, a symbol of colonial hegemony in Southeast Asia. The Petronas Twin Towers, then, serve as a vivid demonstration in steel and glass of the dual face of modern Asia: a region seeking to compete with the advanced nations of the West while still struggling to overcome a legacy of colonial rule. As Asian leaders have discovered, it is a path strewn with hidden obstacles.

At the conclusion of this chapter, you will be able to

- describe the internal tensions between traditionalism and modernism in India and Pakistan;
- detail the struggle for democracy in Southeast Asia;
- explain why Asia has been slow to make changes related to women's equality and freedom;
- outline the factors that contributed to the rise and fall of the "economic miracle" in Japan and South Korea.

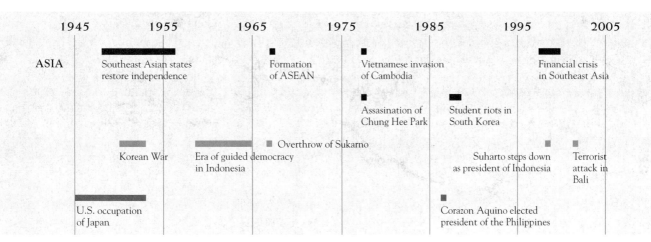

| 1945 | 1955 | 1965 | 1975 | 1985 | 1995 | 2005 |

ASIA

Southeast Asian states restore independence

Formation of ASEAN

Vietnamese invasion of Cambodia

Financial crisis in Southeast Asia

Assasination of Chung Hee Park

Student riots in South Korea

Overthrow of Sukarno

Korean War

Era of guided democracy in Indonesia

Suharto steps down as president of Indonesia

Terrorist attack in Bali

U.S. occupation of Japan

Corazon Aquino elected president of the Philippines

SOUTH ASIA AFTER COLONIAL RULE

In 1947, nearly two centuries of British colonial rule came to an end when two new independent nations, India and Pakistan, came into being. Under British colonial rule, the subcontinent of South Asia had been linked ever more closely to the global capitalist economy. Yet as in other areas of Asia and Africa, the experience brought only limited benefits to the local peoples; little industrial development took place, and the bulk of the profits went into the pockets of Western entrepreneurs.

For half a century, nationalist forces had been seeking reforms in colonial policy and the eventual overthrow of colonial power. But the peoples of South Asia did not regain their independence until after World War II.

How Did the British Transfer Rule to South Asians?

During the 1930s, the nationalist movement in India was severely shaken by disagreements between Hindus and Muslims over minority rights. The outbreak of World War II subdued diverging perspectives, but disagreements erupted again after the war ended in 1945. Battles between Hindus and Muslims broke out in several cities, and Mohammed Ali Jinnah, leader of the Muslim League, demanded the creation of a separate state for each. Meanwhile, the Labour Party, which had long been critical of the British colonial legacy on both moral and economic grounds, had come to power in Great Britain, and the new prime minister, Clement Attlee, announced that power would be transferred to "responsible Indian hands" by June 1948.

But the imminence of independence did not dampen communal strife. As riots escalated, the British reluctantly accepted the inevitability of partition and declared that on August 15, 1947, two independent nations—Hindu India and Muslim Pakistan—would be established. Pakistan would be divided between the main area of Muslim habitation in the Indus River valley in the west and a separate territory in east Bengal over 3000 kilometres to the east. Although Mahatma Gandhi warned that partition would provoke "an orgy of blood,"[1] he was increasingly regarded as a figure of the past, and his views were ignored.

The British instructed the rulers in the princely states to choose which state they would join by August 15, but problems arose in predominantly Hindu Hyderabad, where the *nawab* was a Muslim, and mountainous Kashmir, where a Hindu prince ruled over a Muslim population. After independence was declared, the flight of millions of Hindus and Muslims across the borders led to violence and the death of more than a million people. One of the casualties was

Gandhi, who was assassinated on January 30, 1948, as he was going to morning prayer. The assassin, a Hindu militant, was apparently motivated by Gandhi's opposition to a Hindu India.

With independence, the Indian National Congress, now renamed the Congress Party, moved from opposition to the responsibility of power under Jawaharlal Nehru, the new prime minister. The prospect must have been intimidating. The vast majority of India's 400 million people were poor and illiterate. The new nation encompassed a bewildering number of ethnic groups and 14 major languages. Although Congress leaders spoke bravely of building a new nation, Indian society still bore the scars of past wars and divisions.

The government's first problem was to resolve disputes left over from the transition period. The rulers of Hyderabad and Kashmir had both followed their own preferences rather than the wishes of their subject populations. Nehru was determined to include both states within India. In 1948, Indian troops invaded Hyderabad and annexed the area. India was also able to seize most of Kashmir, but at the cost of creating an intractable problem that has poisoned relations with Pakistan to the present day.

What Were Nehru's Policy Objectives?

Under Nehru's leadership, India adopted a political system on the British model, with a figurehead president and a parliamentary form of government. A number of political parties operated legally, but the Congress Party, with its enormous prestige and charismatic leadership, was dominant at both the central and the local levels. It was ably assisted by the Indian civil service, which had been created during the era of British colonial rule and provided solid expertise in the arcane art of bureaucracy.

Nehru had been influenced by British socialism and patterned his economic policy roughly after the program of the British Labour Party. The state took over ownership of the major industries and resources, transportation, and utilities, while private enterprise was permitted at the local and retail levels. Farmland remained in private hands, but rural cooperatives were officially encouraged. The government also sought to avoid excessive dependence on foreign investment and technological assistance. All businesses were required by law to have majority Indian ownership.

The primary themes of Nehru's foreign policy were anticolonialism and anti-racism. Nehru, along with Egypt's Gamal Abdel Nasser and Yugoslavia's Josip Broz (Tito), was a key figure behind the Non-Aligned Movement, an organization of Third World countries that objected to their being used as Cold War pawns. Under Nehru's guidance, India took a neutral stance in the Cold War on issues of the day, but remained friendly with the Soviets. India sought to provide leadership to all newly independent nations in Asia, Africa, and Latin America. It also sought good relations with the new People's Republic of China. India's neutrality put it at odds with the United States, which during the 1950s was trying to mobilize all nations against what it viewed as the menace of international communism.

Relations with Pakistan continued to be troubled. India refused to consider Pakistan's claim to **Kashmir**, even though the majority of the population there was Muslim. Tension between the two countries persisted, erupting into war in 1965. In 1971, when riots against the Pakistani government broke out in East Pakistan, India took advantage of the situation and intervened on the side of East Pakistan, which declared its independence as the new nation of Bangladesh (see Map 14.1, Plate 29).

> **Kashmir** is a disputed region located in the foothills of the Himalayas. The predominately Muslim Kashmiri have fought for either annexation to Pakistan or, more recently, self-determination, albeit unsuccessfully, from India.

What Challenges Have Nehru's Congress Party Successors Faced?

Nehru's death in 1964 aroused concern that Indian democracy was dependent on the Nehru mystique. When his successor, a Congress Party veteran, died in 1966, Congress leaders selected Nehru's daughter, Indira Gandhi (1917–84)—no relation to Mahatma Gandhi—as the new prime minister. Gandhi was inexperienced in politics, but she quickly showed the steely determination of her father.

Like Nehru, Gandhi embraced democratic socialism and a policy of neutrality in foreign affairs, but she was more activist than her father. To combat rural poverty, she nationalized banks, provided loans to peasants on easy terms, built low-cost housing, distributed land to the landless, and introduced electoral reforms to enfranchise the poor.

Gandhi was especially worried by India's growing population and in an effort to curb the growth rate adopted a policy of enforced sterilization. This policy proved unpopular, however, and, along with growing official corruption and Gandhi's authoritarian tactics, led to her defeat in the general election of 1975, the first time the Congress Party had failed to win a majority at the national level.

A minority government of pro-capitalist parties was formed, but within two years, Gandhi was back in power. She now faced a new challenge, however, in the rise of religious strife. The most dangerous situation was in the Punjab, where militant Sikhs were demanding autonomy or even independence from India. Gandhi did not shrink from a confrontation and attacked Sikh rebels hiding in their Golden Temple in the city of **Amritsar**. The incident aroused widespread anger among the Sikh community, and in 1984, Sikhs among Gandhi's personal bodyguards assassinated her.

> **Amritsar** is an ancient city in Punjab, India, with many revered Sikh shrines, most stunning of which is the Golden Temple, an ornate complex located in the midst of a reinforced lake.

By now, Congress politicians were convinced that the party could not remain in power without a member of the Nehru family at the helm. Gandhi's son Rajiv, a commercial airline pilot with little interest in politics, was persuaded to replace his mother as prime minister. Rajiv lacked the strong ideological and political convictions of his mother and grandfather and allowed a greater role for private enterprise. But his government was criticized for cronyism, inefficiency, and corruption, as well as insensitivity to the poor.

Rajiv Gandhi also sought to play a role in regional affairs, getting involved between the government in Sri Lanka and Tamil rebels (known as the "Elam Tigers") who were ethnically related to the majority population in southern India. At one point, Rajiv switched India's support from the Tamils to the Sri Lankan Singhalese government. The decision cost him his life: while campaigning for re-election in 1991, he was assassinated by a member of the Tiger organization. India faced the future without a member of the Nehru family as prime minister.

During the early 1990s, Congress remained the leading party, but the powerful hold it had once had on the Indian electorate was gone. New parties, such as the Hindu fundamentalist Bharatiya Janata Party (BJP), actively vied with Congress for control of the central and state governments. Growing political instability at the centre was accompanied by rising tensions between Hindus and Muslims that resulted in the death of thousands.

When a coalition government formed under Congress leadership collapsed, the BJP, under Prime Minister A. B. Vajpayee, ascended to power and played on Hindu sensibilities to build its political base. Rajiv Gandhi's Italian-born wife Sonia has taken over the leadership of the Congress Party to improve its political fortunes and won the 2004 elections. Sonia Gandhi, however, passed the torch to Manmohan Singh, who became prime minister.

How Has Pakistan Fared Since Independence?

When in August 1947, Pakistan achieved independence, the unique state united two separate territories over 3000 kilometres apart. West Pakistan, including the Indus River basin and the West Punjab, was perennially short of water and was populated by dry crop farmers and peoples of the steppe. East Pakistan was made up of the marshy deltas of the Ganges and Brahmaputra rivers. Densely populated with rice farmers, it was the home of the artistic and intellectual **Bengalis**.

> **Bengalis** populate a region in India's West Bengal and Bangladesh; this primarily Muslim population has a rich history of artists, critics, and philosophers.

The first years of the new state were marked by intense internal debates over religious, linguistic, and regional issues. Mohammed Ali Jinnah's vision of a democratic state, that would assure freedom of religion and equal treatment for all, was not adopted by successive governments. The new state was also fraught with regional tensions, divisions between east and west. Many in East Pakistan felt that the government, based in the west, ignored their needs. In 1952, riots erupted in East Pakistan over the government's decision to adopt Urdu, a language derived from Indo-European languages and used by Muslims in northern India, as the national language of the entire country. Most East Pakistanis spoke Bengali, an unrelated language. Tensions persisted, and in March 1971, East Pakistan declared its independence as the new nation of Bangladesh. Pakistani troops attempted to restore central government authority in the capital of Dhaka, but rebel forces supported by India went on the offensive, and the government bowed to the inevitable and recognized independent Bangladesh.

The breakup of the union between East and West Pakistan undermined the fragile authority of the military regime that had ruled Pakistan since 1958 and led to its replacement by a civilian government under Zulfikar Ali Bhutto. But now religious tensions came to the fore, despite a new constitution that made a number of key concessions to conservative Muslims. In 1977, a new military government under General Mohammad Zia-ul-Haq came to power with a commitment to make Pakistan a truly Islamic state. Islamic law became the basis for social behaviour as well as for the legal system. Laws governing the consumption of alcohol and the role of women were tightened in accordance with strict Muslim beliefs. But after Zia was killed in a plane crash, Pakistanis elected Benazir Bhutto (b. 1953), the daughter of Zulfikar Ali Bhutto and a supporter of secularism who had been educated in the United Kingdom and the United States. She too was removed from power by a military regime, in 1990, on charges of incompetence and corruption. Reelected in 1993, she attempted to crack down on opposition forces but was removed once again amid renewed charges of official corruption. Her successor soon came under fire for the same reason and in 1999 was ousted by a military coup led by General Pervez Musharraf (b. 1943), who promised to restore political stability and honest government.

In September 2001, Pakistan became the focus of international attention when a coalition of forces arrived in Afghanistan to overthrow the Taliban regime and destroy the al-Qaeda terrorist network. Despite considerable support for the Taliban among the local population, President Musharraf pledged his help to the United States in cracking down on extremists. He also promised to return his country to the secular principles espoused by Mohammed Ali Jinnah and declared a vision of "Enlightened Moderation" that is meant to transform Pakistan into the secular, democratic state it was once intended to be.

POVERTY AND PLURALISM IN SOUTH ASIA

The leaders of the new states that emerged in South Asia after World War II faced a number of problems. The peoples of South Asia were still overwhelmingly poor and illiterate, and the sectarian, ethnic, and cultural divisions that had plagued Indian society for centuries had not dissipated.

How Have Communalism and Sectarianism Marred India?

Perhaps the most sincere effort to create democratic institutions was in India, where the new constitution called for social justice, liberty, equality of status and opportunity, and fraternity. All citizens were guaranteed protection from discrimination on the grounds of religious belief, race, caste, sex, or place of birth.

In theory, then, India became a full-fledged democracy on the British parliamentary model. In actuality, a number of distinctive characteristics made the system less than fully democratic in the Western sense but may also have enabled it to survive. As we have seen, India became in essence a one-party state. By leading the independence movement, the Congress Party had gained massive public support, which enabled it to retain its preeminent position in Indian politics for three decades. The party also avoided being identified as a party exclusively for the Hindu majority by including prominent non-Hindus among its leaders and favouring measures to protect minority groups such as Sikhs, **untouchables**, and Muslims from discrimination.

> **Untouchables** are the lowest group in the outlawed Indian caste system; they are still identified as such, particularly in rural areas.

After Jawaharlal Nehru's death in 1964, however, problems emerged that had been disguised by his adept manoeuvring. Part of the problem was the familiar one of a party too long in power. Party officials became complacent and all too easily fell prey to the temptations of corruption and pork-barrel politics.

Another problem was communalism. Beneath the surface unity of the new republic lay age-old ethnic, linguistic, and religious sectarianism. Because of India's vast size and complex history, no national language had ever emerged. Hindi was the most prevalent, but it was the native language of less than one-third of the population. During the colonial period, English had served as the official language of government, and many non-Hindi speakers suggested making it the official language. But English was spoken only by the educated elite, and it represented an affront to national pride. Eventually, India recognized 14 official tongues.

Divisiveness increased after Nehru's death, and under his successors, official corruption grew. Only the lack of appeal of its rivals and the Nehru family charisma carried on by his daughter Indira Gandhi kept the party in power. But she was unable to prevent the progressive disintegration of the party's power base at the state level, where regional or ideological parties won the allegiance of voters by exploiting ethnic or social revolutionary themes.

During the 1980s, religious tensions began to intensify, not only among Sikhs in the northwest but also between Hindus and Muslims. As we have seen, Gandhi's uncompromising approach to Sikh separatism led to her assassination in 1984. Under her son, Rajiv Gandhi, Hindu militants at Ayodhya, in northern India, demanded the destruction of a mosque built on a holy site where a Hindu temple had previously existed. In 1992, Hindu demonstrators destroyed the mosque and erected a temporary temple at the site, provoking clashes between Hindus and Muslims throughout the country. In protest, rioters in neighbouring Pakistan destroyed a number of Hindu shrines in that country.

In recent years, communal divisions have intensified as militant Hindu groups agitate for a state that caters to the Hindu majority, now numbering more than 700 million people. In the spring of 2002, violence between Hindus and Muslims flared up again over plans by Hindu activists to build a permanent temple at the site of the destroyed mosque at Ayodhya.

Why Didn't Socialism Succeed in India?

Nehru's answer to the social and economic inequality that had long afflicted the subcontinent was socialism. He instituted a series of five-year plans, which led to the creation of a relatively large and reasonably efficient industrial sector, centred on steel, vehicles, and textiles. Industrial production almost tripled between 1950 and 1965, and per capita annual income rose by 50 percent between 1950 and 1980, although it was still less than US$300.

By the 1970s, however, industrial growth had slowed. The lack of modern infrastructure was a problem, as was the rising price of oil, most of which had to be imported. The relative weakness of the state-owned sector, which grew at an annual rate of only about 2 percent in the 1950s and 1960s, versus 5 percent for the private sector, also became a serious obstacle.

India's major economic weakness, however, was in agriculture. At independence, mechanization was almost unknown, fertilizer was rarely used, and most farms were small and uneconomical because of the Hindu tradition of dividing the land equally among all male children. As a result, the vast majority of the Indian people lived in conditions of abject poverty. Landless labourers outnumbered landowners by almost two to one. The government attempted to relieve the problem by redistributing land to the poor, limiting the size of landholdings, and encouraging farmers to form voluntary cooperatives. But all three programs ran into widespread opposition and apathy.

Another problem was overpopulation. Even before independence, the country had had difficulty supporting its people. In the 1950s and 1960s, the population grew by more than 2 percent annually, twice the nineteenth-century rate. Beginning in the 1960s, the Indian government sought to curb population growth. Indira Gandhi instituted a program combining monetary rewards and compulsory sterilization. Males who had fathered too many children were sometimes forced to undergo a vasectomy. Popular resistance undermined the program, however, and the goals were scaled back in the 1970s. As a result, India has made little progress in holding down its burgeoning population, now estimated at more than one billion. One factor in the continued growth has been a decline in the death rate, especially the rate of infant mortality. Nevertheless, as a result of media popularization and better government programs, the trend today, even in poor rural villages, is toward smaller families. The average number of children a woman bears has been reduced from six in 1950 to three today. As has occurred elsewhere, the decline in family size began among the educated and is gradually spreading throughout Indian society.

The **Green Revolution** that began in the 1960s helped reduce the severity of the population problem. The introduction of more productive, disease-resistant strains of rice and wheat doubled grain production between 1960 and 1980. But the Green Revolution also increased rural inequality. Wealthier farmers were able to purchase the necessary fertilizer and pesticides for the new crops, while poorer farmers were often driven off the land. Millions fled to the cities, where they lived in vast slums, working at menial jobs or even begging for a living.

> The **Green Revolution** refers to the introduction of newly developed strains of wheat and rice that could significantly increase agricultural output; it began in the 1960s.

After the death of Indira Gandhi in 1984, her son Rajiv proved more receptive to foreign investment and a greater role for the private sector in the economy. India began to export more manufactured goods, including computer software. The pace of change has accelerated under Rajiv Gandhi's successors, who have continued to transfer state-run industries to private hands. These policies have stimulated the growth of a prosperous new middle class, now estimated at more than 100 million. Consumerism has soared, and sales of television sets, automobiles, videocassette recorders, DVD players, and telephones have increased dramatically. Equally important, Western imports are being replaced by new products manufactured in India with Indian brand names.

Nevertheless, Nehru's dream of a socialist society remains strong. State-owned enterprises still produce about half of all domestic goods, and high tariffs continue to stifle imports. Nationalist parties have played on the widespread fear of foreign economic influence to force the cancellation of some contracts and the relocation of some foreign firms.

As in the industrialized countries of the West, economic growth has been accompanied by environmental damage. Water and air pollution has led to illness and death for many people, and an environmental movement has emerged. Some environmental critics, reflecting the traditional anti-imperialist attitude of Indian intellectuals, blame Western capitalist corporations for the problem, especially since the highly publicized case of toxic gas leakage from the American-owned Union Carbide chemical plant at Bhopal, known as the **Bhopal disaster**. That said, not all the environmental damage in India can be ascribed to industrialization. The Ganges River is so polluted by human overuse that it is risky for Hindu believers to bathe in it.

> The **Bhopal disaster** of 1984 was an industrial disaster that killed hundreds of thousands and made thousands of others ill for years to come. It was caused by the release of toxic gas from a Union Carbide insecticide plant at Bhopal. The disaster became a reference point for raising corporate environmental standards and defending Third World people and workers against unscrupulous foreign companies.

Moreover, many Indians have not benefited from the new prosperity. Nearly one-third of the population lives below the national poverty line. Millions continue to live in urban slums, such as the famous Calcutta (once home to Mother Teresa) where most farm families remain desperately poor. Despite the socialist rhetoric of India's leaders, the inequality of wealth in India is as pronounced as it is in capitalist nations in the West. Indeed, India has been described as two nations: an educated urban India of 100 million people surrounded by over 900 million impoverished peasants in the countryside.

One of the consequences of Rajiv Gandhi's decision to deregulate the Indian economy has been an increase in the presence of foreign corporations, including U.S. fast-food restaurant chains. Their arrival set off a storm of protest in India: from environmentalists concerned that raising grain for chickens is an inefficient use of land, from religious activists angry at the killing of animals for food, and from nationalists anxious to protect the domestic market from foreign competition. A combination of religious and environmental groups have attempted, unsuccessfully, to prevent Kentucky Fried Chicken from establishing outlets in major Indian cities.

How Is India a Traditional and Yet Secular Society?

Drawing generalizations about the life of the average Indian is difficult because of ethnic, religious, and caste differences, which are compounded by the vast gulf between town and country.

Although the constitution of 1950 guaranteed equal treatment and opportunity for all, regardless of caste, and prohibited discrimination based on untouchability, prejudice is hard to eliminate. The untouchables label persists, particularly in villages, where *harijans* (as they were called by Mahatma Gandhi), now called *dalits,* still perform menial tasks and are often denied fundamental human rights.

In general, urban Indians appear less conscious of caste distinctions. Material wealth rather than caste identity is increasingly defining status. Still, colour consciousness based on the age-old distinctions between upper-class

India's Hope, India's Sorrow. In India, as in many other societies in Southern Asia, overpopulation is a serious obstacle to economic development. The problem is particularly serious in large cities, where thousands of poor children are forced into begging or prostitution. Shown here are a few of the thousands of street children in the commercial hub of Mumbai (formerly known as Bombay).

Aryans and lower-class Dravidians remains strong. Class-conscious Hindus still express a distinct preference for light-skinned marital partners.

In few societies was the life of women more restricted than in traditional India. Hindu favouritism toward men was compounded by the local Muslim custom of *purdah* to create a society in which males were dominant in virtually all aspects of life. Females received no education and had no inheritance rights. They were restricted to the home and tied to their husbands for life. Widows were expected to shave their heads and engage in a life of religious meditation or even to throw themselves on their husband's funeral pyre.

After independence, India's leaders sought to equalize treatment of the sexes. The constitution expressly forbade discrimination based on sex and called for equal pay for equal work. Laws prohibited child marriage and the payment of a dowry by the bride's family. Women were encouraged to attend school and enter the labour market.

Such laws, along with the dynamics of economic and social change, have had a major impact on the lives of many Indian women. Middle-class women in urban areas are much more likely to seek employment outside the home, and many hold managerial and professional positions. Some Indian women, however, choose to play a dual role—a modern one in their work and in the marketplace and a more submissive, traditional one at home.

Such attitudes are also reflected in the burgeoning Indian movie industry called **Bollywood**, where aspiring actresses must often brave family disapproval to enter the entertainment world. Before World War II, female actors were routinely viewed as prostitutes or "loose women," and such views are still prevalent among conservative Indian families. Even Karisma Kapoor, one of India's current film stars and a member of the Kapoor clan, which has produced several generations of actors, had to defy her family's ban on its women entering show business.

Courtesy of William J. Duiker

Fetching Water at the Village Well. The scarcity of water will surely become one of the planet's most crucial problems. It will affect all nations, developed and developing, rich and poor. Although many Indians live with an inadequate water supply, these women are fortunate to have a well in their village. More typical is the image of the Indian woman, dressed in a colourful sari, children encircling her as she heads to her distant home on foot, carrying a heavy pail of water on her head.

Bollywood is India's Hollywood located in Mumbai, where hundreds of films are produced each year with low budgets, big names, and melodramatic storylines reflecting India's cultural mosaic.

Nothing more strikingly indicates the changing role of women in South Asia than the fact that in recent years, three of the major countries in the area—India, Pakistan, and Sri Lanka—have had women prime ministers. It is worthy of mention, however, that all three—Indira Gandhi, Benazir Bhutto, and Sirimavo Bandaranaike—came from prominent political families.

Organized efforts to protect the rights of women have been under way in India since the 1970s, when the Progressive Organization for Women (POW) instituted a campaign against sexual harassment and other forms of discrimination against women in Indian society. Like many of their counterparts in other parts of Asia and Africa, however, many activists for women's rights in India are critical of Western feminism, charging that it is irrelevant to their own realities. Although Indian feminists feel a bond

with their sisters all over the world, they insist on resolving Indian problems with Indian solutions. As Indira Gandhi remarked, "To be liberated, a woman should be free to be herself. Rivalry between men and women is unnecessary, is destructive and itself a bondage."

Like other aspects of life, the role of women has changed much less in rural areas. In the early 1960s, many villagers still practised the institution of *purdah*. A woman who went about freely in society would get a bad reputation. Female children are still much less likely to receive an education. The overall literacy rate in India today is less than 40 percent, but it is undoubtedly much lower among women. Laws relating to dowry, child marriage, and inheritance are routinely ignored in the countryside. There have been a few highly publicized cases of *suttee*, although undoubtedly more women die of mistreatment at the hands of their husband or of other members of his family.

Perhaps the most tragic aspect of continued sexual discrimination in India is the high mortality rate among girls. One-quarter of the female children born in India die before the age of 15 as a result of neglect or even infanticide. Others are aborted before birth after gender-detection examinations. The results are striking. In most societies, the number of women equals or exceeds that of men; in India, according to one estimate, the ratio is only 933 females to 1000 males.

Indian society looks increasingly Western in an economic sense, but it is still rooted in traditionalism. As in a number of other Asian and African societies, the distinction between traditional and modern (or native and westernized) can be a matter of the simple dichotomy between rural and urban. The major cities appear modern and westernized, but the villages have changed little since pre-colonial days.

SOUTHEAST ASIA ASPIRES TO INDEPENDENCE

The Japanese wartime occupation had a great impact on attitudes among the peoples of Southeast Asia. It demonstrated the vulnerability of colonial rule in the region and showed that an Asian power could defeat Europeans. The Allied governments themselves also contributed—sometimes unwittingly—to rising aspirations for independence by promising self-determination for all peoples at the end of the war. Although British Prime Minister Winston Churchill later said that the Atlantic Charter did not apply to the colonial peoples, it would be difficult to put the genie back in the bottle.

Some did not try. In July 1946, the United States granted total independence to the Philippines, after a brutal American occupation of the country. The Americans maintained a military presence on the islands, however, and U.S. citizens retained economic and commercial interests in the new country.

The British, too, under the Labour Party, were willing to bring an end to a century of imperialism in the region. In 1948, the Union of Burma received its independence. Malaysia's turn came in 1957, after a Communist guerrilla movement had been suppressed.

The French and the Dutch, however, both regarded their colonies in the region as economic necessities as well as symbols of national grandeur and refused to turn them over to nationalist movements at the end of the war. The Dutch attempted to suppress a rebellion in the East Indies led by Sukarno (1901–70), leader of the Indonesian Nationalist Party. But the United States, which feared a Communist victory there, pressured the Dutch to grant independence to Sukarno and his non-Communist forces, and in 1950, the Dutch finally agreed to recognize the new Republic of Indonesia.

The situation was somewhat different in Vietnam, where the leading force in the anti-colonial movement was the local Indochinese Communist Party (ICP), led by the veteran and Moscow-trained revolutionary Ho Chi Minh. In August 1945, virtually at the moment of Japanese surrender, the Vietminh, an alliance of patriotic forces under secret ICP leadership that had been founded to fight the Japanese in 1941, launched a general uprising and seized power throughout most of Vietnam.

In early September, Ho Chi Minh was declared president of a new provisional republic in Hanoi. In the meantime, French military units began arriving in Saigon, with the permission of the British occupation command there. The new government in Hanoi, formally known as the *Democratic Republic of Vietnam (DRV)* appealed to the victorious Allies for recognition but received no response, and by late fall, the southern part of the country was back under French rule. Ho signed a preliminary agreement with the French recognizing Vietnam as a "free state" within the French Union, but negotiations over the details broke down in the summer of 1946, and war between the two parties broke out in December. At the time, it was only an anti-colonial war, but it would soon become much more (see Chapter 6, page 120).

THE ERA OF INDEPENDENT STATES IN SOUTHEAST ASIA

Many of the leaders of the newly independent states in Southeast Asia (see Map 14.2, Plate 30) admired Western political institutions and hoped to adapt them to their own countries. New constitutions were patterned on Western democratic models, and multiparty political systems quickly sprang into operation.

What Form of Rule Did Southeast Asian States Follow?

By the 1960s, most of these budding experiments in pluralist democracy had been abandoned or were under serious threat. Some had been replaced by military or one-party autocratic regimes. In Burma, a moderate government based on the British parliamentary system and dedicated to Buddhism and nonviolent Marxism had given way to a military government. In Thailand, too, the military now ruled. In the Philippines, President Ferdinand Marcos discarded democratic restraints and established his own centralized control. In South Vietnam (see Chapter 6), Ngo Dinh Diem and his successors paid lip service to the Western democratic model but ruled by authoritarian means.

One problem faced by most of these states was that independence had not brought material prosperity or ended economic inequality and the domination of the local economies by foreign interests. Most economies in the region were still characterized by tiny industrial sectors; they lacked technology, educational resources, capital investment, and leaders trained in developmental skills.

The presence of widespread ethnic, linguistic, cultural, and economic differences also made the transition to Western-style democracy difficult. In Malaysia, for example, the majority of Malays—most of whom were farmers—feared economic and political domination by the local Chinese minority, who were much more experienced in industry and commerce. In 1961, the Federation of Malaya, whose ruling party was dominated by Malays, integrated former British colonies on the island of Borneo into the new Union of Malaysia in a move to increase the non-Chinese proportion of the country's population. Yet periodic conflicts persisted as the Malay government attempted to guarantee Malay control over politics and a larger role in the economy.

The most publicized example of a failed experiment in democracy was in Indonesia. In 1950, the new leaders drew up a constitution creating a parliamentary system and a presidency. Sukarno was elected the first president. President Sukarno of Indonesia was a spellbinding speaker and a charismatic leader of his nation's struggle for independence. Sukarno promoted two of his favourite projects: Indonesian nationalism and guided democracy. The force that would guide Indonesia, of course, was to be Sukarno himself. On guided democracy Sukarno once said,

> Indonesia's democracy is not liberal democracy. Indonesian democracy is not the democracy of the world of Montaigne or Voltaire. Indonesia's democracy is not à la America, Indonesia's democracy is not the Soviet—NO! Indonesia's democracy is the democracy which is implanted in the breasts of the Indonesian people, and it is that which I have tried to dig up again, and have put forward as an offering to you. . . . If you, especially the undergraduates, are still clinging to and being borne along the democracy made in England, or democracy made in France, or democracy made in America, or democracy made in Russia, you will become a nation of copyists![2]

In the late 1950s, Sukarno, exasperated at the continued manoeuvring among devout Muslims, Communists, and the army, dissolved the constitution and attempted to rule on his own through what he called "guided democracy." As he described it, guided democracy was closer to Indonesian traditions and superior to the Western variety. The weakness of the latter was that it allowed the majority to dominate the minority, whereas guided democracy would reconcile different opinions and points of view in a government operated by consensus. Highly suspicious of the West, Sukarno nationalized foreign-owned enterprises and sought economic aid from China and the Soviet Union while relying for domestic support on the Indonesian Communist Party.

The army and conservative Muslims resented Sukarno's increasing reliance on the Communists, and conservative Muslims were further upset by his refusal to consider a state based on Islamic principles. In 1965, military officers launched a coup d'état that provoked a mass popular uprising, which resulted in the slaughter of several hundred thousand suspected Communists, many of whom were overseas Chinese, long distrusted by the Muslim majority. In 1967, a military government under General Suharto was installed.

The new government made no pretensions of reverting to democratic rule, but it did restore good relations with the West and sought foreign investment to repair the country's ravaged economy. But it also found it difficult to placate internal demands for the creation of an Islamic state. In a few areas, including oil and resource-rich western Sumatra, extremists took up arms against the state. Fearing the loss of this valuable area, the Indonesian government has waged a war against opponents.

The one country in Southeast Asia that explicitly rejected the Western model was North Vietnam. Its leaders opted for the Stalinist pattern of national development, based on Communist Party rule and socialist forms of ownership. In 1958, stimulated by the success of collectivization in neighbouring China, the government launched a three-year plan to lay the foundation for a socialist society. Collective farms were established, and all industry and commerce above the family level were nationalized.

Where Has Democracy Succeeded and Failed in Southeast Asia?

In recent years, some Southeast Asian societies have shown signs of evolving toward more democratic forms. In the Philippines, the dictatorial Marcos regime was overthrown by a massive public uprising in 1986 and replaced by a democratically elected government under President Corazon Aquino (b. 1933), the widow of a popular politician assassinated a few years earlier. Aquino was unable to resolve many of the country's chronic economic and social difficulties, however, and political stability remains elusive; one of her successors, former actor Joseph Estrada, was forced to resign on the charge of corruption. At the same time, Muslims in the southern island of Mindanao have mounted a campaign to obtain autonomy or independence that has had some extremists use violence and terror.

In other nations, the results have also been mixed. Although Malaysia is a practising democracy, tensions persist between Malays and Chinese as well as between secular and orthodox Muslims who seek to create an Islamic state. In neighbouring Thailand, the military has found it expedient to hold national elections for civilian governments, but the danger of a military takeover is never far beneath the surface.

In Indonesia, difficult economic conditions caused by the financial crisis of 1997 (see the next section), combined with popular anger against the Suharto government (several members of his family had reportedly used their positions to amass considerable wealth), led to violent street riots and demands for his resignation. Forced to step down in the spring of 1998, Suharto was replaced by his deputy B. J. Habibie, who called for the establishment of a national assembly to select a new government based on popular aspirations. The assembly selected a moderate as president, but he was charged with corruption and incompetence and was replaced in 2001 by his vice president, Sukarno's daughter Megawati Sukarnoputri (b. 1947).

The new government faced a severe challenge, not only from the economic crisis but also from dissident elements seeking autonomy or even separation from the republic. Under pressure from the international community, Indonesia agreed to grant independence to the onetime Portuguese colony of **East Timor**, where the majority of the people are Roman Catholics. But violence provoked by pro-Indonesian militia units forced many refugees to flee the country. Religious tensions have also erupted between

Muslims and Christians elsewhere in the archipelago, and Muslim rebels in western Sumatra continue to agitate for a new state based on strict adherence to fundamentalist - Islam. In the meantime, a terrorist attack directed at tourists on the island of Bali in 2002 provoked fears that Indonesia had attracted terrorist groups throughout the region.

> **East Timor** is a newly independent state (since 2002) that was formerly controlled by Indonesia; earlier, it had been a Portuguese colony.

In Vietnam, the trend in recent years has been toward a greater popular role in the governing process. Elections for the unicameral Parliament are more open than in the past. The government remains suspicious of Western-style democracy, however, and represses any opposition to the Communist Party's guiding role over the state.

Only in Burma (now renamed Myanmar), where the military has been in complete control since the early 1960s, have the forces of greater popular participation been virtually silenced. Even there, however, the power of the ruling regime of General U Ne Win (1911–2002), known as *SLORC,* has been vocally challenged by Aung San Huu Kyi (b. 1945), the admired daughter of one of the heroes of the country's struggle for national liberation after World War II.

What Caused the 1997 Asian Financial Crisis?

The trend toward more representative systems of government has been due in part to increasing prosperity and the growth of an affluent and educated middle class. Although Indonesia, Burma, and the three Indochinese states are still overwhelmingly agrarian, Malaysia and Thailand have been undergoing relatively rapid economic development.

In the late summer of 1997, however, these economic gains were threatened, and popular faith in the ultimate benefits of globalization was shaken as a financial crisis swept through the region. The crisis was triggered by a number of problems, including growing budget deficits caused by excessive government expenditures on ambitious development projects, irresponsible lending and investment practices by financial institutions, and an overvaluation of local currencies relative to the U.S. dollar. An underlying cause of these problems was the prevalence of backroom deals between politicians and business leaders that temporarily enriched both groups at the cost of eventual economic dislocation.

As local currencies plummeted in value, the International Monetary Fund agreed to provide assistance, but only on the condition that the governments concerned

Courtesy of William J. Duiker

One world, One Fashion. One of the negative aspects of tourism is the eroding of distinctive ethnic cultures, even in previously less travelled areas. This village chief from Flores, a remote island in the Indonesian archipelago, seems very proud of his designer sunglasses.

permit greater transparency in their economic systems and allow market forces to operate more freely, even at the price of bankruptcies and the loss of jobs. In the early 2000s, although there were signs that some political leaders recognized the serious nature of their problems and were willing to take steps to resolve them, the political cost of such changes remained uncertain.

What Is ASEAN's Role in Southeast Asia?

In addition to their continuing internal challenges, Southeast Asian states have been hampered by serious tensions among themselves. Some of these tensions were a consequence of historical rivalries and territorial disputes that had been submerged during the long era of colonial rule. Cambodia, for example, has bickered with both of its neighbours, Thailand and Vietnam, over mutual frontiers drawn up originally by the French for their own convenience.

After the reunification of Vietnam under Communist rule in 1975, the lingering border dispute between Cambodia and Vietnam erupted again. In April 1975, a brutal revolutionary regime under the leadership of the **Khmer Rouge** dictator Pol Pot came to power in Cambodia and proceeded to carry out the massacre of more than one million Cambodians. Then, claiming that vast territories in the Mekong delta had been seized from Cambodia by the Vietnamese in previous centuries, the Khmer Rouge regime launched attacks across the common border. In response, Vietnamese forces invaded Cambodia in December 1978 and installed a pro-Hanoi regime in Phnom Penh. Fearful of Vietnam's increasing power in the region, China launched a brief attack on Vietnam to demonstrate its displeasure.

> The **Khmer Rouge** was a Communist party in Cambodia responsible for the terror and murder of more than one million Cambodians in the 1970s.

Courtesy of William J. Duiker

Holocaust in Cambodia. When the Khmer Rouge seized power in Cambodia in April 1975, they immediately emptied the capital of Phnom Penh and systematically began to eliminate opposition elements throughout the country. Thousands were tortured in the infamous Tuol Sleng prison and then marched out to the countryside, where they were massacred. Their bodies were thrown into massive pits. The succeeding government unearthed the remains, which are now displayed at an outdoor museum at the site.

The outbreak of war among the erstwhile Communist allies aroused the concern of other countries in the neighbourhood. In 1967, several non-Communist countries—Indonesia, Malaysia, Thailand, Singapore, and the Philippines—established the **Association of Southeast Asian Nations** (ASEAN). At first, ASEAN concentrated on cooperative social and economic endeavours, but after the end of the Vietnam War, it cooperated with other countries in an effort to force the Vietnamese to withdraw. In 1991, the Vietnamese finally withdrew, and a new government was formed in Phnom Penh.

The **Association of Southeast Asian Nations** (ASEAN) is a cooperative organization that represents the common political, economic, technological, and security interests of member countries in the Asian region.

The growth of ASEAN from a weak collection of diverse countries into a stronger organization whose members cooperate militarily and politically has helped provide the nations of Southeast Asia with a more cohesive voice to represent their interests on the world stage. They will need it, for disagreements with Western countries over global economic issues and the rising power of China will present major challenges in coming years. That Vietnam was admitted into ASEAN in 1996 should provide both Hanoi and its neighbours with greater leverage in dealing with their powerful neighbour to the north.

What Social Issues Prevail in Contemporary Southeast Asia?

The urban-rural dichotomy observed in India also is found in Southeast Asia, where the cities resemble those in the West while the countryside often appears little changed from pre-colonial days. In cities such as Bangkok, Manila, and Jakarta, broad boulevards lined with skyscrapers alternate with muddy lanes passing through neighbourhoods packed with wooden shacks topped by thatch or rusty tin roofs. Nevertheless, in recent decades, millions of Southeast Asians have fled to these urban slums. Although most available jobs are menial, the pay is better than in the villages.

The urban migrants change not only their physical surroundings but their attitudes and values as well. Sometimes the move leads to a decline in traditional beliefs. Belief in the existence of nature and ancestral spirits, for example, has declined among the urban populations of Southeast Asia. In Thailand, Buddhism has come under pressure from the rising influence of materialism, although temple schools still educate thousands of rural youths whose families cannot afford the cost of public education.

Nevertheless, Buddhist, Muslim, and Confucian beliefs remain strong, even in cosmopolitan cities such as Bangkok, Jakarta, and Singapore. This preference for the traditional also shows up in lifestyle. Native dress—or an eclectic blend of Asian and Western attire—is still common. Traditional music, art, theatre, and dance remain popular, although Western music has become fashionable among the young, and Indonesian filmmakers complain that Western films are beginning to dominate the market.

One of the most significant changes that has taken place in Southeast Asia in recent decades is in the role of women in society. In general, women in the region have historically faced fewer restrictions on their activities and enjoyed a higher status than women elsewhere in Asia. With independence, Southeast Asian women gained new rights. Virtually all of the constitutions adopted by the newly independent states granted women full legal and political rights, including the right to work. Today, women have increased opportunities for education and have entered careers previously reserved for men. Women have become more active in politics, and as we have seen, some have served as heads of state.

Yet women are not truly treated as equal to men in any country in Southeast Asia. Sometimes the distinction is simply a matter of custom. In Vietnam, women are legally equal to men, yet until recently no women had served in the Communist Party's ruling politburo. In Thailand, Malaysia, and Indonesia, women rarely hold senior positions in government service or in the boardrooms of major corporations. Similar restrictions apply in Burma, although Aung San Huu Kyi is the leading figure in the democratic opposition movement.

JAPAN: ASIAN GIANT

In August 1945, Japan was in ruins, its cities destroyed, its vast Asian empire in ashes, its land occupied by a foreign army. A decade earlier, Japanese leaders had proclaimed their national path to development as a model for other Asian nations to follow. But their Great East Asia Co-Prosperity Sphere, which had been designed to build a vast empire under Japanese tutelage, had led only to bloody war and ultimate defeat. Half a century later, Japan had emerged as the second greatest industrial power in the world, democratic in form and content and a source of stability throughout the region. Japan's achievement spawned a number of Asian imitators.

What Challenges Has Japan's Liberal Democratic Party Faced?

For five years after the war in the Pacific, Japan was governed by an Allied administration under the command of U.S.

General Douglas MacArthur. The Allied occupation administrators started with the conviction that Japanese expansionism was directly linked to the institutional and ideological foundations of the Meiji constitution. Accordingly, they set out to change Japanese politics into something closer to the pluralistic approach used in most Western nations. The concepts of universal suffrage, governmental accountability, and a balance of power among the executive, legislative, and judicial branches that were embodied in the constitution of 1947 have held firm, and Japan today is a stable and mature democratic society with a literate and politically active electorate and a government that usually seeks to meet the needs of its citizens.

Yet a number of characteristics of the current Japanese political system reflect the tenacity of the traditional political culture. Although post-war Japan had a multiparty system with two major parties, the **Liberal Democratic Party** and the Socialist Party, in practice there was a "government party" and a permanent opposition—the Liberal Democrats were not voted out of office for 30 years. The ruling Liberal Democratic Party included several factions, but disputes were usually based on personalities rather than substantive issues.

> The **Liberal Democratic Party** has been the dominant party in Japan since 1951; it has been plagued by corruption, scandals, and patron-client relations.

That tradition changed suddenly in 1993 when the ruling Liberal Democrats, shaken by persistent reports of corruption and cronyism between politicians and business interests, failed to win a majority of seats in parliamentary elections. Morihiro Hosokawa, the leader of one of several newly created parties in the Japanese political spectrum, was elected prime minister. He promised to launch a number of reforms to clean up the political system. The new coalition government, however, quickly split into feuding factions, and in 1995, the Liberal Democratic Party returned to power. Successive prime ministers failed to carry out promised reforms, and in 2001, Junichiro Koizumi (b. 1942), a former minister of health and welfare, was elected prime minister on a promise that he would initiate far-reaching reforms to fix the political system and make it more responsive to the needs of the Japanese people. His charisma raised expectations that he might be able to bring about significant changes; so far, however, he has had little success.

One of the problems plaguing the current system has been that it continues the centralizing tendencies of the Meiji period. The government is organized on a unitary rather than a federal basis; the local administrative units are called *prefectures*. Moreover, the central government plays an active and sometimes intrusive role in various aspects of the economy, mediating management-labour disputes, establishing price and wage policies, and subsidizing vital industries and enterprises producing goods for export. This government intervention in the economy has traditionally been widely accepted and is often cited as a key reason for the efficiency of Japanese industry and the emergence of the country as an industrial giant.

In recent years, the tradition of active government involvement in the economy has increasingly come under fire. Japanese business, which previously sought government protection from imports, now argues that deregulation is needed to enable Japanese firms to innovate as a means of keeping up with the competition. Such reforms, however, have been resisted by powerful government ministries in Tokyo, which are accustomed to playing an active role in national affairs.

Another problem is related to the fact that the ruling Liberal Democratic Party has long been divided into factions that seek to protect their own interests and often resist changes that might benefit society as a whole. This tradition of factionalism has tended to insulate political figures from popular scrutiny and encouraged the susceptibility to secret dealing and official corruption. A number of senior politicians, including two recent prime ministers, have been forced to resign because of serious questions about improper financial dealings with business associates. Concern over political corruption was undoubtedly a major factor in the defeat suffered by the Liberal Democrats in the summer of 1993, and the issue continues to plague the political scene.

Last but certainly not least, minorities such as the *eta* (hereditary outcastes in traditional Japan, now known as the *burakumin*) and Korean residents in Japan continue to be subjected to legal and social discrimination. For years, official sources were reluctant to divulge that thousands of Korean women were conscripted to serve as **"comfort women"** for Japanese soldiers during the war, and many Koreans living in Japan contend that such condescending attitudes toward minorities continue to exist. Representatives of the "comfort women" have demanded both financial compensation and a formal letter of apology from the Japanese government for the treatment they received during the Pacific War. Negotiations over the issue are under way.

> **"Comfort women"** were primarily Korean women exploited and forced by the Japanese army into military base brothels for sex with Japanese soldiers.

Japan's behaviour during World War II has been an especially sensitive issue. During the early 1990s, critics at home and abroad charged that textbooks printed under the guidance of the Ministry of Education did not adequately discuss the atrocities committed by the Japanese government and armed forces during World War II. Other Asian governments were particularly incensed at Tokyo's failure to accept responsibility for such behaviour and demanded a formal apology. The government expressed remorse, but only in the context of the aggressive actions of all colonial powers during the imperialist era. In the view of many Japanese, the actions of their government during the Pacific War were a form of self-defence. When new textbooks were published that openly discussed instances of Japanese wartime misconduct, including sex slavery, the use of slave labour, and the Nanjing Massacre, many Japanese were outraged and initiated a campaign to delete or tone down references to atrocities committed by imperial troops during the Pacific War.

What Cultural Factors Explain Japanese Economic Successes?

Nowhere are the changes in post-war Japan so visible as in the economic sector, where the nation has developed into a major industrial and technological power in the space of a century, surpassing such advanced Western societies as Germany, France, and Great Britain. Here indeed is the Japanese miracle in its most concrete manifestation.

At the end of the Allied occupation in 1952, the Japanese gross national product was about one-third that of Great Britain or France. Today, it is larger than both put together and well over half that of the United States. Japan is the greatest exporting nation in the world, and its per capita income equals or surpasses that of most advanced Western states. In terms of education, mortality rates, and health care, the quality of life in Japan is superior to that in the advanced nations of the West.

Japan's labour productivity is high, not only because the Japanese are hard workers (according to statistics, Japanese workers spend substantially more time on the job than workers in other advanced societies) but also because corporations reward innovation and maintain good management-labour relations. Consequently, employee mobility and the number of days lost to labour stoppages are minimized (on an average day, according to one estimate, 603 Japanese workers are on strike compared with 11 956 Americans and 611 Canadians). Just as it did before World War II, the Japanese government promotes business interests rather than hinders them. The tradition of loyalty to the firm derives from the communal tradition in Japanese society.

In recent years, the Japanese economy has run into serious difficulties, raising the question as to whether the vaunted Japanese model is as appealing as many observers earlier declared. A rise in the value of the yen hurt exports and burst the bubble of investment by Japanese banks that

had taken place under the umbrella of government protection. Lacking a strong consumerist domestic market, the Japanese economy slipped into a long-term recession that continues today.

These economic difficulties have placed heavy pressure on some of the highly praised features of the Japanese economy. The tradition of lifetime employment created a bloated white-collar workforce and made downsizing difficult. Today, job security is on the decline as increasing numbers of workers are being laid off. Unfortunately, a disproportionate burden has fallen on women, who lack seniority and continue to suffer from various forms of discrimination in the workplace. A positive consequence is that job satisfaction is beginning to take precedence over security in the minds of many Japanese workers, and salary is beginning to reflect performance more than time on the job.

A final factor is that slowly but inexorably, the Japanese market is beginning to open up to international competition. Foreign automakers are winning a growing share of the domestic market, while the government—concerned at the prospect of food shortages—has committed itself to facilitating the importation of rice from abroad. This last move was especially sensitive, given the almost sacred role that rice farming holds in the Japanese mindset.

At the same time, greater exposure to foreign economic competition may serve to improve the performance of Japanese manufacturers. In recent years, Japanese consumers have become increasingly concerned about the quality of some of their domestic products, provoking one cabinet minister to complain about "sloppiness and complacency" among Japanese firms.

Emphasis on the work ethic also remains strong. The tradition of hard work is implanted at a young age within the educational system. Competition for acceptance into universities is intense, and many young Japanese take cram courses to prepare for the "examination hell" that lies ahead. The results are impressive: the literacy rate in Japanese schools is almost 100 percent, and Japanese schoolchildren consistently earn higher scores on achievement tests than children in other advanced countries. At the same time, this devotion to success has often been accompanied by bullying by teachers.

Some young Japanese find suicide the only escape from the pressures emanating from society, school, and family. Parental pride often becomes a factor, with "education mothers" pressuring their children to work hard and succeed for the honour of the family. Ironically, once the student is accepted into college, the amount of work assigned tends to decrease because graduates of the best universities are virtually guaranteed lucrative employment offers. Nevertheless, the early training instils an attitude of deference to group interests that persists throughout life. Some outside

© Barry Cronin Newsmakers/Getty Images

Cool Otaku *Fashion Teens.* Fashion-conscious teenagers have become Japan's most dedicated consumers. With the economy in the doldrums and real estate costs soaring, many young people live with their families well into their twenties, using the money saved to purchase the latest styles in clothing. Avid readers of fashion magazines, these *otaku* ("obsessed") teenagers—heirs of Japan's long affluence—pay exorbitant prices for hip-hop outfits, platform shoes, and layered dresses.

observers, however, believe such attitudes can have a detrimental effect on individual initiative.

One of the more tenacious legacies of the past in Japanese society is sexual inequality. Although women are now legally protected against discrimination in employment, very few have reached senior levels in business, education, or politics, and in the words of one Western scholar, they remain "acutely disadvantaged"—though ironically, in a recent survey of business executives in Japan, a majority declared that women were smarter than men. Women now make up nearly 50 percent of the workforce, but most are in retail or service occupations, and their average salary is only about half that of men. There is a feminist movement in Japan, but it has none of the vigour and mass support of its counterpart in the West.

Japan's welfare system also differs profoundly from its Western counterparts. Applicants are required to seek assistance first from their own families, and the physically able are ineligible for government aid. As a result, less than 1 percent of the population receives welfare benefits. Outside observers interpret this as the product of several factors, including low levels of drug addiction and illegitimacy, as well as the importance in Japan of the work ethic and family responsibility.

Traditionally, it was the responsibility of the eldest child in a Japanese family to care for aging parents, but that system, too, is beginning to break down because of limited housing space and the growing tendency of working-age women to seek jobs in the marketplace. The proportion of Japanese older than 65 years of age who live with their children has dropped from 80 percent in 1970 to about 50 percent today. At the same time, public and private pension plans are under increasing financial pressure, partly because of a low birthrate and a greying population. Japan today has the highest proportion of people older than 65—17 percent of the country's total population of 130 million—of any industrialized country in the world.

SOUTH KOREA: A PENINSULA DIVIDED

While the world was focused on the "economic miracle" occurring on the Japanese islands, another miracle of sorts was taking place across the Sea of Japan on the Asian mainland. In 1953, the Korean peninsula was exhausted from three years of bitter fraternal war, a conflict that took the lives of an estimated four million Koreans on both sides of the 38th parallel and turned as much as one-quarter of the population into refugees. Although a cease-fire was signed at Panmunjom in July 1953, it was a fragile peace that left two heavily armed and mutually hostile countries facing each other suspiciously.

North of the truce line was the People's Republic of Korea (PRK), a police state under the dictatorial rule of Communist leader Kim Il Sung (1912–94). To the south was the Republic of Korea, under the equally autocratic President Syngman Rhee (1875–1965), a fierce anti-Communist who had led the resistance to the northern invasion and now placed his country under U.S. military protection. But U.S. troops could not protect Rhee from his own people, many of whom resented his reliance on the political power of the wealthy landlord class. After several years of harsh rule, marked by government corruption, fraudulent elections, and police brutality, demonstrations broke out in the capital city of Seoul in the spring of 1960 and forced him into retirement.

The Rhee era was followed by a brief period of multi-party democratic government, but in 1961, a coup d'état placed General Park Chung Hee (1917–79) in power. The new regime promulgated a new constitution, and in 1963, Park was elected president of a civilian government. He set out to foster recovery of the economy from decades of foreign occupation and civil war. Adopting the nineteenth-century Japanese slogan "Rich Country and Strong State," Park built up a strong military while relying on U.S. and later Japanese assistance to help build a strong manufacturing base in what had been a predominantly agricultural society. Because the private sector had been relatively weak under Japanese rule, the government played an active role in the process by instituting a series of five-year plans that targeted specific industries for development, promoted exports, and funded infrastructure development. Under a land reform program, large landowners were required to sell all their farmland above 3 hectares to their tenants at low prices.

The program was a solid success. Benefiting from the Confucian principles of thrift, respect for education, and hard work (during the 1960s and 1970s, South Korean workers spent an average of 60 hours a week at their jobs), as well as from Japanese capital and technology, South Korea gradually emerged as a major industrial power in East Asia. The economic growth rate rose from less than 5 percent annually in the 1950s to an average of 9 percent under Park. The largest corporations—including Samsung, Daewoo, and Hyundai—were transformed into massive conglomerates called *chaebols*, the Korean equivalent of the *zaibatsu* of pre-war Japan. Taking advantage of relatively low wages and a stunningly high rate of saving, South Korean businesses began to compete actively with the Japanese for export markets in Asia and throughout the world. The Japanese became concerned about their "hungry spirit" and began refusing to share technology with the South Koreans. Per capita income also increased dramatically. (See Map 14.3, Plate 31.)

> *Chaebols* (Korean for "conglomerates") such as Hyundai, Daewoo, and LG, have been major forces in bringing initial economic success to South Korea.

How Did Government Corruption Hinder South Korea's Democratic Development?

Like many other countries in the region, South Korea was slow to develop democratic principles. Although his government functioned with the trappings of democracy, Park continued to rule by autocratic means and suppressed all forms of dissidence. In 1979, Park was assassinated, and after a brief interregnum of democratic rule, a new military government under General Chun Doo Hwan (b. 1931) seized power. The new regime was as authoritarian as its predecessors, but opposition to autocratic rule had now spread from the ranks of college and high school students, who had led the early resistance, to much of the urban population. Protest against government policies became increasingly frequent. In 1987, massive demonstrations drove government troops out of the southern city of Kwangju, but the troops returned in force and killed an estimated 2000 demonstrators.

With Chun under increasing pressure to moderate the oppressive character of his rule, national elections were finally held in 1989. The government nominee, Roh Tae Woo, won the election with less than 40 percent of the vote. New elections in 1992 brought Kim Young Sam to the presidency. Kim selected several women for his cabinet and promised to make South Korea "a freer and more mature democracy." He also attempted to crack down on the rising influence of the giant *chaebols*, accused of giving massive bribes in return for favours from government officials. In the meantime, representatives of South Korea had made tentative contacts with the Communist regime in North Korea on possible steps toward eventual reunification of the peninsula.

But the problems of South Korea were more serious than the endemic problem of corruption. A growing trade deficit, combined with a declining growth rate, led to a rising incidence of unemployment and bankruptcy. Ironically, a second problem resulted from the economic collapse of Seoul's bitter rival, the PRK. Under the rule of Kim Il Sung's son Kim Jong Il, the North Korean economy was in a state of free fall, raising the spectre of an outflow of refugees that could swamp neighbouring countries. To relieve the immediate effects of a food shortage, the Communist government in Pyongyang relaxed its restrictions on private farming, while Seoul agreed to provide food aid to alleviate the famine.

Courtesy of William J. Duiker

Korean Bridal Couple. Young married couples all over the world enjoy having their wedding photos taken at historical sites. This young Korean bride in a traditional red gown is posing in front of the Pulguksa Temple near Kyongju, the site of the ancient Silla kingdom.

In the fall of 1997, a sudden drop in the value of the Korean currency, the *won,* led to bank failures and a decision to seek assistance from the International Monetary Fund. In December, an angry electorate voted Kim Young Sam (whose administration was tarnished by reports of corruption) out of office and elected his rival Kim Dae Jung to the presidency. But although the new chief executive promised drastic reforms, his regime too has been charged with corruption and incompetence, while relations with North Korea, now on the verge of becoming a nuclear power, remain tense.

CONCLUSION

India and Pakistan took two different political paths after the end of colonialism.

- India's ruling Congress Party followed a socialist path led by Jawaharlal Nehru—a legacy sustained by family members who have become leaders of the party; while committed to Cold War neutrality, India remained in the Soviet ambit.
- India's traditional caste system remains in the shadows of what is meant to be an egalitarian and democratic society.
- During the Cold War, Pakistan was more closely allied to the United States, which fed a persistent rivalry with

India, its socialist neighbour. Pakistan's alliance with the United States was renewed post-9/11 due to Pakistan's role in the American "war on terrorism" in Afghanistan.
- Pakistan followed a more religious path, heeding to conservative elements in its society.

The image of Southeast Asia mired in the Vietnam conflict and the tensions of the Cold War have become a distant memory.

- By the 1990s, a number of ASEAN member countries were on the road to advanced economic development. The remainder are showing signs that they will make similar progress within the next generation.
- While ethnic and religious strains continue to exist within most ASEAN states, political stability and pluralism tend to be on the rise throughout the region.

Whether the unique character of modern Japan and South Korea will endure is unclear, but the attributes of these countries are worthy of study and perhaps emulation.

- Large corporate conglomerates have been important factors in Japanese and South Korean economic success.
- Confidence in the Japanese and South Korean "economic miracle" has been shaken because of the 1997 economic downturn.

- Japanese society has a unique sense of loyalty and willingness to make sacrifices, including to one's employer.
- Japan is a relatively homogeneous society with a strong work ethic and sense of togetherness that has become a prosperous advanced industrial economy.

CRITICAL THINKING QUESTIONS

1. Why are modern and postmodern societies atomized and more individualistic, placing less value on the community and the will of the collective?

2. Are India and Japan true democracies, or are they traditional societies with a democratic façade?

3. Why do many conservatives in the West and East challenge progressive views on gender and sexuality?

4. Economic success in Southeast Asia emerged under political authoritarianism and denial of workers' rights. Are low labour standards a natural part of the early stage of industrial takeoff? Does the West have the right to criticize the East's use of child labour when our own Industrial Revolution was built on the sweat and blood of children?

CHAPTER NOTES

1. Quoted in Larry Collins and Dominique Lapierre, *Freedom at Midnight* (New York: Avon Books, 1975), p. 252.

2. Howard Jones, *Indonesia: The Possible Dream* (New York: Harcourt Brace Jovanovich, Hoover Institute, 1971), p. 237.

Chapter 15

Latin American Dictatorships and Emerging Democracies

Latin American history of the twentieth century is marred by political upheaval and economic turmoil. This region's position in the United States' backyard resulted in its attracting both American and Soviet attention, for better or for worse, and made political rulers ruthless in their quest for both power and foreign economic alliances in the region. Foreign economic interest in Latin America continued well past the end of colonialism. With the Cold War, however, foreign interest in Latin America took a new turn. Supporting ruthless dictators that could further ideological interests became a feature of Latin American foreign relations. The Cuban Revolution demonstrated the benefits of establishing a satellite state near one's adversary; it also demonstrated the costs of losing a friendly regime. For Latin American people and their governments, the Cuban Revolution became a social experiment with populism, socialism, and authoritarianism to be applied in varying forms throughout the region.

At the conclusion of this chapter, you will be able to

- describe how populism, socialism, and state-led economic growth have fared in Latin America;
- explain how the United States has influenced Latin American development;
- outline the factors that have led to the rise and fall of military regimes;
- describe the effects of democratization and economic liberalization on Argentina, Brazil, and Mexico.

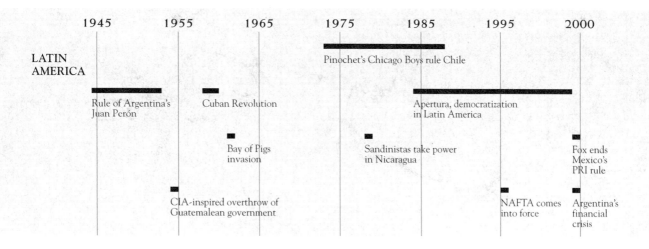

THE MODERN HISTORY OF LATIN AMERICA'S POLITICAL ECONOMY

The Great Depression of the 1930s caused political instability in many Latin American countries that led to military coups and militaristic regimes. But it also helped transform Latin America from a traditional to a modern economy. Since the nineteenth century, Latin Americans had exported raw materials, especially minerals and foodstuffs, while buying the manufactured goods of the industrialized countries, particularly Europe and the United States. Despite a limited degree of industrialization, Latin America was still dependent on an export-oriented economy. As a result of the Great Depression, however, exports were cut in half as Europe and the United States were unable to purchase Latin American goods and Latin American revenues available to buy manufactured goods declined.

In response, many Latin American countries encouraged the development of new industries to produce goods that were formerly imported. In the 1950s, this awakening of Latin American industrial production gained political and intellectual prominence through the work of economist Raúl Prebisch, under the auspices of the United Nations' Economic Commission for Latin America (ECLA). Prebisch's ECLA studies found that Latin America had actually experienced economic growth during the inter-war years, because it was divorced from the industrial core and forced to produce goods that were previously imported. A classic dependency theory argument in favour of divorcing core-periphery relations to spur periphery economic growth (see Chapter 1, page 18) found empirical validity in Latin America's experience. Prebisch and other economists started to advocate a strong state-led industrialization strategy known as **import-substitution industrialization** (ISI). This economic strategy borrowed from the Keynesian belief in the unruliness of market economies and the need for state intervention to rectify market failures. It also promoted the idea of producing manufactured goods locally. Due to a shortage of capital in the private sector, governments often invested in new industries, thereby leading, for example, to government-run steel companies in Chile and Brazil and petroleum companies in Argentina and Mexico.

> **Import-substitution industrialization** (ISI) was an economic and industrial strategy that relied on state investment in the production of consumer goods that had previously been imported, with the expectation of spurring local industrial and economic development.

In Latin America, the state would be the engine of economic growth by investing in its industrial sectors. For many Latin American countries, ISI first produced technologically simple consumer goods like clothing, shoes, and processed foods. As Latin America became increasingly industrialized in its urban centres, people flocked from the rural areas to the cities to participate in the growing workforce. Industrialization prompted urbanization, but more important, it prompted politicization of labourers in urban centres.

Why Did the Failure of Populism in Latin American Countries Usher in Military Regimes?

In the 1960s, however, Latin American countries were still dependent on the United States, Europe, and now Japan for the input goods and advanced technology needed to modernize ISI industries to the second stage of ISI development. The theory behind ISI was that once Latin American countries gained experience in manufacturing goods, eventually they would be able to produce the input goods imported as well; but this goal never materialized as the goods were inefficiently made and of low quality.

According to the ISI strategy, after the domestic market absorbed most locally produced goods, the remainder would be exported. However, poverty conditions in some Latin American countries limited the size of domestic markets. To make matters worse, because the quality of the domestically produced goods was low, many countries were unable to find markets in which to sell them abroad. The second stage of ISI development did not come to pass.

Perhaps the chief problem with ISI was the rising political and social expectations it produced. Labour was now more mobilized then ever, demanding more state redistribution and increased wages. Labour unions and parties gained increased power, attention, and voice in Latin America. In turn, Latin American governments depended on labour support and often complied with their demands by increasing wages, propping up failing companies and industries, and placing price controls on agricultural goods. Urban centres gained from state intervention, while rural areas were neglected or faltered under ISI. Inflation, the constant rise of prices for goods and services, became a dominant feature of Latin American life. In the cities, market prices increased on a daily basis, causing people to constantly consume products and services while cashing out their otherwise depreciated savings. In some cases, people reverted to a barter system, trading goods and service for other goods and services, instead of using paper notes that never kept their value from day to day. Ultimately, the ISI-based system stopped working, and the only group with the capability and political will to change the system was the military.

The economic failures of ISI resulted in takeovers by military regimes that sought to curb the demands of the new industrial middle class and working class that had increased in size and power as a result of industrialization (see Map 15.1, Plate 32). In the 1960s, repressive military regimes in Chile, Brazil, and Argentina abolished political parties and turned to export-oriented economies financed by foreigners while encouraging multinational corporations to come into their countries. These military regimes were the first to experiment with the now prevalent economic ideology of **neoliberalism**. The military leaders were trained technocrats, and some were even American-educated economists, who wanted to remove the so-called subversive elements in their countries. The notorious Chicago-boys of Chile, for example, were economists trained in the influential neoliberal economic school at the University of Chicago. They ultimately promoted ruthless political campaigns to achieve their economic goals. These campaigns included the witch-hunt for leftists, unionists, intellectuals, and artists. The popular uprising of leftist elements grew as opposition to the military's economic policies intensified. Military leaders became increasingly ruthless and repressive, trying to contain social demands for state redistribution and demands for an end to neoliberal economic policies.

> **Neoliberalism** is an economic ideology that emphasizes free market principles and the positive role of individualism, entrepreneurship, and foreign investment in achieving growth.

In the 1970s, Latin American regimes, many of which were military controlled, grew increasingly reliant on borrowing from abroad, especially from banks in Europe and the United States. Throughout the 1970s, declining prices for Latin American countries' commodities and products, coupled with increasing costs of petroleum and oil, put many Latin American countries in precarious economic conditions. At the same time, however, foreign banks' coffers grew as wealth created by petroleum-producing states were deposited into foreign banks. Foreign banks needed to lend these **petrodollars** to make their interest payments, and many Latin American countries soon became some of the foreign banks' preferred clients. Between 1970 and 1982, Latin American debt to foreigners increased from US$27 billion to US$315.3 billion. Among the banks' largest borrowers were Chile, Brazil, Argentina, Colombia, Mexico, and even oil-rich Venezuela. By 1982, a number of governments announced that they could no longer pay interest on their debts to foreign banks, and their economies began to crumble. Most notably, Mexico had announced that it would default on its international debt. The entire international financial system was on the verge of collapse.

To preserve the international financial system, Western states bailed out Mexico with aid and new loans.

> **Petrodollars** are funds that were earned by oil-rich countries in the sale of oil during the 1970s and 1980s; they were deposited in Western banks and then loaned to Third World countries.

Wages fell, and unemployment skyrocketed. Governments were forced to undertake fundamental reforms to qualify for additional loans, reducing the size of the state sector and improving agricultural production in order to stem the flow of people from the countryside to the cities and strengthen the domestic market for Latin American products. Latin American countries became increasingly indebted to international financial institutions, namely the International Monetary Fund (IMF) and World Bank, which required them to undertake further neoliberal economic reforms to qualify for rescheduled debt (new loans to pay off old maturing loans). These neoliberal economic reforms were dubbed **structural adjustment programs** (SAPs), for the structural overhaul used to remove statist and populist elements such as privatizing state-owned industries, dismantling agricultural price controls, liberalizing trade, and downsizing the public sector.

> **Structural adjustment programs** (SAPs) describe the intrusive structural economic conditions required of International Monetary Fund and World Bank loans.

In the 1990s, the neoliberal opening of markets to free trade practices and other consequences of the globalization process began to exert a growing impact on Latin American economies. As some countries faced the danger of bankruptcy, belt-tightening measures undertaken to reassure foreign investors provoked social protests and threatened to undermine the precarious political stability in the region. The "tequila effect" of the 1994 economic crisis of Mexico that spread to the Southern Cone and the currency crisis of Brazil and Argentina demonstrated the vulnerability of economic interconnectedness. While neoliberalism continued, democratization or *apertura* ("opening") progressed as a conciliation to people's socioeconomic hardships. The region's shared neoliberal belief in free markets and free trade also spurred interregional economic cooperation and the rise of trading blocs like the North American Free Trade Agreement (NAFTA), Mercosur, the Andean Group, and the Free Trade Area of the Americas (FTAA).

Other factors have also played important roles in the history of Latin America since 1945. The Catholic Church had been a powerful force in Latin America for centuries, but its hold over people diminished as cities and industrial societies developed. Eventually, the church adopted a middle stance in Latin American society, advocating a moderate capitalist system that would respect workers' rights, institute land reform, and provide for the poor. Some Catholics, however, took a more progressive path to change by advocating **liberation theology**. Influenced by Marxist ideas, advocates of liberation theology believed that Christians must fight to free the oppressed, using violence if necessary. Some Catholic clergy recommended armed rebellions and even teamed up with Marxist guerrillas in rural areas. Other progressive priests worked in factories alongside workers or carried on social work among the poor in the slums. Liberation theology was by no means the ideology of the majority of Latin American Catholics and was rejected by the church hierarchy, including the Vatican. Nevertheless, the Catholic Church continued to play an important role in Latin America by becoming the advocate of human rights against authoritarian regimes.

> **Liberation theology** is a doctrine in Latin America advocated by liberal elements within the Catholic Church; its blend of Christianity and Marxism calls for helping oppressed peoples.

Why Did the Rise of Marxist-Led Insurrections in Latin America Challenge U.S. Hegemony?

The United States continued to cast a large shadow over Latin America. In 1948, the nations of the region formed the **Organization of American States** (OAS), which was intended to eliminate unilateral action by one state in the internal or external affairs of another, while encouraging regional cooperation to maintain peace. The OAS would be a comprehensive regional association that included one of the first international declarations of human rights. Located in Washington, D.C., the OAS was originally designed to build mutual trust and security, but it soon became an instrument of U.S. Cold War policies. The OAS did not end U.S. interference in Latin American affairs and instead became a convenient forum to support its anti-Communist policies. Specifically, the United States repeatedly used the OAS to garner support for its anti-Cuba policies. Although Cuba was a member of the OAS until 1962, it did not participate in OAS affairs and did not vote in the OAS General Assembly.

> The **Organization of American States** (OAS) was formed in 1948 to promote regional cooperation and includes the various countries of Latin America and North America; it has in general been unsuccessful in halting unilateral action by the United States.

OAS members grew increasingly annoyed with U.S. intransigence toward both Cuba and Communist parties and regimes. In 1975, they voted to release members from obligatory sanctions against Cuba. In 1979, they refused to support U.S. efforts to garner support for a resolution denouncing the Nicaraguan Sandinistas. Again, the U.S. failed in 1982 to get OAS members' support for a resolution denouncing the Argentine invasion/reclamation of the Falkland Islands (also called *Malvinas Islands*). Latin America's OAS members reasserted their independence and refused to bend to U.S. pressure to continuously use the OAS as an instrument of their Cold War foreign policies.

The United States repeatedly returned to a policy of unilateral action when it believed that Soviet agents were attempting to use local Communists or radical reformers to establish governments hostile to U.S. interests. In the 1960s, President John F. Kennedy's Alliance for Progress encouraged social reform and economic development by providing private and public funds to elected governments whose reform programs were acceptable to the United States. But the alliance failed to work, and when Marxist-led insurrections began to spread throughout the region, the United States responded by providing massive military aid to anti-Communist regimes, regardless of their oppressive nature. Moreover, the United States returned to the practice of dollar diplomacy (see Chapter 4, page 85) in a number of cases (see the box on page 265).

Until the 1960s, Marxism played a small role in the politics of Latin America. The success of Fidel Castro in Cuba, however, opened the door for other revolutionary movements that aimed to gain the support of peasants and industrial workers and bring social, political, and economic change to Latin America.

For Cubans, What Were the Benefits of the Cuban Revolution?

An authoritarian regime, headed by Fulgencio Batista and closely tied economically to U.S. investors, had ruled Cuba since 1934. Batista, initially elected as a reformer, soon grew to become an oppressive leader. The United States had supported and benefited from Cuba's mono crop export of sugar. As well, American companies and investment were greatly tied to the maintenance of Cuba's economic structure. But, an economy dependent on sugar production made it vulnerable to external economic instability and offered little to modernize the economy. Many Cubans were peasants or cane workers with high rates of seasonal unemployment. The United States benefited from cheap Cuban sugar and from exporting processed and manufactured goods to Cuba; but the Cuban economy was stagnating, and Cubans

THE CASE OF THE UNITED FRUIT COMPANY

In the 1930s, U.S. dollar diplomacy seemed to have ended with the debut of Franklin D. Roosevelt's Good Neighbor Policy. This change in U.S. foreign policy was a relief to many Latin American countries that had been under American tutelage. However, in the 1950s, the case of the United Fruit Company left many decrying renewed U.S. intervention in Latin America as dollar diplomacy with a new vengeance. The neo-colonial interests of the United States in the region became apparent when it intervened to preserve its economic holdings by overthrowing Guatemala's democratically elected government in 1954.

Following the Guatemalan Revolution of 1944, President Jacobo Arbenz succeeded to power in 1950 to usher in a populist regime that favoured an ISI strategy. To accomplish ISI, Arbenz believed that substantial land reforms were first needed to distribute wealth to average peasants and thereby create a consumer base for purchase of ISI products. In 1952, Arbenz instituted land reform laws that would expropriate, or take away holdings of, unused or uncultivated lands from large landowners that would then be distributed to landless peasants. The Arbenz government offered landowners 25-year government bonds as compensation to the landowners.

At the time, the American-owned United Fruit Company owned large tracts of uncultivated land, accounting for 15 percent of its total Guatemalan holdings, and objected to the Arbenz land reform proposal. The United Fruit Company was well connected to the U.S. government, particularly to both Secretary of State John Foster Dulles and his brother, Central Intelligence Agency Director Allen Dulles. The Dulles brothers had been New York City law partners of the legal firm representing the United Fruit Company. Other U.S. government officials, including American UN Ambassador Henry Cabot Lodge and Assistant Secretary of State for Latin America John Moors Cabot, were shareholders in the United Fruit Company. U.S. President Dwight D. Eisenhower approved the State Department and CIA plan to overthrow Arbenz and install a right-wing colonel, Carlos Castillo Armas, who had been previously ousted to Honduras. Eventually, Arbenz was removed by the CIA-backed Castillo and his thugs. The CIA-installed Castillo government quickly reversed the land reform law and returned expropriated holdings to the United Fruit Company. In practice, the Good Neighbor Policy was no more.

---

grew increasingly aware of the inequities in the Cuban-American relationship.

A strong opposition movement to Batista's government developed, led by Fidel Castro and assisted by Ernesto "Che" Guevara (1928–67), an Argentinean who believed that revolutionary upheaval was necessary for change to occur (see the box on page 266). Castro first garnered student and worker support in the cities to overthrow Batista, but when their initial assaults on Batista's regime in both Santiago and Bayamo brought little success, Castro's forces retreated to the Sierra Maestra mountains. Castro would then build an army of peasants that would use guerrilla warfare to try to topple the Batista regime. Castro went to Mexico, where he met and collaborated with Che Guevara, to plan the revolution. As the rebels gained more support in Cuba, including professionals, urban workers, and students, Batista responded with such brutality that he even alienated his own supporters. The dictator fled in December 1958, and Castro's revolutionaries seized Havana on January 1, 1959.

Castro assumed power as head of state and started to institute significant social and economic reforms that were accomplished in the first years of the revolution. One of his noted goals was to redistribute wealth to the impoverished peasants and sugar cane workers. An agrarian reform law in May 1959 nationalized all landholdings over 400 hectares that would be redistributed to landless peasants. Many of the mainly American sugar plantations had in excess of 160 000 hectares. Land redistribution garnered increased peasant support, and the revolution immediately paid off for many Cubans. The Castro government also wanted to raise education levels and literacy rates in the rural areas by building schools, training teachers, and sending revolutionary supporters to the countryside to teach peasants how to read. Eventually, illiteracy was wiped out by creating new schools and establishing teacher-training institutes that tripled the number of teachers within 10 years. The Cuban government also set up universal health care for the country, by building and opening health clinics and hospitals. The state also removed racist segregation laws and practices. Once again, for many of the underprivileged and peasants, the revolution brought immediate social and health benefits.

Relations between Cuba and the United States quickly deteriorated after the agrarian land reforms and after the new

WHO WAS CHE GUEVARA?

The well-known image of Che Guevara that adorns T-shirts and buttons since he shocked and marvelled the masses in the 1950s is imprinted in the minds of many. As a leading member of the revolutionary party, Che fought alongside Fidel Castro in the Cuban Revolution to topple the Batista-led regime. For today's youth, Che, and his image, symbolize revolution, social change, and rebelliousness. For contemporary historians of Latin America, and the Third World more broadly, Che's views represent a radical position about how to push for social and political change. His influence on Latin American movements and parties shook established orders and inspired thousands of others to reject the status quo through violent means.

Ernesto Guevara better known as "Che" Guevara—a nickname which came about because he himself would always call others "Che," the Argentine idiom for "friend" or "pal"—was born on June 14, 1928, in Rosario, Argentina. On a motorcycle, Che took a journey through the mountains of Argentina in which he saw first hand the poverty and distress of peasants. Although Che was a member of Argentina's affluent upper middle class, he became increasingly aware of the hardships endured by the lower classes.

By 1952, Che had been witness to and affected by the National Revolution in Bolivia, where workers demanded reform of the dire state of the country's economy and eventually succeeded in toppling the government in a coup d'état. With economic and social unrest throughout the region, Che became aware of Latin America's position in U.S. foreign affairs, particularly the case of the United Fruit Company in Guatemala. Che was appalled that the American CIA assisted the overthrow of Arbenz's socialist regime, to which Che belonged and supported, in exchange for an American-friendly capitalist government. Che was eventually thrown out of Guatemala by the new regime, but he left with a strengthened belief in the necessity of violence to bring about revolution and political change.

Following the events in Guatemala, Che, a medical graduate of the University of Buenos Aires, worked as a physician at a hospital in Mexico City. From there he met Fidel Castro through a mutual friend, and the two spearheaded a plan to overthrow the government of Cuba. Che left medicine and joined guerrilla forces with less than a hundred men from Mexico, and sailed on a yacht named *Granma* to the southern shores of Cuba. From there the men set up their base in the mountains of Sierra Maestra where they fought against the official army of Cuba. As time passed, land-working peasants who had so far been oppressed and abused by the land-owning classes joined in the rebel forces led by Castro and Che.

After the successful Cuban Revolution, President Castro appointed Che as president of the National Bank of Cuba and Cuba's minister of Industry. Then, by 1967, after some time as a foreign ambassador for Cuba, Che became disillusioned with the Soviet Union and its administration, leading him to formally break ties with the Cuban government in his famous letter to Castro. Che thanked Castro, but told Castro that he wanted to continue his campaign of violent uprisings in other Third World countries. Che, no longer supported by Castro, went on to Congo and then to Bolivia. His final days were spent in Bolivia, where he tried to enlist peasants in a populist revolution. It was there, on October 9, 1967, that Che was captured and murdered by operatives working for the Bolivian government believed to be assisted by U.S. intelligence. His last words were rumoured to have been, "Shoot coward! You are only going to kill a man."

Cuban regime reversed the Batista-regime position of recognizing the Soviet Union. A new level of antagonism arose early in 1960 when a Soviet Union official visited Cuba and established a trade agreement. The Soviets agreed to buy Cuban sugar and provide US$100 million in credits for Cuban industrialization. The warming of Cuban-Soviet relations greatly worried the United States. On March 17, 1960, President Eisenhower directed the CIA to "organize the training of Cuban exiles, mainly in Guatemala, against a possible future day when they might return to their homeland."[1]

Arms from Eastern Europe began to arrive in Cuba, the United States cut its purchases of Cuban sugar, and the Cuban government nationalized U.S. companies and banks. In October 1960, the United States declared a trade embargo on Cuba, driving Castro closer to the Soviet Union. Castro publicly declared Cuba's socialist position and fostered alliances with other socialist states, including China.

On January 3, 1961, the United States broke diplomatic relations with Cuba. The new U.S. president, John F. Kennedy, approved a plan originally drafted by the previous administration to launch an invasion to overthrow Castro's government, but the landing of 1400 CIA-assisted Cubans in Cuba on April 17, 1961, known as the Bay of Pigs, turned into a total military disaster. This fiasco encouraged the Soviets to make an even greater commitment to Cuban independence by attempting to place nuclear missiles in the country, an act that led to a showdown with the United States (see Chapter 6). As its part of the bargain to defuse the missile crisis, the United States agreed not to invade Cuba.

But the missile crisis affected Cuba in another way as well. Castro, who had urged Leonid Khrushchev to stand firm even at the risk of nuclear war with the United States, now realized that the Soviet Union was unreliable. If revolutionary Cuba was to be secure and no longer encircled by hostile states tied to U.S. interests, the Cubans would have to instigate a socialist revolution in the rest of Latin America. Castro believed that once **guerrilla wars** were launched, peasants would flock to the revolutionary movement and overthrow the old regimes. Castro supported revolutionary movements in Guatemala, Nicaragua, Venezuela, and Colombia. Guevara also attempted to instigate a guerrilla war in Bolivia, but was caught and killed by the Bolivian army in the fall of 1967. Castro reaffirmed his commitment to guerrilla warfare and the overthrow of what he viewed to be American cronies in other Latin American regimes. By denouncing other Latin American regimes for their closer ties to the United States, Castro created resentment and enemies even among leftist political parties, which did not share Castro's views on armed uprising. The Cuban strategy of exporting revolutionary ideas had failed to take hold in the region.

> **Guerrilla wars** include untrained and armed militia-like bandits that engage in a low-intensity war by targeting government or regime holdings to spur support among the populace.

In Cuba, however, Castro's socialist revolution proceeded, with mixed results. The Cuban Revolution did secure significant social gains for its people, especially in health care and education. Compared with Latin American countries, Cuban socioeconomic and demographic indicators were impressive. On the economic front, however, Cuban results were mixed. At first, the Castro regime tried the path of rapid industrialization by encouraging agricultural diversification. This included clearing of sugar plantations and attempting to grow cotton. The latter failed as soil and climate conditions were less than favourable. Diversification of agriculture was not reaping the results expected and Castro changed policy directions by fostering closer ties to the Soviet bloc countries where it would

continue to export primary products, including sugar, in exchange for petroleum and manufactured products. Castro's vision of industrializing Cuba and moving away from the dependency on sugar production was not working. Continued economic problems forced the Castro regime to depend on Soviet subsidies and the purchase of Cuban sugar by Soviet bloc countries.

In addition, the U.S. embargo further hindered Cuba's economic relations with other countries and prevented the import of needed consumer goods. All of the Western Hemisphere countries, with exception of Mexico and Canada, had cut economic and diplomatic ties to Cuba after the Cuban Missile Crisis. For many Latin American countries, cutting ties with Cuba ensured U.S. investment and support for counterinsurgency training. For Canada, taking a moderate stance toward Cuba signalled to the world that it followed an independent foreign policy from the United States and that it promoted conciliation and dialogue with would-be rogue states.

Cuban foreign policies were also influenced by the country's increased dependence on the Soviet Union. The American-Soviet *détente* in the 1970s put pressure on Cuba to stop trying to spread its revolutionary fervour in other Latin American countries through small-scale guerrilla movements. Consequently, Cuba resumed its diplomatic ties with other Latin American countries, including Argentina, Chile, and Peru, when ruled by leftist regimes. Throughout the 1980s, Cuba extended its diplomatic relations to other Latin American countries and played an increasingly important role in regional affairs. Outside of Latin America, Cuba exerted its influence upon African nations, such as Angola and Ethiopia, through its military presence and support for Communist regimes. With as many as 50 000 Cuban soldiers in Angola and with the support of the Soviets, Cuba aimed at strengthening the Popular Movement for the Liberation of Angola's (MPLA) bid for power after the withdrawal of Portuguese colonial rule left a political vacuum in 1975. In a struggle against opposition parties such as the National Union for the Total Independence of Angola (UNITA)—supported by South Africa and the United States—as well as the National Front for the Liberation of Angola (FNLA)—also supported by the United States—the Communist MPLA party won power in Angola and was able to establish socialist rule.

Because the majority of Cuban trade was with the Soviet Union and Eastern bloc, the disintegration of the Soviet Union was a major blow to Cuba. Cuba was particularly dependent on subsidized Soviet oil, and this effectively ended with the Soviet demise. The new Russian government in Moscow no longer had a reason to continue to subsidize the onetime Soviet ally. During the 1990s, Castro began to introduce limited market reforms and to allow the circulation of U.S. dollars. Foreign investment laws were relaxed, which attracted businesses from Mexico, Canada, Spain, and Germany. The gradual liberalization of the economy also helped with the Cuban government's plan to promote the Cuban tourism industry.

The end of the Cold War and the Soviet threat did not, however, change American policy toward Cuba. On the contrary, the United States furthered its isolation of Cuba with a strengthened trade embargo. In 1996, the U.S. Helms-Burton Act added new measures to prevent both American and foreign investment in Cuba. The increased economic pressure on Cuba resulted in greater popular demands for political liberalization. Despite economic liberalization, the Cuban regime refused to liberalize the political system, and the Castro regime remained unchallenged as dissidents either fled to the United States or were repressed. The historic visit of Pope John Paul II to Cuba in 1998 helped relax unofficial government sanctioning of religious movements and churches, but mass political mobilization outside of the ruling party remained prohibitive.

Why Did Colombia's Guerrilla Movements Gain Strength?

In 1948, Colombia's populist leader and presidential candidate Jorge Eliécer Gaitán was assassinated, setting off a course of unforeseen pressure for social change. The ensuing decades of turmoil, known as *La Violencia,* claimed the lives of over 200 000 people and embroiled the chiefly rural people in a war against the Colombian government. Rural communities, disconnected and alienated from the increasingly repressive Colombian government, created quasi-independent republics that would cater to the needs of the local farmers.

After the Cuban Revolution, a group of revolutionaries in Colombia's rural communities was inspired by the idea of using guerrilla warfare to unseat the government. In 1964, the Colombian Revolutionary Armed Forces (FARC) was formed by rural peasants with the aim of overthrowing the Colombian government and instituting a leftist policy agenda. The FARC grew increasingly violent as the Colombian government effectively blocked FARC attempts at political participation in the democratic process and as the government grew increasingly repressive and violent toward rural peasants. The FARC did not make much headway until the early 1990s, when the Colombian army occupied FARC strongholds, which further alienated Colombians and led them to turn to the FARC. Meanwhile, the FARC gained rural support for its protection of impoverished farmers cultivating coca (later used in making cocaine), and the U.S. backed and financed Colombian

army intensified its campaign to eradicate coca production. Since the turn of the century, paramilitary groups acting with and without Colombian government support have increased the level of violence in their fight against the FARC.

The United States' "war on drugs" and Plan Colombia include eradicating coca production at its source, thereby making Colombian coca farmers and their FARC protectors key targets. The FARC have also become increasingly violent in their activities by targeting American interests and kidnapping foreign individuals in Colombia, and by attacking and bombing Colombian government installations and officials. Accused of being a terrorist organization profiting from the trafficking of drugs, the FARC continue to attract international attention. In 2005, allegations of Irish Republican Army (IRA) and Venezuelan support of the FARC have made the Colombian crisis international headlines. In the crossfire of this cycle of violence has been the death of hundreds of thousands of innocent Colombian people.

Why Did the Military Overthrow Chile's Marxist President?

Another challenge to U.S. influence in Latin America appeared in 1970 when a Marxist, Salvador Allende (1908–73), was elected president of Chile and attempted to create a socialist society by constitutional means. Chile suffered from a number of economic problems. Wealth was concentrated in the hands of large landowners and a few large corporations. Inflation, foreign debt, and a decline in the mining industry (copper exports accounted for 80 percent of Chile's export income) caused untold difficulties. Right-wing control of the government failed to achieve any solutions, especially since foreign investments were allowed to expand. There was growing resentment of foreign corporations, including Canadian-owned copper companies, but especially American-owned Anaconda and Kennecott, which controlled the copper industry.

In the 1970 elections, a split in the moderate forces enabled Allende to become president of Chile as head of a coalition of Socialists, Communists, and Catholic radicals. A number of labour leaders, who represented the interests of the working classes, were given the ministries of labour, finance, public works, and interior in the new government. As part of Allende's reform policies, the government increased the wages of industrial workers with the hope of creating a stronger consumer base for industrial and manufactured goods. Initially, this move helped Chile's economy grow. Another of Allende's reform policies involved the nationalization of large domestic and foreign-owned corporations. The government was most interested in nationalizing Chile's mining and manufacturing corporations. The proposed nationalization of the copper industry put Chile in direct confrontation with the United States, as both Anaconda and Kennecott were U.S. owned. The final prong of Allende's reform policies included land reform for the benefit of the peasantry.

After nationalizing foreign-owned corporations, the Allende government turned its attention to large domestic corporations, which it started to convert to state-owned enterprises. This move affected firms in the textiles, forestry, and pulp and paper industries. Domestic industrialists and upper-class elites had tolerated Allende's nationalization of foreign-owned corporations, but nationalizing domestic corporations brought growing opposition from the upper and middle classes. Chile's elite and business community (both large and small) began, with covert support from the CIA, to organize strikes and worker lockouts against the government. Businesses were shutting their doors and factories to the workers. Transportation companies refused to move products around the country. Allende's labour supporters were being denied employment and wages. Chile's economic situation continued to worsen as investment and capital left the country. Pressured by the United States, the international donor and financial community also refused to give aid or lend to Chile, further preventing the country from getting finances from abroad.

Allende attempted to stop the disorder by bringing three military officers into his cabinet. They succeeded in ending the strikes, but when Allende's coalition increased its vote in the congressional elections of March 1973, the Chilean army, under the direction of General Augusto Pinochet, decided on a coup d'état. In September 1973, Allende and thousands of his supporters were killed. Whether Allende was murdered by the military or took his own life in his takedown is still a mystery.

Contrary to the expectations of many right-wing politicians and opposition parties, the military remained in power and set up a dictatorship. The regime moved quickly to outlaw all political parties, disband the Congress, and restore many nationalized industries and landed estates to their original owners. The copper industry, however, remained in government hands. Pinochet's regime also adopted a neoliberal economic strategy that sought to remove all remnants of the socialist and planned economy system. Instead of price controls, Chile allowed the free market to determine prices of goods and services. The government decreased its social and public spending, privatizing pensions and education. These measures helped curb inflation which had been extremely high and had negatively distorted prices. After it took power, the military managed to reform the economy, and Chile reported economic growth in the 1970s.

Although Pinochet's regime liberalized the economy and helped the economy initially recover, its flagrant abuse of human rights led to growing unrest against the government in the mid-1980s. Continuous public demonstrations and protest, almost always peaceful, against the Pinochet regime became a regular occurrence in Chile. Some of the protests were organized by labour unions, professionals, intellectuals, artists, and Church movements. After immense public pressure, Pinochet agreed to hold a plebiscite on continuing his rule. The "no" campaign against Pinochet and his military regime won the 1988 plebiscite. In 1989, free elections were held and produced a Christian Democratic president who also advocated free market economics.

The shadow of the Pinochet era continued to hover over Chilean politics, however, as many citizens demanded that the general, then living in exile, be brought to justice for his crimes against humanity. In 2000, he was returned to Chile from Europe and placed on trial for crimes that had allegedly taken place under his rule, including the disappearance of thousands of mainly leftist activists. In 2005, after Pinochet's appeal that he was medically unfit to stand trial and that he held immunity as a former leader, the Chilean Supreme Court upheld a lower court ruling that the 89-year old dictator could stand trial. At the time of writing, Pinochet had been charged for evading taxes on US$26 million that he had hid abroad.

How Did the United States Undermine the Sandinistas?

The United States intervened in Nicaraguan domestic affairs in the early twentieth century, and U.S. marines actually remained there for long periods of time. The leader of the U.S.-supported National Guard, Anastasio Somoza (1896–1956), seized control of the government in 1937, and his family remained in power for the next 43 years. U.S. support for the Somoza military regime enabled the family to overcome any opponents while enriching themselves at the expense of the people and the state.

In 1979, opposition to the regime and the U.S. presence arose from Marxist guerrilla forces known as the *Sandinista National Liberation Front*. The **Sandinistas** named themselves after Augusto César Sandino, who led an uprising against the U.S. marines and the regime in the late 1920s and early 1930s. The Sandinistas were inspired by the Cuban Revolution and Che Guevara's philosophy of guerrilla warfare. They hoped that by encouraging the peasants to revolt against the regime, they could convince others to join the movement. The Sandinistas fought the Somoza regime in both the rural and urban areas. As the brutality and corrupt-nature of the Somoza regime became more apparent, popular support for the Sandinistas grew.

The **Sandinistas** began as a leftist guerrilla force that overthrew a corrupt dictatorship in Nicaragua in 1979; they then formed the Nicaraguan government from 1979 to 1990, but were opposed militarily by the Contras and the administration of U.S. President Ronald Reagan.

By mid-1979, military victories by the Sandinistas left them in virtual control of the country. Inheriting a poverty-stricken nation, the Sandinistas organized a provisional government and aligned themselves with the Soviet Union and Cuba. The Sandinistas organized a fair and honest election in 1984, which they won with high voter turnout. Peasants and the urban poor were particularly strong supporters of the government. The unprecedented elections also helped pave the way for future elections in the country. That said, the democratically elected Sandinistas had significant political opponents that wanted to see their destruction, namely conservatives and elites who wanted greater say in the political and economic process.

The fiercest opponent of the Sandinistas, however, was the United States government. The administrations of Ronald Reagan and George Bush, Sr. viewed neighbouring civil wars and populist uprisings in El Salvador and Guatemala, inspired by the Sandinistas, to be threats in the Western Hemisphere. The U.S. administration believed that Central America faced the danger of another Communist state if the Sandinistas were allowed to continue in power. Consequently, the United States financed the counterrevolutionary **Contras** in a guerrilla war against the Sandinista government.

The **Contras** were right-wing opponents of the leftist Sandinistas in Nicaragua in the 1980s; the administrations of U.S. presidents Ronald Reagan and George Bush supported the Contras with military aid.

The Contras operated out of Honduras and were armed remnants of the Somoza regime. They were also connected to the drug-smuggling trade in Central America. American support for the Contras reflected inconsistency in U.S. policy; it funded the Contras while promoting its so-called war on drugs and "just say no" campaigns. The ultimate scandal, however, was the Iran-Contra Affair where U.S. President Reagan authorized the sale of arms to Iran, arranged through Israeli intermediaries, to finance support for the Contras. Reagan carried out the transactions without the legal approval of Congress, leading to a momentous scandal.

The Contra war in Nicaragua was a classic Cold War proxy war, where the United States financed and armed the Contras, and the Soviets financed and armed the Sandinistas. The greatest loss in the war were the lives of thousands of innocent civilians who were caught in the crossfire. The Contra war and a U.S. economic embargo undermined support for the Sandinistas. Despite popular support for the Sandinistas, the Nicaraguan people knew that continuing Sandinista rule would bring further international intervention to their country. In 1990, the Sandinistas agreed to an election to let the people decide their fate. The Sandinistas lost to a conservative coalition, headed by Violeta Barrios de Chamorro (b. 1929), whose campaign was partly financed and supported by the United States. Despite losing the 1990 elections, the Sandinistas have remained a significant political force in Nicaragua as the dominant opposition to the conservative parties that won subsequent elections.

The Liberal Party, first led by Arnoldo Alemán and then by Enrique Bolaños, won the 1996 and 2001 elections. The Sandinistas led by Daniel Ortega (b. 1945) failed to win power, but have continuously gained electoral support. The future of the Sandinistas' return to political power has received some encouragement and support from neighbouring Venezuelan leftist leader Hugo Chávez. The return of a democratically elected Marxist-led government in Nicaragua remains a strong possibility.

DEMOCRATIC CHANGE IN ARGENTINA, BRAZIL, AND MEXICO

The military became the power brokers of twentieth-century Latin America. Especially in the 1960s and 1970s, Latin American armies portrayed themselves as the so-called guardians of national honour, orderly progress, and security. In the mid-1970s, only Colombia, Venezuela, and Costa Rica maintained democratic governments.

A decade later, pluralistic systems had been installed virtually everywhere except in Cuba, Paraguay, and some of the Central American states. The establishment of democratic institutions, however, has not managed to solve all the chronic problems that have plagued the states of Latin America. Official corruption continued in many countries, and the gap between rich and poor is growing, most notably in Brazil and Venezuela. A leftist regime led by Venezuelan President Hugo Chávez aroused massive support and protests by adopting policies designed to redistribute the wealth in this oil-rich country, reinvigorating the call for populist policies and regimes throughout Latin American .

What Legacy Was Left by Perón?

Fearful of the forces unleashed by the development of industry, the military intervened in Argentine politics in

The Peróns. Elected president of Argentina in 1946, Juan Perón soon established an authoritarian regime that nationalized some of Argentina's basic industries and organized fascist gangs to overwhelm its opponents. He is shown here with his wife, Eva, also known as "Evita," during the inauguration ceremonies initiating his second term as president in 1952.

1930 and propped up the cattle and wheat oligarchy that had controlled the government since the beginning of the twentieth century. In 1943, restless military officers staged a coup d'état and seized power. But the new regime was not sure how to deal with the working classes. One of its members, Juan Perón, thought that he could manage the workers and used his position as labour secretary in the military government to gain favour with them. He encouraged workers to join labour unions and increased job benefits as well as the number of paid holidays and vacations. But as Perón grew more popular, other army officers began to fear his power and arrested him. An uprising by workers forced the officers to back down, and in 1946, Perón was elected president.

Perón pursued a policy of increased industrialization to please his chief supporters—labour and the urban middle class. At the same time, he sought to free Argentina from foreign investors. The government bought the railways; took over the banking, insurance, shipping, and communications industries; and assumed regulation of imports and exports. But Perón's regime was also authoritarian. His charismatic wife, former pauper turned actress, Eva Perón

(or Evita), organized women's groups to support the government. But growing corruption in the Perón government and the alienation of more and more people by the regime's excesses encouraged the military to overthrow him in September 1955. Perón went into exile in Spain.

It had been easy for the military to seize power, but it was harder to rule, especially now that Argentina had a party of *Peronistas* clamouring for the return of their exiled leader. In the 1960s and 1970s, military and civilian governments (the latter closely watched by the military) alternated in power. When both failed to provide economic stability, military leaders decided to allow Juan Perón to return. Reelected president in September 1973, Perón died one year later. In 1976, the military installed a new regime. From 1976 to 1983, the period known as Argentina's *Dirty War,* the military regime was ruthless in eliminating its opponents through torture and killing. During that time, from 10 000 to 30 000 Argentineans "disappeared" and were reportedly taken by the military and murdered. The whereabouts of these people continue to haunt Argentina. Despite numerous pleas, especially from the mothers of those who

Natacha Pisarenko/AP/Wide World Photos

Mothers of Plaza de Mayo walk in Buenos Aires. Since 1977, the mothers of Plaza de Mayo in Argentina have gathered weekly in the main square facing Argentina's Government House demanding information about loved ones who "disappeared" during Argentina's Dirty War at the hands of the repressive military regime.

disappeared (who still stage weekly protests demanding information about their children), the location of those who disappeared remains unconfirmed.

With the economic problems still unsolved, the regime tried to divert people's attention by invading the Falkland Islands (or Malvinas Islands) in April 1982. Great Britain, which had controlled the islands since the nineteenth century, decisively defeated the Argentine forces (see the box on page 273). The loss discredited the military and opened the door once again to civilian rule. In 1983, Raúl Alfonsín (b. 1927) was elected president and sought to reestablish democratic processes.

In 1989, however, Alfonsín was defeated in the presidential elections by the Peronist candidate Carlos Saúl Menem (b. 1930). During his first term, the charismatic Menem won broad popularity for his ability to control the army, to withstand domestic politicking, and to control rampant inflation. Reelected in 1995, Menem furthered his economic policies that helped produce strong economic growth and attract considerable amount of foreign investment, particularly in the Argentine government-issued-bond market. Argentina successfully attracted foreign investment into the bond market because the Argentine currency was pegged to the U.S. dollar—in effect assuring investors that upon exit from the bond market the Argentine currency would retain a high value. But marred by government corruption, continued federal government spending to Peronist-held provinces, increasing foreign debt, and a de facto weakened currency, Argentina was showing signs of economic fatigue.

In 1999, Fernando de la Rúa was elected president on a promise to reduce unemployment—now running at nearly 20 percent—and to bring an end to official corruption of the Peronist party. But with Argentina suffering from low economic growth, rising emigration (a growing number of descendants of European settlers were returning to live in Europe), and shrinking markets abroad, there were signs of trouble. Argentineans and both domestic and foreign businesses wanted to cash out of Argentina before it would collapse. This put pressure on the already embattled value of the Argentine currency, to be further eroded by continued loss of confidence in the economic situation. In December 2001, average Argentineans were lining up in bank queues to withdraw their savings. Similarly, foreign investors and

THE FALKLAND ISLANDS WAR

The Falkland Islands, known as *Islas Malvinas* to Argentineans, are located in the Atlantic Ocean east of Argentina and have been the subject of dispute for many years. First, Great Britain and Spain and later Great Britain and Argentina fought over their sovereignty.

The Falklands are said to have been first sighted in 1592 by an English explorer, and almost 100 years later, they were landed by an English captain who claimed them for Great Britain. Meanwhile, because Argentina believed that the Falklands were under the sovereignty of Spain as per the papal bull of 1493, it claimed them as well. The papal bull divided the region of Latin America into two—all lands west of the Cape Verde Islands belonged to Spain and lands east of the Cape Verde Islands belonged to Portugal—which gave Argentina reason to believe that the Falklands were theirs. After all, Argentina was a former Spanish colony and, following independence, it should claim sovereignty over its territory. Lending itself to this argument was the fact that the Falkands are in close proximity to the Argentine coast.

Officially, the British laid claim to ownership of the Falklands in 1834, when Lieutenant Henry Smith was dispatched there as the first British governor. Once the British defence post was established, the dispute over sovereignty began with Argentina. This matter eventually became a nationalistic sore point within the Argentine political consciousness.

In 1982, a time of political and economic instability within Argentina, Argentine troops, under the military rule of Leopoldo Galtieri, invaded the Falklands and raised the Argentine national flag. The military regime's invasion was intended to divert the nation's attention away from Argentina's political and economic troubles.

In response to Argentina's actions, Great Britain—in an unexpected move—dispatched its navy, air, and armed forces to the region. Rather than take the loss of territory lightly, as many in and out of Argentina had expected it would, Great Britain committed to engage in a battle that lasted some 70 days, and cost the lives of some 250 British soldiers and about 650 Argentineans. Argentina eventually surrendered, with the help of pressure via sanctions put on them by the Reagan administration. The Falklands were relinquished to the British, who still control them.

banks that purchased Argentine bonds denominated, and backed up, in U.S. dollars wanted to cash out of Argentina. In a drastic move, the government decided to prevent people from access to their savings by in effect closing the banks. People took to the streets to protest the government's drastic policies and demanded the resignation of the president. Indeed, the president and members of the government's economic team were forced to quit. To make matters worse, few members of the government wanted the position of interim president, and finding a candidate who could hold the position was difficult at best.

Added to the political chaos, Argentina was in a dire economic situation with its creditors. Failing to get a loan from the IMF and having virtually no access to international credit, Argentina was in technical default to powerful creditors. To make matters worse, the Argentine government announced to its foreign bondholders that it would not live up to the terms of its government-issued bonds. In an April 2003 election, fellow Peronists Néstor Kirchner (b. 1950) and Carlos Menem fought for the presidency. Kirchner campaigned on the slogan of "people first, creditors second"; Menem campaigned on mending relations

with the international financial creditors as a way of reviving foreign economic investment. After the second round of voting, Menem conceded, and Kirchner assumed the presidency and sought to revive public confidence in an economy in paralysis. Kirchner eventually negotiated a loan from the IMF and, in February 2005, holders of Argentine bonds agreed to a deal that would cut 70 percent off their bonds' original face value. Economic recovery resumed in Argentina, but its financial crisis pitted Argentina in a showdown with international financial creditors that tested its government and people.

Why Did Brazil's Socioeconomic Disparities Make Governing Difficult?

After Getúlio Vargas was forced to resign from the presidency in 1945 (see Chapter 4, page 86), a second Brazilian republic came into being. In 1949, Vargas was reelected to the presidency. But he was unable to solve Brazil's economic problems, especially its soaring inflation, and in 1954, after

Down with Banks. This American bank, located in an upscale shopping and banking district in downtown Buenos Aires, is the sight of continued protest, demonstrations, and rallies. Defacing the bank is a near weekly activity of anti-government protests. Nearly two years after the Argentine debt crisis hit, activists continue to mar this and other banks with slogans like "down with politicians" and "thieves," reflecting populist anger with the economic crises, foreign financial interests, and local politicians.

the armed forces called on him to resign, Vargas committed suicide in his presidential palace.

Following the death of Vargas, Juscelino Kubitschek was elected president. Kubitschek embarked on an ambitious plan of rapid industrialization and modernization of Brazil. This included an impressive automobile manufacturing sector, dams, and grand public works projects. His most notable move was relocating the capital from Rio de Janeiro along the coastline to a new city called Brasília, located in the interior. Relocating the capital into the country's hinterland and constructing a capital city from scratch was a formidable task. New roads and infrastructure were built to connect the country to the capital. Brasília was a marvel of modern architecture and urban planning. But, the expenses incurred in building the city and its isolation from bustling Rio de Janeiro and São Paulo are among the perceived

negatives. Kubitschek's modernization of Brazil was epitomized by the construction of Brasília.

Subsequent democratically elected presidents had continued difficulty in controlling inflation while trying to push rapid industrialization, factors that made life difficult for Brazilians. The accompanying social discontent gave rise to a guerrilla movement led by Carlos Marighella. During the 1960s, Marighella led the Action for National Liberation (ALN) against the Brazilian government. As dissidents of Brazil's Communist Party, Marighella and approximately 200 members belonging to the ALN carried out a series of attacks on government offices and American companies in the region. Operating mainly out of São Paulo and Rio de Janeiro, the ALN was comprised of young professionals, students, and intellectuals who disagreed with the version of communism being followed by the government of the day. In an attempt to shake the government's hold on the country, the ALN became notorious for capturing and holding foreign representatives in Brazil. One of the better known cases involved the American ambassador to Brazil in 1969, Charles Elbrick. In an attempt to embarrass the government of Brazil and force them to publicly and violently retaliate, the ALN held on to Elbrick for four days, finally releasing him in exchange for 15 political prisoners being held by the Brazilian government. In the spring of 1964, the military with American support decided to intervene and took over the government. The military suspended democratic elections, greatly circumvented people's civic rights, changed the electoral system to preserve their rule, and closed the Congress. The ALN under the leadership of Marighella struggled against the U.S.-backed military leadership of Brazil for several years prior to the assassination of Marighella in 1969. Marighella also wrote the *Minimanual of the Urban Guerrilla,* which served as a blueprint for guerrilla fighting and set the standard for revolutionary groups throughout Latin America, including the *Tupamaros* of Uruguay.

The armed forces remained in direct control of the country for 20 years, during which time they set a new economic course by cutting back somewhat on state control of the economy and emphasizing market forces. The military also encouraged and attracted foreign multinational corporations at unprecedented levels. The new policies seemed to work on a macroeconomic level, and during the late 1960s, Brazil experienced what has been dubbed an "economic miracle" as it moved into self-sustaining economic growth.

The economic miracle, however, had disappointing results at the microeconomic level, as average Brazilians felt little of the economic growth. Ordinary Brazilians hardly benefited as the gulf between rich and poor, always wide, grew even wider. In 1960, the wealthiest 10 percent of Brazil's population received 40 percent of the nation's income; in 1980, they received 51 percent. At the same time, rapid development led to an inflation rate of 100 percent a year, and an enormous foreign debt added to the problems. Rapid economic growth also carried with it environmental drawbacks. The economic exploitation of the Amazon River basin opened the region to farming, but in the view of some critics threatened the ecological balance not only of Brazil but of the earth itself. By the early 1980s, the economic miracle was turning into an economic nightmare. Overwhelmed, the generals retreated and opened the door for a return to democracy in 1985.

In 1990, national elections brought a new president into office—Fernando Collor de Mello (b. 1949). The new administration promised to reduce inflation with a drastic reform program based on squeezing money out of the economy by stringent controls on wages and prices, drastic reductions in public spending, and cuts in the number of government employees. Collor further reduced spending on the military and defence, weakening the army's power to further intervene in Brazilian politics. But Collor's economic efforts—reminiscent of Menem's in Argentina—were undermined by reports of official corruption, and he resigned at the end of 1992 after having been impeached. In new elections two years later, Fernando Cardoso (b. 1931) was elected president by an overwhelming majority of the popular vote.

Cardoso, a member of the Brazilian Social Democratic Party, introduced measures to privatize state-run industries, to reform social security and the pension system, and to attract foreign investment. Cardoso effectively tackled Brazil's soaring rates of inflation. He rode a wave of economic prosperity to reelection in 1998. But continued economic disparities between the rich and poor, combined with allegations of official corruption and rising factionalism within the ruling party, as well as soaring foreign debt that nearly led to an economic crisis, undermined his popularity, leading to the victory of the Workers' Party in elections held in 2002.

The new president, former machine operator and commoner Luiz Inácio "Lula" da Silva, however, immediately cautioned his supporters that the party's ambitious plans could not be realized until social and financial reforms had been enacted. Lula tackled Brazil's urgent social problems of poverty, AIDS, and hunger. Lula has also committed to accepting IMF advice on macroeconomic policies. Catering to both the poor and the business community has been a tenuous experiment, but Lula made it work. By 2005, Lula effectively lowered unemployment rates, enhanced consumer confidence in the economy, and continuously chipped away at Brazil's massive foreign debt. His popularity and notoriety for straight talk in Brazil, Latin America, and many parts of the Third World is noteworthy.

How Did NAFTA Contribute to the Fall of the PRI?

During the presidency of Lázaro Cárdenas in the 1930s, the Mexican government returned to some of the original populist revolutionary goals by distributing over 17 million hectares of land to landless Mexican peasants, thereby appealing to the rural poor. The basis of the agrarian reforms was a collective land system, called the ***ejido***, which peasants toiled as families or villages. The government supported *ejidos* with financing and other benefits. Peasants could apply to the government to have privately owned farms expropriated and converted into collective *ejidos*. Peasants had to work the land and technically could not mortgage, rent, or sell their *ejidos;* but, their heirs could inherit rights to also work the land under similar terms. Cárdenas expanded the *ejido* system, confiscating an unprecedented amount of private land that was then redistributed to peasants. Cárdenas also nationalized Mexico's oil industry after a Mexican court ruling upheld labour union demands for improved wages that went ignored by foreign-owned oil companies. The state-owned oil company, called Petróleos Mexicanos (or Pemex), became an important source of government income that helped finance Cárdenas's populist policies.

> An ***ejido*** is communal land that is owned by the Mexican government and used by the peasants.

In the 1950s and 1960s, Mexico's ruling party, the **Institutional Revolutionary Party** (PRI), focused on an ISI industrial program. Fifteen years of steady economic growth, increased exports, combined with low inflation, had made these years appear to be a golden age in Mexico's economic development. Even foreign investment returned to Mexico, particularly in the northern industrial belt, in the form of *maquiladoras. Maquiladoras* are primarily American-owned branch-plant manufacturers using cheaper Mexican labour to produce goods for export to the United States. Mexicans flocked to the northern industrial belt to work in the factories. While all of this economic activity and export contributed to the overall growth of the country, the downside was the growing income disparity between rich and poor.

> The **Institutional Revolutionary Party** (PRI) is a populist political party that dominated Mexican politics and the government for much of the twentieth century; democratic elections removed the party from power in 2000.

But at the end of the 1960s, students protested against Mexico's growing income disparity and domination by one-party rule. University students along with other dis-affected groups took to the streets over several months to protest against economic inequalities and the state's political authoritarianism. Mexico was about to host the Olympic games in Mexico City. To show the world that it was a stable place to invest and visit, and had no tolerance for civil disobedience, the PRI took a hard-line with the students by banning protests. The students, however, did not back down and on October 2, 1968, a demonstration by university students in Tlatelolco Square in Mexico City was met by police, who opened fire and killed hundreds of students. Leaders of the PRI became concerned about the need to change the system.

The next two PRI presidents, Luis Echeverría Álvarez (b. 1922) and José López Portillo (b. 1920), introduced political reforms. The government eased rules for the registration of political parties and allowed greater freedom of debate in the press and universities. But economic problems continued to trouble Mexico. Several Mexican businesses and industries were on the verge of bankruptcy and the government stepped in and bought them out to preserve jobs. The Mexican government continued heavily investing in the public sector and in its social welfare policies that cushioned against the negative effects of the deteriorating economy. Sources for government income, however, continued to dry up and the government needed to finance its spending.

In the late 1970s, vast new reserves of oil were discovered in Mexico. As the sale of oil abroad rose dramatically, the government had a new infusion of capital to meet its spending costs. Mexico was also able to attract significant amounts of international finance, much of it in the form of loans of petrodollars. Mexico was clearly overextended, with huge amounts of loans to be serviced and not enough exports to meet its financing needs. Foreign capital and financiers predicted trouble in Mexico's balance sheets and started to withdraw their investments. Mexico quickly was no longer able to make payments on its foreign debt, which had reached US$80 billion in 1982. Western governments and creditors, including the United States and the IMF, came to Mexico's rescue with large financial bailouts. But the government was forced to adopt new economic policies, including the sale of publicly owned companies to private parties as means of paying back the creditors.

The debt crisis and rising unemployment increased dissatisfaction with the government. In the 1988 elections, the PRI's choice for president, Carlos Salinas, who had been expected to win in a landslide, won by only a 50.3 percent majority. The new president continued the economic liberalization of his predecessors and went even further by negotiating the North American Free Trade Agreement (NAFTA) with the United States and Canada. Although

NAFTA was highly controversial in Canada and the United States because of the fear that businesses would move factories to Mexico, where labour costs are cheaper and environmental standards less stringent, some observers asserted that the impact of NAFTA has been less beneficial to Mexico than expected. Reflecting Mexico's continuing economic problems was rising popular unrest in southern parts of the country, where unhappy farmers, many of whom are Amerindians, have grown increasingly vocal in protesting endemic poverty and widespread neglect of the needs of the indigenous peoples, who comprise about 10 percent of the total population of 100 million people.

In the summer of 2000, a national election suddenly ended PRI's 71 years of power. The new president, Vicente Fox (b. 1942), promised to address the many problems affecting the country, including political corruption, widespread poverty, environmental concerns, and a growing population. But he faces vocal challenges from the PRI, which still controls many state legislatures and a plurality in Congress, as well as from the protest movement in rural areas in the south. Calling themselves **Zapatistas** in honour of the revolutionary leader Emiliano Zapata (see Chapter 4, page 86), the rebels demand passage of legislation to protect the rights of the indigenous population and increasing autonomy for regions such as the southern state of Chiapas, where Amerindians make up a substantial percentage of the population. President Fox has expressed his support for legislative action to bring about reforms, but the movement has aroused such a groundswell of support from around the country that he will be under considerable pressure to deal with generations of neglect in solving the problems of Mexico.

> **Zapatistas** are rebels in southern Mexico who desire increased rights for the indigenous population.

LATIN AMERICAN CULTURE

Latin American culture is vibrant, poetic, and romantic. Latin music has a unique rhythm and passion, and reflects a people who enjoy life, value family and friends, and demand progressive change. Latin music and dance are often the pride of many Latin American countries.

In Latin American literature, writers and poets express their political views, which tend to champion the plight of the poor and call for social change. In its many stages, Latin American literature has served to chronicle the history of the land, its people, and its challenges. Those who wrote of the New World and its discovery are considered to be part of the literary classical era. Tales, accounts, and stories of conquest and settlement came in the form of letters from Christopher Columbus to Ferdinand V and from conquerors such as Hernan Cortes of Mexico to King Charles V of Spain. These were Latin America's first writers, and those who would follow would tell tales of battle and write epic poems of heroes lost and victories won, as well as essays and prose on the political and social consciousness of Latin America. The sixteenth century would give rise to one of Chile's most famous writers, Alonso de Ercilla y Zúñiga, who authored the epic poem *La Araucana* that told of the battle fought between the Spaniards who came to the New World as conquerors and the Araucanians, Chile's indigenous people. By the eighteenth century, Latin America's rich literary heritage evolved, becoming more eclectic through works by poets such as José Maria de Heredia of Cuba, who authored romantic pieces that were eventually translated into Portuguese, Italian, German, and English. Banished from Cuba to the United States due to his political and social opposition to its government, Heredia became famous shortly after the publication of a series of poems in 1832 which made him an instant success as a literary figure throughout the Spanish-speaking world of Latin America. By the nineteenth century, other famous romantic writers such as Brazil's national poet, Antônio Gonçalves Dias published pieces such as the "Song of Exile," which can still be recited by many children throughout Brazil today.

What Are the Origins of Latin American Dance?

The fusion of Latin, African, and native cultures underlies what is commonly referred to as *Latin American dance*. The evolution of this dance is best understood in terms of the crossover which took place between the Spanish who colonized this region, the Africans who were imported to the region as slaves, and the native Americans; each imparted upon this art form its own history, stories, and dance movements. As a result of this mix, different Latin American dances arose in different countries: for example, the rumba arose in Cuba, the tango in Argentina, and the merengue in the Dominican Republic and Haiti.

The rumba, much like the rest of Latin dance, is rhythmic in nature, as opposed to a more rigid or staged dance, due to its strong African roots. It is believed to have originated with the African slaves imported to Cuba in the sixteenth century. Seen as one of Latin America's more amorous dances, the rumba is essentially a sexually charged story about a man and a woman told through body movements. In this very fast paced, sensual dance, a man and woman engage in an offensive-defensive struggle between one another. The blanket term *rumba* describes a variety of dances, such as the *son*, the *danzon*, and the *guajira,* which

are performed in specific social strata of Cuban culture. For example, the *son* is most commonly danced among Cuba's middle class and is characterized by a slower pace and less suggestive movements, while the *danzon,* an even slower and more conservative form, is danced among Cuba's upper class.

The tango is another amorous variant of Latin American dance indigenous to Argentina. Much like the rumba, it is dramatic and displays a clash between the sexes. Its roots can be traced back to the poorer neighbourhoods of nineteenth-century Buenos Aires, also known as "Barria de Las Ranas," where immigrants from Europe and Africa came for work. The tango is said to represent a story about love, misery, and disillusionment, emotions that marked the kinds of places where the tango was being danced (mainly in the brothels and bars of Buenos Aires's underworld). Women of decent repute did not tango because of how close both partners danced and because of how obscene the lyrics were thought to be. The tango was considered sinful by most people in Argentina at the time; however, with the economic surge of wealth experienced in Argentina by the early twentieth century, many of Argentina's fortunate vacationed and studied abroad in Paris. It was there that the tango gained popularity. Once Parisians had been introduced to the tango, the dance took off and shed its baggage as an indecent and lowly art form. From then on, the tango came to be known as the pride of Argentina throughout Europe.

The merengue, which can be traced back to the nineteenth century, is a dance native to the Dominican Republic and, to a lesser extent, Haiti. Its origins are somewhat obscure. While many attribute the dance to Dominican folklore, Haiti has also claimed that the dance originated on its side of the shared island. Needless to say, numerous battles have occurred between these neighbouring countries, over claims to shared territory and culture. Shunned for its sexually suggestive nature and daring lyrics, the merengue, which literally means "whipped egg whites and sugar," was made the national dance of the Dominican Republic by its former ruler Rafael Trujillo. Trujillo, who had risen from society's lower class to state leader, ruled the Dominican Republic from the 1930s to the 1960s and made it mandatory for popular bands to include merengue in their performances, since the lyrics were often an oration of class struggles endured by men like him and the masses.

What Was the Focus of Latin American Literature in the Post-War Era?

Post-war writing in Latin America has been vibrant. Nobel Prize–winning writers such as Mario Vargas Llosa, Gabriel García Márquez (b. 1938), Jorge Luis Borges, and Carlos

Even His Royal Highness Likes to Tango! As seen here at the President's Dinner in Argentina on March 9, 1999, Prince Charles takes to the dance floor with Adriana Vasile while visiting in Buenos Aries. The tango, a traditional Latin dance, is often performed by lovers and is considered one of the more amorous and risqué types of Latin dances.

Fuentes are among the most respected literary names of the post-war half century. These authors often use dazzling language and daring narrative experimentation to make their point. The master of this new style is Gabriel García Márquez, from Colombia. In *One Hundred Years of Solitude* (1967), he explores the transformation of a small town under the impact of political violence, industrialization, and the arrival of the U.S.'s United Fruit Company. Especially noteworthy is his use of magical realism, relating the horrendous events that assail the town in a matter-of-fact voice, thus transforming the fantastic into the commonplace. Márquez quickly became known as a writer belonging to

the magic realism movement. The movement was set in motion by a German art critic who coined the term in an effort to describe the fusion of magical elements and the reality of everyday life reflected in art.

Unlike novelists in the West, who tend to focus their attention on the interior landscape within the modern personality in an industrial society, fiction writers in Latin America, like their counterparts in Africa and much of Asia, have sought to project an underlying political message. Many have been inspired by a sense of social and political injustice, a consequence of the economic inequality and authoritarian politics that marked the local scene throughout much of the twentieth century. Some, such as the Peruvian José Maria Arguedas, have championed the cause of Amerindians and lauded the diversity that marks the ethnic mix throughout the continent. Others have run for high political office as a means of remedying social problems. Some have been women, reflecting the rising demand for sexual equality in a society traditionally marked by male domination. The memorable phrase of the Chilean poet Gabriela Mistral—"I have chewed stones with woman's gums"—encapsulates the plight of Latin American women.

CONCLUSION

Latin American countries experimented with state-led policies and nationalist economic strategies that eventually failed. In addition to the economic failures produced by the populist policies, political expectations were raised to levels that politicians could not deliver.

- Entrenched labour interests that continuously raised wages and distorted prices aggravated the failures of the import-substitution industrialization strategy.
- Foreign debt and the policy prescriptions of the International Monetary Fund have aggravated socioeconomic disparities and hardships.

The United States intervened in the domestic affairs of many Latin American countries to either preserve its economic interests or uphold its turf in the Cold War.

- The United States tried to overthrow many leftist governments through direct and indirect means in notable cases in countries such as Cuba, Nicaragua, Chile, and Guatemala.
- The Marxist regime in Cuba has been a continuous thorn in the side of U.S. administrations since the Cuban Revolution. Today, Venezuela's Hugo Chávez and to a lesser extent Brazil's Lula da Silva challenge American foreign policy.

Latin America is rapidly integrating into the world economy, but the political costs of globalization are palpable.

- Argentina's economic crises in 2001 demonstrated the dangers of close integration with world capital markets.
- The fall of Mexico's PRI was precipitated by the failed promises of NAFTA.

CRITICAL THINKING QUESTIONS

1. Latin American society is often described as one obsessed with *machismo* or idolizing macho-like male figures. Does this cultural phenomenon perhaps explain why Latin American regimes revert to military rule when sociopolitical circumstances get complicated?

2. The United States has intervened in Latin American affairs at times to protect its economic and political interests from the expropriation policies of host governments. Should host governments have the right to expropriate property owned by foreign and multinational companies?

3. Even after the end of the Cold War, Cuba remains isolated by the United States. Why does the United States continue the embargo and isolation of Cuba when it is no longer a real threat? Is it a matter of American pride? Who benefits from Cuba's isolation? What message does it send to other would-be rogue states?

4. Neoliberalism purports that private enterprise, domestic and especially foreign multinationals, should be the engines of economic growth and not the state. What are the dangers of depending heavily on foreign investment?

CHAPTER NOTE

1. Dwight D. Eisenhower, *The White House Years: Waging Peace, 1956–1961* (Garden City, N.Y.: Doubleday, 1965), p. 533.

V Beginning a New Millennium

"I haven't the slightest idea who he is. He came bundled with the software."

Chapter 16

Constructing a New World Order

At the end of the twentieth century, both hope and despair were on the rise. In the Western world, social, political, and economic progress seemed to indicate a future of prosperity and growth. On the other hand, in the Third World socioeconomic problems continued to plague many countries as income disparity widened and rates of poverty continued to grow. What would the new century bring? Some have argued that a clash of civilizations, between the Western and Eastern world, will characterize the twenty-first century. Others have argued that technology and globalization offer hope for social, political, and economic progress.

At the conclusion of this chapter, you will be able to

- describe the legacies of the twentieth century, including the Cold War, decolonization, democratization, and modernization;
- explain the effects of globalization at the dawn of the twenty-first century;
- relate the growing importance of multilateralism and international organizations, especially the UN;
- describe the concerns related to the environment and the Technological Revolution in postindustrial society.

THE TWENTIETH CENTURY IN PERSPECTIVE

By 1900, virtually all of Asia and Africa had come under some degree of formal or informal colonial control. World War I weakened the European powers but did not bring the era of imperialism to an end, and the seeds of a second world confrontation were planted at the Paris Peace Conference of 1919, which failed to resolve the problems that had led to the war in the first place. Those seeds began to sprout in the 1930s when Hitler's Germany sought to recoup its losses and Japan became an active participant in the race for spoils in the Pacific region.

As World War II came to a close, the leaders of the victorious Allied nations were presented with a second opportunity to fashion a lasting peace based on the principles of social justice and self-determination. There were several issues on their post-war agenda. Europe needed to be revived from the ashes of the war and restored to the level of political stability and economic achievement that it had seemingly attained at the beginning of the century. Beyond

the continent of Europe, the colonial system had to be dismantled and the promise of self-determination enshrined in the Atlantic Charter applied on a global scale.

During the 1950s and 1960s, the capitalist nations managed to recover from the extended economic depression that had contributed to the start of World War II and advanced to a level of economic prosperity never before seen. The bloody conflicts that had erupted among European nations during the first half of the twentieth century came to an end, and Germany and Japan were fully integrated into the world community. At the same time, the Western colonial empires in Asia and Africa were gradually dismantled, and the peoples of both continents once again recovered their independence.

But if the victorious nations of World War II had managed to resolve several of the key problems that had contributed to a half century of bloody conflict, the ultimate prerequisite for success—an end to the competitive balance-of-power system that had been a contributing factor in both world wars—was hampered by the emergence of a gruelling and sometimes tense ideological struggle between the socialist and capitalist blocs, a competition headed by the only two remaining great powers, the Soviet Union and the United States. While the two superpowers managed to avoid an open confrontation, the post-war world was divided for 50 years into two heavily armed camps in a balance of terror that on one occasion—the Cuban Missile Crisis—brought the world briefly to the brink of a nuclear holocaust. The particular form that the Cold War eventually took—with two heavily armed power blocs facing each other across a deep cultural and ideological divide—was not necessarily preordained, but given the volatility of post-war conditions and the vast gap in mutual understanding and cultural experience, it is difficult to see how the intense rivalry that characterized the East-West relationship could have been avoided.

For the leaders of African and Asian countries after World War II, their concerns included creating a new political culture responsive to the needs of their citizens. For the most part, they accepted the concept of democracy as the defining theme of that culture. Within a decade, however, democratic systems throughout the Third World were replaced by military dictatorships or one-party governments that redefined the concept of democracy to fit their own preferences. Some Western observers criticized the new leaders for their autocratic tendencies, and others attempted to explain the phenomenon by pointing out that after traditional forms of authority were replaced, it would take time to lay the basis for pluralistic political systems. In the interim, a strong government party under the leadership of a single charismatic individual could mobilize the population to seek common goals. Whatever the case, it was clear that many had underestimated the difficulties in building democratic political institutions in developing societies.

The problem of establishing a common national identity was in some ways the most daunting of all the challenges facing the new states of Asia, Middle East, and Africa. Many of these new states were a composite of a wide variety of ethnic, religious, and linguistic groups that found it difficult to agree on common symbols of nationalism. Problems of establishing an official language and delineating territorial boundaries left over from the colonial era created difficulties in many countries. In some cases, these problems were exacerbated by political and economic changes. The introduction of the concept of democracy sharpened the desire of individual groups to have a separate identity within a larger nation, and economic development often favoured some at the expense of others.

From the 1950s to the 1970s, the political and economic difficulties experienced by many developing nations in Asia, Africa, and Latin America led to chronic instability in a number of countries and transformed the Third World into a major theatre of Cold War confrontation. During the 1980s, however, a number of new factors entered the equation and shifted the focus away from ideological competition. China's shift to a more accommodating policy toward the West removed fears of more wars of national liberation supported by Beijing. At the same time, the Communist victory in Vietnam led not to falling dominoes throughout Southeast Asia but to bitter conflict between erstwhile Communist allies Vietnam and China, and Vietnam and Cambodia. It was clear that national interests and historical rivalries took precedence over ideological agreement.

The decline of communism in the final decades of the century brought an end to an era, not only in the Soviet Union but also in much of the rest of the world. For more than a generation, thousands of intellectuals and political elites in Asia, Africa, and Latin America had looked to Marxism-Leninism as an appealing developmental ideology that could rush pre-industrial societies through the modernization process without the painful economic and social inequities associated with capitalism. Communism, many thought, could make more effective use of scarce capital and resources while carrying through the reforms needed to bring an end to centuries of inequality in the political and social arenas.

To many historians, the disintegration of the Soviet Union signalled the end of communism as a competitive force in the global environment. In some parts of the world, however, it has survived in the form of Communist parties presiding over a mixed economy combining components of both socialism and capitalism. Why have Communist political systems survived in some areas while the Marxist-Leninist economic model in its classic form has not? In the first place, it is obvious that one of the consequences of long-term Communist rule was the suffocation of alternative political forces and ideas. As the situation in Eastern Europe has demonstrated, even after the passing of communism itself, Communist parties often appeared to be the only political force with the experience and discipline to govern complex and changing societies.

The wave of optimism that accompanied the end of the Cold War was all too brief. After a short period of euphoria—some observers speculated that the world had reached the "end of history," when the liberal democratic system had demonstrated its longevity and the major problems in the future would be strictly economic—it soon became clear that forces were now being released that had long been held in check by the ideological rigidities of the Cold War. The era of conflict that had long characterized the twentieth century was not at an end; it was simply in the process of taking a different form.

Nowhere was this trend more immediately apparent than in Southeast Asia, where even before the end of the Cold War, erstwhile allies in China, Vietnam, and

Cambodia turned on each other in a conflict that combined territorial ambitions with geopolitical concerns and deep-seated historical suspicions based on the memory of past conflicts. Ideology, it was clear, was no barrier to historical and cultural rivalries. The pattern was repeated elsewhere: in Africa, where several nations erupted into civil war during the late 1980s and 1990s; in the Balkans, where the Yugoslavian Federation broke apart in a bitter conflict that has yet to be fully resolved; and of course in the Middle East, where the historical disputes in the Holy Land and the Persian Gulf have grown in intensity and erupted repeatedly into open war. The irony of this explosion of national, ethnic, and religious sentiment is that it has taken place at a time when it is becoming increasingly evident that the main problems in today's society—such as environmental pollution, overpopulation, and unequal distribution of resources—are shared to one degree or another by all humanity. In a world that is increasingly characterized by global interdependence, how can it be that the world is increasingly being pulled apart?

INTO THE TWENTY-FIRST CENTURY

For four decades, ideological battles were all too frequently submerged in the public consciousness as the two major power blocs competed for advantage. The collapse of the Soviet Union brought an end to the Cold War but left world leaders almost totally unprepared to face the consequences. State leaders, scholars, and political pundits began to forecast the emergence of a "new world order." Few, however, had any real idea of what it would entail. With the division of the world into two squabbling ideological power blocs suddenly at an end, there was little certainty, and much speculation, about what was going to take its place.

Do We Live in a Global Village or Amid a Clash of Civilizations?

One hypothesis that won support in some quarters was that the decline of communism signalled that the industrial capitalist democracies of the West had triumphed in the war of ideas and would now proceed to remake the rest of the world in their own image. Some people cited as evidence the widely discussed book *The End of History and the Last Man,* in which Francis Fukuyama argues that capitalism and the Western concept of liberal democracy, while hardly ideal in their capacity to satisfy all human aspirations, are at least more effective than rival doctrines in achieving those longings and therefore deserve consideration as the best available ideology to be applied universally throughout the globe.[1]

Whether or not Fukuyama's thesis about the **end of history** is true, it is much too early to assume (as he would no doubt admit) that the liberal democratic model has in fact triumphed in the clash of ideas that dominated the twentieth century. Although it is no doubt true that much of the world is now linked together in the economic marketplace created by the Western industrial nations, it seems clear from the discussion of contemporary issues in this chapter that the future hegemony of Western political ideas and institutions is by no means assured, despite their current dominating position as a result of the decline of communism.

> The **end of history** is Francis Fukuyama's thesis that liberal democracy and capitalism should and will dominate.

For one thing, in much of the world today, Western values are threatened or are refuted. In Africa, even the façade of democratic institutions has been discarded as autocratic leaders rely on the power of the gun as sole justification for their actions. In India, the emergence of fragile governments, religious strife, and spreading official corruption has left the future of the world's largest democracy in doubt. Even in East Asia, where pluralistic societies have begun to appear in a number of industrializing countries, leading political figures have expressed serious reservations about Western concepts of democracy and individualism and openly questioned their relevance to their societies. The issue was raised at a meeting of the **Association of Southeast Asian Nations** (ASEAN) states in July 1997, when then Malaysian Prime Minister Mahathir Mohamad declared that the Universal Declaration of Human Rights, passed after World War II at the behest of the victorious Western nations, was not appropriate to the needs of poorer non-Western countries and should be reviewed. A number of political leaders in the region echoed Mahathir's views and insisted on the need for a review. Their comments were quickly seconded by Chinese President Jiang Zemin, who declared during a visit to the United States later in the year that human rights were not a matter that could be dictated by the powerful nations of the world, but rather an issue to be determined by individual societies on the basis of their own traditions and course of development.

> The **Association of Southeast Asian Nations** (ASEAN) is a cooperative organization that represents the common political, economic, technological, and security interests of member countries in the Asian region. Currently, its member countries are Brunei, Cambodia, Indonesia, Laos, Malaysia, Myanmar, the Philippines, Singapore, Thailand, and Vietnam.

It is possible, of course, that the liberal democratic model will become more acceptable in parts of Africa and Asia to the degree that societies in those regions proceed successfully through the advanced stages of the industrial and technological revolutions, thus giving birth to the middle-class values that underlie modern civilization in the West. There is no guarantee, however, that current conditions, which have been relatively favourable to that process, will continue indefinitely, or that all peoples and all societies will share equally in the benefits. The fact is that just as the Industrial Revolution exacerbated existing tensions in and among the nations of Europe, globalization and the Technological Revolution are imposing their own strains on human societies today. Should such strains become increasingly intense, they could trigger political and social conflict.

In *The Clash of Civilizations and the Remaking of World Order,* Samuel P. Huntington has responded to these concerns by suggesting that the post–Cold War era, far from marking the triumph of the Western idea, will be characterized by increased global fragmentation and a **clash of civilizations** based on ethnic, cultural, or religious differences. According to Huntington, cultural identity has replaced shared ideology as the dominant force in world affairs. As a result, he argues, the coming decades may see an emerging world dominated by disputing cultural blocs in East Asia, Western Europe and the United States, Eurasia, and the Middle East, with the societies in each region coalescing around common cultural features against perceived threats from rival forces elsewhere around the globe. The dream of a universal order dominated by Western values, he concludes, is a fantasy.[2]

> The **clash of civilizations** is an argument put forth by Samuel P. Huntington that cultural differences will be the main engine of conflict in world affairs.

Events in recent years have appeared to bear out Huntington's hypothesis. The collapse of the Soviet Union led to the emergence of several squabbling new nations and a general atmosphere of conflict and tension in the Balkans and at other points along the perimeter of the old Soviet empire. Even more dramatically, the terrorist attacks in September 2001 and the invasion of both Afghanistan and Iraq appear to have set the advanced nations of the West and the Muslim world on a collision course.

Some have reconceived Huntington's thesis as a clash of Western civilization led by the United States and Eastern civilization led by the Muslim world. Many have argued that there is a cultural war between the Western liberal-democratic world and the Eastern traditional and conservative world. Benjamin Barber's book ***Jihad vs. McWorld*** highlights this tension between factionalism, tribalism, and

nationalism versus globalization, universalization, and technology. The reaction to globalization would be to return to a lowest common denominator of identity like tribe, ethnicity, and community. In other words, to deal with the alienation of the cosmopolitan and interconnected world, we would return to our root identity. The result of this is a clash of civilization, because only tribalism and factionalism offer individuals cohesion.

> ***Jihad vs. McWorld*** is a book about tribalism versus globalization and the implications for identity.

Huntington's thesis serves as a useful corrective to the complacent tendency of many observers in Europe and the United States to see Western civilization as the zenith and the final destination of human achievement desired by others. In the promotion by Western leaders of the concepts of universal human rights and a global marketplace, there is a recognizable element of the cultural arrogance that was reflected in the doctrine of social Darwinism at the end of the nineteenth century. Both views take as their starting point the assumption that the Western conceptualization of the human experience is universal in scope and will ultimately, inexorably spread to the rest of the world. Neither gives much credence to the view that other civilizations might have seized on a corner of the truth and thus have something to offer.

That is not to say, however, that Huntington's vision of clashing civilizations is necessarily the most persuasive characterization of the probable state of the world in the twenty-first century. In dividing the world into competing cultural blocs, Huntington has probably underestimated the centrifugal forces at work in the various regions of the world. As many critics have noted, deep-rooted cultural and historical rivalries exist among the various nations in southern and eastern Asia and in the Middle East, as well as in Africa, preventing any meaningful degree of mutual cooperation against allegedly hostile forces in the outside world. Differences between the United States and leading European nations over the decision to invade Iraq demonstrate that fissures are growing even within the Western alliance.

Huntington also tends to ignore the transformative effect of the Industrial Revolution and the emerging global informational network. As the Industrial and Technological Revolutions spread across the face of the earth, their impact is measurably stronger in some societies than in others, thus intensifying political, economic, and cultural distinctions in a given region while establishing links between individual societies in that region and their counterparts undergoing similar experiences in other parts of the world. Although the parallel drive to global industrial hegemony in Japan and the United States, for example, has served to divide the two countries on a variety of issues, it has also intensified tensions between Japan and its competitor South Korea and weakened the political and cultural ties that have historically existed between Japan and China.

The most likely scenario for the next few decades, then, is more complex than either the global village hypothesis or its conceptual rival, the clash of civilizations. The world of the twenty-first century will be characterized by simultaneous trends toward globalization and fragmentation, as the inexorable thrust of technology and information transforms societies and gives rise to counterreactions among individuals and communities seeking to preserve a group identity and a sense of meaning and purpose in a confusing world.

Has Multilateralism Been Strengthened?

Under such conditions, how can world leaders hope to resolve localized conflicts and prevent them from spreading into neighbouring regions, with consequences that could bring an end to the current period of economic expansion and usher in a new era of global impoverishment? To some analysts, the answer lies in strengthening **multilateralism** by enhancing the powers of international organizations such as the United Nations (UN).

> **Multilateralism** refers to countries working together through cooperative instruments such as international organizations, regional associations, and international agreements.

The UN and various regional security organizations need to deal effectively with local conflicts. In recent years, the UN has dispatched peacekeeping missions to nearly 20 different nations on 5 continents, with a total troop commitment of more than 40 000 military personnel. During the Cold War, conflicts were often fought among nation-states. The UN peacekeepers were dispatched into disputed territories to keep two nation-states from continuing their war. In the post–Cold War era, however, we have seen fewer *inter*state wars, as we have seen more *intra*state wars. More often now, the UN is asked to keep the peace within the borders of states. These states have included the former Yugoslavia, Somalia, Rwanda, Haiti, Sierra Leone, and East Timor. The post–Cold War reality is that the UN must now intervene in the sovereignty of states to keep warring factions, including the government's army, from killing each other. Canada has been a leading proponent of having the UN include a "responsibility to protect" mandate that would ensure the UN intervenes when human catastrophe appears imminent. The concept of "responsibility to protect" puts into serious question the sanctity of state sovereignty.

Other efforts to expand multilateralism include the newly established International Criminal Court (ICC), which is used to independently try criminals for crimes against humanity. International tribunals to try individuals of war crimes, like Slobodan Milosevic, were used effectively in the past. In the late 1990s, the international community decided to set up a permanent ICC to bring criminals to justice. The North American Treaty Organization (NATO) has also been strengthened after the Cold War through expanded membership of Eastern European countries. NATO has been utilized most recently in Kosovo and Afghanistan. Nearly 100 000 NATO troops are currently attempting to preserve a fragile cease-fire in the Balkans. The challenge is not only to bring about an end to a particular conflict but also to resolve the problems that gave rise to the dispute in the first place. NATO's presence in Afghanistan has expanded the scope of NATO's geographical reach. NATO has established a precedent of moving beyond policing Europe and into other areas of strategic interest to its members.

While multilateral organizations appear strengthened and to be in frequent use, there is some worry that the United States will defy multilateral channels when decisions of the international community do not reflect its interest. The U.S. decision in 2003 to launch an invasion of Iraq while circumventing the UN Security Council, for example, has sparked misgivings about the world's sole superpower. Many worry that U.S. unilateral actions not sanctioned by the UN could undermine global stability and efforts to strengthen multilateralism. Similarly, the United States' decisions not to join the ICC and not to ratify the Kyoto protocol on the environment are all worrying signs that the United States may not be committed to multilateralism, or worse yet, that the United States has neo-imperialist desires, particularly in the Middle East.

Has Economic Globalization Been Triumphant?

After a generation of rapid growth, most of the capitalist states in Europe and North America began in the late 1980s to suffer through a general slowdown in economic performance. This slowdown has in turn given rise to a number of related problems, several with serious social and political implications. These problems include an increase in the level of unemployment; government belt-tightening policies to reduce social services, and welfare and retirement benefits; and in many countries, an accompanying growth in popular resentment against minority groups or recent immigrants, who are used as scapegoats for deteriorating economic prospects.

Desmond Boylan/Reuters/Landov

Raising the American Flag in Iraq. The feared imperialistic aim of the United States in its occupation and then reconstruction of Iraq is best depicted in the image above. American marines raised an American flag over an Iraqi port in the first few days of the invasion of Iraq and in the U.S. march toward Baghdad. The U.S. government quickly ordered the marines to remove the American flag, but deep-seated suspicion of U.S. intentions to politically control the oil-rich region remains. America's self-proclaimed desire to spread democratization in the Middle East, even through the occupation of sovereign countries such as Iraq, is reminiscent of colonialism using indirect rule.

EUROPE: THE TENSION BETWEEN UNITY AND DISUNITY

The problem of economic stagnation has been especially prevalent in Western Europe, where unemployment is at its highest level since the 1930s and economic growth in recent years has averaged less than 1 percent annually. Conditions have been exacerbated in recent years by the need for individual governments to set their financial houses in order so as to comply with the requirements for unification as called for by the Maastricht Treaty of 1992 (see Chapter 8, page 152). For an individual nation to take part in the process, government deficits must not greatly exceed 3 percent of gross domestic product, nor must the national debt greatly exceed 60 percent of total output. Inflation rates must also be cut to minimal levels.

The problem is that many countries are encountering difficulties in adopting the severe economic measures that

are needed to qualify for the transition to economic unity. France, concerned at the potential impact on its own fragile economy, has threatened not to carry out the necessary reforms. In Italy, the refusal of the Communist Party to agree to belt-tightening measures almost led to the fall of the coalition government. Even in Germany, long the healthiest of all major Western European states, reductions in social benefits sharpened tensions between the eastern and western zones and undermined public support for the government of Gerhard Schröder.

But perhaps the most ominous consequence of the new economic austerity has been a rise in anti-foreign sentiment. In Germany, attacks against foreign residents—mainly Turks, many of whom have lived in the country for years—have increased substantially. Conservative forces have turned to the idea of preserving "German culture" as a rallying cry to win the support of Germans concerned over the rapid process of change. In France, hostility to immigrants from North Africa has led to rising support for Jean-Marie Le Pen's National Front, which advocates strict limits on immigration and the ejection of many foreigners currently living in the country. It seems clear that the ethnic animosities that so often fuelled conflict in Europe before World War II have not entirely abated.

By no means do all Europeans fear the costs of economic unity. Official sources argue that it will increase the region's ability to compete with economic powerhouses such as the United States and Japan. But fear of change and a strong legacy of nationalist sentiment have promoted public fears that economic unification could have disastrous consequences. This is especially true in Great Britain and also in Germany, where many see little benefit and much risk from joining a larger Europe.

At the same time, some of the smaller states within the European Union (EU) are afraid that their concerns will be ignored by the larger powers. Such concerns have also emerged in Eastern Europe, where several governments are seeking membership in the EU to improve their own economic conditions.

THE UNITED STATES: CAPITALISM ASCENDANT

In some respects, the United States fared better than other capitalist states as the economic revival that took place in the 1990s enabled the administration of Bill Clinton to reduce budget deficits without having to engage in substantial tax increases or a massive reduction in welfare spending. Even there, however, continued increases in social spending provoked the passage of new legislation to reduce welfare and health care benefits. Nor has the steady growth in the gross domestic product led to increased prosperity for all Americans. Although the rich have been getting richer, the poorest 20 percent of the population has so far seen little benefit. The lack of sustained growth in consumer demand may be a major reason for the economic slowdown that began to appear early in the new century and has brought unemployment levels to the highest rate in recent years.

The United States has not yet witnessed the emergence of significant anti-foreign sentiment on the scale of some countries in Europe, perhaps partly because of the useful effect of a steadily growing economy. Recent history suggests that tolerance toward immigrants tends to decrease during periods of economic malaise, and vice versa. But there are indications that anger against the growing presence of foreign-born residents—especially those who have arrived illegally—is on the rise. Legislation to limit social benefits to non-citizens and to expel illegal aliens has been proposed at the state level and has been debated in Congress. Many American workers, with the support of

labour unions, have vocally opposed the enactment of trade agreements such as the North American Free Trade Agreement (NAFTA) that would allegedly lead to a flight of jobs overseas as U.S. corporations seek to reduce production costs by hiring cheaper labour. Opponents of globalization have become increasingly vocal, leading to violent protest demonstrations at meetings of the World Trade Organization, the World Bank, and the International Monetary Fund.

Yet as in the case of European unity, there is solid economic logic in pursuing the goal of increasing globalization of trade. The U.S. industrial machine is increasingly dependent on the importation of raw materials from abroad, and corporate profits are to a rising degree a consequence of sales of U.S. goods in overseas markets. Although foreign competition can sometimes lead to a loss of jobs—or entire industries—in the United States, the overall effect is likely to be a growing market for U.S. goods in the international marketplace. Moreover, as the case of the automobile industry has demonstrated, increased competition is crucial for maintaining and enhancing the quality of American products.

EAST ASIA: REASSESSING THE "ECONOMIC MIRACLE"

Until quite recently, it was common to observe that the one area in the capitalist world that was in a strong position to advance rapidly in the economic sphere without suffering the social and political strains experienced in the West was East Asia, where Japan and the **"Little Tigers"** appeared able to combine rapid economic growth with a minimum of social problems and a considerable degree of political stability. Pundits in the region and abroad opined that the "East Asian miracle" was a product of the amalgamation of capitalist economic techniques and a value system inherited from Confucius that stressed hard work, frugality, and the subordination of the individual to the community—all reminiscent of the Puritan ethic of the early capitalist era in the West.

> **"Little Tigers"** is a term that describes Taiwan, Singapore, Hong Kong, and South Korea, four states in East Asia that have experienced strong economic development.

There is indeed some similarity between the recent performance of many East Asian societies and early capitalism in the West. Some commentators in East Asia have pointed with pride to their traditional values and remarked that in

The Hong Kong Skyline. Hong Kong reverted to Chinese sovereignty in 1997 after a century of British rule. To commemorate the occasion, the imposing Hong Kong Convention and Exhibition Centre, shown here in the foreground, was built on reclaimed shoreline along Victoria Harbour.

the West such values as hard work and a habit of saving have been replaced by a certain hedonism that values individual over community interests and prizes gratification over future needs. Some observers in the West have agreed with this assessment and lamented the complacency and rampant materialism of Western culture.

As the twentieth century neared its end, however, the argument suddenly became academic, as evidence accumulated that the East Asian miracle itself may be a myth or at least an overstatement of a more complex reality. The financial crisis of 1997 demonstrated that the Pacific nations were not immune to the vicissitudes of capitalism and that overconfidence and lack of attention to fundamentals could be as destructive on one side of the ocean as the other. Mesmerized by the rhetorical vision of the Confucian work ethic and less experienced in riding the choppy waves of the capitalist business cycle, Asian governments and entrepreneurs alike became too complacent in their view that the bull market in

the region would never end. Banks extended loans on shaky projects, and governments invested heavily in expensive infrastructure improvements that exploded budget deficits while promising few financial returns until the distant future. When foreign investors grew wary and began withdrawing their funds, the bubble burst. It has been a sobering experience. As one commentator put it, "It was all too Disneyland; so much glass that was too shiny. Now they are going through a cultural crisis triggered by the economic crisis. These countries have to become more pragmatic."[3]

The economic fundamentals in many East Asian countries are essentially sound, and the region will undoubtedly recover from the current crisis and resume the pace of steady growth that characterized its performance during the last quarter of the twentieth century. But the fiscal crisis of the late 1990s serves as a warning signal that success—in East Asia as in the West—is the product of hard work and can never be assumed.

FROM THE INDUSTRIAL TO THE TECHNOLOGICAL REVOLUTION

As many observers have noted, the world economy as a whole is in the process of transition to what has been called a "postindustrial age," characterized by the emergence of a system that is not only increasingly global in scope but also increasingly technology-intensive. This process, which futurologist Alvin Toffler has dubbed the *Third Wave* (the first two being the Agricultural and Industrial Revolutions), has caused difficulties for people in many walks of life—for blue-collar workers, whose high wages price them out of the market as firms begin to move their factories abroad; for the poor and uneducated, who lack the technical skills to handle complex tasks in the contemporary economy; and even for members of the middle class, who have been fired or forced into retirement as their employers seek to slim down to compete in the global marketplace.[4]

It is now increasingly clear that the **Technological Revolution**, like the Industrial Revolution that preceded it, will have enormous consequences and may ultimately give birth to a level of social and political instability that has not been seen in the developed world since the Great Depression of the 1930s. The success of advanced capitalist states in the second half of the twentieth century was built on the foundations of a broad consensus on the importance of several propositions: (1) the importance of limiting income inequities to reduce the threat of political instability while maximizing domestic consumer demand; (2) the need for high levels of government investment in infrastructure projects such as education, communications, and transportation as a means of meeting the challenges of continued economic growth and technological innovation; and (3) the desirability of cooperative efforts in the international arena as a means of maintaining open markets for the free exchange of goods.

> **Technological Revolution** refers to the postindustrial age in which the use of technology and information is paramount.

As the twenty-first century gains momentum, all of these assumptions are increasingly coming under attack. Citizens are reacting with growing hostility to the high tax rates needed to maintain the welfare state, refusing to support education and infrastructure development, and opposing the formation of trading alliances to promote the free movement of goods and labour across national borders. Such attitudes are being expressed by individuals and groups on all sides of the political spectrum, making the traditional designations of left-wing and right-wing politics increasingly meaningless. Although most governments and

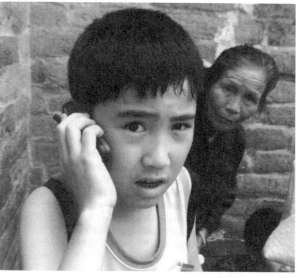

China Calling. As the new century dawns, the entire world is becoming wired, as developing nations realize that economic success depends on information technology. Shown here is a young Chinese boy reporting to his family on a visit to the Great Wall. By 2007 it is estimated that China will be the world's largest user of the Internet, with 300 million individuals on-line. By then, an equal number of Chinese will possess cell phones.

political elites have continued to support most of the programs that underpin the welfare state and the global marketplace, they are increasingly attacked by groups in society that feel they have been victimized by the system. The breakdown of the public consensus that brought modern capitalism to a pinnacle of achievement raises serious questions about the likelihood that the coming challenge of the Third Wave can be successfully met without a growing measure of political and social tension in both the domestic and international arenas.

ONE WORLD, ONE ENVIRONMENT

Another crucial factor that is affecting the evolution of society and the global economy is growing concern over the impact of industrialization on the earth's environment. There is nothing new about human beings causing damage to their natural surroundings. It may first have occurred when Neolithic peoples began to practise slash-and-burn agriculture or when excessive hunting thinned out the herds of bison and caribou in the Western Hemisphere. It almost certainly played a major role in the decline of the ancient civilizations in the Persian Gulf region and later of the Roman Empire.

Greg Baker/AP/Wide World Photos

Never before, however, has the danger of significant ecological damage been as extensive as during the past century. The effects of chemicals introduced into the atmosphere or into rivers, lakes, and oceans have increasingly threatened the health and well-being of all living species. For many years, the main focus of environmental concern was in the developed countries of the West, where most of the global pollution has emanated. This pollution includes industrial refuse, automobile exhaust, and the use of artificial fertilizers and insecticides that have led to urban smog, extensive damage to crops and wildlife, and a major reduction of the ozone layer in the upper atmosphere. In recent decades, however, it has become clear that the environmental problem is now global in scope and demands vigorous action in the international arena.

The opening of Eastern Europe after the revolutions of 1989 brought to the world's attention the incredible environmental destruction in that region caused by unfettered industrial pollution. Communist governments had obviously operated under the assumption that production quotas were much more important than environmental protection. The nuclear power disaster at Chernobyl in the Ukraine in 1986 made Europeans acutely aware of potential environmental hazards, and 1987 was touted as the "year of the environment." Many European states now felt compelled to advocate new regulations to protect the environment, and many of them established government ministries to oversee environmental issues.

For some, such official actions were insufficient, and beginning in the 1980s, a number of new political parties were established to focus exclusively on environmental issues. These **Green movements** and parties have played an important role in making people aware of environmental problems, although they have by no means been able to control the debate. Too often, environmental issues come out second in clashes with economic issues. Still, during the 1990s, more and more European governments were beginning to sponsor projects to safeguard the environment and clean up the worst sources of pollution.

> **Green movements** are politicized groups and parties dedicated to pursuing environmental concerns, usually proposing a sacrifice of economic growth for the betterment of people's health.

In recent years, the problem has spread elsewhere. China's headlong rush to industrialization has resulted in major ecological damage in that country. Industrial smog has created almost unliveable conditions in many cities, and hillsides denuded of their forests have caused severe problems of erosion and destruction of farmlands. Some environmentalists believe that levels of pollution in China are already higher than in the fully developed industrial societies of the West, a reality that raises serious questions about Beijing's ability to recreate the automotive culture of the modern West in China.

Destruction of the rain forest is a growing problem in many parts of the world, notably in Brazil and in the Indonesian archipelago. With the forest cover throughout the earth rapidly declining, there is less plant life to perform the crucial process of reducing carbon dioxide levels in the atmosphere. In 1997, forest fires on the Indonesian islands of Sumatra and Borneo created a blanket of smoke over the entire region, forcing schools and offices to close and causing respiratory ailments for thousands. Some of the damage could be attributed to the traditional slash-and-burn techniques used by subsistence farmers to clear forest cover for their farmlands, but the primary cause was the clearing of forestland to create or expand palm oil plantations, one of the region's major sources of export revenue.

One of the few salutary consequences of such incidents has been a growing international consensus that environmental concerns have taken on a truly global character. Although the danger of global warming—allegedly caused by the release, as a result of industrialization, of certain gases into the atmosphere—has not yet been definitively proved, it had become a source of sufficient concern to bring about an international conference on the subject in Kyoto in December 1997. If, as many scientists predict, worldwide temperatures should increase, the rise in sea levels could pose a significant threat to low-lying islands and coastal areas throughout the world, while climatic change could lead to severe droughts or excessive rainfall in cultivated areas. For the hundreds of thousands killed in the devastating 2004 tsunami (a very large wave created by an underwater earthquake), the growing importance of understanding the environment and its impact on peoples is vital (see the box on page 293).

It is one thing to recognize a problem, however, and quite another to resolve it. So far, cooperative efforts among nations to alleviate environmental problems have all too often been hindered by economic forces or by political, ethnic, and religious disputes. The 1997 Kyoto Climate Conference, for example, was marked by bitter disagreement over the degree to which developing countries should share the burden of cleaning up the environment. As a result, it achieved few concrete results. The fact is that few nations have been willing to take unilateral action that might pose an obstacle to economic development plans or lead to a rise in unemployment. India, Pakistan, and Bangladesh have squabbled over the use of the waters of the Ganges and Indus rivers, as have Israel, Syria, and Jordan over the scarce water resources of the Middle East. Pollution of the Rhine River by factories along its banks provokes

THE 2004 TSUNAMI DISASTER

One of the world's greatest natural disasters occurred on December 26, 2004, claiming the lives of over 300 000 people spanning two continents. The 2004 tsunami, meaning "harbour wave" in Japanese, happened on a Sunday morning approximately 150 kilometres off the coast of Sumatra Island, Indonesia, and was considered the most destructive natural disaster to occur in the region in over 40 years. It registered 9.0 on the Richter scale and touched eight countries spread over Asia and Africa, including India, Malaysia, Somalia, Sri Lanka, Thailand, Maldives, the Seychelles, and Indonesia, with the latter suffering the greatest lost in terms of lives. It cost billion of dollars worth of damage to the region, not taking into account the invaluable lives that were lost that morning.

Scientifically referred to as the Sumatra-Andaman tsunami, it occurred when the tectonic plates of India and Burma collided, one sliding beneath the other. Although tsunamis can be traced back to the Minoan civilization of the eastern Mediterranean in 1480 B.C.E., they have been most common (and destructive) to the Pacific Ocean region off the American West Coast and Hawaii. Because tsunamis have been rare in the Indian Ocean, there were no tsunami regional warning systems in place.

The 2004 tsunami left families completely destroyed as many lost their partners, parents, siblings, and children. Such tragic misfortunes have had a devastating effect on the psyche of those who lived through it. Many people lost everything that morning; within hours homes and entire villages were razed, communities were lost, family members perished, and livelihoods were destroyed. Many of those who died lived in poor fishing communities along the coast. The most vulnerable were the elderly and children, those who were not strong enough to withstand the waves that hit with such ferocity they managed to tear down power lines, uproot train tracks, and bulldoze buildings, homes, boats, cars, and whatever else lay in their path. Many died by drowning, which is the most common cause of death from tsunamis; drowning was also the principle cause of death for countless fishermen who were working in the abundant fishing communities in the region. There were also those who were fascinated by the receding shoreline,

James Nachtwey/VIII/AP/Wide World Photos

The Aftermath of the 2004 Tsunami. **The corpses belonging to some of the over 300 000 people are seen here on the streets of Banda Ache, Indonesia, one of the most ravaged places hit by the tsunami of December 26, 2004.**

walking closer to it, and then finding themselves unable to find higher ground before the first wave hit. At that point, a number of people were helplessly pulled under the water, making escape from the second wave impossible.

Personal accounts of the tragedy were televised, giving the entire world a bird's-eye view of what happened. This level of international awareness coupled with the random nature of the tragedy and the destruction inflicted inspired citizens from all over the world and relief agencies alike to commit aid to the region. Similarly, governments from around the world helped contribute funds and goods to the relief effort. The heightened sense of generosity and concern for the victims of the tsunami renewed hopes of fostering a positive spirit in the global community.

angry disputes among European nations, and the United States and Canada have argued about the effects of acid rain on Canadian forests.

Today, such disputes represent a major obstacle to the challenge of meeting the threat of global warming. Measures to reduce the release of harmful gases into the atmosphere will be costly and could have significant negative effects on economic growth. What is most needed is a degree of international cooperation that would bring about major efforts to reduce pollution levels throughout the world. So far, there is little indication that advanced and developing nations are close to agreement on how the sacrifice is to be divided. International meetings convened to discuss how to implement the agreement hammered out at the Kyoto conference have been mired by the United States' refusal to join the Kyoto accord.

At the root of much of the concern about the environment is the worry that global population growth could eventually outstrip the capacity of the world to feed itself. Concern over excessive population growth, of course, dates back to the fears expressed in the early nineteenth century by the British economist Thomas Malthus, who worried that population growth would increase more rapidly than food supply. It peaked in the decades immediately following World War II, when a rise in world birthrates and a decline in infant mortality combined to fuel a dramatic increase in population in much of the Third World. The concern was set aside for a period after the 1970s, when the **Green Revolution** improved crop yields and statistical evidence appeared to suggest that the rate of population growth was declining in many countries of Asia and Latin America.

> The **Green Revolution** refers to the introduction of newly developed strains of wheat and rice that could significantly increase agricultural output; it began in the 1960s.

Yet some experts question whether increases in food production through technological innovation (in recent years, the Green Revolution has been supplemented by a "Blue Revolution" to increase food yields from the world's oceans, seas, and rivers) can keep up indefinitely with world population growth, which continues today, though at a slightly reduced rate from earlier levels. From a total of 2.5 billion people in 1950, world population rose to 5.7 billion in 1995 and is predicted to reach 10 billion in the middle of this century. Today, many eyes are focused on India, where the population recently surpassed one billion, and on China, where family planning programs have lost effectiveness in recent years and where precious rice lands have been turned to industrial or commercial use.

THE ARTS: MIRROR OF THE AGE

If, as the Spanish tenor Placido Domingo once observed, the arts are the signature of their age, what has been happening in literature, art, music, and architecture in recent decades is a refection of the evolving global response to the rapid changes taking place in human society today. This reaction has sometimes been referred to as *postmodernism*, although today's developments are much too diverse to be placed under a single label. Some of the arts are still experimenting with the modernist quest for the new and the radical. Others have begun to return to more traditional styles as a reaction against globalization and a response to the search for national and cultural identity in a bewildering world.

The most appropriate label for the contemporary cultural scene, in fact, is probably *pluralism*. The arts today are an eclectic hybrid, combining different movements, genres, and media, as well as incorporating different ethnic and national characteristics. There is no doubt that Western culture has strongly influenced the development of the arts throughout the world in recent decades. In fact, the process has gone in both directions as art forms from Africa and Asia have profoundly enriched the cultural scene in the West. One ironic illustration is that some of the best literature in the English and French languages today is being written in the nations that were once under British or French colonial rule. Today, global interchange in the arts is playing the same creative role that the exchange of technology between different regions played in stimulating the Industrial Revolution. As one Japanese composer declared not long ago, "I would like to develop in two directions at once: as a Japanese with respect to tradition, and as a westerner with respect to innovation. . . . In that way I can avoid isolation from the tradition and yet also push toward the future in each new work."[5]

Such a globalization of culture, however, has its price. Because of the penetration of Western culture throughout the Third World, local cultural forms are being eroded or destroyed as a result of contamination by Western music, mass television, and commercial hype. In what has been called the *cocacolaization* of world culture, multinational corporations such as Coca-Cola have pervaded the world, reducing culture to a marketable quality. While American cultural favourites like McDonald's, rock and roll, and Hollywood films are considered merely good marketing by some, others see it as Western cultural imperialism and a real cause for alarm. How does a society preserve its traditional culture when the young prefer to spend their evenings at a Hard Rock Café rather than attend a traditional folk opera or *wayang* puppet theatre? World conferences have been convened to safeguard traditional cultures from extinction, but is there sufficient time, money, or inclination to reverse the tide?

What do contemporary trends in the art world have to say about the changes that have occurred between the beginning and the end of the twentieth century? One reply is that the euphoric optimism of artists during the age of Picasso and Stravinsky has been seriously tempered a century later. Naiveté has been replaced by cynicism or irony as protection against the underlying pessimism of the current age.

One dominant characteristic of the new art is its silence—its reserve in expressing the dissonance and disillusioning events of the past century. It would appear that we entered the twentieth century with too many expectations, hopes that had been fuelled by the promise of revolution and scientific discoveries. Yet, however extraordinary the recent advances in medicine, genetics, telecommunications, computer technology, and space exploration have been, humankind seems to remain as perplexed as ever. It is no wonder that despite the impressive recent advances in science, human beings entered the new millennium a little worn and subdued.

What, then, are the prospects for the coming years? One critic has complained that postmodernism, "with its sad air of the parades gone by,"[6] is spent and exhausted. Others suggest that there is nothing new left to say that has not been expressed previously and more effectively. The public itself appears satiated and desensitized after a century of "shocking" art and, as in the case of world events, almost incapable of being shocked any further. Human sensibilities

have been irrevocably altered by the media, by technology, and especially by the cataclysmic events that have taken place in our times. Perhaps the twentieth century was the age of revolt, representing "freedom from," while the next hundred years will be an era seeking "freedom for."

CRITICAL THINKING QUESTIONS

1. Some non-Western countries do not consider human rights as inalienable rights, but as a manifestation of Western cultural values that do not reflect the values of their cultures. What do you think?

2. Has the West's emphasis on upholding individual rights resulted in the decline of a nurturing community? Has the West rejected the old adage "it takes a village" to properly raise a child?

3. In *Jihad vs. McWorld,* the author discusses the Americanization of the world and the reaction of other countries to Western cultural imperialism. How is globalization a carrier of American values and ideas? What concerns have been raised by the anti-globalization movement?

4. Canada's concept of "responsibility to protect"—the responsibility of states to protect people from avoidable catastrophe—which was proposed to the UN, suggests that governments cannot hide behind the shield of sovereignty when committing crimes against their citizens. There is some agreement on this concept when discussing cases like Sudan and the crisis in Darfur. But could the concept also apply to the government's responsibility to Aboriginal peoples in Canada? How has the Canadian government fared in its "responsibility to protect" Canada's Aboriginal peoples?

Downtown Beijing Today. Deng Xiaoping's policy of four modernizations has had a dramatic visual effect on the capital city of Beijing, as evidenced by this photo of skyscrapers thrusting up beyond the walls of the fifteenth-century Imperial City.

CHAPTER NOTES

1. Fukuyama's original thesis was expressed in "The End of History," *National Interest,* Summer 1989. He has defended his views in Timothy Burns, ed., *After History? Francis Fukuyama and His Critics* (Lanham, Md.: Rowman and Littlefield, 1994). Fukuyama contends—rightly in our view—that his concept of the "end of history" has been widely misinterpreted. We hope we have not done so in these comments.

2. Samuel P. Huntington, *The Clash of Civilizations and the Remaking of the World Order* (New York: Simon & Schuster, 1996). An earlier version was published under the title "The Clash of Civilizations?" in *Foreign Affairs,* Summer 1993.

3. Henny Sender, "Now for the Hard Part," *Far Eastern Economic Review,* September 25, 1997.

4. Alvin Toffler and Heidi Toffler, *Creating a New Civilization: The Politics of the Third Wave* (Atlanta: Turner Publishing, 1995).

5. The composer was Toru Takemitsu. See Robert P. Moran, *Twentieth-Century Music* (New York: Norton, 1991), p. 422.

6. Herbert Muschamp, "The Miracle in Bilbao," *New York Times Magazine,* September 7, 1997, p. 72.

Suggested Readings

1. The Changing Social and Political Order

For a useful introduction to the Industrial Revolution, see D. Landes, *The Unbound Prometheus: Technological Change and Industrial Development in Western Europe from 1750 to the Present* (Cambridge: Cambridge University Press, 1969). More technical but also of value is P. Mathias and J. A. David, eds., *The First Industrial Revolution* (Oxford: Basil Blackwell, 1989). A provocative analysis of the roots of industrialization is D. Landes, *The Wealth and Poverty of Nations: Why Some Are So Rich and Some So Poor* (New York: Norton, 1998).

On the phenomenon of population growth in the West, see T. McKeown, *The Rise of Population* (London: Arnold, 1976). Housing reform is discussed in N. Bullock and J. Read, *The Movement for Housing Reform in Germany and France, 1840–1914* (Cambridge: Cambridge University Press, 1985), and E. Gauldie, *Cruel Habitations: A History of Working-Class Housing, 1790–1918* (London: Allen and Unwin, 1974). On Karl Marx, the standard work is D. McLellan, *Karl Marx: His Life and Thought* (New York: Harper and Row, 1973). On Freud, see P. Gay, *Freud: A Life for Our Time* (New York: Norton, 1988).

For an overview of the final decades of the Chinese Empire, see F. Wakeman Jr., *The Fall of Imperial China* (New York: Free Press, 1975). A stimulating comparison between Western and Chinese experiences with industrialization is K. Pomeranz, *The Great Divergence: China, Europe, and the Making of the Modern World Economy* (Princeton, N.J.: Princeton University Press, 2000). For a recent biography of the Chinese revolutionary Sun Yat-sen, see Marie-Claire Bergère, *Sun Yat-sen* (Stanford, Calif.: Stanford University Press, 1998).

For a reinterpretation of Victorian society, see P. Gay, *Pleasure Wars: The Bourgeois Experience, Victoria to Freud* (New York: Norton, 1998). On the intellectual scene, see William R. Everdell, *The First Moderns: Profiles in the Origins of Twentieth Century Thought* (Chicago: University of Chicago Press, 1997), and Jacques Barzun's impressive overview, *From Dawn to Decadence: 500 Years of Western Cultural Life* (New York: Harper Perennial, 2001). On trends in modern art, see Robert Hughes, *The Shock of the New* (New York: Knopf, 1991).

2. The High Tide of Imperialism in the Non-Western World

There are a number of recent works on the subject of imperialism and colonialism. For a study that focuses on the complex interaction between the colonial powers and the subject peoples, see D. K. Fieldhouse, *The West and the Third World: Trade, Colonialism, Dependence, and Development* (Oxford: Blackwell, 1999). In *Ornamentalism: How the British Saw Their Empire* (Oxford: Oxford University Press, 2000), D. Cannadine argues that it was class, not race, that motivated British policy in its colonies. Also see W. Baumgart, *Imperialism: The Idea and Reality of British and French Colonial Expansion, 1880–1914* (Oxford: Oxford University Press, 1982), and H. M. Wright, ed., *The "New Imperialism": Analysis of Late Nineteenth Century Expansion* (New York: DC Heath, 1976). On the new technology, see D. R. Headrick, *The Tentacles of Progress: Technology Transfer in the Age of Imperialism, 1850–1940* (Oxford: Oxford University Press, 1988).

On the imperialist age in Africa, see T. Pakenham, *The Scramble for Africa* (New York: Random House, 1991). For India, see C. A. Bayly, *Indian Society and the Making of the British Empire* (Cambridge: Cambridge University Press, 1988).

3. War And Revolution: World War I and Its Aftermath

A good starting point for the causes of World War I is J. Joll, *The Origins of the First World War* (London: Macmillan, 1984). Two good recent accounts on the war are M. Gilbert, *The First World War* (New York: Henry Holt, 1994), and J. M. Winter's lavishly illustrated *Experience of World War I* (New York: Oxford University Press, 1989). A good overview by a renowned military historian is J. Keegan, *The First World War* (New York: Knopf, 1999). For a dated but dramatic account, see B. Tuchman, *The Guns of August* (New York: Ballantine Books, 1994). On the inter-war period, see R. I. Sontag, *A Broken World, 1919–1939* (New York: Harper and Row, 1971), and S. Marks, *The Illusion of Peace: Europe's International Relations, 1918–1933* (New York: Palgrave Macmillan, 2003). On the Great Depression, see C. P. Kindleberger, *The World in Depression, 1929–1939,* rev. ed. (Berkeley, Calif.: University of California Press, 1986), and P. Brenden, *The Dark Valley: A Panorama of the 1930s* (New York: Knopf, 2000). For the revolution in musical composition, see R. P. Morgan, *Twentieth-Century Music: A History of Musical Style in Modern Europe and America* (New York: Norton, 1991). For an introduction to modern art, see N. Stangos, *Concepts of Modern Art: From Fauvism to Postmodernism* (London: Thames and Hudson, 1994), and J.-L. Forrier, ed., *Art of the Twentieth Century: The History of Art Year by Year from 1900 to 1999* (Paris: Editions du Chene, 2002).

A good introduction to the Russian Revolution can be found in S. Fitzpatrick, *The Russian Revolution, 1917–1932* (New York: Oxford University Press, 1982), and R. V. Daniels, *Red October* (New York: Charles Scribners Sons, 1967). On Lenin, see R. Service, *Lenin: A Biography* (Cambridge, Mass.: Harvard University Press, 2001), and A. B. Ulam, *The Bolsheviks* (New York: Harvard University Press, 1965).

4. Nationalism, Revolution, and Dictatorship: Africa, Asia, and Latin America from 1919 to 1939

The classic study of nationalism in the non-Western world is R. Emerson, *From Empire to Nation* (Boston: Beacon Press, 1960). For an inquiry into the origins of the concept of nationalism, see B. Anderson, *Imagined Communities* (London: Verso, 1983), and P. Chatterjee, *The Nation and Its Fragments: Colonial and Postcolonial Histories* (Princeton, N.J.: Princeton University Press, 1993).

There have been a number of interesting studies of Mahatma Gandhi and his ideas. For example, see J. M. Brown, *Gandhi: Prisoner of Hope* (New Haven, Conn.: Yale University Press, 1989), and S. Wolpert, *Gandhi's Passion: The Life and Legacy of Mahatma Gandhi* (Oxford: Oxford University Press, 1999).

For a general survey of events in the Middle East, see E. C. Bogle, *The Modern Middle East: From Imperialism to Freedom, 1800–1958* (Upper Saddle River, N.J.: Prentice Hall, 1996). A more specialized treatment is H. M. Sachar, *The Emergence of the Middle East, 1914–1924* (New York: Knopf, 1969). On the early Chinese republic, a good study is L. Yu-sheng, *The Crisis of Chinese Consciousness: Radical Antitraditionalism in the May Fourth Era* (Madison, Wis.: University of Wisconsin Press, 1979). The rise of the Chinese Communist Party is discussed in A. Dirlik, *The Origins of Chinese Communism* (Oxford: Oxford University Press, 1989). Also see L. Eastman, *The Abortive Revolution: China Under Nationalist Rule, 1927–1937* (Cambridge: Harvard University Press, 1974). For an overview of Latin American history in the inter-war period, see E. Williamson, *The Penguin History of Latin America* (Harmondsworth, U.K.: Penguin, 1992). Also see J. Franco, *The Modern Culture of Latin America: Society and the Artist* (Harmondsworth, U.K.: Penguin, 1970).

5. The Crisis Deepens: The Outbreak of World War II

For a general study of fascism, see S. G. Payne, *A History of Fascism* (Madison, Wis.: University of Wisconsin Press, 1996). The best biography of Mussolini is D. Mack Smith, *Mussolini* (New York: Knopf, 1982). Two brief but sound surveys of Nazi Germany are J. Spielvogel, *Hitler and Nazi Germany: A History,* 3rd ed. (Englewood Cliffs, N.J.: Prentice Hall, 1996), and J. Bendersky, *A History of Nazi Germany* (Chicago: Nelson-Hall, 1985). On Hitler, see A. Bullock, *Hitler: A Study in Tyranny* (New York: Harper Row, 1964), and Bullock's recent *Hitler, 1889–1936: Hubris* (New York: Norton, 1999). For an analysis of how Hitler changed Germany, see J. Lucas, *The Hitler of History* (New York: Henry Holt, 1997).

General works on World War II include M. K. Dziewanowski, *War at Any Price: World War II in Europe, 1939–1945,* 2nd ed. (Englewood Cliffs, N.J.: Prentice Hall, 1991), and G. Weinberg, *A World at Arms: A Global History of World War II* (Cambridge: Cambridge University Press, 1994). On the Holocaust, see R. Hilberg, *The Destruction of the European Jews,* rev. ed., 3 vols. (New York: Holmes and Meier, 1985), and L. Yahil, *The Holocaust* (New York: Oxford University Press, 1990). On the war in the Pacific, see R. Spector, *Eagle against the Sun: The American War with Japan* (New York: The Free Press, 1985), and H. Cook and T. Cook, *Japan at War: An Oral History* (New York: New Press, 1992).

6. In the Grip of the Cold War: The Breakdown of the Yalta Agreement

There is a substantial literature on the Cold War. Two general accounts are R. B. Levering, *The Cold War, 1945–1972* (Arlington Heights, Ill.: Harlan Davidson, 1982), and B. A. Weisberger, *Cold War, Cold Peace: The United States and Russia Since 1945* (New York: American Heritage, 1984). Assigning blame for the Cold War to the Soviet Union are H. Feis, *From Trust to Terror: The Onset of the Cold War, 1945–1950* (New York: Norton, 1970), and A. Ulam, *The Rivals: America and Russia Since World War II* (New York: Viking, 1971). Revisionist studies include J. Kolko and G. Kolko, *The Limits of Power: The World and United States Foreign Policy, 1945–1954* (New York: Harper and Row, 1972), and W. La Feber, *America, Russia, and the Cold War, 1945–1966,* 2nd ed. (New York: Viking, 1972). On the end of the Cold War, see W. G. Hyland, *The Cold War Is Over* (New York: Times Books, 1990), and B. Denitch, *The End of the Cold War* (Minneapolis: University of Minnesota Press, 1990).

Recent studies on the Cold War in Asia include O. A. Westad, *Cold War and Revolution: Soviet-American Rivalry and the Origins of the Chinese Civil War* (New York: Columbia University Press, 1993), D. A. Mayers, *Cracking the Monolith: U.S. Policy Against the Sino-Soviet Alliance, 1949–1955* (Baton Rouge, La.: Louisiana State University Press, 1986), and S. Goncharov, J. W. Lewis, and Xue Litai, *Uncertain Partners: Stalin, Mao, and the Korean War* (Stanford, Calif.: Stanford University Press, 1993). For a retrospective account, see J. L. Gaddis, *We Now Know: Rethinking Cold War History* (Oxford: Oxford University Press, 1997). On the role of Vietnam in the Cold War, see F. Logevall, *Choosing War: The Lost Chance for Peace and the Escalation of the War in Vietnam* (Berkeley, Calif.: University of California Press, 1999), W. J. Duiker, *U.S. Containment Policy and the Conflict in Indochina* (Stanford, Calif.: Stanford University Press, 1995), and M. Lind, *Vietnam: The Necessary War* (New York: The Free Press, 1999).

7. The Rise and Fall of Communism in the Soviet Union and Eastern Europe

For a general overview of Soviet society, see D. K. Shipler, *Russia: Broken Idols, Solemn Dreams* (New York: Time Books, 1983). On the Khrushchev years, see E. Crankshaw, *Khrushchev: A Career* (New York: Viking, 1966). Also see S. F. Cohen, *Rethinking the Soviet Experience* (New York: Oxford University Press, 1985). For an internal view, see V. Zubok and K. Pleshakov, *Inside the Kremlin's Cold War: From Stalin to Khrushchev* (Cambridge: Harvard University Press, 1996). For an inquiry into the reasons for the Soviet collapse, see R. Strayer, *Why Did the Soviet Union Collapse? Understanding Historical Change* (New York: ME Sharpe, 1998).

A number of books have appeared on the post-Soviet era in Russia. See, for example, W. Laqueur, *Soviet Union 2000: Reform or Revolution?* (New York: St. Martin's Press, 1990), and C. Freeland, *Sale of the Century: Russia's Wild Ride from Communism to Capitalism* (New York: Crown Publishers, 2000).

For a general study of the Soviet satellites in Eastern Europe, see A. Brown and J. Gary, *Culture and Political Changes in Communist States* (London: Macmillan, 1977), and S. Fischer-Galati, *Eastern Europe in the 1980s* (Boulder, Colo.: Westview Press, 1981). On Yugoslavia, see L. J. Cohen and P. Warwick, *Political Cohesion in a Fragile Mosaic* (Boulder, Colo.: Westview Press, 1983). For an account of the collapse of the satellite system, see T. G. Ash, *The Magic Lantern: The Revolution of '89 Witnessed in Warsaw, Budapest, Berlin, and Prague* (New York: Random House, 1990).

8. Post-War Europe: On the Path to Unity?

For a general survey of post-war European history, see W. Laqueur, *Europe in Our Time* (New York: Viking/Penguin, 1992). The rebuilding of Europe after World War II is examined in A. Milward, *The Reconstruction of Western Europe, 1945–1951* (Berkeley, Calif.: University of California Press, 1984), and M. Hogan, *The Marshall Plan: America, Britain, and the Reconstruction of Western Europe, 1947–1952* (New York: Cambridge University Press, 1987). On the building of common institutions in Western Europe, see S. Henig, *The Uniting of Europe: From Discord to Concord* (London: Routledge, 1997).

For a survey of West Germany, see H. A. Turner, *Germany from Partition to Reunification* (New Haven, Conn.: Yale University Press, 1992). France under de Gaulle is examined in A. Shennan, *De Gaulle* (New York: Longman, 1993). On Great Britain, see K. O. Morgan, *The People's Peace: British History, 1945–1990* (Oxford: Oxford University Press, 1992). On the recent history of Europe, see E. J. Evans, *Thatcher and Thatcherism* (London: Routledge, 1997), S. Baumann-Reynolds, *François Mitterrand* (Westport, Conn.: Praeger, 1995), and K. Jarausch, *The Rush to German Unity* (New York: Oxford University Press, 1994).

On social conditions in Europe, see A. Sampson, *The New Europeans* (London: Heron Books, 1968), and T. G. Ash, *A History of the Present: Essays, Sketches, and Dispatches from Europe in the 1990s* (New York: Random House, 1999). The problems of guest workers and immigrants are examined in J. Miller, *Foreign Workers in Western Europe* (New York: Praeger, 1981). On the development of the environmental movement, see M. O'Neill, *Green Parties and Political Change in Contemporary Europe* (Aldershot, U.K.: Ashgate, 1997).

On the changing role of women in European society, see D. Meyer, *Sex and Power: The Rise of Women in America, Russia, Sweden and Italy* (Middletown, Conn.: Wesleyan University Press, 1987), and C. Duchen, *Women's Rights and Women's Lives in France, 1944–1968* (London: Routledge, 1994). A broader historical view is presented in B. G. Smith, *Changing Lives: Women in European History Since 1700* (Lexington, Mass.: DC Heath, 1989). Also see T. Keefe, *Simone de Beauvoir* (New York: St. Martin's Press, 1998).

For a general view of post-war thought, see R. N. Stromberg, *European Intellectual History Since 1789*, 5th ed.

(Englewood Cliffs, N.J.: Prentice Hall, 1990). On contemporary art, consult R. Lambert, *Cambridge Introduction to the History of Art: The Twentieth Century* (Cambridge: Cambridge University Press, 1981). Also see the bibliography in Chapter 1.

9. Post-War United States: The Rise of a Hegemon

For a general survey of American history, see S. Thernstrom, *A History of the American People,* 2nd ed. (San Diego, Calif.: Harcourt Brace, 1989). The Truman administration is covered in R. J. Donovan, *Tumultuous Years: The Presidency of Harry S Truman* (New York: Norton, 1997). Also see David McCullough's prize-winning biography, *Truman* (New York: Simon Schuster, 1992). On Eisenhower, see S. Ambrose, *Eisenhower: The President* (New York: Simon and Schuster, 1984). For an insider's account of Camelot, see A. Schlesinger Jr., *A Thousand Days: John F. Kennedy in the White House* (Boston: Houghton Mifflin, 1965). On the turbulent decade of the 1960s, consult W. O'Neill, *Coming Apart: An Informal History of America in the 1960s* (Chicago: Quadrangle Books, 1971). On Nixon and Watergate, see J. A. Lukas, *Nightmare: The Underside of the Nixon Years* (New York: Viking, 1976). Other insightful works include B. Glad, *Jimmy Carter: From Plains to the White House* (New York: Norton, 1980), and G. Wills, *Reagan's America: Innocents at Home* (New York: Doubleday, 1987).

On social issues, see W. Nugent, *The Structure of American Social History* (Bloomington, Ind.: Indiana University Press, 1981). Popular culture is treated in R. Maltby, ed., *Passing Parade: A History of Popular Culture in the Twentieth Century* (New York: Oxford University Press, 1989). On the women's liberation movement, see D. Bouchier, *The Feminist Challenge: The Movement for Women's Liberation in Britain and the United States* (London: Macmillan, 1983), and A. Cherlin, *Marriage, Divorce, Remarriage* (Cambridge, Mass.: Harvard University Press, 1981). D. J. Garrow, *Martin Luther King Jr. and the Southern Christian Leadership Conference* (New York: Morrow, 1986), discusses the emergence of the civil rights movement. For the most accessible introduction to American literature, consult *The Norton Anthology of American Literature,* shorter 4th ed. (New York: Norton, 1995). For an overview of American art since the 1960s, see I. Sandler's fascinating *Art of the Postmodern Era* (New York: HarperCollins, 1996).

10. Canada: The Rise of a Middle Power

For general surveys of Canadian history, see D. Morton, *A Short History of Canada* (McClelland and Stewart, 2001),

and D. Francis, D. B. Smith, and R. Jones, *Destinies: Canadian History Since Confederation,* 4th ed. (Toronto: Harcourt Canada, 2000). For a political, economic, and diplomatic survey of post-war Canada, see R. Bothwell, I. Drummond, and J. English, *Canada Since 1945: Power, Politics and Provincialism,* rev. ed. (Toronto: University of Toronto Press, 1989). For a leftist perspective, see A. Finkel, *Our Lives: Canada after 1945* (Toronto: James Lorimer, 1997).

On the prime ministers, see M. Bliss, *Right Honourable Men: The Descent of Canadian Politics from Macdonald to Mulroney* (Toronto: HarperCollins, 2004). The King years are covered in J. L. Granatstein, *Mackenzie King: His Life and World* (Toronto: McGraw-Hill Ryerson, 1977), and *Canada's War: The Politics of the Mackenzie King Government* (Toronto: Oxford University Press, 1975). R. Whitaker's *The Government Party* (Toronto: University of Toronto Press, 1977) is also indispensable. Diefenbaker is well covered in D. Smith, *Rogue Tory: The Life and Legend of John G. Diefenbaker* (Toronto, Macfarlane Walter and Ross, 1995). J. English offers a masterful biography of Pearson in *Shadow of Heaven* (Toronto: Lester and Orpen Dennys, 1989) and *The Worldly Years* (Toronto: Vintage, 1993). Trudeau is well covered in S. Clarkson and C. McCall, *Trudeau and Our Times,* 2 vols. (Toronto: McClelland and Stewart, 1990, 1994) and A. Cohen and J. L. Granatstein, eds., *Trudeau's Shadow* (Toronto: Vintage, 1998). J. Sawatsky, *Mulroney: The Politics of Ambition* (Toronto: Macfarlane Walter and Ross, 1991) is the best text to emerge on the Conservative prime minister, and L. Martin, *Iron Man: The Defiant Reign of Jean Chrétien* (Toronto: Viking, 2003) is the best text on the Liberal prime minister.

On Canadian national identities, see R. Cook, *Canada, Quebec and the Uses of Nationalism* (Toronto: McClelland and Stewart, 1986), and J. R. Saul, *Reflections of a Siamese Twin* (Toronto: Viking, 1997). On Quebec nationalism, see K. McRoberts, *Quebec: Social Change and Political Crisis,* 3rd ed. (Toronto: McClelland and Stewart, 1988), and P.-A. Linteau, R. Durocher, and J.-C. Robert, *Quebec Since 1930* (Toronto: Lorimer, 1991). On Western Canada, see G. Friesen, *The Canadian Prairies,* rev. ed. (Toronto: University of Toronto Press, 1987). For a conservative nationalist view of the 1960s, see G. Grant, *Lament for a Nation* (Toronto: McClelland and Stewart, 1965). Canadian cultural identities are discussed in W. Dodge, ed., *Boundaries of Identity* (Toronto: Lester, 1992), and N. Bissoondath, *Selling Illusions: The Cult of Multiculturalism in Canada* (Toronto: Penguin, 1994). On Aboriginal peoples, see J. R. Miller, *Skyscrapers Hide the Heavens,* rev. ed. (Toronto: University of Toronto Press, 1991).

On Canadian foreign policy, see J. L. Granatstein and N. Hillmer, *Empire to Umpire: Canada and the World*

(Toronto: Copp Clark Longman, 1994). M. Hart, *A Trading Nation: Canadian Trade Policy from Colonialism to Globalization* (Vancouver: University of British Columbia Press, 2002) provides a useful overview of international trade policy. On Canada-U.S. relations, consult the useful overviews by R. Bothwell, *Canada and the United States: The Politics of Partnership* (Toronto: University of Toronto Press, 1992), and J. H. Thompson and S. Randall, *Canada and the United States: Ambivalent Allies,* 2nd ed. (Montreal: McGill-Queen's University Press, 1997). An exceptional overview of the Trudeau years is J. L. Granatstein and R. Bothwell, *Pirouette: Pierre Trudeau and Canadian Foreign Policy* (Toronto: University of Toronto Press, 1990). Also useful are the annual volumes published in the *Canada in World Affairs* and the *Canada among Nations* series.

11. China, Taiwan, and the "Little Tigers"

There are a large number of useful studies on post-war China. The most comprehensive treatment of the Communist period is M. Meisner, *Mao's China, and After: A History of the People's Republic* (New York: The Free Press, 1986). For documents, see M. Selden, *The People's Republic of China: A Documentary History of Revolutionary Change* (New York: Monthly Review Press, 1978).

There are many studies on various aspects of the Communist period in China. For a detailed analysis of economic and social issues, see F. Schurmann, *Ideology and Organization in Communist China* (Berkeley, Calif.: University of California Press, 1968). The Cultural Revolution is treated dramatically in S. Karnow, *Mao and China: Inside China's Cultural Revolution* (New York: Viking, 1972). For an individual account, see the celebrated book by Nien Cheng, *Life and Death in Shanghai* (New York: Grove Press, 1986), and also Liang Heng and J. Shapiro, *Son of the Revolution* (New York: Vintage, 1986). For the early post-Mao period, see O. Schell, *To Get Rich Is Glorious* (New York: Pantheon Books, 1986). On the Tiananmen incident, see L. Feigon's eyewitness account, *China Rising: The Meaning of Tiananmen* (Chicago: IR Dee, 1990). On China's dissident movement, see Liu Binyan, *China's Crisis, China's Hope* (Cambridge: Harvard University Press, 1990), and A. Nathan, *China's Transition* (New York: Columbia University Press, 1999).

On economic and political conditions in post-Mao China, see H. Harding, *China's Second Revolution: Reform after Mao* (Washington, D.C.: Brookings, 1987), K. Lieberthal, *Governing China: From Revolution through Reform* (New York: Norton, 1995), and R. MacFarquhar, ed., *The Politics of China: The Eras of Mao and Deng*, 2nd ed. (Cambridge: Cambridge University Press, 1993). Also see Bruce Gilley,

Tiger on the Brink: Jiang Zemin and China's New Elite (Berkeley, Calif.: University of California Press, 1998). Social conditions are considered in G. Barmé, *In the Red: On Contemporary Chinese Culture* (New York: Columbia University Press, 2000). On the controversial issue of Tibet, see T. Shakya, *The Dragon in the Land of Snows: The History of Modern Tibet Since 1947* (New York: Columbia University Press, 1999). China's changing relationship with the United States is dealt with provocatively in R. Bernstein and R. Munro, *The Coming Conflict with China* (New York: Knopf, 1997).

For the most comprehensive introduction to twentieth-century Chinese art, consult M. Sullivan, *Arts and Artists of Twentieth-Century China* (Berkeley, Calif.: University of California Press, 1996). On literature, see the chapters on Ding Ling and her contemporaries in J. Spence, *The Gate of Heavenly Peace* (New York: Viking, 1981). Also see E. Widmer and D. D. Wang, eds., *From May Fourth to June Fourth: Fiction and Film in Twentieth-Century China* (Cambridge: Harvard University Press, 1993), and J. Lou and H. Goldblatt, *The Columbia Anthology of Modern Chinese Literature* (New York: Columbia University Press, 1995).

On the four Little Tigers and their economic development, see E. F. Vogel, *The Four Little Dragons: The Spread of Industrialization in East Asia* (Cambridge, Mass.: Harvard University Press, 1991), J. W. Morley, ed., *Driven by Growth: Political Change in the Asia-Pacific Region* (Armonk, N.Y.: ME Sharpe, 1993), and J. Woronoff, *Asia's Miracle Economies* (New York: ME Sharpe, 1986). For individual treatments of the Little Tigers, see H. Sohn, *Authoritarianism and Opposition in South Korea* (London: Routledge, 1989), D. F. Simon, *Taiwan: Beyond the Economic Miracle* (Armonk, N.Y.: ME Sharpe, 1992), Lee Kuan-yew, *From Third World to First: The Singapore Story, 1965–2000* (New York: HarperCollins, 2000), and K. Rafferty, *City on the Rocks: Hong Kong's Uncertain Future* (London: Penguin, 1991).

12. Emerging Africa

For a general survey of African history, see J. Reader, *Africa: A Biography of the Continent* (New York: Knopf, 1998), R. Oliver, *The African Experience* (New York: HarperCollins, 1992), which contains interesting essays on a variety of themes, and K. Shillington, *History of Africa* (New York: St. Martin's Press, 1989), which takes a chronological and geographical approach and includes excellent maps and illustrations. Two worthy treatments are B. Davidson, *Africa in History: Themes and Outlines,* rev. ed. (New York: Macmillan, 1991), and P. Curtin et al., *African History* (New York: Longman, 1995).

On nationalist movements, see P. Gifford and W. R. Louis, eds., *The Transfer of Power in Africa* (New Haven, Conn.: Yale University Press, 1982). For a poignant analysis of the hidden costs of nation building, see N. F. Mostert, *The Epic of South Africa's Creation and the Tragedy of the Xhosa People* (London: Jonathan Cape, 1992). For a survey of economic conditions, see *Sub-Saharan Africa: From Crisis to Sustainable Growth* (Washington, D.C.: World Bank, 1989), issued by the World Bank. Also see J. Illiffe, *The African Poor* (Cambridge: Cambridge University Press, 1987). On political events, see S. Decalo, *Coups and Army Rule in Africa* (New Haven, Conn.: Yale University Press, 1990).

On African literature, see D. Wright, *New Directions in African Fiction* (New York: Twayne, 1997), L. S. Klein, ed., *African Literatures in the Twentieth Century: A Guide* (New York: Ungar Publishing, 1986), and C. H. Bruner, ed., *African Women's Writing* (London: Heinemann, 1993).

13. Carving Up the Middle East

Good general surveys of the modern Middle East include A. Goldschmidt Jr., *A Concise History of the Middle East* (Boulder, Colo.: Westview Press, 2001), and G. E. Perry, *The Middle East: Fourteen Islamic Centuries* (Upper Saddle River, N.J.: Prentice Hall, 1996).

On Israel and the Palestinian question, see N. Finklestein, *Image and Reality of the Israel-Palestine Conflict* (London: Verso, 2003), and B. Wasserstein, *Divided Jerusalem: The Struggle for the Holy City* (New Haven, Conn.: Yale University Press, 2001). On U.S. involvement in the Middle East, see R. Khalidi, *Resurrecting Empire: Western Footprints and America's Perilous Path in the Middle East* (Boston: Beacon Press, 2004). The issue of oil is examined in G. Luciani, *The Oil Companies and the Arab World* (New York: St. Martin's Press, 1984). For expert analysis on the current situation in the region, see B. Lewis, *What Went Wrong? Western Impact and Middle Eastern Response* (New York: Oxford University Press, 2001), and P. L. Bergen, *Holy War, Inc.: Inside the Secret World of Osama bin Laden* (New York: The Free Press, 2001).

On the Iranian Revolution, see S. Bakash, *The Reign of the Ayatollahs* (New York: Cambridge University Press, 1984), and B. Rubin, *Iran Since the Revolution* (Boulder, Colo.: Westview Press, 1985). On politics, see R. R. Anderson, R. F. Seibert, and J. G. Wagner, *Politics and Change in the Middle East: Sources of Conflict and Accommodation* (Englewood Cliffs, N.J.: Simon and Schuster, 1993). For a general anthology of literature in the Middle East, see J. Kritzeck, *Modern Islamic Literature from 1800 to the Present* (New York: Holt, Rinehart and Winston, 1970). For a scholarly but accessible overview, also

see M. M. Badawi, *A Short History of Modern Arabic Literature* (Oxford: Oxford University Press, 1993). For an introduction to women's issues, see F. Mernissi, *Beyond the Veil: Male-Female Dynamics in a Modern Muslim Society* (Bloomington, Ind.: Indiana University Press, 1987), and L. Ahmed, *Women and Gender in Islam* (New Haven, Conn.: Yale University Press, 1992).

14. The Emergence of Independent States from South to East Asia

For a recent survey of contemporary Indian history, see S. Wolpert, *A New History of India*, 6th ed. (New York: Oxford University Press, 1999). For two interesting accounts written for nonspecialists, see B. Crossette, *India: Facing the Twenty-First Century* (Bloomington, Ind.: Indiana University Press, 1993), and S. Tharoor, *India: From Midnight to the Millennium* (New York: Arcade Publishing, 1997). Also see P. Brass, *The New Cambridge History of India: The Politics of India Since Independence* (Cambridge: Cambridge University Press, 1990), Ishrat Husain, *Pakistan: The Economy of an Elitist State* (Karachi, Pakistan: Oxford University Press, 1999), and C. Baxter, *Bangladesh: From a Nation to a State* (Boulder, Colo.: Westview Press, 1997). A recent overview, packed with interesting ideas, is S. Khilnani, *The Idea of India* (New York: Farrar, Straus and Giroux, 1998).

On the period surrounding independence, see the dramatic account by L. Collins and D. Lapierre, *Freedom at Midnight* (New York: Avon Books, 1975). On Indira Gandhi, see K. Bhatia, *Indira: A Biography of Prime Minister Gandhi* (New York: Praeger, 1974).

For a useful anthology of Indian fiction since independence, see S. Rushdie and E. West, eds., *Mirror Work* (New York: Henry Holt, 1999), and S. Tharu and K. Lalita, eds., *Women Writing in India*, vol. 2 (New York: The Feminist Press, 1993).

For an introductory survey of modern Southeast Asia with a strong emphasis on recent events, see D. R. SarDesai, *Southeast Asia: Past and Present*, 2nd ed. (Boulder, Colo.: Westview Press, 1989). For a more scholarly approach, see D. J. Steinberg, ed., *In Search of Southeast Asia*, 2nd ed. (Honolulu: University of Hawaii Press, 1985). On Thailand, see P. Phongpaichit and C. Baker, *Thailand's Crisis* (Singapore: Institute of Southeast Asian Studies, 2001). The best overall survey of the Philippines is D. J. Steinberg, *The Philippines: A Singular and a Plural Place* (Boulder, Colo.: Westview Press, 1994). For a recent treatment of politics in Singapore, see R. Vasil, *Governing Singapore: A History of National Development and Democracy* (Singapore: Allen and Unwin, 2000). For insight into the problem of racial divisions in Malaysia, see M. bin

Mohamad, *The Malay Dilemma* (Kuala Lumpur: Federal Publications, 1970).

There is a rich selection of materials on modern Indonesia. On the Sukarno era, see J. Legge, *Sukarno* (New York: Praeger, 1972). On the Suharto era and its origins, see M. Vatikiotis, *Indonesian Politics under Suharto* (London: Routledge, 1993). The most up-to-date treatment of Indonesia in its present state of crisis is G. Lloyd and S. Smith, eds., *Indonesia Today: Challenges of History* (Singapore: Institute for Southeast Asia Studies, 2001). Most of the literature on Indochina in recent decades has dealt with the Vietnam War and related conflicts in Laos and Cambodia. On conditions in Vietnam since the end of the war, see R. Shaplen, *Bitter Victory* (New York: Harper and Row, 1986), a study by a veteran journalist, and W. J. Duiker, *Vietnam: Revolution in Transition,* 2nd ed. (Boulder, Colo.: Westview Press, 1995). For an excellent anthology of contemporary Vietnamese fiction, see *Vietnam: A Traveler's Literary Companion* (San Francisco: Whereabouts Press, 1996).

For a contemporary treatment of economic conditions in Japan, see D. Flath, *The Japanese Economy* (Oxford: Oxford University Press, 2000). Japanese social issues are treated in R. J. Hendry, *Understanding Japanese Society* (London: Routledge, 1987), and T. C. Bestor, *Neighborhood Tokyo* (Stanford, Calif.: Stanford University Press, 1989). Books attempting to explain Japanese economic issues have become a growth industry. The classic account of the Japanese miracle is E. F. Vogel, *Japan as Number One: Lessons for America* (Cambridge, Mass.: Harvard University Press, 1979). For a provocative response providing insight into Japan's current economic weakness, see J. Woronoff, *Japan as—Anything but—Number One* (Armonk, N.Y.: ME Sharpe, 1991). On the role of government in promoting business in Japan, see C. Johnson, *MITI and the Japanese Miracle* (Stanford, Calif.: Stanford University Press, 1982). For the impact of economics on society, see R. J. Smith, *Kurusu: The Price of Progress in a Japanese Village* (Stanford, Calif.: Stanford University Press, 1978).

15. Latin American Dictatorships and Emerging Democracies

For general surveys of Latin American history, see E. B. Burns, *Latin America: A Concise Interpretive Survey,* 4th ed. (Englewood Cliffs, N.J.: Prentice Hall, 1986), and E. Williamson, *The Penguin History of Latin America* (London: Penguin, 1992). Also see T. E. Skidmore and P. H. Smith, *Modern Latin America,* 3rd ed. (New York: Oxford University Press, 1992). On the role of the military, see A. Rouquié, *The Military and the State in Latin America* (Berkeley, Calif.: University of California Press, 1987).

U.S.-Latin American relations are examined in B. Wood, *The Dismantling of the Good Neighbor Policy* (Austin, Tex.: University of Texas Press, 1985). For individual countries examined in this chapter, see L. A. Pérez, *Cuba: Between Reform and Revolution* (New York: Oxford University Press, 1988), B. Loveman, *Chile: The Legacy of Hispanic Capitalism,* 2nd ed. (New York: Oxford University Press, 1988); J. A. Booth, *The End and the Beginning: The Nicaraguan Revolution* (Boulder, Colo.: Westview Press, 1985); J. A. Page, *Perón: A Biography* (New York: Random House, 1983); D. Rock, *Argentina, 1516–1987: From Spanish Colonization to Alfonsín,* 2nd ed. (Berkeley, Calif.: University of California Press, 1987); R. Da Matta, *Carnivals, Rogues, and Heroes: An Interpretation of the Brazilian Dilemma* (Notre Dame, Ind.: University of Notre Dame Press, 1991); and M. C. Meyer and W. L. Sherman, *The Course of Mexican History,* 4th ed. (New York: Oxford University Press, 1991). On Latin American literature, see N. Lindstrom, *Twentieth-Century Spanish American Fiction* (Austin, Tex.: University of Texas Press, 1994).

16. Constructing a New World Order

For divergent visions of the future world order (or disorder), see S. P. Huntington, *The Clash of Civilizations and the Remaking of World Order* (New York: Simon and Shuster, 1996), and F. Fukuyama, *The End of History and the Last Man* (New York: The Free Press, 1992). Also of interest is J. Scott, *Seeing Like a State: How Certain Schemes to Improve the Human Condition Have Failed* (New Haven, Conn.: Yale University Press, 1998). An account of the impact of the fall of communism is contained in R. Skidelsky, *The Road from Serfdom: The Economic and Political Consequences of the End of Communism* (New York: Viking Penguin, 1996). Also see F. Furet, *The Passing of an Illusion: The Idea of Communism in the Twentieth Century* (Chicago: University of Chicago Press, 1999).

On the Technological Revolution and its impact, see A. Toffler and H. Toffler, *Creating a New Civilization: The Politics of the Third Wave* (Atlanta: Turner Publishing, 1997). On the dangers of globalization, see J. E. Stiglitz, *Globalism and Its Discontents* (New York: Norton, 2002). For a fascinating analysis of the contrasting pulls of globalization and diversification in the world today, see B. R. Barber, *Jihad vs. McWorld* (New York: Ballantine Books, 1996).

On current trends in the cultural field, see B. Nettl et al., *Excursions in World Music,* 2nd ed. (Upper Saddle River, N.J.: Prentice Hall, 1997), P. Geyh et al., eds., *Postmodern American Fiction: A Norton Anthology* (New York: Norton, 1998), and D. Damrosch, *What Is World Literature?* (Princeton, N.J.: Princeton University Press, 2003).

Index

Photographs are indicated by *p*. Maps are indicated by plate number.